Ancient Egypt:
The Light of the World
Volume 1

by

Gerald Massey

ISBN: 9781631827891

Ancient Egypt:
The Light of the World
Volume 1

All Rights reserved. No part of this book maybe reproduced without written permission from the publishers, except by a reviewer who may quote brief passages in a review to be printed in a newspaper or magazine.

Cover Art : Paul Amid

Printed December 2020

Published and Distributed By:

Lushena Books
607 Country Club Drive, Unit E
Bensenville, IL 60106

www.lushenabks.com

ISBN: 9781631827891

Printed in the United States of America

ANCIENT EGYPT

It may have been a Million years ago
That Light was kindled in the Old Dark Land
With which the illumined Scrolls are all aglow,
That Egypt gave us with her mummied hand:
This was the secret of that subtle smile
Inscrutable upon the Sphinx's face,
Now told from sea to sea, from isle to isle;
The revelation of the Old Dark Race;
Theirs was the wisdom of the Bee and Bird,
Ant, Tortoise, Beaver, working human-wise;
The ancient darkness spake with Egypt's Word;
Hers was the primal message of the skies:
    The Heavens are telling nightly of her glory,
    And for all time Earth echoes her great story.

PREFATORY

I have written other books, but this I look on as the exceptional labour which has made my life worth living. Comparatively speaking, "A Book of the Beginnings" (London, 1881) was written in the dark, "The Natural Genesis" (London, 1883) was written in the twilight, whereas "Ancient Egypt" has been written in the light of day. The earlier books were met in England with the truly orthodox conspiracy of silence. Nevertheless, four thousand volumes have got into circulation somewhere or other up and down the reading world, where they are slowly working in their unacknowledged way. Probably the present book will be appraised at home in proportion as it comes back piecemeal from abroad, from Germany, or France, or maybe from the Country of the Rising Sun.

To all dear lovers of the truth the writer now commends the verifiable truths that wait for recognition in these pages.

> *Truth is all-potent with its silent power*
> *If only whispered, never heard aloud,*
> *But working secretly, almost unseen,*
> *Save in some excommunicated Book;*
> *'Tis as the lightning with its errand done*
> *Before you hear the thunder.*

For myself, it is enough to know that in despite of many hindrances from straitened circumstances, chronic ailments, and the deepening shadows of encroaching age, my book is printed, and the subject-matter that I cared for most is now entrusted safely to the keeping of John Gutenberg, on this my nine-and-seventieth birthday.

CONTENTS

VOL. I

BOOK   PAGE

I. SIGN-LANGUAGE AND MYTHOLOGY AS PRIMITIVE MODES OF REPRESENTATION 1

II. TOTEMISM, TATTOO AND FETISHISM AS FORMS OF SIGN-LANGUAGE 46
    Fetishism 111

III. ELEMENTAL AND ANCESTRAL SPIRITS, OR THE GODS AND THE GLORIFIED. 120

IV. EGYPTIAN BOOK OF THE DEAD AND THE MYSTERIES OF AMENTA 186

V. THE SIGN-LANGUAGE OF ASTRONOMICAL MYTHOLOGY.
    The Primitive African Paradise 249
    Egyptian Wisdom 269
    The Drowning of the Dragon 287

VI. THE SIGN-LANGUAGE OF ASTRONOMICAL MYTHOLOGY. Part II. 321
    Horus of the Double Horizon 332
    The Making of Amenta. 344
    The Irish Amenta 366
    The Mount of Glory 376

VII. EGYPTIAN WISDOM AND THE HEBREW GENESIS . . 398

VIII. THE EGYPTIAN WISDOM IN OTHER JEWISH WRITINGS 470

LIST OF ILLUSTRATIONS

VOL. I

	PAGE
I. Apt, The First Great Mother	124
II. The Mummy-Babe	219
III. Illustration from a Theban Tomb	289
IV. Hippopotamus and Haunch	311
V. Shu the Kneeler	315
VI. Horus Strangling Serpents	317
VII. Horus on Pisces	343
VIII. Horus the Shoot of the Papyrus	450
IX. Assyrian Cylinder	453
X. The Flaming Sword which Guarded the Tree	455
XI. Horus Bruising the Serpent's Head	462

[The Errata page is omitted; these corrections have been entered into the text]

ANCIENT EGYPT
THE LIGHT OF THE WORLD

SIGN-LANGUAGE AND MYTHOLOGY AS PRIMITIVE MODES OF REPRESENTATION.

BOOK I

THE other day a lad from London who had been taken to the sea-side for the first time in his life was standing with his mother looking at the rolling breakers tossing and tumbling in upon the sands, when he was heard to exclaim, "Oh, mother, who is it chucking them heaps o' water about?" This expression showed the boy's ability to think of the power that was "doing it" in the human likeness. But, then, ignorant as he might be, he was more or less the heir to human faculty as it is manifested in all its triumphs over external nature at the present time. Now, it has been and still is a prevalent and practically universal assumption that the same mental standpoint might have been occupied by primitive man, and a like question asked in presence of the same or similar phenomena of physical nature. Nothing is more common or more unquestioned than the inference that primitive man would or could have asked, "Who is doing it?" and that the Who could have been personified in the human likeness. Indeed, it has become an axiom with modern metaphysicians and a postulate of the Anthropologists that, from the beginning, man imposed his own human image upon external nature; that he personified its elemental energies and fierce physical forces after his own likeness; also that this was in accordance with the fundamental character and constitution of the human mind. To adduce a few examples taken almost at random:—David Hume declares that "there is a universal tendency among mankind to conceive all beings like themselves." In support of which he instances the seeing of human faces in the moon. Reid on the Active Powers (4th Essay) says our first thoughts are that "the objects in which we perceive motion have understanding and power as we have." Francis Bacon had long before remarked that we human beings "set stamps and seals of our own images upon God's creatures and works." (*Exp. History.*) Herbert Spencer argued that human personality applied to the powers of nature was the primary mode of representation, and that the identification of this with some natural force or object is due to identity of name. (*Data of Sociology,* ch. XXIV, 184.) "In early philosophy throughout the world," says Mr. Tylor, "the sun and moon are alive and as it were human in their nature." Professor Max Müller, who taught that Mythology was a disease of language, and that the Myths have been made out of words which had lost their senses, asserts that "the whole animal world has been conceived as a copy of our own. And not only the animal world, but the whole of nature was liable to be conceived and named by an assimilation to human nature." (*Science of Thought,* p. 503.) And "such was the propensity in the earliest men of whom we have any authentic record to see personal agency in everything," that it could not be otherwise, for "there was really no way of conceiving or naming anything objective except after the similitude of the subjective, or of ourselves." (*Ib.,* p. 495.) Illustration of this modern position might be indefinitely multiplied. The assumption has been supported by a consensus of assertion, and here, as elsewhere, the present writer is compelled to doubt, deny, and disprove the popular postulate of the accepted orthodox authorities.

That, said the lion, is your version of the story: let us be the sculptors, and for one lion under the feet of a man you shall see a dozen men beneath the pad of one lion.

"Myth-making man" did not create the Gods in his own image. The primary divinities of Egypt, such as Sut, Sebek, and Shu, three of the earliest, were represented in the likeness of the Hippopotamus, the Crocodile, and the Lion; whilst Hapi was imaged as an Ape, Anup as a Jackal, Ptah as a Beetle, Taht as an Ibis, Seb as a Goose. So was it with the Goddesses. They are the likenesses of powers that were super-human, not human. Hence Apt was imaged as a Water-cow, Hekat as a Frog, Tefnut as a Lioness, Serkh as a Scorpion, Rannut as a Serpent, Hathor as a Fruit-tree. A huge mistake has hitherto been made in assuming that the Myth-Makers began by fashioning the Nature-Powers in their own human likeness. Totemism was formulated by myth-making man with types that were the very opposite of human, and in mythology the Anthropomorphic representation was preceded by the whole menagerie of Totemic Zoötypes.

The idea of Force, for instance, was not derived from the thews and muscles of a Man. As the Kamite Sign-Language shows, the Force that was "chucking them heaps of water about" was perceived to be the wind; the Spirit that moved upon the face of the waters from the beginning. This power was divinised in Shu, the God of breathing Force, whose zoötype is the Lion as a fitting figure of this panting Power of the Air. The element audible in the howling wind, but dimly apprehended otherwise, was given shape and substance as the roaring Lion in this substitution of similars. The Force of the element was equated by the power of the Animal; and no human thews and sinews could compare with those of the Lion as a figure of Force. Thus the Lion speaks for itself, in the language of Ideographic Signs. And in this way the Gods and Goddesses of ancient Egypt were at first portrayed as Superhuman Powers by means of living Superhuman types.

If primitive man had projected the shadow of himself upon external nature, to shape its elemental forces in his own image, or if the unfeatured Vast had unveiled to him any likeness of the human face, then the primary representation of the Nature-Powers (which became the later divinities) ought to have been anthropomorphic, and the likeness reflected in the mirror of the most ancient mythologies should have been human. Whereas the Powers and Divinities were first represented by animals, birds, and reptiles, or, to employ a word that includes all classes, they were portrayed by means of zoötypes. The Sun and Moon were not considered "human in their nature" when the one was imaged as a Crocodile, a Lion, a Bull, a Beetle, or a Hawk, and the other as a Hare, a Frog, an Ape, or an Ibis, as they are represented in the Egyptian hieroglyphics by means of the zoötypes. Until Har-Ur, the Elder Horus, had been depicted as the Child in place of the Calf or Lamb, the Fish, or Shoot of the Papyrus-plant (which was comparatively late), there was no human figure personalised in the Mythology of Egypt.

Primitive or Paleolithic Man was too beggarly poor in possessions to dream of shaping the Superhuman Powers of Nature in the human likeness. There is one all-sufficient reason why he did not; he simply could not. And it is precisely because the Makers of the Myths had not the power to animate the universe in their own likeness that we have the zoömorphic mode of representation as the Sign-Language of Totemism and Mythology. On every line of research we discover that the representation of nature was pre-anthropomorphic at first, as we see on going back far enough, and on every line of descent the zoömorphic passes ultimately into the human representation. Modern metaphysicians have so developed the faculty of abstraction and the disease of Subjectivity that their own mental operations offer no true guidance for generalisations concerning primitive or early man, who thought in things and almost apprehended with the physical sense alone.

They overlook the fact that *imaging* by means of object-pictures preceded the *imagining* so often ascribed to primitive men. These did not busy themselves and bother their brains with all sorts of vagrant fancies instead of getting an actual grasp of the homeliest facts. It was not "Primitive Man" but two German metaphysicians who were looking out of window at a falling shower of rain when one of them remarked, "*Perhaps it is I who am doing that.*" "Or I," chimed in the other.

The present writer once had a cat before whom he placed a sheet of polished tin. The cat saw herself reflected as in a mirror, and looked for a short time at her own image. So far as sight and appearance went, this might have been another cat. But she proceeded to apply the comparative process and test one sense by another, deliberately smelling at the likeness to find out if any cat was there. She did not sit down as a non-verifying visionary to formulate hypotheses or conjure up the ghost of a cat. Her sense of smell told her that as a matter of fact there was no other cat present; therefore she was not to be misled by a false appearance, in which she took no further interest. That, we may infer, was more like the action of Primitive Man, who would find no human likeness behind the phenomena of external nature. Indeed, man was so generally represented by the animals that the appearance could be mistaken for a primitive belief that the animals were his ancestors. But the powers first perceived in external nature were not only unlike the human; they were very emphatically and distinctly more than human, and therefore could not be adequately expressed by features recognisable as merely human. Primitive men were all too abjectly helpless in presence of these powers to think of them or to conceive them in their own similitude. The one primordial and most definite fact of the whole matter was the distinct and absolute unlikeness to themselves. Also they themselves were too little the cause of anything by the work of their own hands to enter into the sphere of causation mentally. They could only apprehend the nature-forces by their effects, and try to represent these by means of other powers that were present in nature, but which were also necessarily superior to the human and were not the human faculties indefinitely magnified. The human being could only impress his own image on external nature in proportion to his mastery over natural conditions. He could not have figured the Thunder-bolt as a Stone-axe in the hands of a destroying Power until he himself had made and could wield the axe of stone as the weapon of his own power. But he could think of it in the likeness of the Serpent already known to him in external nature as a figure of fatal force.

An ignorant explanation of the Egyptian Sign-Language was begun by the Greeks, who could not read the hieroglyphics. It was repeated by the Romans, and has been perpetuated by "Classical Scholars" ever since. But, as the interpreter of Egypt, that kind of scholastic knowledge is entirely obsolete. Ignorance of primitive sign-language has been and is a fertile source of false belief. For example, Juvenal asks, "Who does not know what kind of monsters Egypt insanely worships?" (Sat., 15, 1.) And having seen or heard of the long-tailed Ape in an Egyptian temple, the satirist assumed without question that this animal was set up as an object of worship. He did not know that the Ape itself was the worshipper, as an image in Sign-Language and as the Saluter of the Gods. Ani, the name of this particular Ape, denotes the Saluter, and to salute was an Egyptian gesture of adoration. The Ape or Cynocephalus with its paws uplifted is the typical worshipper as Saluter of the Light. It was, and still is, looked upon in Africa generally as a pre-human Moon-worshipper, who laments and bewails the disappearance of its night-light and rejoices at the renewal and return of that luminary. (Hor-Apollo, B. I, 14. Also Captain Burton, in a letter to the author.) In the Vignettes to the Ritual, Ani the Ape is the Saluter of the rising Sun, that is of Ra, upon the Mount of Sunrise. One of the most profound perversions of the past has been made in misapprehending this primitive sign-language for what is designated "Worship," whether as "Sun-Worship," "Serpent-Worship," "Tree-Worship," or "Phallic-Worship." The Tree, for example, is a type, but the type is not necessarily an object of worship, as misunderstood by those who do not read the types when these are rooted in the ground of natural fact. The forest-folk were dwellers in the trees, or in the bush. The tree that gave them food and shelter grew to be an object of regard. Hence it became a type of the Mother-Earth as the birthplace and abode. Hence Hathor was the hut or house of Horus (Har) in the tree. But worship is a word of cant employed by writers who are ignorant of sign-language in general. Such phrases as "Stock-and-stone worship" explain nothing and are worse than useless. The Mother and Child of all mythology are represented in the Tree and Branch. The Tree was a type of the abode, the Roof-tree; the Mother of food and drink; the giver of life and shelter; the wet-nurse in the dew or rain; the producer of her offspring as the branch and promise of periodic continuity. Was it the Tree then the Egyptians worshipped, or the Giver of food and shelter in the Tree? On the Apis Stele in the Berlin Museum two priests are saluting the Apis-Bull. This is designated "Apis-worship." But the Apis carries the Solar Disk betwixt its horns. This also is being saluted. Which then is the object of worship? There are two objects of religious regard, but neither is the object of adoration. That is the God in spirit who was represented as the Soul of life in the Sun and in the Tree, also by the fecundating Bull. In this and a thousand other instances it is not a question of worship but of sign-language.

Nor did Mythology spring from fifty or a hundred different sources, as frequently assumed. It is one as *a system of representation, one as a mould of thought, one as a mode of expression,* and all its great primordial types are virtually universal. Neither do the myths that were inherited and repeated for ages by the later races of men afford any direct criterion to the intellectual status of such races. A mythical representation may be savage without those who preserve it being savages. When the Egyptians in the time of Unas speak of the deities devouring souls it is no proof of their being cannibals *at the time.* Mythology has had an almost limitless descent. It was in a savage or crudely primitive state in the most ancient Egypt, but the Egyptians who continued to repeat the Myths did not remain savages. The same mythical mode of representing nature that was probably extant in Africa 100,000 years ago survives to-day amongst races who are no longer the producers of the Myths and Märchen than they are of language itself. Egyptian mythology is the oldest in the world, and it did not begin as an *explanation* of natural phenomena, but as a *representation* by such primitive means as were available at the time. It does not explain that the Sun is a Hawk or the Moon a Cat, or the solar God a Crocodile. Such figures of fact belong to the symbolical mode of rendering in the language of animals or zoötypes. No better definition of "Myth" or Mythology could be given than is conveyed by the word "Sem" in Egyptian. This signifies representation on the ground of likeness. Mythology, then, is "representation on the ground of likeness," which led to all the forms of sign-language that could ever be employed. The matter has been touched upon in previous volumes, but for the purpose of completeness it has to be demonstrated in the present work that external nature was primarily imaged in the pre-human likeness. It was the same here as in external nature: the animals came first, and the predecessors of Man are primary in Sign-Language, Mythology, and Totemism.

It is quite certain that if the primitive method had been Conceptual and early man had possessed the power to impose the likeness of human personality upon external phenomena it would have been in the image of the Male, as a type or in the types of power; whereas the primal human personification is in the likeness of the female. The great Mother as the primal Parent is a Universal type. There could be no divine Father in Heaven until the fatherhood was individualised on earth. Again, if primitive men had been able to impose the human likeness on the Mother-Nature the typical Wet-nurse would have been a woman. But it is not so; the Woman comes last. She was preceded by the Beast itself, the Sow, the Hippopotamus, or Lioness, and by the female form that wears the head of the Zoötype, the Cow, Frog or Serpent, on the body of a divinity. Moreover, the human likeness would, of necessity, have included Sex. But the earliest powers recognised in nature are represented as being of no Sex. It is said in the Akkadian hymns, "Female they are not, male they are not." Therefore they were not imaged in the human likeness. The elements of air, earth, water, fire, darkness and light are of no sex, and the powers first recognised in them, whether as destructive or beneficent, are consequently without sex. So far from Nature having been conceived or imaged as a non-natural Man in a Mask, with features more or less human, however hugely magnified, the mask of human personality was the latest that was fitted to the face of external nature. Masks were applied to the face of nature in the endeavour to feature and visibly present some likeness of the operative elemental forces and manifesting powers of Air, Fire, Water, Earth, Thunder and Lightning, Darkness and Dawn, Eclipse and Earthquake, Sand-storm or the drowning waters of the Dark. But these masks were Zoömorphic, not human. They imaged the most potent of devouring beasts, most cunning of reptiles, most powerful birds of prey. In these monstrous masks we see the Primal Powers of Nature all at play, as in the Pantomime, which still preserves a likeness to the primordial representation of external nature that is now chiefly known under the names of Mythology and Totemism. The Elemental powers operant in external nature were superhuman in the past as they are in the present. The Voice of Thunder, the death-stroke of lightning, the Coup de Soleil, the force of fire, or of water in flood and the wind in a hurricane were superhuman. So of the Animals and Birds: the powers of the hippopotamus, crocodile, serpent, hawk, lion, jackal, and Ape were superhuman, and therefore they were adopted as zoötypes and as primary representatives of the superhuman Powers of the Elements. They were adopted as primitive Ideographs. They were adopted for use and consciously stamped for their representative value, not ignorantly worshipped; and thus they became the coins as it were in the current medium of exchange for the expression of primitive thought or feeling.

Sign-language includes the gesture-signs by which the mysteries were danced or otherwise dramatized in Africa by the Pygmies and Bushmen; in Totemism, in Fetishism, and in hieroglyphic symbols; very little of which language has been read by those who are continually treading water in the shallows of the subject without ever touching bottom or attaining foothold in the depths. It is by means of sign-language that the Egyptian wisdom keeps the records of the pre-historic past. The Egyptian hieroglyphics show us the connection betwixt words and things, also betwixt sounds and words, in a very primitive range of human thought. There is no other such a record known in all the world. They consist largely of human gesture-signs and the sounds first made by animals, such as "ba" for the goat, "meaou" for the cat, "su" for the goose, and "fu" for the Cerastes snake. But the Kamite representation by means of sign-language had begun in inner Africa before the talking animals, birds, and reptiles had been translated into the forms of gods and goddesses by the dwellers in the valley of the Nile. The living ideographs or zoötypes were primary, and can be traced to their original habitat and home, and to nowhere else upon the surface of our earth. The cow of the waters there represented the earth-Mother as the great bringer-forth of life before she was divinised as Apt the goddess in human guise, with the head of a hippopotamus. The overseeing Giraffe (or was it the Okapi?) of Sut, the hawk of Horus, the Kaf-Ape of Taht-Aan, the white Vulture of Neith, the Jackal of Anup, and fifty others were pre-extant as the talking animals before they were delineated in semi-human guise as gods and goddesses or elemental powers thus figured forth in the form of birds and beasts or fish and reptiles. The zoötypes were extant in nature as figures ready-modelled, pictures ready-made, hieroglyphics and ideographs that moved about alive: pictures that were earlier than painting, statues that preceded sculpture, living nature-types that were employed when there were no others known to art. Certain primordial types originated in the old dark land of Africa. These were perfected in Egypt and thence dispersed about the world. Amongst them is the Earth as solid ground amidst the water of surrounding space, or as the bringer-forth of life, depicted as a Water-Cow; possibly the Cow of Kintu in Uganda; the Dragon of Darkness or other wide-jawed Swallower of the Light that rose up from the Abyss and coiled about the Mount of Earth at night as the Devourer; the evergreen Tree of Dawn—pre-eminently African—that rises on the horizon, or upon the Mount of Earth, from out the waters of Space; the opposing Elemental Powers beginning with the Twins of Light and Darkness who fought in Earth and Heaven and the Nether World; the Great Earth-Mother of the Nature-powers; the Seven Children of her womb, and various other types that are one in origin and world-wide in their range.

When the solar force was yet uncomprehended, the sinking Sun could be imaged naturally enough by the Beetle boring its way down through the earth, or by the Tortoise that buried itself in the soil: also by the Crocodile making its passage through the waters, or the Golden Hawk that soared up through the air. This was representing phenomena in external nature on the ground of likeness when it could not be imaged directly by means of words. When it is held, as in Australia, that the Lizard first divided the sexes and that it was also the author of marriage, we have to ascertain what the Lizard signified in sign-language, and when we find that, like the serpent or the Frog, it denoted the female period, we see how it distinguished or divided the sexes and in what sense it authorised or was the author of Totemic Marriage, because of its being a sign or symbol of feminine pubescence. It is said by the Amazulu, that when old Women pass away they take the form of a kind of Lizard. This can only be interpreted by knowing the ideographic value in the primitive system of Sign-Language in which the Lizard was a zoötype. The Lizard appeared at puberty, but it disappeared at the turn of life, and with the Old Women went the disappearing Lizard.

The Frog which transformed from the tadpole condition was another Ideograph of female pubescence. This may be illustrated by a story that was told some time since by Miss Werner in the Contemporary Review which contains a specimen of primitive thought and its mode of expression in perfect survival. It happened that a native girl at Blantyre Mission was called by her mistress, a missionary's wife, to come and take charge of the baby. Her reply was, "Nchafuleni is not there; she is turned into a frog." (Werner, Contemporary Review, Sept., p. 378.) She could not come for a reason of Tapu, but said so typically in the language of animals. She had made that transformation which first occurs when the young girl changes into a woman. She might have said she was a serpent or a lizard or that she was in flower. But the frog that changed from a tadpole was also a type of her transformation, and she had figuratively become a frog for a few days of seclusion. Similarly the member of a Totem also became a frog, a beetle, a bull or bear as a mode of representation, but not because the human being changed into the animal. The same things which are said at a later stage by the ideographic Determinatives in the Egyptian hieroglyphics had been expressed previously by the Inner African zoötypes or living Beasts, Birds and Reptiles, as may be seen in the stories told of the talking Animals by the Bushmen. The original records still suffice to show that the physical agencies or forces first perceived were not conceived or mentally embodied in the human likeness, and that external nature offered no looking-glass for the human face.

To take the very illustration adduced by Hume. The original Man in the Moon did *not* depend upon any fancied resemblance to the human face. The Egyptian Man in the Moon, Taht or Tehuti (Greek Thoth), had the head of an Ibis or of the Cynocephalus; both Ibis and Cynocephalus were lunar types which preceded any human likeness, and these were continued as heads to the human figure after this had been adopted. The Man in the Moon, who is Taht (or Khunsu) in Egypt, had a series of predecessors in the Dog or Cynocephalus, the Ibis, the Beetle, the Bull, the Frog, and other ideographic figures of lunar phenomena. As natural fact, the Ibis was a famous Fisher of the Nile, and its familiar figure was adopted as a zoötype of Taht, the lunar God. Where the modern saw the New Moon with the "auld Moon in her arm," the Egyptian saw the Ibis fishing up the old dark orb from out the waters with the crescent of its curving beak, as the recoverer and Saviour of the Drowning Light. The Moon was not looked upon as having any human likeness when it was imaged as (or by) the Cat who saw in the dark; the Hare that rose up by night and went round the horizon by leaps and bounds; the Ibis as the returning bird of passage and messenger of the Inundation; the Frog that transformed from the tadpole; the old Beetle that renewed itself in the earth to come forth as the young one, or the Cow that gave re-birth to the child of light as her calf. The sun was not conceived as "human in its nature" when the solar force at dawn was imaged by the Lion-faced Atum; the flame of its furnace by the fiery serpent Uati; the soul of its life by the Hawk, the Ram, or the Crocodile, which are five Egyptian Zoötypes and a fivefold disproof of the sun being conceived as or considered human in its nature or similitude.

In beginning *ab ovo* our first lesson is to learn something of *the Symbolical Language of Animals*, and to understand what it is they once said as Zoötypes. We have then to use that knowledge in simplifying the mysteries of mythology.

This primitive language is still employed in divers forms. It is extant in the so-called "dead language" of the Hieroglyphics; the Ideographs and Pictographs; in the Totemic types, and figures of Tattoo; in the portraiture of the Nature-Powers which came to be divinised at length in the human likeness as the Gods and Goddesses of Mythology; and in that language of the folk-fables still made use of by the Bushmen, Hottentots, and other Africans, in which the Jackal, the Dog, the Lion, the Crane, the White Vulture and other beasts and birds keep on talking as they did in the beginning, and continue more or less to say in human speech what they once said in the primitive symbolism; that is, they fulfil the same characters in the Märchen that were first founded in the Mythos. It has now to be shown how the Mythical mode of representing natural phenomena was based upon this primitive system of thought and expression, and how the things that were thought and expressed of old in this language continue the primary stratum of what is called "Mythology" to-day.

In the most primitive phase Mythology is a mode of representing certain elemental powers by means of living types that were superhuman like the natural phenomena. The foundations of Mythology and other forms of the ancient wisdom were laid in this pre-anthropomorphic mode of primitive representation. Thus, to summarise a few of the illustrations. The typical Giant Apap was an enormous water-Reptile. The typical Genetrix and Mother of life was a Water-Cow that represented the Earth. The typical Twin-Brothers were two Birds or two Beasts. The typical twin brother and sister were a Lion and a Lioness. The typical Virgin was a heifer, or a vulture. The typical Messiah was a calf, a lamb or Unbu the Branch. The typical Provider was a goose. The typical Chief or Leader is a lion. The typical Artisan is a beetle. The typical Physician is an Ibis (which administered the enema to itself). The typical Judge is a Jackal or a Cynocephalus, whose wig and collar are amusingly suggestive of the English Law-courts. Each and all of these and hundreds more preceded personification in the human image. The mighty Infant who slew the Dragon or strangled serpents while in his cradle was a later substitute for such a Zoötype as the little Ichneumon, a figure of Horus. The Ichneumon was seen to attack the cobra di capella and make the mortal enemy hide its head and shield its most vital parts within the protecting coils of its own body. For this reason the lively, daring little animal was adopted as a zoötype of Horus the young Solar God, who in his attack upon the Apap-Serpent made the huge and deadly reptile hide its head in its own enveloping darkness. But, when the figure is made anthropomorphic and the tiny

Conqueror is introduced as the little Hero in human form, the beginning of the Mythos and its meaning are obscured. The Ichneumon, the Hawk, the Ibis might attack the Cobra, but it was well enough known that a Child would not, consequently the original hero was not a Child, although spoken of as a child in the literalised marvels, miracles, and fables of "the Infancy."

It is the present writer's contention that the Wisdom of the Ancients was the Wisdom of Egypt, and that her explanation of the Zoötypes employed in Sign-Language, Totemism, and Mythology holds good wherever the zoötypes survive. For example, the Cawichan Tribes say the Moon has a frog in it, and with the Selish Indians of North-West America the Frog (or Toad) in the Moon is equivalent to our Man in the Moon. They have a tradition that the devouring Wolf being in love with the Frog (or Toad), pursued her with great ardour and had nearly caught her when she made a desperate leap and landed safely in the Moon, where she has remained to this day. (Wilson, *Trans. of Ethnol. Society*, 1866, New Series, v. 4, p. 304.) Which means that the frog, as a type of transformation, was applied to the changing Moon as well as to the Zulu girl, Nchafuleni.

Sign-language was from the beginning a substitution of similars for the purpose of expression by primitive or pre-verbal Man, who followed the animals in making audible sounds accompanied and emphasised by human gestures. The same system of thought and mode of utterance were continued in mythography and totemism. Renouf says the Scarabeus was "an object of worship in Egypt," as a symbol of divinity. But this is the modern error. If there was a God, and the Beetle was his symbol, obviously it was the divinity that was the object of worship, not the symbol: not the zoötype. Ptah, we know, was that divinity, with the Beetle as a type, and those who read the types were worshippers of the God and not of his symbolic dung-beetle which was honoured as a sign of transformation. When told that the Egyptians were worshippers of the "Bee," the "Mantis," and the "Grasshopper," we recall the words of Hor-Apollo, who says that when the Egyptians would symbolise a mystic and one of the Initiated they delineate a Grasshopper *because* the insect does not utter sounds with its mouth, but makes a chirping by means of its spine. (B. 2, 55.) The grasshopper, then, which uttered a voice that did not come from its mouth, was a living type of superhuman power. And being an image of mystery and superhuman power, it was also considered a fitting symbol of Kagn, the Bushman Creator, or Great Spirit of creative mystery. Moreover, the grasshopper made his music and revealed his mystery in dancing; and the religious mysteries of Kagn were performed with dancing or in the grasshopper's dance. Thus the Initiates in the mysteries of the Mantis are identical with the Egyptian Mystæ symbolised by the grasshopper; and the dancing probably goes back to the time when pre-verbal man was an imitator of the grasshopper, which was a primitive type of mystery, like the transforming frog and the self-interring tortoise. There is a religious sect still extant in England who are known as the "Jumpers," and their saltatory exercises still identify them with the leaping "Grasshoppers" and the "praying Mantis" in the

Mysteries of old. They still "dance that dance." The "Moon belongs to the Mantis," say the Bushmen, which goes to show that the Mantis was not only a Lunar type as the leaper round the horizon, but on account of its power of transformation; and this again suggests the reason why the Mantis should be the zoötype of the Mystæ who transformed in trance, as well as leaped and danced in the mysteries. The Frog and the Grasshopper were earlier leapers than the Hare. These also were figures of the Moon that leaped up in a fresh place every night. It was this leaping up of the light that was imitated in the dances of the Africans who jumped for joy at the appearance of the New Moon which they celebrated in the monthly dance, as did the Congo Negroes and other denizens of the Dark Continent who danced the primitive mysteries and dramatised them in their dances. The Leapers were the Dancers, and the leaping Mantis, the Grasshopper, the Frog, the Hare, were amongst the pre-human prototypes.

The frog is still known in popular weather-wisdom as the prophesier of Rain. As such, it must have been of vastly more importance in the burning lands of Inner Africa, and there is reason to suppose that Hekat, the Consort of Khnum, the King of Frogs, was frog-headed as the prophetess, or foreteller, on this ground of natural fact. Erman says the "Great Men of the South," the "Privy Councillors of the royal orders were almost always invested—I know not why—with the office of Prophet of the frog-headed Goddess Hekat." (*Life in Ancient Egypt,* p. 82, Eng. tr.). The Frog was a prophet of Rain in some countries, and of spring-time in others. In Egypt it was the prophet of the Inundation, hence Hekat was a Consort of Khnum, the Lord of the Inundation, and King of Frogs. Hekat was also the Seer by Night in the Moon, as well as the crier for the waters and foreteller of their coming. From her, as Seer in the dark, we may derive the names of the Witch as the Hexe, the Hag, the Hagedisse; and also that of the dark Goddess Hecate, the sender of Dreams. As prophesier of Rain, or of the Inundation, it was the herald of new life to the land of Egypt, and this would be one reason for its relationship to the resurrection. But, in making its transformation from the tadpole state to that of the frog, it was the figure of a still more important natural fact. This, in the Mythology, was applied to the transformation and renewal of the Moon, and to the transformation of the Mortal into an Immortal in the Eschatology, a type of Ptah, who in one form is portrayed as the frog-headed God. Lamps have been found in Egypt with the Frog upon the upper part, and one is known which has the legend ΕΓΩ ΕΙΜΙ ΑΝΑCΤΑCΙC, "I am the Resurrection." (Lanzone, *Dizionario,* p. 853; Budge, *The Mummy,* p. 266.) In this figure the lamp is an equivalent for the rising Sun, and the frog upon it is the type of Ptah, who in his solar character was the Resurrection and the life in the Mythology before the image passed into the Eschatology, in a Spiritual sense. The frog was a type of transformation, and the Frog-headed Ptah made his transformation in Amenta to rise again as the opener of the Nether Earth. And as he represented the Sun in Amenta, the frog, like the Cynocephalus of Memphis (*Rit.,* ch. 42), was imaged as Golden. Thus we find the Sun in the lower Earth of two depicted in the Golden Frog, and, as stated by John Bell, the

Lamas had an idea that the earth rested on a Golden Frog, and that when the Frog stretched out its foot there was an Earthquake. ("A Journey from St. Petersburgh to Pekin in the year 1719." Pinkerton's *Voyages*, v. 7, p. 369.) Here the frog beneath the earth, like the Tortoise, is Egyptian, and as such we can learn what fact in nature was represented by it as a zoötype of Ptah in the Nether World called the Earth of Eternity, where the typical tadpole that swam the waters made its transformation into the frog that stretched itself out and set foot on land.

It is related in a Chinese legend that the lady, Mrs. Chang-ngo, obtained the drug of Immortality by stealing it from Si Wang Nu, the Royal Mother of the West. With this she fled to the Moon, and was changed into a Frog that is still to be seen on the surface of the orb. (Dennys, *Folk-Lore of China*, p. 117.) As Egyptian, the Mother of the West was the Goddess who received the setting Sun and reproduced its light. The immortal liquor is the Solar Light. This was stolen from the Moon. Chang-ngo is equivalent to the frog-headed Hekat who represented the resurrection. The frog, in Egypt, was a sign of "myriads" as well as of transformation. In the Moon it would denote myriads of renewals when periodic repetition was a mode of immortality. Hekat the frog-headed is the original Cinderella. She makes her transformation into Sati, the Lady of Light, whose name is written with an Arrow. Thus, to mention only a few of the lunar types, the Goddess Hekat represented the moon and its transformation as the Frog. Taht and his Cynocephalus represented the Man and his dog in the Moon. Osiris represented the Lunar Light in his character of the Hare-headed Un-Nefer, the up-springing Hare in the Moon. These are Egyptian Zoötypes, to be read wherever found by means of the Egyptian Wisdom. Amongst other Hieroglyphic Signs in the Language of Animals, the Head of a Vulture signifies victory (doubtless because of the bird's keen scent for blood). The sheathen claw is a determinative of peaceful actions. The hinder part of the Lioness denotes the great magical power. The Tail of a Crocodile is a sign for black and for darkness. An Ape is the ideograph of rage and a fiery spirit, or spirit of fire. The sparrow is a type of physical evil because of its destructive nature in thieving corn—its name of "Tu-tu" signifies a kind of plague or affliction of the fields. (Birch.) The Water-wagtail is a type of moral evil. This bird, as Wilkinson pointed out, is still called in Egypt the father of corruption (aboo fussad). It was regarded as the type of an impure or wicked person, on account of its insidious suggestiveness of immoral motion. The extent to which morals and philosophy were taught by means of these living object-pictures cannot now be measured, but the moralising fables spoken as well as acted by the typical animals still offer testimony, and language is full of phrases which continue the zoötypes into the world of letters, as when the greedy, filthy man is called a hog, the grumpy man a bear, the cunning one a fox, the subtle and treacherous one a snake.

In the Folk-Lore of various races the human Soul takes the form of a Snake, a Mouse, a Swallow, a Hawk, a Pigeon, a Bee, a Jackal, or other animal, each of which was an Egyptian zoötype of some power or soul in Nature before there was any representation of the human Soul or Ancestral Spirit in the human form. Hence we are told that when twins are born the Batavians believe that one of the pair is a crocodile. Mr. Spenser accepts the "belief" and asks, "May we not conclude that twins, of whom one gained the name of crocodile, gave rise to a legend which originated this monstrous belief?" (*Data of Sociology*, ch. 22, par. 175.) But all such representations are mythical and are not to be explicated by the theory of "monstrous belief." It is a matter of Sign-Language. The Batavians knew as well as we do that no crocodile was ever born twin along with a human child. In this instance the poor things were asserting in their primitive way that Man is born with or as a Soul. This the gnosis enables us to prove. One of the earliest types of the Sun as a Soul of life in the water is a Crocodile. We see the Mother who brings forth a Crocodile when the Goddess Neith is portrayed in human shape as the suckler of the young crocodiles hanging at her breasts. Neith is the wet-nurse personified whose child was the young sun-god. As Sebek he was imaged by the Crocodile that emerged from the waters at sun-rise. Sebek was at once the child and the crocodile brought forth by the Great Mother in the mythology. And because the Crocodile had imaged a Soul of Life in water, as a superhuman power, it became a representative, in Sign-Language, of the human Soul. We see this same type of a Soul in external nature applied to the human Soul in the Book of the Dead, when the Osiris in the Nether World exclaims, "I am the Crocodile in the form of a man," that is as a Soul of which the Crocodile had been a symbol, as Soul of the Sun. It was thus the Crocodile was born with the Child, as a matter of sign-language, not as a belief. The crocodile is commonly recognised by the Congo natives as a type of Soul. Miss Kingsley tells of a Witch-Doctor who administered emetics to certain of his patients and brought away young crocodiles. She relates that a Witch-Doctor had been opened after death, when a winged Lizard-like thing was found in his inside which Batanga said was his power. The power being another name for his Soul.

Mr. Spenser not only argues for the actuality of these "beliefs" concerning natural facts, supposed to have been held by primitive men and scientific Egyptians, which vanish with a true interpretation of the mythical mode of representation, he further insists that there seems to be "*ample justification for the belief that any kind of Creature may be transformed into any other*" because of the metamorphosis observed in the insect-world, or elsewhere, from which there resulted "*the theory of metamorphosis in general*" and the notion "*that things of all kinds may suddenly change their forms,*" man of course included. (*Data*, ch. 8, par. 55.) But there was no evidence throughout all nature to suggest that any kind of creature could be transformed into any other kind. On the contrary, nature showed them that the frog was a tadpole continued; that the chrysalis was the prior status of the butterfly, and that the old Moon changed into the New. The transformation was visible and invariable, and the product of transformation was always the same in kind. There was no sign or suggestion of an unlimited possibility in metamorphosis. Neither was there ever a race of savages who did think or believe (in the words of Mr. Spenser) *"that any kind of creature may be transformed into any other,"* no more than there ever were boys who believed that any kind of bird could lay any other kind of bird's egg. They are too good observers for any such self-delusion as that.

Mythical representation did not begin with "stories of human adventure," as Mr. Spencer puts it, nor with human figures at all, but with the phenomena of external nature, that were represented by means of animals, birds, reptiles and insects, which had demonstrated the possession of superhuman faculties and powers. The origin of various superstitions and customs seemingly insane can be traced to sign-language. In many parts of England it is thought necessary to "tell the Bees" when a death has occurred in the house, and to put the hives into mourning. The present writer has known the housewife to sally forth into the garden with warming-pan and key and strips of crape to "tell the Bees," lest they should take flight, when one of the inmates of the house had died. We must seek an explanation for this in the symbolism of Egypt that was carried forth orally to the ends of the earth. The Bee was anciently a zoötype of the Soul which was represented as issuing forth from the body in that form or under that type. There is a tradition that the Bees alone of all animals descended from Paradise. In the Engadine, Switzerland, it is said that the Souls of men go forth from this world and return to it in the form of Bees. Virgil, in the Fourth Book of the Georgics, celebrates the Bee that never dies, but ascends alive into heaven. That is the typical Bee which was an image of the Soul. It was the Soul, as Bee, that alone ascended into heaven or descended from thence. The Bee is certainly one form of the Egyptian Abait, or Bird-fly, which is a guide and pilot to the Souls of the Dead on their way to the fields of Aarru. It was a figure of Lower Egypt as the land of honey, thence a fitting guide to the celestial fields of the Aarru-Paradise. It looks as if the name for the Soul, Ba, in Egyptian, may be identical with our word Bee. Ba is honey determined by the Bee-sign, and Ba is also the Soul. The Egyptians made use of honey as a means of embalming the dead. Thus the Bee, as a zoötype of the Soul, became a messenger of the dead and a mode of communication with the ancestral Spirits. Talking to the Bees in this language was like speaking with the Spirits of the dead, and, as it were, commending the departed one to the guidance of the Bees, who as honey-gatherers naturally knew the way to the Elysian fields and the meads of Amaranth that flowed with milk and honey. The type is confused with the Soul when the Bee is invoked as follows, "almost as if requesting the Soul of the departed to watch for ever over the living":—

> " *Bienchen, unser Herr ist todt,*
> *Verlass mich nicht in meiner Noth.*"

(Gubernatis, *Zoological Myth.*, v. 2, p. 218.) In the Ritual the Abait (as Bee or Bird-fly) is the conductor of Souls to the celestial fields. When the Deceased is asked who conducted him thither, he replies, "It was the Abait-deity who conducted me." He also exclaims, "Hail to thee, who fliest up to heaven to give light to the stars." (Ch. 76. Renouf.) Here the Bee or Bird-fly is a Solar type, and that which represented the ascending sun in the mythology became a type of the Soul in the eschatology. Thus the *inventor* of honey in this world led the way to the fields of flowers in the next.

Modern popular superstition to a large extent is the ancient symbolism in its second childhood. Here is a case in point. The Cock having been a representative of Soul or Spirit, it is sure to be said that the human Soul has entered the Cock by a kind of re-incarnation. Hence we read of a legacy left to a Fowl by a wealthy lady named Silva, of Lisbon, who held that the Soul of her dead husband survived in a Cock. (*Daily Mail*, May 26th, 1892.) So it has been with the zoötypes of other elemental souls that were continued for the human soul, from the Crocodile of the Batavians to the red Mouse of the Germans. Folk-lore is full of fables that originated in this language of signs.

The Jackal in the Egyptian representation is the guide of the Sun upon his pathway in Amenta, who takes up the young child-Horus in his arms to carry him over the waters. In the Hottentot prototype the Jackal finds the Sun in the form of a little child, and takes him upon his back to carry him. When the Sun grew hot the Jackal shook himself and said, "Get down." But the Sun stuck fast and burnt the Jackal, so that he has a long black stripe down his back to this day. (Bleek, *Reynard*, p. 67.) The same tale is told of the Coyote or Prairie-dog, who takes the place of the Jackal in the mythical legends of the Red Men. In the Ritual the Jackal who carried Horus, the young Sun-God, had become the bearer and supporter of Souls. In passing the place where the Dead fall into darkness, the Osiris says, "Apuat raiseth me up." (Ch. 44.) And when the overwhelming waters of the Deluge burst forth, he rejoices, saying, "Anup is my bearer." (Rit., ch. 64.) Here, as elsewhere, the mythical type extant with the earlier Africans had passed into the eschatology of the Egyptians.

The eternal contest betwixt the powers of light and darkness is also represented in the African folk-tales. The Hare (or Rabbit) Kalulu and the Dzimwi are two of the contending characters. The Hare, as in Egypt, is typical of the Good Power, and no doubt is a zoötype of the young up-springing Moon. The Dzimwi is the Evil Power, like Apap, the Giant, the Ogre, the Swallower of the waters or the light. (Werner, "African Folk-Lore," *Contemp. Rev.*, September, 1896.) It is very cunning, but in the end is always outwitted by the Hare. When the Dzimwi kills or swallows the Hare's Mother it is the Dragon of Darkness, or Eclipse, devouring the Lunar light. The Moon-mythos is indefinitely older than the Solar, and the earliest slayer of the Dragon was Lunar, the Mother of the Young Child of Light. Here she is killed by the Dzimwi. Then Kalulu comes with a barbed arrow, with which he pierces the Dzimwi through the heart. This is the battle of Ra and Apap, or Horus and Sut, in the most primitive form, when as yet the powers were rendered non-anthropomorphically. Again, the Monkey who is transformed into a man is a prototype of the Moon-God Taht, who is a Dog-headed Ape in one character and a man in another. A young person refuses several husbands. A Monkey then comes along. The beast takes the skin off his body, and is changed into a Man. To judge from the Egyptian Mythos, the young person was Lunar, and the Monkey changing into a man is Lunar likewise. One of the two won the Lady of Light in the Moon. This was the Monkey that became a Man, as did the Bear in "Beauty and the Beast." In another tale, obviously Luni-Solar, that is with the Sun and Moon as the characters, a girl (that is the Moon) refused a husband (that is the Sun). Thereupon she married a Lion; that is a Solar type. In other words, the Moon and Sun were married in Amenta. This tale is told with primitive humour. When the wedded pair were going to bed she would not undress unless he let her cut off his *tail*. For this remained unmetamorphosed when he transformed into a Man. "When she found out that he was a lion she ran away from that husband." So in a Hindu story a young woman refuses to marry the Sun because he is too fiery-hot. Even in the American Negro stories of Brer Rabbit, Brer Fox, Brer Wolf, and Brer Terrapin the original characters of the typical animals are still preserved as they were in the Egyptian mythology when divinised. The Turtle or Tortoise, the wise and sagacious one, is the hider; the Fox, like the Jackal, Anup, is the cunning one. The Wolf is the swallower, and the Rabbit equates with the Hare, a type of the Good Osiris or of the African Kalulu.

Any number of current superstitions are the result of ignorance concerning the Ancient Wisdom, and one of the worst results bequeathed to us by the past is to be found in our customs of cruelty to dumb animals. These poor victims have had to suffer frightfully for the very service which they once rendered to man as primitive types of expression in Sign-Language. In the Persian and Hebrew laws of Clean and Unclean, many of the animals and birds that were once held sacred in Egypt for their symbolic value are there condemned as unclean, to be cast out with curses; and so the real animals became the outcasts of the mental world, according to the later religion, in the language of letters which followed and superseded the carven hieroglyphics of the earlier time. The Ass has been a shameful sufferer from the part it played in the primitive typology. Beating and kicking the ass used to be a Christian sport practised up and down the aisles of Christian churches, the ass being a cast-out representative of an old Hebrew, and still older Egyptian deity.

The Cat is another sufferer for the same reason. The cat sees by night, and was adopted as a type of the Moon that saw by night and kept watch in the dark. Now, witches are seers and foreseers, and whenever they were persecuted and hounded to death the cat suffered with them, because she had been the type and symbol of preterhuman sight. These were modes of casting out the ancient fetish-images initiated and enforced by the priesthood of a later faith. In Egypt, as Hor-Apollo tells us, the figure of a mouse signified a disappearance. Now, see how cruelly the little animal has been treated because it was a type of disappearance. It was, and may be still, an English custom to charm away disease by making a hole in the shrew-ash or witch-elm tree and shutting up a live shrew-mouse in it. In immuring the mouse in the bole of the tree, the disappearing victim typified or enacted the desired disappearance of the disease. That which had been a symbol in the past is now made use of alive in performing a symbolical action in the present.

Much misery has been caused to human beings as well as animals through the misapplication of certain mythical, that is symbolical characters. Plutarch tells us how the evil Sut (or Typhon) was humiliated and insulted by the Egyptians at certain festivals, "when they abuse red-haired men and tumble an ass down a precipice because Typhon was red-haired and like an ass in complexion." (Ch. 30.) The fact is also notorious in Europe that an evil character has been commonly ascribed to red-haired persons, with no known warrant whatever from nature. They suffer for the symbol. Now for the origin of the symbol, according to the Egyptian Wisdom. Sut, the treacherous opponent of Horus (Osiris in the later Mythos), was the Egyptian Judas. He betrayed his brother to his enemies the Sebau. He was of a red complexion. Hence the Red Ass and the red-haired people were his types. But *the complexion and red hair of Sut were not derived from any human origin.* Sut was painted red, yellowish, or sandy, as representative of the *desert*. He was the original devil in the wilderness, the cause of drought and the creator of thirst. As the Hippopotamus, Sut, like Apt the Mother, was of a red complexion. As the betrayer of his brother Osiris, Sut was brought on with the Jesus-legend in the character of Judas, the traitor; hence in the Miracle-plays and out-of-doors customs, Judas, true to the Sut-Typhonian tradition, is always red-haired or wears a red wig. Thus, in our pictures of the past the typical traitor still preserves his proper hue, but in the belief of the ignorant the clue is lost and the red-haired people come to be the *Viva Effigies* of Sut, the Egyptian Judas, as a human type of evil.

Folk-lore in many lands is the final fragmentary form in which the ancient wisdom—the Wisdom of old Egypt—still survives as old wives' fables, parables, riddles, allegorical sayings, and superstitious beliefs, consecrated by the ignorance which has taken the place of primitive knowledge concerning the mythical mode of representation; and from lack of the lost key, the writers on this subject have become the sheerest tale-bearers whose gossip is full of scandal against primitive and ancient man. But not in any land or language can the Märchen tell us anything directly concerning themselves. They have lost the memory of their meaning. It is only in the Mythos that we can ascertain their original relationship to natural fact and learn that the people who repeat the folk-tales were not always natural fools. It is only in the Egyptian Wisdom that the key is to be found.

One of the most universal of the Folk-Tales which are the débris of Mythology is that of the Giant who had no heart (or spark of soul) in his body. The Apap-Dragon, in Africa, was the first of all the Giants who has no heart in his body, no root in reality, being as he is only the representation of non-existence, drought, darkness, death and negation. To have no heart in the body is an Egyptian expression for lack of understanding and want of nous. As it is said in the Anastasi Papyri of the Slave who is driven with a stick and beaten like the Ass, "He has indeed no heart in his body." It was this lack of Intelligence that made the Giant of the Märchen such a big blundering booby, readily out-witted by clever little Jack, Horus or Petit Yorge, the youthful Solar God; and so easily cajoled by the fair princess or Lunar lady who is held a captive in his dungeon underground. In one of the Tartaro-Legends told in Basque the Hero fights "a body without a soul." When the monster is coming it is said of him "he is about to come, this horrible body without a soul." In another tale the seven-headed serpent, Heren-Suge, bemoans his fate that he hasn't "a spark betwixt his head and tail"; if he had he would burn up Petit Yorge, his lady, his horse, and his terrible dog. In this version the Monster is a serpent, equivalent to the Apap-Reptile or Dragon of drought and darkness, which in the Kamite Mythos has no soul in its body, because it is an image of darkness and negation.

Most of the characters and localities, the scenery and imagery of these Märchen belong to the Egyptian Mythos. The Lake is also African, as the typical great water of those who had never seen the Ocean. It remained the same type with the Egyptians after they did know the Great Green Water of the Mediterranean Sea. In such ways they have preserved their proofs of the Inner African beginnings with an adamantine unchangeableness. The lake of the Goose or Duck is referred to in the Ritual. (Ch. 109.) The Sun was imaged as a Golden Egg laid by the Duck or Goose. The hill or island standing in the lake is the Earth considered as a Mount of the Double Earth in the Kamite Eschatology. The Snake or Dragon in the Lake, or coiling about the Mount or round the Tree, is the Apap-Reptile in the Water of Darkness who coils about the Hill at Sunset (Rit., ch. 108) or attacks the Tree of Life which is an image of the Dawn, the Great Green Sycamore of Hathor. Earth itself was imaged as a Goose that rested on the Nun or the Waters of Space. This was the ancient Mother Goose that every morning laid her Golden Egg. The Sun sinking down into the underworld is described in the Ritual as "the Egg of the Great Cackler:" "The Egg which Seb hath parted from the earth." (Rit., ch. 54.) The Giant with no heart or Soul is a figure of Darkness as the devouring Monster with no Sun (or Soul) in his body. Hence the heart or Soul that was hidden in the Tree, or in the Egg of the Bird far away. The Sun is the Egg that was laid by the Goose of Earth that brought forth the Golden Egg. This Soul of the Giant, Darkness, was not the personal soul of any human being whatsoever, and the only link of relationship is when the same image of a Soul in the Egg is applied to the Manes in the dark of death. The Soul of the Sun in the Egg is the Soul of Ra in the underworld of Amenta; and when the Sun issues from the Egg (as a Hawk) it is the death of Darkness the Monster.

Our forbears and forerunners were not so far beside themselves as to believe that if they had a Soul at all, it was outside of their own bodies hidden somewhere in a tree, in a bird, in an egg, in a hare, in a duck, a crocodile, or any other zoötype that never was supposed to be the dwelling of the human Soul. In the Basque story of Marlbrook the Monster is slain by being struck on the forehead with an egg that was found in a Pigeon, that was found in a Fox, that was found in a terrible Wolf in a forest. (Webster, p. 83.) However represented, it was the Sun that caused the Monster's death. So in the Norse Tales the Troll or Ogre bursts at sight of dawn, because his death was in the Solar orb that is represented by the Kamite Egg of the Goose. The Giant of darkness is inseparable from the young hero or the solar God who rises from Amenta as his valiant conqueror. These being the two irreconcilable enemies, as they are in the Ritual, it follows that the Princess who finally succeeds in obtaining the Giant's secret concerning the hiding-place of his heart in the egg of a bird is the Lunar Lady in Amenta who, as Hathor, was the Princess by name when she had become the daughter of Ra. She outwits the Apap, who is her swallower at the time of the eclipse, and conveys the secret knowledge to the youthful solar hero who overcomes the Giant by crushing his heart in the egg. In fighting with the Monster, the Basque Hero is endowed with the faculty of transforming into a Hawk! The Hawk says to him, "When you wish to make yourself a Hawk, you will say, 'Jesus Hawk,' and you will be a Hawk." The hawk of Jesus takes the place of the Horus-hawk, just as the name of Malboro is substituted for that of the Hero who is elsewhere Petit Yorge=Little Horus. (Webster, *Basque Legends*, pp. 80-83.) Horus, like the Hero of these tales, is human on earth, and he transforms into the Hawk when he goes to fight the Apap-Monster in Amenta. In the Basque version the human hero transforms into a hawk, or, as it is said, "the young Man made himself a hawk," just as the human Horus changed into the Golden Hawk: and then flew away with the Princess clinging firmly to his neck. And here the Soul that was in the egg is identified as the Hawk itself. At least it is when the egg is broken with the blow struck by the Princess on the Giant's forehead that the Hero makes his transformation into the Hawk. In the mythology it was the bird of earth that laid the egg, but in the eschatology when the egg is hatched it is the Bird of Heaven that rises from it as the Golden Hawk. The Hawk of the Sun is especially the Egyptian Bird of Soul, although the Dove or pigeon also was a type of the Soul that was derived from Hathor. In the Märchen the Duck takes the place of the Goose. But these are co-types in the Mythos.

In the Egyptian, Horus pierces the Apap-Dragon in the eye and pins his head to the earth with a lance. The mythical mode of representation went on developing in Egypt, keeping touch with the advancing arts. The weapon of the Basque Hero was earlier than the lance or spear of Horus; it is a stake of wood made red-hot. With this he pierces the huge monster in the eye and burns him blind. The Greek version of this is too well known to call for repetition here, and the Basque lies nearer to the original Egyptian. It is more important to identify the eye and the blazing snake. Horus, the young solar God, is slayer of the Apap by piercing him in the eye. The Apap is the Giant, the Dragon, the serpent of darkness, and the eye of Apap was thought of as the eye of a serpent that was huge enough to coil round the mountain of the world, or about the Tree of life and light which had its rootage in the nether earth. This, on the horizon, was the Tree of dawn. The stake is a reduced form of the tree that was figured in the green of dawn. The typical tree was a weapon of the ancient Horus who is described as fighting Sut with a branch of palm, which also is a reduced form of the tree. The tree of dawn upon the horizon was the weapon of the solar god with which he pierced the dragon of darkness and freed the mountain of earth and the Princess in Amenta from its throttling, crushing, reptilinear coils. This tree, conventionalised in the stake made red-hot in the furnace, formed the primitive weapon with which Horus or Ulysses or the Tartaro put out the Monster's eye, and pierced the serpent's head to let forth the waters of light once more and to free the lady from her prison in the lower world. When the Apap-Monster in the cave of darkness was personified in something like the human shape, the Giant as reptile in the earliest representation passed into the Giant as a Monster in the form of a magnified man called the Cyclops and named Polyphemus. In one of the African Folk-tales the little Hero Kalulu slays the monster by thrusting a huge red-hot boulder down the devourer's throat. This is a type of the red-hot solar orb which the Power of darkness tried to swallow, and thus put out the light.

The lunar lady, as well as the solar hero, is the dragon-slayer in the Basque legends. In one of these the loathly reptile lies sleeping with his head in the lap of the beautiful lady. The hero descends to her assistance in the Underworld. She tells him to "be off." "The Monster" has only three-quarters of an hour to sleep, she says, "and if he wakes it is all over with you and me." It is the Lunar Lady who worms the great secret out of the Monster concerning his death, when he confesses where his heart lies hidden. "At last, at last," he tells her, "you must kill a terrible wolf which is in the forest, and inside of him is a fox, and in the fox is a pigeon; this pigeon has an egg in its head, and whoever should strike me on the forehead with this egg would kill me." The Hero, having become a hawk, secures the egg and brings it to the "young lady," and having done his part hands over the egg and says to her, "At present it is your turn; act alone." Thus it appears that the egg made use of by the Prince to kill the Giant is the Sun, and that made use of by the Princess was the Lunar orb. Here we have "the egg of the sun and the moon" which Ptah is said to have moved in the Beginning. "She strikes the Monster as he had told her, and he falls stark dead." (Webster, "Malbrouk.") The Dragon was known in Britain as the typical cause of drought and the devourer of nine maidens who had gone to fetch water from the spring before he was slain by Martin. These are representative of nine New Moons renewed at the source of light in the Nether World. Dr. Plott, in his History of Cambridgeshire (p. 349), mentions the custom at Burford of making a dragon annually and "carrying it up and down the town in great jollity, on Midsummer Eve," to which he says, not knowing for what reason, "they added a Giant." (Brand, "Midsummer Eve.") Both the Dragon and Giant signified the same Monster that swallowed the water and devoured the givers of light, lunar or solar, the dragon being a zoömorphic type and the Giant hugely anthropomorphic. Instead of saying nine Moons passed into the dark, as a mode of reckoning the months, it might be said, and was said, that Nine Maidens were devoured by the Dragon of darkness. The Myth originated when Darkness was the devouring Giant and the weapon of the warrior was a stone that imaged the Solar orb. In the contest of the young and ruddy hero David with the Giant Goliath the Hebrew Version of the Folk-tale still retains the primitive feature of the stone.

We know the universal Mother as the Evil reptile of the Dark, for ever warring with the Light, that also drinks the water which is the life of vegetation, as the fiery Dragon of Drought. But there is a very primitive version extant amongst the Australian aborigines, the Andaman Islanders, and the red men, in which a gigantic Frog drinks up all the waters in the world. Here the Frog plays the part of the Apap-monster that swallows the waters at sundown and is pierced and cut in pieces coil by coil to set them flowing freely at the return of day, either by the Hawk of Ra or the Cat or by Horus, the anthropomorphic hero. In the Andaman version of the conflict between the bird of Light and the Devil of Darkness the waters are drunk up and withheld by a big Toad. An Iroquois or Huron form of this mythical representation also shows the devouring monster as a gigantic Frog that drank up all the water of the world. The Aborigines of Lake Tyers likewise relate that once on a time there was no water anywhere on the surface of the whole earth. This had all been drunk up and was concealed in the body of a monstrous Frog. The Dragon of the waters is also a denizen of the Holy well in Britain; and here again the evil power of drought and darkness is represented by the Devil in the form of a Frog as presiding spirit of the water. In the well on the Devil's Causeway between Ruckley and Acton there is supposed to be a huge Frog which represents the devil, that is, the hostile power of drought. The proper time for the malevolent Frog to be seen would be when the Well was dried up in times of great drought, hence he is but seldom seen in a rainy climate like ours. (Burne, *Shropshire Folklore*, p. 428.) The Frog still suffers even in this "enlightened land" of ours for supplying a zoötype of the Evil Power. It is yet a provincial sport for country louts to "hike the Toad," that is by jerking it high in the air from the end of a plank as a mode of appealing to Heaven for rain and the kind of weather wanted. Even so, poor Froggy has to walk the plank and suffer in the present for having been a representative in the past of the Monster that drank up all the water. The Orinoco Indians used to keep Toads in vessels, not to worship them, but to have them at hand as representatives of the Power that drank up the Water or kept back the rain; and in time of drought the Toads were beaten to procure the much-desired rain. (Bastian.)

In various countries the Monster of the Dark was represented by an animal entirely black. This in Egypt was the black Boar of Sut. And what these customs signified according to the Wisdom of Egypt they mean elsewhere. When the Timorese are direfully suffering from lack of rain, they offer up a black Pig as a sacrifice. The Black Pig was slain just as Apap was pierced because it imaged the dark power that once withheld the waters of day and now denies the rain, or the Water of Life. In Sumatra it is the Black Cat that typifies the inimical Power which withholds the rain. Women go naked or nearly so to the river, and wade in it as a primitive mode of sacrifice or solicitation. Then a black Cat is thrown into the Water and forced to swim for its life, like the Witch in the European custom.

The Black Goat, the Black Pig, and the Black Cat are all Typhonian types of the same symbolic value as the Black Boar of Sut or the Apap-Dragon. In each case the representative of the dark and evil Power was slain or thrown into the water as a propitiation to the beneficent Power that gave the rain. Slaying the type of Drought was a means of fighting against the Power of evil and making an appeal to the Good Spirit. It was a primitive mode of Casting out Satan, the Adversary, in practical Sign-Language.

The giant or ogre of mythology was a result of humanising the animal types. At first the Apap-reptile rose up vast, gigantic, as the swallowing darkness or devouring dragon. This, when humanised, became the giant, the magnified non-natural ogre of a man that takes the monster's place in later legendary lore. The Apap-dragon coiled about the mount was the keeper of the treasures in the netherworld. So is it with the giant. In "Jack the Giant-killer" it is said "the mount of Cornwall was kept by a huge giant named Cormoran." Jack, our little solar hero, asked what reward would be given to the man who killed Cormoran. "The giant's treasure," they told him, would be the reward. Quoth Jack, "Then let me undertake it." After he had slain the giant, Jack went to search the cave, which answers to the Amenta in the lower earth, in which the treasure was concealed. This was the treasure of light and water that had been hidden by the giant in his lair.

The Aryan fairy-tales and folk-tales can be unriddled in the Kamite Mythos which was based on the phenomena of external nature. It is the Moon, for instance, who was a woman one half the time and a frog or serpent during the other half. In the first character she was Sati, the lady of light. In the second half of the lunation she was the frog that swam the waters of the nether earth and made her transformation as Hekat in Amenta. Some writers have denounced the savage brutality and obscenity of those whom they look upon as the makers of mythology. But in all this they have been spitting beside the mark. Moreover, the most repulsive aspects do not belong to mythology proper, but are mainly owing to the decadence and degradation of the matter in the Märchen. Also to the change which the mythos suffered in passing from the zoömorphic mode of representation. There is neither morality nor immorality so long as the phenomena are non-human and the drama is performed by the primitive actors. But when the characters are humanised or divinised in human form the re-cast may be fatal to the mythical meaning; primitive simplicity is apparently converted into senseless absurdity, and the drama of the nature-powers turned into a masquerade of monsters. Plutarch will furnish us with an illustration which these *idiotai* might have selected for an example. When speaking of the elder Horus who "came into the world before his time" as the phantom-forerunner of the true light, he says that Osiris had accompanied with Isis (his spouse) after her decease. Which looks very ominous for the morals of the "myth-makers" who could ascribe such immorality to their Gods. Is it not a fair deduction from a *datum* like that to infer that the Egyptians were accustomed to cohabit with the corpses of their dead women? Obviously that is one of the possible implications. Especially as Osiris, according to Spencer, was once a man!

But now for an explanation on the plain ground of natural fact. Isis, in one character, was the Mother-Moon, the reproducer of the light in Amenta; the place of conjunction and of re-begettal by the Sun-god, when Osiris entered the Moon, and she became the Woman who was clothed with the Sun. At the end of a lunation the old Moon died and became a corpse—it is at times portrayed as a mummy—in the underworld, and there it was revivified by Osiris, the solar fecundator of the Moon who was the Mother that brought forth the child of light, the "Cripple-deity" that was naturally enough begotten in the dark. (Plutarch.) But worse still. When Osiris lay helpless and breathless in Amenta with a "Corpse-like face" (Rit., ch. lxxiv) his two wives who are likewise his daughters came to cohabit with him, and raise him from the dead, or re-erect him like, and as, the Tat. It is said of Isis she "raised the remains of the God of the resting heart and extracted his seed to beget an heir," or to make him human by reincarnation in the flesh. (*Hymn to Osiris*, *Records*, line 16, p. 102, vol. iv, first series; vol. iv, p. 21, second series.) In this phase it is the female who cohabits with the Corpse of the dead Male. But in neither were the actors of the drama human, although they are humanised in the Märchen. The Mythos is repeated and applied in a Semitic Folk-Tale when Lot's two Daughters are "with Child by their Father." (Gen. xix. 36.) The difference being that Osiris as Father in the Mysteries of Amenta was dead at the time, whereas in the irresponsible Märchen Lot is represented as dead-drunk.

The Myths are not to be explained by means of the Märchen; not if you collect and compare the Nursery-Tales of all the world. But we can explain the Märchen more or less by aid of the Myths, or rather the mythical representations in which we can once more recover the lost key. The Aryan Folk-Tales, for example, are by no means a faithful reflection of the world as it appeared to the primitive mind. They are not a direct reflection of anything; they are refracted mythology, and the representation in mythology is not direct, not literal, but mystical. Egyptian mythology, and all it signifies, lies between the Aryan or other folk-tales and Primitive Man. The Märchen are not the oldest or most primitive form of the Myth; they are the latest. The coinage is the same, but the primitive impress is greatly worn down, and the features are often well-nigh effaced. In the Märchen, the Ancient Wise Woman or old Mother goes on telling her tales, but the memory of their meaning has lapsed by reason of her age. Whereas in the Ritual the representation is still preserved and repeated accurately according to knowledge. The Mythos passes into the Folk-Tale, not the Folk-Tale into the Mythos.

In Egyptian Sign-Language, the earliest language of Mythology, the Sun was represented, in the fulness of its power, by the Lion. When it went down to the Underworld by night or in the winter time it was imaged as the disappearing Mouse. Ra was the Lion: Horus was the Mouse: the blind Shrew-Mouse being a type of Horus darkling in Amenta. Ra as the Solar Lion lost his power in the Underworld and was as the animal in the hunter's toils. Then Horus the Little Hero as the Shrew-Mouse came to deliver the entangled Lion. Under the type of the Mongoose or Ichneumon the little hero attacked the serpent of Darkness: and, as the Mouse, it was the deliverer of the Lion in the Mythos. But when or where the wisdom was no longer taught in the mysteries the Gnosis naturally lapsed. The Myth became a Folk-Tale or a legend of the nursery, and passed into the fable of the mouse that nibbled the cord in two which bound the captured Lion and set the mighty beast at liberty. Thus the Mythos passed into the Märchen, and the Mysteries still clung on for very life in the Moralities.

The Ass in a male form is a type of Tum the Sun-God in Amenta. A vignette to the Ritual shows the Ass being devoured by the serpent of darkness called the eater of the Ass. (Ch. 40.) The Ass then in the Egyptian Mythos represents the Sun-God Tum, Greek Tomos, passing through the nether-world by night. It is Tum in his character of Aiu or Iu who is also represented on the tomb of Rameses the Sixth as a god with the ears of an Ass, hauling at the rope by which the Sun is drawn up from Amenta, the lower Egypt of the mythos. Atum, or Tum, is the Old Man of the setting Sun and Aiu is his Son. Thus the three characters of the Old Man, his Son, and the Ass can be identified with Atum-Aiu=Osiris and Horus; and the nocturnal Sun or the Sun of Winter with the slow motion which constitutes the difficulty of getting the Ass forward in the fable. This difficulty of getting the Ass along, whether ridden by Tum the father or pulled along by his Son, was illustrated in a popular pastime, when on the eighth day of the festival of the Corpus Domini the people of Empoli suspended the ass aloft in the air and made it fly perforce in presence of the mocking multitude. Gubernatis says the Germans of Westphalia "made the Ass a symbol of the dull St. Thomas, and were accustomed to call it by the name of 'the Ass Thomas,' the laggard boy who came the last to school upon St. Thomas's Day." (*Zoological Mythology*, vol. i, p. 362.) But we find an earlier claimant than this for the "Ass Thomas" in Tum, or Tomos, the Kamite Solar God, who made the passage of Amenta very slowly with the Ass, or as it was represented, riding on the Ass; and therefore for the Greek Fable of the old Man and his Ass.

The birth of a Folk-Tale may be seen in the legend of "The Sleeping Beauty." When it was known that the renewing Moon derived her glory from the procreative Sun, their meeting in the Underworld became a fertile source of legends that were mothered by the Myth. The Moon-Goddess is the lovely lady sleeping in Amenta waiting for her deliverer, the Young Solar God, to come and wake her with the Lover's kiss. She was Hathor, called the Princess in her Lunar character; and he was the all-conquering Horus. It was a legend of the resurrection which at first was Soli-Lunar in the Mythos; afterwards a symbolic representation of the Soul that was awakened from the Sleep of death by Horus in his rôle of Saviour or Deliverer of the Manes in Amenta. So the Mythos faded in the fairy-tale.

It is a cardinal tenet of the present work that the Aryan Märchen and European folk-lore were derived from the Egyptian Mythology. This might be illustrated without end. For example, there is a classical tradition or Folk-Tale, repeated by Pliny (*Hist. Nat.*, 7, 3), which tells of a time when a Mother in Egypt bore seven children at one birth. Of course this legend had no origin in natural history. Such a birth belongs to mythology in which the Mother of seven children at a birth was primarily the bringer-forth of seven elemental powers, who can be traced as such, in all their seven characters. The One Great Mother with her seven sons constituted a primary Ogdoad. She survived in a Gnostic form as Achamoth-Ogdoas, Mother of the seven Rulers of the heptanomis. "This Mother," says Irenæus (B. I, ch. v. 2, 3), "they call Ogdoas, Sophia, Earth, Jerusalem." Jerusalem is identified by Jeremiah with the ancient Mother who was the bringer-forth of seven sons as the "Mother of the young men," "she that hath borne Seven," who now giveth up the Ghost. (Ch. xv. 8.) This Mother of seven also appears as the Great Harlot in the Book of Revelation who is the Mother of the Seven Kings which were at the same time seven heads of the Solar Dragon, and also seven Consorts who were born children of the Old Great Mother. There were "the Seven Children of the Thigh" in the Astronomical Mythology. Thus the Ancient Genetrix was the Mother who brought forth Seven Children at a birth, or as a companionship, according to the category of phenomena. Her seven children were the Nature-Powers of all mythology. They are variously represented under divers types because the powers were re-born in different phenomena. We shall find them grouped as seven serpents, seven apes, seven jackals, seven crocodiles, hippopotami, hawks, bulls or rams, who become Seven children of the Mother when the myth is rendered anthropomorphically in the later forms of the Märchen, amongst which there is a Bengalee folk-tale of a Boy who was suckled by seven Mothers. (Lal Behari Day, *Folk-Tales of Bengal*.) And this boy of the Märchen can be identified with child-Horus in the Astronomical Mythos, as "the Bull of the seven cows." The seven cows were grouped in the Great Bear as a seven-fold figure of Motherhood. The cows were also called the seven Hathors who presided over the birth of the child as seven Fates in the Egyptian theology. And in later legends these are the seven Mothers of one child. When he became a child they were the seven women who ministered to him of their substance in a very literal manner. The seven givers of liquid life to the nursling were portrayed as women in Amenta: the seven Hathors who were present as Fates, at child-birth; and as cows in the constellation of the Great Bear. The sucklers might be imaged as seven women, seven cows, seven sows. Thus the Romans had evidently heard of them as a sevenfold form of Rerit the sow, a co-type with the Cow. The Bengalee Folk-tale shows the Egyptian Mythos reduced to the stage of the Aryan Märchen. The typical seven Mothers of the child also survive amongst the other curiosities of Christianity. It is said in the Gospel of the Nativity (ch. viii) that Mary "the virgin of the Lord" had been brought up with seven other virgins in the Temple. Also there are seven women in the Gospels who minister to Jesus of their substance. Again we are able to affiliate the folk-tale with the original Mythos. After which it is of little importance to our inquiry which country the Aryan Märchen came from last. The Seven Hathors or Cows in the Mythos are also the Seven Fates in attendance at the birth of a Child; and in the Babar Archipelago Seven

Women, each of them carrying a sword, are present when a child is born, who mix the placenta with ashes and put it into a small basket, which they hang up in a particular kind of tree. These likewise are a form of the Seven Hathors who were present at Child-birth as the Seven Fates in the Mythos. In such ways the Kamite Mythos passed into the Aryan Märchen.

The Child who had no father had been mythically represented as the Fertiliser of the mother when *in utero*, like Ptah, the God in embryo. Hence he was called the Bull of his Mother. But why the Bull? Because this was not the human Child. It was Horus as the calf, born of the Cow and a pre-human type when the fatherhood was not yet individualised. The Solar God at Sunset made his entrance into the breeding-place of the nether world, and is said to prepare his own generation for rebirth next day, but not in human guise. The bull of his Mother is shown upon the horizon as Horus the calf. But when the persons and transactions are presented anthropomorphically, in accordance with the human terminology the calf which had no Father but was his own bull becomes the child who was born without a father. Thus the Mythos passes into the Märchen or legendary lore, and the child who fecundated his own Mother takes a final form as the Boy-lover of Venus, Ishtar, or Hathor, the divine Mother, and the subject culminated in literature, as (for example) in Shakespeare's poem of "Venus and Adonis," which is at root mythology fleshed in a human form. Again and again the Egyptian Mythos furnishes a prototype that will suffice to account for a hundred Folk-tales. For another instance, take the legend of the Child that was predestined to be a King in spite of the Monster pursuing the Mother, or lying in wait to devour and destroy the infant from before its birth. Har-Ur, or Horus the Elder, was that Child in the mythos. The title of Repa will identify the Child born to be King as that signifies the Heir-apparent, or the Prince who was predestined to become the King. An instructive example of the way in which the Mythos, that we look on as Egyptian, was dispersed and spread in Folk-Tales over the world may be seen in the legend of the combat betwixt a Father and Son. The story has attained to somewhat of an Epical dignity in Matthew Arnold's poem of "Sohrab and Rustum." It is also found in many parts of the world, including New Zealand. Briefly summarised, the story, in legendary lore, is that of the Son who does not know his own Father. In the Maori tale of "Kokako" the boy is called a Bastard. Also in the tale of Peho the child is a Bastard. This is a phrase in later language to describe the boy whose birth was Matriarchal when the Father was unknown individually. But such a legend as this, when found in Folk-Lore, does not come straight out of local Sociology or Ethnology in any country. We have to reckon with the rendering of the natural fact in the Astronomical Mythology of Egypt. In the olden day of indefinite paternity, when the Father was personally unknown it was likewise unknown that the child of light born and reborn in the Moon was the Son of the Solar God. This was a Mythical Son who could not know his own Father. The earliest Son in sociology or mythology did not know his own Father. The elder Horus was the Mother's child, who was born but not begotten. Now, a child whose father is unknown is called a Bastard. Thus Horus was a Bastard born, and it was flung at him by Sut that he was a Bastard. Also in Jewish legend Jesus is called the Mamzer or Bastard. Thus, the child of the Mother only was the Bastard, just as the Mother who was "na wife" came to be called the Harlot. The present writer has no knowledge of a Folk-Tale version of the legend being extant in Egyptian. This does not belong to the kind of literature that was preserved in the sanctity of the coffins and tombs, as was the Book of the Dead. But the essentials are extant, together with the explanation in natural fact, in the ancient Luni-Solar-Mythos. Horus the Bastard was the child of light that was born of Isis in the Moon, when the Moon was the Mother of the child and the Father-source of light was unidentified. But sooner or later there was a secret knowledge on the subject. For instance, in the story told by Plutarch it is said that Taht the Moon-God cleared the character of the Mother by showing that Horus was not a Bastard, but that Ra, the Solar God, was his true Father. It is still continued to be told in various Folk-Tales that the woman was no better than a wanton in her wooing of the man whom she seeks or solicits as her paramour. This character may be traced in the mythology. It is the Lady of Light in the Moon who pursues and seduces the Solar God in the darkness of Amenta, and who exults that she has seized upon the God Hu and taken possession of him in the vale of Abydos where she went to lie down and sought to be replenished with his light. (Ritual, ch. lxxx.) Child-Horus always remains a child, the child of twelve years, who at that age transforms into the Adult and finds his Father. So when he is twelve years of age, the boy Jokull in an Icelandic version of the Folk-Tale goes in search of his Father. They fight and the Son is slain, at least he dies after living for *three nights*. In other versions the fight betwixt Father and Son is continued for three days. This is the length of time for the struggle of Osiris in death and darkness who rises again as Lord of light in the Moon and now is recognised as the Father of Horus who was previously the Mother's child that knew not his Father. Moreover, in the Märchen it is sometimes the Father who is killed in the combat, at other times it is the Son. And, in the Mythos, Osiris the Father rises again upon the third day in the Moon, but at other times he rises as Horus the triumphant Son. A legend like this of the combat between Father and Son does not originate in history, much less does it rise from a hundred different Ethnological sources, as the folk-lorists would have us think. In the Folk-Tales there are various versions of the same subject; the Mythos is one, and in that oneness must the origin be sought for the Märchen. This origin of our Folk-Lore may be found a hundred times over in the "Wisdom" of old Egypt. The Tale of the Two Brothers furnishes a good example of the Egyptian Mythos reappearing in the Folk-Tale. In this there are two brothers named Anup, the elder, and Bata, the younger. Anup has a wife who falls in love with Bata and solicits him illicitly. "And she spoke to him saying, What strength there is in thee, indeed, I observe thy vigour every day." Her heart knew him. She seized upon him and said to him, "Come, let us lie down for a while. Better for thee. . . beautiful clothes." Like Joseph in the Hebrew version, the youth rejected the advances of the lady. He "became like a panther" in his fury at her suggestion. Like Potiphar's wife, she charges him with violating and doing violence to her. We shall have to return to the story. Let it suffice for the present to say that the "tale of the two brothers" in the Märchen is derived in the course of a long descent from the myth of Sut and Horus, the Brothers who were represented later as Anup and Horus, also as the Horus of both Horizons. The elder brother Anup corresponds to Sut, who in one form is Anup; the younger, Bata, to the Sungod Horus of the East. The name of Bata signifies the Soul (ba) of life in the earth (ta) as a title of the Sun that rises again. On this account it is said that Bata goes to "the Mountain of the Cedar," in the flower of which upon the summit lies his heart, or soul, or virile force; the power of his resurrection as the Solar God. Hence Bata says to Anup, "Behold, I am about to become a Bull." And he was raised by Ra to the dignity of hereditary Prince as ruler of the whole land, over which he reigned for thirty years. As myth, such Märchen are interpretable wheresoever they are found. The Solar Power on the two horizons or the Sun with a dual face was represented by Two Brothers who are twins, under whichever name or type, who were earlier than Ra. One is the lesser, darkling and infertile Sun of Night, or of Autumn; the other is the Victor in the Resurrection. These were associated in Amenta with the Moon, the Lady of the lunar light, who is described with them in chapter lxxx of the Ritual as uniting herself with the two Brother-Gods who were Sut and Horus. She is wedded to the one but is in love with the other. Whether as Sut or Elder Horus, her Consort was her impubescent child; and she unites with Hu the Virile Solar God and glories in his fertilising power. She confesses that she has seized upon Hu and taken possession of him in the vale of Abydos when she sank down to rest. Her object being to engender light from his potent Solar source, to illuminate the night, and overthrow the devouring Monster of the dark. This is true mythos which is followed afar off by the folk-lore of the Tale. There was no need to moralise, as this was Egyptian mythology, not Semitic history.

When the Aryan philologists have done their worst with the subject and the obscuration has passed away, it will be seen that the Legend of Daphne was a transformation that originated in the Egyptian Mythos. Ages before the legend could have been poetised in Greece, Daphne was extant as an Egyptian Goddess Tafne or Tefnut by name, who was a figure of the Green Egyptian Dawn. (Birch, *Dictionary of Hieroglyphics*.) The Green Tree was also a type of the Dawn in Egypt. The transformation of the Goddess into the Tree is a bit of Greek fancy-work which was substituted for the Kamite Gnosis of the Myth. Max Müller asked how the "total change of a human being or a heroine into a Tree" is to be explained. Whereas Daphne never was a human being any more than Hathor, in her Green Sycamore, or Tefnut in the Emerald Sky of the Egyptian Dawn. The roots of these things lie far beyond the Anthropomorphic representation, and in a region where the plummet of the Aryanists has never sounded. As the Egyptians apprehended, the foremost characteristic of the Dawn was its dewy moisture and refreshing coolness, not its consuming fire. The tree of dewy coolness, the Sycamore of Hathor, or of Tefnut, was the evergreen of Dawn, and the evergreen as fuel may be full of fire, like the Ash or the Laurel into which Apollo turned the young divinity who was Daphne in Greece and Tafne in Egypt. And if Apollo be the youthful Sun-God, like Horus, on the horizon, who climbs the Tree of Dawn, the dews would be dried by him; otherwise the Tree of Moisture would be transformed into a tree of fire, and assume the burning nature of the Laurel, as in the Greek story. It was the Sun that kindled the fire, and as the Sun climbed up the Tree the Dews of Tefnut dried. It was not the Dawn *quâ* Dawn that was changed into a Laurel, but the cool Green Tree of Dew = Tafne = Daphne, or the Dawn that was dried and turned into the Tree of blazing lustre by the Solar fire, or the Sun, *i.e.*, by Horus or Apollo when personified. The Water of Heaven and the Tree of Dawn precede personification, and the name of Tefnut, from Tef (to drip, spit, exude, shed, effuse, supply), and Nu, for Heaven, shows that Tefnut represented the dew that fell from the Tree of Dawn. She is the giver of the dew; hence the water of dawn is said to be the water of Tefnut. Tefnu gives the moisture from the Tree of Dawn in heavenly dew, but in another character she is fierce as fire, and is portrayed in the figure of a lioness. The truth is, there was Egyptian science enough extant to know that the dew of Dawn was turned into the vapour that was formed into the Green Tree on the horizon by the rising Sun of Morning, and the Kamite Mythos which represented the natural fact was afterwards converted into a Greek fancy, as in numerous other instances.

When once they are identified the myths must be studied in their Egyptian dress. It is my work to point the way, not to elucidate all the Semitic and Aryan embellisments or distortions. But we may depend upon it that any attempt to explain or discuss the Asiatic, American, Australian, and European mythologies with that of Egpyt omitted is the merest writing on the sand which the next wave will obliterate.

Max Müller asked how it was that our Ancestors, who were not idiots, although he has done his utmost to make them appear idiotic in the matter of mythology, came to tell the story of a King who was married to a Frog? His explanation is that it arose, as usual, from a misapplication of names. The Frog was a name given to the Sun, and the name of the frog, Bekha, or Bekhi, was afterwards confused with or mistaken for the name of a Maiden whom the King might have married. In reply to this absurd theory of the mythical origins another writer says it was the nature of savages to make such mistakes, not merely in names but in things; in confusing natural phenomena and in confounding frog-nature with human nature: this confounding confusion being the original staple of "savage Myth." It would be difficult to tell which version is farthest from the actual fact.

Whoever begins with the mythos as a product of the "savage" mind as savages are known to-day is fatally in error. Neither will it avail to begin with idiots who called each other nick-names in Sanskrit. Let us make another test-case of Bekhi the Frog. The Sanskritist does not start fair. He has not learned the language of animals. The mythical representation had travelled a long way before any human king could have got mixed up with a Frog for his wife. We must go back to the Proto-Aryan beginnings, which are Egyptian or Kamite. In Africa we find these things next to Nature where we can get no further back in search of origins. Egypt alone goes back far enough to touch Nature in these beginnings, and, as so often to be said in the present work, Egypt alone has faithfully and intelligently kept the record.

The Frog was a Lunar type on account of its metamorphosis from the Tadpole-condition in the water to the four-legged life on land which type was afterwards applied to the Moon in its coming forth from the waters of the Nun. The name of the Frog in Egyptian is Ka, whence the Lunar Lady, who was represented as a Frog, is designated Mistress Heka or Hekat, who was a consort of the Solar God Khnum-Ra. An inscription in the British Museum tells us that under one of his titles Khnum was called "the King of Frogs." There is no proof, perhaps, of his being a Frog himself, but his son, Ptah, had a Frog-headed form, and his consort, Hekat, is the Froggess. This, then, is the very King by name who was wedded to a Frog, but not as a human being. Such a tale was only told when the Gnosis was no longer truly taught and the ancient myth had been modernised in the Märchen. In the Kamite mythos Khnum has three Consorts, the Goddesses Hekat, Sati, and Ank. We might call them one Wife and two Consorts. The wife is Ank, whose name signifies the Mirror. She personates the Moon as reflector of the Sun. Hekat and Sati are representatives of the dual lunation; Hekat is the Frog of Darkness, and Sati the Lady of Light. As the Frog, Hekat sloughs her frog-skin and reveals her wondrous beauty in the form of Sati, the Woman in glory. These three are the Consorts of Khnum-Ra, who is (1) in Amenta with Hekat, (2) in Heaven with Sati, and (3) in the Moon herself, as the Generator of Light with Ank, or in the Mirror. Khnum-Ra is the nocturnal Sun, and Hekat, his Consort, is a representative of the Moon that transforms in the lower hemisphere, as the tadpole transforms and emerges from the waters in the form of a frog. Khnum, God of the Nocturnal Sun, is King of Frogs in Amenta, the hidden underworld, and it is there that Hekat is his Consort as the Froggess. In the upper Heaven she is the lovely goddess with the arrow of light that was shot from the lunar bow with which her name of Sati (Coptic, Sate) is hieroglyphically written. And every time she re-enters the water of the nether world she transforms into a Frog according to the mythical mode of representing the Moon in Amenta. Thus we can identify the "Sun-Frog" of the Aryan Märchen in the Frog-headed solar God (Ptah) or in Khnum, "the king of frogs," both of whom were solar deities. We can also identify the Frog-maiden in "Mistress Heka," or Hekat, the goddess with a Frog's head, who is one of Khnum's Consorts, the Cinderella (so to say) of the three sisters, who are Ank, Sati, and Hekat, the three goddesses of the myth who survive as the well-known three Sisters of the Märchen. The "Sun-frog" then was Khnum, "the King of Frogs," as the Sun in the night of the underworld, who was wedded to Hekat, the lunar frog in the mythos which supplied the matter for the Märchen.

It is only in this nether world that Sun and Moon can ever meet, and that but once a month, when the Lady of Light transforms into the Frog, or Hekat, which Frog re-transforms into Sati, the Lady of Light, when she emerges from the abyss. The King was not to be seen by his Mistress without the royal garments on, and these were laid aside when the Sun-God entered the nether earth. If the lady dared to look upon her lover in the night she would find him in the shape of the Beast, as in "Beauty and the Beast," which was prohibited; and if the lover looked upon the Maiden under certain conditions she would transfigure into a Frog or other amphibious creature, and permanently retain that shape, as the story was told when the myth was moralised in the Märchen; the exact antithesis of the Frog that transformed into a beautiful Princess, the transformation of Bekhi, and possibly (or certainly) of Phryne, the Frog, whose sumptuous beauty was victoriously unveiled when she was derobed before her vanquished judges. In the different phases of the mythos the young Sun-god might have been met by night as a Crocodile, a Beetle, a Frog, an Eel, or a Bear, for the Bear was also a zoötype of Horus. In one of his battles with Sut he fought in the form of a Bear. It was a law of primitive Tapu that the bride or wife was not to be seen by the lover or husband in a state of nudity. In the story of Melusine the bride is not to be looked on when she is naked. She tells her lover that she will only abide with him so long as he observes this custom of women. This also was the law in the mythical land of Naz, and one man who did look on his wife unveiled was transformed into a monster. Now the veil of the bride is one with that of the virgin Isis, which originated in the loin-cloth or leaf-belt that was demanded by the "custom of women" when the female first became pubescent.

In Egypt, the dog-headed Ape Aani was a zoötype of the moon in her period of eclipse and change, as explained by Hor-Apollo (B. I, 14). The menstruating Ape was a representative of the Sloughing Moon, that is of the veiled bride, the female who was on no account to be looked on in her nudity. The Sun and Moon could not meet below except when the goddess or mistress did vanish from the light of mortals in the world above. The lunar lady in her poor and lonely state goes underground or enters the waters to make her transformation and is invisible during three nights (and days), which correspond to the three days' festival at which Cinderella lost her slipper (the last relic of the magical skin), and won the heart of the fairy prince. The meeting of the sun and moon in Amenta was monthly: once every twenty-eight days, as it was reckoned in the Calendar which, for mystical reasons, counted 13 new moons to the year; and it is these mystical reasons which alone can penetrate to the natural origin of Tapu concerning the custom of women. It was the menses = the mensis; the female period = the lunar. The wife, as we have seen, was not to be looked upon during her monthly period when she was in retirement, like the moon once a month. It was on the sixth day of the New Moon that Osiris re-entered the orb and paid his first visit to the Lady of Light. The Australian deity Pundjel is said to have a Wife whose face he never looks upon. (Smyth, vol. I, 423.) When that representation was first made Amenta was not known as the monthly meeting-place for Moon and Sun by night. It had only been observed that they did not meet by day. Isis, veiled in black, goes down to the nether-world in search of lost Osiris. It was only there they ever met, He as the Bull of Eternity, She as the Cow, a later type than the Frog of Hekat.

This drama of the primitive mysteries, this mythical mode of representing natural fact, is at times more appealing in its touching simplicity than anything to be found amongst the best things that have been "said" in literature. The custom of women which was to be religiously respected being identified, it is easy to see that this led to other customs of Tabu, which were founded and practised as modes of memorising the law intended to be taught and fulfilled.

The mystical Bride who was not to be seen naked was personated by the Wife who wore the bridal veil, or the Wife whose face was never to be seen by her husband until she had borne him a child: or who is only to be visited under cover of the night. For, like the Sun and the Moon, they dwell in separate huts and only meet occasionally and then by stealth, according to the restrictions of Tabu. Hence marriages were made on condition that the woman was not to be seen naked by her husband. When Ivan has burned the frog-skin of the beautiful Helen in the Russian tale, to prevent her from turning into a frog again, she bids him farewell, and says to him, "Seek me in the 27th earth, in the 30th kingdom." (Afanassieff, Story 23.) We have here a reference to the twenty-seven nights of lunar light, the three nights of the moon out of sight, together with the transformation and re-arising on the third day. But the annual conjunction of Sun and Moon at the vernal equinox is indicated in the Vedic version when Urvasi promises to meet her husband on the last night of the year for the purpose of giving birth to the child which was born monthly of the Moon and annually in the soli-lunar rendering of the Mythos. Urvasi says to Pururavas, "Come to me the last night of the year, and thou shalt be with me for one night, and a Son will be born to thee."

The Egyptians have preserved for us and bequeathed the means of interpreting this typology of the early Sign-language. The primitive consciousness or knowledge which has lapsed or got confused in inner Africa, or Australia, India, or Greece, lived on and left its record in their system of signs. If the Australian savage does attribute the earliest marriage-laws to a Crow, he is but saying the same thing as Hor-Apollo (I, 9), who tells us that when the Egyptians denote marriage they depict two Crows, because the birds cohabit in the human fashion, and their laws of intercourse are strictly monogamic. Nor is the Gnosis of the original representation quite extinct. The "Wisdom of Manihiki" is a Mangaian designation of the Gnosis, or knowledge of mythical representation, the secrets of which were limited to a few priests who were the same in the Hervey Isles that the Her-Seshti were to the Wisdom of Egypt. A race so degraded or undeveloped as the Bushmen have their hidden wisdom, their Magic, with an Esoteric interpretation of their dramatic dances and pantomime, by which they more or less preserve and perpetuate the mystic meaning of their religious mysteries. What we do really find is that the Inner African and other aborigines still continue to talk *and think* their thought in the same figures of speech that are made visible by art, such as is yet extant among the Bushmen; that the Egyptians also preserved the primitive consciousness together with the clue to this most ancient knowledge, with its symbolic methods of communication, and that they converted the living types into the later lithographs and hieroglyphics. Animals that talk in the folk-tales of the Bushmen, or the Indians, or the Märchen of Europe, are still the living originals which became pictographic and ideographic in the zootypology of Egypt, where they represent divinities, i.e., naturepowers at first and deities afterwards; then ideographs, and finally the phonetics of the Egyptian alphabet.

No race of men ever yet imagined that the animals talked in human language as they are made to do in the popular Märchen. No men so "primitive" as to think that anyone was swallowed by a great fish and remained three days and nights in the monster's belly, to be afterwards belched up on dry land alive. They were not human beings of whom such stories were told, and therefore those who *first* made the mythical representations were not capable of believing they were human. Put your living representatives of primitive and aboriginal men to the test. Try them with the miracles of the Old or New Testament, presented to them for matters of fact, as a gauge of credulity. What does Dr. Moffat say of his African aborigines? *"The Gospel appeared too preposterous for the most foolish to believe,"* and *"To speak of the Creation, the Fall, and the Resurrection seemed more fabulous, extravagant, and ludicrous to them than their own vain stories of lions and hyænas."* (*Missionary Labours*, p. 245.) But they knew, more or less, that their own legends were mythical, whereas the Christian was vouching for his mythos being historical, and that they could in no wise accept. A Red Indian known to Hearne as a *perfect bigot with regard to the arts and tricks of the jugglers could yet by no means be impressed with a belief in any part of the Christian religion, or the documents and vouchers for its truth.* (Hearne, *Journey among the Indians*, p. 350.) When Robert Drury told the Malagasy for the first time how God created a man, and made a woman from one of his ribs while he was asleep, they said "it was a plain untruth, and that it was a shame to tell such lies with a serious countenance." They at once proceeded to test the statement by reckoning the ribs of a woman and a man. "They said that to talk of what was done before man was made was silly, and that what I had said of God's talking with men and telling them such things had no proof; and the things I pretended to know and talk of were all old women's stories. When I mentioned the resurrection of the body, they told me 'it must be a lie, and to talk to them of burning in fire after this life was an abominable lie.'" (*Madagascar: Robert Drury's Journal, during Fifteen Years' Captivity on that Island.* And *A Further Description of Madagascar*, by the Abbé Alexis Rochon. Edited, with an Introduction and Notes, by Captain Pasfield Oliver, R. A.)

The aborigines do not mistake the facts of nature as we have mistaken the primitive method of representing them. It is we, not they, who are the most deluded victims of false belief. Christian capacity for believing the impossible in nature is unparalleled in any time past amongst any race of men. Christian readers denounce the primitive realities of the mythical representation as puerile indeed, and yet their own realities alleged to be eternal, from the fall of Adam to the redemption by means of a crucified Jew, are little or nothing more than the shadows of these primitive simplicities of an earlier time. It will yet be seen that the culmination of credulity, the meanest emasculation of mental manhood, the densest obscuration of the inward light of nature, the completest imbecility of shut-eyed belief, the nearest approach to a total and eternal eclipse of common sense have been attained beyond all chance of competition by the victims of the Christian creeds. The genesis of delusive superstitions is late, not early. It is not the direct work of nature herself. Nature was not the mother who began her work of development by nursing her child in all sorts of illusions concerning things in general. She did not place her hands upon his eyes and bid him to interpret the world subjectively. Primitive man was not a metaphysician, but a man of common sense. And if limited as a limpet, he clung hard and fast to the rock of reality as the sole ground he had to go upon. The realities without and around were too pressing for the senses to allow him to play the fool with delusive idealities; the intellectual and sentimental luxuries of later hylo-idealists. Modern ignorance of the mythical mode of representation has led to the ascribing of innumerable false beliefs not only to primitive men and present-day savages, but also to the most learned, enlightened, and highly civilized people of antiquity, the Egyptian; for had these natural impossibilities been believed the Egyptians must have shared the same mental confusion, the same manifest delusion concerning nature, the same incapacity for distinguishing one thing from another, as the Pygmy or the Papuan.

It has been asserted that there was little or no prayer in the lower forms of religion. But this would have to be determined by Sign-language rather than by words. Two hands of a person clasped together are equivalent to a spoken prayer. In the Ritual, the speaker says of the God Osiris, "His Branch is of prayer, by means of which I have made myself like him." (Ch. xxviii.) Teru is the Branch, and the same word signifies to adore, invoke, and pray. It was as a mode of praying that the branches of the bedwen or birch were strewn in the ancient British graves. It is the same language and the same sign when the Australian aborigines approach the camp of strangers with a green bough in their hands as the sign of amity equivalent to a prayer for peace and good-will. Acted Sign-language is a practical mode of praying and asking for what is wanted by portraying instead of saying. A green branch of a symbolic Tree is dipped in water and sprinkled on the earth as a prayer for rain. New Caledonian wizards dig up a skeleton and pour water on the dead bones to denote the great need of a revivifying rain. Amongst the rock-drawings of the Bushmen there is a scene in which it is apparent that a hippopotamus is being dragged across country as a symbolic device for producing rain. Naturally the water-cow is an African zoötype of water. In Egypt she imaged the Great Mother who was invoked as the wateress. Not only are the four naked natives dragging the water-cow overland; two of them also carry the water-plant, probably a lotus, in their hands, as a symbol of the water that is so greatly needed. It was a common mode of primitive appeal for savages to inflict great suffering on the representative victim to compel the necessary response. In this case, as we read the language of signs, they are intending to compel the nature-power to send them water, the female hippopotamus or water-cow being the image of that power. This would be dragged across the land as a palpable mode of forcing the Great Cow of Earth to yield the water, in the language that was acted. The appeal to the Power beyond was also made with the human being as the suffering victim. In Transylvania, girls strip themselves stark naked, and, led by an elder woman who is likewise naked, they steal a harrow and carry it across a field to the nearest brook; then they set it afloat and sit on the harrow for an hour in making their appeal. The Pawnee Victim (or the Khond Meriah) made appeal to the cruel Powers as the intercessor and suppliant on behalf of the people by her wounds, her tears and groans, her terrible tortures purposely prolonged in slowly dying, her torn tormented flesh agape with ruddy wounds, as in the later Mysteries where the Victim was held to be divine. Pathetic appeal was made to the Nature-Power or Elemental Spirit, chiefly the Goddess of Earth as food-giver, by means of the suffering, the moans, the tears, the prayers of the Victims. This was employed as a Moving-Power, often cruel enough to search the heavens for the likeness of a pitying human heart. The ears of dogs were pinched by the Mexican women during an eclipse to make them howl to the Power of Light. Meal-dust is thrown into the eyes of the Sacred Turtle by the Zunis to make it weep. The Australian Diererie solicit the Good Spirit for rain by bleeding two of their Mediums or divinely-inspired men, supposed to be persons of influence with the Moora-Moora or Good Spirits, who will take heed of their sufferings and send down rain. The scene described by Gason (*The Native Tribes of South Australia*, p. 276) should be compared with that in the 1st Book of Kings, ch. xviii, where the Priests of Baal cut and slash their flesh with knives and lances and limp around the altar with their bleeding wounds as a mode of invoking heaven for rain. Such customs were universal; they were supplicating in the dumb drama of Sign-language for the water or the food that was most fervently desired. The Guanches used to separate the lambs from their mothers, so that their bleatings might make a more touching appeal to the superhuman Powers. When the corn of the Zulus was parched with continual drought they would hunt for a particular Victim called the "Heaven-Bird," as the favourite of the Gods, kill it and cast it into a pool of water. This was done that the heart of heaven might be softened for its favourite, and weep and "wail for it by raining; wailing a funereal wail." (Callaway, *Religious System of the Amazulu*, p. 407.) The idea is to make the Heavens weep at sight of this appeal, that is representation, of the suffering people, and elicit an answer from above in tears of rain. The customs generally express the need of water and the suffering endured from long-continued drought.

When the Chinaman raises his little breast-work of earth with bottles stuck in it muzzle outward, looking like guns in position, to scare away the devils or evil Nature-Powers, he is threatening them and protecting his dwelling in Sign-language—signs which they are supposed to understand. Making the sign of the Cross or ringing the bells subserves the same purpose in the religion of Rome. When the church-bells were rung in a thunderstorm it was intended to scare off evil spirits just as much as was the Chinaman's futile fortification.

The Intichiuma ceremonies of the Arunta Tribes are amongst the most primitive now extant upon the surface of the earth. These are performed as sacred mysteries in various modes of Sign-language, by which the thought, the wish, the want is magically expressed in act instead of, or in addition to, words. The obvious object of these most ancient mysteries of magic is the perennial increase of food, more expressly of the animal or plant that gives its name to the totem of those who perform the particular rites. The members of the Witchetty-Grub Tribe perform a mystery of transformation in relation to the grub which is an important article of diet. With magical incantations they call upon the grub to lay an abundance of eggs. They invite the animals to gather from all directions and beg them to breed in this particular feeding-ground of theirs. The men encase themselves in the structure intended to represent the chrysalis from which the grub emerges in re-birth, and out of this they crawl. In trying to interpret the dumb drama of these Totemic Mysteries we have to learn what is thought and meant to be expressed chiefly by what is done. Thus we see the mystery of transformation is acted magically by the men of the Witchetty-Grub Totem for the production of food in the most primitive form of a prayer-meeting or religious service; and the Powers are solicited, the want made known by signs, especially by the sign of fasting during the performance. They shuffle forth one after another in imitation of animals newly born. Thus they enact the drama or mystery of transformation in character.

The primary phase of what has been continually miscalled "Phallic Worship" originated in the idea and the symbolism of Motherhood. The Earth itself as producer of food and drink was looked upon as the Mother of life. The Cave in the Earth was the Womb of the Bringer-forth, the uterine symbol of the Genetrix. The Mother in Mythology is the Abode. The sign of the female signified the place of birth: the birth-place was in the cave, and the cleft in the rock or entrance to the Mother-earth was the earliest phallic type identified throughout external nature. The Cave, the Cavern, or Cleft in the rock was an actual place of birth for man and beast, and therefore a figure of the uterus of the Mother-earth. Hence the mount of earth, or the rock, was made a type of the Earth-mother in the stone seat of Isis, or the conical pillar of Hathor. The Stone-Image of the mount of earth as *Mons Veneris* was identified at times as female by the κτείς being figured on it, as it was upon the conical stone of Elagabalus: or the impression of Aphrodite which was pointed out upon the Black Stone at Mecca by Byzantine writers. The *Cteis* or Yoni was the natural entrance to or outrance from the Mount, and all its co-types and equivalents, because it was an emblem of the Mother who brought forth her children from the earth.

The natives of Central Africa have a widespread tradition that the human race sprang out of a soft stone. This goes far towards identifying the stone as a symbol of the earth; especially the stone with a hole in it that was made use of in the Mysteries as the emblem of a second or spiritual birth. The Yao, of Central Africa, affirm that Man, together with the animals, sprang from a hole in the rock. This birthplace, with the Arunta of Australia, is represented by the stone with a hole in it, from which the children emanate as from the womb of Creation. In their magical ceremonies they represent a woman by the emblematic figure of a hole in the earth. (N.T., p. 550.) Also a figure of the Vulva as the Door of Life is imaged on certain of their Totems. The Esquimaux Great Mother Sidné is the earth itself as producer of life and provider of food, who is a figure of the Mother.

The origin of so-called "Phallic worship" then began with the earth herself being represented as the Womb of Universal Life, with the female emblem for a figure of the Birth-place and Bringer-forth. Not that the emblem was necessarily human, for it might be the sign of the Hippopotamus, or of the Lioness, or the Sow; anything but worshipful or human. The mythical gestator was not imaged primarily as a Woman, but as a pregnant Water-Cow, size being wanted to represent the *great*, *i.e.*, enceinte, Earth-mother, and her chamber of birth. But, under whatsoever type, the Mother was the abode, and the oval image drawn by the cave-dwellers on their walls as the universal figure of the female proves the type to have been uterine. The Female was the dwelling and the door of life, and this was her image "in all the earth." The likeness was also continued in the oval burial-place as sign and symbol of re-birth, and lastly as the oval window or the door in architecture; the Vesica in Freemasonry. The Mother's Womb was not only a prototype of the tomb or temple; it also represented the house of the living.

"When the magistrate of Gwello had his first house built in wattle and daub, he found that the Makalanga women, who were engaged to plaster it, had produced, according to a general custom, a clay image of the female member in relief upon the inside wall. He asked them what they did that for. They answered benevolently that it was to bring him good luck. This illustrates the pure form of the cult of these people, who recognize the unknown and unseen power by reverencing its manifestation (in this instance) on the female side of the creative principle." (Joseph Millerd Orpen, *The Nineteenth Century*, August, 1896, pp. 192-3.) They knew the natural magic of the emblem if the European did not. Also, they were identifying the woman with the abode. In Bent's book he gives an illustration of an iron-smelting furnace, conventionally showing the female figure and the maternal mould. "All the furnaces found in Rhodesia are of that form, but those which I have seen (and I have come upon five of them in a row) are far more realistic, most minutely and statuesquely so, all in a cross-legged sitting position, and clearly showing that the production or birth of the metal is considered worthy of a special religious expression. It recognized the Creator in one form of his human manifestation in creation." This is lofty language. "We call the same thing by another name in our part of the country."

The God Seb is the Egyptian Priapus, who might be termed a Phallic deity. But he is the Earth-God and Father of Food; the God of Fructification associated with plants and fruits, flowers and foliage, which are seen issuing from his body. He is the "Lord of Aliment," in whom the reproductive powers of earth are ithyphallically portrayed. But the potency represented by Seb was not human, although the human member is depicted as a type of the begetter or producer. The enemies of Ra are repulsed by the phallus of Horus. When the Apap-monster is overthrown it is said, "Thy phallus, O Horus, acts forever. Thy phallus is eternal." (Rit., XXXIX, 8.) Where Herakles employs his club against the Hydra, the phallus was the typical weapon used by Horus against the Apap-dragon. Apap was the Image of Evil as negation, sterility, non-production; and the weapon of Horus symbolized the virile power of the procreative sun. Again, it is said the phallus of Osiris is agitated for the destruction of the rebels, and it dooms the beast Baba to be powerless during millions of years. (Rit., xciii, 1.) The Lion and phallus are elsewhere identical as zoötype and type of the solar force when it is said the luminous lion in its course (the sun) is the phallus of Ra. (Rit., xvii.) As this was solar and not human, it will account for the enormous size of the image carried in the processions of the Phallus. (*Herodotus*, B. 2, 48.)

Hippolytus, in his account of the Naaseni, speaks of the hidden mystery manifested by the phallic figure which held a "first position in the most ancient places, being shown forth to the world, like a light set upon a candlestick." This identifies the male emblem with its solar origin as symbol of the Sun. It is something to know that when the long sperm candles are set up in the religious Mysteries to-day, the Ritualists are not doing this to the praise and glory of the human member, but are making use of a type which has been continued in the darkest Christian ignorance of pre-Christian origins.

A still more curious but kindred case of survival occurs in Australia, where it is a custom yet extant amongst the aborigines for the widow of a deceased person of importance to wear the phallus of her dead husband suspended round her neck for some time, even for years, after his death. This is not an action directly natural, but one that is dominated and directed by some religious sentiment, however primitive, which makes the action symbolical, and Egypt, who used such types, intelligently interprets them. By wearing the phallus the widow was preserving it from decaying in the earth, and in wearing it she was preserving that type of resurrection which Isis in her character of the Widow sought so sedulously to preserve in a typical image. (Plutarch, *Of Isis and Osiris*.) In the Turin Ritual (ch. xciii.) the Manes prays that the Phallus of Ra may not be devoured by the powers of evil at a feast of fiends. In Egyptian Resurrection-scenes the re-arising of the dead or inert Osiris is indicated by the male emblem, re-erection being one with resurrection. It is thus the dead are raised or re-erected as Spirits and the power of rising again is imaged in the life-likeness as by the figure of Amsu-Horus. Thus interpreted few things could be more pathetic than the poor Widow's devotion to her dead husband, in wearing the emblem as a token of his future resurrection. In point of time and stage of development the Widow in Australia is the natural prototype of the Widow divinized as Isis who consecrated the phallus of Osiris and wore it made of wood. It is in such ways as this the Wisdom of Old Egypt will enable us to read the most primitive Sign-language and to explicate the most ancient typical customs, because it contains the gnosis or science of the earliest wisdom in the world. The "Language of Animals" is obviously Inner African. It is employed especially by the Bushmen and Hottentots. Just as obviously was it continued by the dwellers in the valley of the Nile. Beyond the hieroglyphics are the living types, many of which were continued as Egyptian, and these have the same significance in Egypt that they had in Inner Africa, and still say the same things in the language of words that they said as zoötypes. It appears as if the many links that we thought broken past mending in the long chain of human evolution were preserved in Egypt. There is a Kamite tradition mentioned by Plutarch that previous to the time when Taht first taught a language of words to the human race they used mere cries like the pre-human animals. We know that Homo imitated the cries of the zoötypes because he continued to do so in the Totemic Mysteries. We know that the Ape was one of the most prominent zoötypes. Now the God Taht who is here called the creator of speech, and whose name of Tehuti is derived from Tehu, a word for speech and to tell, is portrayed in the form of the Kaf-Ape. The Kaf-Ape is the clicking Cynocephalus; and it is recognized as the Clicker who preceded the Speaker; the animal from whom the later language came. Whence the Kaf-headed Taht-Ani is the figure of the God who taught mankind their speech and made the hieroglyphics, which ultimately led to letters. This type of language, speech, the word, the mouth, the tongue, carries us back to the pre-lingual Clickers, and establishes the link betwixt them and the Clicking Ape in tracing the origin and line of descent for human speech. The Cynocephalus, then, represents a pre-human source of speech, and is personified in Taht-Ani as the Divine Speaker. We may look upon the Clicking Ape as one of the animals whose sounds were repeated by his successor Man. The Egyptian record testifies to his pre-eminence. Possibly the Ape, as typical talker, Sayer or Divine Word, may account for the tradition current among the negroes in West Africa, also in Madagascar, that the Apes once talked and could do so yet, but they conceal their faculty of speech for fear they should be made to work. The Ass was also honoured like the Ape of Taht-Ani as a saluter of the Gods or Nature-Powers. It was a great past-master of pre-human sounds, as the pre-human utterer of the vowels in their earliest form. (Nat. Genesis.) The Egyptians call the Ass by the name of Iu, Aiu, and Aai, three forms of one primary diphthong in which the seven vowel-sounds originated. Iu signifies to come and go, which might aptly describe the Ass's mode of producing the voice. Aiu or Iu with the A protheic shows the process of accretion or agglutination which led to the word Aiu, Iao, Ioa, Iahu becoming extended to the seven vowels finally represented in the fully drawn-out name of Jehovah, which was written with the seven vowels by the Gnostics. The English attribute the dual sound of "hee-haw" to the Donkey, and, if we omit the aspirate, "ee-aw" is near enough as a variant and the equivalent of Iu, Aiu, or Aai, as the name given to itself by the Ass which was registered in language by the Egyptians. The animal with his loud voice and long-continued braying was an unparalleled prototype of the Praiser and Glorifier of the Gods or Nature-Powers. He uttered his vowel-sounds at the bottom and top of the octave which had only to be filled in for the Ass to become one of the authors of the musical scale. Such were two of the Sayers in the language of animals, as zoötypes, as pictographs of ideas; as likenesses of nature-powers; as words, syllables, and letters; and what they said is to be read in Totemism, Astronomy, and Mythology; in the primitive symbolism of the aborigines, and in the mystical types and symbols now ignorantly claimed to be Christian.

It is but doing the simplest justice to these our predecessors in the ascending scale of life and evolution to show something of the *rôle* they once played and the help they have rendered to nascent, non-articulate man in supplying the primary means of imaging the superhuman forces surrounding him; in lending him their own masks of personality for Totemic use before he had acquired one of his own, and in giving shape and sound and external likeness to his earliest thought, and so assisting him on his upward way with the very means by which he parted company from them. Whosoever studies this record by the light that shineth from within will surely grow more humanly tender towards the natural zoötypes and strive henceforth to protect them from the curse of cruelty, whether inflicted by the fury of the brutal savage or the bloody lust of the violating vivisectionist. This zoömorphic mode of representation offers us the key by which we can unlock the shut-up mind of the earliest, most benighted races so far as to learn more or less what they mean when they also talk or act their unwritten language of animals in Totemic customs and religious rites, and repeat their Märchen and dark sayings which contain the *disjecta membra* of the myths. It is as perfect for this purpose of interpreting the thought of the remotest past, become confused and chaotic in the present, as in the alphabet for rendering the thought of the present in verbal language.

Homo was the finisher but by no means the initial fashioner of language. Man was preceded by the animals, birds, and reptiles, who were the utterers of pre-verbal sounds that were repeated and continued by him for his cries and calls, his interjections and exclamations, which were afterwards worked up and developed as the constituents of later words in human speech into a thousand forms of language. Thinking, by man or animal, does not depend upon speech. Naming is not necessary for reflecting an image of the place or thing or person in the mirror of the mind. Thought is primarily a mental mode of representing things. Without true images of things, there is no trustworthy process of thought. Doubtless many blank forms may be filled in with a word as a substitute for thinking; but words are not the image of things, nor can they be the equivalent of the mental representation which we call thinking. It is the metaphysician who thinks, or thinks he thinks, in words alone—not the Poet, Dramatist, or natural man. The Argus-eyed Pheasant did not think in words but in images and colours when she painted certain spots upon the feathers of her young progeny. Thought is possible without words to the animals. Thought was possible without words to inarticulate man and the mere clickers. The faculty of thinking without words is inherent in the dumb, and it is impossible that such faculty should be extinct or not exercised by articulate man. Much thinking had been acted without words before the appearance of Man upon the planet. Also by Homo while as yet there were no words but only cries, ejaculations, and animal sounds. The dog can think without words. To make its hidden meaning heard, how pleadingly he will beseech without one sound of human speech. So it is with the human being. As an example, let us suppose we are going upstairs to bed in the dark. In doing this we do not think "*S t a i r s*,"—"*B a n i s t e r*,"—"*L a n d i n g*," handle of door, Candle-stick, Matches. We act the same as if we saw, only the vision is within and the dark without. We see the stair and feel for it with the foot. We see the banister mentally and clutch it with the hand. Internal seeing and external touch concern us a thousandfold more than words, and these give us a sensible hold of outer things. Thought does not need to spell its way in letters. We are thinking all the while as a process of mental representation, and do not go on words when we are not called upon to speak.

The Bull and Cow said "Moo"; the Cow with us is still called a "Moo-Cow" in nursery language. The Goat and Ram said "Ba." The Goose in hissing cried "Su." The Hippopotamus in roaring said "Rur" or "Rur-rur." Various others in uttering sounds by nature were giving themselves the names by which they were to be known in later language. The name of the Cat in Egyptian is Mau or Miau. This, then, was one of the self-namers, like the Goose Su. Philologists may tell us that "Mu" and "Ba" and "Su" are not words at all. In Egyptian they are not only words but things, and the things are named by the words. Such words are a part of the primary sound-stuff out of which our later words were coined. Moreover, they are words in the Egyptian language. In that we find the word Ba signifies to be, Ba therefore is a form of to be. Also it is the name for the Ram and the Goat, both of whom are types of the Ba-er or Be-ing, both of whom say "Ba." The Cow says Moo. Mu (Eg.) means the mother, and the mythical mother was represented as a moo-cow. The Ibis was one of the self-namers with its cry of "Aah-Aah," consequently Aah-Aah is one name of the bird in the Egyptian hieroglyphics, and also of the moon which the Ibis represented.

It is but natural to infer that the Totemic Mother would make her call with the sound of the animal that was her Totemic zoötype. Her zoötype was her totem, and her call would identify her with her totem for the children of each particular group. But where the moo-cow made its gentle call at milking-time, the water-cow would roar and make the welkin ring. And the wide-mouthed roarers would be imitated first perforce, because most powerful and impressive. They roared on earth like the thunder or Apap-reptile in the darkness overhead. In the hieroglyphics the word rur is equal to roar in English, or to ruru, for the loud-roarer in Sanskrit; and the greatest type of the roarer under that name is Rurit the hippopotamus, whose likeness was figured in heaven as the Mother of the Beginnings. When the Cat cried "miau" it did not exactly utter the letters which now compose the word, but contributed the primary sounds evolved by the animal in its caterwauling; and the phonetics that followed were evolved in perfecting the sounds. The shaping of primary into fully developed sounds, and continuing these in words, was the work of the dawning human intelligence. So with other pre-human sounds that were produced by animals before the advent of Man.

According to the hidden Wisdom, which is now almost a dead letter, there are reasons why we should be particular in sounding the letter H as an aspirate. In the hieroglyphics one H or Ha-sign is the fore-part of a Lion, signifying that which is first, beginning, essence, chief, or Lord; and Shu the power of Breathing-force is represented by a panting lion. This, then, is the "Ha," and in expelling the breath it makes the sound of Ha. Thus the Lion says "Ha," and is the figure of breathing-force; and this one of the origins in language survives in the letter H—*when properly aspirated.* It is a dark saying of the Rabbins that *"All came out of the letter H."* The Egyptian zoötypes and hieroglyphics are the letters in which such dark sayings were written and can still be read. The letter H, Hebrew He, Egyptian Ha, is the sign of breath, as a Soul of Life, but as the hieroglyphics show, even the breath that is first signified was not human. The earliest typical breather is an animal. The panting lion imaged the likeness of the solar force and the breath of the breeze at dawn, as an ideographic zoötype of this especial Nature-power. On the line of upward ascent the lion was given to the god Shu, the Egyptian Mars. On the line of descent the ideographic type passes finally into the alphabet for common everyday use as the letter H. The supremacy of the lion amongst animals had made it a figure of firstness. And in the reduced form of the hieroglyphics the forepart of the lion remained the sign of the word "Ha," which denotes priority. The essence of all that is first and foremost may be thought in this likeness of the lion.

Amongst the natural zoötypes which served at first as ideographs that were afterwards reduced to the value of letters in the final phonetic phase, we see that beast, bird, fish, and reptile were continued until the written superseded the painted alphabet. These pictorial signs, as Egyptian, include an

- A. from Am, or Hab, the Ibis.
- A. from Akhu, a Bird.
- A. from Akhem, the Eagle.
- A. from An (Variant Un), the Hare.
- Aa. from Khaa, the Calf.
- B. from Ba, the Bird of Soul.
- B. from Ba, a Nycticorax.
- B. from Ba, the Goat or Ram.
- F. from Fu, the Puff-adder.
- H. from Ha, the panting Lion.
- H. from Hem or hum, the Grasshopper.
- K. an erect serpent.
- K. from Ka, an Ape.
- K. from Kam, the Crocodile's Tail.
- Kh. or Q. from Kha, the Fish.
- Kh. or Q. the Calf.
- M. from *Mu,* the Owl.
- M. from Mau, the Cat or Lion.
- M. from Mu, the Vulture.
- N. from Neh, the Black Vulture.
- N. from the Lizard.
- N. from the Fish.
- N. from the Crocodile.
- P. from Peh, the Lioness.

P.	from Pa, a Water-fowl.	*T.*	from Ta, the Nestling.
R. or *L.*	from Ru, the Lion.	*T.*	from the Hoopoe.
R.	from Ru, the Snake.	*T.*	from Tet, the Ibis.
R.	from Ru, the Grasshopper.	*U.*	from the Duckling.
S.	from Su, the Goose.	*U.*	from Un, the Hare.
S.	from Sa, the Jackal.	*U.*	from Ur, the Finch.
T.	from Tet, the Snake.		

The zoötypes serve to show the only ground on which a divine origin could have been ascribed to language on account of the pre-human and superhuman sounds. Several of these are representative of Powers in nature that were divinized. They uttered the sounds by which they were self-named, and thus the Language of Animals might become the language of the Gods. The zoötype of Apt the Roarer was the Hippopotamus, and Apt of Ombos was "the Living Word." The zoötype of Taht, as God of Speech and Writing, was the Clicking Ape. A zoötype of the nocturnal Sun as Atum-Ra was the Ass. The Goose that said "Su" was a zoötype of Seb the God of Earth. Ka is the Egyptian name for the Frog; this was obviously self-conferred by the call of the animal, and the Frog was made a zoötype of Power divinized in Ptah the God of Transformation and Evolution.

It is obvious that Homo in making his gestures either continued or imitated sounds that were already extant in the animal world, such as the clicks of the Cynocephalus, and other sounds which can be identified with their zoötypes, the animals that uttered the sounds before man had come into being. We know that monkeys have an uncontrollable horror of snakes, and no doubt primitive man had a similar feeling. Now, supposing the primitive man in a difficulty wished to warn his fellows of the presence of a snake, and had no words to convey the warning with, what would he do? What could he do but make use of the imitative faculty which he possessed in common with the ape? He would try to utter some signal of warning in an imitative manner! The sound would have to be self-defining *i.e.,* a snake-sound for a snake. It is usually said that snakes hiss. But the Africans represent them as puffing and blowing rather than hissing, as we have it expressed in the name of the *puff*-adder. When the snake swelled and distended itself, reared up and puffed, it made the sound which constituted its own audible sign: and the human being would naturally repeat that sound as his note of warning to anyone in danger. The apes will do so much, for they will swell and puff and thrust out the mouth, expel their breath and spit at sight of the snake. This representative sound turned into a note of warning would in time be accompanied by a gesture that portrayed to the eye some visible likeness to the thing signified by the sound. To do this the mimic would swell and puff out his cheeks in puffing out his breath. He would thus become the living likeness of the puff-adder, both to eye and ear. The man would represent the audible image and visible likeness of the snake, and such a representation would belong to the very genesis of gesture-language and natural hieroglyphics. Further, we have the means of proving that such was the process in the beginning. The puff-adder, the cerastes or horned snake, remains the Egyptian hieroglyphic sign for the phonetic figure or letter F, the syllabic Fu, which was an ideographic fuff or puff-adder. The swelling, puffing, fuffing snake is self-named and self-defined in the first or ideographic stage—it then becomes *fu* in the second or syllabic stage, and finally is the letter F of modern language, where it still carries the two horns of the hieroglyphic snake. Here we see the survival of the snake as one of the mystical authors of language, like the Ape, the Ass, the Goose, the hissers, purrers, grunters, roarers previously described.

Sometimes the zoötypes are continued and remain apparent in the personal name. Some neighbours of the present writer, who are known by the name of Lynch, have a Lynx in their coat-of-arms, without ever dreaming that their name was derived from the Lynx as their totem, or that the Lynches were the Lynxes. This is one of numerous survivals of primitive totemism in modern heraldry. Again, the Lynx is one of the animals which have the power of seeing in the dark. The Moon is an eye that sees by night, or in the dark. This was represented as the eye of the Lynx or the Cat, the Seer being divinized as a Lynx in Mafet, an Egyptian Goddess. The seeing power thus divinized is marked in later language by the epithet "Lynx-eyed." Lastly, there are something like 1,000 Ideographic signs in the Egyptian hieroglyphics, and only 26 letters in our alphabet. So few were the sounds, so numerous the visible signs of things and ideas. We now know that man had a language of gesture-signs when he was otherwise dumb, or could only accompany his visible signs with clicks and other ape-like sounds, which he kept on repeating with intention until they were accepted at an exchangeable value as the first current coinage or counters of speech before words. The Zoötypes were also continued in the religious Mysteries to visibly and audibly denote the characters assumed in this primitive drama. Just as the Zulu girl could not come to her mistress because she was now a Frog, so the Manes in Amenta exclaim, "I am the Crocodile." "I am the Beetle!" "I am the Jackal!" "I am the God in Lion-form!" These express his powers. They are also the superhuman forms taken by the superhuman powers, Power over the water, Power of transformation, Power of resurrection, Power of seeing in the dark of death, together with others, all of which are assumed because superhuman. In assuming the types he enters into alliance with the powers, each for some particular purpose, or, rather, he personates them. When surrounded by the enemies of the Soul, for example, he exclaims, "I am the Crocodile-God in all his terrors." This has to be read by the Osirian Drama. Osiris had been thus environed by the Sebau and the associates of the evil Sut when he lay dismembered in Sekhem. But he rose again as Horus. In this case the Crocodile-type of terror was employed: and down went the adversaries before the Almighty Lord—thus imaged in Sign-language. The Masquerade continued in later Mysteries with the transformation of the performers in the guise of beasts, birds, and reptiles, had been practised in the Mysteries of Amenta, where the human Soul in passing through the Nether World assumed shape after shape, and made its transformation from the one to the other in a series of new births according to the Kamite doctrine of metempsychosis, which was afterwards perverted and turned into foolishness in India and in Greece. In this divine drama the Soul from earth is assimilated to the zoötypes or is invested in their forms and endowed with their forces which had figured forth the earlier Nature-powers in the mythology. The Egyptian Ritual is written in this language of animals, and never was it read in the past, never will it be in the future, unless the thinking can be done in the Ideographic types of thought. Merely reading the hieroglyphics as phonetics is but a first lesson in Sign-language.

TOTEMISM, TATTOO AND FETISHISM AS FORMS OF SIGN-LANGUAGE

BOOK II

WITH due search we shall find that the unwritten and remotest past of primitive man is not immemorial after all that may have been lost by the way. Most obscure conditions have been more or less preserved and represented in the drama of primitive customs; in the mirror of mythology and the Sign-language of Totemism. Ceremonial rites were established as the means of memorizing facts in Sign-language when there were no written records of the human past. In these the knowledge was acted, the Ritual was exhibited, and kept in ever-living memory by continual repetition. The Mysteries, totemic or religious, were founded on this basis of action. Dancing, for example, was a mode of Sign-language in all the mysteries. To know certain mysteries implied the ability to dance them, when they could not be otherwise expressed. The Bushmen say that the Mantis-Deity Kagn taught them the Mysteries of dancing under the type of the "Praying Mantis" or the leaping grasshopper. Primitive men had observed the ways and works of Nature, and imitated all they might as a means of thinking their meaning when they could not talk. They danced it with the Grasshopper, they writhed and swelled and puffed it with the Serpent; they panted it with the Lion, roared it with the Hippopotamus, hummed it with the insects, pawed and clicked it with the Ape. In short, they acted in accordance with the example of their forerunners on the earth. They not only wore the skins of animals and feathers of birds, they made their motions in Totemic dances and imitated their cries as a primary means of making themselves understood. From the beginning in the far-off misty morning of the past, dancing in the likenesses of animals was a Totemic mode of demonstration. Amongst the earliest deities of Egypt are Apt and Bes, who issue forth from Inner Africa as dancers in the act of dancing the mystery of the phallic dance, and in the skins of animals. The Arunta Tribes of Central Australia dance the Unthippa Dance in the ceremony of young-man-making at the time of circumcision. This tells the story of the way they came in what is known as the "Range all along." (Spencer and Gillen, *Native Tribes of Central Australia,* p. 442.) It is said to be the dance of the Unthippa Women in the Alcheringa who were beings of both sexes and who danced all the way "until their organs were modified and they became as other women are." This denotes the status of the pre-Totemic people who were as yet undivided by the Totemic Rites of Puberty which are now illustrated in the mystery of the dance. In the Initiation ceremonies of the males described by Messrs. Spencer and Gillen (p. 381), a special dance of the women follows the making of the youth into a man who is now welcomed by them into the ranks of the elders. "A number of young women come near. Each one is decorated with a double horse-shoe-shaped band of white pipe-clay which extends across the front of each thigh and the base of the abdomen. A flexible stick is held behind the neck and one end grasped by each hand. Standing in a group, the women sway slightly from side to side, quivering in a most remarkable fashion, as they do so, the muscles of the thighs and the base of the abdomen." The object of the decoration and movement is evident. It is to incite the youths and prepare them for connubium. At this period of the ceremonies a general interchange and a lending of women also takes place. "This women's dance goes on night after night for perhaps two or three weeks." The men sing the "Corroboree Song" whilst the women dance the mystery of young-man making, and show the object and mode of it. In this case white pipe-clay was substituted for the white Undattha-Down with which the female was usually embellished. Here the customs of the Totemic Mysteries naturally suggest that a primary object in putting on fur and feather or down, and dancing in the skin of the Totemic Animal at the festival of pubescence, was to dramatize the coming age for sexual intercourse when this was determined by the appearance of the pubes whether of the female or the male.

There had been a pre-Totemic period of promiscuity in which there was no regulated intercourse of sexes, no marriage by the group, or of one half the group with the other half. At that time, or in the pre-eval state, the earth as yet was undivided into South and North; the Mythical Cow was not yet cut in twain, or the mother separated into the Two Women. Much is told us by tradition if we can but interpret truly. It says the race of beings was not then divided, and had but one leg to go or stand on, meaning there was but one stock. All the earth, in later phrase, being of one blood and of one language. The sexes were not yet divided by the lizard, as female pubescence was quaintly figured. There was no cutting of the male or opening of the female with the firestick or the stone knife by which the sexes were divided, or made, or in the latter phrase "created" into men and women. These were the "Inapertwa" beings in the Alcheringa who preceded women and men and were pre-Totemic. These were the Unopened or the Uncircumcised, who had to be transformed into women and men by cutting and opening; that is by introcision and circumcision, or subincision, by which they were made into women and men in becoming Totemic. Dancing then was a dramatic mode of rendering the mysteries of primitive knowledge in visible Sign-language. With the Tshi-speaking peoples "Soffa," the name of the priest, signifies "the dancing man." The African Acholi in their dances, says Sir H. Johnston, imitate animals "most elaborately." An African potentate has been known to dance for some ten or fifteen minutes together in receiving a distinguished European visitor, like Richard Burton, before he had represented all his own titles of honour and claims to admiration in the language of dance and gesture-signs. With the Bechuanas each Totem has its own special dance, and when they want to know the clan to which a stranger may belong they will ask "What dance do you dance?" as an equivalent for the question "To what clan do you belong?" These dances are continued in the Initiatory ceremonies of Totemism. They tend to show that the shapes and sounds and movements of the Totemic animals were imitated in the primeval pantomime by way of proclaiming the clan to which the particular group belonged. The Totemic type was thus figured to sight in gesture-language before it could be known by name. Admission into the Dacota Clan was effected by means of the great Medicine Dance. The Medicine Men of the Iroquois have four dances which are sacred to themselves, no other person being allowed to dance these Mysteries. The first is the "Eagle-Dance," the second the "Dark Dance" (performed in the dark); the other two are the "Pantomime Dance" and the "Witches' Dance." (*Myths of the Iroquois.* Bureau of Ethnology. Second Annual Report, 1880-81, p. 116.) The Eagle being the Bird of Light, the Sun-Bird, we may infer that the first two dances told the story of the Beginning with Light and Darkness, which was thus rendered in gesture-language and continued to be memorized in that fashion by those who danced such primitive Mysteries. We also learn from the sacred dances of the aborigines in the character of the Bear, the Wolf, the Seal, the Crab, or other animal that the gesture-language included an imitation of the Totemic zoötype. The Mandan Indians dance the Buffalo-dance, the heads of the dancers being covered with a mask made of the Buffalo's head and horns. In other dances of the Dog and Bear totems, the dancers acted in the characters of the animals. The Llamas of Thibet dance the Old Year out and the New Year in whilst wearing their animal masks. The Snake-dance is still performed by the Moqui Indians of Arizona (Bourke, *Snake-Dance of the Moquis,* p. 116), and also amongst the Australian aborigines when they "make the Snake" in their sacred procession of the Mysteries (Howitt). It was a common Totemic custom for the brothers and sisters to perform their commemorative ceremonies or mysteries in the likeness of the Totemic-animal. In the Australian Rites of Initiation the teachings and moral lessons are conveyed in object-lessons pantomimically displayed. The various Totems are indicated by the language of gestures. The "Rock-Wallabies" are initiated by jumping with the knees slightly bent and the legs kept wide apart. The Kangaroos hop about in the likeness of the Totemic animal. The howlings of a pack of dingoes or wild dogs are heard afar off as if in the depth of the forest. The sounds grow less and less distant. At length the leader of the band rushes in on all fours followed by the others. They run after each other on all fours round the fire, imitating the actions of wild dogs in the Dingo dance. (A. W. Howitt on some Australian Ceremonies of Initiation.) With the Inoits at their religious fêtes and anniversaries of the dead, the biographies of the departed are told to the spectators in dumb show and dancing. With the Kakhyens of Northern Burmah it is the custom to dance the ghost out of the house at the time of the funeral. The Egyptian mourners also accompanied the Manes on the way to Amenta with song and dance, as may be seen in the Vignettes to the Book of the Dead, where the text deals with the mysteries of the Resurrection. The same Mystery is expressed in the Black Fellow's jumping up a White Fellow when he rises from the dead. It used to be the custom in Scotland for dancing to be kept up all night long after a funeral (Napier, *Folk-lore of West Scotland,* p. 66). Not as a desire of getting rid of the Spirit, but as an act of rejoicing in dancing the Resurrection of the Spirit. The on-lookers often wonder why the performers in Gaelic and Keltic dances should, when furiously dancing, give forth such inhuman shouts and shrill blood-curdling cries. But there is nothing likelier than that these are remains of the "Language of Animals," and a survival of the primitive Totemic practices. Leaping in the air with a shout while dancing had a special dramatic significance. What this was may be inferred from the Egyptian Funeral Scenes. That which had survived as the Dance of Death in the Middle Ages was the earlier Dance of the Resurrection, or the rising again from the dead. The dancing occurs in the presence of the mummy when this has been raised to its feet and set on end, which is then a figure of the risen dead. The rising again was likewise imitated in the dance. Hence the women who are seen to be jumping with curious contortions on some of the bas-reliefs are acting the resurrection. It is their duty and delight to "dance that dance" for the departed (Papyrus of Ani). Thus, Sign-language, Totemism and Mythology were not merely modes of representation. They were also the primitive means of preserving the human experience in the remoter past of which there could be no written record. They constitute the record of pre-historic times. The most primitive customs, ceremonial rites and revels, together with the religious mysteries, originated as the means of keeping the unwritten past of the race in ever-living memory by perennial repetition of the facts, which had to be acted from generation to generation in order that the knowledge might become hereditary. This is a thesis which can be fully proved and permanently established. Before ever a Folk-tale was told or a legend related in verbal speech, the acting of the subject-matter had begun, dancing being one of the earliest modes of primitive Sign-language. Not "trailing Clouds of Glory" have we come from any state of perfection as fallen angels in disguise with the triumphs of attainment all behind us, but as animals emerging from the animal, wearing the skins of animals, uttering the cries of animals, whilst developing our own; and thus the nascent race has travelled along the course of human evolution with the germ of immortal possibilities in it darkly struggling for the light, and a growing sense of the road being up-hill, therefore difficult and not to be made easy like the downward way to nothingness and everlasting death.

It is now quite certain that speech was preceded by a language of animal cries, accompanied by human gestures because, like the language of the clickers, it is yet extant with the Aborigines, amongst whom the language-makers may yet be heard and seen to work in the pre-human way. The earliest human language, we repeat, consisted of gesture-signs which were accompanied with a few appropriate sounds, some of which were traceably continued from the predecessors of Man. A sketch from life in the camp of the Mashona chief Lo Benguela, made by Bertram Mitford, may be quoted, much to the present purpose:—

" 'He comes—the Lion!' and they roared.

" 'Behold him—the Bull, the black calf of Matyobane!'—and at this they bellowed.

" 'He is the Eagle which preys upon the world!'—here they screamed; and as each imitative shout was taken up by the armed regiments, going through every conceivable form of animal voice—the growling of leopards, the hissing of serpents, even to the sonorous croak of the bull-frog—the result was indescribably terrific and deafening." ("The Triumph of Hilary Blachland," by Bertram Mitford, p. 28.) In this Sign-language, which was earlier than words, the Red Men acted their wants and wishes in expressive pantomime whilst wearing the skins of the animal that was pursued for food. They "laid their case" as it were before the Powers previous to the hunt. Each hunt had its especial dance which consisted in the imitation of the motions, habits, and cries of the animals to be hunted. They climbed like bears, built like beavers, galloped about like buffaloes, leaped like roes, and yelped like foxes. (Chateaubriand, "Voyage en Amer.," p. 142.) Travellers have detected a likeness betwixt the scream of the Prairie-dog and the speech of the Apache Indians, who will imitate the animal so perfectly as to make it respond to them from the distance. On the night of the Lunar festival, when waiting for the Moon to rise, they will invoke her light with a concert of cries from their brethren of the animal world, which include the neighing of the Horse, the whinnying of the Mule, the braying of the Ass, the screech of the Coyote, the call of the Hyena, the growl of the Grizzly Bear, when this Totemic orchestra performs its nocturnal overture in the Language of Animals. The Zuni Indians in their religious service imitate the cries of the beasts which are imaged as their fetishes in ceremonial rites at the council of Fetishes. They sing a very long hymn or prayer-chant, and at the close of each stanza the chorus consists of the cries which represent their Deities, called the Prey-Gods, in the guise of their Totemic Animals. Hall, in his "Life with the Esquimaux," tells us how the Inoit look up to the Bear as superior to themselves in hunting the seal. Because, as they say, the Bear *"talks* sealish," and can lull the animal to slumber with his incantation. The Inoit have learned the secret of Bruin, and repeat his language all they can to fascinate, decoy, and magically overcome the seal and capture it, but they are still beaten by the Bear. Dr. Franz Boaz has recently discovered the remains of a very primitive tribe of Aborigines near the boundary betwixt Alaska and British Columbia. They are called the Tsutsowt, and are hunted to death by the Indians like wild beasts. They formerly consisted of two Clans that rigidly observed the ancient law of Totemic connubium, no woman being allowed to marry within her own Clan. At present there is but one Clan in existence, and the men of this Clan have been forced to seek for wives among the Indians of Nass river. These Tsutsowt apparently talk in bird-language. They cheep and chirrup or whistle in their speech with a great variety of notes.

The Supreme Spirit, Tharamulun, who taught the Murrung tribes whatever arts they knew, and instituted the ceremonies of Initiation for Young-man-making, is said to have ordered the names of animals to be assumed by Men. (Howitt, "On Some Australian Beliefs.") Before the names could be assumed, however, the animals were adopted for Totems, and the earliest names were more or less the cries and calls of the living Totems. The mothers would be known by their making the cry of their Totemic animal, to which the children responded in the same pre-human language. The Sow (say) is the mother, the children are her pigs. The mother would call her children as a sow, and the children would try to repeat the same sounds in response. The Totemic Lioness would call her kittens by purring, and the cubs would respond by purring. The Hippopotami, Lions, and other loud roarers would grow terrible with the sounds they made in striking dread into the children. When as yet they had no names nor any art of tattooing the Totemic figures on the flesh of their own bodies, the brothers and sisters had to demonstrate who they were, and to which group they belonged by acting the character of the zoötype in the best way they could by crying or calling, lowing, grunting, or puffing and posturing like the animals in this primitive pantomime or *bal masqué*. Thus the sign to the eye and the sound to the ear were continued *pari passu* in the dual development of Sign-language that was both visual and vocal at the same time when the brothers and sisters were identifying themselves, not with nor as the animals, but *by means of them,* and by making use of them as zoötypes for their Totems. The clicks of the Pygmies, the San (Bushmen), the Khoi-Khoi (Hottentots), and the Kaffirs constitute a living link betwixt the human beginner and his predecessor the Ape. The Bushmen possess about the same number of clicks as the *Cynocephalus* or Dog-headed Ape. The Monkey-Mother also menstruates; another link betwixt the Ape and the human female. The Clickers born of her as blood-mother would be known by their sounds as Monkey-Men. Taht-Aani is a Totemic monkey-man raised to the status of a divinity in Egypt. Hanuman is the same in India, where the Jaitwas of Rajputana claim to be the descendants of the Monkey-God. And the Ape-Men, imitating the *Cynocephalus,* would be on the way to becoming the human Clickers. Very naturally, naming by words would follow the specializing by means of the Totemic types, as we have Tree the type, and Tree the name; Bull the type, and Bull the name; Dove the type, and Dove the name; Lynx the type, and Lynch the name. An instance is supplied by Frederick Bonney in his notes on the customs of the River Darling Aborigines, New South Wales, which is also to the point. He observed that the children are *named* after animals, birds, and reptiles, and the name is a word in their language *meaning the movement or habit of one of them.* (*Journal Anthrop. Institute,* May, 1883). The sound may be added. The Totem (say) is an animal. First it was a figure. And from this a name was afterwards drawn, which at times, and probably at first, was the voice of the animal.

The earliest formation of human society which can be distinguished from the gregarious horde with its general promiscuity of intercourse between the sexes is now beginning to be known by the name of Totemism, a word only heard the other day. Yet nothing later than the Totemic stage of Sociology is fundamental enough as ground to go upon in discussing Sign-language, Mythology, and Fetishism, or in tracing the rootlets of religion; and the study of the subject has but just commenced. It had been omitted, with all its correlates and implications, from previous consideration and teachings concerning the prehistoric past and present status of the scattered human family. On this line of research the inquiries and explorations which go back to this tangible beginning are now the only profitable studies. The results of these alone can be permanent. All the rest were tentative and transitory. But "No satisfactory explanation of the origin of Totemism has yet been given." So says the writer of a book on the subject. (Frazer, J. G., "Totemism.")

The author of "Primitive Marriage," who first mooted the subject in England, could make nothing of it in the end. According to his brother, in a preface to "The Patriarchate" McLennan gave up his hypothesis and ceased to have any definite view at all on the origin of Totemism. Nevertheless, McLennan was right in his guess that the so-called "animal-worship of the Egyptians was descended from a system of Totems or Fetishes" (Budge, "The Gods of the Egyptians," vol. I, p. 29), though "Worship," we protest again and again, is not the word to employ; in this connection it is but a modern counterfeit. The Totem, in its religious phase, was as much the sign of the Goddess or the God as it had been of the Motherhood or Brotherhood. It was an image of the superhuman power. Thus the Mother-earth as giver of water was imaged as a water-cow. Seb the Father of Food was imaged by the goose that laid the egg. Horus the bringer of food in water was imaged by the fish or papyrus shoot. These, so to say, were Totems of the Nature powers. But when it came to "worship" it was the powers that were the objects of supreme regard, not the Totems by means of which the powers were represented; not the water-cow, the goose, the fish, the shoot, but the Goddess Apt, and the Gods Seb, Sebek- and Child-Horus. It is in the most primitive customs that we must seek for the fundamental forms of rites and ceremonies. It is in Totemism only that we can trace the natural genesis of various doctrines and dogmas that have survived to be looked upon as a divine revelation especially vouchsafed to later times, in consequence of their having been continued as religious Mysteries without the guidance of the primitive Gnosis.

The human past in its remoter range might be divided into two portions for the purpose, and described as pre-Totemic and Totemic. The first was naturally a state of promiscuity more or less like that of the animals, when there were neither Totems, nor Law of Tabu, nor covenant of blood, nor verbal means of distinguishing one person from another. The only known representatives of this condition now living are the Pygmies of the Central African Forests. By Totemism we mean the earliest formation of society in which the human group was first discreted from the gregarious horde that grovelled together previously in animal promiscuity. The subject, however, has various aspects. The term has many meanings which have to be determined by their types. Many years ago the present writer sought to show that Totemism, Mythology, Fetishism, and the hieroglyphic system did not originate in separate systems of thought and expression, as any modern "ism" sets up for itself, but that these had a common rootage in Sign-language, of which they are various modes or forms. Totemism originated in Sign-language rather than in Sociology, the Signs being afterwards applied for use in Sociology as they were in Mythology and Fetishism. The name "Totem" is supposed to have originated in the language of the North American Indians. The word Totem exists in the Ojibway language for a sign, a symbol, mark, or device of the group, Gens, or Tribe. The Rev. Peter Jones, an Ojibway, spells the word "Toodaim." Francis Assikinack, an Ottawa Indian, renders it by *Ododam*. The Abbé Thavenet, quoting from the Algonkin language, gives *nind Otem* for "my tribe," and *kit Otem* for "thy tribe." The root of the word as here rendered is Tem or Dem. The name and things thus denoted are found to be universal for a group, a gathering, a collection, a total of persons, animals, huts or houses. The Magar Thum is the Phratry or Clan, of which there were twelve altogether. The Attic township was called a Dem. The Sanskrit Dama is the home; Greek Domos, Latin Domus, Sclavonic Domu, English Dome. Itembe=the dome is the roof in Niamwezi. In Zulu the Tumu is an assemblage. In Maori, the *Tamene* is a collection of people. Also the Toma is a cemetery like the Scottish Tom, and the Tumuli where the dead were gathered together. Tomo, in archaic Japanese, denotes a gathering of persons who are companions. In Assyrian, likewise, the Timi are the companions. As is usual in the present work, we turn to Egypt to see what the great Mother of Civilisation has to say concerning the Tem and the Totem.

Τωμ (Tom) in Coptic signified joining together as in the Tem. The word "Tem" has various applications in Egyptian. It signifies Man, Mankind, Mortals, also to unite, be entire or perfect. Moreover, it is a name for those who are created persons, as in making young men and young women in the Totemic ceremonies, of which more hereafter. If ever the word "created" could be properly applied to the Making of Men and to those who were grouped together, it is in Totemism. In Egyptian, Tem, or Tem-t, is not only a Total and to be totalled. The sign of Tem-t in the Hieroglyphics is the figure of *a total composed of two halves* ⊗; thus the Tem is one with the Total, and the Total comprised two halves at the very point of bifurcation and dividing of the whole into two; also of totalling a number into a whole which commences with a twofold unity. And when the youths of the Aborigines on the River Darling are made men of in the ceremonies of puberty—that is, when they are created Men—they are called Tumba. (F. Bonney.) It would seem as if the word "Tem" for the total in two halves had been carried by name as well as by nature to the other side of the world, for two classes in St. George's Sound are universally called Erinung and Tem. The whole body of natives are divided into these two moieties. The distinctions, says Nind, are general, not tribal. They agree, however, with the Arunta division into two classes of the Churinga at the head of the Totems which represent the sub-divisional distinctions. (Scott Nind, *Journal of Royal Geographical Society*, vol. I, 1832.) The Egyptian Tem is also a place-name as well as a personal name for the social unit, or division of persons. The Temai was a District, a Village, a Fortress, a Town or a City, on the way to becoming the Dom, as we have it in the heirdom and the kingdom, for the whole or total that is governed by a King. But the group-name for people preceded the group-name for a collection of dwellings, whether for the living or the dead. Here the "Tem" is a total, as we have it in English for a "team" of horses, a brood of ducks, a litter of pigs. Egypt itself had passed out of the Totemic stage of Sociology in monumental times, but the evidences for its prehistoric existence are visibly extant in the place-names and in the mirror of Mythology which reflects aloft a pre-monumental past of illimitable length. In Egypt the Zoötypes of the Motherhoods and Companionships had become the Totems of the Nomes. Thus we find the Nome of the Cow; the Nome of the Tree; the Nome of the Hare; the Nome of the Gazelle; the Nome of the Serpent; the Nome of the Ibis; Nome of the Crocodile; Nome of the Jackal; Nome of the Siluris; Nome of the Calf; and others. These show the continuity of Totemic Signs. Also the status of Totemic Sociology survived in Egypt when the Artizans and Labourers worked together as the Companions in Companies; the Workmen in the Temple and the Necropolis were the Companions; the Rowers of a Ship were a Company like the Seven Ari or "Companions" on board the bark in the Mythical representation. These companions are the Ari by name, and the Totemic Ari can be traced by name to Upper Egypt, where Ariu, the land of the Ari, is a name of the seventeenth Nome. (Brugsch.) At a remote period Egypt was divided into communities the members of which claimed to be of one family, and of the same seed—which, under the Matriarchate, signifies the same Mother-blood, and denotes the same mode of derivation on a more extended scale.

So ancient was Totemism in Egypt that the Totems of the human Mothers had become the signs of Goddesses, in whom the head of the beast was blended with the figure of the human female. The Totems of the human Mothers had attained the highest status as Totems of a Motherhood that was held to be divine, the Motherhood in Nature which was elemental in its origin. So ancient was Totemism in Egypt that the Tems were no longer mere groups, clans, or brotherhoods of people, or a collection of huts like the Tembs of the Ugogo. The human groups had grown and expanded until the primitive dwelling-places had become great cities, and the burial-mounds of still earlier cities; the zoötype of the Motherhood and the Brotherhood had become the blazon of the kingdom. If we take the City to be the Egyptian Temai, the Lion was the Totem of the Temai in Leontopolis; the Hare was the Totem of the Temai in Unnut; the Crocodile was a Totem of the Temai in Crocodilopolis; the Cat in the Temai of Pi-Bast (Bubastes); the Wolf was the Totem of Lycopolis; the Water-Cow of Teb; the Oxyrhynchus of Pi-Maza; the Apis of Ni-ent-Hapi; the Ibis of Hermopolis; the Bull of Mendes; the Eel of Latopolis; the dog-headed Ape of Cynopolis.

When Egypt comes into sight, the Tems have grown into the Temais and the Totems into the signs of Nomes, and she has left us the means of explaining all that proceeded in the course of her long development from the state of primitive Totemism in Africa: the state which more or less survives amongst the least cultured or most decadent races that have scattered themselves and sown the Kamite Wisdom which they carried as they crawled about the world; and, as the evidence shows, when this identifiable Wisdom of the Ancient Motherhood was first carried forth from Egypt, she was in the most ancient Totemic stage of Sociology. The "Tem," then, in the last analysis, as Egyptian, is a Totality in two halves, also a total of "Created Persons," that is, of those who were constituted Persons or companions in the Tem or Group by means of the Totemic Rite. In other languages the Tem, Deme, or Timi are the Group, or Brotherhood. And in the languages of the Red Men, the Dodam, Otem, or Ododem is the *symbol of the group* of Brotherhood or Motherhood, who were known by their Totem. Totemism really originated in the Sign-language of Inner Africa. Some thirty different Totems have been enumerated as still extant amongst the natives of Uganda and Unyoro, and each Totem is connected with a birthplace or place of origin for the family in relation to the Elemental Ancestry (Johnstone), which is the same as with the Arunta in Australia. But a great mistake has hitherto been made in supposing that a sign called the Totem had its origin in Sociology. The primitive type now generalized under the name of "the Totem" was employed for various purposes as a factor in Sign-language. It might be personal, sexual, sociological or religious. It might be the sign of legal sanction, or a type of Tabu. It might identify the human Mother or the superhuman power that was invoked for water, for food and shelter as the Mother-earth.

Since the brief jottings on "Totemism" were made in the "Natural Genesis" (section 2) much water has passed beneath the bridge. A flood of light has been poured out on the subject by Messrs. Spencer and Gillen in their invaluable work on the Native Tribes of Central Australia. The Wisdom of the Egyptians is supplemented most helpfully by the traditions of the Arunta. The Gods and Goddesses may have been relegated to the "Alcheringa," but much of the primitive matter has been preserved at a standstill which had been transfigured by continual growth in Egypt. It is shown by the Arunta and other Australian tribes that certain Totemic districts were identified by or with the food they produce, as the district of the Kangaroos, the district of the Emus, or the district of the Witchetty-Grubs. The Arunta tribes are distributed in a large number of small local groups, each of which is supposed to possess a given area of country, and therefore of the food grown in it. Generally the group describe themselves by the name of some animal, bird, or plant. One area belongs to the group who call themselves Kangaroo-Men; another belongs to the Emu-Men; another to the Hakea-flower-Men; another to the people of the Plum-tree. (N.T., pp. 8-9.) The tribal area of the Australian Euahlayi is likewise divided into hunting-grounds in relation to food. According to Sir George Grey, the natives say that the Ballaroke family derived their name from the Ballaroke, a small opossum, on account of their having subsisted on this little animal; and of the Nag-Karm Totem he tells us the Nagarnook family obtained their name from living principally in former times upon this fish. These, then, were food-totems. So likewise are the Witchetty-Grub, the Kangaroo, and the

Emu of the Arunta groups. Scott Nind also tells us that the tribes of the Torndirrup and Moncalon classes are in a measure named from the kind of game or food found most abundant in the district (*Journal of Royal Geographical Society,* 1832), which is the same as saying that the members of the Emu-totem were named from the Emu-bird, or the Kangaroos from the Kangaroo-animal, naming from food being sub-divisional and later than the descent from the Tree and Rock or the Churinga of the two primary classes. The most important ceremonies of the Arunta are performed for the sake of food, that is for increasing the supply of the plant, animal, bird, or insect which is the Totem of the particular group that enacts the rite and makes the magical appeal. The Emus perform, propitiate, and plead for abundance of Emus. The Witchetty-Grub people ask for plenty of Beetles. These not only eat their Totem, they are also its protectors. The Totem was eaten ceremonially as a type of the food that was asked for, with its likeness drawn upon the ground in the blood of the brotherhood.

It is obvious that both in Australia and Inner Africa the primitive Totemic mapping-out includes that of food-districts, and that the special food of certain districts was represented by the Totem of the family or tribe. At the time of the 6th Egyptian Dynasty one family branch of the Hermopolitan princes owned or possessed the Nome of the Hare whilst another governed the Nome of the Gazelle. (Maspero, "Dawn of Civilisation," Eng. tr., p. 523.) These in the primitive stage would be the food-districts of the totemic Hares and Gazelles, and this status has been preserved in Australian Totemism with the ownership retained by the group. The totemic origin of the zoötypes assigned to the Egyptian Nomes is shown when the animals were not to be eaten as common food. As Plutarch says, the inhabitants of the Oxyrhynchus Nome did not eat a kind of Sturgeon known as the Oxyrhynchus. (Of Isis and Osiris, p. 7.) Also, the people of Crocodilopolis would not eat the flesh of the Crocodile.

The notions of Totemism previously entertained have been upset by the new evidence from Australia, which tends to prove that the Totem was first of all eaten by the members of the group as their own especial food. Hence they were appointed its preservers and cultivators, and were named after it. According to the present interpretation, the Totem primarily represented the maternal ancestor, the mother who gave herself for food and was eaten, and who as the mythical Great Mother in Egypt was the Goddess Hathor in the Tree; the suckler as Rerit the Sow, the Nurse as Rannut the Serpent, the enceinte Mother as Apt, who was fleshified for eating as the totemic Cow. The object of certain sacred ceremonies associated with the Totems is to secure the increase of the animal or plant which gives its name to the Totem. Each totemic group has its own ceremony and no two of them are alike, but however they may differ in detail the most important point is that one and all have for their main object the purpose of increasing the supply of food; not food in general, but the particular food that is figured by their Totem. For example, the men of the Emu-totem perform their special ceremony and pour out the oblation of blood in soliciting plenty of Emu. There can be no mistake in the kind of food that is piously besought, as a likeness of the Emu-bird is portrayed on the ground in the blood of the tribe to indicate the Power that is appealed to. Thus, in the very dawn of ownership by the group, when property was common and not several, the Totem would be a sign of that which came to be called property as the special food of the totemic family or clan. A group of totemic Kangaroos would be the owners and eaters of the Kangaroo in their locality. A group of totemic Emus would be the owners and eaters of the Emu. Those whose Totem was the Tree would eat the fruit of the Tree, a Totem being the veritable image of the food. The women of the Grass-seed Totem fed upon the Grass-seed in the Alcheringa. The women of the Hakea-totem always fed upon the Hakea-flower in the Alcheringa. After the men of the Witchetty-Grub have performed the Intichiuma ceremony for increase of food, the Grub becomes Tabu to the members of the Totem, and must on no account be eaten by them until the animal is abundant and the young are fully grown. If this rule should be broken it would nullify the effect of the ceremony. (N.T., p. 203.) If the Witchetty-Grub men were to eat too much of their Totem, the power of performing the ceremony for plenty would depart. At the same time, if they were not to eat a little of the totemic animal it would have the same effect as eating too much. Hence the sacred duty of tasting it at certain times. The people of the Emu-totem very rarely eat the eggs. If an Emu-man who was very hungry found a nest of eggs he would eat but one. The flesh of the bird may be eaten sparingly, and only a very little of the fat, eggs and fat being more tabu than the meat. "The same principle holds good through all the totems. A carpet-snake man will eat sparingly of a poor snake, but he will scarcely touch the reptile if it be fat." (N.T., p. 202.) That was left, like the finest grain, for seed. So the members of the Irriakura-totem do not eat their Totem for some time after the ceremony of Intichiuma. The man of the Idnimita-totem, a large long-horned beetle, may not eat the grub after Intichiuma until it becomes abundant. It is the same with the men of the Bandicoot Totem. But when the animal becomes plentiful, those who do not belong to the Totem go out in search of one, which when caught is killed and some of the fat put into the mouth of the Bandicoot-men, who may then eat a little of the animal. (Pp. 204-7.) Again, the Arunta have a custom or ceremony in which the members of any local group bring in stores of the totemic plant or animal to their men's camp and place them before the members of the Totem. Thus, as Messrs. Spencer and Gillen remark, "clearly recognizing that it is these men who have the first right of eating it" (p. 210), because it was their Totem. In this social aspect, then, Totemism was a means of regulating the distribution of food, and in all likelihood it must have included a system of exchange and barter that came to be practised by the family groups. In this phase the Totem was a figure of the especial kind of food that was cultivated and sought to be increased by the magical ceremonies of the group. If we were to generalize, we should say that in the beginning the "food" represented by the Totem, whether animal or vegetable, was both cultivated or cared for, and eaten by the members of that Totem. In scarcity, it was eaten less and less, and was more and more prohibited to the brotherhood, for social, religious or ceremonial reasons, and that this was certainly *one of the origins in Totemism*. The Totem as food may partly explain the totemic life-tie when the human brother is taught to take care of the animal and told to protect it because his life is bound up with the animal's so closely that if it dies he too must die.

Totemism, however, does not imply any worship of animals on the part of primitive men. It is the sheerest fallacy to suppose that the most undeveloped aborigines began to worship, say, fifty beasts, reptiles, insects, birds, or shrubs, because each in some way or measure fulfilled one of fifty different *conceptions* of a divinity that was recognized beneath its half-hundred masks. Moreover, if primitive men had begun by *worshipping* beasts and holding their deadliest foes *religiously sacred* as their *dearest friends;* if they had not *fought* with them for very existence inch by inch, every foot of the way, to conquer them at last, they never could have attained supremacy over their natural enemies of the animal world. It would be going against all known natural tendency for us to imagine that human nature in the early stage of Totemic sociology was confused with that of the lower animals. The very earliest operation of the consciousness which discreted the creature with a thumb from those who were falling behind him on four feet was by distinguishing himself from his predecessors: and the degree of difference once drawn, the mental landmark once laid down, must have broadened with every step of his advance. His recognition of himself depended on his perceiving his unlikeness to them, and it can be shown how the beasts, birds, reptiles, and fishes were first adopted as zoötypes on account of their superhuman and superior power in relation to the various elements, and therefore because of their unlikeness to the nature of the human being. The ancestral animal then is neither an ideal nor imaginary being as a primitive parent supposed to have been a beast, or a bird, a plant, or a star, any more than the first female as head of the Gaelic Clan Chattan was a great cat, or was believed to be a Great Cat, by the brothers in the Clan Sutherland.

However ancient the mythical mode of representing external nature, some sort of sociology must have preceded mythology and been expressed in Sign-language. Actuality was earlier than typology. Thus amongst the American Indians we find that Earth, Water, Wind, Sun, and Rain are Totems, without being, as it were, put into type by mythology. This, which can be paralleled in Africa and Australia, points to a beginning with the elements of life themselves as the objects of recognition which preceded the zoötypes; the elements of water, earth, air, and vegetation. It need scarcely be re-asserted that Totemism was a primitive means of distinguishing the offspring of one Mother from the offspring of the other; the children of the Tree from the children of the Rock, the hippopotami from the crocodiles, the serpents from the swine. The earliest sociology touches on promiscuity at the point of departure from the human horde when the Mother was the only parent known. The Mother comes first, and from that point of departure the Egyptian representation reflects the sociology in the Mirror of the Mythos. In the pre-Totemic stage, there was one Mother as head of the family. This is repeated in Egyptian Mythology. In Totemism the Motherhood is divided between two sisters, or a Mother and an elder sister. This is repeated in Egyptian mythology. In Totemism the dual Motherhood is followed by the brotherhoods. This is repeated in Egyptian Mythology, beginning with the Twin-Brothers Sut and Horus, or the Black Vulture and the Golden Hawk, which are equated by, or continued as, the Crow and Eagle-Hawk of Karween and Pundjel in Australia. In Totemism the two Brothers are followed by four or six in a group, and these are consorts of the sisters in group-marriage. So is it in the Egyptian Mythos. In this way Mythology will lend its search-light to show the backward path of prehistoric Totemism.

At a very early stage the boys became the Consorts of the Mother. When of age they would enter into connubium with her, the eldest being first. Incest at the time was naturally unknown, it being the same with them as with the animals. This status is reflected in the Mirror of Mythology. For example, there is evidence that the eldest Son was the earliest representative or outline of a Father and that he cohabited with his own Mother on purpose to keep pure the Mother-blood. This is an African institution. The queens of Cape Gonzalves and Gaboon are accustomed to marry their eldest Sons as a means of preserving pure the royal blood. It was a very stringent law and custom with the Yncas of Peru that the heir to the kingdom should marry his eldest sister. (Bastian, *Der Mensch in der Geschichte,* vol. III, p. 293; Wearne, S., *Journey to the Northern Ocean,* p. 136.) This custom also is reflected in Egyptian Mythology. Indeed, so perfectly have the prehistoric sociological conditions been preserved by the Egyptians in their Mythical rendering of the natural fact that the very beginning in heaven is with the first departure from utter promiscuity as it was on earth. The Genetrix as typical Woman is both Mother and Consort to her own Children. Hence Apt, the old first Mother of Gods and Men, was called the "Great Mother of him who is married to his Mother." That is, of Horus as the Crocodile-headed Sebek. Sut, the male Hippopotamus, was also both Son and Consort of the same first Mother. As Hor-Apollo says, "when the male Hippopotamus arrives at its prime of life it consorts with its own Mother." This was the status of Sebek-Horus, who was termed the husband of his Mother. The earliest powers born of the Earth-mother were thought of as fecundating her in utero; Sut as the Hippopotamus, Sebek as the Crocodile, Shu as the Lion, Elder Horus as the Child. The tradition of the sons who consorted with the Mother is to be detected in the story told of Mars by Herodotus (b. ii, 64). He describes an Egyptian festival which the priests informed him was instituted to celebrate or commemorate the ravishing of his Mother by the God Mars. Now Mars, in Egypt, is the warrior Shu, who was one of the sons that cohabited with the Mother. Thus Sut, Horus, and Shu are all three described in this pre-Totemic character. There were seven altogether of these Sons who were Consorts of the Mother in Mythology, and who reappear with the Old Harlot and partake of her cup of fornication in the Book of Revelation. At a later time both Sut and Horus were denounced as "Violators of their Mother." When Isis uttered the cry of "No Crocodile," Horus had violated his Mother, and it was the Mother who effected the "Act of Salvation" by refusing the incestuous intercourse of Son and Mother, whether of the uterine Son or only of the same Totem, which in this case was the Crocodile. (*Magic Papyrus,* p. 7.) With Sut as Violator, it was the Hippopotamus; with Horus the Crocodile, with Shu the Lion. Thus, in the mirror of Egyptian Mythology human promiscuity is reflected when the Great Mother's own Sons are her Consorts. Polyandry is represented when brothers and sisters couple together, as did Shu and Tefnut. The African marriage of one male with two sisters is reflected in the mythos when Osiris is the consort of Isis and Nephthys.

If we take the word "Totem" to indicate a sign, the earliest sign or symbol to be identified in Totemism was related to the fact of feminine pubescence. This was the Word that issued out of silence in the Beginning. The earliest law of covenant or tabu was based upon the transformation that occurred at the time when the girl became a woman ready for connubium. This was the mystery of a transformation that was a primal source of all the transformations in the folk-tales of the world. The girl became a woman as a natural fact. This had to be expressed in the visible language already drawn from external nature. We are told by Theale, the Cape historian, that the only festival celebrated by the Zulu-Kaffirs to-day is one that is kept when the girl becomes pubescent. This, was indeed the mother of mystery, the mystery of all mysteries ever solemnized or celebrated by the people of the past. It was a time of rejoicing because the girl had come of age and was now ready to be welcomed into communal connubium by the whole group of grown-up males. When the female had attained pubescence and become of age the opening period, as it is commonly designated, was proclaimed, and confirmation given in various modes of Sign-language. The fact was tattooed on the person. A cicatrice was raised in the flesh. Down was exhibited as a sign of the pubes. The Zulu women published their news with the *Um-lomo* or mystical mouth-piece. The act may be read on behalf of the women by assuming the operation to have been female from the first, and then passed on to the boys. The girl in her initiation joins the ranks of the Motherhood. She has attained her opening period. The tooth is knocked out to visualize the opening. One of the signs of readiness shown by the Arunta women was the erection of the sacred Pole immediately after the ceremony of introcision had been performed. A Purulu woman of the Achilpa Totem (in the mythical past) is said to have had a large Nurtunja. This when erected stood so high as to be seen by the men a long way off. *The woman showed her Undattha or down* (typical of the pubes and pubescence) and the men performed the rite upon her, and then they all had intercourse with her. (N.T., p. 407.) The special fact then signified by the raising of her Nurtunja, or sacred pole, was that her womanhood was now accomplished. This may explain why no Nurtunja is used but once, a fresh one being made for every ceremony. Also why Churinga were hung upon the pole to intimate her Totem.

The name for a Totem (in Luganda) is Muziro, which signifies something tabooed: "something I avoid for medical or other reasons." This tends to identify the Totem in one of its aspects as a teacher of Tabu in relation to the primitive mystery of female nature.

The fact is that the Sign-language of Totemism was in existence long before two groups of people were distinguished from each other by two different signs or zoötypes. Sign-language is far older than any form of Totemic sociology. The signs now known as Totemic were previously extant; they had served other uses, and were continued for other purposes. The very first thing to regulate in primitive marriage was the time at which the pubescent girl was marriageable. This was determined primarily by nature and secondly by the preparatory rite. As shown by the Australian customs, no girl was marriageable until the rite of introcision had been performed upon her person. Her Totem followed the Totemic rite as her heraldic badge. Thus a first division was made to indicate the fit and protect the unfit from savage assault, when the Totem was individual and feminine. So in the mysteries of Artemis no young woman was considered marriageable until she had danced in the bear-skin at the Mysteries; the Bear-skin that symbolized the pubes or pubescence, as did the down of birds or the skin of the serpent. The natural *raison d'être,* the primary need for the Totem, was in its being a sign of feminine pubescence. In a state of sexual promiscuity the first thing to be determined was the Mother-blood. This was manifested at the period of puberty, and the Totem was adopted as the symbol of motherhood. The manifestor was now a frog, a serpent, a she-bear, or as we say, a Woman, to be distinguished by her Totem. The Totem then was the sign of "Earth's first blood" on this most primitive natural ground. When the Australian black described the Churinga-like sacred stones of New South Wales as "All same as bloody brand," he meant the blood-brand, or Totemic mark, and thus identified the Mother-Totem with the Mother-blood. The different motherhoods were recognized as different Mother-bloods which were visibly discriminated by the different Mother-Totems. The recognition of the Mother-blood, even in the undivided horde, would naturally lead to the Blood-motherhood which we postulate as fundamental in Totemism. At first no barrier of blood was recognized. The brothers and sisters of the same mother intermarried, although they were, or because they were originally, of the same one blood. When the nations of the earth were all of one blood it was the blood of the Mother, who in her mystical aspect is the Virgin-Mother of the Mythos and the Eschatology. On entering the ranks of the motherhood the girl assumed her sign which signified that she was now a woman. In being made Totemic she was recognized by her zoötype—that is, by the reptile, beast, or bird of the Totem into which she had first made her transformation at the time of puberty. In various legends it was said that in making this transformation the young women were changed into beasts. Once on a time a young girl in Arcadia transformed into an animal. It is common in the folk-tales for the female to change into a hyena, a tigress, a serpent, a lioness, or some other beast or reptile. It was the same with the Zulu-Kaffir girl who became a frog. When her change occurred she was no longer a tadpole of a girl, but a full-blown frog, and in the human sense a woman. The beginnings were very lowly in Sign-language. It had been awesomely remarked that the serpent had the faculty of sloughing its skin and renewing itself. Hence it is said by the Kaffirs that when the girl makes her change she is visited by the great serpent, or, in other legends, she is said to change into a serpent. In the Arunta tradition the two females who are the founders of Totemism and finishers of the human race made their transformation into the lizard. (N.T., p. 389.) The native women of Mashonaland also tattoo themselves with the lizard-pattern that is found on their divining tablets when they come of age. (Bent., p. 305.) Thus the lizard in one instance, the serpent in another, the frog in a third, is the type of beast or reptile into which the young woman is said to transform at the particular period. Hence the lizard, frog, and serpent remain as fetishes with the aborigines. Both lizard and frog were continued in Egypt, but the serpent there attained supremacy. At the coming of age the girl changed into a lizard, a frog, or a serpent as a mode of indicating her status as a woman, whether in nature or in Totemism. Thus three different types, the lizard, frog, and serpent, are identified as figures of the fact in nature, with the "beast" or reptile into which the young girl made her transformation in the mysteries of motherhood which formed the mould of other later mysteries in Totemism and mythology; the types of which were worn by the Goddesses as well as by the Egyptian women. The amulet of Isis which she tied round her neck when she had conceived Child-Horus corresponded to the Totemic sign of the pubescent Virgin. It was of blood-red stone and it imaged the blood of Isis. (Plutarch, c. 65.) The girl was changed into the woman at the time of puberty, therefore the Totem was a type of motherhood. In a sense it was the Crown of Maternity which in Egypt was represented by the serpent of renewal. In attaining this type the girl became a lizard or the Zulu maiden was said to be visited by the great serpent. The serpent that visited the Kaffir maiden was also a Totem of the Virgin-goddess Rannut, in the Kamite mythos, and this was doubled to be worn by the Egyptian Queens as the symbol of Maternity or a Totem of the dual Motherhood, in the characters of Girl and Woman, Maid and Mother, Virgin and Gestator. We may now affirm that Totemism was founded on the nature of the female as a mode of showing when the maiden might be admitted into the ranks of Motherhood, and the young girl made her transformation into the animal and became a frog, a lizard, serpent, crocodile, bear, lioness, cat or other zoötype as the bringer-forth of human offspring in the mask. Which animal was represented would depend upon the Totem of the Motherhood or the Group of Males. And here it may be asserted that for the first time we touch another of the several tap-roots of Totemism.

The Totem has sometimes been called the "original Ancestor," as if it were a representative of the human Father. But the sole original Ancestor in sociology, in Totemism, in mythology, is the Mother; and the female Totems of the Motherhood on earth were repeated as the Totems of the Mother in heaven, or in the Astronomical Mythology. One object of the Totem being worn in the form of the Skin, the badge of tattoo, or the crest, was to signify the "blood" which *could only be determined by the Motherhood,* so that the children of the same Totem could or should not intermarry because they were or were not of one blood. It follows, therefore, that the earliest Totems must have signified the Mother as a means of identifying the one blood of her children. Descent from the Mother, identified by her Totem, is indicated from one end of Africa to the other, when the Egyptian Pharaoh wears the tail of the Cow, the Kaffir chief or Bushman the tail of the Lioness, and the Hottentot is the Son of the yellow Lion-tail. So is it in the Egyptian Mythology where, the priority of the Mother-Totem is well exemplified. Shu is also a Son of the Lion-tail, the She-Lion, and he carries the Ur-Heka or Great Magical Power on his head. This is the hinder-part of the Lioness; and the tail of a Lioness on his head denotes the Lioness as a Mother-Totem from which the child traces his descent as a lion. The earliest human being individualized was necessarily the Mother. She and her children formed the primal family, whose tie was that of Blood-Motherhood, a tie that must have been already common with the horde in pre-Totemic times, the one blood of Motherhood being the original source of all Blood-Brotherhood. The primary form of human personality (*personâ*) was that attained by woman under the Matriarchate as the Mother. Fortunately Providence placed the Mother first and secured her on the side of procreant nature, for the perpetuation of the race. It has been cast up against Woman that she is Mother first and Consort afterwards, and that the Maternal instinct reigns supreme. But Woman was the Mother ages earlier than she could be the wife. The Mother had the start by many thousand years. The child was known as hers from the beginning. The husband was not. Her function was that of breeder for the group and bearer for the Tribe, and not for love of the individual. She fulfilled the Ideal of Primitive Man as the Woman of infinite capacity, like the Lioness, Hippopotamus, or other huge Titanic type of superhuman power and size. She may have had her individual likes and dislikes, but was grimly governed in the grasp of stern Totemic Law. It was perforce her duty to provide pasturage for "forty feeding as one," or the whole tribe, not to cultivate her own personal preferences. The Mother necessarily grew predominant in the duality of her nature. And still the noblest nature yet evolved is hers whose desire for maternity is dual, and who blends most perfectly the love of the Mother and Wife in one.

The solution of the problem now propounded is that the secret of the Totemic Sphinx, in its ultimate secrecy, originated with the Totem being *first of all* a sign of feminine pubescence, and a personal means of making known the natural fact; that it thus became a blazon of the Mother-blood and primal family group; which tends to corroborate the suggestion now sought to be established that the Totem was a figure of the female from the beginning, and that this was followed by a long and manifold development in the application of the Sign to the Motherhoods and Brotherhoods, and to the inter-marriage of the groups now called Totemic.

There are two classes of tradition derived from Totemism concerning the descent of the human race. According to one, human beings were derived from the Totemic animals, or Birds, as the Haidahs in Queen Charlotte Sound claim descent from the Cow. According to the other, the Totemic zoötypes are said to have been brought forth by human mothers. The Bakalai tribes of Equatorial Africa told Du Chaillu that *their women gave birth to the Totemic animals,* we have seen how, and that one woman brought forth a Calf, others a Crocodile, a Hippopotamus, a Monkey, a Boa, or a Boar. (Du Chaillu, *Explorations and Adventures in Equatorial Africa*, p. 308.) The same statement as this of the Bakalai is made by the Moqui Indians, who affirm that the people of their Snake-Clan are descended from a woman who gave birth to Snakes. (Bourke, *Snake-dance of the Moquis*, p. 177.) In various savage myths we have seen how the animals are descended from human mothers. This is a complete reversal of the supposed belief that the human race is descended from beasts, birds, reptiles, and all the other Totemic types, and tends to show that the primary Totems were representatives of the Mothers, whence the alleged descent of the Totemic animals from human originals which of necessity were female; when the Women as the authors of Totemism brought forth the types. Because the Mother was the primal personality it followed that the earliest human group was a Motherhood. The Clan at first was Matriarchal. This is still extant in the Oraon Maharis, which are the Motherhoods by name. (Dalton, *Ethnology of Bengal*, p. 63.) When there was no individual fatherhood yet determinable, descent was in the female line, from the Mother to the Eldest Daughter. These became the typical "Two Women" in Totemism and the "Two Mothers" in Mythology because they had been the Two Mothers in the primitive Sociology, as the Mother and the Eldest Daughter of the human family. The primary human group was naturally uterine. The family first formed were the children of one Mother, and the human pact or tie was founded on the one blood of the Mother; the Blood-Motherhood which determined the Blood-Brotherhood. According to Schoolcraft, the Totems of the Algonquins denote the Mothers. The Emu, which is also "The Woman," Ngalalbal, is a Mother-Totem of the Kurnai in Australia. When the Euahlayi tribe of Australia take their Totem-names from their Mothers, and are divided into two groups as the Light-blooded and the Dark-blooded, this indicates a twofold derivation from the one Mother-blood, whether pre-Totemic or Totemic. If we take the Bear as a Mother-Totem, we can understand the Ainu of Japan when they say their earliest ancestor was suckled by a Bear. In that case the Totemic Mother was a She-Bear, and the fact was memorized when the Ainu women suckled the young Bear that was to be killed and solemnly eaten at the annual festival. Besides which, when the She-Bear was eaten in place of the human Mother the sex of the Totem was determined by her being invested with a necklace and adorned with eardrops like a woman.

It is the same when the Snake-Clan of Arizona claim descent from a Woman who gave birth to Snakes. She was the Mother of that Totem and the Snakes were her children. But there was a Mother in Mythology who did give birth to the Totem-animals, and who is confused at times with the human Motherhood. This was the Mother-earth, who was represented by the snake as renewer of vegetation in the Goddess Rannut. Egyptian Mythology is a mirror of Totemism from the beginning with the human Mother who was the primal parent. And as it was in Totemism so is it in the Mythology and Eschatology of Egypt. In the beginning was the Great Mother, because the first person recognised in Totemism was the Mother. The Totemism of Egypt was the basis of all its Mythology and Eschatology, but that stage of sociology was almost *silted* under and hidden out of sight as one of the several strata of Egypt's buried past. The Indians who trace their descent from the Spirit-Mother and a Grizzly Bear acknowledge that the Bear, like that of the Ainos, was a She-Bear, and consequently a Mother-Totem. The Tugas claimed descent from a She-Wolf, and the Tufans from a She-Dog. Descent from the Mother or in the female line was universally recognized by the aborigines. From this it follows that the zoötypes first represented the Motherhoods; and when the males came to the fore the same animal would serve two purposes. As female it would represent the motherhood; as male the brotherhood. A tribe of Indians still living in North-West America claim to have descended from a Frog. If this was a Totem of the Motherhood, the descent would be the same as if it were from the Goddess Hekat, only their sign is simple Frog, whereas the Frog had been elevated in status by becoming an image of the Mother as Mistress Hekat, the *Froggess* who typified the Divine Mother in the transforming Moon. The divine Cow of the Todas is an extant type of the Great Mother as the giver of food, equivalent to Hathor, the Egyptian Venus, the Cow that protected her Son with her body, primarily when the Mother was a Water-Cow. The Toda Palal or High Priest obviously personates the Divine Son, and is the dispenser of blessings to the world for the divine Motherhood that was represented by the Cow.

No race on earth so ignorant but that it has claimed descent from the Mother. And this human descent being the recognized fact in Totemism form the remotest times, the descendants from the Mother who could be, and was, identified as their own flesh and blood and breath, the Mother who gave visible birth to the human offspring, and no other, from the womb, never could have claimed an actual descent from animals, reptiles, birds, trees, stones and other objects, animate and inanimate. An Australian tribe considered themselves to have been Ducks who at one time were changed into Men. In that case the Duck would be a Totem of the Mother as the means of tracing their descent in the female line. When they became Men the descent would be reckoned from the Male Progenitor. The Bygahs have a tradition that the *foster-mother* of the first Man was a Milch-Tigress, and therefore, as we show, a Mother-Totem. In this statement the foster-mother is distinguished from the human Mother and is identified by means of her Totem as the Tigress and Lioness, or Sow or Water-Cow, or any other female zoötype. The Hyena was a Mother-Totem of Inner Africa. The Wanika in East Africa reverence this animal as ancestral. When a Hyena dies it is bewailed by the whole people. The mourning for a chief is said to be nothing compared with the death of a Hyena (New, Charles, *Life and Wanderings*, p. 122), because, as we hold, of its being a maternal zoötype. It is certain that the hippopotamus was a Mother-Totem with the natives of the Zambesi, who have now the greatest horror of touching its flesh. Livingstone's pilot would go without food rather than cook it in the same pot which had contained any of the meat. (Livingstone, *Zambesi*.) As Herodotus tells us, the first Mother of the Scyths was a Serpent-woman. With the Kings of Abyssinia the line of descent was traced from the Serpent, which was therefore a Mother-Totem. The process of divinizing the power by means of the type had begun in Africa beyond Egypt. The vulture in Ashanti is the same sign of royalty as with the Egyptians. In Coomassie, says Ellis, "vultures are considered birds sacred to the Royal Family. This is not in the same way as the leopard is to the leopard family; but rather that these birds have been despotically declared to be sacred," which means that they are exceptionally sacred by being the totem of the Royal Family, or, as in Egypt, of royal and divine Maternity. Any molestation of this bird was punishable with death. (Ellis, A. B., *The Tshi-speaking People*, p. 213.) It is a Mother-Totem like the vulture of Neith, which was both royal and divine, as the Bird of Blood, the Mother-blood, the royal blood.

The Mother was the primal parent, and the Totem was a means of distinguishing one mother and one group of children from another before these were divided in the two classes of the Two Mothers. Single Motherhood was naturally known to the gregarious horde. Which means that the earliest Totems were types of the female. This is shown in the Egyptian Mythology, that mirror of the Matriarchate. "Your Mother" knew her children and they knew their Mother. "My Mother" knew her children, and they knew their Mother. But without some permanent sign the children would go forth like the beasts from the lair and the birds from the nest, and even this one natural link of relationship must have been lost in the undistinguishable horde. That sign was the Totem as the earliest mode and means of identifying the Mother and of memorizing the descent of the children upon any line of the original Matriarchate. The mother's sign then was the Totem of her own children, male and female, differentiated by sex. "Your Mother" was known by her Totem; "My Mother" by her Totem—to each other's children. The Mother's Totem was naturally recognized by her own children. If "Your Mother" was a Lioness, the male offspring knew themselves as her young Lions. If "My Mother" was a Hippopotamus, her children knew themselves as Hippopotami, or Bulls of the Cow if male. The Mother was always human beneath the Totemic mask which was needed, adopted, and worn to distinguish one human mother from the rest, so that she could be identified by others who were not her children. Thus the first "Two Women," the "My Mother" and "Your Mother" of the Kamilaroi, were recognized as the Emu and Iguana, and these became the Totems of their children.

The Arunta in their isolation have preserved some relics of a primitive tradition of the pre-Totemic and pre-human state in what they term the "Alcheringa." In this the mythical ancestors, the Nooralie, or Mura-Mura of other tribes, are supposed to have lived. At that time, or in that condition, nothing human had been evolved, distinct from other forms of life. As it is said, in those days there were neither men nor women, only rudimentary creatures waiting to be humanized. The Alcheringa represents a mythical past which did not commence with those who have no clue to the origins. It is a past that was inherited and never had any contemporary existence for them. These rudimentary beings the Arunta call "the Inapertwa, or imperfect creatures." We know what was meant by the term because it is still applied to the girls who have not been opened and the boys who have not undergone the rite of circumcision or sub-incision. Such beings still remained the same as the Inapertwa creatures because they had not yet been made into men and women. The sexes were not then divided at puberty or, in other words, had not yet become Totemic. The Arunta tradition tells us further that the change from pre-human to human beings, and from the pre-Totemic to the Totemic status, was effected by Two Beings who were called the Ungambikula, a word which signifies "out of nothing" or "self-existing." Though these two are not designated Women, they are two females. There being no men or women in those days, only the rudimentary Inapertwa, it was the work of the Ungambikula to shape the Inapertwa creatures into women and men, with their lalira, or great stone knives, made of quartzite. These Two Beings were the primitive creators of men and women from the undistinguishable horde of the imperfect Inapertwa as founders of Totemism (N.T., p. 388), by means of the Totemic rites. They are said to have changed the Inapertwa into human beings belonging to six different Totems—(1) The Akakia, or Plumtree. (2) The Inguitchika, or Grass-seed. (3) The Echunpa, or Large Lizard. (4) The Erliwatchera, or Small Lizard. (5) The Atninpirichina, or Parakeet. (6) The Untaina, or Small Rat. The Two Beings having done their work of cutting and carving which was to establish Totemism, then transformed themselves into lizards. Hence it was the lizard of Australian legend that was reputed to have been the author of marriage, because the lizard was an emblem of the feminine period.

It will be shown by degrees what the nature of these rudimentary creatures was, and what is their relation to the human race and to Totemism. The same primeval tradition is to be found in the Mangaian myths of creation. In this the beings born of Vari-ma-te-takere, the originator of all things, the very-beginning, dwelt in the Mute-land at the bottom of Avaiki. There was no verbal language in this land of the Great Mother. You could not provoke an angry answer there. The only language known in the Mute-land is said to be that of signs—"such as nods, elevated eyebrows, grimaces, and smiles." (Gill, p. 6.)

> " Avaiki is a land of strange utterance,
> Like the sighs of a passing breeze;
> Where the dance is performed in silence,
> *And the gift of speech is unknown.*" (Native song).

The Mother and Daughter of the Mangaian version take the place of the two female ancestresses in the Arunta legend. Also, one name of the daughter in another of the islands was Papa or Foundation. In this also the six Totems are equated by six parts of Avaiki, the body of the Great Mother (Mother-earth), who is said to pluck off six portions of her flesh, from the right and left sides of her body, with which to form her children. The tradition is one and universal with many variants. It is fundamentally the same in the mythology of the Californian Indians, who tell us that at first their ancestors walked on all fours. Then they began to put forth some members of the human body, such as a finger or a toe, until they were perfected like the Inapertwa when these were made into men and women. They missed their tails, which they lost as the result of having to sit up. It was a result of this derivation of the children from the mothers illustrated by means of Totemic zoötypes that the aborigines in various Asiatic and European countries were despised and derided by later races as "The Men with Tails." When the Burmese call the Karens "Dog-men," and the Airyas of India call the aborigines "Monkey-men" they are naming them derisively in accordance with the primitive Totemic status. Nothing is more common than for the later lighter races to accredit the old dark races with the possession of tails, as a continuation of the Totemic likeness. They were the beast men, or their descendants from the earlier Totemic times and status. The Kickapoos tell a humorous story of their ancestors who once were in possession of tails which they afterwards lost. Then the impudent frog would send every morning and ask them how they felt without their tails, much to the amusement of the bear, who used to listen and shake her fat sides with laughter at the joke. As the frog had likewise lost its tail in the process of becoming a frog from a tadpole we may see in this the particular Totemic type of the Kickapoos that lost their tails. The tail or hinder part is naturally a Mother-Totem. The tail of the lioness carried on his head is the Mother-Totem of Shu. The Egyptian kings were men with tails. They wore the tails of the lioness and the cow, which were two forms or zoötypes of the mythical mother, Neith the Milch-Cow (earlier, Apt, the Water Cow) and Tefnut, the Lioness. Here the tails of the lioness and cow were worn by the human lion or bull who at one time sported his Mother-Totem in the shape of the typical animal's tail. Various tribes on the Upper Nile are the wearers of artificial tails made of hair, straw, or fibre of hemp, in place of the earlier skin. On grand occasions the Egyptian judges and other dignitaries wore the tails of jackals made of horsehair. In Egyptian symbolism the jackal represents the judge; and the tail of horsehair still survives with us as the queue of the judge's wig. The fox in Europe took the place of the jackal as the zoötype of the lawyer, and this preserves the character of Anup, the jackal, as the sign of council and of cunning or wiseness on the part of those who "wear fur," or the later silk.

One supreme and primary object of Totemism was the preservation of the Mother-blood in aboriginal purity. This gave priority and unparalleled importance to maternal Totems like those of the Serpent and Vulture of the Mother which were symbols of royal and divine maternity in Egypt. The most profoundly primitive of all the ancient mysteries was that of the Mother-blood. At the same time it was the most profoundly natural. By this mystery it was demonstrated that blood was the basis of womanhood, of motherhood, of childhood, and in short, of human existence. Hence the preciousness of the Mother-blood. Hence the customs instituted for its preservation and the purity of racial descent. Only the mother could originate and preserve the nobility of lineage or royalty of race. And the old dark race in general has not yet outlived the sanctity of the Mother-blood which was primordial, or the tabu-laws which were first made statutable by means of the Mother's Totem.

In the Egyptian system of representation there are Seven Souls or life-forces recognized in nature. Six of these were pre-human, elemental powers, born of the primary Great Mother when there was as yet no human soul distinguished from the six that were the souls, such as light, or air, earth, or water, and animal or vegetable life. The seventh soul alone was human. This was the soul of blood brought forth by a Goddess in the human likeness. The earliest soul considered to be human, the soul that was made flesh in the Child-Horus, was born of the Mother-blood, the blood of Isis, and, as such, was distinguished from the earlier elemental powers, otherwise the six Totemic and pre-human souls. The Blood-Mother was imaged as the Virgin Neith who was represented in one phase by the vulture that was fabled, like the pelican, to pierce its thigh and give its offspring her own blood for nourishment. (Hor-Apollo, B. I, 11.) This was as the conceiver of a soul that was incarnated by the Blood-Mother. The blood that was considered to be the soul of life, in a series of seven souls, is the blood of the female—not the typical blood of the male; the blood of Isis, not the blood of Adam, Atum, or Belus; and it can be shown that the human race, distinguished from the preliminary people, originated in the Mother-blood. This was a demonstration made by nature herself on grounds as permanent as they were primitive. The reproduction of human life and the means of descent were dependent on the Mother-blood. By this same means the Mother also attained her supremacy, the Matriarchate being based upon the Mother-blood that was to be so preciously preserved and memorized. According to the Egyptian wisdom, the salvation of the human race was effected by the blood of Isis. Salvation was perpetuation. Isis was the Virgin-Mother, and hers also was the Mother-blood. The blood of the Mother, who was primarily the Virgin, being the earliest recognized source of human life, thence came the doctrine of a Virgin-Mother and the saving blood in the Eschatology. This Mother-blood originated with the Virgin at the time of puberty. It passed into the racial Mother-blood in the phase of fulfilment with marriage. The Virgin, represented in the Egyptian Mystery, was the maiden who conceived; in her second character she was the bringer-forth. These Two Mothers were imaged by the double Uræus-crown of Maternity. The mythical Virgin-Mother had a very natural origin. She represents the pubescent female who was the fount and source in nature for the one original blood. The blood of Isis was the Virgin-blood. She was the Mother of Life in the mythical representation, and in the first of two characters she is the Virgin-Mother, when her sister Nephthys is the Bringer-forth or Nurse of the child. The sacredness of the Virgin-blood, the earliest Mother-blood, will help to account for the sanctity of the pre-pubescent virgins who were so carefully secluded from the outer world at the time of its primary manifestation. Among the Ot-Danons of Borneo the pre-pubescent girl is sometimes shut up during seven years awaiting her sign of the Virgin-Motherhood. This is born in blood, and she is consequently looked upon as one newly born into life. She is led forth to breathe the air, and is shown the sun, the water, and the trees. Then the event is celebrated by the sacrifice of a slave, and her body is painted with his blood. This was the Blood-Mother as a Virgin, in the first of the two characters assigned to the female. Thus, the Two Women in Totemic Sociology were the Virgin and the Mother. It is the same in the Mythology, and lastly in the Eschatology. The first of the Two was the pubescent Virgin who conceives: the second is she who brings forth. Hence the doctrine of a Double Motherhood. Ra is said to be united to his "Double Mother." One of the Ptolemies claims to be the Beloved of the "Double Divine Mother." The Double Mother was also the Double Sister in another relationship with Horus. "I am thy Double Sister," says Isis to Osiris. (P. Pierret, Panthéon Eg., 28.) In this duality Isis is the Blood-Mother and Nephthys the Milch-Mother; hence she is called the Nurse. Isis is at once the Great Mother and also the Virgin-Mother who keeps the primary place in the Mythos because the Virgin preceded the bringer forth of the child as source itself. This double Motherhood is also assigned to Jesus in the Gospels with the Two Mothers as two sisters: the first being the Virgin Mary, the second, Mary the wife of Cleopas.

In modern times the blood in certain families is considered to be royal, and royal blood is the blood to be sacredly or very carefully preserved from any base admixture, although the origin of royal blood is hitherto unknown. Under the Matriarchate there could be no blood-royal by derivation from the Male. There was but one blood, that of the Mother. It was impossible at first for the males to transmit. There was but one means of descent for the race. This was the Mother-blood. Hence the primitive customs for preserving it in purity and sanctity. The Mother-blood was not only known as the "one blood" of the race, it also denoted the "one flesh" or one stock. Descent from the Mother connoted the one blood or one flesh. It would be a way of preserving the Mother-blood in Totemism for the brother and sister *of the same Totem* to intermarry; the same Totem being a determinative of the Motherhood, as the means of identifying the original Mother-blood. Messrs. Spencer and Gillen tell us that the Arunta traditions point to a time "in the Alcheringa" when it was the normal condition for the male to cohabit with a woman of the same Totem as his own. The evidence points back to a time when the brother and sister of the same Totem always married each other. It was long sought to keep the Mother-blood intact by the intermarriage of the uterine brothers and sisters. These used to cohabit, and such intercourse was at one time considered to be not only natural and proper, but was esteemed as preferable. The Kalangs of Java are what is now termed Endogamous, and when a girl is asked in marriage the man "must prove his descent from their peculiar stock." That is originally the one stock of the Mother-blood. People of this stock were known both in Africa and Australia as the one-legged people, those who were the undivided primitive Endogamists. Prolonged efforts were made by the "Endogamists" to preserve the Mother-blood or the "one flesh," as it was called by the aborigines of Victoria, who say of a man that takes a woman of his own group to wife, he has *"fallen* into the same flesh." (Dawson, *Australian Aborigines*, p. 28.) It was a custom long continued by the Egyptians to preserve the Mother-blood by the marriage of the brother and sister, a custom that was sacred to the Royal family, thus showing that the Mother-blood transmitted by the elder sister was the Royal blood. The Goajiros of Colombia in South America have divided and subdivided into a score of Totemic groups, but they all preserve the descent in the female line, and therefore from the Mother-blood. For, if a member wounds himself with his own knife he is not allowed to spill any of his own blood without paying for it. His family on the Mother's side demand blood-money in compensation for *their* loss. There was no individual property in the Mother-blood. This belonged to the family or tribe. It happens with the Gonds of Central India that they have lost much of their pure blood by intermixture with the Hindu race. Hence, at the installation of a rajah his forehead must be touched with a drop of blood drawn from the body of a pure aborigine of the tribe to which the rajah belongs. (Forsyth, J., *Highlands of Central India,* p. 137.) Intermarriage has now come to be called Endogamy in opposition to Exogamy, or marriage outside the group. But the family traced from the Mother-blood was earlier than the Totemic tribe. When the children of one and the same mother intermarried, a kind of Endogamy, however limited, would be founded. And when the children of one mother were compelled to marry the children of another mother a sort of Exogamy was established.

The Mother was the foundress of the family, consisting of herself and children. The foundation of the human structure was in blood, the blood of the Mother. The fact was commemorated in blood-sacrifice when the victim was immured, or the blood was poured out at the base of the building; the custom, like others, is a mode of memorial that was continued in Sign-language when the origin and meaning of the act were inexplicable. The Mother-blood, we repeat, was primary, and various customs, rites, or ceremonies show the purpose that was intended to keep the one first blood, that of the Mother, intact. Each family would be proud and prefer their own fount of source, and endeavour to keep it pure. Hence the marriage of the uterine brother and sister was a mode of preserving the Mother-blood. Hence also the eating of the Mother living was a way of preserving her blood to the consanguineous group. The Mother eaten sacramentally was the earliest victim of blood-sacrifice. In this great cruel rite the body was eaten living to preserve the Mother-blood. Eating the Mother was the primitive Eucharist in which the Mother was the Host whose flesh was torn in pieces like the later bread, and whose blood was drunk religiously as is the later wine. Blood was the life, and this was given by the Mother in her life and death. The human Mother was then in the position of the Totemic zoötype that was substituted for the parent and eaten by the brothers in a later sacrificial rite. It is not uncommon for the communicants who partake of the Sacrament to hold that they have eaten the body and drunk the blood of God himself, and this belief survives in Christianity, as witnessed by the hymn which is sung after taking the Sacrament, beginning with—

> "Jesus, Mighty Saviour,
> Thou art *in us* now."

To emphasize the fact still more, it is sometimes requested that those who have not eaten the God should sing the word "with" instead of "in." (Instance quoted in *British Weekly,* Sept. 1895.) The Eucharistic rite of the Mexicans was called Teoqualo, or "God is eaten"; and to eat the God as represented was to share the nature of the divinity. In like manner the Namaquas eat the flesh and drink the blood of the lion and tiger to partake of their superhuman strength. The Tierra del Fuegians explained that they ate the white man on purpose to share in his superior power. The Kamilaroi will eat the heart and liver of a brave man in order that they may partake of his spirit. The Mother was eaten on the same principle, but, as the Mother, she was eaten sacramentally in the primitive family meal. The custom of "killing the God," the priest, the royal personage, the virgin or divine animal, and eating the victim at a sacrificial meal was rooted in this very primitive practice of the children eating the body of the Mother and drinking her blood in what may be termed the primordial Eucharist. The Mother was the earliest of the sacrificial victims that for special reasons were only allowed to live a certain number of years, at the end of which time the giver of life was eaten in honour by her children as the most primitive sacramental food. The Mother was eaten at the family sacrament because, in the first place, she was the Mother. But there were other motives at work. She was sacrificed comparatively young to preserve her from the effects of age, from grey hairs and wrinkles, from disease, decrepitude, and bodily decay. The children were preserving her from the worms of earth and from the prowling beasts of prey, and probably from the change of life at the departure of the lizard. In eating the body of her who had been the food-giver, they were returning her as food to the family, and in partaking of her blood, the precious Mother-blood, they were giving back the soul (of blood) to the life of the family or brotherhood. Some races, like the Indian, will not eat the blood of an animal, for fear the soul of the animal should enter the human body. But this was a reason, in religious cannibalism, for the eating of the Mother-blood in order that her soul of life which was her blood might re-enter the family or brotherhood, or be "contained" by them. The Mother was not turned into a sacrifice, or the blood preserved on her own personal account, so much as on account of the family or tribe to which the blood belonged. Dawson tells us that only those who had died a violent death were eaten by the aborigines of the Port Fairy District, Western Australia. And then they were eaten "as a mark of affectionate respect, in a solemn service of mourning for the dead." (James Dawson, *Australian Aborigines.*) The dead were eaten as a sign and token of mourning for those who were taken away before their time; and thus religious cannibalism is resolved into a solemn mourning for the dead; and the significance would be the same when the funeral feast was furnished by the body and blood of the Mother. The Fijians, among other races, used to put their mothers to death before they had attained old age. There is an account in Wilkes's exploring expedition of the putting to death of a mother (p. 211, abbreviated). She was walking about as gay and lively as anyone, when one of her boys invited Mr. Hunt to the funeral. Her two sons considered she had lived long enough. They had prepared her funeral feast, and were now going to kill and bury her. They were doing this from love of their mother, and said that none but themselves, her own sons, could perform so sacred an office. Among the wandering Birhors of India, who are cannibals, the parents *in articulo mortis* will beg their children to kill and eat them; and this is done as an act of filial piety. (Réclus, *Primitive Folk*, Eng. tr., p. 249.) At the British Association meeting for 1895 it was testified by Capt. Hynde that one of the finest races of the Congo Negroes are still in the habit of eating the old and decrepit members of their families. Now, as the Mother was the earliest parent known and honoured, it was she who would be eaten by the children in the earliest form of a funeral meal. According to Herodotus (4, 26), it was a custom observed by the Issedones to eat the dead bodies of their parents. But, we repeat, the Mother was the only parent known at first, therefore the only one that could be knowingly eaten as the parent. The Mongols and other races considered it impious for any part of the sacrifice to remain uneaten or unconsumed. Terrible penalties were inflicted for such sacrilege. Now, there is nothing like the eating of the Mother with honour that can so plausibly explain the origin of such a custom. The Mother as sacrifice would be "very sacred indeed," and to eat the body wholly and entirely, including the bones and viscera, would be giving the proof of the highest honour and the profoundest affection which at the time was humanly possible. Nothing was considered unclean, because it was the Mother. At first the body of the human Mother was religiously eaten as the most primitive Eucharistic Meal. Her flesh thus eaten was the sacred food, and her blood was the drink when these were devoured warm with life. Her representative, the Totemic zoötype, was adopted later, and torn piecemeal, to be eaten in a similar manner. This tearing of the "host" in pieces tooth and nail was continued in the Egyptian, Greek, and other mysteries; and so it comes about that the body of Osiris or the Christ was torn in pieces as flesh in the form of bread, and every one of the communicants must drink of the wine as blood. Hence the commandment: "Drink ye all of it." And here it may be remarked that the sacrificial victim in the Gospel is eaten alive, or, at least, the Last Supper is solemnized before the victim was crucified. We next see the group of communicants extending beyond the inner circle when, as related by Angas, the different parts of the body were apportioned according to the human relationship, the choicest portions being given to those who had been nearest and dearest to the departed in this life. It was from affection the children ate their parent, but the ceremony of devouring her alive was awesome and cruel. It had to be performed, from motives that sufficed to establish the custom, but she was not eaten because the act was cruel. Still, the cruel ending of her life made her become a sacrificial victim, and as she was eaten piously, the meal was sacramental and the prototype of all the sacraments in which the Totemic zoötypes or the Divine Son succeeded as the victim sacrificed at the Eucharistic Meal. The Mother gave her life back to the family or tribe whilst living. She was literally eaten alive. In accordance with the law of Tabu, it was the custom for everyone to share and share alike all round in killing and eating the sacrifice.

This was so when the victim was a fawn or a kid. But no victim was so naturally calculated to raise the initial difficulty of striking the first blow in a form so acutely cruel as the Mother. This must have verily necessitated the practice of all the participants falling on the victim together to avoid the sense of individual blood-guiltiness. Everyone must partake of the body, everyone must tear the flesh and lap the blood; everyone must share the responsibility of the awful act. The Mother was not only eaten physically. There was a primitive kind of spiritual communion celebrated in the rite which raised it to a religious status. The body and blood were supposed to be converted into spirit. The theory is explicitly expressed in the Greek statement that "the dead was raised again in the same sacrifice." "All tasted the sacrificial flesh, so that the life of the victim was renewed in the lives of those who ate it." (Theophrastus in Porph., *De Abst.*, II, 29. Cited in *Encyclopædia Brit.*, v. XXI, p. 137, Ninth ed.) And this, of course, applied to the Mother as well as to any other victim whose flesh was eaten as a sacrifice. In eating the flesh and blood of the Mother, the Brothers were absorbing her soul of life and she was being converted into a spirit. The idea survives in the Alcestis. As pointed out by Percy Gardner (*Sepulchral Relief from Tarentum*, p. 21), the heroine of the drama "is scarcely dead before she is invoked by the chorus as a superhuman Power able to give and to withhold favours, now that she has been transubstantiated."

Eating the human Mother as the Eucharist at the family meal led naturally to eating the Mother of Life who gave herself in food that men might live; the Mother who was represented by the Ainu She-Bear, the Acagchemen Panes-Bird, the crucified Great Mother of the Cypriotes, or by the blood of Isis in Egypt, and who, under various mythical or Totemic types, was the renewer of life by offering up her own; the earliest type of voluntary sacrifice which preceded that of Horus the Saviour-Son or of Osiris in a later Eucharist. The human Mother was eaten actually, not as a Totemic type. The "Great Mother" was eaten by proxy as Totemic: Rerit or Shaat was annually eaten as the Sow; Hathor was eaten as the Heifer; the female being the Totem of the Mother, whether human or divine. The Goddess Tari Pennu is a form of the Earth-Mother who was worshipped by the Kolarians of Bengal, and made fecund periodically by oblations of blood at her festival of reproduction when the human doctrine was repeated and reapplied to external nature and she was fertilized with blood. The offering was at times the flesh and blood of a virgin. A young girl, called the Meriah, was stripped stark naked and bound with cords to a maypole crowned with flowers, and ultimately put to death with horrible tortures, torn in pieces, and partly eaten. (Réclus, *Primitive Folk*, pp. 311-315.) In the Khond sacrifice of the Meriah we have another form of the Great Mother. She was fastened to the stake by her hair and forced to become a figure of the crucified, for her arms were extended cross-wise by four priests, who pulled her legs apart to complete the figure. She was the cross, the crucified and the Christ or Charis in one.

The theory now substantiated is that the earliest Totems were zoötypes of the Mothers, that the Mother was the earliest victim eaten at the family meal, and that the human sacrifice was commuted by the substitution of the Totemic animal at a later stage of development. Thus, we hear that the sacrificial offering made to the river Nile was first of all a human virgin, and afterwards a sacred animal. Also, when the Panes-Bird of the Acagchemens is said to have been a woman previously, or elsewhere, we see the bird has been substituted for the human victim in the Eucharistic rite as representative of the Great Mother. The Emu was the bird of Earth in Australia, like the Goose in Egypt. As layer of the egg it represented Earth, the Mother of Food. Now the Emu, in the Kurnai mythology, is also called "the Woman," or Mother, who, like Neith, was imaged as the Giver of Food. And when the Arunta members of the Emu Totem propitiate the power solicited by them for the increase of food, the blood which they shed from their own veins is not simply poured forth on the ground. A small prepared plot of soil is saturated with blood and allowed to dry, and on this the bird is outlined to represent the food of the Totem for which they are asking. The Emu is a type of the Earth-Mother to whom the oblation of blood is offered, and who is thus identified by the bird as their provider or providence, who had been "the Woman" previously. The human Mothers had been eaten sacramentally to preserve the family blood in all its primal, that was virginal, purity. At a later stage, when the Totemic animal was religiously eaten periodically as the sacrificial victim, this had come to represent the Great Mother, the Earth-Mother, the Mother who was propitiated and pleaded with for provender; the Mother of Food who was eaten vicariously with the Totem as her type of food. Blood was the ancient life and Motherhood the fount of source. Blood was the earliest human tie. Then the Blood-Brotherhood succeeded and gradually superseded the Blood-Motherhood. A group of progenitors, or brothers of the blood, began to usurp the place of the Ancestresses as parental powers on the way to finally establishing the Patriarchate.

Civilization first began with the conditions of the pre-Totemic people, who were pre-human. According to the traditions of the Arunta, they had no stone knife, no fire-stick, no rites or ceremonies of pubescence. Indeed, there were no men or women then extant. The nascent race was not yet humanized; it had to be created by becoming Totemic. This tradition of the human origin, which can be universally corroborated, is, in its way, a primitive version of the so-called "Creation of Man" that comes to us belated in the Book of Genesis. It tends to show that human beings, "Created Men" of the Egyptian "Tem," were a birth of Totemism. The traditions of the Arunta affirm that Totemism originated with "Two Women" who, as here suggested, were the Mother and the Eldest Daughter in the human family, the first two persons who were recognized as ancestral types of the Virgin who conceived and the Mother who brought forth. There is ample evidence to show that Totemism was founded by "Two Women," *the* "Two Women" who were the mythical Ancestresses of the Race. These are represented by the two females who prepared young girls for sexual intercourse at the period of pubescence, by performing the opening rite of introcision, and who were consequently the typical founders of Totemism.

The Arunta say it had been found that many of the younger women died in consequence of unlimited promiscuous intercourse with men who were unrestrained and women unprepared by the opening rite when there was as yet no law of tabu. The opening rite was preparatory and considered necessary to befit the young women for sexual intercourse, and also to protect them previously from savage treatment. Therefore we argue that it was devised by the Mothers for the protection of the daughters. The women of the Hawk Totem are said to have made certain men "ashamed of their excesses." (Spencer and Gillen, N.T., p. 416.) The men were monstrous in their size and savagery, and necessitated the Totemic rites. It is related of the "Two Women," here called the Elder and the Younger Sisters, that they were "considerably alarmed at the Ulpmerka Men." But when the pubescent rites had been performed, the women were no longer afraid, and all the men had free access to them (p. 315). In order that the fears of the "Two Women" might be allayed the Ulpmerka made a large nurtunja, or Totem-pole, upon which the sacred emblems called the Churinga were suspended. "After this had been shown to the women they were no longer timid." One of the Two was then decorated with the *down of birds* and a small nurtunja, of a blunt, conical shape, was set upon her head for ornament, and the men danced round her, shouting *"Wah! Wah!"* Then she was taken and laid beside the large nurtunja, which was fixed upright in the ground. The operation of opening the vulva, *Atna ariltha-Kuma,* was then performed by means of a large stone knife. After this the intercourse was lawful and all the men had access to her. The same ceremony was repeated in the initiation of the second or younger woman. Sexual intercourse till then had been promiscuous, and there was no standing on ceremony or waiting till the females came of age for rape to be enforced. The first two females were made into women by means of the opening rite in which they were prepared for Totemic connubium. One of these, the elder one, operated on the younger, and then the two women became the first Ancestresses of the Race who were constituted such by the opening rite that was performed at puberty. These were the Two Women of the Lizard Totem. There were only "Two Women" originally among the Plum-tree Ulpmerka Men, that is the uncircumcised. At first they were unopened. Then they were operated on, and all the men had access to them, first with one, and then with the other (p. 315). These were the Two Women with whom semi-promiscuity was regulated by the division into the two classes with which dichotomous-Totemism began. These Two Women are variously described as coming to introduce the rite of pubescence by means of which the girls were made into women and the uncircumcised males into men. This is performed by them at different halting places.

Under the Matriarchate, racial descent was reckoned by the Mother-blood, therefore the Mother was the earliest Woman known. The eldest daughter was the primary channel of descent. Therefore the eldest daughter was the second woman of the primal Two. A score of mothers or daughters would not change the type of the two women first known as the Mother and Eldest Daughter or the Two

Sisters. Thus amongst the primitive or archaic traditions of the human race there is a legend of descent from "Two Women" called the "Ancestresses." This is extant in Africa and in Australia: in Totemism and Mythology. The Arunta have several traditions or fragments of tradition concerning these two typical women in the sociology of Totemism. There were "Two Women" in the Alcheringa or Mythical Past. Two Women of the Opossum Totem. (p. 403). Two Women of the Magpie Totem (p. 404). Two Women of the Hakea Totem (p. 436). Two Women of the Kangaroo Totem (p. 464). Two Women who accompanied the Men of the Plum-tree in the Alcheringa, as Two Sisters, Elder and Younger (pp. 149, 315). The starting point of the Hakea-flower Totem is from Two Female Ancestors (p. 122). These Two Women are called the elder and the younger. All the men had access to both of them as soon as they had undergone the opening rite.

Thus the Arunta trace the origin of Totemism in its sociological aspect to the rites of puberty that were adopted for utility when the pre-human creatures were first changed into women and men by means of the rites. These were first performed upon Two Women of the Lizard Totem, one being described as the Elder, the other as the Younger Sister. The lizard is the sign of feminine pubescence and especially the Mother's Totem in Africa and Australia. Hence it was honoured as the author of primitive marriage. The Two Women are the Ancestresses of the human race because they were the first two females to undergo the preparatory rite that changed them into Totemic women fitted for social intercourse in communal connubium. This feminine duality evolved in the sociology had been divinized as the Great Mother in mythology both in Australia and in Africa. In the Osirian cult Isis and Nephthys are at once the Two Mothers, Two Sisters, and Two Wives of Osiris. Isis is the Virgin-Mother, the Blood-Mother, the one of Two who conceives but does not bring forth the Child. Nephthys represents the Goddess who does bring forth and who is the Nurse by name. These are also called the Mother and Sister as well as the Two Sisters and the Two Wives. In short, they are the Two human Ancestresses of the Race who were divinized in Mythology. Thus the Two Women who were the Authors of Totemism are the Two Ancestresses who may be described either as Two Mothers, Two Sisters elder and younger, Mother and Daughter, or the Virgin and Gestator, in the various legends, because they are the typical Two that were from the beginning when the Mother and Eldest Daughter were the means of descent during the Matriarchate. With the Nairs of Malabar, whose manners are very primitive, the brothers obey their eldest sister. Next to the mother she is the ruler of the family. And in former times, on great ceremonial occasions, the reigning prince himself yielded precedence to his eldest daughter. She was one of the only "Two Women." The Mother being the first person in the human family, the eldest sister was the second as next available for sexual intercourse; and these became the mythical "Two Women" from whom the Australian natives claim descent. These represent the female duality that brought on the Mother-blood. In some of the legends the Mother passes into the Two Ancestresses as the Mother and Sister, instead of Mother and Daughter. At others they are the Two Sisters. Isis is designated the Mother, and Nephthys the Sister. Demeter is the Mother, and Persephone or Kore is the Daughter. The two were often called the Mother and Daughter. It may seem a long way from the Greek Mother and Daughter to the Polynesian Mythology, but as a form of the feminine ancestors they are originally the same in the human sphere. In the Australian ceremonies of initiation there is what Howitt terms the feminine "duality" of Ngalalbal, in the "Wives of Daramulun." This female duality is the analogue of the two sisters, Isis and Nephthys, who were the two consorts of Horus or Osiris in the Egyptian mythos. These Two Sisters are the same Two Mothers of the typical child in Australia as in Africa. Daramulun, like Horus, is the child of the Two Mothers, "The Ngalalbal-dance," says Howitt, "is rendered very effective through being preceded by the 'duality' of Ngalalbal, the wives of Daramulun." These are seen to glide from the forest past the fire and to disappear in the gloom beyond to a slow and rather melancholy air sung by the audience, which may be rendered, "Ngalalbal, you two coming from afar, where are you going to?" (Howitt, *Australian Ceremonies of Initiation*.) Ngalalbal, the wife of Daramulun, was originally represented by the Emu, and is at the same time "the Woman" who divides into the Two Women. Thus the human source of descent follows the pre-human here, as in the Egyptian Mythos. And in the duality of Ngalalbal we have the two wives who are the two sisters of Horus in the Osirian myth. This feminine duality was one of the secret mysteries in Australia as in Africa. Communal marriage, as practised in Totemism, had been reduced in Egypt to the system of two wives; the one being known as the Hemet or Wife, the other as the Neb.t-Paru or Mistress of the House. This was also an Inner-African marriage institution. The first corresponded to Isis the Wife; the second to Nephthys the Mistress of the House. The Wives of Osiris were also his Sisters. Isis says to Osiris, "I am thy double Sister." This she was in the two characters of Isis and Nephthys, because the Great Mother *qua* Mother duplicated in the two females as ancestresses. Hence the "Double Divine Mother" who is mentioned in the texts. Not that Osiris was supposed to have married two Blood-Sisters, but that sister was the earlier name for the Wife, because there was a Totemic Sisterhood corresponding to the Totemic Brotherhood. This dual symbolism extant amongst the Australian aborigines, had been divinized and preserved in the Mythology of Egypt, because it was once extant in the Sociology. In these Two Sisters who were Two Wives one sees the Totemic consorts reduced to that number as the sisters of one brother, on the way to complete monogamy. At an earlier social stage, which we find among the Namaqua Hottentots, two chiefs had four wives in common among them. This was a departure from the equality of the more primitive communal connubium in which four brothers were husbands to four sisters, as in Africa, or ten brothers to ten sisters, as in Britain.

There would have been two Ancestresses to the human race in the Hebrew Genesis if the legend had been properly reported. In the extra-biblical tradition Adam had two wives, Lilith and Chavah, but

Lilith, the more mystical female of the two, has been damned by orthodoxy as the demoniacal destroyer of children = she who did not bring forth. In a more mystical phase the female duality of nature was pre-pubescent and pubescent. It is mentioned here because the dogma of a Virgin-Mother originated in this natural reality, and because the two divine women Isis and Nephthys also represent the Virgin and the Mother in this mystical character. Isis was the Virgin and Nephthys was Matrona; the Virgin who conceived, and Matrona who brought forth the child. Female nature of itself divides into the two phases of Girlhood and Womanhood; the Virgin and the Mother, the one being the Mother of blood, the other the Milch-Mother of the child. Such was the origin of a double Motherhood which is personified in the Egyptian mythos. In one cult the Goddess Neith is the Mother who conceives the child, and Sekhet is the Bringer-forth. Now, Neith was the mystical Virgin, whilst Sekhet was the Goddess of sexual passion. But in the Osirian cult this female duality was represented by Isis the Virgin and Nephthys the Nurse. These are the Two human Ancestresses (Tiriti) divinized, but not merely as two sisters in sociology.

The marital or sexual relations were at first promiscuous. Then there was a division of the gregarians into two communities or classes in which the primal promiscuity was regulated for group-marriage with the totality divided in two halves, and subdivided afterward by the Totems, which were extended more and more until they reached the radius of the "Upper Ten" or the Chinese "hundred families." As will bear repeating, to the confusion of various writers, the Arunta have traditions of a time when a man always married a sister of his own Totem. This, as tribal, followed the marriage of the brother and sister of the blood in natural endogamy: the same intermarriage that is found in African Totemism. There was a time, the Arunta also say, when "under the old system" all the Purula women were eligible as wives to a Panungo man, whereas under the new system only one half of the women were marriageable to him (*Native Tribes,* p. 421), those of the other half being strictly forbidden to him. This shows that utterly promiscuous intercourse was followed and superseded by the division of the whole into two halves; which we take to have been the intercourse that was sacred to the brother and sister of the blood within the matriarchal family, and which was afterwards divided into the first two exogamic intermarriageable groups. As testified to by the latest witnesses, the "fundamental feature" in the organism of the Australian tribes is "the division of the tribe into two exogamous intermarrying groups" (p. 55). In the Urabunna Tribe, which may be taken as typical, "the whole tribe is divided up into two exogamous intermarrying classes, respectively called Matthurie and Kirarawa. These two classes are subdivided into *two sixes* as Totemic groups. "All descent is counted from the Mother both as regards class and Totem" (p. 60). And "the men of one half of the tribe must marry the women of the other half," in marriage by the group, no such thing as individual marriage being known. One of the Australian aborigines who had travelled far and wide has stated that "he was furnished with temporary wives by the various tribes amongst whom he sojourned in his travels; that his right to these women was recognized as a matter of course; and that he could always ascertain whether they belonged to the *division* into which he could legally marry, though the places were 1,000 miles apart and the languages were quite different." (Fison and Howitt, p. 53.) Starting from the beginning with the Two Classes, one man at that stage was entitled to half the women. As we find, the two divisions spread out over great parts of the land. Totems were added and further divisions made when the two were divided into four and the four into eight, but if the man belonged to one of the primary two classes, his right to half of the women corresponding to his Totem would still hold good if they were scattered over all the country. His range in the communal marriage would be more circumscribed if his were one of the well-known four Totems, and become still more limited if it were only one of the eight into which the two were so frequently subdivided in Australia and America. On certain festival occasions the women of all the Totems are held as common property or there is partial promiscuity of the sexes by a return from the subdivisional arrangement to that of the first Two Classes; as when a man will lend his wife to a stranger, always provided that he belongs to the *same class* as himself (N.T., p. 93), the class that was anterior to the Totem. This common right of all the tribal brothers of one class to all the women of the other even from the beginning, when there were but two, will explain certain perplexing marriage customs of later times, when the marriage of individuals was slowly taking the place of marriage between groups or classes; which may be termed customs of exemption from the primitive communal connubium, such as the right of the tribal elders to act the part of Baal-Peor, and the *droit du seigneur* still extant, although commutable, in the island of Jersey.

As a natural fact, the human race originated from the Mother-earth in Two Classes. They were the forest-folk and the Troglodites born of the Tree and the Rock; and such a fact was sure to have been preserved in the Kamite Record. In the very first stage they were the children of Earth, or the Earth-Mother. The Mother is then divided or followed by the Two Women who are distinguished from each other by their emblems of the Birth-place: the Tree and the Rock, or stone with a hole in it, which is an image of the Mother-earth. We can now compare the wood and stone Churinga of the Arunta with other emblems of the Tree and Rock of earth.

The Australian Totemic system begins with being Dichotomous. There is a Division of the Whole in two halves. The Arunta erect two Totem-posts or sacred poles, one for the south and one for the north, by which the division is most carefully distinguished. There are Two Ancestresses or self-existent female founders; Two kinds of Churinga made of wood and stone; Two Women of the Lizard Totem. There are several instances in which the first departure from promiscuity remains final because it has never been outgrown. This is so in the case of the two classes still extant and still recognizable, which held good for marital rights all over the continent. The whole universe was divided into two primary classes of things, corresponding to the two primary Totemic classes of the Australian aborigines.

The Port Makay Tribe in Queensland divided all Nature between their two primary Motherhoods; the dichotomous system founded on the twofold character of the Mother as Virgin and Gestator whom the Egyptians had divinized as She who conceived and She who brought to birth. The Totems commonly follow the two divisions as the signs of subdivisions. Indeed, it appears that we get a glimpse here and there of the two divisions without any Totems following them, as if the most rudimentary organization had extended no further. The Banks Islanders, for example, appear to have been divided into two primary classes, and to have had no sub-divisional Totems. Reading Totemism by aid of the Egyptian wisdom, it is evident that the two classes, the two kinds of Churinga (wood and stone), the two Poles (North and South), the two women, represent the Motherhood that was duplicated in the two female ancestors; and that the Totems of the sub-divisions represent the blood-brotherhoods, thus affiliated to the Mother-blood, which were followed finally by the blood-fatherhood. The Arunta beginning is immeasurably later than the Egyptian tradition preserved in the astronomical mythology. Their beginning is in fact with Totemism. This was preceded by a period or condition of existence called "the Alcheringa" or the far-off past of the mythical ancestors of whose origin and nature they have no knowledge but have preserved the tradition.

The twofold division was fundamental and universal in Egypt. Beginning with the two Egypts and the two Tiruti, they had the two halves, North and South, divided by the Equinoctial line: the two earths upper and lower, the two houses of earth and heaven, the two houses of government, the two houses of the treasury, the two granaries, the two fields of sacrifice. The War Department was twofold. The property of the State and of the Temple was divided into two parts. An endeavour to recover the Kamite mythology from the traditions of the Arunta may look like fishing the infinite, but deep-sea dredgers sometimes find strange things. The Ritual preserves a record of the fact that in the primary division of the total or the whole earth in two halves, the boundaries of South and North were determined by two trees. Hence, when the Sun, or Solar God, rises in the East, he is said to issue forth from betwixt the two sycamores of the North and South. This division of the oneness in space into North and South in locality has been curiously preserved by the Arunta Tribes, who make use of the two Poles in their religious or Totemic ceremonies, one the Nurtunja, is erected in the North; the other, called the Waninga, is made use of in the South. (P. 627.) These are equivalent to the Kamite two sycamore-trees of the North and South, as types of the original division of the earth, and of the later earth and heaven; also called the two trees in the garden of the beginning. This primordial division of the whole into two classes still persists in the Christian scheme of the future life, where the dichotomous arrangement of the promiscuous multitude is continued as from the first. There are to be only two classes of people in the world to come, and only two Totems, the sheep and the goat, to distinguish those who are still described in gesture-language as being the one on the right hand, the other on the left;

which is a re-beginning hereafter in exact accordance with the first Totemic bifurcation of the human race on earth.

In the course of time, as human consciousness increased, the Mother would be made exempt from the primitive promiscuous intercourse. Here it may be observed that much of the early wisdom was secreted in the Totemic Tabus that were recited to the initiates in the mysteries of young-man and young-woman-making. The Buffalo-clan of the Omaha Indians are prohibited from eating a calf whilst it is red, but when it turns black the animal may be eaten. This, as we understand it, was a mode of memorial by means of Tabu. There was a similar prohibition in the Red Maize clan. The youngsters of the sub-clan are told that if they were to eat of the red maize they would break out in running sores all round the mouth. Nothing is more common in the initiation of Australian youths than for these to be solemnly warned against eating forbidden food. They are not to eat the emu, that is a Totem which represents the Mother—as did other forms of prohibited food, including the tree. Thus eating the fruit of the forbidden tree is violating the Mother or female, in one of the phases known to be prohibited. If, as herein advanced, the Totem first represented the Mother, we may find a root-reason why it came to be prohibited from being eaten, excepting as a sacrament at the religious festival of promiscuity once a year. We know that in the Totemic Mysteries it was the Mothers or female elders who inducted the boys into a knowledge of connubium. This probably registers the fact that, when the boys became pubescent, the Mothers showed their own way, in the early state of promiscuity. And the likelihood is that the Mother was made Tabu to her own children as the earliest law of prohibition from what came to be considered unnatural sexual intercourse which had been at one time natural. They were prohibited from "eating of her" in this sense, and the mode of memorizing the law would be by not eating of the zoötype which represented the Mother. The Hindu does not eat the cow, the Jew does not eat the swine, and this is because these represented the Mother as a Totemic sign, and the typical Great Mother in the Mythology. Descent from the Mother was represented by descent from the Totem. Thus, if the Totem were a cow, and it was said in a mystery, thou shalt not eat of the cow, when it was intended to repudiate the primitive practice, the command would signify in Sign-language, "Thou shalt not eat the Mother." She was now forbidden food, whether as the cow, the sow, the emu, or the tree, the same as with the red calf, which represented the child. According to Bailey, the custom of the Veddahs "sanctions the marriage of a man with his younger sister." But to "marry an elder sister or aunt would, in their estimation, be incestuous," whereas "marriage with the younger sister is considered to be natural." It was in fact the proper marriage. To understand this, we may assume that the elder sister of two stands for the Mother, and that the Tabu was originally directed against connubium betwixt the son and the Mother, whereas the marriage of a brother and sister, blood or tribal, was allowed as the only proper connection now for preserving the Mother-blood without committing incest.

If the Totem is a means of Tabu, as we know it to have been, and the Mother or the Sister is represented by the Totem, then the human female is aimed at under various Totemic types. Thou shalt not eat the calf whilst it is red would convey protection for the pre-pubescent girl. There are twenty different kinds of game forbidden to the Narrinyeri youths in their initiation; also any food belonging to women is prohibited. This would include the animal which constituted the Totem that was first of all the sign of the Mother herself, as the cow, the sow, the mouse, or other female zoötype. Thus, when, as Plutarch tells us, the Egyptians thought that if a man should drink the milk of a sow his body would break out in sores, it should be remembered that the sow was a Totem of the Mother, and the human Mother was masked by the sow. Various Tabus are expressed in Sign-language, which has to be interpreted. A prohibition against eating the Mother would be expressed by not eating the food or animal that was her Totem. Say the Totem was a type of the Mother, who was at one time eaten, and was represented by the cow, and afterwards the custom was prohibited, the law of Tabu in that case would be conveyed to the initiate in the primitive mysteries by the injunction "Thou shalt not eat the cow," or cohabit with the Mother. Various Tabus were certainly conveyed in that way. Thou shalt not eat the cow, Hindu and Toda Tabu; Thou shalt not eat the sow, Jewish Tabu; Thou shalt not drink the milk of the sow, Egyptian Tabu; Thou shalt not eat the hare, Damara Tabu; Thou shalt not go near or look on the crocodile, Bechuana Tabu; Thou shalt not eat the calf while it is red, Omaha Tabu; Thou shalt not touch the Mother-blood, common Tabu; Thou shalt not eat the *female* of any animal, Kurnai Tabu; Thou shalt not eat the fruit of the tree of knowledge, Biblical Tabu; Thou shalt not eat the Totem, common Tabu. We might add "Thou shalt not marry a deceased wife's sister," as a Christian Tabu. Thus not eating the cow or other female-totem— like the sow or the panes-bird—would originally mean not conjoining with the Mother, whereas not eating the calf whilst it was red would be a mode of protecting or of safeguarding the impubescent girl.

The Totemic festival of fructification naturally had a phallic character, as it was sexual from the first. It was not only performed at seed-sowing and harvest, on behalf of food. Long before corn was cultivated in the name of Isis or Demeter, there was a general rejoicing at the time when the youth was made into a man and the girl into a woman. The general rejoicing at the girl's coming of age was in celebration of her entering into connubium, which was communal, as she was then open and accessible to all the males, at least on this occasion when she entered the ranks of womanhood as common property, which was afterwards made several by development of the marriage-law. Marriage began as a recognized, if regulated, right of all the brothers to ravish every maiden as she came of age, and thus to make a woman of her for tribal connubium. And the primitive rite, though commuted, was continued in the later ceremonies. Various customs tend to show that capture in marriage originated as a mode of rescuing or ransoming the woman from the clutch of the general community in which the female was common to all the males of the group. In the special marriage of individual pairs the woman had to be captured and carried off from the group—only instead of being captured we might say "rescued" by the individual (and his friends) from being the promiscuous property of the community. Hence the custom of compensation to the group (or, later, parents) for permitting the female to become private property in personal marriage. The primitive rite of connubium was first consummated by all the males of the Totemic group, not by an individual husband. The customs show that communal connubium involved connection with the whole brotherhood as a rite of marriage after the general promiscuity had been modified. For instance, with the Australian Kunandaburi tribe when a girl became marriageable, on natural grounds, her affianced husband, accompanied by his male contemporaries, fetched her from her parents, and the marriage was consummated there and then, not by the husband, but by the whole of his confrères; the *jus primae noctis,* including all his Totemic brethren. Mr. O'Donnell, who furnished the information, says it included all the males present in camp without exception of class, Totem or kin, and was fulfilled for several days. (Howitt, *Mother-right to Father-right,* J. A. S., Feb. 7, 21, 1882.) This was communal connubium once for all, but only once, in place of the older custom of continual promiscuity. In the Sonthal marriage, which also takes place by the group once a year, all the candidates for matrimony live together for six days in promiscuous intercourse. After which, only separate couples are held to have established their right to marry. (*The People of India,* by J. F. Watson and J. W. Kaye, vol. I, p. 2.) Thus there was a rite of promiscuity observed as a propitiatory preparation for individual marriage. This was to be seen at the temple of Belit in Babylon, where the women offered themselves to all men promiscuously before they were free to marry. It was a mode of releasing the woman from a bondage imposed upon her in the past. It is said of this custom in the Epistle of Jeremy—"The women also *with cords about them,* sat in the ways burning bran for incense: but if any of them, drawn by some that passeth by, lie with him, she reproacheth her fellow that she was not thought as worthy as herself *nor her cord broken*" (*Book of Baruch,* 6, 43). When the Attic maidens danced as bears at the Brauronia in the ἀρκτεια of Artemis, it was a mode of making them individually marriageable, and the mode was evidently in accordance with the Totemic ritual as in the mysteries of Belit. This will also explain the crave for human blood, which was attributed to the goddess, on the ground that the blood was that of the Virgins thus consecrated by the most ancient practice of promiscuity, or all-for-all.

In various ways the Totemic or tribal organization fought hard and long against the woman becoming private property. The males considered, with Prudhomme, that property was robbery, and individual ownership in marriage had many modifications in the course of being eventually established.

In the south of Malayalam a married woman is permitted to have twelve other husbands as lovers besides the man to whom she is legally bound, but she must play the game fairly and not exceed the number allowed. With the Esquimaux or Inoits the primitive communal marriage still obtains in spite of their being monogamists in appearance. As M. Réclus remarks, adultery is a daily escapade with the women as well as the men. The "members of the Marital Association keep running accounts and open large credits" with each other. When the wind blows from the south every woman is out on the rampage after other men, but each wife must lawfully couple with the man to whom the husband would willingly have lent her, and who will lend his own wife in return. They hold that all were made for all. The sin against nature is for the lawful wife to seek connubium with a bachelor, who can make *no return in kind* to the husband. (Réclus, *Primitive Folk,* Eng. tr., p. 32. Ross, Second Voyage.) The custom is African. Sir Harry Johnston mentions a curious mode of weighing out even-handed justice in cases of adultery. Amongst the A-nyanja if a man is caught in the act he is compelled to get another man as substitute to cohabit with *his* wife before he can return to her; he must also pay his substitute for this service four yards of cloth, or make an equivalent present, otherwise the substitute can claim and carry off the wife as his own property. (*Brit. Cent. Africa,* p. 415.)

It was not the men alone who resisted the change. According to Petherick, the mother of the bride, among the Hassanyeh Arabs, protests against "binding her daughter" to a due observance of that chastity which matrimony is expected to command for more than two days in the week at a time. (Petherick, J., *Egypt, the Soudan, and Central Africa.*) Various ways of limiting the primitive promiscuity, and at the same time of securing elasticity in the marriage tie, might be cited. For example, the Spaniards found a curious custom current in Lancerota. A woman there had several husbands, but "a husband was considered as such *only during a lunar revolution.*" (Spencer, *Data,* 298.) Thus one woman was limited to one man for a month, and the marital relations were changeable with the moon. That which was once the woman's right is still sought for as a privilege when the Esthonian women claim to repeat the rites of the ancient saturnalia, such as dancing in a state of nudity at the festival of spring. With us the Matriarchate still survives on Friday, the woman's day, and in February, the month in which the women claim the right to choose their husbands every leap-year. On certain festive occasions there is a total or partial return to the pre-eval status of the sexes. This return occurs at the phallic festival or primitive Agapæ. In a corroboree of the Arunta, which lasts for ten days or a fortnight at a time, there is a partial return to promiscuity, or the sexual licence which the natives say was a practice of the Alcheringa, or old, old times. (N.T., pp. 96-101.) This does not stand alone. According to the report of Mr. Kühn in *Kamilaroi and Kurnai* (by L. Fison and A. W. Howitt, pp. 285-7), the men of the Turra tribe were not debarred from sexual intercourse with women of their own Totem in the orgies of the grand corroboree. This shows the same return to utter promiscuity for the time being as in all other celebrations of the phallic festival when the only law was that of all for all. It was a return *pro tem.* to the most ancient usage, which is represented in mythology by the old first Mother in connubium with her own sons. The primitive customs were established as a means of memorizing that which could not otherwise be registered. Thus the Arunta danced the history of their descent from the time when the race was not divided by the Lizard. And thus the state of promiscuous intercourse was repeated in the religious mysteries, including those of the Christian Church. According to a Latin myth, the saturnalia of ancient Rome was held in commemoration of the sexual promiscuity that once obtained. Such customs constituted the record of prehistoric if not primitive man. That is why their performance is so permanent and so universal.

A change in the human descent from the Motherhood to the Fatherhood is apparent in the Egyptian Mythology as early as the time of Ptah, the father of Atum-Ra. The Mother, human or divine, was primordial. Next came the sisters. Then the brothers, the same in mythology as in Totemism. Previous to the dynasty of Ptah there were seven brothers born of the sevenfold Motherhood, when there was as yet no father individualized. Six of these were pre-human, for instance, Sut the Male-Hippopotamus, Sebek the Crocodile, Shu the Lion, Hapi the Ape, Apuat the Jackal, Kabhsenuf the Hawk; and one, the Elder Horus, was human, as the child of Isis, the blood-Mother. The seven souls are commonly reckoned as 6+1. The six are pre-anthropomorphic. They were powers of the elements represented by the zoötypes, such as the soul of earth that was imaged by the beast of earth; the soul of water by the crocodile; the soul of breathing-force by the lion; the soul of fire by the ape; the soul of vegetation by the serpent. The seventh soul was human. This was imaged in Child-Horus, who became the chief of the Seven and leader of the Company.

The Dog-rib Indians preserve a tradition, which is also repeated along the Pacific coast from Alaska to Oregon, that the ancient Mother of the human race was a woman who was mated with a dog. The woman gave birth to six pups, which used to throw off their skins at will when they were alone, and play in human shape. This, in its quaint way, is another form of the mystery of the six as prehuman souls which culminated in the seventh soul that attained the human status together with the anthropomorphic type. In the Mangaian "Mute-land," at the root of all beginning, there are "Two Women," called the Mother and her Daughter. This beginning was at the bottom of the hollow cocoa-nut shell called Avaiki. Vari is the name of the mythical Great Mother. Tu-Metua is the daughter. Her name, which signifies "Stick-by-the-parent," is knowingly natural. Another point. She is the last product of the Great Mother, the only female child, and is called her support, her beloved child. These two are the ground and basis of a world in six divisions.

Now, there came a time in Egypt when the brothers, who had previously been the children of the Mother, were called the sons of Ptah, and all their powers were comprehended in the unity of the God who was portrayed as both Father and Mother in one person. In the Texts, Ptah is called "the husband of his Mother," which shows the polygamous Patriarch who afterwards entered the monogamic state with Sekhet Mer-Ptah for his single consort. (Maspero, *The Dawn of Civilisation,* p. 106, note, Eng. tr.) It has been previously shown that the custom of couvade was a dramatic mode of affiliating the offspring to the father which had previously derived its descent from the Mother. (*Nat. Genesis.*) It is certain that in this the male impersonates the Mother because he acts as if in gestation with the child and sometimes undergoes a fictitious parturition. But the supreme peculiarity of this primitive mystery is that the male parent not only acts the part of the Mother, but also of the father; both parents in one person. It is in this sense only that Sut, who was the first-born of the Seven, is called in later language a Father of the Gods. (Rit., ch. 8.) In Akkad or Babylonia, the group of seven males is divided into Ea as a father with his six sons. It is the same among the Zuni Indians, whose fetish deities are seven in number, that is six, with a form of God the Father as the supreme one. These were the rulers of the six regions or mountains, with Po-shai-an-kia in the centre as the head over all. (Cushing. Second Annual Report, Bureau of Ethnology, Washington, 1883.)

A soul of life in man, animal, and vegetable was at one time held to be derived by the transformation and embodiment of some external force in animal guise. Hence came the anima or soul of wind that was humanized in breathing, whether as the soul of man or animal. At length it was observed that a human soul of flesh was formed or embodied in the Mother-blood, as it was written in the secret Book of Nature. This was the earliest soul of man that was discreted from the external elements of life, which formed the rudimentary and pre-human beings who are to be met with in the legends of the aborigines the whole world over. These were also known to the Semites as pre-Adamic people; the Admu, the Kings of Edom, which brings us back to the Egyptian root of the matter in the word *Tum* or *Tem*. Tem, we repeat, signifies Mankind, mortals created persons, which were created mystically from the soul of Adam in Hebrew, or Atum in Egyptian, the earlier form of which name in the Ritual is "Tum." The race of Tum, Atum, or Admu identify their origin in nature, with the soul of blood by the Adamic name. And, sociologically, the "Creation of Man" *qua* man was a birth of Totemism. The creation of man in the Egyptian genesis is late when measured by the mythology. Atum represents the primal being who was the earliest evolved as perfect man. As Sun-God he is designated Ra in his first sovereignty, the solar mythos being last of all. This, with Atum as Supreme God in the human likeness, was preceded by the lunar and the stellar mythos; by the Mother-earth and all her Elemental Powers. We shall frequently find the time-gauge of the past in Egypt when it is nowhere else recoverable on earth.

The subject of the Hebrew beginnings is fundamentally the same, as will be seen when we can reach the root. It is the evolution of the human race from the pre-human conditions that were actual in nature and not, as alleged, the abortions of a false belief. This was the subject dramatized, danced and taught in all the mysteries of gesture-language and Totemic ceremonies by means of which the unwritten past was commemorated and indurated by ceaseless repetition of the acted drama.

The so-called Legends of Creation would be more correctly termed the legend of human Evolution, although in a different sense from that of Darwinian development. As Semite, they came to us in the latest and least genuine form, with no clue to any true interpretation. In a Maori myth, Man was created by the God Tiki from red clay. This he kneaded with his own blood, or with red water from the swamps. Man is Atum in Egyptian, Admu in Assyrian, Adam in Hebrew; and this was the creation of the human Being discriminated from the preliminary and pre-human Beings of the Mythos and the Märchen in legendary lore. It was the soul of blood distinguished from the earlier souls or forces of the external elements, which were the six preceding the human soul as supreme one. The origins in mythology are very natural underneath the mask. Indeed, they are a hundredfold more natural than the pretended explanations of their modern misinterpreters. Primitive naturalists had only the light of nature for guidance, and by this they went.

The creation of man, or, as the earlier versions have it, of men and women, was mystical in one sense, in another it is Totemic. As before said, the history of the race might be roughly divided into pre-Totemic and Totemic, pre-human and human. This, when reflected in the mirror of Egyptian Mythology, is pre-Atumic, or, in the Semitic version, pre-Adamic and Adamic. The same legend of a later origin for mankind is also Mexican. When there were no human beings on the earth certain of the lower powers solicited help from the supreme gods in the work of creation, or of a re-beginning. They are instructed to collect the remains of the former race, and these will be vivified by the *blood of the Gods*. In this version the god who plays the part of Atum, Adam, or Belus procures a bone from the burial-place, and on this the gods drop the blood drawn from their own bodies. Whereupon there is a new creation, namely, that of mankind. (Mendieta, *Hist. Ecl. Ind.*, p. 77.) Here, as elsewhere, the human soul of blood is derived from source as male instead of from the earlier motherhood. So in the Book of Genesis the second creation of Adam is based upon the bone called a rib which is extracted from the male.

It is in Atum, the Son of Ptah, that man was perfected. In him the Matriarchate is completely superseded by the Father-Right or derivation from the Fatherhood. Now the change in the human descent from the Mother-blood to the Father-blood is obviously commemorated in the mysteries or ceremonial rites of the Arunta. In the operation of young-man-making two modes of cutting are performed upon the boy by which he becomes a man and a tribal father. The first of these is commonly known as circumcision, or lartna, by the Arunta; the other ceremony of initiation, which comes later, is the rite of sub-incision called ariltha. The second cutting is necessary for the completion of the perfect man. Indeed, some of the more stalwart young men undergo the cruel rite a second or even a third time (N.T., p. 257.) to prove their manhood. With this trial-test the youth becomes a man; a fathership is founded, and, as certain customs show, the Motherhood is in a measure cast off at the time or typically superseded by the fatherhood. Nature led the way for the opening-rite performed upon the female, therefore we conclude that this preceded the operation performed upon the men, and we suggest that this was a custom established, like that of couvade, in the course of commemorating the change from the Matriarchate to the Father-right.

The rite is Inner African. It is universally practised by the Fan (or Fang) Tribes. An uncircumcised native is not considered as a man either for fighting, working, or inheriting, but is regarded as a nonentity and not allowed to marry. The rite proves the reality of manhood. (Nassau, *Fetishism in West Africa,* p. 12.)

We have previously traced the custom of couvade to Ptah, and now propose to trace the rite of ariltha or sub-incision to the full-formed father Atum, who was his son. When the Arunta perform the rite of sub-incision, which follows that of the primary operation, a slit is cut in the penis right down to the root. The natives have no idea as to the origin of the practice. (N.T., p. 263.) But as the practice proves, it is performed as an assertion of manhood, and is a mode of making the boy into a man, or creating man. Now, at this time it was customary to cast the Motherhood aside by some significant action, that is at the time when the fathership is established in the initiation ceremony. And in the Arunta rite of sub-incision the operating Mura first of all cuts out an *oval-shaped* piece of skin (from the male member) which he flings away. (p. 257.) The oval shape is an emblem of the female all the world over, and this we take to be another mode of rejecting the mother and of attributing begettal to the father, as it was attributed in the creation by Atum-Ra, who was both male and female (as the one All-Parent). The human soul was preceded by the elemental forces of external nature which were typified in a tradition that is universal. The soul that followed these as human was then born of blood, at first of Mother-blood, the blood of Isis, which was followed by a creation from the Father-blood. In the Babylonian legend concerning the generation of mankind attributed to Oannes by Berosos, the beginning is with hideous beings in the abyss, which are described as human figures mixed with the shapes of beasts. "The person who was supposed to have presided over them was a woman named Omoroca." This is the Great Mother who at first was Mother-earth. "Belus came and cut the woman asunder," which in Totemism is the dividing of the one woman, or the type in two. At the same time he destroyed the animals in the abyss. Thus the pre-human period was succeeded by the Matriarchate and the two female Ungambikula, who in the Arunta tradition cut and carved the rudimentary creatures into Totemic men and women. Then Belus the deity "cut off his own head: upon which the other gods mixed the blood with the earth; and from thence men were formed." Thus the source of life, or a soul of blood was changed from the female to the male deity who in the Egyptian theology is Atum-Ra, or Tum, the image of created man, or of man who was created from the soul of blood that is at first female and afterwards was fathered on the male. This creation of man or Tum is represented in the "Book of the Dead" (ch. XVII). The God, as Father, takes the Mother's place; the Matriarchate terminates in the mythology of Egypt. Tum is described as giving birth to Hu and Sa, as the children of Him who now unites the Father with the Mother as divinity in one person.

Hu denotes matter, Sa (or Ka) signifies spirit. This creation, then, is from blood and spirit; "the double primitive essence" first assigned to Ptah. The change from the Mother-blood to the Father-source is the same in the Kamite legend as in the Semitic version, but the *modus operandi* was different. Belus produces the blood by cutting off his own head, whereas in the Ritual Father Atum draws the blood from the genitalia of a divine being who is both male and female blended in the formation of the Father-Mother, from whom the soul of blood was now derivable. The drops of blood are described as issuing from the person of Atum when he performed the rite of "sub-incision" or of mutilation on himself in the generation now attributed to the solar deity, considered to be male as well as female, or, finally, male instead of female. Thus the Arunta are still performing a blood-covenant in the rite of ariltha on the male which is attributed to Atum-Ra in the Egyptian mythos and by which he demonstrates the parentage of the children Hu and Sa, in the course of changing the descent from the Matriarchate to the Patriarchate. The primitive essence of human life was blood derived from the female source, with Nature herself for the witness. In the later biology it was derived from the "double primitive essence" of Ptah that was continued in Atum and his two children Hu and Sa. Thus the basis of being was shifted from the Mother-blood to that of blood and spirit assigned to the Fatherhood.

From the "cutting" of the male member now attributed to Atum-Ra we infer that the rite of circumcision and of sub-incision was a mode of showing the derivation from the human father in supersession of the Motherhood, and that in the Arunta double-cutting the figure of the female was added to the member of the male. Nor is this suggestion without corroboration. In his ethnological studies (p. 180.) Dr. Roth explains that "in the Pitta-Pitta and cognate Boulia dialects the term *Me-Ko ma-ro* denotes "the man with a Vulva," which shows that the oval slit WAS cut upon the penis as a figure of the female and a mode of assuming the Motherhood. In the Hebrew Book of Genesis this carving of the female figure on the person of the male—in the second creation—has been given the legendary form of cutting out the woman from the body of the male. Adam is thus imaged in the likeness of the biune Parent. The foundation of Jewish Monotheism was laid in the blood of the new covenant which followed the cult of the female. It is noticeable that when the Jewish child is circumcised it is said of him that he is made to "enter into the covenant of Abraham," that is of the Great Father in Israel. Moreover, the man who stands sponsor as the godfather is called the Master of the Covenant. (Godwyn, *Moses and Aaron*, p. 216.) This may possibly explain the re-circumcising of the children of Israel. If, as the history asserts, they dedicated to the female in the earlier time and were afterwards circumcised in a covenant made with the deity as God the father, re-circumcising would be a means of denoting a change in the rite, when the people were circumcised on the Hill of Foreskins. "And this is the cause why Joshua did circumcise" (*Joshua*, ch. V, 2, 4). The two covenants would thus tally with the two forms of the ceremony performed in first circumcision by the Arunta and in sub-incision, which is re-circumcising in the rites of the same people. Thus, there were two covenants, one sealed in the blood of the female, one in the blood of the male, and both were applied to the deity according to the sex.

This mode of affiliation to the male deity is likewise obvious in the legend of the Guatemalans, who besought the Quiché God Tohil to favour them with the element of fire. This he gave them on condition that they united themselves to him by drawing blood "beneath the girdle." (Bancroft, v, 547.) That is by drawing it from the *membrum virile* in a covenant of blood. When they did this they received the fire from Heaven which was derived direct from God the father as begetter who was Atum-Ra in Egypt, and God the father in spirit as well as in flesh and blood.

The cause of a mystical relationship that was recognized between man and the animals may now be traced on grounds less lofty than that of the supposed divine incarnations, and more natural than that of an animistic interfusion which led to a confusion of identity and personality. The animals were first recognized as powers in themselves, but they were also adopted as the living visible symbols of elemental powers that were superior to the human as a means of representing natural phenomena. They were further adopted into the human family as Totemic types with religious rites that gave them all the sanctity of the blood-covenant and made them typically of one flesh with the human brothers. Thus they were doubly adopted; and this led to their becoming later living fetishes as the naturalized representatives of superhuman powers, though not as the direct object of human worship. The life-tie assumed between Totemic man and the Totemic animal or zoötype was *consciously assumed,* and we can perceive by what process and on what ground the assumption was made. The zoötype being adopted as a badge of distinction, the primeval coat of arms, it was a custom for the human beings to enter into a brotherhood of blood. That is, the men who were not born of the same mother, or of two sisters, could extend the natural tie of blood by a typical rite to others who were born of different mothers. In this way, the larger kin, clan, or tribe was formed on the basis of brotherhood under some totemic sign. Now if the animal becomes of kin to the human brother by virtue of a covenant intentionally made in the blood of both, that proves the kinship did not exist before. The relationship did not spring from any root in nature, or any false belief, but was ordained for the purpose, and is consequently limited to the particular beast and brotherhood. The bull is only kinsman to those whom he serves as a Totem, an image of the ancestor and a type of the fraternity. So is it with all the other zoötypes which had been employed from before the time when the individual fatherhood was known. There is no necessary confusion of identity. If men had abstained from eating the animals on the ground of kinship and intercommunion of nature, because of a confusion or identification of themselves with the beasts, they ought to have abstained from eating any, whereas they ate them all in turn, exceptions being made solely on the artificial ground of the Totemic motherhood or brotherhood. The beast only became of the "same flesh" with the particular family because it had been adopted as their Totem, ancestral animal, or foster-brother of the blood-covenant, and not on account of any belief that they descended from this or the other non-human parent with a different progenitor for every separate group. Even in the human relationship the being "of one flesh" shows that the system represents a later extension of the same family that first derived from one mother, the mode of extension being by the blending of blood, the re-birth, the drinking of the covenant, and eating of the fetish. But there was nothing promiscuous in this arrangement, which had been made on purpose to avoid promiscuity. They did eat, and did not tolerate being eaten by, each other's Totems. The relationship of men with beasts was most deliberately adopted, and the partnership was held with the strictest regard to the law of limited liability. Thus the blood-brotherhood with the beasts was not based on any belief that they were on a level with the human being, nor on any mental confusion respecting their oneness of nature. At least it was not that which first rendered the animals tabu, or made them sacred to men.

The typical character of the Totemic animal was continued in various ways; putting on the skin was a mode of assimilating the wearers to the powers beyond the beast, the superhuman forces which the animals represented in visible symbolry. Hence on going to battle they wore the skins and acted the *rôle* of the animals, birds, and reptiles, as their link of alliance with the superhuman nature-powers that were over all. In like manner the God Shu, the warrior of the gods, the Egyptian Mars, does battle whilst wearing the superhuman power of the Lioness on his head—and the moon-god, Taht-Aan, is clothed with the power of the great Ape, the ideograph of superhuman rage, when he fights against the demons of darkness by night on behalf of the suffering Solar God. The mage or medicine-man was wrapped up in the skin of the Totemic beast for the purpose of communing with the spirits of the dead. Thus the trance, the transformer, and the transformation, the beast, the nature-power, and the human ghost, got mixed up together. Such being the fact, it is easy to identify the foundation of the faith of ignorant belief that the medicine-men had everywhere the power of transforming into wolves, hyænas, or tigers themselves; and that belief would cause the fear lest they should apply this power of metamorphosis to others, and ultimately create a belief in their power to transform human beings into animal shapes. The only veritable power of metamorphosis possessed by the ancient medicine-men or mages, the witches or wizards, was that of inducing the condition of trance either in others or in themselves. This was and is a fact in Nature with which the primitive races were profoundly well acquainted. But those who are ignorant of such phenomena will be apt to mistake a surface appearance for the underlying reality, and must find it difficult, if not impossible, to distinguish between the true cause and a false belief. In the mysteries they changed place and shape and nature with the beasts of prey. They masked themselves in the skins of animals, reptiles, and birds, and sat at feast in those forms to devour the sacrifice when the Totemic animal was slain for the Eucharistic rite. In that way they transformed and were said to change themselves into wolves or tigers, bears or crocodiles, to partake of this most primitive rite of transubstantiation. For it did become a religious ceremony and a mode of entering into alliance and communion with the powers first apprehended as superhuman. When the ghastly, grim reality had passed into the legendary phase we are told, as Plato tells us in the Republic, that those who ate of the human sacrifices offered to the Wolf were transformed into wolves. Herodotus likewise relates that the Neurian wizards changed themselves into wolves for a few days once a year. First, the men who ate the flesh of the Beast had changed themselves into wolves to eat it, according to the mode of masking. Next it was said that by eating human flesh men would become Were-wolves, and lastly we have the Were-wolf as a man who is supposed to turn into the wolf on purpose to devour human flesh. Such are the tricks of typology, based on the primitive simplicity and the agnostic misinterpretation of later times when the mythos passes into the fable which deposits these types of the were-wolf, the mermaid, the cockatrice, the serpent-woman, the vampire, or the ghoul. In the latest phase of this transformation and transubstantiation it is the flesh of a supposed historical personage that is eaten and his blood that is drunk with the view of effecting a transformation into Horus or the Christ. It was a masquerade; but the men beneath the masks originally knew that they were acting in characters which they themselves had created. They wore skins in a typical transformation; they clothed or tattooed themselves with the signs of superhuman powers for a definite purpose, and not because they were returning to the condition of beasts from which they came, or expected to be saved by doing so. The masking and metamorphosis were but modes of the mysteries which included the mystery of Trance. This primitive drama is not yet played out. The rites and doctrines are also to be identified at times as survivals in religious ritual. A startling illustration may be seen in a collection of English hymns (1754), where these lines occur:—

"What greater glory could there be
Than to be clothed with God?
He drew His skin upon my skin,
His blood upon my blood."

The skin is likewise assumed by the Manes as their Totem in the other life, different ideas being expressed by different kinds of skin. In the Ritual (ch. 145, 31) the speaker who has just been baptized and anointed in process of regeneration when he transforms into the likeness of Horus the adult says he has the skin of a Cat for his badge. The cat being a seer in the dark, the skin shows that he is no longer as the sightless Horus, but is the Horus with the second sight or beatific vision. With the Red Indians the skin of the Totemic animal is placed at the side of a man who is dead or dying. It has also been stuffed at times and hung above the grave. The sign is the same for the dead man as for the dead animal. In each instance the skin means renewal, repetition, resurrection for another life. It has been a common custom for the dead to be buried in the skin of an animal, or in shoes or boots made from the skin of an animal. When Field-Marshal the Duke of Wellington was buried in St. Paul's Cathedral his boots were taken with him to the tomb, and in a sense he was buried in the skin. The significance of the skin is everywhere the same. The slipper thrown after the newly-wedded has the same meaning. Leather is made from the skin that denotes a renewal of life, and the act expresses the desire for the couple to be blest with children. We have seen that the skin was equivalent to the animal as a type of renewal. This may afford us a clue to the custom of swearing oaths in making covenants on the skin, which would be like swearing by the future life, the hope of immortality, or "by the eternal God." The earliest masks were formed of the head and skin of the Totemic zoötype. They also represented the invisible powers, and finally became the heads of goddesses and gods. Masks were assumed when deities or spirits were represented in the mysteries. Thus, when a mask is put on by the Inoit girl at the time of her first menstrualia it denotes the presence of the Nature-power that reveals itself in this particular way as one of the mysteries of Nature. The masks that were worn in certain mysteries were derived from the Totemic zoötypes, not from the human face. Hence their superhuman ugliness at times. These masks were used as portraits of the powers beyond the Totem, and in the Inoit mysteries, when the controlling spirit of a Shaman was consulted, it was customary for the mask which represented the particular power invoked to be laid upon the Shaman's face, and this mask was the skin of a victim that moment killed. (Réclus, *Prim. Folk,* Eng. tr., p. 87.) A tribe of the hill-men near Darjeeling, in India, still retain the huge and hideous masks that represent the powers of Nature. These are worn on the heads of priests when performing their elaborate religious rites. One of these images the god who looks after their spears and helps to drive them home. Which shows the character of the masks as effigies of the Nature-powers is not forgotten. (Paragraph and picture in the London *Daily Mail,* Nov. 20, 1896.) We have seen that the change made by the young girl into an animal at puberty was an origin of wearing the mask. This we assume to have been primary. Next, the practice was continued in Matriarchal Totemism. Then the customs of cutting in sub-incision, of wearing the skin, and of becoming the Totemic beast, are applied to the male in the later mysteries of young-man-making.

The Totemic mysteries survived as eschatological in the Osirian religion. For example, when Horus the child, who was born of the Mother only, under the divine Matriarchate, makes his transformation into Horus the adult, who rises from the dead in Amenta, it is in the character of the Anointed son of the Father. Anointing had then become the mode of showing the Glory of the Father in the person of the Son. This was imaged with the holy oil upon the face of Horus. He who had been Horus the mortal in the flesh, is now Horus in spirit personalized and established as the Anointed Son. The typical Anointed originated as the youth who was made a man of at the period of puberty, at which time the Mother's child assumed the likeness of the father at the time of his Totemic rebirth. The boy who was initiated into the mysteries of the Australian Blacks was equally made the Anointed in however primitive a fashion. When his probation terminated, and the stringent rules of his novitiate were relaxed, he was rubbed by an old man with fat that was taken from the Totemic animal which was previously forbidden food. He was not permitted to eat the female of any animal, nor the emu, that primordial Mother-Totem, and he becomes a free man by having the fat of the animal smeared over his face. In fact he is made a figure of the Anointed. The Kurnai youth was made a free man of when anointed with fat. With the Adamanese the bodies of the initiates are smeared over with the melted fat of pork and turtle in the ceremony of free-man-making. (E. H. Man, *Aboriginal Inhabitants of the Andaman Islands,* p. 62.) The boy was anointed when he made his change into the adult. Horus was anointed when he transformed from the mortal Horus to the Horus in spirit who rose again from the dead. And this anointing is still practised in the extreme unction of the Roman Catholic rite that is administered when the dying are about to pass into the future life. This again correlates with, and is a survival of, the aboriginal custom of placing a lump of fat in the mouth of the dead, by which act they were made into a form of the Anointed preparatory to their resurrection. The mummies exhumed at Deir el-Bahari show that the faces had been painted and anointed for burial. "The thick coats of colour which they still bear are composed of ochre, carmine (or pounded brick) and animal fat." (Maspero, *Dawn of Civilisation,* Eng. Tr., p. 54, note 5.) These are also forms of the Anointed One, who was made so by extreme unction more primitively applied to Osiris the Karast-Mummy.

The art of Tattooing was likewise a Totemic mode of Sign-language. This also corroborates the feminine origin of the signs, as when some of the aborigines such as the Ainu of Japan, and the Siberian Chukchi, only tattooed their women. "Tattoo the women and not the men," is the command that was given in the Wisdom of Manihiki. The Totem is sometimes tattooed on the person of the clansman, as it was by the Iroquois, the Ojibways, and other tribes of the Red Men. The Indians of San Juan Capistrano practised a peculiar mode of tattoo. A figure of the personal Totem was made of crushed herbs on the right arm of the novice. The paste was then set on fire and the figure of the Totem burned into the flesh. At an earlier stage before the art of tattoo had been mastered it was the custom to cut the flesh and raise cicatrices to pattern. This was especially practised by the Australian aborigines, and the tribal badges thus figured in the flesh were sometimes representations of the Totem. (*Kamilaroi and Kurnai,* by Fison and Howitt, p. 66.) Herbert Ward, who suffered the ceremony of establishing the covenant of blood-brotherhood with Mata Mwiki, a Bangala chief, in 1886, found that the skin of the Bangalas was tattooed or slashed and cicatriced in conformity with the Totemic or tribal pattern and that the patterns varied with the different tribes. (Herbert Ward, *Five Years with the Congo Cannibals,* 1890.) The Esquimaux indicate the particular Inoit tribe by different ways of trimming the hair; the women by the figures tattooed on their faces. The Aleuts at one time tattooed the figures of birds and fishes upon their skins. The women told Hall that they tattooed their faces as a mark of high distinction. It was so, as a sign of womanhood. The custom of tattooing the Totemic token upon the body may be traced in survival through all the later mysteries as a mode of identifying the initiates with their particular community. It is more than probable that the habit of the ancient Britons mentioned by Roman writers in staining their bodies with woad really refers to the system of Totemic Tattoo, as is indicated by the description of the Picts found in Claudian's *De Bello Getico* (XXIV, 417-18), *"ferroque notatas porlegit examines Picto moriente figuras."* This is shown by an initial letter in the *Book of Kells*—a facsimile of which has been published by the Palæographical Society, containing the figure of a man quite naked, the body being covered all over with significant marks just as the hieroglyphics are described by Boece, who affirms that in "all their secret business the ancient Britons wrote with cyphers and figures of beasts made in manner of letters" which he identifies with the hieroglyphics of Egypt. Thus the woad-bedaubed men stigmatized as savages become the more intelligent illustrators of Totemic times and customs who wore the stigmata of Tattoo, and the Picts or painted men are the men who carried the Totemic marks either painted or branded on the living book of their own bodies. They were not merely dyeing their flesh for decoration, but making figures for use that could be read by others at sight. Even the raising of cicatrices in the flesh which preceded tattooing was an Egyptian custom. On the bas-reliefs of the Temples at Philæ and Ombos the bosoms of goddesses and queens are scored with long incisions which, starting from the circumference, united in the centre round the nipple of the breast. (Maspero.)

In Totemism the Mother and Motherhoods, the Sisters and Sisterhoods, the Brothers and Brotherhoods, the girl who transformed at puberty, the Mother who was eaten as a sacrifice, the two women who were ancestresses, were all of them *Human,* all of them actual, in the domain of natural fact. But when the same characters have been continued in mythology, they are superhuman. The Mother and Motherhoods, the Sisters and Sisterhoods, the Brothers and Brotherhoods, have been divinized. The realities of Totemism have supplied the types to mythology as goddesses and gods that wear the heads or skins of beasts to denote their character. The Mother, as human in Totemism, was known as the Water-Cow, and this became a type of the Great Mother in mythology and polytheism. But it is the type that was continued, *not the human Mother.* The Mother as first person in the human family was first person in the Totemic sociology. Thence came the Great Mother in mythology who was fashioned in the Matriarchal mould. But with this difference: it is the human Mother underneath the mask in Totemism. It is *not* the human Mother who was divinized as the Great Provider in mythology. Totemism is not derived from mythology, but it has been mixed up with it because the same Sign-language was employed in both. Thus, the Mother was human in the mask of Totemism and is superhuman in the mask of mythography. This was the Great Mother who was the First Person, as the "only one," according to the Egyptian Wisdom.

They were not seven human mothers or sisters who were constellated in the fields of Heaven as seven Hathors or seven Cows. These were the Mothers of food, who were givers of life in the form of the Cow, when the Seven Stars in Ursa Major supplied the numerical figure of Plenty. Thus there are two kinds of Motherhoods that have to be most carefully discriminated one from the other; the first is human, the last is superhuman. The human Mother might be represented by or as the Totemic cow, serpent, frog, or vulture. Nevertheless they were not human Mothers who were divinized in those same likenesses as the Egyptian goddesses Isis, Rannut, Hekat, and Neith. But the human Mother who was eaten at the sacramental meal did supply *a type* of the superhuman Mother in external nature, who also gave herself as a voluntary sacrifice for human food and sustenance; the Mother of life in death who furnished the eucharist that was eaten in the religious mysteries. The human Mother had been an actual victim, eaten as a sacrifice. The superhuman Mother or goddess was eaten *typically,* or by proxy. Hence she who was the giver of food and life to the world came to be eaten sacramentally and vicariously, that is, in some Totemic victim, by whose death her sacrifice was symbolically represented.

There were different types of the sacrificial victim at different stages of the Eucharist. At one stage it was the Red Calf as the type of Horus, the child. At another it was Osiris as the Bull or Ox. The victim, speaking in the Book of the Dead, exclaims, "I am the Bull of the sacrificial herd" who identifies his body with the "mortuary meal." But in Egypt the Great Mother was eaten as the Cow that represented the goddess Hathor or Isis; also as the Sow which represented the goddess Shaat or Rerit; two of the types that were figures of the Great Mother who thus gave her body and blood for human food that was eaten as a voluntary sacrifice of her own maternal self. Herodotus notwithstanding, the cow had been a type of sacrifice in Egypt. Moreover, it was the Red Cow or Red Heifer, the same as in the Hebrew Ritual. As already shown, the Mother-types and Totems were primary and the Red Cow was a type of the Blood-Mother from the time when she was the Red Water-cow of the first Mother Apt, who was succeeded by Hathor, as the Milch-Cow.

It is sometimes difficult to distinguish between the human Mother in Totemism and the Great Mother in Mythology, because the same types were employed for both. Besides which, as Earth was the bringer-forth of all living things, she was also a Mother to the human race in common with the other forms and elements of life. For instance, as the bringer-forth of life she was the Mother of animal food; the giver of grass-seed; of tubers and plants in the soil, and of food in the fruitful tree. As the Crocodile, the Serpent, the Goose, the Emu, or the Witchetty-Grub, she was the layer of the egg, and thus a Mother to be ultimately divinized as the Great Mother who was superhuman, in the Kamite Mythology; Apt, the Hippopotamus; Rerit, the Sow; Neith, the Crocodile; Rannut, the Serpent; Uati, the Papyrus; Hathor, the Fruit-tree; Isis, the Field. The human Mother was the suckler of her children. This image of Maternity was likewise given to the Earth as the Nursing-mother, who was the giver of liquid life in water. But the Earth as wet-nurse or layer of the egg for food could not be so directly rendered. Hence the need of Sign-language in the mythical representation of superhuman phenomena. The human Mother had brought forth her children in the forest and from the cave in the rock; in consequence of which, as natural fact, the tree and the hole in the stone, or the ground, have each continued ever since to represent the human birth-place in the image of the female figured as the superhuman Mother, the Great Mother-earth. It was not the human Mother that was the object of worship or of propitiation with the offering of blood. This was the typical Mother; the Great or pregnant Mother; the Mother of food and sustenance; the Mother who for ages on ages was not imaged in the human shape because she was superhuman. In modern phraseology the primitive "seekers after God" were seekers after food and drink and physical sustenance. The Giver of these elements was the Earth itself, or herself, when depicted in the image of the Mother as the Nurse of life.

Nothing simpler has been recovered from the past than the religious system of the Arunta Tribes of Central Australia, who, in their sacred rites, are self-portrayed as seekers after food. An important ceremony, that was designed to bring success in kangaroo-hunts, consisted in the letting of blood. Thus the blood was an offering to secure plenty of food. (N.T., p. 193, note.) In certain of the Intichiuma ceremonies blood is poured out freely as an offering on behalf of food. These ceremonies are performed for the purpose of insuring the increase of the animal or plant which gives its name to the Totem, the emu, the beetle, the kangaroo, or others. The blood was poured out on the earth as an oblation to the Earth-mother, even though she was only represented by the Emu-bird. The earliest religion, so to call it, was a cultus of the Mother who was propitiated as the "Only One" who was in the beginning. This was the primal providence or provider as the Great Mother, the Mother-earth, who was invoked with offerings of blood for food and drink. In Egypt she was given several characters. She was Abt; Khebt, or Ta-Urt, the Hippopotamus-headed; Rerit, or Shaat, the many-teated Sow; Hathor, the Cow; Rannut, the Serpent-woman, and others related to the phenomena of external nature as the source of life, of food and water.

The root of the whole matter was fecundity, and the goddess, who in later times was called the Mother of love in Egypt, originated in the giver of plenty as the goddess of fecundity. But the fecundity at first was that of Earth, the provider of food and drink. Hence, she was imaged by the Suckler who gave the image of life as Shaat the Sow, or Hathor the Cow. At this stage that which has been so often generalized by the phrase "Phallic worship" was propitiation of what we call Mother Nature=Mother-earth divinized, or idealized as superhuman in the likeness of the large-uddered Cow or the multimammalian Sow, which were figures in a cult of fecundity; the first and foremost object of the "worship" being the food and drink that were supplied by the Mother-earth who gave her life in sacrifice that men might live.

The Mother-earth, Dhurteemah, is still the primordial deity with the Bygah tribes of Seonee, India. They offer food to her as provider at every meal before they call on any other god or goddess. With the Babylonians Nin-Ki-Gal, the Great Lady, is another form of the Earth-Mother. As Miss Kingsley shows, this primitive Earth-Mother of African origin still survives in Africa as the Earth-Goddess Nzambi, the Great Mother. There is "aye a something" that shows the stage of the beginning is still extant as Inner African, from which the thought and symbolism of Egypt were developed. In her account of "Fetish" according to different schools Miss Kingsley tells us the Earth-Goddess Nzambi is the paramount feature in the "Fetishtic" religion. "She is the Great Mother." "Round her circle almost all the legends, in her lies the ultimate human hope of help and protection, or, in modern phrase, salvation." (Kingsley, M. H., *West African Studies*, pp. 154, 155.) Previously the same writer had said "the school of Nkissi is mainly concerned with the worship of the mystery of the Power of Earth; Nkissi-nsi." (Kingsley, *West African Studies*, p. 137.)

Now "the mystery of the power of earth," or Nkissi-nsi, as Egyptian, is expressed by the word Kep, which is a name of the old Earth-Mother, Ta-Urt. The word Kep signifies mystery, to be mysterious; the mystery of fermentation, the mystery of fertilization, and of water as the source of life. This is as it was in Africa from the first; and as it was in the beginning so it remained in Egypt, allowing for development, to the last, for Apt, the old first Mother-earth, survives in the eschatology of the Ritual, still keeping her hippopotamus form, as "the Mistress of divine protections" and rekindler of the light of life from the spark when it had gone out in the dark of death. Thus, she who had brought to birth as the Mother-earth lived on as the bringer to rebirth for another life in the phase of eschatology. (Renouf, *Book of the Dead,* ch. 137 A, 137 B. Notes. Also Vignette in Nebseni.)

The old first great mother, then, one of whose names is Khebt, was the Mother-earth in her primary character, and if we go back far enough we find the type is universal. The Mother-earth gave birthplace and food to all the children born of her. Isis, represented as the Sekhet or field, was still the Mother-earth. With the Algonkins, Mother-earth was the great grandmother of all. Mamapacha, worshipped by the Peruvian tribes, was the Mother-earth.

Following the pathetically-primitive custom of ceremonially eating the mother in honour, as the first giver of food, a cult emerges from the darkness of the past upon the way to worship; the worship of the Mother with young, who was the pregnant, therefore the great, Mother. This was a cult of supplication, propitiation, and thankfulness for food and liquid life, which made its offerings to the Mother-earth as the provider of plenty. Mother-earth is the Great Mother of the Moqui Indians, "Our Grandmother" with the Shawnees, and the Grandmother of the Karens in Burmah. Tari-Pennu is the Mother-earth to the Khonds of Orissa. The Finnish goddess, consort of Ukko, is the Mother-earth. The Esquimaux old Mother Gigone was the Mother-earth; Gae was the Greek Mother-earth; Ops was the Roman Earth-Mother, whom we look on as a form of the Egyptian goddess Apt, or Ap. The ancient Germans worshipped Mother Hertha, who is identical by name with the earth, and also with Ta-Urt, the Egyptian Mother-earth. There was a primitive kind or class of people known as earth-born aborigines, like the San of the Khoi-Khoi and the Chinese Miautze. These children of earth who came forth from the forest and the cave would naturally be divided first for recognition in two categories as the Children of the Tree and the Rock, which are spoken of by Hesiod as the two origins of mortals, both tree and rock being representatives of the earth as birthplace. This cult of the Earth-worshippers may account for the Earth-eaters, who still survive in Africa and also with the Indians of California. The tradition is common with the people of several countries that they issued originally from the ground. But to restore the lapsed meaning we have to read Earth for ground, and then identify the earth with one of her types as the Mother of all, who is the Great Mother in mythology. According to S. Powers, the Californian Indians think that their Prairie-Dog ancestors were moulded directly from the soil. If so, they have lost the clue which survives in mythology. The Coyote as a burrower in the ground is a type of the Mother-earth that was made the totem of the Coyote Indians. The birth of the human race from the Mother-earth is indicated both directly and indirectly in the legends of the Kaffirs. In these men issued from the ground, from the cleft in the rock, or a bed of reeds. Others say that Unkulunkulu split them out of a stone. It is still said of a great chief by the Zulus that he was not born; he was belched up by a Cow. The Cow, like the cloven stone, or the tree, was a female type of the Mother-earth. Thus represented, the earth becomes a rock, from which issued the race of men, or in the words of Isaiah, it is the rock whence they were hewn (ch. li, 1) and the hole of the pit from whence they were digged. Also, as the rock was a type of the earth, the Great Mother, we can see how and wherefore in a following stage the stone pillar or the hole-stone should become a figure of the mythical Genetrix as it was of Hathor and the Paphian Venus; and why the stone seat should be an emblem of the Earth-Mother Isis as a figure of foundation. With the Bushmen the Earth-Mother has become the typical "Old Woman" of later language. Earth as the superhuman Mother is denoted in the Quiché legend in which it is said the human race descended from a cave-dwelling woman or female. Cave, pit, and cavern were the uterus, so to say, of Mother-earth as the place of coming forth, the Unnu, or opening of Neith; the Ununait of Hathor as the solar birthplace. Very naturally the mount was typical of Mother-earth in which the cave was a place of birth for man and beast. "The citizens of Mexico and those of Tlatelolco were wont to visit a hill called Cacatepec, because, as they said, it was their Mother" (Bancroft). Molina states that the principal sacred place or Huaca of the Mexican Yncas was that of the hill Huanacauri, from whence their ancestors were held to have commenced their journey (Spencer, *Data of Sociology,* ch. XXIV, 186). The mount with the cave in it was a natural figure of the Mother-earth to the Troglodites who were born and there came to consciousness. When the Navajos issued from the womb (euphemistically from the bowels) of a great mountain near the San Juan River, that mountain is an image of the Mother-earth. The Oneida, Ojibway, and Dacotah Indians, who claim derivation from a sacred stone, at the same time trace their descent from the *mountain of the race*.

Naturally, the cave as birthplace of the Earth-Mother was identified with the uterine abode. We might say identified by it, that is by the emblem scrawled upon the rock from time immemorial. This figure, or similitude of the female, called the symbol of wickedness "in all the land" by Zechariah (ch. 5, 8), portrayed through all the world, has ever been most prominent in the primitive art of the aborigines from Africa to Australia. Not as an object of worship, nor of degradation, but as a likeness of the human abode depicted in the birthplace of the Cavemen. The superhuman type of the motherhood appears in symbolism as the Cleft, the Gap, the Cave, as well as the Tree, the Sow, the Water-Cow, Crocodile, Lioness, and other zoötypes. The human mother comes into view by means of her emblem, the hieroglyphic Ru or door of life in the divinized motherhood as the *Vesica Piscis* of later iconography. There is no getting outside of nature, either in the beginning or in the end. With the Arunta tribes of Central Australia a gorge among the hills at some local totem-centre is identified as the place of emanation from the Earth-Mother. This is exactly in keeping with the Gorge of Neith, whence issued the "younglings of Shu" as spirits of breathing-force. Local tradition tells that at the Emily Gap, near to Alice Springs, "certain Witchetty-Grubs became transformed into Witchetty-Men" (N.T., p. 123). Otherwise stated, the elemental souls passed into the mothers of that ilk to be specialised in the human form instead of becoming animal, bird, or reptile. If we take Hathor as the abode of birth, that is, the Mother-earth as the birthplace and the bringer-forth of life, the stone or conical pillar of Hathor was a type of this birthplace. Now, let us turn for a moment to the Erathipa-stone of the Arunta for the proof that the stone with an opening in it was a Totem of the Mother-earth, the stone out of which the Zulus say the human race was split in the beginning. There is no mistaking the nature of the Arunta stone. It is a representative image of the Mother in the very simplest form. According to the tradition, spirit-children issue from a hole in the Erathipa-stone. Over this aperture a black band is painted with charcoal. This completes that figure of the female which has been portrayed in all the earth as a symbol of the human mother applied to her who was externalized as the superhuman mother, the primeval birthplace. The Fijian pillar-stones were girdled round the waist with the primitive Cestus or Liku of hair, to typify pubescence and identify the motherhood. It is common for the Tree to be draped in female attire and hung with feminine ornaments, as when the Israelite women wove hangings for the Asherah. Two female figures of stone and wood are to be found not only in the Arunta Churinga, but at the head of all human descent and all the "stock-and-stone" worship of the world. They are recognized by Homer when Penelope says to Ulysses, "Tell me thy lineage, and whence thou art, for thou dost not spring from the ancient Tree nor from the Rock" (*Odyss.* 19, 163), meaning that he must be an immortal, whereas these are two types of an origin that is of the earth. Hesiod also (*Theog.* 30, 35) speaks of the Tree and Rock as being amongst the mysteries of the beginning pertaining to the ever-living, blest immortals. The earlier name of the chief sanctuary in Israel, called Bethel, was Luz, or the Almond Tree. Bethel was the place of the stone-pillar, as the abode of the God, and Luz, the locality of the Tree. These, we repeat, are two primary and universal types of the feminine abode, represented by the Two Women in Australia and the Two Divine Sisters in Egypt. They are classed together also as objects of abhorrence in the later casting out of the primitive types. "Woe unto them that saith to the *Wood* Awake! to the dumb stone, *Arise!*" in the making of idols (Hab. ii, 19). "The *Stone* shall cry out of the wall, and the *beam* out of the timber shall answer it" (Hab. ii, 11). The wood and stone of the Australian Churinga, which are Totemic types, are excommunicated in Israel as idols when they were no longer understood as symbols. They came to be looked upon as deities in themselves, set up for worship. Both Cæsar and Lucanus state that the gods of the Gauls were pillar-*stones* and tree-*trunks*. Nevertheless, these were not the gods. In Egypt both the Pillar and Tree were pedestals for the gods, and both were blended in the tree-pillar, or Tat of Ptah. As images of the Mother both were the Beth or abode, as Bringer-forth of the Divinity or Spirit which was the object of worship, as was the God of Jacob in the Conical Pillar and of Horus in the Tree. These two primordial and universal types of origin are coupled together in Logion V. of the ΛΟΓΙΑ ΙΗϹΟΥ (p. 12). "Raise the Stone, and there thou shalt find me; cleave the wood, and there am I." To raise the stone is to erect an altar. The Wood is one with the Tree. The Stone was raised and the Tree prepared for worship, because they were types of the Divine Abode, which represented the Two Women or Sisters who were the Two Mothers or Bringers-forth of the Race in the beginning. The perception that life was born of the Earth must have been as primordial as it was natural, and that which brings to birth is the Mother. Thus the race of human beings, in common with the animals, was born of Mother-earth. In Central Africa the natives claim that they came from a hole in the rock (Duff Macdonald). It is indeed a common African tradition. The stone or rock crops up continually as an emblem of the Earth or solid ground. The Earth itself was brought to a point and focussed in the ceremonial stone on which the offering was made. For instance, when the members of the Hakea-flower Totem perform their mystery to solicit food, one of the young men opens a vein in his arm and lets the liquid flow over the ceremonial stone until it is entirely covered with blood. A rock near Gouam, in the Marcian Islands, is locally regarded as the ancestor of the human race. The African birthplace denoted by the rock of earth and the forest-tree is indicated by the tradition of the Ovaherero which relates that Men were born from the Omumborombonga Tree, and that sheep and goats issued from a flat rock. (Reiderbecke, Rev. H., *Missionary Labours*, p. 263.) Now, the Great Goddess who was "worshipped" with the gory rites of many lands originated as the Mother-earth who was fertilized with blood, and with the definite object of procuring food. This was the superhuman Mother who gave her own life in food, and to whom blood was offered as a propitiatory sacrifice for sustenance. Also in this rite the blood was poured out freely on the earth itself, as life for life. The Intichiuma ceremonies of the Arunta amply show that human blood was poured out on the earth as a sacrificial offering for food. Plenty of blood was shed for plenty of food. It was a mode of magical invocation that is still practised in the mysteries of black magic for the evocation of spirits. Food was the supreme object sought by primitive folk, and the giver of food and drink was propitiated and besought for more. This was naturally the Mother—the Mother-earth; the Mother in the water, in the tree, in the animals that were eaten. Hence the Intichiuma ceremonies of the Arunta are still performed for the increase of the animal or plant which gives its type (or name) to the Totem. "The sole object of these ceremonies is that of increasing the total food supply." (*Native Tribes*, p. 169.) The Arunta of the Emu-totem pour out their blood lavishly upon the earth in asking for plenty of Emu, an image of which is painted on the ground to be deluged with blood. On the other hand, the men of the Witchetty-Grub totem, in praying for food, will paint their totem on the body of each man in red ochre, which is a local substitute for blood. Then they represent the mystery of transformation, from matter to spirit, from death to life, and await the emergence of the fully-developed insect from the cocoon of the chrysalis (N.T., pp. 175-6). In the one case blood was offered actually, in the other symbolically, but in both it was offered for continuance and increase of food. Thus the Intichiuma ceremony is a festival celebrated for the increase of food, especially of the totem that was eaten solemnly at the thanksgiving meal. Also the Corroboree of promiscuous intercourse takes place at this festival of invocation for plenty of food. And *the drama of reproduction is humanly enacted, as it were, in aid of production in external nature.*

The "blood of the martyrs" was not only the "seed of the Church" in later ages; the flesh and blood of the victim offered in sacrifice were also buried in the earth as seed for the future harvest. In West Africa it was a custom for a man and woman to be killed with spades and hoes in the month of March, and for their bodies to be buried in the middle of a newly-tilled field to secure a better crop. The Marimos, a Bechuana tribe, offer up a human victim for the welfare of their crops. The man chosen for a sacrifice is taken to the field and slain amongst the wheat, according to their phrase, to serve as *seed*. The custom was not only African. The Pawnee Indians offered the flesh and blood of a sacrificial victim at the time of seed-sowing. As late as the year 1837 a captive Sioux girl was sacrificed by them at the time of planting the maize. The flesh was torn in morsels to be buried in the earth, and the corn was sprinkled with drops of her propitiating blood. The appeal for food and drink was natural and universal. According to the ancient wisdom, this appeal was made to the Mother-earth as the source of life, who was imaged as the giver of sustenance in various forms, but first and foremost as the superhuman suckler, the Sow, the Water-Cow, or Milch-

Cow. Egypt has registered the permanent proof that a superhuman power was first besought for food and drink in the person of the Great Mother. The human mother who was eaten sacramentally had supplied the type for the Great Mother in mythology. The sacrifice was offered to the goddess on the hill-top, on the altar-stone, in the field or granary, or under the green tree, as these were different types of the Earth-Mother. The palm-tree that is being fecundated on the Mesopotamian monuments represents the Mother-earth as source of food, one form of which is the produce of the tree. The tree is female. The cone held in the hand of the Geni is an emblem of the male, or solar power by which the earth is fertilized. Earth is the mother of food, the universal matrix; the tree is but a type, like other representatives of the bringer-forth. The sacrifice portrayed beneath the tree upon the Hindu monuments is frankly phallic (Moor's *Hindu Pantheon*).

Under whatsoever type or name, the so-called "tree-worship" or "phallic worship" is a festival of fertilization, celebrated in propitiation of the earth-goddess, who is the genetrix besought for food and sustenance, and blood was the primitive oblation made to the Mother-earth. This, however, was *not the only one,* as is shown by the invocatory rites.

The ancient Mother still survives amongst the Western Inoits in the same primeval character of Mother-earth; she who is the bringer of food, and who when in a merry mood will play at raining down melted fat in her capacity of the Great Mother who is pregnant with plenty, and who is designated Mother Plenty. We are not likely to get much nearer to primitive nature than amongst these Esquimaux, who still perform the mystery of generation and celebrate their Arctic Agapæ at the annual festival of fecundity. In one of the scenes the Shamans enact *the resurrection of life as the reproduction of food.* The prey is hunted to death with savage cries. Whilst fleeing from the pursuers the man in a mask, who acts the part of the animal seizes hold of a brand from the fire and hurls it aloft to the roof, so that when it falls back to the ground it throws out a shower of live sparks. What does this portend? asks Réclus. The answer is that, "surrounded as it is by its persecutors, the quarry forgets its danger to reproduce its species, an exploit which all the spectators greet with acclamation." It is not enough to kill the prey; it must also reproduce itself, so that its race may not die out or food become scarce. This festival was universal once. It was celebrated all over the world as a drama of reproduction—first and foremost for the reproduction of food. The resurrection of food by reproduction in animal life is thus enacted at the Inoit festival, as it has been acted in a hundred other mysteries, Intichiuma, Eucharists, Corroborees, and religious revels. By the dim glimmer of this distant light we see the victim's death was followed with the act of a begettal to new life. It was a drama of reproduction in which the sacrificial victim from the first had represented food—the new food of another year, or of another life in the religious mysteries. It was, we repeat, a drama of reproduction, in which the victim that died and was eaten as the Eucharist was symbolically reproduced in the Corroboree that followed. From very early times the sacrifice of a victim was solemnized, and followed by the phallic feast, whether in the Corroboree of the Arunta or the Christian Agapæ. First the sacrificial victim is slain and eaten, *ante lucem,* at the evening meal or Last Supper, and next the festival of reproduction was celebrated in the Agapæ. This reproduction was performed by universal promiscuity from a time when paternity was impersonal and the relationship of the sexes was that of all for all, when boundless licence was the only law befitting the Great Mother. This promiscuity is also recognizable when Tertullian repeats the charges that were brought against the conduct of the Christians at their festivals: *"Dicimur scleratissimi de sacramento infanticidii et pabulo inde, et post, incesto convivium quod eversores luminum"* (Tertullian, *Apologeticum,* ch. vii.).

We now come to the secondary cause of what has been called "phallic worship." The first we found in Earth herself being imaged and propitiated as the Great Mother in the pre-anthropomorphic mould when she was represented by the Water-Cow, the Sow, the Goose, or other figure of food. Long before the god Seb was divinized as "the Father of Food," the Earth was Mother of Food and gave drink as the wet-nurse, with the Sow as suckler of her children, and the cave in the rock as her womb.

The goddess Hathor, the Egyptian Venus, was the fairest representative of Mother-earth. She was propitiated as the Mother of Plenty, like the Inoit Sidné, and was imaged in the likeness of the cow or sow, as the figure of food and fecundity. She was also the goddess of generation, maternity, and child-birth, as well as of music and the dance, of loveliness and love. Length of time and the course of development have to be allowed for. The Greek Venus in her nudity is immeasurably distant from the goddess Hathor offering her milk to the glorified. Nevertheless, the Mother of Food was primary as Mother-earth, and the Goddess of Love explains the phallic nature of the later cult of fertilization.

The most exact and comprehensive title for the religion designated phallic worship would be the Cult of the Great Mother, taking Hathor for the type, who was the womb of life as Mother-earth, the suckler as the cow, the giver of food, shelter, and water as the tree, and who in the course of time became the Goddess of Love, of fecundity and child-birth. Moreover, *in the later phallic cult the type had been changed from the cow to the human female.* The primitive simplicity of "Hathor worship" was just that of the infant pulling and mumbling at the mother's nipples, when the source of milky plenty was portrayed as superhuman in the likeness of the cow or sow; and when the representation became anthropomorphic this simplicity was lost.

The Cow or Sow was superseded by the Woman in the temples as the more alluring type of the great goddess. It is most naïvely-pitiful to see how the sex became the human organ of the superhuman power offering itself as Hathor in the Asherah-tree or as the house of God; acting the goddess as the great harlot of the cult in its debasement and deterioration. This, we repeat, was mainly a result of the representation becoming anthropomorphic. The Great Mother was the ideal in the minds of the devotees, she whose size had been imaged by the hippopotamus, whose sexual force had been represented by Sekhet as the lioness in heat. Thus, when the type was humanized the female of the greatest capacity would present the nearest likeness to the divinity, and be held most worthy of her at the festival of fertilization. The Great Mother, when represented in the human form, becomes the harlot of promiscuous intercourse who brought much revenue to the religious house by her capacity for performing the rite on behalf of the Great Mother in her tree-tent or rock-cave, or later sanctuary. Carver in his *Travels* relates that when amongst the Naudowessies he saw they paid uncommon respect to one of their women, who was looked up to, if not worshipped, as a person of high distinction, because on one occasion she invited forty of the principal warriors to her tent, provided them with a feast, and treated them all as her husbands. This, the Indians said, was an ancient custom by which a woman might win a husband of the first rank. (Lubbock, *Origin of Civilization,* p. 101.) She, like the Water-Cow, would be a type of the Great Mother, or Goddess of Fecundity, represented by the woman capable of entertaining all the males of the Totem at one time as the Great Mother indeed. It was as representatives of the Great Mother that the temple prostitutes attained pre-eminence in various lands, and afterwards were highly honoured as the servants of the goddess.

The Great Mother in the Mount was represented by such goddesses as Astarte, whose Ephebæ and Courtesans received her devotees in grottoes and caves that were hollowed out for the purpose in the Syrian hillsides. The temple of Hathor at Serabit-el-Khadem, discovered by Professor Petrie in the Peninsula of Sinai, was based originally on a cave in the rock, which was the Great Earth-Mother's earliest shrine. In England there is or used to be a mild return to sexual promiscuity once a year. The confusion or "mingling on the Mound" was practised on the hill, though not in a very Belialistic way. In the present writer's youth it was an Easter pastime for the lads and lasses to meet upon the "Beacon," the "Steps," or some other sacred hill—equivalent to the Mound, and kiss and romp and roll each other down the hill-side in a scene of fine confusion, and with much soiling and tearing at times of pretty frocks that had to be put on quite new for the saturnalia. All young folk were sweethearts in a kind of sexual promiscuity on Easter Day. In its way this was a form of the phallic festival and the return to promiscuity that was celebrated at the time of year when a reproduction of the fruits of the earth was dramatized and all the inimical influences that made for sterility, drought, and famine were figuratively driven away. As Herodotus relates, some 700,000 people used to assemble at Bubastis to celebrate the annual festival of the Great Mother Bast, who was known as the goddess of strong drink and sexual passion. The women who exposed their persons on the boats to the watchers on the shore were exhibiting the natural lure to signify that they were free to all comers, for this occasion only, in the service of the goddess, who was a lioness in heat. They were going to celebrate the great festival of reproduction. He says that when the barges passed the river-side towns some of the women danced on board, others stood up and exposed their persons to those who were watching them from the banks of the Nile. (B. 2, 60.)

The phallic festival was periodically celebrated in honour of the Great Mother, the first supreme power in nature personalized as the goddess of fertility, the giver of food and drink, the celebration being in accordance with primitive usage and the promiscuous sexual intercourse of pre-Totemic times. The phallic festivals were chiefly repeated at the equinoxes—that is, at seed-time and harvest. The equinox was a figure of equality of all things being on a level. This fact is expressed in the names of our Fairs and Evens. Promiscuity was a mode of making things fair and even in the sexual saturnalia. High and low, rich and poor, young and old, "commingled on the mound," the hill, the high places. It was a world in which old maids and bachelors were not allowed, and there was at most a six months' lease for private ownership in womankind (from one equinox to the other). Hence we learn from the witches' confessions that women were the strongest supporters of the "Sabbath." Laws of Tabu were violated with impunity for this occasion only. At this time, and no other, men and women of the same Totem cohabited promiscuously. The Asherah is a sacred simulacrum of the goddess whose desire was to be for ever fecundated. And when the women of Israel set up the Asherah and wore the hangings for curtains of concealment (II. Kings xxiii. 7) they became the representatives of the Great Mother who is denounced by the biblical writers as the Great Harlot, but who was a most popular Mother in Israel, and Sekhet her own second self in Egypt.

There is every reason for concluding that the unlimited excess indulged in promiscuity at the phallic festival was designed to represent the desire for an illimitable supply of food, the boundlessness of the one being dramatically rendered by the latitude and licence of the other. It was a magical mode of the mysteries in which the meaning was expressed in act as a primitive form of Sign-language addressed to the superhuman Power as the Great Mother. The customs of the savage, or, as we prefer to say, the aborigines, are modes of memorizing. For ages on ages their only means of keeping an historic record of the past, the sole mode of memorial, have been the customs; and with what faithful persistence these have been fulfilled. Promiscuous connubium is recognized by the Arunta as the condition that obtained in the remotest times. They connect it with the custom of exchanging wives at the Corroboree, saying this was the practice of the Alcheringa (N.T., pp. 96, 99). That was in the time beyond which nothing is or can be known, because nothing was formulated in the lawless state of utter promiscuity. Howitt relates that on one occasion, when the *Aurora Australis* was more alarming and portentous in appearance than usual, the Kurnai tribe beheld it with great terror, and betook themselves to intersexual communism by the exchange of wives as a mode of warding off the calamity supposed to be impending. (Howitt on some Australian beliefs.)

The root origin, then, of what has been called the phallic religion is also to be traced in a periodic celebration of the festival of reproduction, which was first applied to the renewal of food in the flesh of animals and the fruits of the earth, this reproduction being rendered in the grossest human guise on the hugest scale, and in the most prodigious manner befitting the Great Mother in communal connubium with all her sons together. The festival of fertilization is a survival from the far-off past when the Mother-earth was the All and the Only One, to be propitiated as the giver of food. Being the Mother, she was represented by the female, who was at first pre-human, and finally human. Thenceforth woman was the living type of the mythical Great Mother, instead of the Cow or Sow, the Goat or the She-Bear; and at this festival all womankind were one in imaging the Mother who from the beginning had been the All-One. Nothing was recognized but the female, the typical organ of motherhood, which imaged the earth as mother of sustenance; the mother, who was propitiated and solicited in various ways, by oblations of blood and other offerings, was also invoked in the likeness of the human female to be fertilized in human fashion. She was the Great Mother, the All-One, and nothing less than the contributions of all could duly, hugely, adequately represent the oblation. In Drummond's *Œdipus Judaicus,* pl. 13, there is a drawing from the Mithraic monuments according to Hyde, which shows that the seed-sowing at the festival of fertilization was illustrated in the human fashion by the male, and that the Earth-Goddess was fecundated as the female, who was represented by the women in the orgie of promiscuity. The mystery of reproduction was acted in the festival, as the vicarious mode of fecundating the Great Mother and Good Lady, by the bountiful sowing of human seed. It was a primitive mode of representing her, on behalf of whom all womenkind contributed vicariously. Call it "worship," "phallic worship," or any other "worship," the supreme object of devotion at first was food and drink, which were represented by the earth in crop, the tree in fruit, the animal pregnant with young; by the Mammalia, the Water-Cow, the Sow, the Milch-Cow, the Goose, the Emu, the Kangaroo; and lastly by the goddesses and the women who represented Mother-Earth as Apt or Isis, Nin-Ki-Gal or Demeter, when the latter had been objectified in Hathor, the goddess of love, or Sekhet, the goddess of sexual communion, as divinity in female form. As it is said of Pepi in the Texts, "Thy sister Isis hath come to thee rejoicing in thy love. Thou hast had intercourse with her, and hast made her to conceive." (Budge, *Book of the Dead,* Introduction, p. 134.) In these celebrations the woman took the place of the goddess. At the time when the begetters were not yet individualized a single pair of actors would have conveyed but little meaning. The soul of procreation was tribal, general, promiscuous, and the mode of reproduction in the most primitive mysteries was in keeping therewith. Reproduction by the soul of the tribe was rendered by all the members contributing to fecundate the Great Mother. Hence the phallic saturnalia, in which the reproduction of food, especially in the future life of the animals, and the continuation of the species were dramatized in a primitive phallic festival which survived eventually as the "love-feast" of the Christian cult.

Many examples could be cited of this custom, which was universal as it was primitive, and which may be looked upon as the festival of reproduction that represented the begettal of future food in human fashion and in connubium as it were with the Great Mother, the Mother-Nature, or the Mother-earth, like Pepi with his divine sister Isis. In India to-day young girls are married to the Gods. The doctrine is the same in the Roman Cult when the Virgins are the dedicated Brides of Christ. In the earlier rite it was the Males who, like the Pharaoh Pepi, were married to the divine Mother who was personated by the women in the mysteries of the primitive religion. At such a time, whatsoever their status attained in civilization, the people lapsed *pro tem.* into a state of general promiscuity. The women lost all feeling of modesty and became raging Bacchantes. Men and women were more furious than animals in the indulgence of their passion at this wild debauch. As described by M. Réclus, divinized Mother-earth had to be stirred from her winter sleep by naïvely-lascivious spectacles for the purpose of exciting the spirit of fecundity. She was represented by young wantons of women, who danced and frolicked indescribably or lay down and scraped the ground with their heels, caressed it with their hands, and offered their embraces like so many naked Danæas wooing the fertilizing sun. In this saturnalia there was a general reversion to the practice of an earlier time somewhat analogous to the throw back of atavism in race, with this difference: the intentional lapse in moral status was but temporary, although periodically recurrent. It was a stripping off, or rather bursting out, of all the guises and disguises, trappings, ties, and stays of civilization, and running *amok* in all the nudity of nature.

There is a pathos of primitive simplicity in some of the appeals thus made in the lower ranges of the cult that is unparalleled in literature. The Thotigars of Southern India, at the festival of sowing seed, will insist that their wives shall make themselves common to all comers as an incitement for the Mother-earth to follow their example. The husbands improvise shelters by the road-side and stock them with provisions for their wives, and call upon the passers-by to "procure the public good and ensure an abundance of bread" (Réclus, *P. F. P.,* p. 283). *A propos* of this same festival, Israel is charged by Hosea with having become a prostitute by letting herself out for hire upon the *corn-floor!* "Thou hast gone a-whoring from thy God; thou hast loved hire upon every corn-floor" (ch. ix, 1). In this case the harlot was a representative of the Mother-earth as goddess of corn who was being fertilized by proxy on the grand scale in the phallic festivities, which included connubium upon the corn-floor, as well as on the hill, under the green tree, or in the embrace of the earth itself.

Phallic religion, then, as here maintained, did not originate in a worship of the humans sex. The Great Mother, pregnant with plenty, was the object of propitiation and appeal, as the bringer to birth and the giver of food. This was the superhuman mother in mythology, and not the human parent, as in Totemism. "Phallic worship" originated in the cult of the motherhood. It was the Mother who was honoured; her body and blood were sacredly eaten in the primitive Eucharist, if not as an act of adoration, it was an act of primitive homage and affection. The type was then applied to Mother-earth as the giver of life, of food and drink, the Great Mother in mythology who was thus fertilized and fecundated as it were dramatically in the human fashion for increase of food.

The drama of reproduction also involved the mystery of resurrection and rebirth applied to the periodic renewal of food which was represented in character by the victim. Reproduction was represented in various modes of resurrection, including the dance. It was a common custom for the skin of the animal, bird, or reptile to be preserved entire and suspended on a pole as the sign of reproduction for another life. This might be the skin of the Ainu bear, who is invoked to "come back soon into an Ainu" whilst being offered up as a sacrifice. They then rejoice and sing, and *both* sexes dance in ranks as bears. Judging from other forms of the primitive Agapæ, we surmise that what is meant by the sexes dancing in ranks as bears is that the performers at this festival coupled together in the skins of the bear for the reproduction of their future food, which in this case was the bear, but elsewhere might be the buffalo, the bull, the boar, or other Totemic animal that was slain and eaten sacramentally. The resurrection acted in the mysteries of Amenta still continues the Totemic type when the reproducer is Osiris, the Bull of Eternity. It was the same festival of reproduction when the goat was the sacrificial type as when it was the bear, or calf, or lamb, or other zoötype that was eaten, food being the primitive object in propitiating the superhuman Power. It was the mystery of reproduction and renewal of the animal for future food, whether this were the bear, the bull, the goat, the turtle, or any other Totemic type. The secret of the mystery is that food was the object of the festival of reproduction, and the Great Mother was propitiated for abundance of food. Sexual intercourse was known to be a mode of reproduction, and the performers not only danced in Totemic guise as animals, they acted the characters. In this mad festival of fertilization for the production of food men also dressed and acted as women; women dressed and acted as men, the function of each being thus apparently doubled. We know that in the Totemic mysteries the performers wore the skins of animals as a mode of acting in character, and when they acted thus in pairs it would inevitably give rise to statements that men and animals commingled in dark rites without distinction of nature. Now, the goat was a Jewish type, Totemic or religious, and the Jews were reputed to be goat-worshippers after the animal had been made a symbol of the evil Sut in Egypt. But the goat was at one time good, as a giver of food in flesh and milk, when those of the Totem would dance in the skin of the goat and be denounced by later ignorance as "worshippers" of the Shedim or of Satan. Thus amongst the mysteries that were continued by the primitive Christians is this of reproduction, which was first applied to food and finally to the human soul. Hence they were charged with "running after heifers," just as the Jews were denounced for running after she-goats. The root of the whole matter is that in this festival of fructification the animals which are eaten for food are represented by the Totemic actors in the skins as reproducing themselves for food hereafter. The fact is disclosed by the Inoit ceremony in which the prey must reproduce itself before the sacrificial victim dies, so that the species shall live on and future food may be secured. The mystery was the same the wide world round. The early Christians had to be admonished against "running after heifers" in their mysteries performed at "Christmas and on other days." This was the survival of a primitive custom that, like all others, had its genesis in the nature that was blindly groping in the gloom with dark religious rites. The fact was patent in all the mysteries that promiscuous sexual intercourse was an act which came to be called religious. The Agapæ did not originate with what is termed Christianity, but was one of the most primitive institutions of the human race, which began as the festival of fertility when the invocation of the superhuman Power was for food and sustenance addressed to the Good Lady, the Earth-Goddess, the Great Mother, in her several elemental characters. It was a festival of fructification at which she was represented by the human female, the more the merrier, the primary object being future food far more than human offspring, and it was this desire that gave the touch of religious feeling to the orgy of the sexes in which the seed was sown broadcast, so to say, for future harvest.

Following Totemism, we find that Fetishism takes up the tale of development in Sign-language. By Fetishism the present writer means the reverent regard for amulets, talismans, mascots, charms, and luck-tokens that were worn or otherwise employed as magical signs of protecting power. Fetishism has been classified as the primal, universal religion of mankind. It has also been called "the very last corruption of religion." (Max Müller, *Nat. Rel.*, p. 196.) But it will not help us to comprehend the position of the primitive races by simply supposing them to have been in an attitude of worship when they were only groping mentally on all fours. On the contrary, we consider the so-called "fetishes" to be a residual result of Sign-language and Totemism, and do not look on Fetishism as an organized religious cult. The name of Fetishism was given by de Brosses, in his work on the cult of the fetish gods, published in 1760. The word fetish is said to be derived from a root which yields our word faith. *Feitico*, in Portuguese, is the name for an amulet, a talisman, or magical charm. The word would seem to have been adopted by the West Coast natives and applied to their gru-grus, ju-jus, enquizi, or mokisso, which are worn for mental medicine as the representative type of some protecting superhuman power. But Fetishism did not originate with the Portuguese. Also the same root-word is found in the Irish as *fede*. An ancient Irish wedding-ring in the shape of two hands clasped together was called a *fede*. This too was a fetish, as a sign of fidelity or faith. The same thing was signified by the Egyptian "Sa" for the amulet or magical charm. The word "Sa," variously illustrated, denotes protection, aid, backing, defence, virtue, soul, efficacy. An earlier form of the word is Ka: there was a divinity named Sau, or Ka, who was the god of fetish-figures which are identifiable as amulets, charms, knots, skins, and other things that were worn as types of protective power. In Egypt, Sa or Ka was the author or creator of the types which became fetishtic. (Rit., ch. xvii.) Nothing can be more pathetic than the appeal that was made to Sa, the god of amulets. The word Sa also signifies touch. Thus the protecting power appealed to as the god of the fetish was the god of touch. The amulet brought the power nearer to be laid hold of, and made its presence veritable to this sense. Thus, Fetishism was a mode of Sign-language which supplied a tangible means of laying hold of the nature powers that were to some extent apprehended as superhuman without being comprehended. Hence the talisman, the amulet, or magical charm is worn as something tangible, a thing to *touch* or clutch hold of, on purpose to keep in touch with the power represented by the fetish. This god of touch is still extant in the Church of Rome, as well as his amulets and charms, the cross, the rosary, and other fetish figures that are yet worn for protection, and are touched in time of need, to establish the physical link with the invisible Power with which it may be thought desirable to keep in touch.

But, it was not, as de Brosses said in his early generalization, that *anything* would serve promiscuously for a fetish. On the contrary, there was no fetish without some special symbolic value known to those who read these natural hieroglyphics. We see by the Zunis that one great reason for making fetish images and honouring them was that the so-called worship was a mode of laying hold upon the powers which they represented. This is common. The images are a means of taking tangible possession of the powers themselves through their hostages. The devotees thus have them in their power, and hold them as it were in captivity, to control, command, and even coerce or punish them. Hence the gods were sometimes beaten in the shape of their fetish images. The appeal was not always prayerful. Certain magical formulæ in the Egyptian Ritual were repeated as words of command. In saluting the two lions, the double-uræi and the two divine sisters, the deceased claims to *command* and compel them by his magical art (xxxvii, 1).

Magic is the power of influencing the elemental or ancestral spirits. Magical words are words with which to conjure and compel; magical processes were acted with the same intent. If the process consisted in simply tying a knot, it was a mode of covenanting and establishing a bond with the object of compelling fulfilment. The Fetishism of Inner Africa, with its elemental powers, its zootypology, its science of magic and mental medicine, its doctrine of transformation, its amulets and charms, came to its culmination in the typology, the mythology, the magic, the religious rites and customs of Egypt. Egypt will show us the final phase and perfect flower of that which had its rootage in the remotest past of humanity in the Dark Continent. Wearing the fetish as a charm, a medicine, a visible symbol of power, is common with the Negro races. Many of them delight in wearing a beltful of these around the body. If the Negro has to bear a heavier load than usual, he will clap on a fresh fetish for every pound of extra weight—thus adding to his burden by his mode of outsetting the weight, because the fetishes represent a helpful power. If he has to carry 100 pounds weight he will want, say, half-a-dozen fetish images in his girdle. But if the weight be doubled he will require a dozen fetishes to enable him to sustain it. His fetishes represent power in various forms, whether drawn from the animal world or human, whether the tokens be a tooth, a claw, a skin, a horn, hair, a root, a bone, or only a stone. They represent a stored up power, for the Negro has faith in his fetishes, and that acts as a potent mental influence. If he has only a gree-gree of cord, he will tie it into knots, and every knot is the sign of increase in power according to his reckoning. When it was known what the type or fetish signified as a representative figure, it could make no direct appeal to religious consciousness, nor evoke a feeling of reverence for itself, any more than the letters of the alphabet. Mere fetishism in the modern sense only comes in with ignorance of Sign-language. The Arunta have an emblem in their Churinga which is a very sacred fetish. This is associated with the Alcheringa spirits. When there is a battle the Churinga is supposed to endow its owner with courage. "So firm is their belief in this, that if two men were fighting, and one of them knew that the other carried a Churinga whilst he did not, he would certainly lose heart and without doubt be beaten" (Spencer and Gillen). We know that the Inner African custom of carrying a number of amulets and charms strung upon the body for protection was continued in ancient Egypt, because we see it employed in the equipment of the dead for their journey through the nether world. When the deceased enters the presence of the Typhonian powers in Amenta he exults in being prepared with "millions of charms," or fetish images, which friendly hands have buried with his body, such as the terrible Eye of Horus, the Beetle of Transformation, the Tablet of Tahn, the Sceptre of Felspar, the Buckle of Stability, the Ankh-cross of Life, and other types of protecting power. With his fetishes outside and inside of his mummy, he exclaims, "I clothe and equip myself with thy spells, O Ra!" and so he faces the darkness of death in defiance of all the evil powers. Each amulet or fetish signifies some particular way of protecting, of preserving, transforming, reproducing, or renewing life, and re-establishing him for ever, the sun being representative of the power that revivifies for life eternal. We learn from the chapter on bringing the charms of a person in Hades that the amulets, spells, and talismans are equivalent to the powers of the mind, heart, and tongue of the deceased. He says, "I have made the gods strong, bringing all my charms to them" (ch. 23). In the chapter on stopping the crocodiles that come to make the deceased "lose his mind" in Amenta, we see how the earlier zoötypes that once represented the powers of destruction have still kept their place, and can be turned to good account by him, as when the deceased cries, "Back, Crocodile of the West! There is an asp in my belly! There is a snake in my belly!"—the one being the symbol of royal supremacy, the other of transformation into new life. The primitive mode of portraying the powers in nature that were superior to the human was continued in this typology of the tomb. Thus the Manes cling to powers beyond the human, which were first represented by the natural types that have now become fetishtic; a means of claiming alliance with them and of clothing themselves in death with their shield of protection and panoply of power. In spirit-life the deceased clutches at the same types that were fetishes in this life, and holds on by the same assistance. He not only clothes himself with their images as talismans and spells, he transforms into their likeness to personate their superhuman forces. Thus he can pass underground as a tortoise, a beetle, or a shrewmouse; make way through the mud or the nets as an eel, through the water as a crocodile, through the dark as a jackal, or see in it as a cat; fly swiftly as a swallow, and soar through the air or solar fire as the golden hawk; shed his past life like the tail of the tadpole that turns frog, or slough it like the skin of the serpent. In making his passage by means of manifold manifestations he exclaims, "I have flown as a hawk," "I have cackled as a goose," "I am the swallow" (as the soul of swiftness). He runs through the zoötypes which represented the powers of the soul in various stages of development, and says: 1. I am the jackal. 2. I am the hawk. 3. I am the great fish. 4. I am the phœnix. 5. I am the serpent. 6. I am the ram. 7. I am the sun. In this passage the deceased transforms into these zoötypes of the nature powers in order that he may go where the merely human faculties would fail to carry him through. He assumes their power by wearing representative images or fetishes—by impersonation of their parts and by incorporation of these potencies which are beyond the human, and therefore superhuman. Hence the exclamation, "I have incorporated Horus"—*i.e.*, the youthful god who was for ever re-born in phenomenal manifestation as representative of the eternal in time, in whose likeness the mortal transformed into an immortal to realize the type. The Ritual contains many references to magic as a mode of transformation. The Osiris says: "My mouth makes the invocation of magical charms. I pray in magical formulæ" (31, 2-3). That is the precise explanation of the primitive modes of invocation and evocation, "I pray in magical formulæ." And these magical formulæ were acted, performed, and signified by a thousand things that were done in place of being said: "My magical power gives vigour to my flesh" (64, 27). "Masters of Truth, who are free from evil, living for ever, lend me your forms. Give me possession of your magical charms," "for I know your names" (72, 1, 2). Chapter 64, is spoken of as a hymn that caused the reader to go into a state of ecstasy. "He no longer sees, no longer hears, whilst reciting this pure and holy composition" (50, 33), which obviously points to the condition of trance that was attributed to the magical power of the formulæ. Urt-Hekau, great in magical words of power, is a title of Isis, who was considered the very great mistress of spells and magical incantations. It is said of her: "The beneficent sister repeateth the formulæ and provideth thy soul with her conjurations. Thy person is strengthened by all her formulæ of incantation."

It is the power beyond the type that goes far to account for the origin and persistence of fetishism. The African knows well enough that the power is not necessarily resident in the fetish, which fails him continually and in the times of greatest need. But his trust is in the power that is represented by the fetish, the power that never dies, and therefore is eternal.

The magical incantations which accompany the gesture signs also prove that the appeal, whether in dumb show or in words, was being made to some superior superhuman force—that is, one of the elemental powers in mythology which became the goddesses and gods in the later eschatology. The hawk will show us how a fetish image was educed from a type or sign of superhuman force. The bird in Egypt was a symbol of the Horus sun on account of its swiftness and its soaring power. It was used to signify height, excellence, spirit, victory. And just as letters are reduced ideographs, so the hawk's foot and kite's feather will denote the power first represented by the bird itself, and as such they are worn upon the person. They are the visible signs of swiftness or upward flight, and therefore a true medicine or *fetish* to speed one on. Also, when superhuman powers in nature were represented by the superhuman types or zoötypes, it was not that the deceased changed into an animal or bird or reptile, either in this life or the next, when he is self-assimilated to the type. When the deceased in the Ritual says, "I am the lion," he is clothing himself in the strength of the great power that had been represented by the lion, which might be that of Shu or of Atum-Ra. The wearers of the fetish images, whether on earth or in Amenta, are affiliated or assimilated to the power beyond by means of the type, whether this is represented by wearing the whole skin or a piece of it, the horn, the hoof, the tooth, or tail of the animal, the feathers of the bird or rattle of the snake. Thus, the horn of the bull, or a portion of it, might be worn to assimilate the wearer to Osiris, "the Bull of Eternity." An old Fan hunter gave Miss Kingsley a little ivory half-moon which was specially intended "to make man see bush," otherwise for her to see her way in the night of the forest (*Trav.* p. 102). So the eye of Horus which images the moon is given to the deceased for his night-light in the darkness of death. Horus presents the (solar) eye by day and Taht the lunar eye by night (Rit., ch. 144, 8). The eye was an emblem of great magical and protecting power. With many of the West Coast Africans the eye-balls of the dead, more particularly of Europeans, constitute a great medicine, fetish, or charm. Dr. Nassau told Miss Kingsley that he had known graves to have been rifled in search of them (Kingsley, M. H., *Travels in West Africa*, p. 449).

The amulets, charms, and tokens of magical power that were buried with the Egyptian dead became fetish on account of what they imaged symbolically, and fetishtic symbolism is Sign-language in one of its ideographic phases. The Usekh-collar indicated being set free from the bandages and rising again from the dead in the glorified form of the Sahu-mummy. The Tam-sceptre signified union with the loved and lost. As Egyptian, one of the fetish figures buried with the dead is the sign of the corner or angle, named *Neka* Γ. It is the mystical corner-stone of the Masonic builder, and a sign of building on the square, for which the symbol stands. Building on the square, or a fourfold foundation, is to build for ever. Paul speaks as a Mason or a gnostic when he makes the mystical Christ the "chief corner-stone" in the temple that is builded "for an habitation of God in the spirit" (*Eph.* ii. 20-22). The Ankh-cross signified the life to come, that is, the life everlasting. The Shen-ring imaged continuity for ever, in the circle of eternity. The heart of green basalt showed that the deceased in this life was sound-hearted. The beetle Kheper typified the self-reproducing power in nature which operates by transformation according to the laws of evolution. The jackal-headed User-sceptre was buried as an image of sustaining power, the vertebral column of Sut or Osiris that supported the heavens. The Tat, a pillar or tree-trunk, was an emblem of stability and type of the god Ptah as the fourfold support of the universe. We have heard much of the savage who was able to secrete his soul in a stone or a tree, but without the gnosis by which alone such nursery-tales could be explained. Now, in one of the numerous changes made by the Osiris in Amenta he transforms into a stone (Rit., ch. 161), saying "*I am the tablet of felspar.*" This was the Uat-amulet that was placed in the tomb as a type of that which was for ever green, fresh and flourishing, equivalent to the green jade found in Neolithic graves. In this an evergreen was, so to say, made permanent in stone, and buried with the dead as a type of eternal youth. The deceased exclaims, "I am the column of green felspar" (Rit., ch. 160), and he rejoices in the stone being so hard that it cannot be crushed or even receive a scratch, saying, "If it is safe, I am safe; if it is uninjured, I am uninjured." The power of this amulet was in its impenetrable hardness, which represented eternal permanence for the soul which it imaged. One of the most sacred fetishes in Egypt was an amulet of red stone, which represented the blood of Isis. That is the mother-blood in theology—the blood by which salvation came, to give eternal life—a sublimated form of the mother-blood in totemism, which came to give the human life. Isis, moreover, is the virgin divinized. We speak of the blood tie between mother and child. This was first figured by means of the totem, and naturally the figure became a fetish. The Egyptians, being more advanced, were able to manufacture fetishtic types like the Ankh-image of life, the Tat-emblem of stability, the Nefer-amulet of good luck, the Scarabæus of transformation, the serpent of eternity.

It must have been a work of proud accomplishment for primitive man when first he made a string of hair or of any fibrous material, and could tie a knot in it. We might say primitive woman, hers being the greater need. It is the goddess Ankh who wears the hemp-stalks on her head, the goddess Neith who is the knitter divinized. The knotted tie is one of the most primitive and important of all the African fetishes to be found in Egypt. It is the gree-gree of Inner Africa. The Ankh-tie itself is originally merely a piece of string called a strap. It is the sign of dress, of undress, to tie or fasten, and of linen hung up to dry. The tie in Egypt takes several forms in the Ankh, the Tet, the Sa. The Ankh denotes life. The Sa has ten loops or ties, which in the language of signs might signify a period of ten lunar months. The Tet-tie, now a buckle, represents the blood of Isis, the saving blood, the soul of blood derived from the virgin mother, which was imaged in the human Horus. The tie was the earliest form of the liku or loin-belt first worn by the female as the mother of life at the period that was indicated by nature for propagation and connubium. Necklaces were worn by the Egyptian women to which the tie-amulet of Isis formed a pendant, and indicated her protecting power. In others the amulet suspended was the Ankh of life, or the heart (Ab); the Tat-sign of stability, or the Neferu-symbol of good luck. These were all fetishes that were worn to establish the personal *rapport* and alliance with the respective powers, which are known by name when divinized.

Fetishes generally are objects held in honour as the representatives of some power that was worshipped when the feeling had attained that status. Thus a stone may be the sacred symbol of eternal duration; the frog a living symbol of the power of transformation;

the serpent a symbol of the power of self-renewal; the crocodile a zoötype of the power that could see when itself was unseen. The sword-fish is sacred to the Negroes of Guinea. This they do not eat. But the sword when cut off and dried becomes a fetish. That is as a type of the superhuman power whose symbol is the sword. In the final phase amulets, charms, talismans, mascots, and tokens became fetishtic through being adopted and worn as visible or secret signs of some protecting power. They are as much ideographs as any others in the Egyptian hieroglyphics and as a mode of representation they belong to the ancient language of pre-verbal signs.

In Egypt the great First Mother Apt was propitiated as the "Mistress of Protection." And the "protection" was signified by types of permanence and power that were natural at first, then artificial when the horn and tooth were succeeded by the ivory that was carved into amulets and charms, which objectified the power of protection for the living or the dead. The power of Apt was portrayed in nature by the hippopotamus, and a tooth of the animal would symbolize its strength. Hence we find that figures of the animal were shaped in ivory, or stone, to be worn as types of the "Mistress of Protection." Figures of hippopotami carved out of red stone have been discovered lately in the prehistoric sites of Egypt, which were obviously intended to be worn as amulets.

Thus the fetish was at first a figure of the entire animal that represented the protecting power as the superhuman Mother Apt (*Proc. S. of B. A.,* xxii, parts 4 and 5, p. 460). Afterwards the tooth, the horn, the hoof would serve to image the power when worn upon the person of the living or buried with the mummy of the dead. A tooth is one of the most primitive types of power. Lions' teeth are worn by the Congo blacks as talismans or amulets. Crocodiles' teeth are worn by the Malagasy; dogs' teeth by the Sandwich Islanders; tiger-cats' teeth by the Land Dyaks; boars' teeth by the Kukis; hogs' teeth by the natives of New Guinea; sharks' teeth by the Maori. All these were fetish types as images of superhuman strength. When the Esquimaux Angekok goes forth to battle with the evil spirits and influences inimical to man, he arms himself with the claws of bears, the beaks of birds, the teeth of foxes, and other types of the nature powers which were primarily represented by the zoötypes that bequeathed these, their remains, to the repertory of fetishism. Thus the primitive Inner African mode of representation was not only preserved in the wisdom of Egypt, it became eschatological in one phase just as it remained hieroglyphical in the other, and in both it was the outcome and consummation of African Sign-language.

That which has been designated telepathy and the transference of thought by the Society for Psychical Research was well known amongst the aboriginal races, and that knowledge was utilized in their system of mental magic, or what the red men term their medicine. The earliest medicine was mental, not physical, not what we term physic. The effects that were sought for had to be educed by an influence exerted on the mind, rather than by chemical qualities found in the physics. Hence the fetishes of the black or red aborigine are his medicine by name as well as by nature. These things served, like vaccination, traction-buckles, or "tar-water and the Trinity," as fetishes of belief so long as that belief might last. They constituted a mental medicine, and an access of strength or spiritual succour might be derived from the thought. Belief works wonders. Hence the image of power becomes protective and assisting; it supplies a medicine, as it is termed, a medicine to the mind; and the fetishes, therefore, are properly called a medicine. Thus the earliest healing power was mental. It was the influence of mind on mind, that operated chiefly by suggestion. This was extant before the time of drugs, when mental influence was considered magical, and the man whose power was greatest was the mage or the magician. When the fetish-monger came to think that the healing or helping power resided in the fetish itself, one of two things had occurred. Either the devotee had lost sight of the original representative value of the fetish, and in his ignorance had gone blind with superstition, or it had been discovered that certain natural products did contain stimulating properties and healing virtues in themselves, and thus the medicine of physics began to supplement the more primitive mental medicine of the earlier fetishism. But the mass of fetishes do not possess their power intrinsically or inherently; they have only a representative value, which continues to make successful appeal to belief long after it has passed out of knowledge. Thus we have the fetishism of a primitive intelligence mixed up and confused with the fetishism of later ignorance. The first mental medicine was derived by laying hold of the nature powers in some typical or representative way. For example, the fire-stone from heaven was a sign of primary power. This was worn as a mental medicine at first, but it becomes physic at a later stage when, as with the Burmese, a cure for ophthalmia is found in the scrapings of thunderbolts or meteoric stones. A medicine of immense power for the muscles is still made by the Chinese from the bones of a tiger which have been dug up after lying some months in the earth and ground into a most potent powder, whilst the blood and liver of the same animal supplies a medicine of mighty power—*i.e.*, to the mind that can derive it by typical transference from the tiger. It is one of the most curious and instructive studies to trace this transformation of the earliest mental medicine into actual physics. For example, the nose-horn of the rhinoceros is an African fetish of the greatest potency. This represents the power of the animal, and when carried as a fetish, charm, or amulet it is a type of the power looked upon as assisting and protecting no matter where this power may be localized mentally. The rhinoceros being a persistent representative of power in and over water, its horn would naturally typify protection against the drowning element for boatmen and sailors. In the next stage the medicine is turned into physic by the horn being ground down and swallowed as a powder. Our familiar hartshorn derived its primal potency as a mental medicine from the horn of the deer, which was adopted as a type of renovation on account of the animal's having the power periodically to shed and renew its horns, and the horn itself as an emblem of renovation was a good mental medicine long before essences were extracted or drugs compounded from it in the chemistry of physics. One might point to many things that supplied the mental medicines of fetishism before they were ground down or calcined for the physic prescribed by our learned leeches of later times, who played the same ignorant part in dealing with these leavings of the past in this department of physics that the priests have played with the sweepings of ancient superstitions with which they have so long beguiled and ignorantly doctored us. The mode of assuming power by wearing of the skin as a fetish is still extant. The skin was worn as the only genuine garment of the magician or sorcerer. As we read in the *Discovery of Witchcraft,* the wizard's outfit included a robe furred with foxskin, a breastplate of virgin parchment, and a dry thong of lion's or hart's skin for a girdle. The skin also survives as a part of the insignia worn in our law courts, colleges, and pulpits, where it still serves in Sign-language to determine a particular status; it likewise survives as the cap and tails on the head of the clown in a less serious kind of pantomime. Some years since the present writer was making an inquiry at the Regent's Park Zoological Gardens respecting the sloughing of the serpent, when the attendant thought it was the "slough" of the serpent that was wanted. The writer then learned that this cast-off skin of the reptile was still sold in London as a charm, or fetish, a medicine of great potency, and that the sum of £5 was sometimes paid for one.

The fetishes acquired their sacred character, not as objects of worship, but from what they had represented in Sign-language; and the meaning still continued to be *acted* when the language was no longer read. The serpent was a symbol of renewal and self-renovation from the first, and thus the slough or skin remains a fetish to the end. We are so bound up together, the past with the present, and the doctrine of development is so vitally true, that we cannot understand the significance of a thousand things in survival which dominate or tyrannize over us to-day, until we can trace them back to their origin or learn something satisfactory about their primal meaning and the course of their evolution. Many queer customs and beliefs look unreasonable and irrational now which had a reason originally, although their significance may have been lost to us. Many simplicities of the early time have now become the mysteries of later ignorance, and we are made the victims of the savage customs bequeathed by primitive or prehistoric man, now clung to as sacred in our current superstition. It was a knowledge of these and kindred matters of the ancient mysteries that once made sacred the teachers of men, whereas it is the most complete ignorance of the natural beginnings that characterizes the priestly caste to-day concerning the primitive customs which still survive and dominate both men and women in the fetishism which has become hereditary now.

ELEMENTAL AND ANCESTRAL SPIRITS, OR THE GODS AND THE GLORIFIED.

Book III

THE Fetishism and Mythology of Inner Africa, left dumb or unintelligible, first became articulate in the Valley of the Nile. Egypt alone preserved the primitive gnosis, and gave expression to it in the language of signs and symbols as mouthpiece of the old dark land. From her we learn that amulets, talismans, luck-tokens, and charms became fetishtic, because they represented some protecting power that was looked to for superhuman aid, and that this power belonged to one of two classes of spirits or superhuman beings which the Egyptians of the Ritual called "the Gods and the Glorified." The first were elemental powers divinized. The second are the spirits of human ancestors, commonly called the ancestral spirits. The present object is to trace the origin of both, and to distinguish betwixt the one and the other, so as to discriminate elsewhere betwixt the two kinds of spirits, with the Egyptian wisdom for our guide.

According to the historian Manetho, who was a master of the secrets that were known to the Hir-Seshta, the keepers of chronology in Egypt had reckoned time and kept the register for a period of 24,900 years. This period Manetho divides under three divine dynasties with three classes of rulers, namely, the "Gods," the "Heroes," and the "Manes." The reign of the gods was subdivided into seven sections with a deity at the head of each. Now, as will be shown, the "Gods" of Egypt originated in the primordial powers that were derived at first from the Mother-earth and the elements in external nature, and these gods became astronomical or astral, as the Khus or Glorious Ones in the celestial Heptanomis, or Heaven in seven divisions.

In their stellar character they became the Seven Glorious Ones whom we read of in the Ritual (ch. 17), who were seven with Horus in Orion; seven with Anup at the pole of heaven; seven with Taht, with Ptah, and finally with Ra and Osiris, as the Seven Lords of Eternity. These two divine dynasties, elemental and Kronian, were followed in the list of Manetho by the Manes or ancestral spirits. In his Hibbert Lectures, Renouf denied the existence of ancestor-worship in Egypt. Nevertheless, he was entirely wrong. The New Year's Festival of the Ancestors determines that. This is referred to in the Calendar of Esné. It was solemnized on the 9th of

Taht, the first month of the Egyptian year, and was then of unknown antiquity.

The Egyptians entertained no doubt about the existence, the persistence, or the personality of the human spirit or ghost of man; and as we understand Manetho's account of the Egyptian religion in the times before Mena, the worship of the ghosts or spirits of the dead was that which followed the two previous dynasties of the elemental powers of earth and the Kronidæ in the astronomical mythology. For the present purpose, however, the three classes mentioned fall into the two categories of beings which the Egyptians designated *"the Gods and the Glorified."* The gods are superhuman powers, whether elemental or astronomical. The glorified are the souls once mortal which were propitiated as the spirit-ancestors, here called the Manes of the dead. Not that the Egyptian deities were what Herbert Spencer thought, "the expanded ghosts of dead men." We know them from their genesis in nature as elemental powers or animistic spirits, which were divinized because they were superhuman, and therefore *not* human. Sut, as the soul of darkness; Horus, as the soul of light; Shu, as the soul of air or breathing force; Seb, as soul of earth; Nnu (or Num), as soul of water; Ra, as soul of the sun, were gods, but these were not expanded from any dead men's ghosts. Most emphatically, man did not make his gods in his own image, for the human likeness is, we repeat, the latest that was applied to the gods or nature-powers. Egyptian mythology was founded on facts which had been closely observed in the ever-recurring phenomena of external nature, and were then expressed in the primitive language of signs. In the beginning was the void, otherwise designated the abyss. Darkness being the primordial condition, it followed naturally that the earliest type in mythical representation should be a figure of darkness. This was the mythical dragon, or serpent Apap, the devouring reptile, the monster all mouth, the prototype of evil in external nature, which rose up by night from the abyss and coiled about the Mount of Earth as the swallower of the light; who in another phase drank up all the water, as the fiery dragon of drought. The voice of this huge, appalling monster was the thunder that shook the firmament (Rit., ch. 39); the drought was its blasting breath that dried up the waters and withered vegetation. As a mythical figure of the natural fact, this was the original Ogre of the North, the giant who had no heart or soul in his body. Other powers born of the void were likewise elemental, with an aspect inimical to man. These were the spawn of darkness, drought and disease. In the Ritual they are called the Sami, demons of darkness, or the wicked Sebau, who for ever rose in impotent revolt against the powers that wrought for good. These Sami, or black spirits, and Sebau supplied fiends and spirits of darkness to later folklore and fairyology; and, like the evil Apap, the offspring also are of neither sex. Sex was introduced with the Great Mother in her hugest, most ancient form of the water cow, as representative of the Mother-earth and bringer forth of life amidst the waters of surrounding space. Her children were the elemental powers or forces, such as wind and water, earth and fire; but these are not to be confused with the evil progeny of Apap. Both are elemental in their origin, but the first were baneful, whereas the latter are beneficent.

When the terrors of the elements had somewhat spent their force, and were found to be non-sentient and unintelligent, the chief objects of regard and propitiation were recognized in the bringers of food and drink and the breath of air as the elements of life. Those were the beneficent powers, born of the Old Mother as elemental forces, that preceded the existence of the gods or powers divinized. The transformation of an elemental power into a god can be traced, for example, in the deity Shu. Shu as an elemental force was representative of wind, air, or breath, and more especially the breeze of dawn and eve, which was the very breath of life to Africa. Darkness was uplifted or blown away by the breeze of dawn. The elemental force of wind was imaged as a panting lion couched upon the horizon or the mountain-top as lifter up of darkness or the sky of night. The power thus represented was animistic or elemental. Next, Shu was given his star, and he became the Red God, who attained the rank of stellar deity as one of the seven "Heroes" who obtained their souls in the stars of heaven. The lion of Shu was continued as the figure of his force; and thus a god was born, the warrior-god, who was one of the Heroes, or one of the powers in an astronomical character. Three of these beneficent powers were divinized as male deities in the Kamite Pantheon, under the names of Nnu, Shu, and Seb. Nnu was the producer of that water which in Africa was looked upon as an overflow of very heaven. Shu was giver of the breath of life. Seb was divinized, and therefore worshipped as the god of earth and father of food. These three were powers that represented the elements of water, air, and earth. Water is denoted by the name of Nnu. Shu carries the lion's hinder part upon his head as the sign of force; the totem of Seb is the goose that lays the egg, a primitively perfect figure of food. These, as elemental powers or animistic souls, were life-givers in the elements of food, water, and breath. Not as begetters or creators, but as transformers from one phase of life to another, *finally* including the transformation of the superhuman power into the human product. There are seven of these powers altogether, which we shall have to follow in various phases of natural phenomena and on divers radiating lines of descent. Tentatively we might parallel:—Darkness = Sut; light = Horus; breathing power = Shu; water = Nnu (or Hapi); earth = Tuamutef (or Seb); fire = Khabsenuf; blood = Child-Horus. These were *not* derived from the ancestral spirits, once human, and no ancestral spirits ever were derived from them. Six of the seven were pre-human types. The seventh was imaged in the likeness of Child-Horus, or of Atum, the man. Two lists of names for the seven are given in the Ritual (ch. 17, i., 99-107), which correspond to the two categories of the elemental powers and the Glorious Ones, or Heroes. Speaking of the seven, the initiate in the mysteries says, "I know the names of the seven Glorious Ones. The leader of that divine company is An-ar-ef the Great by name." The title here identifies the human elemental as the sightless mortal Horus—that is, Horus who was incarnated in the flesh at the head of the seven, to become the first in status, he who had been the latest in development. In this chapter of the Ritual the seven have now become astronomical, with their stations fixed in heaven by Anup, whom we shall identify as deity of the Pole. "They do better," says Plutarch, "who believe that the legends told of Sut, Osiris, and Isis do not refer to either gods or men, but to certain great powers that were superhuman, but not as yet divine" (*Of Isis and Osiris,* ch. 26). The same writer remarks that "Osiris and Isis passed from the rank of good demons (elementals) to that of deities" (ch. 30). This was late in the Kamite mythos, but it truly follows the earlier track of the great powers when these were Sut and Horus, Shu and Seb, and the other elemental forces that were divinized as gods.

In the astronomical mythology the nature-powers were raised to the position of rulers on high, and this is that beginning which was described by Manetho with "the gods" as the primary class of rulers, whose reign was divided into seven sections, or, as we read it, in a heaven of seven divisions—that is, the celestial Heptanomis. Certain of these can be distinguished in the ancient heavens yet as figures of the constellations which became their totems. Amongst such were the hippopotamus-bull of Sut, the crocodile-dragon of Sebek-Horus, the lion of Shu, the goose of Seb, the beetle of Kheper (Cancer), and other types of the starry souls on high, now designated deities, or the Glorious Ones, as the Khuti. The ancient mother, who had been the cow of earth, was elevated to the sphere as the cow of heaven. It was she who gave rebirth to the seven powers that obtained their souls in the stars, and who were known as "the Children of the Thigh" when that was her constellation. These formed the company of the seven Glorious Ones, who became the Ali or Elohim, divine masters, time-keepers, makers and creators, which have to be followed in a variety of phases and characters. The Egyptian gods were born, then, as elemental powers. They were born as such of the old first Great Mother, who in her character of Mother-earth was the womb of life, and therefore mother of the elements, of which there are seven altogether, called her children. The seven elemental powers acquired souls as gods in the astronomical mythology. They are given rebirth in heaven as the seven children of the old Great Mother. In the stellar mythos they are also grouped as the seven Khus with Anup on the Mount. They are the seven Taasu with Taht in the lunar-mythos, the seven Knemmu with Ptah in the solar mythos. They then pass into the eschatology as the seven souls of Ra, the Holy Spirit, and the seven great spirits glorified with Horus as the eighth in the resurrection from Amenta.

The Egyptians have preserved for us a portrait of Apt (Kheb, or Ta-Urt), the Great Mother, in a fourfold figure, as the bringer forth of the four fundamental elements of earth, water, air, and heat. As representative of the earth she is a hippopotamus, as representative of water she is a crocodile, and as the representative of breathing force she is a lioness, the human mother being imaged by the pendent breasts and procreant womb. Thus the mother of life is depicted as bringer forth of the elements of life, or at least four of these, as the elemental forces or "souls" of earth, water, fire, and air, which four are imaged in her compound corpulent figure, and were set forth as four of her seven children. Apt was also the mother of sparks, or of souls as sparks of starry fire. She was the kindler of life from the spark that was represented by the star. This, we reckon, is the soul of Sut, her first-born, as the beneficent power of darkness. The power of water was imaged by Sebek-Horus as the crocodile. The power of wind or air, in one character, was that of the lion-god Shu; and the power of the womb is the Child-Horus, as the fecundator of his mother. These, with some slight variations, are four of the seven powers of the elements identified with the mother as the bringer forth of gods and men, whom we nowadays call Mother Nature. Six of the total seven were represented by zoötypes, and Horus was personalized in the form of a child. Evidence for a soul of life in the dark was furnished by the star. Hence the soul and star are synonymous under the name of Khabsu in Egyptian. This was an elemental power of darkness divinized in Sut, the author of astronomy. Evidence for a soul of life in the water was furnished by the fish that was eaten for food. This elemental power was divinized in the fish-god Sebek and in Ichthus, the mystical fish. Evidence for a soul of life in the earth was also furnished in food and in periodic renewal. The elemental power was divinized in Seb, the father of food derived from the ground, the plants, and the goose. Evidence for a soul of life in the sun, represented by the uræus-serpent, was furnished by the vivifying solar heat, the elemental power of which was divinized in Ra. Evidence for a soul of life in blood was furnished by the incarnation, the elemental power of which was divinized in elder Horus, the eternal child. Six of these seven powers, we repeat, were represented by zoötypes; the seventh was given the human image of the child, and later of Atum the man. Thus the earliest gods of Egypt were developed from the elements, and were not derived from the expanded ghosts of dead men. Otherwise stated, the ancestral spirits were not primary.

Apt, the First Great Mother.

Dr. Rink, writing of the Eskimo, has said that with them the whole visible world is ruled by supernatural powers or "owners," each of whom holds sway within certain limits, and is called his Inua (viz., its or his Inuk, which word signifies "man" and also owner or inhabitant). This is cited by Herbert Spencer as most conclusive evidence that the agent or power was *originally* a human ghost, because the power may be expressed as the Inuk, or its man—"the man in it—that is, the man's ghost in it." The writer did not think of the long way the race had to travel before "the power" could be expressed by "its man," or how late was the anthropological mode of representing the forces of external nature. "The man" as type of power belongs to a far later mode of expression. Neither man nor woman nor child was among the earliest representatives of the elemental forces in external nature. By the bye, the Inuk is the power, and in Egyptian the root Nukh denotes the power or force of a thing, the potency of the male, as the bull; thence Nukhta is the strong man or giant. Sut was a Suten-Nakht. Horus was a

Suten-Nakht, but neither of them was derived from man. The elements themselves were the earliest superhuman powers, and these were thought of and imaged by superhuman equivalents. The power of darkness was not represented by its man, or the ghost of man. Its primal power, which was that of swallowing all up, was imaged by the devouring dragon. The force of wind was not represented by its man, but by its roaring lion; the drowning power of water by the wide-jawed crocodile, the power of lightning or of sunstroke by its serpent-sting, the spirit of fire by the fiery-spirited ape. In this way all the elemental forces were equated and objectified before the zoötype of Sign-language was changed for the human figure or any one of them attained its "man" as the representative of its power. The earliest type of the man, even as male power, was the bull, the bull of his mother, who was a cow, or hippopotamus. Neither god nor goddess ever had been man or woman or the ghost of either in the mythology of Egypt, the oldest in the world. The Great Mother of all was imaged like the totemic mother, as a cow, a serpent, a sow, a crocodile, or other zoötype, ages before she was represented as a woman or the ghost of one. It is the same with the powers that were born of her as male, six of which were portrayed by means of zoötypes before there was any one in the likeness of a man, woman, or child. And these powers were divinized as the primordial gods. The Egyptians had no god who was *derived from a man*. They told Herodotus that "in eleven thousand three hundred and forty years [as he reckons] no god had ever actually become a man" (B. 2, 142). Therefore Osiris did not originate as a man. Atum, for one, was a god *in the likeness of a man*. But he was known as a god who did not himself become a man. On the other hand, no human ancestor ever became a deity. It was the same in Egypt as in Inner Africa; the spirits of the human ancestors always remained human, the glorified never became divinities. The nearest approach to a deity of human origin is the god in human likeness. The elder Horus is the divine child in a human shape. The god Atum in name and form is the perfect man. But both child and man are entirely impersonal—that is, neither originated in an *individual* child or *personal* man. Neither was a human being divinized. It is only the type that was anthropomorphic.

The two categories of spirits are separately distinguished in the Hall of Righteousness, when the Osiris pleads that he has made "oblations to *the gods* and funeral offerings to *the departed*" (Rit., ch. 125). And again, in the chapter following, the "oblations are presented to *the gods* and the sacrificial meals to *the glorified*" (ch. 126).

A single citation from the chapter of the Ritual that is said on arriving at the Judgment Hall will furnish a brief epitome of the Egyptian religion as it culminated in the Osirian cult. "I have propitiated the great god with that which he loveth; I have given bread to the hungry, water to the thirsty, clothes to the naked, a boat to the shipwrecked. *I have made oblations to the gods and funeral offerings to the departed,*" or to the ancestral spirits (Rit., ch. 125). The statement shows that the divine service consisted of good works, and primarily of charity. The gods and the glorified to whom worship was paid are: (1) The Great One God (Osiris); (2) the Nature-Powers, or Gods; and (3) the Spirits of the Departed. But the order in development was: (1) The Elemental Forces, or Animistic Nature-Powers; (2) the Ancestral Spirits; (3) the One Great God over all, who was imaged phenomenally in the Kamite trinity of Asar-Isis in matter, Horus in soul, Ra in spirit, which three were blended in the Great One God. In the Hymn to Osiris (line 6) the ancestral spirits are likewise discriminated from the divine powers or gods. When Osiris goes forth in peace by command of Seb, the God of Earth, "the *mighty ones* bow the head; the *ancestors* are in prayer." These latter are the commonalty of the dead, the human ancestors in general, distinguished from the gods or powers of the elements that were divinized in the astronomical mythology. In one of the texts the "spirits of the king," the ever-living Mer-en-Ra, are set forth as an object of religious regard superior in status to that of the gods, by which we understand the ancestral spirits are here exalted above the elemental powers as the objects of propitiation and invocation. The Egyptian gods and the glorified were fed on the same diet in the fields of divine harvest, but are entirely distinct in their origin and character. The glorified are identifiable as spirits that once were human who have risen from the dead in a glorified body as Sahus. The gods are spirits or powers that never had been human. We know the great ones, female or male, from the beginning as elemental forces that were always extant in nature. These were first recognized, represented, and divinized as superhuman. The ghost, when recognized, was human still, however changed and glorified. But the Mother-earth had never been a human mother, nor had the serpent Rannut, nor Nut, the celestial wateress. The god of the Pole as Anup, the moon god Taht, the sun god Ra, had never been spirits in a human guise. They were divinized, and therefore worshipped or propitiated as the superhuman powers in nature, chiefly as the givers of light, food, and drink, and as keepers of time and season. These, then, are the goddesses and gods that were created by the human mind as powers that were impersonal and non-human. Hence they had to be envisaged with the aid of living types. Spirits once human manifest as ghosts in human form. It follows that the gods were primary, and that worship, or extreme reverence, was first addressed to them and not to the ancestral spirits, which, according to H. Spencer and his followers, had no objective existence. Neither is there any sense in saying the Egyptian deities were *conceived* in animal forms. This is to miss the meaning of Sign-language altogether. "Conception" has nought to do with Horus being represented by a hawk, a crocodile, or a calf; Seb by a goose, Shu by a lion, Rannut by a serpent, Isis by a scorpion. The primary question is: Why were the goddesses and gods or powers presented under these totemic types, which preceded the anthrotype in the different modes of mythical representation? Three of the seven children born of the Great Mother have been traced in the portrait of Apt, the old first genetrix, as Sut the hippopotamus, Sebek the crocodile, and Shu the lion. But there was an earlier phase of representation with her two children

Sut and Horus, who were born twins. It is the same in the Kamite mythology as in external nature. The two primary elements were those of darkness and light: Sut was the power of darkness, Horus the power of light. In one representation the two elements were imaged by means of the black bird of Sut and the white bird, or golden hawk, of Horus. Thus we can identify two elemental powers, as old as night and day, which are primeval in universal mythology; and these two powers, or animistic souls, were divinized as the two gods Sut and Horus with the two birds of darkness and light, the black vulture and the gold hawk depicted back to back as their two representative types or personal totems.

The beginning with these two primal powers is repeated in the mythology of the Blacks on the other side of the world. With them the crow and hawk (the eagle-hawk) are equivalent to these two birds of darkness and light; and according to the native traditions, the eagle-hawk and crow were first among the ancestors of the human race. That is as the first two of the elemental powers which became the non-human ancestors in mythology. They are also known as the creators who divided the Murray Blacks into two classes or brotherhoods whose totems were the eagle-hawk and crow, and who now shine as stars in the sky. (Brough Smyth, v. I, 423 and 431.) This is the same point of departure in the beginning as in the Kamite mythos with the first two elemental powers, viz., those of darkness and light. These two birds are also equated by the black cockatoo and the white cockatoo as the two totems of the Mûkjarawaint in Western Australia. The two animistic souls or spirits of the two primary elements can be paralleled in the two souls that are assigned to man or the Manes in the traditions of certain aboriginal races, called the dark shade and the light shade, the first two souls of the seven in the Ritual. These, as Egyptian, are two of the seven elements from which the enduring soul and total personality of man is finally reconstituted in Amenta after death. They are the dark shade, called the Khabsu, and the light shade, called the Sahu. A Zulu legend relates that in the beginning there were two mothers in a bed of reeds who brought forth two children, one black, the other white. The woman in the bed of reeds was Mother-earth, who had been duplicated in the two mothers who brought forth in space when this was first divided into night and day. Another version of the mythical beginning with a black and white pair of beings was found by Duff Macdonald among the natives of Central Africa. The black man, they say, was crossing a bridge, and as he looked round he was greatly astonished to find that a white man was following him (*Africana*, vol. I, p. 75). These are the powers of darkness and daylight, who were portrayed in Egypt as the Sut-and-Horus twins, one of whom was the black Sut, the other the white Horus, and the two "men" were elementals. The natives on the shores of Lake Rudolf say that when it thunders *a white man* is born. But the white man thus born is the flash of light or lightning imaged by an anthropomorphic figure of speech.

The aborigines of Victoria likewise say the moon was a black fellow before he went up into the sky to become light, or white. Horus in Egypt was the white man as an elemental power, the white one of the Sut-and-Horus twins, who is sometimes represented by an eye that is white, whereas the eye of Sut was black. In the mythos Horus is divinized as the white god. The children of Horus, who are known to mythology as the solar race, are the Khuti. These are the white spirits, the children of light. The solar race at last attained supremacy as chief of all the elemental powers, and in the eschatology the Khuti are the glorious ones. The Khu-sign is a beautiful white bird. This signifies a spirit, and the spirit may be a human ghost, or it may be the spirit of light, otherwise light imaged as a spirit; thence Horus the spirit of light in the mythology, or the glorified human spirit, called the Khu, in the eschatology. The symbols of whiteness, such as the white down of birds, pipeclay, chalk, flour, the white stone, and other things employed in the mysteries of the black races and in their mourning for the dead, derive their significance from white being emblematic of spirit, or the spirits which originated in the element of light being the white spirit. The turning of black men into white is a primitive African way of describing the transformation of the mortal into spirit. It is the same in the mysteries of the Aleutians, who dance in a state of nudity with white eyeless masks upon their faces, by which a dance of spirits is denoted. With the blacks of Australia the secret "wisdom" is the same as that of the dark race in Africa. According to Buckley, when the black fellow was buried the one word *"Animadiate,"* was uttered, which denoted that he was gone *to be made a white man*. But this did not mean a European. Initiates in the totemic mysteries were made into white men by means of pipeclay and birds' down, or white masks, the symbols of spirits in the religious ceremonies. This mode of transformation was not intended as a compliment to the pale-face from Europe. Neither did white spirits and black originate with seeing the human ghost. Horus is the white spirit in the light half of the lunation, Sut in the dark half is "the black fellow," because they represent the elements of light and darkness that were divinized in mythology. Hence the eternal contention of the twins Sut and Horus in the moon. It is common in the African mysteries for the spirits to be painted or arrayed in white, and in the custom of pipeclaying the face, on purpose to cause dismay in battle, the white was intended to suggest spirits, and thus to strike the enemy with fear and terror. Also, when spirits are personated in the mysteries of the Arunta and other tribes of Australian aborigines, they are represented in white by means of pipeclay and the white down of birds. It is very pathetic, this desire and strenuous endeavour of the black races, from Central Africa to Egypt, or to the heart of Australia, to become white, as the children of light, and to win and wear the white robe as a vesture of spiritual purity, if only represented by a white mask or coating of chalk, pipeclay, or white feathers. Many a white man has lost his life and been made up into medicine by the black fellows on account of his white complexion being the same with that assigned to the good or white spirits of light. In a legend of creation preserved among the Kabinda it is related that God made all men black. Then he went across a great river and called upon all men to follow him. The wisest, the best, the bravest of those who heard the invitation plunged into the wide river, and the water washed them white. These were the ancestors of white men. The others were afraid to venture. They remained behind in their old world, and became the ancestors of black men. But to this day the white men come (as spirits) to the bank on the other side of the river and echo the ancient cry of "Come thou hither!" saying, *"Come; it is better over here!"* (Kingsley, M. H., *Travels in West Africa,* pp. 430, 431.) These are the white spirits, called the white men by the black races, who originated in the representation of light as an elemental spirit, the same term being afterwards applied to the white bird, the white god, and the white man. This legend is also to be found in Egypt. As the Ritual shows, there was an opening day of creation, designated the day of "Come thou to me." The call was made by Ra, from the other side of the water, to Osiris in the darkness of Amenta—that is, from Ra as the white spirit to Osiris the black in the eschatology. But there was an earlier application of the saying in the solar mythos. In the beginning, says the best-known Egyptian version, the sun god Temu, whose name denotes the creator god, having awoke in the Nnu from a state of negative existence, appeared, as it were, upon the other side of the water, a figure of sunrise, and suddenly cried across the water, "Come thou to me!" (as spirits). Then the lotus unfolded its petals, and up flew the hawk, which represented the sun in mythology and a soul in the eschatology. Thus Tum the father of souls, being established in his spiritual supremacy, calls upon the race of men to come to him across the water in the track of sunrise or of the hawk that issued forth as Horus from the lotus. From such an origin in the course of time all nature would be peopled with "black spirits and white," as animistic entities, or as the children of Sut and Horus; as the black vultures or crows of the one, and the white vultures or gold hawks of the other. Thus we have traced a soul of darkness and a soul of light that became Egyptian gods in the twin powers Sut and Horus, and were called the dark shade and the light of other races, the two first souls that were derived as elementals. The anima or breath of life was one of the more obvious of the six "souls" whose genesis was visible in external nature. This was the element assigned to Shu, the god of breathing force. In the chapter for giving the breath of life, to the deceased (Rit., ch. 55) the speaker, in the character of Shu, says: "I am Shu, who conveys the breezes, or breathings. I give air to these younglings as I open my mouth." These younglings are the children whose souls are thus derived from Shu, when the soul and breath were one, and Shu was this one of the elemental powers divinized as male.

Messrs. Spencer and Gillen have shown that up to the present time the Arunta tribes of Central Australia do not ascribe the begettal of a human soul to the male parent. They think the male may serve a purpose in preparing the way for conception, but they have not yet got beyond the incorporation of a soul from the elements of external nature, such as wind or water—that is, the power of the air or of water, which was imaged in the elemental deity. Spirit children, derivable from the air, are supposed to be especially fond of travelling in a whirlwind, and on seeing one of these approaching a native woman who does not wish to have a child will flee as if for her life, to avoid impregnation. (*Native Tribes*, p. 125.) This doctrine of a soul supposed to be incorporated from the elements is so ancient in Egypt as to have been almost lost sight of or concealed from view beneath the mask of mythology. The doctrine, however, was Egyptian. The insufflation of the female by the spirit of air was the same when the goddess Neith was impregnated by the wind. With the Arunta tribes it is the ordinary woman who is insufflated by the animistic soul of air. In Egypt, from the earliest monumental period, the female was represented mythically as the Great Mother Neith, whose totem, so to call it, was the white vulture; and this bird of maternity was said to be impregnated by the wind. "Gignuntur autem hunc in modum. Cum amore concipiendi vultur exarserit, vulvam ad Boream aperiens, ab eo velut comprimitur per dies quinque" (Hor-Apollo, B. I, 11).

This kind of spirit not only entered the womb of Neith, or of the Arunta female; it also went out of the human body in a whirlwind. Once when a great Fijian chieftain passed away a whirlwind swept across the lagoon. An old man who saw it covered his mouth with his hand and said in an awestruck whisper, "There goes his spirit." This was the passing of a soul in the likeness of an elemental power, the spirit of air that was imaged in the god Shu, the spirit that impregnated the virgin goddess Neith. According to a mode of thinking in external things which belonged to spiritualism, so to say, in the animistic stage, the human soul had not then been specialized and did not go forth from the body as the Ka or human double. It was only a totemic soul affiliated to the power of wind, which came and went like the wind, as the breath of life. To quote the phrase employed by Messrs. Spencer and Gillen, a spirit-child was *incarnated* in the mother's womb by the spirit of air. The doctrine is the same in the Christian phase, when the Holy Spirit makes its descent on Mary and insufflates her, with the dove for totem instead of some other type of breathing force or soul. There is likewise a survival of primitive doctrine when the Virgin Mary is portrayed in the act of inhaling the fragrance of the lily to procure the mystical conception of the Holy Child. This is a mode of inhaling the spirit breath, or anima, the same as in the mystery of the Arunta, but with the difference that the Holy Spirit takes the place of the spirit of air, otherwise that Ra, as source of soul, had superseded Shu, the breathing force. Such things will show how the most primitive simplicities of ancient times have supplied our modern religious mysteries.

We learn also from the Arunta tribes that it is a custom for the mother to affiliate her child thus incorporated (not incarnated) to the particular elemental power, as spirit of air or water, tree or earth, supposed to haunt the spot where she conceived or may have quickened. (N. T., pp. 124 and 128.) Thus the spirit-child is, or may be, a reincorporation of an Alcheringa ancestor, who as Egyptian is the elementary power divinized in the eschatology, and who is to be identified by the animal or plant which is the totemic type of either. Not that the animal or plant was supposed by the knowers to be transformed directly into a human being, but that the elemental power or superhuman spirit entered like the gust that insufflated the vulture of Neith or caused conception whether in the Arunta female or the Virgin Mary. The surroundings at the spot will determine the totem of the spirit and therefore of the spirit-child. Hence the tradition of the Churinga-Nanga being dropped at the place where the mother was impregnated by the totemic spirit, which, considering the sacred nature of the Churinga, was certainly a form of the Holy Spirit. The spirit of air rushed out of the gap between the hills; or it was at the water-hole, or near the sacred rock, or the totemic tree, that the mother conceived, and by such means the child is affiliated to the elemental power, the animistic spirit, the Alcheringa ancestor, as well as to the totemic group. The mother caught by the power of wind in the gap is the equivalent of divine Neith caught by the air god Shu and insufflated in the gorge of Neith. The element of life incorporated is the source of breath, or the spirit of air, which would have the same natural origin whether it entered the female in her human form, or into that of the bird, beast, fish, or reptile. It was the incorporation of an elemental spirit, whether of air, earth, water, fire, or vegetation.

In popular phraseology running water is called living water, and still water is designated dead. There is no motion in dead water, no life, no force, no spirit. Contrariwise, the motion of living water, the running spring or flowing inundation, is the force, and finally the soul of life in the element. Air was the breath of life, and therefore a soul of life was in the breeze. In the deserts of Central Africa the breeze of dawn and eve and the springs of water in the land are very life indeed and the givers of life itself, as they have been from the beginning. These, then, are two of the elements that were brought forth as nature powers by the earth, the original mother of life and all living things. When the supreme life-giving, life-sustaining power was imaged as a pouring forth of overflowing energy the solar orb became a figure of such a fountain head or source. But an earlier type of this great welling forth was water. Hence Osiris personates the element of water as he who is shoreless. He is objectified as the water of renewal. His throne in heaven, earth, and Amenta is balanced upon water. Thus the primary element of nutriment has the first place to the last with the root-origin of life in water. Birth from the element of water was represented in the mysteries of Amenta by the rebirth in spirit from the water of baptism. It is as a birth of water that Child-Horus calls himself the primary power of motion. Also "the children of Horus" who stand on the papyrus plant or lotus are born of water in the new kingdom that was founded for the father by Horus the son. This too was based upon the water. Hence two of Horus's children, Tuamutef and Kabhsenuf, are called the two fishes (Rit., ch. 113), and elsewhere the followers of Horus are the fishers. One of the two lakes in Paradise contained the water of life. It was designated the Lake of Sa, and one of the meanings of the word is spirit, another is soil or basis. It was a lake, so to say, of spiritual matter from which spirits were derived in germ as the Hammemat. This lake of spirit has assuredly been localized in Europe. The superstition concerning spirits that issue from the water is common, and in Strathspey there is a lake called Loch Nan Spoiradan, the Lake of the Spirits.

When spirit-children were derived from the soul of life that was held to be inherent in the element of water, they would become members of the water-totem—unless some pre-arrangement interfered. For example, a water-totem is extant in the quatcha-totem of the Arunta tribe. A child was conceived one day by a lubra of the Witchetty-grub clan who happened to be in the neighbourhood of a quatcha, or water locality. She was taking a drink of water near to the gap in the ranges where the spirits dwell, when suddenly she heard a child's voice crying "Mia, mia!" the native term for relationship, which includes that of motherhood. She was not anxious to have a child, and therefore ran away, but could not escape. She was fat and well-favoured, and the spirit-child overtook her and was incorporated willy-nilly. In this instance the spirits were Witchetty-grub instead of water spirits of the quatcha-totem locality, otherwise, if the totem had not been already determined locally, this would represent the *modus operandi* of the elemental power becoming humanized by incorporation. The water spirit is a denizen of the water element, always lying in wait for young, well-favoured women, and ready to become embodied in the human form by the various processes of drinking, eating, breathing, or other crude ways of conversion and transformation.

The several elements led naturally to the various origins ascribed to man from the ideographic representatives of earth, water, air, fire, such as the beast of earth, the turtle or fish of water, the bird of air, the tree or the stone. The Samoans have a tradition that the first man issued from a stone. His name was Mauike, and he is also reputed to be the discoverer of fire. Now the discoverer of fire, born of a stone, evidently represents the element of fire which had been found in the stone, the element being the animistic spirit of fire, to which the stone was body that served as type (Turner, *Samoa*, p. 280, ed. 1884). The derivation of a soul of life from the element of fire, or from the spark, is likewise traceable in a legend of the Arunta, who thus explain the origin of their fire-totem. A spark of fire, in the Alcheringa, was blown by the north wind from the place where fire was kindled first, in the celestial north, to the summit of a great mountain represented by Mount Hay. Here it fell to the earth, and caused a huge conflagration. When this subsided, one class of the Inapertwa creatures issued from the ashes. These were "the ancestors of the people of the fire-totem," the people born from the element of fire (N. T., p. 445). The tradition enables us to identify an origin for children born of fire, or the soul of fire, that is, the power of this element. Moreover, it is fire from heaven. It falls as a spark, which spark falls elsewhere in the fire-stone. These particular Inapertwa, or pre-human creatures, were discovered by two men of the Wungara or wild-duck totem, and made by them into men and women of the fire-totem. Such, then, are the offspring of fire or light, where others are the children of air or of water, as one of the elemental or animistic powers; and the pre-human creatures became men and women when they were made totemic. The transformation is a symbolical mode of deriving the totemic people from the pre-human and pre-totemic powers which were elemental.

There is a class of beings in the German folk-tales who are a kind of spirit, but not of human origin, like so many others that are a product of primitive symbolism, which came to be designated elementals because they originated in the physical elements. These little earth-men have the feet of a goose or a duck. Here the Kamite wisdom shows how these are the spirits of earth who descended from Seb, the power, spirit, or god of earth, whose zoötype in Egypt was the goose. Thus the earth god or elemental power of the mythos becomes the goose-footed earth man of the Märchen and later folk-lore, which are the *débris* of the Kamite mythology. The cave-dwellers in various lands are likewise known as children of the earth. Their birthplace may be described as a bed of reeds, a tree, a cleft in the rock, or the hole in a stone. Each type denotes the earth as primordial bringer forth and mother of primæval life. Children with souls derived from the element of earth are also represented by the Arunta as issuing from the earth *viâ* "the Erithipa stone." The stone, equal to the earth, is here the equivalent for the parsley-bed from which the children issue in the folk-lore of the British Isles. The word Erithipa signifies a child, though seldom used in this sense. Also a figure of the human birthplace is very naturally indicated. There is a round hole on one side of the stone through which the spirit-children waiting for incorporation in the earthly form are supposed to peep when on the look-out for women, nice and fat, to mother them. It is thought that women can become pregnant by visiting this stone. The imagery shows that the child-stone not only represents the earth as the bringer forth of life, but that it is also an emblem of emanation from the mother's womb. There is an aperture in the stone over which a black band is painted with charcoal. This unmistakably suggests the pubes. The painting is always renewed by any man who happens to be in the vicinity of the stone (N. T., p. 337). These Erithipa stones are found in various places. This may explain one mode of deriving men from stones, the stone or rock in this case being a figure of the Mother-earth.

In such wise the primitive representation survives in legendary lore, and the myth remains as a tale that is told. Earth, as the birthplace in the beginning, was typified by the tree and stone. A gap in the mountain range, a cleft in the rock, or the hole in a stone presented a likeness to the human birthplace. The mystery of the stone affords an illuminative instance of the primitive mode of *thinging* in Sign-language, or thinking in things. Conceiving a child was thought of as a concretion of spirit, and that concretion or crystallization was symbolized by means of the white stone in the mysteries. It is the tradition of the Arunta tribe that when a woman conceives, or, as they render it, when the spirit-child enters the womb, a Churinga-stone is dropped, which is commonly supposed to be marked with a device that identifies the spirit-child, and therefore the human child, with its totem. Usually the Churinga is found on the spot by some of the tribal elders, who deposit it in the Ertnatulunga, or storehouse, in which the stones of conception are kept so sacredly that they must never be looked upon by woman or child, or any uninitiated man. "Each Churinga is so closely bound up with the spirit individual (or the spirit individualized) that it is regarded as its representative in the Ertnalutunga" or treasury of sacred objects. In this way the Arunta were affirming that, when a child was conceived of an elemental power, whether born figuratively from the rock or tree, the air, the water, or it may be from the spark in the stone that fell with the fire from heaven, or actually from the mother's womb, it was in possession of a spirit that was superhuman in its origin and enduring beyond the life of the mortal. This was expressed by means of the stone as a type of *permanence*. Hence, when the stone could not be identified upon the spot, a Churinga was cut *from the very hardest wood* that could be found. The stones were then saved up in the repository of the tribe or totemic group, and these Churingas are the stones and trees in which primitive men have been ignorantly supposed to keep their souls for safety outside of their own bodies by those who knew nothing of the ancient Sign-language.

A magical mode of evoking the elemental spirit from material substance survives in many primitive customs. Whistling for the wind is a way of summoning the spirit or force of the breeze, which was represented in Egypt as the power of a panting lion. Touching wood or iron, or calling out "Knife!" to be safe, is an appeal to the elemental spirit as a protecting power. Setting the poker upright in front of the grate to make the fire burn is a mode of appeal made to the spirit of fire in the metal. This, like so many more, has been converted to the superstition of the cross. The Servians at their Coledar set light to an oak log and sprinkle the wood with wine. Then they strike it and cause sparks to fly out of it, crying, "So many sparks, so many goats and sheep! so many sparks, so many pigs and calves! so many sparks, so many successes and so many blessings!" (Hall). These in their way were seekers after life, the elemental spirit of life in this instance being that of fire from the spark. The element of fire was evoked from both wood and stone. It was their spirit-child. Now, it is a mode of magic to evoke a spirit from these by rubbing the wood or stone, or the totems made from either. And this way of kindling fire is applied by the Arunta for the purpose of calling forth the spirits of children from the Erithipa stones, which are supposed to be full of them. By rubbing a man can cause them to come forth and enter the human mother. Clearly the *modus operandi* is based on rubbing the stone or wood, to kindle fire from the spark that signified a germ or soul of life.

Another mode of evoking the spirit of and from an element may be illustrated by a Kaffir custom. When the girls have come of age and have suffered the opening rite of puberty, it is the Zulu fashion for the initiate to run stark naked through the first plenteous downpour of water, which is characteristically called a "he-rain," to secure fertilization from the nature power. In this custom a descent of the elemental spirit for incorporation is by water instead of fire (or earth, air, or light), but the principle is the same in primitive animism. Whichever the agent, there is a derivation from a source that is superhuman, if only elemental. It was the elemental powers that supplied pre-human souls in the primitive sociology. These we term totemic souls, souls that were common to the totemic group of persons, plants, animals, or stones, when there was no one soul yet individualized or distinguished from the rest as the human soul. They could not be "the souls of men" that were supposed to inhabit the bodies of beasts and birds, reptiles and insects, plants and stones, when there were no souls of men yet discreted from the pre-human souls in old totemic times. The human lives, or souls, are bound up with the totemic animal or bird, reptile or tree, because these represented the same animistic nature power from which the soul that is imaged by the totem was derived. The soul in common led to the common interest, the mysterious relationship and bond of unity betwixt man and animal and elemental powers, or the later gods. It was this totemic soul, common to man and animal, which explains the tradition of the Papagos that in the early times "men and beasts talked together, and a common language made all brethren." (Bancroft, vol. III, p. 76.) In the primary phase the soul that takes shape in human form was derived directly from the element as source of life. In a second phase of representation the powers of the elements were imaged by the totemic zoötypes. Thence arose the universal tradition, sometimes called belief, of an animal ancestry in which the beasts, birds, reptiles, fish, plants, trees, rocks, or stones were the original progenitors of the human race, through the growing ignorance of primitive Sign-language. Spirit-children derived from the elemental power of air are described in the Ritual as "the younglings of Shu," the god of breathing-force. And as the lion was the totem of Shu, the children would or might be derived from the lion as their totemic type. Germs of soul might ascend from the water of life in the celestial Lake of Sa, or soul, as the children of Nnu. The children of Horus are emanations from the sun. As such they have their birth in heaven to become incorporate on the earth, Child-Horus being first, according to the eschatology. It is because the sun was looked upon at one stage as the elemental source of a soul that its power could be, as it was, represented by a phallus. Thence also arose the belief that the sun could impregnate young women. This will partly explain why the female at the time of first menstruation must not be looked on by the sun. The young and fat Arunta woman, fleeing to escape from the embraces of the wind for fear of being impregnated with the elemental spirit-child, suggests a clue. She did not wish to bear a child, therefore she fled from the elemental power. In the other case the maiden must not be caught, for fear a soul should be made incarnate under the new conditions. For this reason the young girls were taught that terrible results would happen if they were *seen by the sun* in their courses; and they were consequently kept in the shade, or were instructed to hide themselves when the time arrived. They were not merely secluded at puberty, but were shut up sometimes darkly for years together, and suspended on a stage betwixt earth and heaven, as Tabu, until the period of pubescence came, at which moment they must not be shone upon by the sun, nor breathed on by the air, nor must they touch the elements of earth or water. They were secluded and consecrated for puberty, and were shut up from the elements to which generation had been attributed by the early human thought, a superior element of soul being now recognized in the blood of the virgin.

Blood was the latest element of seven from which a soul of life was derived. This followed the soul of air, water, heat, vegetation, or other force of the elements, and a soul derived from blood was the earliest *human* soul, derived from the blood of the female. Not any blood, not ordinary menstrual blood, but that blood of the pubescent virgin who was personalized in the divine virgin Neith, or Isis, or Mary. In the Semitic creation man, or Adam, was created from a soul of blood. Blood and Adam are synonymous, and the previous races, "which are but spittle," had derived their souls, in common with the animals, from the elements of external nature that were represented by totems, not by the blood of the mother nor the ancestry of the father. Several forms of an external soul had been derived from the elements of earth, air, and water, and at length a human soul was differentiated from the rest. This was the soul of blood which has been traced to the pubescent virgin. The virgin mother in mythology is only typical, but the type was founded in the natural fact that the mother-blood originated with the virgin when the blood was held to be the soul of life. This, to reiterate, was the pubescent virgin ready for connubium. The virgin Neith was represented by that bird of blood, the vulture, who was said to nurse her young on her own blood. The virgin Isis was portrayed as the red heifer, when Child-Horus was her red-complexioned calf. The first rendering, then, was pre-anthropomorphic, and at last the human likeness was adopted for the soul of blood, and this was imaged in Child-Horus as the soul born in the blood of Isis, the divine blood-mother, who was the typical virgin. This was the creation of man in the mythology, who was Atum the red in the Egyptian, Adam in the Hebrew version; and in man this seventh soul was now embodied in the human form.

The human soul never was "conceived as a bird," but might be imaged as a bird, according to the primitive system of representation. The golden hawk, for instance, was a bird which typified the sun that soared aloft as Horus in the heavens, and the same bird in the eschatology was then applied to the human soul in its resurrection from the body. Hence the hawk with a human head is a compound image, not the portrait of a human soul. The celestial poultry that pass for angels in the imagination of Christendom have no direct relation to spiritual reality. A feathered angel was never yet seen by clairvoyant vision, and is not a result of revelation. We know how they originated, why they were so represented, and where they came from into the Christian eschatology. They are the human-headed birds that were compounded and portrayed for souls in Egypt, and carried out thence into Babylonia, Judea, Greece, Rome, and other lands.

In the *Contes Arabes,* published by Spitta Bey, the soul of a female jinn who has become the wife of a human husband goes out of her as a beetle, and when the beetle is killed the female dies. Again, in a German tale the soul of a sleeping girl is seen to issue from her mouth in the form of a red mouse, and when the mouse is killed the maiden dies. In both cases we find Egyptian symbolism surviving in folk-lore. The red mouse was a zoötype of the soul of blood, the soul derived from the mother of flesh, and, being such, it was consecrated as an image of Child-Horus, who was born in the blood of Isis; and because it was the figure of an elemental soul in the ancient symbolism, the mouse remained the emblem of the human soul in the Märchen of other nations. The scarabæus placed in the chest of the deceased to signify another heart was given to the Manes in Amenta, and the giving of this other heart to the Manes was dramatically represented on the earth by inserting the beetle in the embalmed body as a typical new heart, the beetle being a type of transformation in death. According to Renouf in *Parables in Folk-lore,* we have here the notion of "a person's life or soul being detached from the body and hidden away at a distance." "The person," he continues, "does not appear to suffer in the least from the absence of so essential a part of himself." (*Proceedings Soc. Bib. Arch.,* April 2, 1889, p. 178.) But this is not the genesis of the idea. What we find in folk-lore is not contemporary evidence for current beliefs. In this the ancient wisdom is continually repeated without knowledge, and the symbols continue to be quoted at a wrong value. The soul or heart of the witch, the jinn, or the giant never was the soul of a mortal. The Arabic jinns originate as spirits of the elements. They appear in animal forms because the primary nature powers were first represented by the zoötypes; hence such animals as jackals, hyenas, serpents, and others are called "the cattle of the jinn." No human soul was ever seen in the guise of a mouse or a beetle, hawk or serpent, turtle, plant or tree, fire-stone or starry spark, if but for the fact that no one of the souls had been discreted separately *as a human soul* from the elemental, animistic, or totemic powers which were pre-human. It was on the ground of a pre-human origin for such souls that a doctrine of pre-existence, of transmigration, of reincarnation for the soul could be and was established, *i.e.,* because it was not the personal human soul. This account of an elemental origin for the earliest souls of life may help to explain that pre-existence of the soul (erroneously assumed to be the human soul) which crops up in legendary lore. In the *Book of the Secrets of Enoch* it was declared that "Every soul was created eternally before the foundation of the world." (*Sclavonic Enoch,* ch. 23, 5.) The pre-existence of souls is an Egyptian doctrine, but not of human souls already individualized and possessing each a personal identity. They were the elemental souls, not the ancestral human spirits. The Egyptian Hamemmat survived in Talmudic tradition as a class of pre-human beings. It was held as a Jewish dogma that the souls which were to enter human bodies had existed before the creation of the world in the Garden of Eden, or in the seventh, *i.e.,* the highest, heaven (Chagiga, 12 b). So the primordial powers in the Ritual are identifiable with the divine ancestors who preceded Ra (ch. 178, 22), and who are called the ancestors of Ra. "Hail ye, chiefs, ancestors of Ra!" Elsewhere they are the seven souls of Ra, when Atum-Ra becomes the one god in whom all previous powers are absorbed and glorified. The religious ceremonies of the Arunta date from and represent the doings of these ancestors in the Alcheringa at a time when the ancestor as kangaroo was not directly distinguishable from the kangaroo as man. The derivation of souls from elemental and pre-human powers is marked when the Arunta claim that each individual is a direct reincarnation of a totemic ancestor who is still living in the Alcheringa. And, as the same origin is assigned for the totemic animal, it follows that the man and animal are brothers, born of the same ancestral and pre-human soul (N. T., p. 202). This is indicated when it is said that the spirit kangaroo enters the kangaroo animal in just the same way in which the spirit kangaroo man enters the womb of the kangaroo woman (N. T., p. 209). These totemic souls are the pre-human ancestors of the Arunta tribes who lived in their pre-human as well as prehistoric past. "Every native thinks that his (mythical) ancestor in the Alcheringa was the descendant of, or is immediately associated with, the animal or plant" "which bears his totemic name." So intimately in the native mind are these ancestors associated with the totemic types that "an Alcheringa man says of the kangaroo totem that it may sometimes be spoken of either as a man kangaroo or a kangaroo man" (N. T., pp. 73, 119, and 132). The present explanation is that these ancestors in the Alcheringa originated in the superhuman nature powers or elemental souls that were first represented by the totems which are afterwards (or also) representative of the totemic motherhood. Thus the origin of the totemic men, in this phase, was not from the tree or animal of the totem whose name they bore, but from the elemental power or pre-human nature-soul from which both the man and animal derived a soul of life in common, as it was in the Alcheringa or old, old times of the mythical ancestors which in other countries, as in Egypt, have become the gods, whereas in Australia, Inner Africa, China, India, and elsewhere they remained the ancestors derived from animals, plants, and other zoötypes that were totemic and pre-human. The derivation and descent of human souls from these superhuman elemental nature powers was at first *direct;* afterwards they were represented by totemic zoötypes in ways already indicated and to be yet more fully shown. Thus a clan of the Omahas were described as the wind people. The Damaras have kept count of certain totemic descents (or eandas) from the elemental powers when they reckon that some of their people "come from the sun" and others "come from the rain" (Galton, *Narrative,* 137); others come from the tree. The progenitor, as male, may and does take the mother's place in later ages, but the bringer forth was female from the first. So is it with the types. Hence the mount, the tree, the cave, the water-hole, the earth itself were naturally female; indeed, we might say that locality is feminine as the birthplace, and the elemental power was brought forth as male. In Scotland, persons who bore the name of "Tweed" were supposed to have had the genii of the River Tweed for their ancestors (Rogers, *Social Life in Scotland,* III, 336), which denotes the same derivation from the elemental source, in this instance the spirit of water, as when the Arunta of the water-totem claim descent by reincorporation from the elemental ancestor in the Alcheringa, or as it might be in the Egyptian wisdom, from the God Nnu, or Num, or Hapi, the descent being traceable at first by the totem, and afterwards by the name.

Primitive man has been portrayed in modern times as if he were a philosophic theorist. He has been charged with imagining all sorts of things which never existed, as if that were the origin of his spirits and his gods, whereas the beginning was with the elemental powers. These were external to himself. There was no need to imagine them. They *were*. And with this cognition his theology began. Primitive men were taught by the consistency of experience. However primitive, they neither had nor pretended to have the power of taking the soul out of the body when in peril, and depositing it for safety in a tree, or stone, or any other totemic type. Such a delusion belongs to the second childhood of the human race rather than to the first. It never was an article of faith even with the most benighted savages, as will be exemplified. Bunsen was one of those who have cited the "Tale of the Two Brothers" to prove "how deep-seated was the Egyptian belief in the transmigration of the *human* soul." But, as before said, Bata, the hero of the transmigrating soul, is not a human being! He is a folk-lore form of the mystical hero, the young solar god who issued in the morning or the spring-time from the typical tree of dawn. In like manner the golden hawk, in the Ritual, brings *his* heart = soul from the Mountain of the East, where it had been deposited in the tree of dawn upon the horizon. Externalizing the heart or soul in this way was not the act of men who were out of their minds or beside themselves, but simply a mode of symbolism which remains to be read in order that the error based upon it may be dispelled. When the nature powers are represented as human in the folk-tales they assume a misleading look, and primitive thought is charged with puerilities of the most recent fashion. It is these elemental souls that have been mixed up with the human soul by Hindus and Greeks, by Buddhist, Pythagorean, and Neo-Platonist, and mistaken for the human soul in course of transmigration through the series which were but representatives of souls that were distinguished as non-human by those who understood the types. The mantis, the hawk, the ram, the lion, and others in the Ritual are types of souls, may be of human souls, but not on this earth. Such were types of elemental powers first, and next they were continued as indicators of the stages made in the seven transformations of the Manes in Amenta, the earth of eternity. This imagery was first applied to the powers of external nature, and when it is continued in a later phase the mythical characters become mixed up and confounded with the human in the minds of those who know no better, or who are at times too knowing ever to know. Once a year the Santals "make simple offerings to a ghost [or spirit] who dwells in a Bela-tree" (Hunter). This is taken by Herbert Spencer to show that the spirit in the tree was derived from the human ghost, which, according to his theory, never existed save in dreams. He points to certain Egyptian representations of "female forms" "emerging from trees and dispensing blessings" (*Data,* ch. 23, 182). But in no case has the female any human origin or significance. The females are Hathor and Nut, who personate the divine mother, not the human mother, in the tree, as the giver of food and drink provided by the Mother-earth. As to the "ghost in the tree," neither was that derived from the human spirit or the shadow seen in dreams. Egypt will tell us what it signified, and thereby prove that it did not originate in the human ghost or the Spencerian phantom born of sleep. "Plant worship," says the same writer, "is the worship of a spirit originally human." "Everywhere the plant spirit is shown by its conceived human form and ascribed human desires to have originated from a human personality." In reply to this it can be shown from the oldest representations known, viz., those of Egypt, that the anthropomorphic mode of rendering was not primary, but the latest of all. Rannut, the goddess of plant life, was depicted as a serpent, before the human figure was assigned to her, the sloughing, self-renovating serpent being a zoötype of renewal in a variety of phenomena, including vegetation. Nut in a female form gives the water of life from the tree, but she was previously Heaven itself in very person or Heaven typified as giver of the water from the tree or milk from the cow. Neither Nut nor Rannut was derived from a spirit originally human, but from a power in external nature that was known to be superhuman. Hathor in the tree was a divinity not derived from any mortal personality, and her figure of the divine female in the tree was preceded by that of the wet-nurse as a milch-cow and still earlier as the water-cow. In the Osirian mysteries the so-called "corn spirit" is derived from the water. At Philae the god=the corn spirit is represented with stalks of corn springing from his mummy, and, according to the inscription, this is Osiris of the mysteries who springs from the returning waters—as the bringer of food in the shape of corn. In a vignette to the Book of the Dead the power of water also is portrayed in "the Great Green One," a spirit represented by the hieroglyphic lines that form a figure of water. This when divinized is Horus as the shoot of the papyrus plant, or the branch of endless years—a type of the eternal manifested by renewal in food produced from the element of water in the inundation (Pap. of Ani, p. 8). What the picture intimates is that water was the source of life to vegetation, and the figure in green arising from the element of water is the spirit of vegetation that was divinized in Horus as the "shoot" or "natzar,"—a figure that survives as "Jack" in the green who dances in the pastimes on May-day. Nowhere in the range of Egyptian symbolism does "the plant spirit" originate in or from a human personality. Mighty spirits were supposed to dwell in certain trees by the Battas of Sumatra, who would resent and revenge any injury done to them. Such mighty spirits or powers of the elements had grown up, as Egyptian, to become the goddesses and gods, as Hathor and Nut in the sycamore, Isis in the persea tree, Seb in the shrubs and plants, Horus in the papyrus, or Unbu in the golden bough.

A soul of self-renewing life in the earth or the tree had been imaged by the serpent, a soul of life in the water had been imaged by the fish, a soul of life in the air by the bird, the elements being represented by the zoötypes which afterwards became totemic and finally fetishtic. Thus, if the tree were the Nanja of an Australian tribe it would stand for the life of the tribe and be the totem of the pre-human soul. And when the human soul had been discreted as an individual soul from the general or tribal soul, the sacred tree which imaged the life or soul of the tribe might be claimed to represent the soul of a man. This was what did occur. A definite case is known to Messrs. Spencer and Gillen in which a black fellow earnestly pleaded with a white man not to cut down a particular tree, because it was the Nanja-tree, and he feared that if it were destroyed some evil would befall him personally. The tree *quâ* tree had been a type of self-renewing superhuman power, then a tribal totem bound up with the life of the tribe, and lastly it is said that the man believed his separate or discreted soul was in the tree, which furnished a place of refuge when his tree soul (or Miss Kingsley's "bush soul") was in danger.

The reader may depend upon it that primitive man who fancied he had a separate soul which he could hide for safety in a tree, a stone, or an egg is a very modern product indeed, the sheerest reflex image of his misinterpreters, who are but speculative theorists that have never mastered the language of the primitive signs. As already said, the supposed transmigration of human souls, of turtles, or of other zoötypes was impossible when as yet there was no human soul. The soul that might transmigrate was pre-human, elemental, and totemic; a soul that was divisible according to its parts and elemental powers, but common to life in general and in all its forms in earth and water, air and tree, to man and reptile, fish, insect, bird, and beast. When the sacred bear is killed for food at Usu, Volcano Bay, by the Ainu, they shout, "We kill you, O bear! Come back soon into an Ainu." That is as food, which in a sense is the transmigration of soul, but it is that elemental soul of food which is represented by the bear of eternity, and not a human soul. There was a doctrine of the transmigration of soul, or souls that were not human, to warrant the language of the Zuni Indian which he addressed to the turtle: "Ah! My poor dear lost child, or parent, my sister or brother to have been! Who knows which? May be my own great-grandfather or mother." (Cushing, F. H., *Century Magazine,* May, 1883.) This, however, was no transmigration of human souls. We repeat, at that primitive stage of thought no soul was specialized as human. There were only animistic or totemic souls; and if the element derived from should be water and the totem be the turtle, the type would represent the soul that was common to both man and animal, as brother turtles of the water totem, the elemental power over all being imaged as the turtle that was eternal, one of the mystical ancestors in the Arunta Alcheringa, or one of the gods in Egypt. Moreover, when once the soul of blood born of woman had been discriminated as a human soul *it was no longer possible to postulate a return of that same soul to the pre-human status.* It was discreted for ever from the soul of the animal, fish, bird, and reptile. The kangaroo-man would no longer have the same soul as the kangaroo. There was no ground for thinking that the human soul would be reincorporated or reincarnated in the body of the beast or reptile, and therefore no foundation for the doctrine of reincarnation which has been applied to human souls, and consequently misapplied by modern reincarnationists who do not know one soul from another. But the metempsychosis of soul or souls did survive as a doctrine long after the *human* species had been discreted and individualized, and when the primitive significance was no longer understood. Readjustment of the standpoint was made in the Egyptian wisdom, but seldom if ever elsewhere. Thus, in Buddhist metaphysic the soul continued to pass (theoretically) through the same "cycle of necessity" with the totemic souls which had been the pre-human creatures of the elements, like the "Inapertwa" of the Arunta. As a result of the soul, here termed totemic, having been at one time common to men and animals and the elemental powers, this led to a perplexing interchange of personality, or at least of shape, betwixt the superhuman powers, the men, and animals in the primitive mysteries and in the later folk-tales or legendary lore, in which we seem to hear the very aged mother-wisdom, or her misinterpreters, maundering in a state of dotage.

It must be borne in mind that the earliest mode of becoming was not by creating, but by transforming. For instance, when Ptah is imaged as the frog, or beetle, he is the deity as transformer, but when portrayed as the *embryo in utero* he images the creator or creative cause. A drama of transformation was performed in the totemic mysteries. The boy became a man by being changed into an animal, which animal was his totemic representative of the providing and protecting power. This was a mode of assimilating the human being to the divine or superhuman power when it had been imaged in the elemental stage by means of the particular totemic zoötype, whether animal, bird, fish, insect, reptile, or plant. We gather from the magical practices of the western Inoits that when the sorcerer or spirit medium clothes himself in the skin of animals, the feathers of birds, teeth of serpents, and other magical emblems it is done to place himself *en rapport* with the kings of the beasts and the powers of the elements, for the purpose of deriving superhuman aid from these our "elder brothers." This, of course, was the natural fact that has been described as making the transformation into animal, bird, or reptile. Spirit mediums, as sorcerers and magicians, witches and wizards, are great transformers who make their transformations in the mystery of trance. In that state they were assimilated to and united in alliance with one or other of the primordial powers, each of which was represented by its totemic zoötype. There were spirit mediums extant when the superhuman powers were elemental (not the ancestral spirits), and these were imaged by the animals and other zoötypes. Thus the spirit mediums in alliance with certain of these powers might be said to assume their likeness as animals, just as in modern times the witch is reputed to transform into a cat or hare, or the wizard into a wolf. The blacksmiths in Africa, who are thought to work by spirit agency, are supposed in Abyssinia to transform themselves into hyenas. The sorcerers and witches, otherwise the spirit mediums, of the Mexicans were said to transform themselves into animals. The Khonds affirm that witches have the power of transforming themselves into tigers.

Again, when the goddess Neith and the Arunta women were insufflated by the wind the soul was thus derived directly from the element. But when the bird is introduced as the white vulture of Neith or the dove of Hathor the insufflation may be attributed to the bird of air or soul. So with the element of water. The descent of soul may be direct from the element or derived from some type of the element. For example, the Karens hold that the waters are inhabited by beings whose proper shape is that of dragons or crocodiles, but occasionally these appear as men and take wives of the children of men, as do the sons of heaven in the Book of Enoch. Indeed, it is quite possible that this self-incorporation of the elemental powers in a human form through the mothers is the source of the Semitic legend relating to the sons of God who cohabited with the daughters of men. Of course, the phrase "sons of God" belongs to a later nomenclature. The elemental powers knew no God the Father. These in the Book of Enoch are the seven primary powers that were the Holy Watchers once in heaven and the heirs of life eternal, but whose origin was as powers of the elements such as pursued the Arunta daughters of men. And, whether elemental or astronomical, they were seven in number. They are charged with having forsaken their lofty station and with acting like the children of earth. They have "lain with women" and "defiled themselves with the daughters of men." In the Book of Enoch the seven have acquired the character that was attained by the elemental powers, and have to be followed in the phase of legendary lore which obfuscates the ancient wisdom, though far less so than does the Book of Genesis. It was not as astronomical powers that the story could be told of the seven. But as elemental forces pursuing nice fat women—like the Arunta spirits of air—to incorporate themselves they could be described as beings who polluted themselves with women; they being spiritual or superhuman, whereas the daughters of men were of the earth earthy. This legend was represented finally in literature by what has been termed "the loves of the angels." The complexion of these external spirits is likewise elemental. Their various colours are copied straight from nature, and not from the complexion of human beings. The spirit of darkness was black. The spirit of light was white. The spirit of water or vegetation was green. The spirit of air was blue. The spirit of fire was red. The spirit of the highest god upon the summit of the seven upward steps is golden, as Ra the divine or holy spirit in the final eschatology. Thus we can trace the black spirits and white, red spirits and grey, green, or blue, to an elemental origin and show that the spirit as a green man, a blue man, a black man (where there are no blacks), a white man (where there are no whites), a red man, or a golden child was derived directly from the elements and not from a ghost that was called into existence by the wizardry of dreams. When human spirits were recognized and portrayed the same types and colours were used. The human spirit issuing from the red flesh in death is painted blue. Not because spirits were seen to be of that complexion when "all was blue," but because the spirit of air or anima had been an elemental spirit in the blue. The spirit in green (vegetation) remains the "green man" as wood spirit in Europe. The spirit of darkness is black as the bogey man, the black Sut in Egypt. The Zuni Indians described by Mr. Cushing have a system of praying to the seven great spirits, or nature gods, by means of the seven different colours which are painted on their prayer-sticks. Six of these colours represent the six regions into which space was divided, the four quarters, together with the height and depth or zenith and nadir. The powers thus localized are called the "makers of the paths of life," on account of their relationship to the supreme one of the seven, who sits at the centre of all, and who is the only one of them portrayed in the human form as the highest of the seven. Each of these has its own proper complexion, and the fetishes that represent the human powers are also determined by colours in the material from which they are modelled or the pigment with which they are painted. The particular power prayed to is identified to the ear by imitating the roar or cry of the beast that served for zoötype, as well as to the eye by its own especial colour. And here it may be possible to trace what might be termed the "golden prayer" of the Zunis. In the ceremonies of their ancient mysteries an ear of corn is typical of renewal in a future life. In praying for plenty of food two ears of corn are laid on the body of a dead deer close to the heart. "Prayer meal" made from maize is held in the hand and scattered on the fetish image of the deer, whilst the prayer is addressed to the deer divinity or prey-god, as the power beyond the fetish. The corn-pollen is offered so that the spirit may clothe itself in yellow or in the wealth of harvest gold. If this prayer in yellow (equivalent to a prayer-book bound in gold, or at least gilt-edged) were addressed to the corn god by the Zuni when he prays for his daily bread and offers the flower of the yellow maize, the colour of the offering would identify it with the colour of the fetish, and therefore with the yellow lion as a zoötype of the vivifying sun that ripened the corn to clothe the earth with vegetable gold. Like the Zuni Indians, the Tibetans still pray in accordance with a scheme of colours. A prayer was lately found upon a "praying wheel" addressed "To the yellow god, the black god, the white god, and the green god. Please kindly take us all up with you, and do not leave us unprotected, but destroy our enemies." Some such colour scheme is apparent in Egypt when Horus is the white god, Osiris is the god in black, Shu the god in red, Amen the god in blue, Num the god in green.

In the Egyptian series of colours yellow likewise represented corn, which gave the name to the "yellow Neith." The nature gods were appealed to and invoked in want or sickness as a primitive kind of doctors who were looked to as superhuman and whose powers were medicines. The power of the deer god was the deer medicine, and each medicine represented the special power that was besought in hunting each particular beast. These are the kind of "spirits" that were prayed to in colours by primitive races of men, and these colours, like the glorified globes in the druggist's window, represented the powers of the different spirits as medicines. The native doctors of New Guinea have a scale of colours with which they paint their patient with the complexions of corresponding spirits. Different colours denoted different spirits of healing forces in nature that were representative of the seven elements and seven localities of the spirits. When the Omaha medicine-men are acting as healers of the sick they will use the movements and cry with the voices of their totemic animals. Not because the animals were a source of healing power in themselves, but because the totems had a spiritual relationship and were the representatives of powers beyond the human. Thus, in one case the spirits prayed to are identified by their colours, and in the other by their totemic zoötypes. If we interpret this according to Egyptian symbolism, when the sick person was suffering from asthma he would plead his suit in blue to the god of air or breathing-force whilst panting like a sick lion, and the medicine would be equivalent to a blue pill. In case of fever he would pray in green to the god in green, that is, to the water spirit, and would be going to the green god for a drink, as the thirsty soul in our day might seek the sign of the Green Dragon or the Green Man. And if he prayed in red it would be to the red Atum, or Horus, the child that was born red in the blood of Isis, as the saviour who came apparelled in that colour. The main object at present, however, is to distinguish animism from spiritualism by tracing the difference betwixt the elemental souls and the ancestral spirits, although animism is a most unsatisfactory title. The "anima" signifies one of the seven elemental souls, but does not comprehend the group. Here is one of several clues. The animistic nature powers were typified; the ancestral spirits are personalized. The elemental powers are commonly a group of seven, but spiritualism has no experience nor knowledge of seven human spirits that visit earth together, or traverse the planetary chain of seven worlds; nor is there any record of the dream personages coming and going in a group of seven, or in seven colours, not even as a septenary of nightmares born of seven generations of neurotic sufferers from sevenfold insomnia. In animism, mediums could not interview the serpent, bull, or turtle of eternity in spirit form. On the contrary, the animistic powers have had to be objectified and made apparent by means of these totemic types. Thus, in animism there are no spirits proper—that is, no spirits which appear as the doubles of the dead or phantasms of the living. It may be allowed that the spirits of the elements—of air, water, earth, fire, plant or tree—were in a sense ancestral, though not ancestral spirits. But the one were pre-human, the others are originally human. These animistic powers in the Arunta Alcheringa are called the ancestors who reproduce themselves by incorporation in the life on earth in the course of becoming man or animal. It was inevitable that there should be some confusion here and there betwixt the elemental souls and the ancestral spirits when the power to differentiate the one from the other by means of the type was lost or lapsing. It was Kalabar "fash," the natives told Hutchinson, that the souls of men passed into monkeys. The Zulus also say there are Amatonga or ancestral spirits who are snakes, and who come back to visit the living in the guise of reptiles. Such "fash," however, is just the confusion that follows the lapse of the most primitive wisdom. Both the monkey and the snake had been totemic types not only of the human brotherhoods, but also of the elemental powers or souls. Thus there was an elemental soul of the snake-totem and the ancestral spirits of that same ilk; and the snake remained as representative of both, to the confounding of the animistic soul with the ancestral spirit at a later stage. But those who kept fast hold of the true doctrine always and everywhere insisted that their ancestral spirits did not return to earth in the guise of monkeys, snakes, crocodiles, lions, hawks, or any other of the totemic zoötypes. They did not mistake the "souls" of one category for "spirits" in the other, because they knew the difference. The same distinction that was made by the Egyptians betwixt the superhuman powers and the Manes, or the gods and the glorified, is more or less identifiable all the world over.

Thus, the origin of spirits and of religion is twofold. At first the elemental powers are propitiated; next the ancestors are worshipped. The earliest form of a religious cult was founded in evocation and propitiation of the great Earth-mother, the giver of life and birth, of food and water, as the primary power in mythology, who was represented in Egypt by her zoötypes the water-cow of Apt; the fruit-tree of Hathor, the sow of Rerit, the serpent of Rannut, who was first besought in worship as "the only one," the great goddess, the Good Lady, the All-Mother who preceded the All-Father. The gods and goddesses of the oldest races were developed from these superhuman nature powers which originated with and from the earth as the Universal Great Mother, and not from the ancestral human spirits. Also the one is universally differentiated from the other. The two classes of gods and spirits, elemental and ancestral, are still propitiated and invoked by the natives of West Africa. As Miss Kingsley tells us, one class is called *the Well-disposed Ones*. These are the ancestral spirits, which are differentiated from the other class, that is referred to as *"them,"* the generic name for non-human spirits. (*West African Studies*, p. 132.)

The religion of the Yao is now pre-eminently a worship of the ancestral spirits, but "beyond and above the spirits of their fathers and chiefs localized on the hills, the Yao speak of others that they consider superior; only *their home is more associated with the country which the Yao left in the beginning*." (Duff Macdonald, vol. i., p. 71.) This was that land of the gods who were the primordial elemental powers, the old home or primeval paradise of many races.

The Yao also distinguished clearly betwixt the elemental power and its zoötype. "It is usual," says Mr. Macdonald, "to distinguish between the spirit and the form it takes. A spirit often appears as a serpent. When a man kills a serpent thus belonging to a spirit he goes and makes an apology to the offended god, saying, 'Please, please, I did not know that it was your serpent!' " (*Africana*, vol. i., pp. 62, 63.) The Thlinkeets emphatically assert that the ancestor of the wolf clan does not reappear to them in the wolf form. The Maori likewise are among those who distinguish betwixt the Atuas that represent the ancient nature powers and the spirits which reappear as spectres in the human form. They recognize the difference between the totemic type and the ancestral human spirit. It is our modern metaphysical explanation and the vague theories of universal animism that confuse the gods and ghosts together, elemental spirits with human, and the zoötypes with the pre-totemic ancestors. The Ainu people recognize two classes of gods and spirits. The first are known as the "distant gods," those who are remote from human beings. The others are the "near at hand," corresponding to the spirit ancestors of other races. (Batchelor, Rev. Y., *The Ainu of Japan*, p. 87.) The Shintoism of the Japanese shows the same dual origin of a cult that is primitive and universal, which was based first on a propitiation of the nature powers, and secondly on the worship of ancestral spirits. The number and the nature of these powers as the Great Mother and the seven or the eight Kami are the same in Japan as in the land of Kam. The Veddahs of Ceylon, who worship "the shades of their ancestors and their children," also hold that "the air is peopled with spirits; that every rock, every tree, every forest, and every hill, in short every feature of nature, has its *genius loci*." Here again we have the two classes of ancestral spirits, human in origin, and the animistic spirits derivable from the elements. The "gods" of the Samoans were those elemental powers that were represented by the zoötypes. "These gods," says Turner, "are supposed to appear in some visible incarnation, and the particular thing (or living type) in which the god appeared was to the Samoan an object of veneration. It was, in fact, his 'idol' (or his totem). One, for instance, saw his god in the eel, another in the shark, another in the lizard," and so on through all the range of external nature. (Turner, *Samoa*, p. 17, ed. 1884.)

With the Eskimo the nature spirits are quite distinct from the ghosts of human beings. Some of the former are allowed to the common people as objects of religious regard, but it is the spirits of human beings, the dead ancestors or relatives of the living, who inspire or otherwise manifest through the abnormal medium called the Angekok. Everywhere it is the reappearing spirits of the dead, and they alone, who can demonstrate a continuity of existence for the living. The original powers or gods of the elements that were represented by the zoötypes are very definitely discriminated by the Tongans from the spirits of human beings. They do not mix up or confuse their gods with their ghosts. Their primal gods were not ghosts. These do not come as apparitions in the human likeness, or as shadows of the dead. When they appear to men, it is said to be in their primitive guise of lizards, porpoises, water-snakes, and other elemental totemic types; whereas the ghosts of nobles and chiefs, who alone are supposed to have the power of coming back, or of being on view, are not permitted to appear in the shape of lizards, porpoises, and water-snakes, the representatives of the original gods. So the Banks Islanders recognize and distinguish two classes of supernatural powers, in the spirits of the dead and those that never have been human. These are their gods and ghosts, the gods and the glorified. The nature powers are called Tamate, the ghosts are designated Vui. As with the Tongans, the Papuan ghosts of the nobles are nearest in status to the great or primary powers, but are not to be confounded with them; being of different origin in this world, they do not blend together in the next. This shows that in both cases the gnosis is not quite extinct. (Codrington, *Journal Anthrop. Institute*, February, 1881.) Kramer tells us that the Niassans worship both gods and ancestors, and that the two kinds of super-human beings are never confounded by them. The two are kept perfectly distinct, and each has a different terminology. (Cited by Max Müller in *Anthropological Religion*, Lecture X.) This distinction made betwixt the elemental gods and the ghosts of ancestors is shown by the Institutes of Menu. "Let an offering to the gods be made at the beginning and end of the Sraddha. It must not begin and end with an offering to ancestors, for he who begins and ends it with an oblation to the Pitris quickly perishes with his progeny." (Works of Sir W. Jones, vol. iii., pp. 146-7.) Amongst all the "spirits," the apparition or ghost is solely human. There is no pretence of seeing the ghosts of animals. The great spirit or great bear of the Ainus remains a bear. The great spirit as the turtle of the Zunis remains a turtle. The great spirit of the Samoans remains an owl. Their representatives are the bear, the turtle, the owl, and not the apparition of a bear, a turtle, or an owl. The zoötypes have no spiritual manifestations or phantasms. Only the souls of human beings reappear as ghosts. Thus we demonstrate that the worship of human ancestors alone was not the primary phase of religious worship.

We must needs be careful not to get the "divinity" confounded with the "divine personage." But we may say there was no killing of the god, the tree spirit, the corn spirit, or the spirit of vegetation, in the Frazerian sense, and of putting the deity to death to save him from old age, disease, and decay, and magically bringing him to life again in a more youthful form. This is another result of mixing up the two classes together by the modern non-spiritualist. The aborigines knew better. The death of the sacred bird, with the Samoans, was "not the death of the god. He was supposed to be yet alive, and incarnate in all the owls in existence." (Turner, *Samoa*, p. 21.) So was it with the turtle of the Zunis, the panes-bird of the Acagchemen Indians, and the bull of Osiris, called "the Bull of Eternity." In killing the goose of Seb or the calf of Horus, the bull of Osiris or the meriah of the Khonds, the partakers of the sacrament had no more thought of killing the god or nature power as a mode of rejuvenation than they had of killing the earth which produced the food.

Also the spiritual theory will most satisfactorily explain the motive for killing and eating the divine personage, whether as the mother or the monarch, whilst the victim was comparatively young, in good health, and wholly exempt from any bodily infirmity. The slaying and eating were performed as a religious rite and a mode of spiritual communion. This implies a sacrificial offering to the gods or spirits, which had to be as pure and perfect as possible. In the rubrical directions of the Hebrew ritual it is expressly commanded that the sacrificial offering shall be presented "without blemish" otherwise it is unacceptable to the Lord. The death or dying down of the food-producing power as Osiris was a fact of annual occurrence in external nature. This death of the self-devoted victim was solemnized and mourned over in the mysteries, where the chief object of celebration was the resurrection of Osiris, as the sun from the nether world, or the returning waters of the inundation; or as Horus in the lentiles, or Unbu in the branch of gold, or the human soul resurgent from the mummy in the mysteries of Amenta. This was the divinity who has to be distinguished from the typical divine personage. We learn from the eschatology, by which the mythology was supplemented and fulfilled, that there were seven food-givers altogether in a female form. These are grouped as the seven Hathors, or milch-mothers, in the mythology called "the providers of plenty" for the glorified elect, in the green pastures Aarru, or the Elysian Fields. The earliest representation being totemic and pre-human, the mythical mother was portrayed by means of the zoötype.

The wet-nurse was imaged as a cow or a sow. The mother of aliment was figured in the tree. The earth itself was imaged as the goose, or other zoötype, which laid the egg for food. The Red Men say "the bear, the buffalo, and the beaver are manitus (spirits) which furnish food." (Schoolcraft, *Indian Tribes,* vol. v., 420.) They were totems of the elemental powers that were propitiated as the givers of food. Now, the first giver of food and drink was the Mother-earth, who was represented by the zoötypes which furnished food and drink. The elemental spirits as producers of food may be seen in the Aztec "popul vuh" as "they that gave life," a group of primordial powers, with such names as shooter of the coyote, opossum, and other animals with the blow-pipe—a naïve way of describing the superhuman providers of food in the character of the hunter. The Zuni "prey-gods" are also propitiated as superhuman powers in animal forms, the gods of prey that are the givers of food. (Amer. Bureau of Ethnology, 1880-81.) In the Arunta stage of mythical representation there are no goddesses or gods. The powers of the elements were not yet divinized; they are only known, like the human groups, by their totemic types. Whereas in the wisdom of ancient Egypt we can identify the elemental powers and trace them by nature and by name into the phase of divinities, whether as goddesses or gods.

Thus we are enabled to reach back to the superhuman powers in totemism that preceded the gods and goddesses in mythology. Instead of gods and goddesses, the Arunta tribe have their mythical ancestors, who were kangaroos, emus, beetles, bandicoots, dingoes, and snakes, as totemic representatives of elemental forces, especially those of food and drink, in the primordial Alcheringa, who were incorporated or made flesh on earth in both men and animals. In the Egyptian eschatology these primordial powers finally became the Lords of Eternity. But from the first they were the ever-living ones under pre-anthropomorphic totemic types. Osiris, for example, remains in the Ritual as "the Bull of Eternity." Atum was the Lion of Eternity. And when both had been personified in the human likeness the zoötype still survived. Thus the beast, the bird, the fish, which represented the powers of the elements, which were of themselves ever-living, furnished natural types of the eternal. Again, the human descent from the elemental powers is indicated by the tradition of the Manx which asserts that the first inhabitants of their island were fairies, and that the little folk, called the good people, still exist among them and are to be seen dancing on moonlight nights, the same as in the Emerald Isle:—

> "Wee folk, good folk,
> Trooping altogether;
> Green jacket, red cap,
> And white owl's feather."

In relation to spiritism, the present demonstration has hitherto been limited to the animistic "spirits" or elemental powers that were pre-human, superhuman, and entirely non-human. We now come to the spirits of human origin which manifest as phantoms of the living and as doubles of the dead.

The origin of the "gods" was in the powers of the elements, with a magical evocation and propitiation of these powers ever manifesting in external nature, especially as givers of food and drink, with the ritual based on blood. But the most essential part of religion assuredly originated in the worship of the ancestral spirits. Only there must be the spirits of human origin discriminated from the animistic spirits or elemental powers as the *raison-d'être* of the worship. The feeling of fear and dread of the destroying powers was followed at a later stage of development by the natural affection for the mothers, the fathers, and children, who were universally propitiated as the ancestral spirits. Spiritualism proper begins with the worship of ancestral spirits, the spirits of the departed, who demonstrate the continuity of existence hereafter by reappearing to the living in phenomenal apparition, the same to the races called civilized as to those who are supposed to "believe in ghosts" because they are savages. Herbert Spencer proclaims that "the first traceable conception of a supernatural being is the *conception* of a ghost" (*Data*, p. 281). Here in passing we may note that the word "supernatural," continually employed by the agnostics, belongs, like many others, to an obsolete terminology which has no meaning for the evolutionist. There was no supernatural when there could have been no definition of the natural. In the present work the word *superhuman* is made use of as being more exact. The elemental powers were superhuman, yet they were entirely natural.

A brief but comprehensive account of Inner African spiritualism is given by the author of *Three Years in Savage Africa,* who says: "The religion of the Wanyamwezi is founded mainly on the worship of spirits called the 'Musimo.' Their ceremonies have but one object, the conciliation or propitiation of these spirits. They have no idea of one supreme power or God—personal or impersonal—governing the world, and directing its destinies or those of individuals. They believe in the earthly visitation of spirits, especially to announce some great event, and more generally some big disaster. Thus they tell how the Chief Mirambo one day met a number of Musimo carrying torches, who invited him to follow them into the forest, which he did. Once there, they attempted to dissuade him from proceeding with a war which he was then contemplating, and in which he subsequently lost his life. The dead in their turn become spirits, under the all-embracing name of Musimo. The Wanyamwezi hold these Musimo in great dread and veneration, as well as the house, hut, or place where their body had died. Every chief has near his hut a Musimo hut, or house of the dead, in which they are supposed to dwell, and where sacrifices and offerings must be made. They are constantly consulting oracles, omens, and signs, and attach great importance to them." When desirous of consulting the spirits, "the party betakes itself to the Musimo house, in front of which the Mfumu (medium) stands with the others arranged in a circle behind him. The Mfumu then holds a kind of religious service: he begins by addressing the spirits of their forefathers, imploring them not to visit their anger upon their descendants. This prayer he offers up kneeling, bowing and bending to the ground from time to time. Then he rises and commences a hymn of praise to the ancestors, and all join in the chorus. Then, seizing his little gourd, he executes a *pas seul,* after which he bursts into song again, but this time singing as one inspired. Suddenly he stops and recovers himself. All this time, except when chanting, the spectators observe a most profound stillness. After a brief interval of silence the Mfumu proceeds to publish the message which he has just received from the Musimo. This he does by intoning in a most mournful and dreary manner. The congregation then retire, and wind up the proceedings with a noisy dance in the village." (Lionel Décle, *Three Years in Savage Africa,* pp. 343-345.) According to Giel, the pigmies of the Ituri Forest, at the lowest point in the ascent of man, propitiate and invoke the spirits of their ancestors; they also build little huts for them to rest in and make offerings of food to their spirit visitants (Giel, W. E., *A Yankee in Pigmy Land*). The Lendu to the west of Lake Albert, who are worshippers of the ancestral spirits, are accustomed to carry rough wooden dolls supposed to represent the departed, and place them in the deserted huts in which their dead lie buried (Johnston).

African spiritualism, which might be voluminously illustrated, culminated in the Egyptian mysteries. The mystery teachers were so far advanced as phenomenal spiritualists, and say so little about it in any direct manner, that it has taken one who owns to having had a profound experience of the phenomena many years to come up with them in studying the eschatology of the Ritual. If spiritualism proper is based on phenomenal and veritable facts in nature, as it is now claimed to be, then the past history of the human race has to be rewritten, for it has hitherto been written with this the most important of all mental factors omitted, decried, derided, or falsely explained away. Current anthropology knows nothing of man with a soul that offers evidence for a continuity of its own existence. The Egyptians had no more doubt about it than the Norsemen who used to bring legal actions against the spirits of the dead that came back to haunt and torture the living, and were accused on evidence and adjudged to be guilty. There is a like case in a papyrus translated by M. Maspero (*Records of the Past,* vol. xii., 123). In this an Egyptian widower cites the spirit of his deceased wife to a law court, and forbids her to torment or persecute him with her unwelcome attentions. He asks what offence did he ever commit in her lifetime that should warrant her in causing him to suffer now. He speaks of the evil condition he is in, and of the affidavit he has made. This writing is directed to the gods of Amenta, where it is to be read in judgment against her. M. Maspero suggests that the writ would probably be read aloud at the tomb, and then tied to the statue of his wife, who would receive the summons in the same way that she was accustomed to receive the offerings of prayer and food by proxy at certain times of the year. The Egyptians were profoundly well acquainted with those abnormal phenomena which are just re-emerging within the ken of modern science, and with the hypnotic, magnetic, narcotic, and anæsthetic means of inducing the conditions of trance. Their rekhi or wise men, the pure spirits in both worlds, are primarily those who could enter the life of trance or transform into the state of spirits, as is shown by the determinative of the name, the phœnix of spiritual transformation.

Ancestor worship is made apparent in the Book of the Dead by the speaker in the nether world, who asks that he may behold the forms of his father and his mother in his resurrection from Amenta (ch. 52). And when he attains the domain of Kan-Kanit on Mount Hetep, where the joy is expressed by dancing, he prays that he may see his father and intently view his mother (Rit., ch. 110). It is said of one of the magical formulæ, "If thou readest the second page it will happen that if thou art in the Amenta thou wilt have power to resume the form which thou hadst upon the earth" (*Records of the Past,* vol. iv., 131-134). In one of the Egyptian tales the writer describes the dead in the tombs conversing about their earth life, and as having the power of leaving the sepulchre and mixing once more with the living on this earth. The Egyptian Book of the Dead is based upon a resurrection of the soul in Amenta and its possible return to the earth at times, for some particular purpose, as the double or ghost. The deceased when in Amenta prays that he may emerge from the world of the dead to revisit the earth (Rit., ch. 71). He asks that he may come forth with breath for his nostrils and with eyes which can see, and that he may shine upon his own ka-image from without, not that he may become a soul within an idol of wood or stone. The persistence of the human soul in death and its transformation into a living and enduring spirit is a fundamental postulate of the Egyptian Ritual and of the religious mysteries. The burial of the mummy in the earth is coincident with the resurrection of the soul in Amenta, which is followed by its purifications and refinings into a spirit that may be finally made perfect. In the opening chapter the departing soul of the deceased pleads that he may be conscious in death, to see the lords of the nether world and to inhale the "incense of the sacrificial offerings made to the divine host—sitting with them." He prays: "Let the priestly ministrant make invocations over my coffin. Let me hear the prayers of propitiation." Not as the dead body, but as a living spirit (ch. 1). He also pleads that when the Tuat is opened he may "come forth to do his pleasure upon earth amid the living" (ch. 2). The Egyptians know nothing of death except in the evil that eats out the spiritual life. The dead are those that do not live the spiritual life, no matter where. These are called the twice dead in the spirit world. It will suffice to show how profound the spiritualism must have been when the prayers and invocations are made, the oblations and the sacrifices are offered, not to the person of the deceased (who is represented by the dead mummy), but to the ka-image of his eternal soul, which was set up in the funeral chamber as the likeness of that other spiritual self to whose consciousness they made their religiously affectionate appeal. They make no mistake as to the locality of consciousness. Their funeral feast was a festival of rejoicing, not of mourning. When Unas makes his passage it is said, "Hail, Unas! Behold, thou hast not departed dead, but as one living thou hast gone to take thy seat upon the throne of Osiris" (Budge, *Gods of Egypt,* vol. I, 61). The sacred rites were duly paid to the departed not merely "in memory of the dead," but for the delectation of the re-embodied ka that lived on in death. The dead were designated the ever-living. The coffin was called the chest of the living. No eye might look on the prepared mummy in its last resting place but the eye of its spiritual owner, who came back to see that it was properly preserved in sepulchral sanctity, a small aperture being left in the wall of the Serdab through which the returning spirit alone might pass, to see the mummy, when it returned on a visit to the earth. We learn from the vignettes to the Ritual that the soul might revisit the earth when it had attained the status of the Ba, which is imaged as the hawk with a human head. In this shape it descends and ascends the ladder or staircase that was erected as the way up from the Kâsu or burial place to the boat of souls.

In the first stage of continuity hereafter the soul persists visibly as the shade. This form of the Manes is commonly associated with the mummy in the tomb where it received the mortuary meals that were offered to the dead. It was held by some that the shade remained as warder of the mummy, or corpse, and never left the earth. When the deceased has passed the forty-two tribunals of the Judgment Hall he is told that he can now go out of the Amenta and come in at will as an enfranchized spirit. It is said to the Osiris, "Enter thou in and come forth at thy pleasure like the Glorified Ones; and *be thou invoked each day upon the Mount of Glory*" (Rit., ch. 126, 6). He has now become one of the glorified, the spirits who are appealed to as protectors—that is, the ancestral spirits, the host of whom he joins to become the object of invocation and propitiation or of worship on the Mount of Glory. The clairvoyants in the Kamite temples were designated seers of the gods and the spirits. In speaking of his forced exclusion from office in the Temple of Amen, Tahtmes the Third says: "So long as I was a child and a boy I remained in the Temple, but not even as a seer of the god did I hold office" (*Egypt under the Pharaohs,* Brugsch, Eng. trans., vol. I, p. 178). In the "Second Tale of Khamuas" there is a contest between the Ethiopian and Egyptian magicians. Amongst other tests of superiority, the Ethiopians bring writing as a challenge to the Court of Pharaoh. This has to be read without opening the letter or breaking the seal. Then said Si-Osiris to his father, "I shall be able to read the letter that was brought to Egypt without opening it, and to find what is written on it without breaking its seal." The father asks what is the sign that he can do this. Si-Osiris answers, "Go to the cellars of thy house: every book that thou takest out of the case I will tell thee what book it is and read it without seeing it." This he does, and then he shows the superiority of Egyptian magic over the sorceries of the Ethiopians by reading the contents of the letter without opening it or breaking the seal. (Griffith, *Stories of the High Priests of Memphis,* pp. 51-60.)

The mode in which the clairvoyant faculty was made use of in the mysteries for seeing into the world beyond death is also illustrated by the priest who is portrayed as the dreamer with the dead. He is called the Sem-priest, and is represented as being in the tomb and sleeping the sleep in which he was visited by the glorified. The recumbent Sem awakes when the other officiating ministrants arrive at the sepulchre. His first words are, "I see the Father in his form entire." That is Osiris in his character of Neb-er-ter. In his demise Osiris was represented as being cut in pieces, by his enemy Sut, as a mode of depicting death to the sight of the initiates. That which applied to Osiris also applied to the dead in Osiris. They were figuratively cut in pieces as the tangible equivalent for abstract death. "I see the Father in his form entire" was the formula of the Sem-priest as sleeper and seer in the tomb and as witness and testifier that the dead in Osiris were living still. "How wonderful! He no longer existed." And now, "What happiness! He exists, and there is no member missing to the Manes" (*i.e.*, the human soul in Amenta). (Prof. E. Lefébure, *Proc. Soc. Bib. Arch.*, vol. xv., pt. 3, p. 138.)

All ancestor worshippers have been spiritualists in the modern sense who had the evidence by practical demonstration that the so-called dead are still living in a rarer, not less real form. The ancestral spirits they invoke and propitiate were once human, not the elemental or animistic forces of external nature, which under the name of spirits have been confused with them. Their belief in a personal continuity has ever been firmly based on phenomenal facts, not merely floated on ideas. The evidence that deceased persons make their reappearance on the earth in human guise is universal; also that the doubles of the dead supplied both ground and origin for a worship of ancestral spirits that were human once in this life and still retained the human likeness in the next, and manifested in the human form. The Karens say the Lâ (or ghost) sometimes appears after death, and cannot then be distinguished from the deceased person. In the opinion of the Eskimo the soul (or spirit) exhibits the same shape as the body it belonged to (Rink), but is of a more subtle and ethereal nature, as is the Egyptian Sahu or spiritual body. The Tonga Islanders held that the human soul was the finer, more aëriform, part of the body—the essence that can pass out as does the fragrance from a flower. The islanders of the Antilles found that the ghosts vanished when they tried to clutch them. The Greenland seers described the soul as pallid, soft, and intangible when they attempted to seize it. "Alas! then," says Achilles, as he tries to embrace the spirit of Patroclus, "there is indeed in the abodes of the shades a spirit and an eidōlon, but it is unsubstantial." Mr. Cushing tells us that, whatsoever opinions the ancestors of the Zunis may have held regarding the so-called "transmigration of souls," their belief to-day relative to the future life is spiritualistic. When a corpse had been burnt by the Hos they still called upon the spirit to come back to the world of the living. It is held by them that the spirit lives on, although the dead body is reduced to ashes. The author of *Africana* testifies that the Central African tribes among whom he lived were unanimous in saying there is something beyond the body which they call spirit or pure spirit, and that "every human being at death is forsaken by the spirit." Hence they do not worship at the grave. "All the prayers and offerings of the living are presented to the spirits of the dead" (vol. I, p. 59). It is common for the Yao to leave an offering beside the head at the top of their beds intended for the spirits who it is hoped will come and whisper to the sleeper in his dreams. Their spirits appear to them in sleep and also in waking visions, which are carefully discriminated from dreams of the night by them as by all intelligent aborigines, and not confused the one with the other, as is generally done by the European agnostic. (Duff Macdonald, *Africana,* vol. I, pp. 60-61.) The Banks Islanders pray to their dead men, and not to the elemental powers or animistic spirits. The Vateans call upon the spirits of their ancestors, whom they invoke over the kava bowl—that is, the divine drink which is taken by the seers for the purpose of entering into rapport with the spirits. When the Zulu King Cetewayo was in London he said to a friend of the present writer, "We believe in ghosts or spirits of the dead because we see them." But when asked whether the Zulus believed in God, he said they had not seen him. For them the ghost demonstrates its own existence; the god is but an inference, if necessary as a final explanation of phenomena. The ghost can be objectively manifested; the deity must be ideally evolved. The Amazulu say the same thing as Cetewayo: "We worship those whom we have seen with our eyes, who lived and died amongst us. All we know is that the young and the aged die and the shade departs." These shades were propitiated. That is the universal testimony of all races, savage or civilized. They believe in ghosts because they see them. The ghost is the supreme verity in universal spiritualism. As Huxley says, "there are savages without God in any proper sense of the word, but there are none without ghosts" (*Lay Sermons and Addresses,* p. 163). The colossal conceit of obtuse modern ignorance notwithstanding, the ghost and the faculty for seeing the ghost are realities in the domain of natural fact. The seers may be comparatively rare, although the clairvoyant and seer of spirits (as a product of nature) is by no means so scarce as either a great painter or great poet. These abnormal faculties are human, and they can be increased by cultivation. Their existence is for ever being verified like other facts in nature, and the truth is ultimately known by the experience which is for ever being repeated. It is a funeral custom of the Amandebele, one of the Bantu tribes, to introduce the spirit of a deceased person to his father, his grandfather, and other relatives, of whose conscious existence and personal presence no doubt is entertained. These are matters of life and death with the primitive races. The spirits come to announce the death of individuals. They see the ghost, they hear its message, and they die to the day or hour foretold. "I could give many instances which have come within my own knowledge among the Fijians," says Mr. Fison (*Kamilaroi and Kernai,* p. 253). Mr. Spencer tells us that "Negroes who when suffering go to the woods and cry for help to the spirits of dead relatives show by these acts the grovelling nature of the race" (*Data of Sociology,* ch. 20, par. 151). Whether the spirits are thought to be a reality or not, this appears one of the most natural and touching of human acts, aspiring rather than grovelling, especially as the relative addressed is so commonly the mother, the African mama. But is it grovelling to cling to the loved and lost?—to turn for comfort to the dear ones gone, and seek a little solace if only in the memory that leaned and rested on them in the solitude of their suffering? Here the "great teacher of our age" is far behind the nigger. He did not know that the "spirits of dead relatives" are and always have been a demonstrable reality, and those who do not *know* have no authority for giving judgment on the subject. They who have no dead lost friends to feed, to invoke, or to love may look on such ceremonies as savage or insensate, but to those who have, and who still offer them the food of affection, such actions are but the primitive exhibition of our modern spiritualism in its simple childhood, and they have for us something of the tender and touching charm of infancy, even when the first has now become a sort of second childhood through length of time and lapse of knowledge and loss of memory.

The Peruvians declared that the reason why they buried property with their departed friends was because they had seen those who had long been dead walking adorned with the clothes and jewels which their friends had buried with them. West African Negroes have been so sure of their conscious continuity hereafter that when they were slaves in far-off lands they have killed themselves on purpose to revisit and re-live in their old homes. We have it on the authority of Livingstone that the Manyema tribe of Africans exulted in the assurance that after death the suffering ones would be able to come back when they were set free to return and haunt and torture those who had sold them into slavery during their life on earth. Mariner mentions the case of a young Tongan chief who was pursued by the spirit of a dead woman. She, having fallen in love with him, besought him to die and go to her; and he died accordingly. The Karens hold that the dead are only divided from the living by a thin white veil which their seers can penetrate. The Kaffirs when fighting used to leave open spaces in their line of battle for their dead heroes to step into and stop the gap in fighting for them shoulder to shoulder and side by side.

First of all, there is a class of customs intended to prevent the dead from returning in spirit. The living will do anything in their power by way of propitiation, bribery, and flattery for the dead not to come back. All they needed in this life was supplied to them for the next: food, drink, clothes, horses, weapons, slaves, and wives in abundance. For if the dead were in need of anything it was feared that they might pursue and haunt the living. The Zulu Kaffirs say that diseases are caused by the spirits of the dead to compel the living to supply them with offerings of meat and drink. It was a custom of the Fijians to pour out water after the corpse to hinder the ghost from coming back, water being the element opposed to breath, to spirit or spirits—"a running stream they daurna cross!" The Siamese break an opening through the wall of a house, pass the coffin through, and carry the corpse round the house three times to prevent the spirit from finding its way back. The Hottentots make a hole in the wall of their hut and carry the dead body through it, closely building it up immediately afterwards. We may smile, but until lately we had the relic of a belief as simple. We used to run a stake through the bodies of our suicides, buried at the cross-roads, to pin them to the cross and not allow them to walk or wander as ghosts. This custom of barring the passage back was practised by black men, red men, yellow men, and white men—therefore it was universal. An Australian aborigine will cut the right thumb off the hand of his dead enemy, so that the returning ghost shall not be able to handle a spear or club if he should come back. Many other races purposely maimed their dead. When

Clytemnestra put her husband to death she took the precaution of having him "arm-pitted"—that is, of having his hands cut off and bound fast under his arms, which was a Greek mode of doing an irretrievable injury to the ghost of the dead.

Nor was the feeling of fear limited to those whom they had any reason to dread. On the death of a nursing child the Iroquois take two pieces of cloth, steep them in the milk of its mother, and place them in the hands of the dead little one so that it may not return in spirit from need of food to haunt and trouble the bereaved parent. They also think that the sleeping infant holds intercourse with the spirit world, and it is a custom for the mother to rub the face of the living child with a pinch of ashes at night to protect it from nocturnal spirits. In Lapland the mothers, when committing infanticide, cut out the tongues of the little ones before casting them away in the forest, lest the poor innocents should be heard crying and calling on them in the night. The Chinook Indians declare that the dead wake at night and get up in search of food. The Algonkins bring food to the grave for the nourishment of the shade which remains with the body after death. In doing this they had an object, which was the ghost in reality and not a hallucination to be resolved into nothingness by any philosophy of dreams. The Iroquois maintained that unless these rites of burial were performed the spirits would return to trouble their relatives and friends. In one of the cuneiform texts it is taught that the Manes which are neglected by their relatives on earth succumb to hunger and thirst. As it is said, "He whose body is left forgotten in the fields, his soul has no rest on earth. He whose soul no one cares for, the dregs of the cup, the remains of the repast, that which is thrown among the refuse of the street, that is all he has to nourish him." (Maspero, *Dawn of Civilization*, Eng. tr., p. 509.) The necessity that was felt for providing the dead with food will account for the Buddhist doctrine of non-immortality for the man who has no children. In this way; the manes needs provisioning. The proper person to supply them is a son, and he who dies without a son to perform the sacrifice may be left like the poor souls in the Assyrian story who succumb to hunger and thirst and thus die out altogether as neglected starvelings. It is said in the Dattaka-Mimansa, *"Heaven awaits not one who is destitute of a son."* The Inoits likewise have a custom of giving a new-born son the name of someone who has lately died, in order "that the departed may have rest in the tomb" (Rink, *Eskimo Tales*). This is a mode of adopting a son for the service of the dead where the deceased may have had no son to make the offerings. Of all the charitable institutions on the earth's surface, the most remarkable, surely, is that of the Chinese Taoists called the *Yu-Lan-Ui,* or *"association for feeding the dead,"* which collects supplies for the sustenance of the needy spirits who have no relations on earth to offer sacrifices to these paupers of the other world. In the Egyptian Book of the Dead the deceased prays that he may take possession in Amenta of the funeral meals that were and continue to be offered to him by his living friends on earth. "Let me have possession of my funeral meals. Let me have possession of all things which are ritualistically offered for me in the nether world. Let me have possession of the table (of offerings) which was made for me on earth, the solicitations which were uttered for me that he (I) may feed upon the bread of Seb." This is the refrain to a kind of litany. (Rit., ch. 68, Renouf.) In the vignettes to the Ritual and other scenes it is noticeable how the female mourners expose their breasts and as it were offer their nipples to the mummy on its way to the deadhouse (Papyrus of Ani). This agrees with the scene in a funeral procession of the Badyas, in which the women lean over their dead companions and squeeze their milk into the mouth of the deceased. King Teta in the Pyramid texts exults in Amenta that he is not left to suffer from hunger and thirst as a Manes. He is not like one of those poor starvelings who are forced to eat the excrements and swallow the filth that is, as it were, the sewage of the life on earth. "Hateful to Teta are hunger and thirst," and from these he does not suffer. He is supplied with pure food and drink in plenty. (Teta, ii, 68-9.) Homer describes the spirits as rushing to lap or breathe the blood poured out in sacrifice. When Odysseus entered Hades and the blood was poured out, the shades that drank of it revived and spoke. The Zuni Indians of to-day reverence certain images or fetishes of the ancestral souls or spirits, which images they treat as their representatives of the dead. These are dipped into the blood that is offered in sacrifice. Whilst performing this rite they will say, "My father, this day thou shalt refresh thyself with blood; with blood shalt thou enlarge thy heart!" The Indians of Virginia used to put children to death for a certain class of spirits to suck the blood, as they said, from the left breast. The Mexicans, who would sacrifice 50,000 human beings in one year, held that human blood was the only efficacious offering, and the purest was the most acceptable. Hence the sacrifice of infants and virgins. Offering the blood of the innocent to save the guilty, or those who feared for themselves, would lead to a doctrine of substitution and vicarious atonement which culminated as Christian in the frightful formula, "Without blood there is no remission of sin!" Not merely human blood this time, but the ichor of a divine being who was made flesh on purpose to pour out the blood for the divine vengeance to lap in the person of a gory ghost of God. "My father! This day shalt thou refresh thyself with blood!" That doctrine is but an awful shadow of the past—the shadow, as it were, of our earth in a far-off past that remains to eclipse the light of heaven in the present and darkens the souls of men to-day through this survival of savage spiritualism direfully perverted. The blood first offered as life for the dead was not given for the remission of sin.

The Peruvians spread the funeral feast, "expecting the soul of the deceased" to come and eat and drink. The Bhils, among the hill tribes of India, offer "provision for the spirit." The North American Indians paid annual visits to the place of the dead, and made a feast to feed the spirits of the departed. The Amazulu prepare the funeral meal and say, "There then is your food, all ye spirits of our tribe; summon one another. I am not going to say, 'So-and-so, there is your food,' for you are jealous. But thou, So-and-so, who art making this man ill, call the spirits: come all of you to eat this food." (Callaway, *Amazulu*, 175.) There were economical reasons against carrying the worship back too far when worship consisted mainly in making offerings. A Yao will excuse himself from giving even to his own grandfather. He gives to his father, and says, "O father! I do not know all your relatives. You know them all: invite them to feast with you." (Duff Macdonald, *Africana,* vol. I, p. 68.) Thus he makes his offering once for all, and saves expenses.

The funeral custom is almost universal for the mortuary meal to be made to feed the *spirits* of the departed, and communion with the ancestral spirits was an object of the totemic Eucharist. The sacrifices offered to the dead, the burial rites and funerary ceremonies, generally imply the existence of a living consciousness to which the piteous appeal was made. The fact becomes visible in the mysteries of Amenta. And one of the greatest acts of sacrifice for the dead is shown in the funeral feast. In their funeral ceremonies the Yucatanese *fasted for the sake* of the dead. Now fasting for the sake of the dead in the most primitive sense was going without food that it might be given to the ghosts or spirit ancestors. The living fasted that the Manes might be fed. And herein lies the true *rationale* of the funeral fast. This was no doubt the motive for the Haker-festival of the Egyptians, when the provisions were laid upon the altar as an offering to Osiris in his coffin. The word Haker denotes both a festival and a fast; it also signifies starving, and starving with the view of giving the food thus saved to the spirits of the dead would be a *really religious sacrifice.* This festival that was celebrated by starving or fasting on behalf of the dead comes to its culmination in the season of Lent as a fast of forty days. In this originally the food of the living would be given as a sacrificial offering to the dead, or the ancestral spirits, or to the god who gave his life in food for men and animals. Here the Egyptian Lent or season of fasting for forty days is in the true position, as it followed and did not precede the death of Osiris. To have any real meaning, the fast which was ordained as a sacrifice of food for the dead was naturally celebrated after and not before the death, to constitute a funeral offering and "to make that spirit live." Going without the food and giving it as a sacrificial offering to the dead assuredly affords the proper explanation of the funeral festival that was celebrated as a solemn fast which finally passed into the Christian Eucharist. The offering of blood to the dead is explained on the ground that the blood is the life; and the more blood shed, the more the life offered, the more precious the sacrifice. Further, the Tahitians thought the gods fed on the spirits of the dead, and therefore frequent sacrifices of human beings were made to supply them with spiritual diet. Blood, the liquid of life, was drink; spirit, the breath of life, was food. This should be compared with the Egyptian legend of Unas, who is fed on the spirits of gods. Also with the account of Horus-Sahu, the wild hunter, of whom it is said that he ate the great gods for his breakfast, the lesser ones for his dinner at noon, and the small ones for his evening meal. The doctrine is identical with that of the Tahitians. Prayers for the dead are continued when the offerings of food have ceased. The fasting survives when the practice has become a meaningless farce. The oblation of blood is still a religious rite. For flagellation that causes the blood to flow is closely akin to the self-gashings, lacerations, amputations, and immolations of primitive mourners who made their personal sacrifice in this way at the grave. Also blood and spirit as an offering to the dead are still represented by the sacramental wine and bread.

Here it may be remarked that when modern ritualists swing their censers heavenwards and fill the church with clouds of incense, the rite, so far as it has any fundamental significance, is an act in the worship of the ancestral spirits. Breath, like blood, is an element of life, and this was represented by the smoke of the fire-offering and by fragrance-breathing incense in the primitive ritual of Inner Africa, that was continued in ancient Egypt and afterwards in Rome. A breath of life is offered in the ascending fumes to give the spirits life, because the breath was once considered to be the soul of life. This was one of the elemental souls. Incense, truly typical and properly compounded in the Christian ritual, ought to include the *seven elements* in one soul of breathing life as an offering to the spirits of the dead, because the elemental souls were seven in number, and because the seven souls contributed to the making of the one eternal spirit. It has been said that savages believe their weapons to have souls in common with themselves, and therefore when they bury their dead they not only bury their weapons, they also break them, to set free the souls of the weapons to accompany the spirits of the warriors. The supposed reason is purely gratuitous and ignorantly European. The interpreters know nothing of the ancient Sign-language as it was enacted in such typical customs as these. The breaking of the weapons or other things when offered to the dead is done as *a sign of sacrifice*. The object of the offering is sacrifice, and no sacrifice could be too great, no property too precious, as an offering to the spirits of the dead. When Mtesa, King of Uganda, died, over £10,000 worth of cloth was buried with him as a sacrificial offering (Lionel Décle, *Three Years in Savage Africa,* p. 446, note).

Herbert Spencer could find no origin for the idea of an after-life save the conclusion which the savage draws from the notion suggested by dreams (Spencer, *Facts and Comments,* p. 210). But whatsoever dreams the savage had, they would become familiar in the course of time. He would learn that dreams had no power to externalize themselves in apparitions, had there been no ghosts or doubles of the dead. He would also learn readily enough, and the lesson would be perpetually repeated, that howsoever great his success when hunting in his dreams of the night, there was no game caught when he woke next morning. Clearly no reliance could be placed on dreams for establishing the ghost, any more than on the result of other dreams. Moreover, the same savage that is assumed to have panned out on dreams for a false belief also reports that he sees the spirits of the dead by abnormal vision and has the means of communicating with them. But all the credulity of all the savages that ever existed cannot compete or be compared with the credulity involved in this belief or assumption that the ghost itself, together with the customs, the ceremonies, the religious rites of evocation and propitiation, the priceless offerings, the countless testimonies to the veritability of abnormal vision, the universal practices for inducing that vision for the purpose of communicating with spiritual intelligences, had no other than a subjective basis, and a false belief that the dream-shadow was the sole reality. Now, can one conceive anything more fatal to the claims made on behalf of evolution as a mode of nature's teaching than this assumption that man has universally been the victim of an illusion derived from a baseless delusion? If primitive men were the victims of a delusion which has been continued for thousands of years in defiance of all experience and observation, what guidance or trust could there be in evolution; or how are we to distinguish between the false product and the true if man dreamed the ghost into being when there was no ghost, if he has been so far the victim of his own Frankenstein as to found the whole body of his religious beliefs and customs on that which never existed? Primitive man was not a hundredth part so likely to be the victim of hallucination or diseased subjectivity as the modern. External Nature is not hallucinative; it is the scene of continuous education in primal or rudimentary and constantly recurring realities. His elemental spirits or forces were real, and not the result of hallucination; why not his ancestral spirits? Primitive or archaic man was not metaphysician enough to play the fool with facts in this way, to say nothing of his manufacturing facts from the phantasies and vanishing stomachic vapours from which dreams are continually made. A dreamer by night who became the condenser of his dreams by day, and then manufactured the ghost that no one ever saw or handled or heard or "smelt out," which ghost had no existence in verifiable reality, and yet had the power to haunt mankind inside of them for ever after! The aborigines knew better, whereas the agnostics do not know.

It is not the people that see visions who are the visionaries. The true visionaries are the subjective-minded metaphysicians, who do not know a dream of the night from a vision of the day, and who can most easily blend the object and subject in one. The Kurnai distinguish betwixt the imagery of dreams and the spirits seen by open vision. They say that whereas anyone may be able to communicate with "ghosts" during sleep, it is only the spirit mediums or wizards who can do so in waking hours. (Howitt.) A priest of the Fijian god Ndengei, describing his passing into the state of trance, said, "My own mind departs from me, and then, when it is truly gone, my god speaks through me" (Williams, *Fiji,* p. 228). Unless a profound fanatic, a modern medium would not call the spirit that controlled him God, but the spirit of a person that had once been human and now was one of the ancestral spirits. There is nothing in all nature but the fact that will adequately account for the universal fear of the ghost. It is the fact alone that gives any rational explanation of the inarticulate faith. When once we admit the fact as operative reality the costly customs, the libations of life, the mysteries of belief, the propitiations of fear and proofs of affection, are all duly motived or amply explicated. Modern science has let loose a deluge of destruction that is fatal to the ignorant beliefs and the false faiths derived from misinterpreted mythology, but it will not efface one single fact nor uproot a single reality in nature. Gods and goddesses may defeature and dislimn, to pass away as fading phantoms of the nature powers, but the human ghost remains, and remains to-day as ever, or more than ever, to the civilized as well as to the savage.

And if, as we maintain, these phenomena are a part of nature's reality, the methods of science once applied to them can but verify the fact and establish its veridical character. There is no possible way of knowing the truth except by interrogation of the phenomena themselves, not merely in the physical domain, but also in the region of intelligence, where you meet with an operator who has to be taken into partnership. The spiritualistic phenomena also confute the assertion of Spinoza to the effect that personality has no foothold in the world outside ourselves, for these intelligences whom we call "spirits" are persons. They appear in the visible, audible, tangible, and palpable forms of personality. Not only as the persons who are called "the dead," but also as phantoms of the living, eidōlons, recognizable feature by feature, of individuals who were not yet dead. The ghost of the living as a visible reality has been seen out of the body in this life, as Goethe saw his other self, which tends to double the evidence for the existence of the ghost of the dead. The English Society for Psychical Research has collected over a thousand cases of the phantasms of the living.

The "science of religion" with the ghost left out is altogether meaningless. The ghost offers the one unique objective proof of spiritual existence, and the doings and sayings of the ghost, whether it be apparent or concealed, still furnish the data of modern as of ancient spiritualism.

Religion proper commences with and must include the idea of or desire for another life. And the warrant for this is the ghost and the faculties of abnormal seership. It has been urged by some writers that religion began with the worship of death and the apotheosis of the corpse. But ancestor worship in all lands was a worship of the ancestral spirits, not a cultus of the corpse. The spirits were the ancestors; the ancestors were spirits. The awe excited by the dead is caused by the active ghost of the dead, not by the motionless corpse. The sacrifices offered to the dead are made to propitiate the living ghost of the dead, not the corpse. It was the fact that the ghost might return and did return and make itself apparent, with the power to manifest displeasure or revenge, that made the *revenant* so fearsome in the early stages of "ghost worship." Dread of the ghost and the desire to placate so uncanny a visitant will account for propitiation of the ghosts.

The truth is that the Christian is the one and only religion in the world that was based upon the corpse instead of the resurrection in spirit. In no other religion is continuity in spirit made dependent on the resurrection of the earthly body. The Christians mistook the risen mummy in Amenta for the corpse that was buried on earth, whereas the Egyptian religion was founded on the rising again of the spirit *from* the corpse as it was imaged in the resurrection of Amsu-Horus transforming from the mummy-Osiris, and by the human soul emerging alive from the body of dead matter. There is no instance recorded in all the experiences of spiritualists ancient or modern of the corpse coming back from the tomb. And this religion founded on the risen corpse is naturally losing all hold of the world. It has failed because immortality or the continuity of personality could not be based upon a reappearing corpse. The so-called worship of ancestors depended entirely on the ancestors being considering living, conscious, acting and recipient spirits, and not as corpses mouldering in the earth. This furnished the sole *raison-d'être* for all the sacrificial offerings, the life, the blood, the food, the choicest and costliest things that could be given to the dead. Those whom we call "the dead" were to them the veritable living in superhuman forms possessing superhuman powers. The Egyptian Amenta is the land of the ever-living. Sacrifices to the dead were not senselessly offered to the senseless corpse, but to the spirit personage that was its late inhabitant, still alive, and supposed to be needing material nourishment from the well-known elements of life. In an Australian funeral ceremony it was customary for the relatives of the deceased to cut themselves until the corpse and burial place were covered with their blood. This was done, they said, to give the dead man strength and enable him to rise in another country. (Brough Smyth, vol. ii, p. 274.) By which they meant a survival of the living spirit, not a resurrection of the buried body. The *corpse* is not, and could not be, the starting point of worship when the sacrifice was eaten quiveringly alive, with the flesh warm and the blood welling forth from every wound. That is when there was no corpse, and neither was there any death. The life was taken and converted into other life, the life of the children, tribe, or clan, and was continued on that line. It was also continued on another line in the spirit life. Again we say there was no death in our modern acceptation of the term. The burial customs, rites, and ceremonies one and all, from the remotest times, were founded in the faith that the departed still lived on in spirit. In the earliest mode of interment known the dead were buried for rebirth. The corpse was bound up in the fœtal likeness of the embryo in utero, and placed in the earth as in the mother's womb, the type being continued in the womb-shaped burial vase of the potters. This, however, did not denote a resurrection of the body, but was symbolical of rebirth in spirit. Not only were the dead elaborately prepared for the spiritual rebirth; many symbols of reproduction and emblems of the resurrection were likewise buried in the tomb as amulets and fetish figures of protecting power. The corpse and spirit are distinguished in the resurrection scenes of the Egyptian Ritual by the black shade laid out upon the ground and the ka-image of continued life. The corpse and spirit are shown together as the twofold entity when the Chinese, amongst others, kindle candles round the coffin, "to give light to the spirit which remains with the corpse" (Doolittle, *Social Life of the Chinese*, p. 126). One Egyptian picture shows the ba-soul nestling to the body on the funeral couch in an attitude of the tenderest solicitude, with its hands placed over the non-beating heart of the mummy (Maspero, pp. 198-199). The Australian Kurnai likewise hold that the ghost of the deceased comes back to take a look at its mortal remains. A native speaking of this to Howitt said, "Sometimes the Murup comes back and looks down into the grave, and it may say, "Hallo, there is my old 'possum rug, there are my old bones." (Howitt, *On some Australian Beliefs*.) The Fijians practise one of the naïvest customs for preventing a deceased woman from manifesting as an apparition. In life her only garment was the *liku* or waist-fringe which she wore as a cover for her nakedness. In death the little apron is purposely left upon her body with the strings untied, so that if the poor thing should rise up with a desire to return, her only bit of clothing will fall from her, and she will be forced, from delicacy of feeling, to crouch down again in shame and confusion, and thus be unable to show herself to the living. (Fison, *Notes on Fijian Burial Customs*.)

Now it was known that no Fijian corpse had ever risen and returned from the tomb. It was also *known* that the consciousness thus appealed to was not that of the corpse. This therefore was an appeal in Sign-language pathetically made to the Manes or spirit of the departed not to come back and trouble the living. When the bodies of the dead (or living) were buried at the base of a building, it was not for any service that could be rendered by the rotting body, but for the spirit to become a protecting power. In Siam when a new city gate was erected the first four or eight people passing were seized and buried beneath it as "guardian angels." Under the gates of Mandalay human victims were buried alive to furnish "spirit watchers." Everywhere the spirit or ghost, not the corpse, is the object of religious regard. And as no corpse was ever known by any race of people to return from the grave, the practices that were intended to prevent the dead from coming back were not aimed at the corpse, to whom they did not apply, but to the alleged living consciousness of the spirit that was represented by the double. Hence the custom of eating or of burying the victim whilst alive.

Brough Smyth describes a Birraark or medium as lying on his stomach beside the dead body whilst speaking to the sprit of the deceased, receiving and reporting the messages given to him by the dead man (*Aborigines of Australia,* vol. I, 107). The Birraark of the Kurnai were declared to be initiated into their mysteries by the spirits or mrarts whom they met in the bush, and it was from the spirits of the dead they obtained their replies when they were consulted by members of the tribe (*ibid.,* p. 254). Spirits of the dead appear to the living and address them in their own language, as when the Eskimo mother comes back to her boy by day to cheer him and says, "Be not afraid; I am thy mother, and love thee still" (Crantz, vol. i, 209). The Mandan Indians arrange the skulls of their dead in a circle. The widows know the skulls of their former husbands, and the mothers know the skulls of their children. The skulls so placed form the spirit-circle in which the women sit for intercourse with the souls of the departed. "There is scarcely an hour in a pleasant day but more or less of these women may be seen sitting or lying by the skull of their child or husband, talking to it in the most pleasant and endearing language that they can use (as they were wont to do in former days), and seemingly getting an answer back" (Catlin, *N. A. Indians,* vol. I, p. 90). John Tanner bears witness to the reality of these phenomena amongst the Indian Medamen. He was himself inducted into the state of abnormal seership, and saw a spirit in the shape of a young man, who said to him, "I look down upon you at all times, and it is not necessary you should call me with such loud cries." (*Narration,* p. 189, New York, 1830.) The Marian Islanders held that the spirits of the dead returned to talk with them.

The dead bodies of their ancestors were desiccated and kept in their huts for the purpose of spirit-communion, and oracles were supposed to be given from their skulls. This tends to identify at least one motive for making and preserving the mummy. A custom of the Acagchemen Indians is peculiarly enlightening in relation to totemic spiritualism. At seven years of age the children are, or used to be, thrown into a trance by the medicine-men in order that they might learn from their spirit guides which of the zoötypes, beast, bird, reptile, or what not, was to be adopted for the child's own personal totem. This, according to the present reading of the data, was a mode of identifying the particular power represented by the totemic zoötype, and a means of affiliating the child, now become an individual, to the power (the later god) for the protection thus sought, and this power was figured and visualized by the totemic zoötype. Thus the personal totem which was seen by the child in trance was a prototype of the spiritual support extended to the novice by a protector in the spirit world. So when the Inoit novice had prepared his body to become the temple of some spirit, he would call upon the genius (or ka) to take up its abode with him. The spirit invoked sends some totemic animal, an otter or badger or other zoötype, for him to kill and flay and clothe himself with the skin. By this means he is supposed to obtain the power of running wild or of making his transformation into the animal that images the superhuman power. The tongue of the beast is then cut out and worn as the medicine, the fetish, charm, or gree-gree of the initiate. This again, to all appearance, is equivalent to the Child-Horus becoming the Word.

We now turn to the chief human agent in the production of abnormal phenomena, namely, the spiritual medium. As usual, we make use of the Egyptian wisdom for guidance in the past. A human soul had been discreted and discriminated from the animistic and totemic souls and personalized in Horus as the Child of the Blood-Mother. This was Horus in the flesh, or in matter. A divine soul was then imaged as the Horus who had died and risen again in spirit from the dead. The powers previously extant had been united and continued as "the Seven Souls of Ra." We read of these in the Ritual, where they are the seven elemental powers that were divinized as the "Ancestors of Ra," those who preceded him in time, but are now "in his following." (Rit., ch. 178, 22, 34, 180, 36.) Ra is the self-originated invisible and eternal being, the father in spirit who is not to be apprehended save through the mediumship of Horus the son; that is, Horus in spirit who bears witness for the father in his resurrection from the dead by testifying to the hidden source of an eternal life, the Horus who says in the Ritual, ch. 42, "I am the Everlasting One: Witness of Eternity is my name." In him the human Horus divinized in death became the spirit medium of the father-god. Ra the Holy Spirit was now the source of a divine descent for human souls, who were consequently higher in status than the earlier gods that were but elemental powers, and higher than the mother-soul which had been incarnated in the human Horus. These were ever-living souls, and born immortals, who were looked upon in many lands as divine beings manifesting in the human form. A spirit that lived for ever was now the supreme type of the human soul. The king who never dies, that is, the divine personage in human form, now took the place of the turtle that never died, or the Bull of Eternity, or any other totemic type of the elemental and pre-human soul. The king who never dies impersonates the immortal in man, who was the royal Horus in the Kamite eschatology. "The king is dead, long live the king!" is an ancient doctrine of human Horus dying to rise again as royal Horus the ever-living, who was the typical demonstrator of a life eternal as Horus the born immortal. The king who ever lives is a human figure of the immortal born from the dead. Egyptian kings were not directly deified. The human Ra was an image of the divine Ra, a likeness of the superhuman power. In various texts the Pharaoh is called the ka of the god, the image and likeness, and to that the worship was indubitably directed. It was as the living representative of divinity that the Ra or Pharaoh was adored by the Egyptians. In this character the king himself is portrayed in the act of worshipping his own ka, or divine eidōlon—the god imaged within and by himself. In both cases the worship was no mere flattery of the mortal man; it was meant for the ever-living immortal. The Pharaoh was the representative of Ra on earth. So was it in Africa and beyond. The Master of Whiddah said of himself, "I am the equal of God; such as you behold me, I am his complete portrait" (Allen and Thompson's *Narrative,* vol. i., 228). This as Egyptian would be the ka-image of the god. The person who, as reckoned, now inherited a soul that was thought to be immortal verily shared in a nature that was superior to any of the elemental forces, such as those of wind and earth and water, even the sun, or the blood of Isis, the highest of them all; and over these the spirit-born, or second-born, assumed the mastery or claimed supremacy. They themselves were of spiritual origin, and as spirits they were superhuman on a higher plane than any merely animistic powers, who, like the Polynesian Tuikilakila Chief of Somosomo, also claimed to be a god. Mendieta in his report of the Mexican gods tells us: "Others said that only such men had been taken for gods who *transformed* themselves or (who) appeared in some other shape and did or spake something while in that shape beyond (the ordinary) human power" (Mendieta, *Historia Ecclest. Indiana,* 1870, p. 84). The Mexicans were here speaking of their trance-mediums. They entered the state of trance for their transformation, and in that condition manifested superhuman or spiritual powers that were looked upon as divine. Amongst all races of people such men were divinized under whatsoever name, as mediums, mediators, and links betwixt two worlds. In this phase the transformers were those who entered the state of trance. This asserted superiority over the powers of the elements is one cause of the claims made by or accredited to the divine mediums, preposterous enough at times, with regard to their superhuman control of the elements as rain-makers and rulers of the weather. The supernormal faculty of the seer and sorcerer is the sole root of reality from which the fiction springs. The Mexican kings, on assuming the sovereignty, were sworn to make the sun shine, the clouds to give forth rain, the rivers to flow, and the earth to produce abundantly (Bancroft, vol. ii., 146). The Inoit Angekok has to play the part of "great provider" to the people, as master of the elements on which plenty of food depends, the water for fish and the air for returning birds of passage. Such mediums were a sort of titular, not actual, masters over the elemental powers, as a result of their asserted higher origin. A line of priest-kings founded on this basis of divinity was at one time extant in the island of Niué, in the South Pacific. Being the representative of deity, the monarch was made responsible for the growth of food, and in times of dearth he was put to death because of a failure in the crops. So exigent were the people that at last no one would consent to become king, and so the monarchy expired. (Turner, *Samoa*.)

The immortal in man being more immediately demonstrated by spiritual manifestation and the abnormal phenomena of trance and interior vision, the mediums were the first divine persons who demonstrated the facts of spirit existence and spirit intercourse. And such were the earliest born immortals. They had the witness within. But those who were not mediums had to attain assurance as best they could; they had to make use of the others. Paul speaks of not being certain of his own immortality. But he presses on to see if by any means he may attain to the resurrection from the dead. This led to a doctrine of conditional immortality that was universal, and to a theory of the mediums or mediators being divine personages or born immortals, like the second Horus, who was the first fruits of them that previously slept. The earliest guidance then was spiritual on this ground. The aboriginal priest-king or divine person was looked to as a ruler and leader in this world on account of his abnormal relationship to the other. He was the demonstrator of a soul that was the first considered to be ever-living. This divine descent was based upon the derivation from the god in spirit who was now superior to all other gods, and who in the Egyptian religion is Ra the Holy Spirit. The three highest ranks in Egypt were the divine, the royal, and the noble, and the three were distinguished from each other by their peculiar type of beard. Thus the loftiest rank was spiritual, and this primacy originated not in men becoming bishops, but in their possessing those spiritual powers and faculties which have been repudiated and expurgated by the Churches of orthodox Christianity, but which were looked upon of old as verily divine. We also learn from Synesius's *Logos Aiguptios,* quoted by Heeren (Ideen, vol. ii., Egypt, p. 335), that in electing a monarch, whereas the vote of a soldier was reckoned as one, the vote of a prophet or seer was counted as one hundred. The Egyptian priesthood pre-eminently exemplifies the idea that the incarnating power made use of certain persons as sacred agents, male or female, for such a purpose. Hence the higher order of priests were known as fathers in god. They were supposed to share in the divine nature, with power to communicate the holy spirit to others who desired to partake of its benefits. The insufflation of the Holy Spirit with the laying on of hands by modern religious impostors who do but parody the ancient custom without knowledge is a relic of the sacred rite. The spiritualistic medium was originally revered not because he was a priest or king, not on account of his earthly office, but because of his being an intercessor with the superhuman powers on behalf of mortals. Among the Zulu Kaffirs the mere political chief has been known to steal the medicines and fetish charms, the information and the magical vessel of the diviner and seer, on purpose to confer the sacred authority on himself and then to put the spiritual ruler to death and take his place, which is similar to the method of the Christians in getting rid of the pagans and stealing the appurtenances of their religion, and ruling without their "open vision." Among the Hottentots the "greatest and most respected old men of the clan" are the seers and prophesiers, or the mediums of spirit intercourse. Their practical religion, says Dr. Hahn, consists of a "firm belief in sorcery and the arts of the living medicine-man on the one hand, and on the other belief in and adoration of the powers of the dead" (Hahn, *Tsuni Goam,* p. 24). That is the religion of all ancient spiritualism distinguished from animism, and it is universal amongst the aboriginal races. The spirits of the dead are accepted as operative realities. They are dreaded or adored according to the mental status of the spiritualists, and the sorcerers, magi, the medicine-men, the witches, and witch doctors are the spirit mediums employed as the accepted and established means of communication. Also witches, wizards, sorcerers, shamans, and other abnormals who had the power of going out of the body in this life were feared all the more after death by many tribes because they had demonstrated the facts which caused such fear and terror; they had also been their exorcists and layers of the ghost whose protective influence was now lost to the living. One way of denoting that such beings were heavenly or of divine descent was signified by the custom of not allowing them to touch the ground with their feet. This was not an uncommon kind of tabu applied to the divine personage as representative of the god. It was a mode of showing that he was not of the earth earthy, and therefore he was heavenly, or something betwixt the earth and heaven, like Horus, who was "the connecting link" in spirit (Rit., ch. 42). It was because he was reckoned of divine descent that the king or other form of the ruler was not allowed to show the ordinary signs of age, decay, and decrepitude, nor to die a natural death like any mere mortal, but was put to death in his prime whilst robust and vigorous, and, as the saying is, "full of spirit." The Japanese Mikado was carried on men's shoulders because it was detrimental to his divinity for him to go afoot. One account of him says, "It was considered as a shameful degradation for him even to touch the ground with his foot" (Pinkerton's *Voyages and Travels,* vol. VII, p. 613). These were the divine kings, like the Egyptian Ank, the everlasting ones, the born immortals among men. This mode of doing honour and conferring dignity has its survivals in the custom of "chairing" or carrying the hero of the hour on the shoulders of those whose desire is to elevate him beyond a footing of equality with themselves on common ground; also in the practice of taking the horses out of the hero's carriage, when human beings take the place and position of the beasts.

It may be that there were other reasons than the one assigned upon a previous page for the crucial seclusion of the girls at the period of puberty. It is probable that they were at the same time initiated in the mysteries of mediumship. Seeing that it was a practice for pubescent lads to be initiated into the mysteries of seership and made mediums of at the time they were made into men, it is more than probable that the girls were also inducted into the mysteries of trance at the time of their pubescent transformation. This would explain the extreme length of time during which the girls were often secluded from all eyes save those of their female overseers. We hear of the boys being kept in their isolation and practised upon until they did see. Why not the girls? Clairvoyance was "the vision and the faculty divine," the "beatific vision" of all the early races. It was sought for and cultivated, prized and protected, as the most precious of all human gifts, and the possessor was held to be divine. The girls who were secluded for the serpent's visit would, as spirit mediums, become the oracles of the serpent wisdom, and as mediums they would attain to primitive divinity. Moreover, when the typical serpent visits the Basuto virgin her limbs are plastered over with white clay and her face is covered by a mask. This denotes her transformation into a superior being of a spiritual order, which she would become as a spirit medium. This suggestion finds support from a story that is told by the Kirgis of Siberia. The daughter of a khan was kept shut up in a dark iron house so that no man might look upon her. She was attended by an old woman. When the girl attained her maidenhood she said to the old woman, "Where do you go so often?" "My child," said the old woman, "there is a bright world. In that bright world your father and mother live, and all sorts of people dwell; that is where I go." Obviously this other world was entered in the state of trance as well as at the time of death. The maiden said, "Good mother, I will tell nobody, but show me that bright world." So the old woman took the girl out of the dark iron house. But when the girl saw the bright world she fainted and fell. And the eye of God fell on her and she conceived. This was evidently in the hypnotic swoon that was induced by the aged woman, who thus initiated the maiden into the mysteries of mediumship at the period of her puberty. (Radloff, W., cited in *The Golden Bough* [1st edn., 1890], vol. ii., p. 237.)

According to Mansfield Parkyns, the greater number of the mediums or possessed persons among the Abyssinians were women. It is the same to-day in modern spiritual phenomena. Also in ancient Egypt the woman was held to be the superior medium as seer and diviner. Duff Macdonald (vol. i., p. 61) says of the Yao people: "Their craving for clearer manifestations of the deity is satisfied through the prophetess. She may be the principle wife of the chief. In some cases a woman without a husband will be set apart for the god (or spirit). The god comes to her with his commands at night. She delivers the message in a kind of ecstasy. She speaks (as her name implies) with the utterance of a person raving with excitement. During the night of the communication her ravings are heard resounding all over the village." It was as a medium for spirit communication that the witch or wise woman attained her pre-eminence in the past and her evil character in the present. Witchcraft is but the craft of wisdom; witches were the wise in a primitive sense and in ways considered to be magical for assignable reasons. But witchcraft and wizardry, magic and "miracle," would be meaningless apart from primitive spiritualism. The witch as abnormal seer and revealer was the most ancient form of the mother's wisdom. The spirit medium was the nearest approach to a human divinity. He or she was the born immortal who demonstrated the existence in this life of a soul or spirit beyond or outside of the body for a life hereafter. And as he or she was the demonstrator of that soul, they were the first to be accredited with the possession of such a soul, and this possession constituted him or her as born immortal. The Tongans hold that it is not everyone who possesses a spiritual part capable of living a separate existence in Bolutu, the Tongan Amenta. Only the Egi or chiefs are credited with the possession of enduring souls in the life on earth. The status of these souls of the nobles is well shown when it is said they cannot return to earth in the old totemic guise of lizards, water-snakes, or porpoises. Not these, but the ghost, or double, is the one witness for the ever-living souls. (Mariner, *Tonga Islands,* vol. ii., pp. 99-105.) The Fijians, amongst others, declare that only the select few have souls which are inherently immortal. Thus, when the ordinary Egyptian entered Amenta he, like Paul, was by no means certain of his enduring soul. This had to be attained, and his pilgrimage and progress to that end are portrayed in the drama of the Ritual, as will be hereafter shown. It is quite common for the old dark races to be despised and badly treated by the more modern as the people who have no souls. They are not looked upon as human beings, but are denounced as wild beasts, reptiles, monkeys, dog-men, bush-men, men with tails, and it is here explained how it was they had no souls. They were the preliminary people, who only had totemic souls which were born of the elements and only represented the elemental or pre-human soul. An arresting instance is mentioned by Howitt in which a group of the Australian aborigines ceased to use their own totemic name and called their children after a celebrated seer or medium. In doing this they were affiliating the fatherless ones to a higher type than that of the old totemic elemental soul. This was the soul whose origin was held to be divine, as demonstrated by the supranormal faculties of the Birraark or spirit medium. The Incas of Peru were a superior race, who had souls, whereas the aborigines were looked down upon as the people without souls. The Incas, on account of this superior soul, were also born immortals or the ever-living ones, whose name of the Inca agrees with that of the Egyptian Ank, the king, or the Ankh, as the ever-living. Such persons did not originate in kings and emperors or as earthly rulers merely mortal. Under whatsoever personal title or type, the divine or semi-divine character was primarily derived from intercourse with spirits or the gods, and the consequent extension of human faculty in the abnormal phase of mediumship. The people of East Central Africa, says Santos (1586), "regard their king as the favourite of the souls of the dead, and think that he learns from them all that passes in his dominions." This identifies the king in this case with the spiritual medium, and points to the origin of the priest-king in the same character. The Fitaure of the Senegambian Sereres, who is the chief and priest in one, is a spirit medium, with power over the souls of the living and the spirits of the dead. "Every West African tribe," says Miss Kingsley, "has a secret society—two, in fact, one for men, one for women. Every free man has to pass through the secret society of his tribe. If during this education the elders of the society discover that a boy is what is called in Calabar an *ebumtup* (a medium), a person who can see spirits, they advise that he should be brought up to the medical profession." (Kingsley, *W. A. S.,* p. 214.) In Kimbunda the Sova or chief is the religious centre of his tribe. He is their wise man, their seer, their supreme man of abnormal powers. The religion, according to Magyar, consists in making sacrifices to the ghosts of their ancestors, the richest offerings being made to the Sova. The faculty of seeing and foreseeing formed the basis of their power over the common people. The mchisango or witch-doctor of the Yao and other Central African tribes, who is called by Stanley the "gourd-and-pebble man," is the person sought by the people in all their profoundest perplexities. The man of mental medicine still keeps his place and holds his own against the doctors who deal in physics (*Africana,* vol. i., p. 43). He invokes his spirits by means of a rattle made of a dried gourd with small pebbles inside it. "Some of these diviners," says the Rev. Duff Macdonald, "are the most intelligent men in the country." The same account is given by Messrs. Spencer and Gillen of the Arunta spirit mediums and medicine-men in Central Australia.

The divine man was the diviner, the seer, the sorcerer, the spirit medium with all the early races. In the Marquesan and the South Sea Islands the divine man was supreme, whether he was a priest, a king, or only a person of inferior birth and station. If he had the supernormal faculty, the mana, he was the human representative of divinity on that account. "Among the Solomon Islanders," says Mr. Codrington (*J. Anth. Inst.,* x., 3), "there is nothing to prevent any man becoming a chief, if he can show that he is in possession of the mana—that is, the abnormal, mediumistic, or supernormal power." The Egyptian magical power will explain the mana of the Melanesians, described by Dr. Codrington as a power derived from all the powers of nature that were recognized. They are not in the mental position of thinking they can derive their mana directly from a god that is postulated as the one spiritual source of power. The powers recognized in nature are various, and were recognized because they were superhuman though not supernatural. Hence their influence was solicitously sought to augment the human. The unseen powers were operant in nature from the first as elemental forces which man would like to wield if he only knew the way to gain alliance with them and to share the power. "The mana," says Dr. Codrington, "can exist in almost anything. Disembodied souls or supernatural beings have it and can impart it, and it belongs essentially to personal beings who originate it, though it may act through the medium of water, or a stone or a bone" (p. 119). That is, it can be gathered from the powers that were pre-personal and elemental, as well as from the ancestral spirits who are personal. The Melanesian gathering his mana may be seen in the Manes of the Egyptian Ritual in the act of collecting his magical power. Here the mana is magical, and it is described as the great magic Ur-heka which is formulated for use as the word of power that can be directed at will by the Manes in possession of it. The soul of the deceased has great need of this superhuman power in his passage through Amenta. It is by means of this he opens the doors that are closed against him, makes his transformations, and conquers the direst of all difficulties. He collects his magical charm or word of power from every place and thing in which it exists and from which it rays out (ch. 24, 2, 5). "Behold," he exclaims, "I bring my magical charms which I have collected from every quarter," more persistently than the hounds of chase and more swiftly than the light. In this way he is drawing influence from the nature powers as well as from the ancestral spirits.

At a later stage of the present inquiry it will be shown how the Egyptian eschatology was formulated in the mould of the mythology. The typical seven souls in the one are repeated *as a type* in the other. The seven elemental powers were continued as the seven souls of Ra, and are described as "the ancestors of Ra." Thus, when the personality of the deceased is reconstituted in Amenta for the after life, it is on the foundation of these seven external souls, the highest of which is represented by the "Ka." The seventh in the series of souls was personified in the human Horus, and this is the first soul to rise again and to be repeated after death as Horus in spirit. When it is said of the Egyptian king that spirit constitutes his personality, he is Horus in spirit, the representative of Ra—the *ka,* or living likeness of the god on earth. The ka-image, then, is the type of this, the enduring personality. With the Pelew Islanders the divine man is a spirit medium called a korong—that is, if the power be permanent; in other words, if he is naturally a medium, he is a korong. But they distinguish betwixt the born korong and a person who may be temporarily possessed. The office of korong is not hereditary, and when the korong dies the manifestation of the spirit or the divine afflatus in another medium is eagerly awaited. This is looked upon here, as elsewhere, as a new incarnation of the god, which shows that the reincarnation was one of *the power and not the personality* of the korong. It was the power of seership, not the individual soul of the seer, that returned in the new avatar; hence the same power was not dependent on the return of the same person. The power may be manifested by some one of very lowly origin, but he is forthwith exalted to the highest place as a divine being. Those who are ignorant of the facts of abnormal experience are entirely "out of it," both as students and teachers of anthropology. The most important of all data concerning the origins of religion have to be omitted from their interpretation of the past of man, or, what is far worse, obfuscated with false or baseless explanations.

The wizards who are reverenced by the Australian Kurnai are those who can "go up aloft" and bring back information from the spirits of the departed commonly known in many lands as "the ancestral spirits."

The spiritual medium ruled as a seer, a sorcerer, a diviner, a healer, who foresaw and uttered oracles, revealed superior knowledge by supernal power, and was looked up to as a protector, a guardian spirit, because he was held to be in league with the spirit world; very divinity in a human form. The divine kings, the spiritual emperors, the gods in human guise, the "supernatural" beings, the intercessors for common people, whether male or female, were incalculably earlier than the physical force hero, the political ruler, or the ritualistic priest. Hence it is amongst the most undeveloped races, like the African and Melanesian, that these preserve their early status still. We have a survival of this status of the spirit medium in a modified form when the priest is called in as exorcist of spirits because he represents the wise man or wizard, in whom Latinity has taken the place of the ancient wisdom. Thus when the ghost of Hamlet's father appears, Marcellus says, "Thou art a scholar; speak to it, Horatio!" Some of the most degraded aborigines among the dark race of India still keep the position of superior people in relation to the neighbouring tribes on account of their being the masters of magical arts and the mediums of spirit intercourse. The Burghers of the Neilgherry Hills have the custom of getting one of the neighbouring tribe of Curumbars to sow the first handful of seed and to reap the first sheaf of corn, evidently for mystical reasons, as the Curumbars are reputed to be great sorcerers, and therefore the influence sought is spiritualistic which they are accredited with possessing. From the first sheaf thus reaped cakes are made to be offered as an oblation of first-fruits and eaten together with the flesh of a sacrificial animal in a sacramental meal. (Harkness, *Description of a Singular Aboriginal Race inhabiting the Summit of the Neilgherry Hills*, p. 56.) Spirit mediums being considered divine beings, or immortals in a mortal guise, like the Manushya Devah, have been looked to as the purveyors of a diviner essence than the protozoa of the ordinary mortal male for the procreation of children. "Roman ladies," says Réclus, "flung themselves into the arms of the thaumaturgists, whom they took for quasi-divine beings able to bestow intenser pleasure and superior progeny." The medium was looked upon as a being loftily transcendent, a channel of communication for the gods and the glorified in their intercourse with mortals. The Eskimos are not only willing but anxious that their Angekoks or spirit mediums should have sexual intercourse with their wives, so that they may secure children superior to those of their own personal begetting. The Angekok is looked upon as a medium for the descent of the holy spirit, and as such he is chosen to initiate young girls into the mystery of marriage. Those men who afterwards take the young woman for wives consider this connection with the divine man a preparatory purification for motherhood. With other races it was looked upon as a religious rite for the bride to cohabit with the holy man or medium on the night before her marriage. There are instances, as on the Malabar coast, in which the bridegroom fees the holy man to lie with his wife the first night after marriage. With the Cambodians, the right to spend the first night with the bride was the prerogative of the priest. The Burmese great families have each their spiritual director, to whom they send their daughter before her wedding night, and, according to the official phrase, "pay him the homage of the flower of virginity." A Brahman priest complained to Weitbrecht the missionary that he was the spiritual purifier in this sense to no fewer than ten different women (*Journal des Missions Evangélistiques*, 1852), not one of whom was his own wife. According to Wilken, the Arabs act in the same way in order that the offspring may be ennobled. This practice—this desire for being ennobled—may have led to its being claimed as a right, the *jus prima noctis,* or right of the feudal lord to sleep the first night with his vassal's new-made bride. The primitive religious feeling would give the profoundest sanction to the phallic rite. Descending from the chief as a medium to the man whose supremacy was acknowledged on account of his courage, we find it was a custom with the Spartans for a husband to select a hero or brave man to lie with his wife to beget heroic offspring. The offices of king, priest, or clergyman remain, but the vision and the faculty divine have fled. The king survives without the seal of sovereignty, the priest without his spiritual influence, divines without divinity. The religious doctors still practise, but they are no longer of the healing faculty. The curates cannot cure. False diplomas take the place of the genuine warrant. The once living link considered to be the ever-living one is now the missing link betwixt two worlds. Indeed, this was prepensely broken by the Christians, and that spiritualism was cast out as devilish which all gnostics held to be divine. Blindness through believing a lie has taken the place of the "open vision" which was sought of old. The priests remain as mediums, without the mediumistic faculty; but they still take the tithe and receive payment for performing the magical rites as qualified intermediaries betwixt the gods and men or women. Nor is the belief in their spiritual potency as fathers in God entirely extinct.

The theory and practice of magic were fundamentally based on spiritualism. The greatest magician or sorcerer, witch or wizard, was the spirit medium. The magical appeal made in mimetic Sign-language was addressed to superhuman powers as the operative force. The spirits might be elemental or ancestral, but without the one or the other there was no such thing as magic or sovereignty. In one of its most primitive aspects magic was a mode of soliciting and propitiating the superhuman elemental powers or animistic spirits, the want, the wish, the intention, or command being acted and chiefly expressed in Sign-language. In another phase it was the application of secret knowledge for the production of abnormal phenomena for the purpose of consulting the ancestral spirits. The hypnotic power of the serpent over its victims was recognized as magical. This is shown in the Ritual when the speaker says to the serpent that "goeth on his belly" (ch. 149), "I am the man who puts a veil (of darkness) on thy head." "I am the great magician." "Thine eyes have been given to me, and through them I am glorified." He has wrested the magical power called its strength from the serpent by taking possession of its eyes, and by this means he is the great magician.

Black magic has its secrets only to be muttered in the dark. In the mysteries of the Obeah and Voudou cults it was held that the starveling ghosts could be evoked by offerings of blood, and that they were able to materialize the more readily and become visible in the fumes of this physical element of life. Other mysteries of primitive spiritualism might be cited. For example, Miss Kingsley, who was so profoundly impressed on the subject of African "fetishism," mentions a class of women who had committed adultery with spirits, and who were recognized as human outcasts by the natives of West Africa, and consequently accursed (*West African Studies,* p. 148).

Sexual commerce betwixt human sensitives and spirits is known alike to the aboriginal races and to modern mediums. Telepathic communication of mind with mind directed by the power of will even without words was a mode of magic practised by the primitive spiritualists. All that is nowadays effected under the names of hypnotism, mesmerism, or human magnetism was known of old as magic. In Egyptian the word Heka, for magic, means to charm, enchant, or ensnare; it also signifies thought and rule—*ergo,* thought as ruling power was a mode of magic; and the God Taht, the ruling power of thought, the thinker personified, was the divine magician, mainly as the transformer in the moon. One mode of exercising magical power practised by Australian medicine-men, though not limited to them, is to point at the person who is being operated on with a stick or bone. This is done to render the person unconscious. Therefore the "pointing-stick" thus used is a kind of magic wand, equivalent to the disk of the modern mesmerist intended to fix attention and induce the condition of coma. Pointing with the stick was naturally preceded by pointing with the fingers, as in modern hypnotism. The "magnetic fluid" of the modern mesmerist was known to the African mystery-men from time immemorial. This again corresponds to the magical fluid of the Egyptians called the "Sa," which was imparted from one body to another by the laying on of hands or making passes as in hypnotizing. The Sa was a sort of ichor that circulated in the veins of the gods and the glorified. This they could communicate to mortals, and thus give health, vigour, and new life. Maspero says the gods themselves were not equally charged with the Sa. Some had more, some less, their energy being in proportion to the quantity. Those who possessed most gave willingly of their superfluity to those who lacked, and all could readily transmit the virtue of it to mankind. This transfusion was most easily accomplished in the temples. "The king or any ordinary man who wished to be impregnated presented himself before the statue of the god, and squatted at its feet with his back to the statue. The statue then placed its right hand on the nape of his neck, and by making passes caused the fluid to flow from it and to accumulate in him as in a receiver." By transmitting their Sa of life to mortals the gods continually needed a fresh supply, and there was a lake of life in the northern heaven, called the Lake of Sa, whither they went to draw the magical ichor and recruit their energies, when exhausted, at this celestial fount of healing. (Maspero, *The Dawn of Civilization,* Eng. tr., p. 110.) Khunsu Nefer-hetep, the great god, giver of oracles in Thebes, was the caster-out of demons, the driver-away of obsessing spirits; and in the story of "The Possessed Princess" his statue is sent for by the Chief of Bakhten to exorcise an evil spirit that has taken possession of his daughter. This is effected by the god imparting the Sa, from the magical power of which the evil demon flees. (*Records,* vol. iv., p. 55.)

Magic has been described as a system of superstition that preceded religion. But magical ceremonies and incantations are religious, inasmuch as they are addressed to superhuman powers. Magical ceremonies were religious rites. If religion signifies a propitiation or conciliation of powers superior to man, it is not necessarily opposed to magic, which supplied the most ready means of influencing such powers that were postulated as extant. Various modes of so-called "sympathetic magic" have been practised in making a primitive appeal to the powers. The Tshi-speaking people have a magical ceremony, the name of which denotes an invocation to the gods for pity and protection. In time of war the wives of the men who are with the army dance publicly stark naked through the town, howling, shrieking, gesticulating, and brandishing knives and swords like warriors gone insane. And from head to foot their bodies are painted of a dead-white colour. (Ellis, A. B., *The Tshi-speaking Peoples,* p. 226.) Dancing in a state of nudity was a mode in which the women showed the natural magic of the sex. Being all in white, they danced as spirits in the presence of the powers, whether sympathetic or not, whilst soliciting aid and protection for their men engaged in battle. In magic there was also a sense of binding as the root idea of religion, far beyond the meaning of the word *re-ligio* in Latin. The bond or tie had been magical before it was moral, as we find it in the "bonds of gesa" and other modes of binding by means of magical spells. One mode of compelling spirits was by the making of a tie, and of tying knots as a mode of acting the desire or of exhibiting controlling power. The most primitive and prevalent type of the African gree-gree is a magical tie. The magic of this proceeding was on the same plane as the utterance of the "words that compel," only the intent was visibly enacted in the language of signs, howsoever accompanied in the language of sounds. The character of the fetish-man was continued by the Christian priest. According to the promise made to Peter in the Gospels, it is said, "Whatsoever thou shalt bind on earth shall be bound in heaven; and whatsoever thou shalt loose on earth shall be loosed in heaven" (Matt. xvi. 19). And thus in the latest official religion the power to bind, tie up, and make fast was reconferred on Rome, where theological beliefs became identical with spiritual and intellectual bondage.

This attitude of controlling, commanding, and binding of the superhuman powers by means of magic also points to the lowly origin of these nature powers which became more and more inferior and of less and less account in later times when they were superseded by other "spirits" or gods, and the practices of magic were less and less appropriate to a deepening sense of the divine.

The earliest human soul which followed those that were derived from the external elements had not attained the power of reproduction for an after-life, on which account the likeness of the Elder Horus in the mythos is *an impubescent child*. But when he makes his transformation in death Horus has acquired the reproducing power, as shown by his figure of the virile male, portrayed in the person of Amsu, who arises from the tomb in ichthyphallic form. In the eschatology the reproducing power is spiritual. It is the power of resurrection and of reappearing as a spirit—that is, the divine double of the human soul, which was tabulated as the eighth in degree. The soul that could reappear victoriously beyond the grave was a soul that could reproduce itself for "times infinite," or for eternity. When Horus rose again from the dead as the divine double of the human Horus he exclaims, "I am he who cometh forth and proceedeth. I am the everlasting one. I am Horus who steppeth onwards through eternity. (Rit., ch. 42.) "I am the link." This is he who had passed and united a soul that was elemental with the spirit that was held to be divine. This is the soul beyond the human, which has power to reproduce itself in spirit and prove it by the reappearance of the Ka or double of the dead. The Kamite Ka is portrayed in the Egyptian drawings as a spiritual likeness of the body, to identify it with the soul of which it is the so-called double—the soul, that is, which has the power to duplicate itself in escaping from the clutch of death, and to reappear in rarer form than that of the mortal, as the soul or spirit outside the body to be seen in apparition or by the vision of the seers. The ardent wish of the deceased in Amenta to attain the power of appearing once more on the earth is expressed again and again in the Ritual as the desire to become a soul or spirit that has the power to reproduce itself in apparition, or as the double of the former self, which was imaged in the Ka; the desire for continual duration after death, or in other words for everlasting life, also *with the power to reappear upon the earth among the living*.

"*My duration*" the speaker calls his Ka (ch. 105). All life through it was an image of the higher spiritual self, divine in origin and duration. The speaker continues, "May I come to thee (the Ka) and be glorified and ensouled?" It was a soul that could be drawn upon and lived on in this life as a sort of food of heaven and sustenance for a future life. The Ka was propitiated or worshipped—that is, saluted with oblations—as a divine ideal. It was the Ka of the god that was "propitiated according to his pleasure." (Rit., ch. 133.) It was the Ka of the Pharaoh that was worshipped as the image of Ra. So when the Manes propitiates the Ka-image of himself it is not an offering to his mortal self, but to that higher spiritual self which was now held to be an emanation of the divine nature, and which had the power of reappearing and demonstrating continuity after death. The Kamite equivalent for eternal life is the permanent personality which was imaged by or in the Ka. With the Tshi-speaking tribes the Ka is called the Kra, which name answers to the Kla of the Karens. The Kra, like the Ka, is looked upon as the genius or guardian spirit who dwells in a man, but whose connection with him terminates when the Ka transforms or merges into the Sisa or enduring spirit. According to Ellis, "when a man dies his Kra becomes a Sisa, and the Sisa can be born again to become a Kra in a new body" (*Tshi-speaking Peoples*, p. 149.) The Ka was common to Inner Africa as a statue or portrait of the spiritual man. Whilst the mummy of a king of Congo was being made, an image of the deceased was set up in the palace to represent him, and was daily presented with food and drink. This was his living likeness, his spiritual double, which the Egyptians called the Ka. And this, not the dead corpse, was propitiated with the offerings. The object of worship or propitiation was the Ka, not the mummy. The Ka imaged the ghost or double itself, and not a spirit supposed to be residential in the mummy. The Esquimaux, the Lapps, and other northern races also preserved the Egyptian Ka, especially in relation to the Shaman or Angekok, who has his Ka or double like the Egyptian priest. With this he unites himself in soul when about to divine and make his revelations in the state of trance.

Uniting with the Ka or genius is a mode of describing his entrance into the spirit or the entrance of the inspiring spirit into him. The practice of the Mexicans and others, who made an image of the dead and placed it on the altar and offered oblations to it, shows that their effigy also represented the Ka or spiritual likeness. Amongst many races an image of the deceased person was set up to receive the oblations of food and drink. All primitive spiritualists held that in death the spirit rose again and lived on still, and for this reason the Ka statue was erected in the funerary chamber as it had been in the forest hut. A black shadow of the body cast upon the ground could not demonstrate the existence of an eternal soul; neither could the hawk or serpent or any other symbol of force. But the Ka is the double of the dead. It is a figure of the ghost. The Ka, then, was an image of the only soul of all the series that ever could be seen outside the human body. This was wholly distinct from the soul of life in a tree, a plant, a bird, a beast, or a reptile, because it was an apparition of the human soul made visible in the human form. The Battas of Sumatra have the seven souls like the Egyptians. One of these is outside the body, but when it dies, however far away it may be from the man, he also dies, his life being bound up with it. But the origin and significance of the Ka, together with the doctrine of its propitiation, are explicitly stated in the rubrical directions to ch. 144 of the Ritual. At this stage of his spiritual progress the deceased has reached the point where the mummy Osiris has transformed into the risen Horus, the divine one who is the eighth at the head of the seven great spirits. Thus, in the mysteries of Amenta, human Horus dies to rise again as lord of the resurrection and to manifest as double of the dead. He is divinized in the character of the ghost, and as such he becomes the spirit medium for his father, the holy spirit; his "Witness for Eternity," who is called the only-begotten and anointed son. In this character the deceased is Horus in spirit, ready for the boat of Ra. An effigy of the boat was to be made for the deceased. Amongst the other instructions given it is said that "a figure of the deceased is to be made" in presence of the "gods." This figure is the Ka. Hence the oblations of flesh and blood, bread and beer, unguents and incense, are to be offered; and it is stated that this is to be done to make the spirit of the deceased to live. It is also promised that the ceremony, if faithfully performed, will give the Osiris strength among the gods and cause his strides to increase in Amenta, earth, and heaven. Thus the Ka image to which the offerings were made was representative of the deceased who lived on in the spirit, whether groping in the nether world, or walking the earth as the ghost, or voyaging the celestial water in the boat of Ra on his way to the heaven of eternity. Naturally enough, the sustenance of life was offered to feed the life of those who were held to be the living, not the dead. Amongst the other things it is commanded that four measures of blood shall be offered to the spirit or Ka image of the deceased. The doctrine is identical with that of the other races who gashed and gored their bodies to feed the spirits of the departed with their blood, because the blood was the life, and because it was the life they desiderated for their dead. In the same rubrical directions it is ordered that incense shall be burned in presence of the Ka image as an offering to the spirit of Osiris-Nu, and in Sign-language incense represents the breath of life; in that way another element of life besides blood was offered the deceased "to make that spirit live." And the offerings are to be presented to the Ka image of the deceased. Thus the Egyptian wisdom witnesses and avouches that the primitive practices of offering food and drink to the dead, and more especially the soul of life in blood, were based upon the postulate that the so-called dead were living still in spirit form. And, obviously enough, the sustenance of life was offered to feed the life of those who were held to be living because seen to be existing in the likeness that was represented by the human figure of the spirit-Ka.

It is one of the various delusions recrudescent in our day that theology began with the self-revelation to the world of a one and only god. No delusion or mania could be a grosser birth of modern ignorance, more especially as the "only one" of the oldest known beginning was female and not male; the mother, not the father—the goddess, not the god.

The Egyptians gave a primary and permanent expression to the dumb thought of the non-speaking, sign-making races that preceded them in the old African home. But they did not begin by personifying any vague infinite with a definite face and form, nor by worshipping an abstraction which is but the shadow of a shade, and not the image of any substance known. In the Book of the Dead (ch. 144) the adorations are addressed to the Great Mother Sekhet-Bast as the supreme being, she who was uncreated by the gods and who was worshipped as the "Only One"; she who existed with no one before her, the only one mightier than all the gods, who were born of her, the Great Mother, the All-Mother when she was the "Only One." By a cunning contrivance this Great Mother is shown to be the only one who could bring forth both sexes. As Apt, and again as Neith, the genetrix or creatress is portrayed as female in nature, but also having the virile member of the male. This was the only one who could bring forth both sexes. She was figured as male in front and female in the hinder part (Birch, *Egyptian Gallery*). Here we may refer to the Arunta traditions of the Alcheringa ancestors relating to the beings who were half women and half men when they first started on their journey, but before they had proceeded very far their organs were modified and they became as other women are (N. T., p. 442).

The mother was indeed the *Only One* in the beginning, however various her manifestations in nature. She was the birthplace and abode. She was the Earth-mother as the bringer forth, the giver of food and drink who was invoked as the provider of plenty. As the Great Mother she was depicted by a pregnant hippopotamus. As a crocodile she brought the water of the inundation. As Apt the water-cow, Hathor the milch-cow, or Rerit the sow she was the suckler. As Rannut she was the serpent of renewal in the fruits of earth. As the Mother of Life in vegetation, she was Apt in the dom-palm, Uati in the papyrus, Hathor in the sycamore-fig, Isis in the persea-tree. In one character, as the Mother of Corn, she is called the Sekhet or field, a title of Isis; all of which preceded her being imaged in the human likeness, because she was the mother divinized. This is the "only one" who is said to have been extant from the time when as yet there had been no birth (Brugsch, *Theosaurus In. Eg.,* p. 637). The mother gave birth to the child as Horus, who came by water in the fish, the shoot of the papyrus, the branch of the tree, and other forms of food and drink that were most sorely needed. Hence the child as bringer was a saviour to the land of Egypt.

In the beginning of the Egyptian theology, then, the Word was not the god, but the goddess. The fecundity, the power, the glory, and the wisdom of the primordial bringer forth were divinized in the Great Mother, who was worshipped at Ombos as the "Living Word." In one of her many forms she is the lioness-headed Sekhet-Bast, who was the object of adoration in Inner Africa as "the Only One." Following the mythical mother, the son became her word or logos, and in Sebek-Horus the Word was god. This was in the mythology that preceded the eschatology. The earliest mode of worship recognizable was in propitiation of the superhuman power. This power of necessity was elemental, a power that was objectified by means of the living type; and again of necessity the object of propitiation, invocation, and solicitation was the power itself, and not the types by which it was imaged in the language of signs.

But, if we use the word worship at all, then serpent worship is the propitiation of the power that was represented by the serpent as a proxy for the superhuman force. The power might be that of renewal in the fruits of earth which was divinized in the serpent goddess Rannut or in the serpent of the inundation. "Tree worship" was the propitiation of a power in nature that was represented by the tree and by the vegetation that was given for food. Although the votive offerings were hung upon its branches, the tree itself was not the object of the offering, but the power personified in Hathor or Nut as giver in the tree. Waitz tells the story of a negro who was making an offering of food to a tree, when a bystander remarked that a "tree did not eat food." The negro replied: "Oh, the tree is not fetish; the fetish is a spirit and invisible, but he has descended into this tree. Certainly he cannot devour our bodily food, but he enjoys its spiritual part, and leaves behind the bodily part which we see." This, then, was not tree worship as commonly assumed; the tree was not the object of religious regard. There was a spirit or power beyond that manifested in the tree. In like manner, earth worship was the propitiation of the power in nature that was worshipped as the Great Mother, the bringer forth and nurse of life, the "only one" who was the producer of plenty. The most primitive man knew what he wanted. The objects of perpetual desire and longing were food and fecundity.

It has been shown that the Egyptian gods were primarily the elemental powers, and how the ancestral spirits became the glorified elect in the Egyptian eschatology. It is now possible to trace the one god of the Osirian religion as the final outcome from the original rootage, the culmination and consummate flower of all.

Before the human father could be personalized as the progenitor it would seem that causation was represented by the embryo in utero, the child, whom the Egyptians called the fecundator of the mother. The eternal child is thus addressed in one of the solar litanies: "O, thou beautiful being, who renewest within thyself in season as the disk within thy mother Hathor"; as "the Heir of Eternity, self-begotten and self-born." According to the Ritual, life was apprehended as a mode of motion or renewal coming of itself, in the water welling from the earth, the vegetation springing from the water, or, more mystically manifested, in the blood of the pubescent virgin. The type of this self-motion is the eternal, ever-coming child. Hence Child-Horus claims to be "the primary power of motion" (Rit., ch. 63A). This was as the child of her who came from herself, the seventh soul that was imaged as Horus, the mortal who was incarnated in the virgin blood. There is another curious thing worth noting. The seven elemental powers or animistic souls were all male, and male only, which may account for the tradition that women have no souls, unless they derive them from the male; whereas the second Horus, Horus in spirit, represented a soul of both sexes, as the typical witness for the parent in heaven. With the Egyptians (of the Ritual) real existence and enduring personality were spiritual, and these were imaged by the Ka type of an existence and personality which could only be attained in spirit. The Ka image represented an enduring or eternal soul as a divine ideal that was already realized, even in this life, by the born immortals who were mediums of the spirit. But for others it was a type of that which had to be attained by individual effort. On entering Amenta the soul of the deceased was not necessarily immortal. He had to be born again as a spirit in the likeness of Horus divinized. Thus the man of seven souls was said to be attended or accompanied all life through by the Ka likeness of an immortal spirit, which was his genius, guardian, guide, or protector, to be realized in death, when he rose again and manifested as the Ka or cidōlon of the dead—that is, as the ghost, the eighth man, the man from heaven, the Christ or risen Horus of the gnosis.

The process of compounding the many gods in one is made apparent when Osiris says, "I am one, and the powers of all the gods are my powers" (Rit., ch. 7). In the course of unifying the nature powers in one, the mother goddess with the father god was blended first in Ptah, the biune being, as a type of dual source such as was illustrated by the customs of couvade and subincision, in which the figure of the female was assumed by the man with a vulva or the divinity as parturient male, the type that was repeated in both Atum and Osiris, as well as in Brahma and Jehovah. In the inscription of Shabaka from Memphis, Ptah, in one of his divine forms, is called "the mother giving birth to Atum and the associate gods" (line 14).

The highest of the elemental powers was divinized as solar in the astronomical mythology. This was the Elder Horus, who had been the soul of vegetation in the shoot of the papyrus plant as product of the inundation. As the young sun god he was now the calf or child upon the Western Mount and leader of the seven glorious Khuti (Rit., ch. 17). In his second advent, at his resurrection from Amenta, he became the Horus in spirit, Horus of the resurrection, he who arose hawk-headed on the Eastern Mount. This was Atum-

Horus, he in whom the spirit or ghost was blended with the elemental power in Atum-Ra, who had attained the status of the holy spirit in the Egyptian eschatology. The eighth was now the highest of the series as the god who demonstrated the power of resurrection by his rising from the dead, first as the sun, next as the soul which was represented by the Ka as the image of the reappearing other self. The gods were thus "essentialized in the one" (as Thomas Taylor phrased it): the seven in Horus the mortal, the eight in Horus of the resurrection, the nine in Ptah, or, as Damascius observed, "speaking Chaldaically," "in the paternal peculiarity" (*Iamblichus on the Mysteries,* by Thomas Taylor, note, p. 74, ed. 1895). This god was impersonated as the one in Atum-Ra, the "Holy Spirit." There was no god personified as the father in spirit until the All-One was uniquely imaged in Atum-Ra as the first wearer of the Atef crown, and in him the god in spirit was *based upon the ghost* instead of the earlier elemental soul. Not only was the "paternal peculiarity" represented in Atum as a begetter, he was the begetter of souls, or rather of soul and spirit; the one being personalized in his son Hu, the other in his son Sa (or Ka). The soul of man the mortal had been derived from the seven elemental powers, including the mother blood (Rit., ch. 85). This was divinized in Horus, who was Atum as the child (Tum) the first Adam in the Hebrew creation. The soul of man the immortal was now derived from Atum-Ra, the father in spirit, and imaged in Nefer-Atum, the Hebrew second Adam. This was Horus of the resurrection as an eighth soul, the outcome of the seven. The soul with power to reproduce itself in death was now an image of eternal life as Horus who became the resurrection and the life to men.

The one god in spirit and in truth, personified in Atum-Ra, was worshipped at Annu as Huhi the eternal, also as the Ankhu or ever-living one in the character and with the title of the Holy Spirit. He is described as *the divinized ghost.* Hence it is said that "it is Atum who nourishes the doubles" of the dead, he who is first of the divine ennead, *"perfect ghost among the ghosts"* (Hymn to Osiris, lines 3 and 4.) There was no father god or divinized begetter among the seven primordial powers. They were a company of brothers. Ptah was the first type of a father individualized as the father who transforms into his own son, and also as a father and mother in one person. Ra, as the name implies, is the creator god, the god in spirit founded on the ghost. He is god of the ancestral spirits, the first to attain that spiritual basis for the next life which the Ka or double in this life vouched for after death. Hence Atum-Ra was deified as "the perfect ghost among the ghosts," or the god in spirit at the head of the nine. The elemental souls were blended with the human in the deity Ptah, and in Atum-Ra, his successor, the ancestral spirit was typified and divinized as a god in perfect human form, who became the typical father of the human race and of immortal souls proceeding from him as their creator, who is now to be distinguished from all previous gods which had reproduced by transformation and by reincorporation or incarnation of the elemental powers.

Thus the gods of Egypt originated in various modes of natural phenomena, but the phenomena were also spiritual as well as physical, the one god being ultimately worshipped as the holy spirit. Both categories of the gods and the glorified were, so to speak, combined and blended in the one person of Atum-Ra, who imaged the highest elemental power as soul of the sun in the mythology, and was divinized as Ra the holy spirit, the ghost of ghosts, in the Egyptian eschatology. The reappearing human spirit thus supplied the type of an eternal spirit that was divinized and worshipped as the Holy Ghost in Egypt and in Rome.

Maspero has said of Egypt that she never accepted the idea of the one sole god beside whom there is none other (*The Dawn of Civilization,* Eng. tr., p. 152). But here the "one god" is a phrase. What is meant by the phrase? Which, or who, is the one god intended? Every description applied to the one god in the Hebrew writings was pre-extant in the Egyptian. Atum-Ra declares that he is the one god, the one just or righteous god, the one living god, the one god living in truth. He is *Unicus,* the sole and only one (Rit., chs. 2 and 17), beside whom there is none other; only, as the later Egyptians put it, he is the only one from whom all other powers in nature were derived in the earlier types of deity. When Atum is said to be "the Lord of oneness," that is but another way of calling him the one god and of recognizing the development and unification of the one supreme god from the many, and acknowledging the birth of monotheism from polytheism, the culmination of manifold powers in one supreme power, which was in accordance with the course of evolution. In the Ritual (ch. 62) the Everlasting is described as Neb-Huhi Nuti Terui-f, the Eternal Lord, he who is without limit. And, again, the infinite god is portrayed as he who dilates without limit, or who is the god of limitless dilation, Fu-nen-tera, as a mode of describing the infinite by means of the illimitable. And it is this Nen-tera that we claim to be at the root of the word Nnuter or Nûter. Here the conception is nothing so indefinite or general as that of power. Without limit is beyond the finite, and consequently equal to the infinite. Teru also signifies time. The name, therefore, conveyed the conception of beyond time. Thus Nnuter (or Nuter) denoted the illimitable and eternal in one, which is something more expressive than mere power. Power is of course included, and the Nuter sign, the stone axe, is a very primitive sign of power.

Of this one supreme god it is said in the Hymn to the Nile or to Osiris, as "the water of renewal": "He careth for the state of the poor. He maketh his might a buckler. He is not graven in marble. He is not beheld. He hath neither ministrants nor offerings. He is not adored in sanctuaries. No shrine is found with painted figures. There is no building that can contain him. He doth not manifest his forms. Vain are all representations." (*Records of the Past,* vol. iv.) Also, in the hymn to the hidden god Amen-Ra, a title of Atum, he is saluted as "the one in his works," "the one alone with many hands, lying awake while all men sleep to seek out or consider the good of his creatures," "the one maker of existence," "the one alone without a peer," "king alone, single among the gods" (*Records of the Past,* vol. ii., 129). Surely this is equivalent to the one god with none beside him, so far as language can go. The Egyptians had all that ever went to the making of the one god, only they built on foundations that were laid in nature, and did not begin *en l'air* with an idea of the "sole god" in any abstract way. Their one god was begotten before he was conceived. Egypt did not accept the idea. She evolved and revealed it from the only data in existence, including those of phenomenal spiritualism which supplied the idea of a holy ghost that was divinized in the likeness of the human—the only data, as matter of fact, from which the concept could have ever been evolved; and but for the Egyptians, neither Jews nor Christians would have had a god at all, either as the one, or three, or three-in-one. There is no beginning anywhere with the concept of a "one god" as male ideationally evolved. But for thousands of years before the era called Christian the Egyptians had attained the idea, and were trying to express it, of the one god who was the one soul of life, the one self-generating, self-sustaining force, the one mind manifesting in all modes of phenomena; the self-existent one, the almighty one, the eternal one; the pillar of earth, the ark of heaven, the backbone of the universe, the bread of heaven and water of life; the Ka of the human soul, the way, the truth, the resurrection, and the life everlasting; the one who made all things, but himself was not made.

But, once more, what is the idea of the one god as a Christian concept? The one god of the Christians is a father manifesting through one historic son by means of a virgin Jewess. Whereas the father was the one god of the Egyptians in the cult of Atum-Ra which was extant before the monuments began ten thousand years ago. Only, the son of the one god in Egypt was *not historic nor limited to an individual personality*. It was the divine nature manifesting as the soul of both sexes in humanity. The one god of the Christians is a trinity of persons consisting of the Father, Son, and Holy Spirit, and these three constituted the one god in the religion which is at least as old as the coffin of Men-Ka-Ra, who is called "Osiris living eternally, king of the double earth," nearly six thousand years ago.

Finally, in the Egyptian theology Osiris is Neb-Ua, the one and only lord. All previous powers were united in his power. Where Ra had seventy-two names denoting his attributes, Osiris has over one hundred and fifty. All that was recognized as beneficent in nature was summarized in Osiris. All the superhuman powers previously extant were combined and blended in the final form of the all-in-one—the motherhood included. For in the trinity of Osiris, Horus, and Ra, which three are one, the first person is imaged in the likeness of both sexes. Osiris as male with female mammæ is a figure of the nourisher and source of life, who had been from the beginning when the mother was the "only one." The one god of the Egyptian theology culminated as the eternal power of evolution, reproduction, transformation, renewal, and rebirth from death to life, on earth in food, and to a life of the soul that is perpetuated in the spirit. The oneness of the godhead unified from all the goddesses and gods was finally compounded in this supreme one inclusive deity, in whom all others were absorbed—Horus and Sut, as twins of light and darkness; the seven elemental powers, as the seven souls;

Nnu, father of the celestial water, as the water of renewal in Osiris; Seb, the father of food on earth, as the father of divine food or bread of heaven in Amenta. The mother and father were combined in Ptah as the one parent. Atum-Horus assumed the form of man, as son of Seb on earth; Osiris-Sekeri that of the mummy in Amenta, as god the ever-living in matter; and Ra, bird-headed, as an image of the holy spirit. Horus the elder was the manifestor as the eternal child of Isis the virgin mother and his foster-father Seb, the god of earth; and at his second advent in Amenta Horus became the son of the father in heaven as a final character in the Osirian drama. Taht gave place to Osiris in the moon, Ptah to Osiris in the Tat, Anup to Osiris as the guide of ways at the pole. It is said in the Hymn to Osiris that "he contains the double ennead of the double land." He is "the principle of abundance in Annu"; he gives the water of renewal in the Nile, the breath of life in the blessed breezes of the north, the bread of life in the grain. And, lastly, he is the food that never perishes; the god who gives his own body and blood as the sacramental sustenance of souls; the Bull of Eternity who is reincorporated periodically as the calf, or, under the anthropomorphic type, as Horus the ever reincarnating, ever-coming child who rose up from the dead to image an eternal soul. Such was the god in whom the all at last was unified in oneness and as One.

EGYPTIAN BOOK OF THE DEAD AND THE MYSTERIES OF AMENTA.

Book IV

The Egyptian Book of the Dead contains the oldest known religious writings in the world. As it comes to us it is mainly Osirian, but the Osirian group of gods was the latest of all the divine dynasties, although these, as shown at Abydos (by Prof. Flinders Petrie), will account for some ten thousand years of time in Egypt. The antiquity of the collection is not to be judged by the age of the coffins in which the papyrus rolls were found. Amongst other criteria of length in time the absence of Amen, Maut, and Khunsu supplies a gauge. The presence and importance of Tum affords another, whilst the persistence of Apt and her son Sebek-Horus tells a tale of times incalculably remote.

As a key to the mysteries and the method of the book it must be understood at starting that the eschatology or doctrine of Last Things was founded in the mould of the mythology, and that the one can only be unraveled by means of the other. Moreover, there is plenty of evidence to prove that the Ritual was based on the mythology, and not the mythology upon the Ritual. The serpent, of darkness, was the evil reptile in mythology. In theology it becomes the deluder of mankind. Here the beginning was with darkness itself, which was the deceiver from the first. The serpent, being a figure of darkness, was continued by theology as the official adversary of souls in the eschatological domain. The eschatology of the Ritual, then, can only be comprehended by means of the mythology. And it is the mythos out of view that has made the Ritual so profoundly difficult to understand. Reading it may be compared with a dance seen by a deaf man who does not hear the music to which the motion is timed, and who has no clue to the characters being performed in the dumb drama. You cannot understand what they are doing and saying as Manes in another world without knowing what was thought and said by human beings in this concerning that representation of the nature powers, the gods and goddesses, which constitutes mythology.

Amenta is a huge fossil formation crowded with the dead forms of a past life in which the horny conspectuities of learned ignorance will only see dead shells for a modern museum. As a rule, Egypt is always treated differently from the rest of the world. No Egyptologist has ever dreamed that the Ritual still exists under the disguise of both the gnostic and canonical gospels, or that it was the fountain-head and source of all the books of wisdom claimed to be divine. In the mythology—that is, in the primitive mode of rendering the phenomena of external nature—Osiris as light-giver in the moon was torn in fourteen pieces during the latter half of the lunation by the evil Sut, the opposing power of darkness. He was put together again and reconstituted by his son, beloved Horus, the young solar god. This representation could not have been made until it was known that the lunar light was replenished monthly from the solar source. Then Horus as the sun god and the vanquisher of Sut, the power of darkness, could be called the reconstituter of Osiris in the moon. In that way a foundation was laid in natural fact according to the science of mythology, and a mystery bequeathed to the eschatology which is doctrinal. For as it had been with the dismembered, mutilated god in the mythos, so it is with the Osiris deceased, who has to be reconstructed for a future life and put together bit by bit as a spiritual body in one of the great mysteries of Amenta. In the mythos Har-Makhu was the solar god of both horizons, or the double equinox, who represented the sun of to-day that rose up from the nether world as conqueror of darkness to join the west and east together on the Mount of Glory, as the connecting link of continuity in time betwixt yesterday and to-morrow. The type was continued in the eschatology, when Har-Makhu became the Horus of the greater mysteries, Horus of the religious legend who suffered, died, and was buried in Amenta, and who rose again from the dead like the winter sun, as Horus in spirit, lifting aloft the insignia of his sovereignty. This was he who made the pathway, not merely betwixt the two horizons, but to eternal life, as son of Ra, the holy spirit in the eschatology. The intermediate link in the mythos, which "connects the solar orb with yesterday," is now the intermediary betwixt the two worlds and two lives in time and eternity. This is he who exclaims, "I am the link! I am the everlasting one! I am Horus who steppeth onwards through eternity" (Rit., ch. 42.) This was he who, in the words of the gnostic Paul, "broke down the wall of partition" and "made both one," "that he might create in himself one new man" and "reconcile them both in one body," even as the double Horus, Har-Sam-Taui, was made one when blended and established as one person in another mystery of Amenta (Rit., ch. 42).

The mythology repeated in the Ritual is mainly solar and Osirian, but with glimpses of the lunar and the stellar mythos from the beginning. For example, Apt the ancient genetrix, as goddess of the Great Bear constellation, and leader of the heavenly host, was the kindler of the starry sparks by night in the mythology. In the eschatology she is continued as the mistress of divine protections for the soul, and she who had been the kindler of the lights in the darkness of night was now propitiated as rekindler of life from the spark in the dark of death (Rit., ch. 137B). Ra in the mythos is the solar god represented by the sun in heaven, and in the eschatology he became the god in spirit who is called the holy spirit and first person in the trinity which consisted of Atum the father god, Horus the son, and Ra the holy spirit; the three that were also one in the Osirian cult, first as three forms of the solar god and next as three forms of the god in spirit. It is thus we are enabled to trace the formation of the Egyptian eschatology in the mould of the mythology.

There is no death in the Osirian religion, only decay and change, and periodic renewal; only evolution and transformation in the domain of matter and the transubstantiation into spirit. In the so-called death of Osiris it is rebirth, not death, exactly the same as in the changes of external nature. At the close of day the solar orb went down and left the sun god staring blankly in the dark of death. Taht the moon god met him in Amenta with the eye of Horus as the light that was to illuminate the darkness of the subterranean world. In the annual rendering on the third day light was generated by renewal in the moon. Thus Osiris rose again, and a doctrine of the resurrection on the third day was bequeathed to the eschatology. The sun in sinking was buried as a body (or mummy) in the nether world of Amenta. When rising again at dawn it was transformed into a soul, a supreme elemental soul, that preceded the god in spirit. This was in the mythology. In the eschatology the same types were reapplied to the human soul, which was imaged in the flesh as the inarticulate, blind, and impubescent Horus, who died bodily but was preserved in mummy form to make his transformation into the luminous Sahu, when he rose again in glory as Horus the divine adult. "*I am the resurrection and the life*" is the perfect interpretation of an Egyptian picture that was copied by Denon at Philæ. (*Egypt*, vol. II, pl. 40, no. 8, p. 54.) (Lundy, fig. 183.) Divine Horus is portrayed in the act of raising the deceased Osiris from the bier by presenting to him the Ankh sign of life. He was the life in person who performed the resurrection, and therefore is "*the resurrection and the life.*" As such he simply stands for a soul considered to be the divine offspring of god the father, not for any historical character that makes preposterous pretensions to possess miraculous power. Previously he had been the resurrection and the life as *solar vivifier in the physical domain,* or otherwise stated in the mythology. It was this difference betwixt the mythology and eschatology that constituted the lesser and the greater mysteries. The lesser in their origin were partly sociological. They were the customs and the ceremonial rites of totemism. The greater mysteries are eschatological and religious. For instance, the transformation of the youth into the adult or the girl into a woman in the totemic mysteries was applied doctrinally to the transformation of the soul in the mysteries of Amenta. With the more primitive races, such as the Arunta of Australia, the mysteries remain chiefly totemic and sociological, though interfused with the religious sentiment. The greater mysteries were perfected in the Egyptian religion, to be read of in the Ritual as the mysteries of Amenta.

From the beginning to the end of the written Ritual we shall find it is based upon the mythical representation which was primary. The mythical representation was first applied to the phenomena of external nature, and this mode of representation was continued and re-applied to the human soul in the eschatology. Egyptian myths, then, are not inventions made to explain the Ritual. Totemic representation was earlier. This mode was continued in the mythology. Ritual arose from the rendering becoming religious in the phase of eschatology, and did not originate as an explanation of mythology and totemism. But not until the different phases are discriminated can the Ritual be read, that which has been founded on it understood, or the mental status of the thinkers ascertained. In the mythology the solar god, who in his primary form was Ptah (Khepr), is the maker of a complete circle for the sun as founder and opener of the nether earth, this solar pathway being a figure of for ever, a type of the eternal working in time. In the eschatology the god in spirit who is Ra the holy spirit is "the god who has created (or opened out) eternity" (Rit., ch. 15). The one is on the physical basis, the other on the spiritual plane. In the mythology the seven primordial powers that pass through various phases, elemental, stellar, or lunar, always in a group of seven, finally become the seven souls of Ra, who attained supremacy as the sun god in mythology and also as the holy spirit. Thence came the doctrine of the seven souls in man, as seven gifts of the holy spirit in the eschatology. In the mythical representation Sothis on New Year's Day was the bringer forth of the child that was mothered by Hathor or Isis. The type is employed in the eschatology of the Ritual when the Manes in Amenta prays for rebirth as a pure spirit and says, "May I live (or rise up and go forth) from between the closed knees of Sothis." The rebirth of the child in Sothis was the renewal of the year, Sothis being represented in the feminine character by Hathor as the bringer forth from betwixt her knees or, as elsewhere rendered, her kheptu, *i.e.,* her thighs. So the Manes are reborn from between the thighs of Nut in the mysteries of Amenta, and here the visible birthplace of spirits perfected is localized in Sothis, the opener of the year and bringer of the babe to birth upon the horizon or the mount of glory. In this way the skies of night were made luminous with starry lore that was mythical in the astronomy and the words of a divine wisdom in the later eschatology when the mysteries were represented in Amenta. Instead of flashlights showing pictures on the housetops of a city after dark, the stars were used by the Egyptians to illustrate the mysteries that were out of sight. The triumph of Horus over Sut or over the Apap dragon of drought and darkness was illustrated in the stellar mythos when in the annual round Orion rose and the Scorpion constellation set upon the opposite horizon. The Egyptian nearing death could lie and look upon a future figured in the starry heavens. As it was with Osiris or Horus so would it be with him. The way had been mapped out, the guiding stars were visible. His bier or coffin of new birth could be seen in the mesken of the mother. He rose again in spirit as the babe of Sothis. "He joined the company of the holy Sahus" in Orion with the pilot Horus at the look-out of the bark. He saw the golden isles in a heaven of perpetual peace to which the pole was the eternal mooring post. Whilst he was passing from this life the bark of Ra was making ready for his soul to go on board.

The foundation of Amenta itself has yet to be delineated. It is a tangible threshold to the other world, the secret but solid earth of eternity which was opened up by Ptah when he and his seven Knemmu erected the Tat pillar that was founded in the winter solstice as the figure of a stability that was to be eternal. In the mythos the Tat is a type of the sun in the winter solstice that has the power of returning from the lowest depth and thus completing the eternal road. In the eschatology it is the god in person as Ptah-Sekeri or Osiris, the backbone and support of the universe. Horus erecting the Tat in Sekhem was raising Osiris from the sepulchre, the father re-erected as the son in the typical resurrection and continuity of the human spirit in the after life. The figure of Amsu-Horus rising in the resurrection or "coming forth," with member erect, has two characters, one in the mythology, one in the eschatology. In the mythology he images the phallus of the sun and the generative force that fecundates the Mother-earth. In the eschatology the image of erection is repeated as a symbol of resurrection, and in this phase the supposed phallic god, the figure of regenerative force, is typical of the resurrection or re-erection of the mortal in spirit.

Horus the child with finger to mouth is portrayed in the sign of the Scales at the autumn equinox, the point at which the sun begins to lessen and become impotent. This the Egyptians termed the "little sun," which when personified was infant Horus, who sank down into Hades as the suffering sun to die in the winter solstice and be transformed to rise again and return in all his glory and power in the equinox of Easter. This was matter of the solar mythos, also of life in vegetation and in the water of the inundation. In the eschatology Horus the child is typical of the human soul which was incarnated in the blood of Isis, the immaculate virgin, to be made flesh and to be born in mortal guise on earth as the son of Seb, and to suffer all the afflictions of mortality. He descended to Amenta as the soul sinking in the dark of death, and as the soul he was transfigured, changed, and glorified, to rise again and become immortal as a spirit perfected according to the teachings in the eschatology. A brief list will show how certain zoötypes that were founded in the mythological representation were continued in the eschatology:—

Type of power.	*Mythical.*	*Eschatological.*
The beetle	= The sun as transformer	= The god as self-evolver
The serpent	= Renewal	= Eternal life
The ibis	= Messenger	= Word or logos
The jackal	= Seer in the dark	= Guide in death
The heifer	= The moon	= Virgin mother
The hawk	= Soul of the sun	= Ra the divine spirit
Fish, calf, or lamb	= Youthful solar god re-born	= The messiah

In the mythology the Apap reptile lies in the Lake of Darkness, where the sun goes down, as the eternal adversary of the light with which it is at war all night and all the winter through. He seeks to bar the way of the sun in the nether world. In the eschatology it is the human soul instead of the sun that has to struggle with the opposing monster in making the passage of Amenta. The same scenery served, as already shown, to illustrate the mystery in a religious and spiritual phase.

Chapter 64 of the Ritual is known to have been extant in the time of King Septi, of the first dynasty, the Usaiphais of Manetho. That was over 6,000 years ago. It is a chapter from the Book of Life "to be recited on coming forth to day, that one may not be kept back on the path of the Tuat, whether on entering or in coming forth; for taking all the forms which one desireth, and that the person may not die a second time." If this chapter be known, the person is made triumphant on earth (as in the nether world), and he performeth all things which are done by the living. The chapter was then so ancient that it had been lost sight of, and was discovered "on a plinth of the god of the Hennu (or Sekru) bark, by a master builder in the time of King Septi the Victorious." When this chapter was composed the primary nature powers had been unified in the one god, who was represented as the lord of two faces, who "seeth by his own light," the "Lord of Resurrections, who cometh forth from the dusk, and whose birth is from the House of Death." That is, as the solar god who was Atum on one horizon and Horus on the other; hence the lord of two faces. The supreme god thus described is the father in one character, the son in the other. The Manes speaking in the character of the son says of the father, "He is I, and I am he." At that time the earth had been tunnelled by Ptah and his pigmy workers, and a spirit world created on the new *terra firma* in the earth of eternity, over which the solar god effused his radiance nightly when he lighted up the Tuat with his indescribable glories (ch. 15). The "Lord of Resurrections" as a solar god had then become the lord of resurrections as the generator of ever-living souls. Egyptian theology, then, was based upon the mythology which preceded it and supplied the mould. So is it with the Hebrew and Christian theology. But here is the difference betwixt them. The mythology remained extant in Egypt, so that the beginnings of the theology could be known and tested, and were known to the mystery teachers, and the origins referred to for the purpose of verification. The commentary which has been partially incorporated with the text of chapter 17 survives to show the development of the theology from mythology and the need of explanations for the Ritual to be understood; at it was the necessary explanations which constituted the gnosis or wisdom of the "mystery teachers of the secret word," whereas the Hebrew and Christian theologies have been accepted minus the necessary knowledge of the origins, the means of applying the comparative method and checking false assumptions. In Christianity the mysteries have been manufactured out of mist, and it has been taken for granted that the mist was impenetrable and never to be seen through, whereas the mysteries of the Ritual can be followed in the two phases of mythology and eschatology. The main difference betwixt the mythos and the eschatology is that the one is represented in the earth of time, the other in the earth of eternity. And if we take the doctrine of a resurrection from the dead, the soul that rose again at first, in mythology, was a soul of the returning light, a soul of life in vegetation, or other of the elemental powers; a soul in external nature. For instance, a soul of life, as source of drink, was apprehended in the element of water, seen also in the plant and figured in the fish. The superhuman type was divinized in Horus. A soul of life, as source of breath, was apprehended in the breeze, and imaged as the panting of a lion. The superhuman type was divinized in Shu. A soul of food was apprehended in the earth, and represented by the goose that laid the egg. The superhuman type was divinized in Seb.

In the Masonic and all other known mysteries, ancient or modern, the initiate has his eyes bandaged so that he may enter the reception room blindfold. This figure, in the Egyptian mysteries, is Horus in the dark, sometimes called the blind Horus, An-ar-ef. In the mythos Horus is the sun in the darkness of Amenta and the depths of the winter solstice. He is the prototype of "blind Orion hungering for the morn," and of Samson "eyeless in Gaza." The character was founded in the mythical representation of natural phenomena, and was afterwards continued in the eschatology. The same type serves in the two categories of phenomena which are here distinguished as the mythical and the eschatological. In the latter the sightless Horus images the human soul in the darkness of death, where it is blind from lack of outer vision. This duality may serve to explain the twofold rendering of the eyes. According to the hieroglyphic imagery, Horus is without eyes or sightless in one character. He is also portrayed in another as the prince of sight, or of double sight. This, according to the mythos, is a figure of the risen sun and of dawn upon the coffin-lid of Osiris in Amenta. In the eschatology it is Horus, lord of the two eyes, or double vision—that is, of second sight—the seer in spirit with the beatific vision which was attained by him in death. The change from one character to the other is represented in the mysteries by the unbandaging of the initiate's eyes, which are intentionally dazzled by the glory of the lights. The Egyptian Book of the Dead is the one sole record of this two-fold basis of the mysteries.

Enough has now been cited to show the method of the Ritual and the mode in which the eschatology of the Egyptian religion was founded in the mould of the pre-extant mythology. The Book of the Dead is the Egyptian book of life. It is the pre-Christian word of God. This we learn from the account which it gives of itself. It is attributed to Ra as the inspiring holy spirit. Ra was the father in heaven, who has the title of *Huhi,* the eternal, from which we derive the Hebrew name of Ihuh. The word was given by God the father to the ever-coming son as manifestor for the father. This was Horus, who as the coming son is Iu-sa or Iu-su, and, as the prince of peace, Iu-em-hetep. Horus the son is the Word in person. Hence the speaker in the character of Horus says, "I utter his words—the words of Ra—to the men of the present generation, and I repeat his words to him who is deprived of breath" (ch. 38). That is, as Horus, the sayer or logos, who utters the words of Ra the father in heaven to the living on earth, and to the breathless Manes in Amenta when he descends into Hades or the later hell to preach to the spirits in prison. The word or the sayings thus originated with Ra the father in heaven. They were uttered by Horus the son, and when written down in hieroglyphics by the fingers of Taht-Aan for human guidance they supplied a basis for the Book of the Dead. It had been ordained by Ra that his words, such as those that bring about "the resurrection and the glory" (Rit., ch. 1), should be written down by the divine scribe Taht-Aan, to make the word truth, and to effect the triumph of Osiris against his adversaries; and it is proclaimed in the opening chapter that this mandate has been obeyed by Taht. The Ritual purports to contain the gnosis of salvation from the second death, together with the ways and means of attaining eternal life, as these were acted in the drama of the Osirian mysteries. Hence the Osiris says that freedom from perdition can be assured by means of this book, in which he trusts and by which he steadfastly abides. The object of the words of power, the magical invocations, the funeral ceremonies, the purgatorial trials, is the resurrection of the mortal to the life which is everlasting. This opening chapter is described as the "words" which bring about the resurrection on the Mount of Glory, and the closing chapters show the deceased upon the summit of attainment. He has joined the lords of eternity in "the circle of Osiris," and in the likeness of his own human self, the very "figure which he had on earth," but changed and glorified (ch. 178). Therefore the most exact and comprehensive title for the Book of the Dead now put together in 186 chapters would be "The Ritual of the Resurrection." The books of the divine words written down by Taht are in the keeping of Horus the son, who is addressed as "him who sees the father." The Manes comes to him with his copy of the writings, by means of which he prevails on his journey through Amenta, like Pilgrim with his roll. He exclaims: "O thou great seer who beholdest his father! O keeper of the books of Taht! Here am I glorified and filled with soul and power, and provided with the writings of Taht," the secrets of which are divine for lightening the darkness of the nether earth (Rit., ch. 94). With these the Manes is accoutred and equipped. The Word of god personified in Horus preceded the written word of god and when the words of power were written down by Taht the scribe of truth, they were assigned to Horus as the logia of the Lord, and preserved as the precious records of him who was the word in person; first the word of power as the founder, then the word in truth or made truth, as the fulfiller. The divine words when written constituted the scriptures, earliest of which are those ascribed to Hermes or Taht, the reputed author of all the sacred writings. And now we find that both the word in person and the written word, together with the doctrine of the word according to the ancient wisdom, are more or less extant and living still in the Egyptian Book of the Dead. The magical words of power when written down by Taht became the nucleus of the Ritual, which is late in comparison with the astronomical mythology and other forms of Sign-language, and belongs mainly to the Osirian religion.

The mystical word of power from the first was female. Apt at Ombos was worshipped as "the Living Word." The supreme type of this power borne upon the head of Shu is the hinder part of a lioness, her sign of sexual potency. The thigh or khepsh of Apt is also the typical Ur-heka, and it is a symbol of the great magical power. The Ur-heka or magical sign preceded words, and words preceded the writings. Great magical words of power are ascribed to Isis, whose word of power in the human sphere was personified in Horus the child, her word that issued out of silence. This is the word that was made flesh in a mortal likeness, the soul derived from blood. Child-Horus, however, manifests in divers phenomena as the Word-of-Power emaned by Isis, in the water, in vegetation, in food, and lastly in the virgin mother's blood. The first Horus was the Word-of-Power, the second is the Word-made-Truth in Horus, Ma, t-Kheru, by doing it. Horus the Word-of-Power was the founder, who was followed by Horus the Fulfiller. This title does not merely mean the Word of Truth, the True Logos (Celsus), or the True Voice (Plutarch), but denotes the Word-made-Truth or Law by Horus the Victorious, the father's own anointed son, who fulfilled the Word of Power. It is Horus the Word-of-Power personalized as a little child who survives as the miraculous worker two or three years old in the apocryphal gospels. He is credited with doing these infantine marvels as the Word-of-Power in person. He also utters the word of power in performing his amazing miracles.

The magical words were orally communicated in the mysteries from mouth to ear, not written to be read. They were to be gotten by heart. In the Book of the Dead memory is restored to the deceased through the words of power that were stored up in life to be remembered in death. The speaker in chapter 90 says: "O thou who restorest memory in the mouth of the dead through the words of power which they possess, let my mouth be opened through the words of power which I possess." That is, by virtue of the gnosis, memory was restored by the deceased remembering the divine words. Now, Plato taught that a knowledge of past lives in a human pre-existence was restored to persons in this life by means of memory. The origin of the doctrine is undoubtedly Egyptian, but it was made out by a perversion of the original teaching. This restoration of or through memory occurs to the Manes in Amenta after death, and the things remembered appertain to the past life on earth. Plato has misapplied it to the past lives and pre-existence of human beings dwelling on the earth. The words of power were not only spoken. They were likewise represented in the equipment of the mummy, sometimes called its ornaments, such as the word of salvation by the blood of Isis with the red Tet-buckle, the word of durability by the white stone, the word of resurrection by the scarabæus, the word of eternal life by the cross, called the ankh. These were forms of the magical words expressed in fetish figures.

The Manes in Amenta begins his course where he left off on earth when his mouth was closed in death; it is opened once more for him by Ptah and Tum, and Taht supplies him with the great magical words of power that open every gate. These were written on the roll of papyrus that is carried in his hand by the pilgrim who makes his progress through the nether regions in the subterranean pathway of the sun. The so-called Book of the Dead, then, here quoted as the Ritual for the sake of brevity, is the Egyptian book of life: life now, life hereafter, everlasting life. It was indeed the book of life and salvation, because it contained the things to be done in the life here and hereafter to ensure eternal continuity (Rit., ch. 15, hymn 3). The departing soul when passing away in death, or, as the truer phrase is, when setting into the land of life, clasps and clings to his roll for very life. As the book of life, or word of salvation, it was buried in the coffin with the dead when done with on earth. It showed the way to heaven objectively as well as subjectively, as heaven was mapped out in the astral mythos. The Manes enters Amenta with a papyrus roll in his hand corresponding to the one that was buried in his coffin. This contains the written word of truth, the word of magical power, the word of life. The great question now for him is how far he has made the word of god (Osiris) truth and established it against the powers of evil in his lifetime on the earth. The word that he carries with him was written by Taht-Aan, the scribe of truth. Another word has been written in his lifetime by himself, and the record will meet him in the Hall of Justice on the day of weighing words, when Taht will read the record of the life to see how far it tallies with the written word and how far he has fulfilled the word in truth to earn eternal life. The sense of sin and abhorrence of injustice must have been peculiarly keen when it was taught that every word as well as deed was weighed in the balance of truth on the day of reckoning, called the Judgment Day. The questions confronting the Manes on entering Amenta are whether he has laid sufficient hold of life to live again in death? Has he acquired consistency and strength or truth of character enough to persist in some other more permanent form of personality? Has he sufficient force to incorporate his soul anew and germinate and grow and burst the mummy bandages in the glorified body of the Sahu? Is he a true mummy? Is the backbone sound? Is his heart in the right place? Has he planted for eternity in the seed-field of time? Has he made the word of Osiris, the word that was written in the papyrus roll, truth against his enemies?

The chapters for opening the Tuat, for dealing with the adversary in the nether world, for issuing forth victoriously and thus winning the crown of triumph, for removing displeasure from the heart of the judge, tend to show the ways of attaining the life everlasting by acquiring possession of an eternal soul. The Manes is said to be made safe for the place of rebirth in Annu by means of the books of Taht's divine words, which contain the gnosis or knowledge of the things to be done on earth and in Amenta. The truth is made known by the words of Horus which were written down by Taht in the Ritual, but the fulfilment depends on the Manes making the word truth by doing it. That is the only way of salvation or of safety for the soul, the only mode of becoming a true being who would endure as pure spirit for ever. The Egyptians had no vicarious atonement, no imputed righteousness, no second-hand salvation. No initiate in the Osirian mysteries could possibly have rested his hope of reaching heaven on the Galilean line to glory. His was the more crucial way of Amenta, which the Manes had to treat with the guidance of the word, that step by step and act by act he must himself make true. It is said in the rubrical directions of chapter 72 that the Manes who knew it on earth and had it written on his coffin will be able to go in and out by day under any form he chooses in which he can penetrate his dwelling-place and also make his way to the Aarru fields of peace and plenty, where he will be flourishing for ever even as he was on earth (Rit., 72, 9, 11). If chapter 91 is known, the Manes takes the form of a fully-equipped spirit (a Khu) in the nether world, and is not imprisoned at any door in Amenta either going in or coming out. Chapter 92 is the one that opens the tomb to the soul and to the shade of a person, that he may come forth to day and have the mastery over his feet. The book of giving sustenance to the spirit of the deceased in the under world delivers the person from all evil things (Rit., 148). There was another book wherewith the spirits acquired strength by knowing the names of the gods of the southern sky and of the northern sky (chs. 141-3). The Ritual was pre-eminently a book of knowledge or of wisdom, because it contained the gnosis of the mysteries. Knowledge was all-important. The Manes make their passage through Amenta by means of what they know. The deceased in one of his supplications says: "O thou ship of the garden Aarru, let me be conveyed to that bread of thy canal, as my father the great one who advanceth in the divine ship, *because I know thee*" (ch. 106, Renouf). He knew because, as we see by ch. 99, he had learned the names of every part of the bark in which the spirits sailed. Knowledge was power, knowledge was the gnosis, and the gnosis was the science of the mystery teachers and the masters of Sign-language. Ignorance was most dire and deadly. How could one travel in the next world any more than in this without knowing the way? The way in Amenta was indicated topographically very much in keeping with the ways in Egypt, chief of which was the water-way of the great river. Directions, names, and passwords were furnished in writing, to be placed with the mummy of the deceased. Better still, if these instructions and divine teachings were learned by heart, had been enacted and the word made truth in the life, then the Book of the Dead in life became the book of life in death. The word was given that it might be made truth by doing it as the means of learning the way by knowing the word. The way of life in three worlds, those of earth, Amenta, and heaven, was by knowing the word of god and making it true in defiance of all the powers of evil. According to this earlier Bible, death came into the world by ignorance, not by knowledge, as in the Christian travesty of the Egyptian teaching. As Hermes says: "The wickedness of a soul is ignorance. The virtue of a soul is knowledge" (Divine Pymander, B. iv., 27, 28). There was no life for the soul except in knowing, and no salvation but in doing, the truth. The human soul of Neferuben in the picture is the wise or instructed soul, one of the Khu-Akaru: he is a master of the gnosis, a knower or knowing soul, and therefore not to be caught like an ignorant fish in the net. Knowledge is of the first importance. In all his journeyings and difficulties it is necessary for the deceased to *know*. It is by knowledge that he is lighted to find his way in the dark. Knowledge is his lamp of light and his compass; to possess knowledge is to be master of divine powers and magical words. Ignorance would leave him a prey to all sorts of liers in wait and cunning enemies. He triumphs continually through his knowledge of the way, like a traveller with his chart and previous acquaintanceship with the local language; hence the need of the gnosis of initiation in the mysteries. Those who knew the real name of the god were in possession of the word that represented power over the divinity, therefore the word of power that would be efficacious if employed. Instead of calling on the name of god in prayer, they made use of the name as the word of god. And as these words and mysteries of magic were contained in the writings, it was necessary to know the writings in which the gnosis was religiously preserved to be in possession of the words of power. Hence the phrases of great magical efficacy in the Ritual are called "the words that compel." They compel the favourable action of the super-human power to which appeal is made. To *make* magic was to *act* the appeal in a language of signs which, like the words, were also intended to compel, and to act thus magically was a mode of compelling, forcing, and binding the superhuman powers. Magic was also a mode of covenanting with the power apprehended in the elements. The *quid pro quo* being blood, this was a most primitive form of blood-covenant. Giving blood for food was giving life for the means of living.

The Ritual opens with a resurrection, but this is the resurrection in the earth of Amenta, not in the heaven of eternity. It is the resurrection of a body-soul emerging in the similitude of the moon-god from the dark of death. The first words of the Ritual are, "O Bull of Amenta [Osiris], it is Taht, the everlasting king, who is here!" He has come as one of the powers that fight to secure the triumph of Osiris over all his adversaries. After the life on earth there was a resurrection in Amenta, the earth of eternity, for the human soul evolved on earth. It was there that the claim to the resurrection in spirit and to life eternal in heaven had to be made good and established by long and painful experiences and many kinds of purgatorial purification, by which the soul was perfected eventually as an ever-living spirit. The word of promise had to be performed and made truth indeed, for the Ma-Kheru of immortality to be earned and endless continuity of life assured. Everyone who died was in possession of a body-soul that passed into Amenta to become an Osiris or an image of the god in matter, although it was not every one who was reborn or regenerated in the likeness of Ra, to attain the Horushood, which was portrayed as the *hood* of the divine hawk. Emergence in Amenta was the coming forth of the human soul from the coffin and from the gloom of the grave in some form of personality such as is depicted in the Shade, or the Ba, a bird of soul with the human head, which shows that a human soul is signified. Osiris the god of Amenta in a mummy form is thus addressed by the Osiris N. or Manes: "O breathless one, let me live and be saved after death" (ch. 41). This is addressed to Osiris who lives eternally. Though lying as a mummy in Amenta, breathless and without motion, he will be self-resuscitated to rise again. Salvation is renewal for another life; to be saved is not to suffer the second death, not to die a second time. According to Egyptian thought, the saved are the living and the twice dead are the damned. Life after death is salvation of the soul, and those not saved are those who die the second death—a fate that could not be escaped by any false belief in the merits of Horus or the efficacy of the atoning blood. There was no heaven to be secured for them by proxy.

The Ritual is not a book of beautiful sentiments, like the poetic literature of later times. It is a record of the things done by the *dramatis personæ* in the Kamite mysteries. But now and again the beauty of feeling breaks out ineffably upon the face of it, as in the chapter by which the deceased prevails over his adversaries, the powers of darkness, and comes forth to the day, saying, "O thou who shinest forth from the moon, thou that givest light from the moon, let me come forth at large amid thy train, and be revealed as one of those in glory. Let the Tuat be opened for me. Here am I." The speaker is in Amenta as a mummy soul appealing to the father of lights and lord of spirits that he may come forth in the character of Horus divinized to delight the soul of his poor mother. He wishes to capitalize the desires of those who "make salutations" to the gods on his behalf. These in modern parlance would be the prayers of the priests and congregation (ch. 3) for his welfare and safety in the future life, otherwise for his salvation. In the chapter by which one cometh forth to day he pleads: "Let me have possession of all things soever which were offered ritualistically for me in the nether world. Let me have possession of the table of offerings which was heapt for me on earth—the solicitations which were uttered for me, 'that he may feed upon the bread of Seb,' or the food of earth. Let me have possession of my funeral meals," the meals offered on earth for the dead in the funerary chamber (ch. 68).

The chief object of the deceased on entering Amenta is the mode and means of getting out again as soon as possible upon the other side. His one all-absorbing interest is the resurrection to eternal life. He says, "Let me reach the land of ages, let me gain the land of eternity, for thou, my Lord, hast destined them for me" (ch. 13). Osiris or *the* Osiris passed into Amenta as the lord of transformations. Various changes of shape were necessitated by the various modes of progression. As a beetle or a serpent he passed through solid earth, as a crocodile through the water, as a hawk through the air. As a jackal or a cat he saw in the dark; as an ibis he was the knowing one, or "he of the nose." Thus he was the master of transformations, the magician of the later folk-tales, who could change his shape at will. Taht is termed the great magician as the lord of transformations in the moon. Thus the deceased in assuming the type of Taht becomes a master of transformation or the magician whose transformations had also been made on earth by the transformers in trance who pointed the way to transformation in death. When Teta comes to consciousness on rising again in Amenta he is said to have broken his sleep for ever which was in the dwelling of Seb—that is, on the earth. He has now received his Sahu or investiture of the glorious body.

Before the mortal Manes could attain the ultimate state of spirit in the image of Horus the immortal, he must be put together part by part as was Osiris, the dismembered god. He is divinized in the likeness of various divinities, all of whom had been included as powers in the person of the one true god, Neb-er-ter, the lord entire. Every member and part of the Manes in Amenta has to be fashioned afresh in a new creation. The new heart is said to be shaped by certain gods in the nether world, according to the deeds done in the body whilst the person was living on the earth. He assumes the glorified body that is formed feature by feature and limb after limb in the likeness of the gods until there is no part of the Manes that remains undivinized. He is given the hair of Nu, or heaven, the eyes of Hathor, ears of Apuat, nose of Khenti-Kâs, lips of Anup, teeth of Serk, neck of Isis, hands of the mighty lord of Tattu, shoulders of Neith, back of Sut, phallus of Osiris, legs and thighs of Nut, feet of Ptah, with nails and bones of the living Uræi, until there is not a limb of him that is without a god. There is no possibility of coming back to earth for a new body or for a re-entry into the old mummy. As the Manes says, his "soul is not bound to his old body at the gates of Amenta" (ch. 26, 6). Chapter 89 is designated the chapter by which the soul is united to the body. This, however, does not mean the dead body on earth, but the *format* or bodily type of the mummy in Amenta. "Here I come," says the speaker, "that I may overthrow mine adversaries upon the earth, *though my dead body be buried*" (ch. 86, Renouf). "Let me come forth to day, and walk upon my own legs. Let me have the feet of the glorified" (ch. 86). At this stage he exclaims, "I am a soul, and my soul is divine. It is the eternal force." In chapters 21 and 22 the Manes asks for his mouth, that he may speak with it. Having his mouth restored, he asks that it may be opened by Ptah, and that Taht may loosen the fetters or muzzles of Sut, the power of darkness (ch. 23). In short, that he may recover the faculty of speech. In the process of transforming and being renewed as the new man, the second Atum, he says, "I am Khepera, the self-produced upon his mother's thigh." Khepera is the beetle-type of the sun that is portrayed in pictures of the goddess Nut proceeding from the mother's khepsh. The name of the beetle signifies becoming and evolving, hence it is a type of the becomer in making his transformation. The mouth being given, words of power are brought to him, he also gathers them from every quarter. Then he remembers his name. Next the new heart is given to him. His jaws are parted, his eyes are opened. Power is given to his arms and vigour to his legs. He is in possession of his heart, his mouth, his eyes, his limbs, and his speech. He is now a new man reincorporated in the body of a Sahu, with a soul that is no longer bound to the Khat or dead mummy at the gates of Amenta (ch. 26). He looks forward to being fed upon the food of Osiris in Aarru, on the eastern side of the mead of amaranthine flowers.

In one phase of the drama the deceased is put together bone by bone in correspondence to the backbone of Osiris. The backbone was an emblem of sustaining power, and this reconstruction of deceased is in the likeness of the mutilated god. The speaker at this point says, "The four fastenings of the hinder part of my head are made firm." He does not fall at the block. There are of course seven cervical vertebræ in the backbone altogether, but three of these are peculiar, "the atlas which supports the head, the axis upon which the head turns, and the *vertebræ prominens,* with its long spiral process" (ch. 30, Renouf). No doubt the Osiris was rebuilt upon this model, and the four joints were fundamental, they constituted a four-fold foundation. In another passage the Osiris is apparently perfected "upon the square," as in the Masonic mysteries. It is the chapter by which one assumes the form of Ptah, the great architect of the universe. The speaker says, "He is four times the arm's length of Ra, four times the width of the world" (Rit., ch. 82, Renouf), which is a mode of describing the four quarters or four sides of the earth, as represented by the Egyptians. There were seven primary powers in the mythical and astronomical phases, six of whom are represented by zoötypes, and the seventh is imaged in the likeness of a man. This is repeated in the eschatology, where the highest soul of seven is the Ka-eidōlon with a human face and figure as the final type of spirit which was human on the earth and is to be eternal in the heavens. The Manes who is being reconstituted says, "The [seven] Uræus divinities *are my body*. . . . My image is eternal" (ch. 85), as it would be when the seven souls were amalgamated into one that was imaged by the divine Ka. The seven Uræus divinities represented the seven souls of life that were anterior to the one enduring soul. In the chapter of propitiating one's own Ka the Manes says, "Hail to thee, my Ka! May I come to thee and be glorified and made manifest and *ensouled?*" (ch. 103)—that is, in attaining the highest of the souls, the unifying one. These souls may be conceived as seven ascending types of personality. The first is figured as the shade, the dark soul or shade of the Inoits, the Greenlanders, and other aboriginal races, which is portrayed personally in the Ritual lying darkly on the ground. The shade was primary, because of its being, as it were, a shadow of the old body projected on the ground in the new life. It is portrayed as a black figure stretched out in Amenta. In this way the earth shadow of the body in life served as the *type* of a soul that passed out of the body in death. This may explain the intimate relationship of the shade to the physical mummy, which it is sometimes said to cling to and remain with in the tomb, and to draw sustenance from the corpse so long as it exists. Thus the shade that draws life from the dead body becomes the mythical prototype of the vampire and the legendary ghoul. It may be difficult to determine exactly what the Egyptians understood by the khabit or shade in its genesis as a soul, but the Inoit or Aleutians describe it as "a vapour emanating from the blood"; and here is wisdom for those who comprehend it. The earliest human soul, derived from the mother when the blood was looked upon as the life, was a soul of blood, and the Inoit description answers perfectly to the shade in the Egyptian Amenta. Amongst the most primitive races the typical basis of a future personality is the shade. The Aleutians say the soul at its departure divides into the shade and the spirit. The first dwells in the tomb, the other ascends to the firmament. These, wherever met with, are equivalent to the twin-souls of Sut the dark one, and Horus the soul of light. For we reckon the Egyptian seven to be earliest and old enough to account for and explain the rest which are to be found dispersed about the world. The soul as shade or shadow is known to the Macusi Indians as the "man in the eyes," who "does not die." This is another form of the shadow that was not cast upon the ground. Dr. Birch drew attention to the fact that whilst the deceased has but one Ba, one Sahu, and one Ka, he has two shades, his Khabti being in the plural (*Trans. Society of Bib. Arch.*, vol. VIII, p. 391). These two correspond to the dark and light shades of the aborigines. They also conform to the two souls of darkness and light that were imaged by the black vulture and the golden hawk of Sut and Horus, the first two of the total septenary of powers or souls. The shade, however, is but one-seventh of the series. The other self when perfected consists of seven amalgamated souls. Some of the Manes in Amenta do not get beyond the state of the shade or Khabit; they are arrested in this condition of mummied immobility. They do not acquire the new heart or soul of breath; they remain in the egg unhatched, and do not become the Ba-soul or the glorified Khu. These are the souls that are said to be eaten by certain of the gods or infernal powers. "Eater of the shades" is the title of the fourth of the forty-two executioners (ch. 125). The tenth of the mystical abodes in Amenta is the place of the monstrous arms that capture and carry away the Manes who have not attained a condition beyond that of the shade or empty shell. The "shells" of the theosophists may be met with in the Ritual. The Manes who is fortified with his divine soul can pass this place in safety. He says, "Let no one take possession of my shade [let no one take possession of my shell or envelope]. I am the divine hawk." He has issued from the shell of the egg and been established beyond the status of the shade as a Ba-soul. With this may be compared the superstition that in eating eggs one should always break up the empty shell, lest it should be made evil use of by the witches. There are wretched shades condemned to immobility in the fifth of the mystical abodes. They suffer their final arrest in that place and position, and are then devoured by the giants who live as eaters of the shades. These monsters are described as having thigh-bones seven cubits long (ch. 149, 18, 19). No mere shade has power enough to pass by these personifications of devouring might; they are the ogres of legendary lore, who may be found at home with the ghoul and the vampire in the dark caverns of the Egyptian under world. These were the dead whose development in spirit world was arrested at the status of the shade, and who were supposed to seek the life they lacked by haunting and preying upon human souls, particularly on the soul of blood. In its next stage the soul is called a Ba, and is represented as a hawk with a human head, to show that the nature of the soul is human still. This is more than a soul of shade, but it was not imagined nor believed that the human soul as such inhabited the body of a bird. In one of the hells the shades are seen burning, but these were able to resist the fire, and it is consequently said, "The shades live; *they have raised their powers.*" They are raised in status by assimilating higher powers.

Following his taking possession of the soul of shade and the soul of light the Osiris is given a new heart, his whole or twofold heart. With some of the primitive folk, as with the Basutos, it is the heart that goes out in death as the soul that never dies. Bobadilla learned from the Indians of Nicaragua that there are two different hearts; that one of these went away with the deceased in death, and that it was the heart that went away which "made them live" hereafter. This other breathing heart, the basis of the future being, is one with the Egyptian heart by which the reconstituted person lives again. The heart that was weighed in the Hall of Judgment could not have been the organ of life on earth. This was a second heart, the heart of another life. The Manes makes appeal for this heart not to bear evidence against him in presence of the god who is at the balance (chs. 30A and 30B). The second is the heart that was fashioned anew according to the life lived in the body. It is said to be the heart of the great god Tehuti, who personated intelligence. Therefore it would seem to typify the soul of intelligence. Hence it is said to be young and keen of insight among the gods, or among the seven souls. The physical representation comes first, but it is said in the text of Panchemisis, "The conscience or heart (Ab) of a man is his own god" or divine judge. The new heart represents rebirth, and is therefore called the mother (ch. 30 A); and when the deceased recovers the basis of future being in his whole heart he says, although he is buried in the deep, deep grave, and bowed down to the region of annihilation, he is glorified (even) there (ch. 30 A, Renouf).

Now if we take the shade to image a soul of blood, the Ba-hawk to image a soul of light, and the hati-heart to represent a soul of breath, we can perceive a *raison d'être* for the offering of blood, of lights, and of incense as sacrifices to the Manes in three different phases or states. Blood was generally offered to the shades, as we see in survival among the Greeks and Romans. The shade was in the first stage of the past existence, and most needing in Amenta the blood which was the life on earth and held to be of first necessity for the revivifying of the dead as Manes or shades. The Sekhem was one of the souls or powers. It is difficult to identify this with a type and place in the seven. *Pro tem.* we call it fourth of the series. It is more important to know what force it represents. The name is derived from the word khem, for potency. Khem in physics signifies erectile power. The man of thirty years as typical adult is khemt. Sekhem denotes having the power or potency of the erectile force. In the eschatological phase it is the reproducing, formative power of Khem, or Amsu, to re-erect, the power of erection being applied to the spirit in fashioning and vitalizing the new and glorious body for the future resurrection *from* Amenta. The Khu is a soul in which the person has attained the status of the pure in spirit called the glorified, represented in the likeness of a beautiful white bird; the Ka is a type of eternal duration in which the sevenfold personality is unified at last for permanent or everlasting life.

It is the Khu that is thus addressed in the tomb as the glorified one: "Thou shalt not be imprisoned by those who are attached to the person of Osiris [that is, the mummy], and who have custody of souls and spirits, and who shut up the shades of the dead. It is heaven only that shall hold thee." (Rit., ch. 92.) The shade of itself could never leave the tomb. For this reason it was commonly held that the shade remained with the corpse or mummy on the earth. But here the tomb, the mummy, and the shade are not on earth; they are in Amenta. Without the Ba-soul, the shade remains unvivified. Without the Sekhem, it lacks essential form or power of re-arising. Without the Khu-spirit the person does not ascend from the sepulchre or prison-house of the nether world. But when this has been attained the deceased is glorified. If chapter 91 is known, "he taketh the form of a fully-equipped Khu [spirit] in the nether world, and does not suffer imprisonment at any door in Amenta, either in coming in or going out" (Renouf, ch. 91). It is only when the Manes is invested as a Khu that he ascends to the father as a son of god. So we gather from the following words addressed to Horus by the person who is now a Khu: "O mighty one, who seest thy father, and who hast charge of the books of Taht, here am I. I come, and am glorified and filled with soul and power, and am provided with the scriptures of Taht," his copy of the book of life, his light in the darkness of Amenta. He now ascends to Ra his father, who is in the bark, and exclaims again and again, "I am a powerful Khu; let thy soundness be my soundness" (Renouf, ch. 105). When the deceased has been made perfect as a Khu, he is free to enter the great house of seven halls (ch. 145). Likewise the "house of him who is upon the hill," and who is "ruler in the divine hall." The great house is the heaven of Osiris based upon the thirty-six gates or duo-decans of the zodiac. The other is the house of Anup at the summit of the mount in Annu. "Behold me," he exclaims; "behold me. I am come to you, and have *carried off and put together my forms,*" or constituent parts of the permanent soul, which were seven altogether. These are: (1) The Khabit or dark shade; (2) the Ba or light shade; (3) the breathing heart; (4) the Sekhem; (5) the Sahu; (6) the Khu; (7) the Ka. When the Manes has become a Khu, the Ka is still a typical ideal ahead of him; so far ahead or aloof that he propitiates it with offerings. In fact, he presents himself as the sacrificial victim that would die to attain conjunction with his Ka, his image of eternal duration, his type of totality, in which the seven souls were permanently unified in one at last. The Ka has been called the double of the dead, as if it simply represented the *Doppel-ganger*. But it is not merely a phantom of the living or personal image of the departed. It serves also for the apparition or *revenant;* it is a type rather than a portrait. It is a type that was pre-natal. It images a soul which came into existence with the child, a soul which is food and sustenance to the body all through life, a soul of existence here and of duration for the life hereafter. Hence it is absorbed at last in the perfected personality. It is depicted in the Temple of Luxor, where the birth of Amenhetep III, is portrayed as coming from the hand of god. The Ka of the royal infant is shown in the pictures being formed by Khnum the moulder on the potter's wheel. It is in attendance on the person all life through, as the genius or guardian angel, and the fulfilment of the personality is effected by a final reunion with the Ka. As already shown, when divine honours were paid to the Pharaoh the offerings were made to his Ka, not to his mortal self. Thus the Manes in Amenta makes an offering of incense to purify himself in propitiation of his Ka (ch. 105). There is a chapter of "providing food for the Ka." Also the mortuary meal was eaten in the chamber of the Ka, the resurrection chamber of the sepulchre. Food was offered to the Ka-eidōlon as the representative of the departed, instead of directly to the spirits of the ancestors. It was set up there as receiver-general of the offerings. Also the food was presented to it as a type of the divine food which sustained the human soul. Thus, when the divine sustenance is offered by the god or goddess to the soul of the mortal on the earth, or to the Manes in Amenta, it is presented by the giver to the Ka. Certain priests were appointed to be ministers to the Ka, and these made the offerings to the Ka of the deceased on behalf of the living relatives. This is because the Ka was the type of personality, seventh of the seven souls attained as the highest in which the others were to be included and absorbed. In the vignettes to chapter 25 of the Ritual (Naville, *Todt., Kap.* 25, vol. I, p. 36) the deceased is shown his Ka, which is with him in the passage of Amenta, not left behind him in the tomb, that he may not forget himself (as we might say), or, as he says, that he may not suffer loss of identity by *forgetting his name*. Showing the Ka to him enables the Manes to recall his name in the great house, and especially in the crucible of the house of flame. When the deceased is far advanced on his journey through Amenta, his Ka is still accompanying him, and it is described as being the food of his life in spirit world, even as it had been his spiritual food in the human life. "Thou art come, Osiris; thy Ka is with thee. Thou feedest thyself under thy name of Ka" (128, 6). When the Osiris has passed from the state of a shade to the stage of the Ka, he will become what the Ritual designates a fully equipped Manes who has completed his investiture. As a Sahu he was reincorporated in a spiritual body. As a Khu he was invested with a robe of glory. As a sacred hawk with the head of a Bennu he was endowed with the soul of Horus (ch. 78). It was here he exclaimed "Behold me; I am come to you [the gods and the glorified], and have carried off my forms and united them." But in chapter 92 he was anxiously looking forward to the day of reckoning, when he said, "Let the way be open to my soul and my shade, that I may see the great god within his sanctuary on the day of the soul's reckoning," "when all hearts and words are weighed." He is not yet one of the spirits made perfect, being neither judged nor justified. He has to pass his last examination, and is now approaching the great hall of judgment for his trial. He says, "I am come that I may secure my suit in Abydos," the mythical re-birthplace of Osiris. This is the final trial of the long series through which he has hitherto successfully passed (Rit., ch. 117, Renouf). He has now arrived at the judgment hall. It has been asserted that the deeds which the deceased had done here on earth in no wise influenced the fate that awaited the man after death (Maspero, *Egyptian Archæology,* Eng. tr., p. 149). But how so, when the new heart which was given to the deceased in Amenta, where he or she was reconstituted, is said to be *fashioned in accordance with what he has done in his human life?* And the speaker pleads that his new heart may *not be fashioned according to all the evil things that may be said against him* (Rit., ch. 27). He is anxious that the ministrants of Osiris in the Neter-Kar, "who deal with a man *according to the course of his life,*" may not give a bad odour to his name (ch. 30 B). And again he pleads, "Let me be glorified through my attributes; let me be estimated according to my merits" (ch. 72). It is plainly apparent that the future fate of the soul was dependent on the deeds that were done in the body, and the character of the deceased was accreted according to his conduct in the life on earth.

The jury sitting in the judgment hall consisted of forty-two masters of truth. Their duty was to discover the truth with fierce interrogation and the instinct of sleuth-hounds on their track. Was this Manes a true man? Had he lived a true life? Was he true at heart when this was tested in the scales? His viscera were present for inspection, and these keen scrutinizers in their animal-headed forms were very terrible, not only in visage, for they had a vested interest in securing a verdict of guilty against the Manes, inasmuch as the viscera of the condemned were flung to them as perquisites and prey, therefore they searched with the zeal of hunger for the evidence of evil living that might be found written on this record of the inner man. Piecemeal the Manes were examined, to be passed if true, to be sent back if not, in the shape of swine or goats or other typhonian animals, and driven down into the fiery lake of outer darkness where Baba the devourer of hearts, the Egyptian "raw-head-and-bloody-bones," was lying in wait for them. The highest verdict rendered by the great judge in this most awful Judgment Hall was a testimony to the truth and purity of character established for the Manes on evidence that was unimpeachable. At this *post-mortem* the sins done in the body through violating the law of nature were probed for most profoundly. Not only was the deceased present in spirit to be judged at the dread tribunal, the book of the body was opened and its record read. The vital organs, such as the heart, liver, and lungs, were brought into judgment as witnesses to the life lived on earth. Any part too vitiated for the rottenness to be cut off or scraped away was condemned and flung as offal to the powers who are called the eaters of filth, the devourers of hearts, and drinkers of the blood of the wicked. And if the heart, for example, should be condemned to be devoured because very bad, the individual could not be reconstructed for a future life.

In order that the Osiris may pass the Great Assize as one of the justified, he must have made the word of Osiris truth on earth against his enemies. He must have lived a righteous life and been just, truthful, merciful, charitable, humane. In coming to the Hall of Judgment or Justice to look on the divine countenance and be cleansed from all the sins he may have committed he says, "I have come to thee, O my Lord. I know thee. Lord of Righteousness is thy name. I bring to thee right. I have put a stop to wrong." His plea is that he has done his best to fulfil the character of Horus-Makheru. Some of his pleas are very touching. "He has not exacted from the labourer, as the first-fruits of each day, more work than was justly due to him. He has not snatched the milk from the mouths of babes and sucklings. He has not been a land-grabber. He has not damned the running water. He has caused no famine, no weeping, no suffering to men, and has not been a robber of food. He has not tampered with the tongue of the balance, nor been fraudulent, mean, or sordid of soul. There is a goodly list of pre-Christian virtues besides all the theoretical Christian ones. Amongst others, he says, "I have propitiated the god with that which he loveth." This was especially by the offering of *Maat,* viz., justice, truth, and righteousness. "I have given bread to the hungry, water to the thirsty, clothes to the naked, and a boat to the shipwrecked" (ch. 125). Yet we have been told that charity and mercy were totally unknown to the pagan world. He asks the forty-two assessors for the great judge not to go against him, for he did the right thing in Tamerit, the land of Egypt. His heart is weighed in the scales of justice. He passes pure, as one of those who are welcomed by Horus for his own faithful followers, the blessed of his father, to whom it is said, "Come, come in peace." Horus the intercessor, advocate, or paraclete, now takes him by the hand and leads him into the presence of Osiris in the sanctuary. The Manes in the Judgment Hall is black-haired, as seen in the pictures of Ani (Papyrus of Ani, pl. 4). But when he kneels before Osiris on the throne his hair is white. He has passed as one of the purified and is on his way to join the ranks of the just spirits made perfect, who are called the glorified. The attendants say to him, "We put an end to thy ills and we remove that which is disorderly in thee through thy being smitten to the earth" in death. These were the ills of mortality from which he has now been freed in spirit. Here occurs the resurrection of the Osiris in the person of Horus, and it is said, "Ha, Osiris! thou hast come, and thy Ka with thee, which uniteth with thee in thy name of Ka-hetep" (ch. 128). An ordinary rendering of "Ka-hetep" would be "image of peace" = type of attainment; but as the word hetep or hepti also means number seven, that coincides with the Ka being an image of the septenary of souls, complete at last to be unified in the hawk-headed Horus.

In the book or papyrus-roll for invoking the gods of the Kerti, or boundaries, we find the speaker has now reached the limit of Amenta. He says, "I am the soul of Osiris, and rest in him" (ch. 127). He is hailed as one who has attained his Ka and received his insignia of the resurrection. It is now said to the Osiris, "Ha, Osiris! thou hast received thy sceptre, thy pedestal, and the flight of stairs beneath thee" (Rit., ch. 128). The sceptre was the hare-headed symbol of the resurrection first carried by Ptah the opener. The pedestal is the papyrus of Horus, and the stairs denote the means of ascent from Amenta to the summit of the Mount of Glory. He is now prepared and empowered to enter the bark of Ra which voyages from east to west by day and from west to east by night. Before entering the bark the Osiris has attained to every one of his stations in Amenta previously to sailing for the circumpolar paradise upon the stellar Mount of Glory.

Chapter 130 is the book by which the soul is made to live for ever on the day of entering the bark of Ra, which means that it contains the gnosis of the subject. It was made for the birthday or re-birthday of Osiris. Osiris is reborn in Horus as the type of an eternal soul. Hence the speaker says, in this character, "I am coffined in an ark like Horus, to whom his cradle [or nest of reeds] is brought." He is reborn as Horus on his papyrus, an earlier figure on the water than the bark of Ra. He prays, "Let not the Osiris be shipwrecked on the great voyage; keep the steering tackle free from misadventure." When he entered Amenta the deceased in Osiris bore the likeness of the god in mummy form. Before he comes forth from the lower Aarru garden he can say, at the end of certain transformations in type and personality, "I am the soul of Osiris, and I rest in him" (ch. 127). This is in the character of Horus. "I am Horus on this auspicious day" at the "beautiful coming forth from Amenta." He has reached the boundary, and now invokes the god who is in his solar disk, otherwise in the bark of Ra. He died in Osiris to live again in Horus, son of god, or in his likeness. Chapters 141 and 142 begin the book of making the Osiris perfect. And this, as the Ritual shows, was in the likeness of Horus the beloved sole-begotten son of Ra, the god in spirit. Now, when the Manes had included his Ka in the name of Ka-hetep (Rit., ch. 128) it is said to the deceased (in the Pyramid texts, Teta, 284, Pepi I, 34), "Horus hath brought to pass that *his* ka, which is in thee, should unite with thee in thy name of Ka-hetep," which shows the Ka within him was the image of Horus divinized. This corroborates the suggestion that the ka-type was derived from Ka (later Sa) the son of Atum-Ra, who was earlier than Horus as the son of Osiris. Thus the divine sonship of humanity which was personified in Horus, or Iu, or Sa, was also typified in the ka-image of a higher spiritual self; and when the Manes had attained the status of a spirit perfected it was in the form of the divine son who was the express image of the father god. He was Horus the beloved, in all reality, through perfecting the ideal type in his own personality.

He now enters the divine presence of Osiris-Ra to relate what he has done in the character of human Horus, Har-Tema, and Har-Makheru on behalf of his father which constitutes him the veritable son of god. When the Manes had attained the solar bark he has put on "the divine body of Ra" and is hailed by the ministrants with cries of welcome and acclamations from the Mount of Glory (ch. 133). In travelling through the under-world he had passed from the western horizon of earth to the east of heaven, where he joins the solar boat to voyage the celestial waters. There is a change of boat for the night. Hence the speaker says he is "coming in the two barks of the lord of Sau" (ch. 136 B, Renouf). There may be some difficulty about the exact position of the chapter numbered 110 in the Ritual, but there is no difficulty in identifying the fields of peace upon the summit of Mount Hetep as the lower paradise of two, which was the land of promise attainable in Amenta. This was the sub-terrestrial or earthly paradise of the legends. When the Manes comes to these elysian fields he is still in the earth of eternity, and has to prove himself an equal as a worker with the mighty Khus (Khuti), who are nine cubits high, in cultivating his allotment of arable land. The arrival at Mount Hetep in this lower paradise or heaven of the solar mythos precedes the entrance to the Judgment Hall which is in the domain of the Osiris below, and the voyage from east to west in the Matit and the Sektit bark of the sun, therefore it is not in the ultimate heaven or the upper paradise of eternity upon Mount Hetep. We see from the Pyramid texts (Pepi I, lines 192, 169, 182, Maspero, *Les Inscrip. Des Pyramids de Sakkarah*) that there were two stages of ascent to the upper paradise, that were represented by two ladders: one is the ladder of Sut, as the ascent from the land of darkness, the other is the ladder of Horus, reaching to the land of light. King Pepi salutes the two: "Homage to thee, O ladder of Sut. Set thyself up, O ladder of God. Set thyself up, O ladder of Sut. Set thyself up, O ladder of Horus, whereby Osiris appeared in heaven when he wrought protection for Ra." Pepi likewise enters heaven in his name of the ladder (Budge, Book of the Dead, Intro., pp. 117, 118). The Manes also says, in ch. 149, "I raise my ladder up to the sky, that I may behold the gods."

But, having traced the reconstruction of the deceased for a future life, we now return, to follow him once more from the entrance to Amenta on his journey through the under-world. His mortal personality having been made as permanent as possible in the mummy left on earth, the Manes rising in Amenta now sets out to attain the personality that is to last for ever. He pleads with all his dumbness that his mouth may be opened, or, in other words, that his memory, which he has lost awhile, may be given back to him, so that he may utter the words of power (chs. 21-23) with which he is equipped. The ceremony of opening the mouth after the silence of death was one of the profoundest secrets. The great type of power by means of which the mouth is opened was the leg of the hippopotamus goddess, the symbol of her mightiness as *primum mobile* in the Great Bear having been adopted for this purpose in the eschatology. The ceremony was performed at the tomb as well as in Amenta by the opener Ptah as a mystery of the resurrection. And amongst the many other survivals this rite of "opening the mouth" is still performed in Rome. It was announced in a daily paper not long since (the *Mail*, August 8th, 1903) that after the death of Pope Leo XIII and the coronation of Pius X "a Consistory would be held to close and open the lips of the cardinals newly created," or newly born into the purple. The Osiris also prays that when his mouth is opened Taht may come to him equipped with the words of power. So soon as the mouth of the Manes is freed from the fetters of dumbness and darkness (or muzzles of Sut) and restored to him, he collects the words of power from all quarters more persistently than any sleuth-hound and more swiftly than the flash of light (chs. 23, 24, Renouf). These words of power are magical in their effect. They paralyze all opposition. They open every door. The power is at once applied. The speaker says, "Back, in retreat! Back, crocodile Sui! Come not against me, who live by the words of power!" (ch. 31). This is spoken to the crocodiles or dragons who come to rob the Manes and carry off the words of power that protect the deceased in death. The magical mode of employing the words of power in the mysteries of Taht is by the deceased being assimilated to the character and assuming the superhuman type as a means of protection against the powers of evil. The speaker in the Ritual does not mistake himself for the deity. He is the deity *pro tem.* in acted Sign-language, and by such means is master of the magical power. It is the god who is the power, and the magician employs the words and signs which express that power; but instead of praying to the god he makes use of the divine words attributed to the god, and personates the god as Horus or Ra, Taht or Osiris, in character. He puts on the mask of a crocodile, an ibis, a lion, or other zoötype of the primary powers, and says to his adversaries: I am the crocodile (= Sebek), or, I am the lion (= Atum), or, I am Ra, the sun, protecting himself with the Uræus serpent, and consequently no evil thing can overthrow me (ch. 32). Repeating ch. 42 was a magical way of escaping from the slaughter which was wrought in Suten-Khen, and the mode of magic was for the deceased in his rebirth to become or to be assimilated to the divine child in his rebirth. He tells the serpent Abur that he is the divine babe, the mighty one. Not a limb of him is without a god. He is not to be grasped by arms or seized by hands. "Not men or gods, the glorified ones or the damned; not generations past, present, or to come, can inflict any injury on him who cometh forth and proceedeth as the eternal child, the everlasting one" (Rit., ch. 42), or as Horus, the son of Isis. These divine characters are assumed by the Manes when he commands his enemies to do his bidding. According to the magical prescriptions, in fighting the devil, or the evil Apap, a figure of the monster was to be moulded in wax with the name inscribed upon it in green (Budge, *Proceedings Soc. of Arch.,* 1866, p. 21). This was to be spat upon many times, spurned with the foot, and then flung into the fire, as a magical mode of casting out the devil. When the Apap reptile is first encountered and addressed in the Ritual it is said, "O one of wax! who takest captive and seizest with violence and livest upon those who are motionless, let me not become motionless before thee" (Rit., ch. 7). This is because the presence of the devouring monster is made tangible by the image of wax which represents the power addressed, that is otherwise invisible. The ideal becomes concrete in the figure that is thus magically employed. It is in this magical sense that the opening chapters of the Ritual are declared to contain the "words of power" that bring about the resurrection and the glory of the Manes in Amenta. This mode of magic is likewise a mode of hypnotism or human magnetism which was universally common with the primitive races, especially the African, but which is only now being timidly touched by modern science. The power of paralyzing and of arresting motion was looked upon as magical potency indeed. Hypnotic power is magical power. This is described as being taken from the serpent as its strength. In one passage (Rit., ch. 149) the serpent is described as he "who paralyzes with his eyes." And previously, in the same chapter, the speaker says to the serpent, "I am the man who covers thy head with darkness, and I am the great magician. Thine eyes have been given to me, and I am glorified through them. Thy strength [or power] is in my grasp." This might be termed a lesson in hypnotism. The speaker becomes a great magician by taking possession of the paralyzing power in the eyes of the serpent. The description seems to imply that there had been a contest betwixt the serpent-charmer and the serpent, and that the man had conquered by wresting the magical power from the reptile. The Manes has much to say about the adversary of souls whom he meets in Amenta. This is the Apap of darkness, of drought and dearth, disease and death. It is the representative of evil in physical phenomena which was translated as a figure from the mythology into the domain of eschatology. In chapter 32 the "Osiris standeth up upon his feet" to face and defy the crocodiles of darkness who devour the dead and carry off the words of power from the glorified in the under-world. They are stopped and turned back when the speaker says: "I am Atum. All things which exist are in my grasp, and those depend on me which are not yet in being. I have received increase of length and depth and fulness of breathing within the domain of my father the great one. He hath given me the beautiful Amenta through which the living pass from death to life" (ch. 32). Thus the Osiris appears, speaks, and acts in the characters of a drama previously extant in the mythology. He comes forth: As the bull of Osiris (ch. 53 A); as the god in lion form, Atum (ch. 54); as the jackal Ap-uat, of Sothis or Polaris; as the divine hawk, Horus (ch. 71); as the sacred hawk (ch. 78); as the lotus of earth (ch. 81); as the bennu-bird or phœnix-soul of Ra (ch. 83); as the shen-shen or hernshaw (ch. 84); as the soul that is an image of the eternal (ch. 85); as the dove or swallow (ch. 86); as the crocodile Sebek (ch. 88); as the khu, or glorified spirit (ch. 91); and many more. But the individual is shown to persist in a human form. He comes forth by day and is living after death in the figure, but not as the mummy, that he wore on earth. He is portrayed staff in hand, prepared for his journey through the under-world (Naville, *Todt.*, Kap. 2, vignette). Also the ka-image of man the immortal is portrayed in the likeness of man the mortal. The human figure is never lost to view through all the phantasmagoria of transformation (Naville, *Todt.*, vignettes to Kap. 2 and 186). From beginning to end of the Ritual we see it is a being once human, man or woman, who is the traveller through the netherworld up the mount of rebirth in heaven, at the summit of the stellar paradise, where the effigy of the earthly personality was ultimately merged in the divine image of the ka, and the mortal puts on immortality in the likeness of the dear old humanity, changed and glorified. This shows the ghost was founded on a human basis, and that it continued the human likeness in proof of its human origin.

Resurrection in the Ritual is the coming forth to day (Peri-em-hru), whether FROM the life on earth or TO the life attainable in the heaven of eternity. The first resurrection is, as it were, an ascension from the tomb in the nether earth by means of the secret doorway. But this coming forth is *in,* not *from,* Amenta, after burial in the upper earth. The deceased had passed through the sepulchre, emerging in the lower earth. He issues from the valley of darkness and the shadow of death. Osiris had been cut to pieces in the lunar and other phenomena by the evil Sut, and the limbs were gathered up and put together by his son and by the mother in Amenta, where he rose again as Horus from the dead. And whatsoever had been postulated of Osiris the mummy in the mythology was repeated on behalf of the Osiris in the eschatology.

Osiris had originated as a god in matter when the powers were elemental, but in the later theology the supreme soul in nature was configurated in a human form. Matter as human was then considered higher than matter unhumanized, and the body as human mummy was superior to matter in external nature. Also the spirit in human form was something beyond an elemental spirit; hence the god as supreme spirit was based, as already shown, upon the human ghost, with matter as the mummy. Osiris as a mummy in Amenta is what we might call the dead body of matter invested with the limbs and features of the human form, as the type to which the elemental powers had attained in Ptah, in Atum, and in the human-featured Horus, which succeeded the earlier representation by means of zoötypes. Osiris is a figure of inanimate nature, personalized as the mummy with a human form and face, whilst being also an image of matter as the physical body of the god. The process applied to the human body first in death was afterwards applied to the god in matter, in the elements, or in the inert condition at the time of the winter solstice, awaiting corpse-like for his transformation or transubstantiation into the young and glorious body of the sun, or spirit of vegetation in the spring. The solar god as the sun of evening or of autumn was the suffering, dying sun, or the dead sun buried in the nether earth. To show this, it was made a mummy of, bound up in the linen vesture without a seam, and thus imaged in a likeness of the dead who bore the mummy form on earth, the unknown being represented by the known. The sun god when descending to Amenta may be said to mummify or *karas* his own body in becoming earthed or, as it were, fleshed in the earth of Ptah. Hence the mummy-type of Ptah, of Atum, and Osiris, each of whom at different stages was the solar god in mummied form when buried in Amenta. It has now to be shown how it was brought about that the final and supreme one god of the Egyptian religion was represented as a mummy in the earth of eternity, and why the mystery of the mummy is the profoundest of all the mysteries of Amenta. An essential element in Egyptian religion was human sympathy with the suffering god, or the power in nature which gave itself, whether as herself or himself, as a living sacrifice, to bring the elements of life to men in light, in water, air, vegetation, fruit, roots, grain, and all things edible. Whence the type was eaten sacramentally at the *thanksgiving meal*. This feeling was pathetically expressed at "the festival of the staves," when crutches were offered as supports for the suffering autumn sun, otherwise the cripple deity Horus, dying down into Amenta and pitifully needing help which the human sympathizers tried to give. Can anything be more pathetic than this address to the sufferer as the sun god in Amenta: "Decree this, O Atum, that if I see thy face [in glory] I shall not be pained by the signs of thy sufferings." Atum decrees. He also decrees that the god will look on the suppliant as his second self (Rit., ch. 173; Naville).

The legend of the voluntary victim who in a passion of divinest pity became incarnate, and was clothed in human form and feature for the salvation of the world, did not originate in a belief that God had manifested once for all as an historic personage. It has its roots in the remotest part. The same legend was repeated in many lands with a change of name, and at times of sex, for the sufferer, but none of the initiated in the esoteric wisdom ever looked upon the Kamite Iusa, or gnostic Horus, Jesus, Tammuz, Krishna, Buddha, Witoba, or any other of the many saviours as historic in personality, for the simple reason that they had been more truly taught. Mythology was earlier than eschatology, and the human victim was preceded by the zoötype; the phenomena first rendered mythically were not manifested in the human sphere. The natural genesis was in another category altogether. The earliest Horus was not incorporated in a human form. He represented that soul of life which came by water to a dried-up, withering world upon the verge of perishing with hunger and with thirst. Here the fish or the first-fruit of the earth was the sign of his incorporation in matter; hence the typical shoot, the green ear, or the branch that were imaged in Child-Horus. The saviour who came by water was Ichthys the fish. The saviour who came in fruit as product of the tree was the Natzer. The saviour who came by spirit was the soul of the sun. This was the earliest rendering of the incorporation of Horus as the primary life and light of the world made manifest in external nature, before the doctrine was applied to biology in the human domain, where Horus came by blood, as the mode of incarnation in the human form. In the later myth Osiris is the deity who suffered as the winter sun, assailed by all the powers of darkness. He also suffered from the drought as imaged in the fire-breathing Apap-reptile, and in other ways as lord of life in water, vegetation, and in various forms of food. This suffering deity or provider was the god in matter. Ra is the god in spirit, Osiris in matter. Not only in the matter of earth, but also in the human form—the form assumed by Horus as the child of earth, or Seb. Osiris, the great sufferer in the dead of winter, was not simply the sun, nor was Osiris dead, however inert in matter, lying dumb in darkness, with non-beating heart. He was the buried life of earth, and hence the god in matter imaged in the likeness of a mummy waiting for the resurrection in Amenta. Such was the physical basis in the mythos of the mystery that is spiritual in the eschatology. Mummy-making in Egypt was far older than the Osirian cult. It was at least as old as Anup the divine embalmer of the dead. Preserving the human mummy perfectly intact was a mode of holding on to the individual form and features as a means of preserving the earthly likeness for identifying the personality hereafter in spirit. The mummy was made on purpose to preserve the physical likeness of the mortal. The risen dead are spoken of in the Ritual as "those who have found their faces." The mummy was a primitive form of the African effigy in which the body was preserved as its own portrait, whereas the ka was intended for a likeness of the spirit or immortal—the likeness in which the just spirit made perfect was to see Osiris in his glory. Both the mummy and the ka were represented in the Egyptian tomb, each with a chamber to itself. From the beginning there had been a visible endeavour to preserve some likeness or memento of the earthly body even when the bones alone could be preserved. Mummy-making in the Ritual begins with collecting the bones and piecing them together, if only in a likeness of the skeleton. It is at this stage that Horus is said to collect the bones of his father Osiris for the resurrection in a future life by means of transubstantiation. The same primitive mode of preparing the mummy is implied when it is said to the solar god on entering the under-world, "Reckon thou thy bones, and set thy limbs, and turn thy face to the beautiful Amenta" (ch. 133, Renouf). Teta, deceased, is thus addressed, "O Teta, thou hast raised up thy head for thy bones, and thou hast raised up thy bones for thy head." Also the hand of Teta is said to be like a wall as support of Horus in giving stability to his bones. Thus the foundation was laid for building the mummy-type as a present image of the person who had passed.

Amongst other types, the Yucatanese made little statues of their fathers. The head was left hollow, so that the ashes of the cremated body might be placed in the skull, as in an urn; this, says Landa, was then covered "with the skin of the occiput taken from the corpse." The custom is akin to that which has been unearthed in the European bone caves, where the skulls of the adult dead are found to have been trepanned, and the bones of little children inserted instead of human ashes. In Sign-language the bones of the child were typical of rebirth in a future life. The desire to live and the longing for a life after death, in earlier times, are inexpressible, and the efforts made to give some kind of expression to the feeling are ineffably pathetic. D'Acugna relates that it was a custom with the South American Indians to preserve and keep the dead bodies of relatives in their homes as long as was possible, so as to have their friends continually before their eyes. For these they made feasts and set out viands before the dead bodies. Here, in passing, we would suggest that in the Egyptian custom as described by both Herodotus and Plutarch it was not the dead mummy that was brought to table as a type of immortality, but the image of the ka, which denoted what the guests would be like after death, and was therefore a cause for rejoicing. Carrying the ka image round the festive board was just a Kamite prototype of the elevation and carrying round of the host for adoration in the Church of Rome. Indeed, the total paraphernalia of the Christian mysteries had been made use of in Egyptian temples. For instance, in one of the many titles of Osiris in all his forms and places he is called *"Osiris in the monstrance"* (Rit., ch. 141, Naville). In the Roman ritual the monstrance is a transparent vessel in which the host or victim is exhibited. In the Egyptian cult Osiris was the victim. The elevation of the host signifies the resurrection of the crucified god, who rose again in spirit from the *corpus* of the victim, now represented by the host. Osiris in the monstrance should of itself suffice to show that the Egyptian Karast (Krst) is the original Christ, and that the Egyptian mysteries were continued by the gnostics and Christianized in Rome. The mode of conveying the oral wisdom to the initiate in the mysteries of young man making was continued in the mystery of mummy making. Whilst the mummy was being prepared for burial, chapters of the Ritual were read to it, or to the conscious ka, by an official who was known as the man of the roll. Every Egyptian was supposed to be acquainted with the formulæ, from having learned them during his lifetime, by which he was to have the use of his limbs and possession of his soul restored to him in death, and to be protected from the dangers of the nether-world. These were repeated to the dead person, however, for greater security, during the process of embalming, and the son of the deceased, or the master of the ceremonies, took care to whisper to the mummy the most mysterious parts, which no living ear might hear with impunity. (Maspero, *The Struggle of Nations,* Eng. trans., pp. 510, 511.)

But it is an error to suppose with some Egyptologists, like M. de Horrack, that the new existence of the deceased was begun in the old earthly body (*Proceed. Society of Bib. Archæology,* vol. vi, March 4, 1884, p. 126). The resurrection of the dead in mummy form may look at first sight as if the old dead corpse had risen from the sepulchre. But the risen is not the dead mummy, it is a type of personality in the shape of the mummy. It is what the Ritual describes as the mummy-form of a god. The Manes prays , "May I too arise and assume the mummied form as a god," that is, as the mummy of Osiris, the form in which Amsu-Horus rose, a type of permanent preservation, but not yet one of the spirits made perfect by possession of the ka. It was this mistake which led to a false idea that the Egyptian held the dogma of a corporeal resurrection of the dead which became one of the doctrines that were fostered into fixity by the A-Gnostic Christians. The Osiris as mortal Manes, or Amsu-Horus as divinity, does rise in the mummy form, but this is in another life and in another world, not as a human being on our earth. It has the look of a physical resurrection in the old body, and so the ignorant misinterpreters mistook it and founded on it a corporeal basis for the future life. In the Christian scheme the buried dead were to rise again in the old physical *corpus* for the last judgment in time at the literal ending of the world. This was another delusion based on the misrendering of the Egyptian wisdom. The dead who rose again in Amenta, which was the ground floor of a future state of existence, also rose again for the judgment; but this took place in the earth of eternity which was mistaken by the Christians for the earth of time, just as they had mistaken the form of the risen sahu for the old body of matter that never was supposed to rise again by those who knew. The earthly mummy of the deceased does not go to heaven, nor does it enter the solar boat, yet the Osiris is told to enter the boat, his reward being the *seat which receives his sahu or spirit mummy* (Rit., ch. 130). Clearly this can only refer to the spiritual body, as the earthly mummy was left on the earth outside the gates of Amenta. Not only is the corporeal mummy not placed on board the boat of souls, the deceased was to be represented by a statue of cedar wood anointed with oil, or, as we might say, *Christified* (134, 9, 10). There is no possible question of a corporeal resurrection. The object, aim, and end of all the spiritualizing processes is to become non-corporeal in the earthly sense—that is, as the Ritual represents it, to defecate into pure spirit. The word sahu (or the mummy) is employed to express the future form as well as the old. But it is a spiritual sahu, the divine mummy. Even the bones and flesh of souls are mentioned, but these are the bones of Osiris, the backbone of the universal frame, and the flesh of Ra. The terms used for the purpose of divinizing are antipodal to any idea of return to corporeality as a material mummy. The mummy of the Manes is a sahu of the glorified spirit. This state of being is attained by the deceased in chapter 73: "I am the *beloved son* of his father. I come to the state of a sahu of the well-furnished Manes." He is said to be mummified in the shape of a divine hawk when he takes the form of Horus (78, 15, 16), not as the earthly mummy in a resurrection on our earth. The resurrection of Osiris was not corporeal. The mummy of the god in matter or mortality rises from the tomb transubstantiated into spirit. So complete is the transformation that he is Osiris bodily changed into Horus as a sahu or spirit. The Egyptians had no doctrine of a physical resurrection of the dead. Though they retained the mummy *as a type of personality,* it was a changed and glorified *form* of the earthly body, the mummy that had attained its feet in the resurrection. It was the Karast mummy, or, word for word and thing for thing, Amsu-Horus was the Kamite Christ who rose up from the mummy as a spirit.

Also it is entirely false to represent the Egyptians as making the mummy and preserving it for the return of the soul into the old earthly body. That is but a shadow of the true idea cast backwards by Christianity. Millions of cats were made into mummies and sacredly preserved around the city of Bubastes, but not with the notion of a bodily resurrection. They were the totems of the great cat clan or its metropolis, the Egyptian "Clan Chattan," which had become symbols or fetishes of religious significance to later times when the totemic mother as the cat, the seer by night, was divinized in the lunar goddess Pasht, and the worshippers embalmed her zoötype, not because they adored the cat, but because the deess herself was the Great Mother typified by the cat. Both the mother and the moon were recognized beyond the cat, which was their totemic zoötype and venerated symbol. Osiris was the mummy of Amenta in two characters; in one he is the khat-mummy lying laid out with corpse-like face upon the funeral couch, in the other he is the mummy risen to his feet and incorporated in the glorious body. These two characters were continued as the *Corpus Christi* and the risen Christ in Rome. Hence in the iconography of the catacombs the Egyptian mummy as Osiris-sahu, and as Horus the new-born solar child, are the demonstrators of the resurrection for the Christian faith, where there is no testimony whatever to an historical event. Any time during the last 10,000 years the mummy made for burial in the tomb was imaged in the likeness of Osiris in Amenta, who, though periodically buried, rose again for ever as the type of life eternal. In making the mummy of Osiris the Egyptians were also making an image of the god who rose again in spirit as Osiris-sahu or as Horus divinized, the risen Christ of the Osirian cult. When the lustrations were performed with water in Tattu and the anointings with oil in Abydos, it was what may be termed a mode of Christifying or making Horus the child of earth into Horus the son of god who became so in his baptism and anointing that were represented in the mysteries. The first Horus was born of the virgin, not begotten. The second Horus was begotten of the father, and the child was made a man of in his baptismal regeneration with the water and with unction, with the oil of a tree or the fat of a bull.

We have now to show that in making the mummy the Egyptians were also making the typical Christ, which is the anointed. The word karas, kares, or karis in Egyptian signifies embalmment, to embalm, to anoint, *to make the mummy. Kreas, creas,* or *chros,* in Greek denotes the human body, a person or carcase, more expressly the flesh of it; *cras,* Gaelic and Irish, the body; Latin, *corpus,* for a dead body; these are all preceded by the word karas or karast, in Egyptian, with the risen mummy for determinative of the meaning. Each body that had been embalmed was karast, so to say, and made into a type of immortality in the likeness of Osiris-sahu or Horus, the prototypal

Christ. It will be made apparent by degrees that the religion of the Chrestoi first began at Memphis with the cultus of the mummy in its two characters, which represented body and spirit, or Ptah in matter and Kheper (Iu-em-hetep) in spirit. Hence the hawk as bird of spirit issuing from the karast-mummy was an image of the resurrection. The origin of the Christ as the anointed or "karast" will explain the connection of the Christ name and that of the Christiani with unction and anointing. Horus the Kamite Christ was the anointed son. The oil upon his face was the sign of his divinity. This supplied a figure of the Christ to Paul when he says that for those who *"put on Christ"* "there can be no male and female, for ye are one [man or mummy] in Christ Jesus" (Gal., iii. 28). The Christ was "put on" metaphorically in the process of anointing which originated with the making of the mummy. Whether the dead were represented by the bones invested with a coating of blood, of flesh-coloured earth, or by the eviscerated and desiccated body that was bandaged in the cloth of a thousand folds, the object was to preserve and perpetuate the deceased in some permanent form of personality. The Egyptians aimed at making the mummy imperishable and incorruptible, as an image of durability and continuity, a type of the eternal, or of Osiris-karast in the likeness of a mummy. Hence the swathe without a seam and of incredible length in which the mummy was enfolded to represent unending duration. Some of these have been unwound to the extent of seven or eight hundred yards, and one of them is described as being a thousand yards in length. But, however long, it was made without a seam. This vesture is alluded to in the chapter of the golden vulture. The chapter is to be inscribed for the protection of the deceased on "the day of his burial in the cloth of a thousand folds" (Rit., ch. 157, 3).

This cloth was the seamless swathe of the Egyptian *karast,* which became the vesture or "coat without a seam woven from the top throughout" (John xix. 23) for the Christ. Even the poorest Egyptian, whose body was steeped in salt and natron and anointed with a little cedar oil, was wrapped in a single piece of linen equally with the mummy whose swathe was hundreds of yards in length, because the funeral vesture of Osiris, his body of matter, was without a seam. The dead are often called "the bandaged ones." On rising from the tomb the deceased exclaims triumphantly, "O my father! my sister! my mother Isis! I am freed from my bandages! I can see! I am one of those who are freed from their bandages to see Seb" (158, 1). Seb denotes the earth, and the Manes is free to visit the earth again, this time as the ghost or double of his former self. Covering the corpse with the transparent tahn, or golden gum, was one way of turning the dead body into a type of the spiritual body which was imaged as the glorified. One cannot doubt that this was a mode of showing the transformation of the Osirian dead mummy into the luminous body called the sahu of Osiris when he was transfigured but still retained the mummy form in Amsu-Horus at his rising from the sepulchre. Mummies buried in the tomb at Medum had been thus enveloped. This was one form of investiture alluded to in the Ritual as distinguished from the mummy bandages. One of these mummies is now to be seen in the Royal College of Surgeons.

"The mode of embalming," says Prof. Petrie, "was very singular. The body was shrunk, wrapped up in linen cloth, then modelled all over with resin (or tahn) into the natural shape and plumpness of the living figure, completely restoring all the fullness of the form, and this was wrapped round with a few turns of the finest gauze." (Petrie, *Medum,* Intro., ch. 2, pp. 17 and 18.) There was no coffin present in the tomb. The mummy thus invested with the tahn had been buried in this primitive kind of glass case, in which the form and features could be seen either directly or by means of the modelling. The tahn, gum or resin, as a natural product from the tree, preceded glass, and would be fashioned for the earlier monstrance. Remodelling the dead in the likeness of the living form by means of the pellucid tahn is a mode of making the glorified body on earth that was imaged by the sahu in Amenta, and thus the mummy here attains the twofold type of the Osiris Khat, or corpse, and the Osiris-sahu, or the glorified in spirit. In the Christian agglomerate of Egyptian doctrines and dogmas, rites and symbols, the pellucid tahn may, we think, be recognized in the sacred monstrance of the Roman ritual. This is a show-case in which the host or *Corpus Christi* is placed to be uplifted and exhibited. The eye of Horus is yet visible in the *lanula* or crescent-shaped crystal of the monstrance which holds the consecrated bread. The name of this show-case is derived from the Latin *monstrare,* "to show," and this had been the object of the mummy makers in employing the transparent tahn.

In the eschatological or final phase of the doctrine, to make the mummy was to make the typical anointed, also called the Messu, the Messiah, and the Christ. Mes or mas, in the hieroglyphics, signifies to anoint and to steep, as in making the mummy, and messu in Egyptian means the anointed; whence Iah the Messu becomes Messiah in Hebrew. There was a previous form of the anointed in the totemic mysteries of young man making. When the boy attained the age of puberty he was made into the anointed one at the time of his initiation into the way of a man with a woman. It was a custom with certain Inner African tribes to slit the urethra of the boy and lubricate the member with palm oil. This was a primitive way of making the anointed at puberty. Australian aborigines are also known to slit the prepuce cover for the same purpose. At this stage of the mystery the anointed one is the adult youth who has attained the rank of begetter full of grace and favour, or is khemt, as it was rendered in Egyptian. Tertullian claims that the name of the Christians came from the unction received by Jesus Christ. This is in perfect keeping with the derivation of the typical Christ from the mummy which was anointed so abundantly with oil in its embalmment. It is said of the woman who anointed Jesus in Bethany, "In that she poured the ointment upon my body, she did it *to prepare me for my burial*" (Matt. xxvi. 12). She was preparing the mummy after the manner of Anup the embalmer, who prepared Osiris for his burial and resurrection. But it was only as a dead mummy and not a living man that the gnostic Jesus could have been embalmed for burial.

We now proceed to show that Christ the anointed is none other than the Osiris-karast, and that the karast mummy risen to its feet as Osiris-sahu was the prototypical Christ. Unhappily, these demonstrations cannot be made without a wearisome mass of detail. And we are bound for the bottom this time. Dr. Budge, in his book on the mummy, tells his readers that the Egyptian word for mummy is *ges,* which signifies to wrap up in bandages. But he does not point out that ges or kes, to embalm the corpse or make the mummy, is a reduced or abraded form of an earlier word, karas (whence krst for the mummy). The original word written in hieroglyphics is krst, whence kas, to embalm, to bandage, to knot, to make the mummy or karast (Birch, *Dictionary of the Hieroglyphics,* pp. 415-416; Champollion, *Gram. Egyptienne,* 86). The word krs denotes the embalmment of the mummy, and the krst, as the mummy, was made in the process of preparation by purifying, anointing, and embalming. To karas the dead body was to embalm it, to bandage it, to make the mummy. The mummy was the Osirian *Corpus Christi,* prepared for burial as the laid-out dead, the karast by name. When raised to its feet, it was the risen mummy, or sahu. The place of embalmment was likewise the krs. Thus the process of making the mummy was to karas, the place in which it was laid is the karas, and the product was the krst, whose image is the upright mummy = the risen Christ. Hence the name of the Christ, Christos in Greek, Chrestus in Latin, for the anointed, was derived, as the present writer previously suggested, from the Egyptian word krst. Karas also signifies the burial-place, and the word modifies into Kâs or Châs. Kâsu the "burial place" was a name of the 14th Nome in Upper Egypt. A god Kâs is mentioned three or four times in the Book of the Dead, "the god Kâs who is in the Tuat" (ch. 40). This was a title of the mummy Osiris in the funerary dwelling. In one passage Kâs is described as the deliverer or saviour from all mortal needs. In "the chapter of raising the body" (178) it is said of the deceased that he had been hungry and thirsty (on earth), but he will never hunger or thirst any more, "for Kâs delivers him" and does away with wants like these. That is, in the resurrection. Here the name of the god Osiris-Kâs written at full is Osiris the Karast—the Egyptian Christ. Not only is the risen mummy or sahu called the karast, Osiris as lord of the bier is the Neb-karast equivalent to the later Christ the Lord, and the lord of the bier is god of the resurrection from the house of death. The karast is literally the god or person who has been mummified, embalmed, and anointed or christified. Anup the baptizer and embalmer of the dead for the new life was the preparer of the karast-mummy. As John the Baptist is the founder of the Christ in baptism, so Anup was the *christifier* of the moral Horus, he on whom the holy ghost descended as a bird when the Osiris made his transformation in the marriage mystery of Tattu (Rit., ch. 17). We read in the funeral texts of Anup being "Suten tu hetep, Anup, neb tser khent neter ta *krast*-ef em set" (Birch, *Funeral Text,* 4th Dynasty). "Suten hept tu Anup tep-tuf khent neter ha am ut neb tser *krast* ef em as-ef en kar neter em set Amenta" (Birch, *Funeral Stele of Ra-Khepr-Ka,* 12th Dynasty). Anup gives embalmment, krast; he is lord over the place of embalmment, the kras; the lord of embalming (krast), who, so to say, makes the "krast." The process of embalmment is to make the mummy. This was a type of immortality or rising again. Osiris is krast, or embalmed and mummified for the resurrection. Passage into life and light is made for the karast-dead through the embalmment of the good Osiris (Rit., ch. 162)—that is, through his being karast as the mummy type. Thus the Egyptian krast was the pre-Christian Christ, and the pictures in the Roman Catacombs preserve the proof. The passing of the karast into the Christ is depicted in the gnostic iconography. It is in the form of a child bound up in the swathings of a diminutive Egyptian mummy, with the halo and cross of the four quarters round its head, which show its solar origin. It is the divine infant which has the head of Ra in the Ritual who says, "I am the babe; I renew myself, and I grow young again" (chs. 42 and 43). The karast mummy is the type of resurrection in the Roman Catacombs because the karast was the prototypal Christ. It is the Egyptian karast as thing and word that supplied and will explain the Greek Christ, Christos, Krstos, or Latin Chrestus,

The Mummy-Babe

and account for the *Corpus Christi,* the anointed, the Saviour, doctrinally, typically, actually in every way except historically, and of that the karast, Krstos, or Christ is entirely independent. "Henceforth," said a dignitary of the Church of England the other day, "Christianity has done with the metaphysical Christ." But there is no physical Christ except the karast mummy, which was Osiris when laid out and lying down in death, and Horus of the resurrection standing up as Amsu risen from the sepulchre, having the whip hand over all the powers of darkness and the adversaries of his father.

Say what you will or believe what you may, there is no other origin for Christ the anointed than for Horus the karast or anointed son of god the father. There is no other origin for a Messiah as the anointed than for the Masu or anointed. Finally, then, the mystery of the mummy is the mystery of the Christ. As Christian, it is allowed to be for ever inexplicable. As Osirian, the mystery can be explained. It is one of the mysteries of Amenta, with a more primitive origin in the rites of totemism.

We now claim sufficient warrant for affirming that Christ the anointed is a mystical figure which originated as the Egyptian mummy in the twofold character of Osiris in his death and in his resurrection: as Osiris, or mortal Horus, the karast; and Osiris-sahu, or Horus divinized as the anointed son. The Christ or karast still continues to be made when the sacrament of extreme unction is administered to the dying as a Roman Catholic rite. Though but a shadow of the primitive reality, it perpetuates the "sacred mystery" of converting the corpse into the sahu, the transubstantiation of the inert Osiris by descent of Ra; the mortal Horus, child of the mother, into Horus the anointed son of god the father. "Extreme unction," the seventh of the holy sacraments, is indeed a Christian rite.

It will now be necessary to give an account of certain other mysteries of Amenta and doctrines of the Ritual. The Egyptians celebrated ten great mysteries on ten different nights of the year. The first was the night of the evening meal (literally the last supper), and the laying of offerings on the altar. It is the night of provisioning the Lord's table. Osiris had been overcome by Sut and the Sebau, who had once more renewed their assault upon Un-nefer when they were defeated and exterminated by his faithful followers. Therefore this was also the night of the great battle when the moon god Taht and the children of light annihilated the rebellious powers of darkness. On the second night the overthrown Tat-Cross, with Osiris in it, or on it, was again erected by Horus, Prince of Sekhem, in the region of Tattu, where the holy spirit Ra descends upon the mummy and the twain become united for the resurrection. On the third night the scene is in Sekhem; the mystery is that of the blind Horus or of Horus in the dark, who here receives his sight. It is also the mystery of dawn upon the coffin of Osiris. We might call it the mystery of Horus the mortal transfiguring into Horus the immortal. On the fourth night the four pillars are erected with which the future kingdom of god the father is to be founded. It is called "the night of erecting the flag-staffs of Horus, and of establishing him as the heir of his father's property." The fifth scene is in the region of Rekhet, and the mystery is that of the two sisters with Isis watching in tears over her brother Osiris, and brooding above the dead body to give it the warmth of new life. On the sixth night the glorious ones are judged, the evil dead are parted off, and joy goeth its round in Thinnis. This is the night of the great festival named *Ha-k-er-a,* or "Come thou to me," in which the blending of the two souls was solemnized as a glorious mystery by a festival at which there was much eating and drinking. The mystery of the seventh night was that of the great judgment on the highway of the damned, when the suit was closed against the rebels who had failed once more and were ignominiously defeated. After the verdict comes the avengement. The eighth is the night of the great hoeing in Tattu, when the associates of Sut are massacred and the fields are manured with their blood. The ninth is called "the night of hiding the body of him who is supreme in attributes." The mystery is that of collecting the remains of Osiris, whose body was mutilated and scattered piecemeal by Sut, and of *hiding it.* The mystery on the tenth night presents a picture of Anup, the embalmer, the anointer, or christifier of the mummy. This is in Rusta, the place of resurrection from Amenta. It may be the series is not in exact order, but that does not interfere with the nature of the mysteries. In each of the ten acts of the drama the suffering Osiris and the triumph over all his adversaries are portrayed as mysteries in a prototypal miracle-play or drama that was held to be divine. The chapter of these ten mysteries was recited penitentially for the purification of the Manes and the coming forth after death (Rit., ch. 18, rubric). With this we may compare the fact that the Jewish new year is ushered in with ten days of penitence.

The altar or communion-table thus provisioned was the coffin lid. This also was continued in the ritual of Rome, for it is a fact that the earliest Christian altar was a coffin. According to Blunt's *Dictionary of Doctrinal and Historical Theology* (p. 16), this was a hollow chest, on the lid or *mensa* of which the Eucharist was celebrated. This, as Egyptian, was the coffin of Osiris that constituted the altar on which the provisions were laid in Sekhem for the eucharistic meal. Hence the resurrection is described as "dawn upon the coffin of Osiris." Therefore he rose in spirit from the mummy in the coffin, beneath the lid which constituted the table. This was the body supposed to be eaten as the Eucharist, which was represented by the provisions that were laid upon the altar for the sacramental meal. The first of the ten great mysteries is the mystery of the eucharist, and we find that the primitive Christian liturgies are all and wholly restricted to the eucharist as the one primordial sacrament of the Christian Church. The first of the Osirian mysteries is the primary Christian sacrament. "Provisioning the altar" was continued by the Church of Rome. "The mysteries laid upon the altar" which preceded" the communion of the body and blood of Christ" were then eaten in the eucharistic meal (Neale, Rev. J. M., *The Liturgies,* Introd., p. 33). Thus we see in the *camera obscura* that the provisions laid on the altar or table represented the flesh and blood of the victim about to be eaten sacramentally. The night of the things that were laid upon the altar is the night of the great sacrifice, with Osiris as the victim. The things laid on the altar for the evening meal represented the body and blood of the Lord. These, as the bread and wine, or flesh and beer, were transelemented or transubstantiated by the descent of Ra the holy spirit, which quickened and transformed the mummy Osiris into the risen sahu, the unleavened bread into the leavened, the water into wine. Osiris, the sacrifice, was the giver of himself as "the food which never perishes" (Rit., ch. 89).

The Christian liturgies are reckoned to be the "most pure sources of eucharistical doctrine." And liturgy appears to have been the groundwork of the Egyptian ritual. It is said by one of the priests (Rit., ch. 1), "I am he who reciteth the liturgies of the soul who is lord of Tattu"—that is, of Osiris who establishes a soul for ever in conjunction with Ra the holy spirit in the mysteries of Amenta. In one character Osiris was eaten as the Bull of Eternity, who gave his flesh and blood as sustenance for humanity, and who was the divine providence as the provider of food. The eating of the mother was also continued in the eucharist, Osiris being of both sexes. This was typically fulfilled in one way by converting the bull into an ox. The duality was also imaged in the bread and beer or wine, which is the mother blood in a commuted guise. It is said of the body that was eaten in "the Roman mysteries" that it is "the body which bestows on us, *out of its wounds,* immortality and life, and the beatific vision with the angels, and food and drink, and life and light, the very bread of life, the true light, eternal life, Christ Jesus." "Wherefore this entrance symbolizes at the same time both the second advent of Christ and His sepulture, for it is He who will be our beatific vision in the life to come," as Horus of the second sight, all of which was portrayed of Osiris and fulfilled. (Neale, *The Liturgies,* Introd., p. 30.) Blood sacrifice from the beginning was an offering of life, hence the life offering. When the mother was the victim her blood was offered as life to the ancestral spirits. It was also life to the brotherhood, and partaking of it in communion constituted the sacrament. So in the Christian Eucharist the blood is taken to be the life, and is partaken of as the life, the "life of the world" (Neale, *Liturgy of Basil the Great*), "the divine life that is the life everlasting, the new life that is for ever" (Neale, *Liturgy of St. Chrysostom,* ii). The bread broken in the Christian sacrament represents a body that was "*broken, immolated, and divided.*" This does not apply to the body of Jesus, according to the "history." But it does apply to the body of Osiris, which was "broken, immolated, and divided" by Sut, who tore it into fourteen fragments. The altar table, or coffin lid, was provisioned with these parts of the broken body to be typically eaten as the Eucharist on the night "when there are at the coffin the thigh, the head, the heel, and the leg of Un-nefer." Moreover, when the mother was eaten as the sacrifice, the flesh and blood were warm with life. She was not eaten in cold blood. It was the same with the Meriah of the Kolarians, and also with the totemic animal. The efficacy lay in the flesh being eaten alive, and the blood being drunk whilst it was warm with life which constituted the "living sacrifice." This type of sacrifice was also continued in the Christian Eucharist. *Hot water was at one time poured into the chalice with the wine at the consecration of the elements, to give it the warmth of life* (Neale, *Liturgy of St. Chrysostom,* p. 120.) Even the act of tearing the flesh of the victim's body piecemeal is piously perpetuated by the breaking instead of cutting the bread for the Christian sacrament. The lights upon the coffin of Osiris are represented in the Roman ritual by a double taper, the *dikerion,* reputed to signify "*the advent of the Holy Spirit,*" which corresponds to the descent of Ra the holy spirit on the inert body of Osiris in Tattu, where the two souls are blended to become one in Horus of the resurrection.

The flabellum or fan is a mystical emblem in the Egyptian mysteries. For one thing, it signified the shade or spirit. Fans are frequently portrayed for souls of a primitive type. (Birch, *Trans. Soc. Bib. Arch.,* vol. VIII, p. 386.) Souls burning in the hells are imaged by flabella. These fans were brought on in the Oriental Church. In the Clementine liturgy they are ordered to be made of peacocks' feathers (Neale, p. 76, Introd., pp. 29, 30). They are called fans of the Holy Spirit, and were carried in procession with the "veil that was wrapped about the body of the Lord Jesus" like the folds of gauze that were wrapped round the mummy at Medum. But the fan or shade = spirit had been reduced in status, and was then used as a flapper for whisking the flies away from the sacrifice (Durandus, iv, 33-8; Neale, Introd., p. 29). It is not pretended that the second advent is historical, nevertheless it is portrayed in the mystery of the Eucharist by the descent of the Holy Spirit. The second advent is the coming forth of Horus in spirit from the mummy or corpse which was his image in the human form. The first is in being made flesh and putting on the likeness of mortality, the second is in making his transformation into a spirit, as the type of immortality. The marriage of Cupid and Psyche is a fable that was founded on this union of the two souls which we have traced in the Ritual as the soul in matter, or the human soul, and the soul in spirit. Cupid, under another name, is Eros, whilst Eros and Anteros are a form of the double Horus, Eros in spirit, Anteros in matter, and the blending of the two in the mysteries was the marriage of Cupid and Psyche in the mystery of Tattu. Now here is another of those many mysteries which have no origin in historic Christianity. The agapé was celebrated in connection with the eucharist. This was not founded at the time of the Last Supper, nevertheless it was held to be a Christian sacrament. Paul in speaking of the love-feast at Corinth as a scene of drunken revelry (I. Cor. ii. 20-22), recognizes the celebration of two suppers, which he is desirous of having kept apart, one for the church, and one for the house. These two are the eucharist and the agapé. Ecclesiastical writers differ as to which of the two ought to be solemnized first, but there is no question that two were celebrated in connection with each other. In his attack on the licentiousness of the Christian agapé Tertullian asks the wives, "Will not your husbands know what it is you secretly take before other food?" and again, "Who will without anxiety endure her absence all night long at the Pascal solemnities?" "Who will without some suspicion of his own let her go to attend that Lord's banquet which they defame?" (Keating, Y. F., *The Agape and the Eucharist,* p. 70.) As Egyptian, we can identify the two, and thus infer the order in which they stood to each other. Whether both were called suppers or not, the Egyptians celebrated the last supper of Osiris on the last night of the old year, and the mesiu, or the evening meal, on the first night of the new year. And this duality was maintained by the gnostics and continued by the Christians. These are two of the Osirian mysteries, and in the list of the ten great mysteries there are two nights of provisioning the altar—that is, two nights of a feast or memorial supper. One is held in Annu, the other in Sekhem, with the resurrection in Tattu coming between the two. In Sekhem the blind Horus receives his sight, or his beatific vision of the divine glory, which was seen when he had pierced the veil hawk-headed in the image of Ra. Provisioning the altar in Sekhem is designated "dawn upon the coffin of Osiris" (Rit., ch. 18). The eucharist was a form of the mortuary meal in which the death of Osiris was commemorated by the eating of the body and the drinking of the blood. The agapé, or phallic feast, was a mode of celebrating the re-arising of Horus, Prince of Sekhem, as portrayed by the re-erection of the Tat. This accounts for the sexual orgie of the agapé, a primitive form of which was acted by the Eskimo in the festival of reproduction. In their mysteries this was the reproduction of food. In the Egyptian it was the regeneration and resurrection of the soul that was celebrated at the agapé. The death, of course, came first. This was on the night of the great sacrifice, and the eucharist was eaten in commemoration. Then followed the triumph in Tattu and the regenesis of the soul, which was acted by the "holy kiss" or blending of the sexes in the feast of love, as a dramatic rendering of this union betwixt the human nature and divine, or of the brother and sister, Shu and Tefnut. In the totemic mysteries of young man making begettal was included in the *modus operandi,* and in this the women invoked the spirit of the male for the new birth. The phallic festival of promiscuous intercourse still survived when the mysteries became religious, whether in Egypt, Greece, or Rome. In these Osiris was resuscitated as Horus the only begotten son, the women being the begetters or regenerators. In the evocations of Isis and Nephthys we hear them calling on the lost Osiris to come back to them in the person of the son. They plead that the lamp of life may be relighted, or more literally that the womb may be replenished. "Come to thine abode, god An," they cry. "Beloved of the Adytum! Come to Kha" (a name of phallic significance), "oh, fructifying Bull." This is in the beneficent formulæ that were made by the two divine sisters, Isis and Nephthys, to effect the resurrection of Osiris, which are said to have been composed by them on the twenty-fifth day of the month Koiak, December 22nd. They are magical evocations of the god addressed to the inert Osiris, who is caused to rise again by Isis in his ithyphallic form. Most pathetic in its primitiveness is the picture of the two divine sisters, or mothers, Isis and Nephthys, watching by the dead or inert brother who is Osiris in death and Horus in his resurrection, crooning their incantations, brooding bird-like over the germ of life in the egg, and breathing out the very soul of their own life in yearning for him, until the first token of returning consciousness is given, the earliest sign of the resurrection is made in response to the vitalizing warmth of their affection. These evocations follow the night of "the last supper" and the battle with Sut and the Sebau. "Oh, come to thine abode!" the two dear sisters cry. "Come to thy sister! Come to thy wife! Come to thy spouse!" they plead whilst stretching out their longing arms for his embrace. "Oh, excellent Sovereign, come to thine abode. Rejoice; all thine enemies are annihilated. Thy two sisters are near to thee, protecting thy funeral couch, calling thee in weeping, thou who art prostrate on thy funeral bed. Thou seest our tender solicitude. Speak to us, Supreme Ruler, our Lord. Chase away all the anguish which is in our hearts." These in the funeral scenes are the two women watching in the tomb (*Records,* vol. ii., 119). Then was the only son of god begotten of the holy spirit Ra. The "pair of souls" were blended in the Horus of a soul that was to live for ever, or to taste eternal life. The marriage rite was acted, and the marriage feast was celebrated in this prototypal ceremony that was continued in the Agapé of the Osirian and the Christian cult.

The Christian dogma of a physical resurrection founded on the historic fact of a dead corpse rising from the grave can be explained as one of the Kamite mysteries which were reproduced as miracles in the Gospels. If we take the original representation in the solar mythos, the sun in the under-world, the diminished, unvirile, impotent or suffering sun was imaged as Ans-Ra, the solar god bound up in linen, as the mummified Osiris. The type remained for permanent use, but when the transformation had been effected the mummy vanished. The sepulchre was empty. The sun of winter or of night did not remain in Hades. Neither did it come forth as the dead body or unbreathing mummy of Osiris. Osiris, the hidden god in the earth of Amenta, does not come forth at all except in the person of the risen Horus, who is the manifestor for the ever-hidden father. To issue thus he makes his transfiguration which constitutes the mystery, not the miracle, of the resurrection. Osiris defecates and spiritualizes. The mummy as *corpus* is transubstantiated into the sahu, the mortal Horus into the immortal, and the physical mummy disappears. But it did not disappear because the living Horus rose up and walked off with the dead body of Osiris. When the transformation took place the type was changed in a moment, in the "twinkling of an eye." The mummy Osiris transubstantiates, and makes his transformation into Osiris-sahu. As the Ritual expresses it, "he is renewed in an instant" in this second birth (ch. 182). The place was empty where the mummy had lain upon the bier, and the body was not found. This change is described when it is said in the litany of Ra, he "raises his soul and hides his body." Thus the body was hidden in the resurrection of the soul. "Hiding his body" is consequently a name of Horus, "emanating from Hes" as a babe in the renewal of Osiris. Concealing the body of dead matter was one way of describing the transubstantiation in texture and the transfiguration in form. This was one of the greater mysteries.

When Horus rent the veil of the tabernacle he had become hawk-headed, and consequently was a spirit in the divine likeness of Ra the holy ghost. Therefore the tabernacle was the body or mummy, "the veil of flesh" (Neale, *Liturgy of St. James,* pp. 46-7) from which he had emerged. The speaker in the Ritual says, "I am the hawk in the tabernacle, and I pierce through the veil"—that is, when he is invested with the soul of Horus and disrobes himself of the mummy (Rit., ch. 71, Renouf) or the veil which represented the flesh, as did the veil of gauze when folded round the mummy in the pyramid at Medum. The "holy veil" was carried in the Christian mysteries, together with the "holy gifts" and "fans of the spirit," and this is said to represent "the veil that was wrapped about the body of the Lord Jesus" (Neale, *The Liturgies,* Introd., p. 30, "Prayer of the Veil.") This (in the *Liturgy of St. James,* Neale, p. 46) is "the veil of the flesh of Christ," therefore the veil of the body or temple of the spirit that was rent in the resurrection by Horus when he "pierced through the veil." He rends or pierces through the veil, saying, "I am the hawk in the tabernacle, and I pierce through the veil. Here is Horus!" who comes forth to the day as a hawk (ch. 71). In the form of a divine hawk the risen one is revealed and goes forth as a spirit. In the Gospel the loud cry is immediately followed by the going forth as a spirit. "And behold, the veil of the sanctuary was rent in twain from the top to the bottom. And the earth did quake, and the rocks were rent and the tombs were opened, and many bodies of the saints that had fallen asleep were raised" (Matt. xxvii. 45-53). Horus now takes his seat at the table of his father Osiris, with those who eat bread in Annu. He gives breath to the faithful dead who are raised by him, he who is the resurrection and the life. The same scene is apparently reproduced by John. Jesus makes his apparition to the disciples at what looks like the evening meal, although the meal is not mentioned. Jesus is the breather. "He breathed on them and said, Receive ye the Holy Spirit"—which in the Ritual is the breath of Atum-Ra, the father, imparted by Iu the son, or by Horus to the faithful dead. The scene has now been changed from Amenta to the earth of Seb by those who made "historic" mockery of the Egyptian Ritual, and sank the meaning out of sight where it has been so long submerged. More of this hereafter. Enough at present to indicate the way that things are tending. In this divine drama natural realities are represented with no perniciously destructive attempt to conceal the characters under a mask of history. Majestically moving in their own might of pathetic appeal to human sympathy, they are simply represented for what they may be worth when rightly apprehended. But so tremendous was this tragedy in the Osirian mysteries, so heart-melting the legend of divinest pity that lived on with its rootage in Amenta and its flowerage in the human mind, that an historic travesty has kept the stage and held the tearful gaze of generation after generation for nineteen hundred years.

Amenta, the earth of eternity, is the land of the mysteries where Taht, the moon god, in the nether night was the great teacher of the sacred secrets together with the seven wise masters. The passage through Amenta is a series of initiations for the Osiris deceased. He is inducted into the mysteries of Rusta (1, 7, 9), the mysteries of the Tuat (130, 27), the mysteries of Akar (148, 2, 3). He knows the mysteries of Nekhen (113, 1). Deceased invokes the god who dwells in all mysteries (14, 1); deceased learns the mystery of the father god Atum, who becomes his own son (15, 46); he is the mysterious of form (17, 91) and the mysterious of face, like Osiris (133, 9). "I shine in the egg," says the deceased, "in the land of the mysteries." Chapter 162 contains the most secret, most sacred, the greatest of all mysteries. Its name is the book of the hidden dwelling—that is, the book of Amenta or the ritual of the resurrection. Obscure as these mysteries may seem, on account of the form—that of dramatic monologue and soliloquy—and the brevity of statement, we can recognize enough to know that these are the originals of all the other "mysteries," Gnostic, Kabalistic, Masonic, or Christian. The dogma of the incarnation was an Egyptian mystery. Baptismal regeneration, transfiguration, transubstantiation, the resurrection and ascension, were all Egyptian mysteries. The mystery of an ever-virgin mother; the mystery of a boy at twelve years of age transforming suddenly into an adult of thirty years, and then becoming one with the father, as it had been earlier in the mysteries of totemism; the mystery in which the dead body of Osiris is transubstantiated into the living Horus by descent of the bird-headed holy spirit; the mystery of a divine being in three persons, one of which takes flesh on earth as the human Horus, to become a mummy as Osiris in Amenta, and to rise up from the dead in spirit as Ra in heaven. These and other miracles of the Christian faith were already extant among the mysteries of Amenta. But the meaning of the mysteries could only be known whilst the genuine gnosis was authentically taught. This had ceased when the Christian Sarcolatræ took possession of the "Word-made-flesh," and literalized the mystical drama as a more tangible-looking human history, that was set forth in the very latest of the Gospels as a brand-new revelation sent from God, and personally conducted in Palestine by the "historic Jesus."

When Bendigo, the pugilist, became converted he proposed to take up preaching as his new profession. And when it was objected that he didn't know anything and couldn't read or write, he replied that he "expected to pick up a good deal by listening round." So was it with the early Christians. They could neither read nor write the ancient language, but they picked up a good deal by listening round. "You have your man upon the cross," said one of them to the Romans; "why do you object to ours?" Their man upon the cross being identical with Osiris-Tat or the ass-headed Iu. It is said of Taht as a teacher of the mysteries, "And now behold Taht in the secret of his mysteries. He maketh purifications and endless reckonings, piercing the firmament and dissipating the storms around him and so it cometh to pass that the Osiris hath reached every station," and, we may add, attained his immortality through the teachings communicated in the mysteries of Taht (Rit., ch. 130, Renouf). The 148th chapter of the Ritual recounts some of the most secret mysteries. It was written to furnish the gnosis or knowledge necessary for the Manes to get rid of his impurities and acquire perfection in the "bosom of Ra" the holy spirit.

At the entrance to the mysterious valley of the Tuat there is a walled-up doorway, the first door of twelve in the passage of Amenta. These twelve are described in the Book of Hades as twelve divisions corresponding to the twelve hours of darkness during the nocturnal journey of the sun. The first division has no visible door of entrance. The rest have open doors, and the twelfth has double doors. It is hard to enter, but made easy for the exit into the land of eternal life. Here is the mystery: how to enter where there is no door and the way is all unknown? It is explained to the Manes how divine assistance is to be obtained. When the stains of life on earth are effaced the strength is given for forcing the entrance where there is no door, and in that power the Manes penetrates with (or as) the god (Rit., ch. 148, 2, 3). Thus Horus was the door in the darkness, the way where no entrance was seen, the life portrayed for the Manes in death. The secret entrance was one of the mysteries of Amenta. It was known as "the door of the stone," which name was given to their Necropolis by the people at Siut, the stone that revolved when the magical word or "open sesame" was spoken. The entrance to the Great Pyramid was concealed by means of a movable flagstone that turned on a pivot which none but the initiated could detect. This, when tilted up, revealed a passage four feet in breadth and three and a half feet in height into the interior of the building. This was a mode of entrance applied to Amenta as the blind doorway that was represented by the secret portal and movable stone of later legends. The means of entrance through what appeared to be a blank wall was by knowing the secret of the nicely adjusted stone, and this secret was communicated to the initiates with the pass-word in the mysteries.

Horus begins his work by carrying out the divine plans of his father Osiris on earth. He makes firm the battlements to protect Osiris against the assaults of all the powers of darkness. He makes the word of Osiris truth against his enemies. He opposes Sut, his father's adversary, to the death. He makes war upon the evil Apap, that old serpent, and overthrows the powers that rise up in rebellion, which are called the rebels in the Ritual, who are ever doomed to failure in the fight betwixt them and the father, who is now represented by Horus his beloved son, Horus of the resurrection, who is himself the door in death as the means of entrance to Amenta. He covers the naked body of the breathless one. He opens the fountains of refreshment for the god of the non-beating heart (ch. 1). He wages battle on the "eater of the arm" (ch. 11) and the black boar Sut, two types of the power of dearth, death, and darkness. He protects his father from the devouring crocodiles (ch. 32), from the serpents Rerek, Seksek, and Haiu, also from the apshait, an insect that preys upon the buried mummy (chs. 33, 34, 36). He says, "I have come myself and delivered the god in his dismembered condition. I have healed the trunk and fastened the shoulder and made firm the leg" (ch. 102), *i.e.*, in reconstructing the mummy. He restores to Osiris his sceptre, his pedestal, and his staircase from the tomb (ch. 128). He says, "I have done according to the command that I should come forth in Tattu, to see Osiris" (ch. 78). He has kept the commandment that was given him by the father. The Manes in Amenta tell of "the fortunes of that great son whom the father loveth," and how he had "pierced Sut to the heart," and how they had "seen the death." They also tell of the "divine plans which were carried out by Horus, in the absence of his father," when he represented Osiris on the earth (ch. 78). With his work accomplished, both on earth and in Amenta, Horus of the resurrection goes to see his father, and they embrace each other. Horus addresses his father, here called Ra-Unnefer-Osiris-Ra. He exclaims: "Hail, Osiris! I am thy son Horus; I have come. I have avenged thee. I have struck down thy enemies. I have destroyed all that was wrong in thee. I have killed him who assailed thee. I stretched forth my hand for thee against thy adversaries. I have brought thee the companions of Sut with chains upon them. I have ploughed for thee the fields. I have irrigated for thee thy land. I have hoed for thee the ground. I have built for thee the lakes of water. I have turned up the soil of thy possessions. I have made sacrifices for thee of thy adversaries. I have made sacrifices for thee of thy cattle and thy victims. I have bound thy enemies in their chains. I have sowed for thee wheat and barley in the field of Aarru. I have mowed them there for thee. I have glorified thee. I have anointed thee with the offering of holy oil. I have established for thee thy offerings of food on the earth for ever." (Rit., ch. 173, excerpt from Naville's rendering in Renouf's Book of the Dead.) All this and more he claims to have done. "I have given thee Isis and Nephthys." The two divine sisters, the consorts of Osiris, the mothers and protectors of Horus, are thus brought back by him to the father. They have been with him from the beginning on earth in the hall of Seb; with him in his conception and incarnation by Isis and his nursing by Nephthys. They were his ministering angels, in attendance on him as protectors from the cut-throat Sut, or the monster Apap, who sought to slay the child or destroy it in the egg; with him in the agony of his blindness when torn and bleeding in the garden of Pa; with him as watchers in the tomb until he wakes; with him in his resurrection from Amenta. They are with him when he ascends to the father as conqueror of death, as ruler of the double earth and lord of the kingdom which he and his disciples or children have established for ever. The work attributed to Horus, the divine exemplar, was to be fulfilled by his followers in the double earth of time and eternity. That was the object of the mysteries. It is in the character of the divine Horus that the human Nebseni says to Osiris, "Thou one God, behold me. I am Horus thy son. I have fought for thee. I have fought on thy behalf for justice, truth, and righteousness. I have overcome thine adversaries." He also claims to have done the things that Horus did as set forth in the writings or represented in the drama, and thus fulfilled the ideal of self-sacrificing sonship in very reality, making the word of Osiris truth against his enemies. And it was but the word even when personified, which to be of any actual efficacy must be made truth in human life, in conduct, and in character (Pap. of Nebseni, Rit., ch. 173, Budge).

If there be any revelation or inspiration in a great ideal dramatically portrayed, the Egyptians found it in their divine model set forth in Horus:

> Horus the saviour, who was brought to birth
> As light in heaven and sustenance on earth.
> Horus in spirit, verily divine,
> Who came to turn the water into wine.
> Horus, who gave his life, and sowed the seed
> For men to make the bread of life indeed.
> Horus the comforter, who did descend
> In human fashion as the heavenly friend.
> Horus the word, the founder in his youth.
> Horus, fulfiller as the word made truth.
> Horus the lord and leader in the fight
> Against the dark powers of the ancient night.
> Horus the sufferer with his cross bowed down,
> Who rose at Easter with his double crown.
> Horus the pioneer, who paved the way
> Of resurrection to eternal day.
> Horus triumphant with the battle done,
> Lord of two worlds, united and made one.

It was the object of their loftiest desires to grow in his likeness whilst looking lovingly upon his features, listening to his word, and fulfilling his character in their own personal lives. A mythical model may be no more than an air-blown bladder for learning to swim by. The reality lies in learning to swim. This was how the ideal Horus served the Egyptians. They did not expect him to swim for them and carry them and their belongings as well, but learned to swim for themselves.

There is nothing in all poetry considered as the flower of human reality more pathetic than the figure of Horus in Sekhem. He has grappled with the Apap of evil and wrestled with Sut—the devil or Satan—and been overthrown in the passage of absolute darkness. Blind and bleeding from many wounds, he continues to fight with death itself; he conquers, rises from the grave like a warrior with one arm! Not that he has lost an arm; he has only got one arm free from the bonds of death, the bandages of the mummy made for the burial. But he lives, he rises again triumphant, lifting the sign of the Dominator aloft; and in the next stage of transformation he will be altogether free from the trammels of the mummy to become pure spirit, in the likeness of the father as the express image of his person.

It is a common Christian belief, continually iterated, that life and immortality were brought to light, and death, the last enemy, was destroyed, by a personal Jesus only nineteen centuries ago, whereas the same revelation had been accredited to Horus the anointed and to Iu-su the coming son for thousands of years before, with Horus or Iu-su as the impersonal and ideal revealer who was the Messiah in the astronomical mythology and the Son of God in the eschatology. The doctrine of immortality is so ancient in Egypt that the "Book of Vivifying the Soul for Ever," "said over a figure of the enlightened dead," was not only extant some 6,000 years ago in the time of Husapti, fifth king of the first dynasty, it was then so old that the true tradition of interpretation was at that time already lost. The Egyptian Christ-Jesus or Horus, as revealer of immortality, was the ideal figure of a fact known to the ancient spiritualists, that the soul of man or the Manes persisted beyond death and the dissolution of the present body, and the drama of the mysteries was their *modus operandi* for teaching the fact, with Horus (or Iu-su) as typical manifestor. In this character he was set forth as the first fruits of them that slept, the only one that came forth from the mummy on earth, as the sahu mummy in Amenta; the only one, however, as a type that prefigured potential continuity for all, the doctrine being founded on the ghost as the phenomenal apparition of an eternal reality.

The Egyptians, who were the authors of the mysteries and mythical representation, did not pervert the meaning by an ignorant literalization of mystical matters, and had no fall of man to encounter in the fallacious Christian sense. Consequently they had no need of a redeemer for the effects of that which had never occurred. They did not rejoice over the death of their suffering saviour because his agony and shame and bloody sweat were falsely supposed to rescue them from the consequences of broken laws; on the contrary, they taught that everyone created his own karma here, and that the past deeds made the future fate. The morality was a thousandfold loftier and nobler than that of Christianity, with its delusive doctrine of vicarious atonement and propitiation by proxy. Horus did such or such things for the glory of his father, but not to save the souls of men from having to do them. There was no vicarious salvation or imputed righteousness. Horus was the justifier of the righteous, not of the wicked. He did not come to save sinners from taking the trouble to save themselves. He was an exemplar, a model of the divine sonship; but his followers must conform to his example, and do in life as he had done before they could claim any fellowship with him in death. Except ye do these things yourselves, there is no passage, no opening of the gate, to the land of life everlasting.

The Christian cult is often said to be founded on the "mysteries of the incarnation." But what teacher of the spurious mysteries has ever been able to tell us anything of their natural genesis? What has any bibliolater ever known about the word that was in the beginning? The word which issued out of Silence? The word of life that came by water, by blood, and in the Spirit? For him such language has never been related to any phenomena extant in nature. The wisdom of old Egypt only can explain the typical word and its relationship to a so-called revelation. The doctrine of the incarnation is Egyptian, and to the Egyptian wisdom we must appeal if we would understand it. No other word was ever made flesh in any other way than in Horus, who was the logos of the Mother Nature as the Child-Horus, the khart, or inarticulate logos, and the word that was made truth in the adult phase of his character as Horus Mat-Kheru, the second Horus, the paraclete and direct representative of the father in heaven. The incarnation, which is looked upon as a central mystery of the Christian cult, had no origin and can have no adequate or proper explanation in Christianity. Its real origin, like those of the other Egyptian dogmas and doctrines, was purely natural; it was prehistorical and non-personal, and as the mystery of Horus and his virgin mother, who were equally prehistorical and non-historical, it had been the central mystery of the Egyptian faith for ages, utilized by the ancient teachers for all it ever was or could be worth, and was continued by the teachers of historic Christianity in ignorance of its origin and only true significance, or with a criminally culpable suppression of the gnosis by which alone the inexplicable latter-day mysteries could have been explained.

The primitive mysteries were founded on the facts in nature which are verifiable to-day as from the first, whereas the mysteries of the Christian theology have been manufactured, shoddy-like, from the leavings of the past by the *modus operandi* of miracle. These remain to-day unverified because they are for ever unverifiable. We know how Horus came by water on his papyrus; how then did he come by blood? The child had been incorporated in the fish, the shoot, the branch, the beetle, calf, or lamb, as the representative type; and in his incarnation Horus came by blood, but not by the blood shed on a tree, or the tat-cross. He came to earth by blood as representative of the human soul that came by blood. The Ritual tells us that the gods issued out of silence (ch. 24). This was portrayed in the Osirian system when the infant Horus is depicted pointing with his finger to his mouth, making the sign of silence as it was understood in all the mysteries. Horus is not the ordinary child or khart of the hieroglyphics. He images the logos, the word of silence, the virgin's word, that gave a dumb or inarticulate utterance to the mystery of the incarnation. The doctrine of the incarnation had been evolved and established in the Osirian religion at least 4,000 and possibly 10,000 years before it was purloined and perverted in Christianity. It was so ancient that the source and origin had been forgotten and the direct means of proof lost sight of or obliterated except amongst the gnostics, who sacredly preserved their fragments of the ancient wisdom, their types and symbols and no doubt, with here and there a copy of some chapters of the Book of the Dead done into Greek or Aramaic by Alexandrian scribes. The doctrine of salvation by the blood of Isis connoted the idea of coming into existence by means of the mother's blood, or mystically the blood of the virgin mother. In primitive biology all birth and production of human life was first derived from the mother's blood, which was afterwards informed by the soul of the fatherhood. The lesson first taught by nature was that life came by blood. Procreation could not occur until the female was pubescent. Therefore blood was the sign of source as the primary creative human element. Child-Horus came by the blood of the virgin Isis, in that and no other way. Jesus, the gnostic Christ, also came by blood that way, not only according to the secret doctrine of John, for the Musselmans have preserved a fragment of the true gnosis. In the notes to ch. 96 of the Koran, Sale quotes the Arabic tradition that Jesus was not born like any other men from blood concreted into flesh, but came *in the flow, or in the flowing blood*—that was, in the virgin's blood first personalized in Horus, who was made flesh as the virgin's child. The doctrine of the incarnation was dependent on the soul of life originating in the mother blood, the first that was held specifically and exclusively human on account of its incarnation. This was the soul derived from a mother who was the mystical virgin in biology, and who was afterwards mystified by theology as the mother of god, the eternal virgin typified in the likeness of the totemic. The blood mother had been cognized sociologically as the virgin. Thence came the doctrine of a virgin mother as a type. Blood was the mother of a soul now differentiated from the external souls as human. First the white vulture of the virgin Neith, next the red heifer of the virgin Isis, then the human virginity, supplied the type of an eternal virgin, she in whom the mystery of maternal source was divinized as the virgin mother in the eschatology.

Thus "incarnation" proper begins with the soul that came into being by means of the virgin blood. This was the child of the mother only, the unbegotten Horus, who was an imperfect first sketch of the soul in matter that assumed the form of human personality as Horus the mortal, who was blind and maimed, deaf and dumb and impotent, because it was a birth of matter or the mother only, according to the mythical representation. The mother being the source and sustenance of life with her own blood, this led to a doctrine of salvation by the blood of Isis the divinized virgin. Thus the mystical blood mother was the earliest saviour, not the male. The elder Horus was her child who came by blood. He was her blood child in the eschatology; hence the calf, as his type, was painted red upon the tablets. As the Child-Horus he was an image of her suffering in the human form; thence Horus the child of blood became a saviour through suffering, in a mystery which had a natural origin. This origin can be followed in the Christian iconography when, as Didron shows, a figure of Jesus was portrayed upon the cross, as a little child of two years, naked, and with its body painted red all over, as was the Horus-calf upon the tablets. A curious instance of salvation by the blood of Isis is given in the Ritual. In a vignette to ch. 93, the saving and protecting power of the red tet-buckle, which is an image of the blood of Isis, is shown. A pair of human hands are outstretched from this amulet to grasp the arms of the Manes and prevent him from going toward the east, as that way lies the tank of flame, or hell in modern phrase. In the Gospel account of the incarnation the "word" was "made flesh," but the blood basis of the doctrine has been omitted. Salvation through the blood of Isis was imaged by the red tet-amulet that was put on by her when she had conceived her blood child. This salvation was effected when the child was brought into existence. According to the Ritual, the salvation of the Manes is in living on hereafter. He pleads that he may live and be saved after death (ch. 41), and he wore the tet-buckle in his coffin as the sign of his salvation by the blood of Isis.

Further, how did a purificatory power come to be associated with blood so that one of the horrible dogmas of later theology could be expressed in lines like these:—

> "There is a fountain filled with blood
> Drawn from Immanuel's veins,
> And sinners plunged beneath that flood
> Lose all their guilty stains"?

The natural genesis of such a monstrous doctrine can be traced on two lines of descent. One of these has its starting-point in the theological victim being slain as a scapegoat in a sacrifice that was held to be piacular. The blood of the sin offering thus acquired the character of the atoning blood. According to the Christian doctrine, "All things are cleansed with blood, and apart from the shedding of blood there is no remission" (Heb. ix. 22). On the other line of descent, the idea of purification by blood was derived from a human origin, and not merely from the blood of the animal that was slain as a sacrifice for sin. This is one of the origins that were unfolded to the initiated by the teachers of the secret wisdom in the mysteries. The earliest form of the purifying blood was female. It was first the blood of the virgin mother, the blood of Isis, the blood of the incarnation, the flowing blood, the element in which Horus manifested when he came by blood, the blood on which the rite of purification was founded as a natural mode of cleansing. This is the one sole origin in the whole realm of nature for the blood which cleanseth, and it was in this feminine phase that a doctrine of purification by blood was established for the use of later theology when the sacrificial victim had been made a male who was held to have shed the atoning, purifying, saving blood upon a tree. There was no other way by which a soul was ever saved by blood than this act of salvation effected by the virgin mother. There never was any other incarnation than this of Horus in the blood of Isis, and no other saviour by blood was possible in the whole domain of unperverted nature. Neither could the transaction be made historical, nor the saviour personal, not if every tree on earth were cut into the figure of a cross with the effigy of a bleeding human body hung on every bough. Purification by means of blood then originated in the blood of Isis, the virgin mother of the human Horus, who, as the red child, calf or lamb, personated that purification by blood which became doctrinal in the eschatology. To substitute the blood of a Jew shed on a cross as a means of making the purification for sins and the mode of cleansing souls in the "blood of the lamb" for the natural purification of the mother was the grossest form of profanity, inconceivably impious to those who knew the mystical nature of the doctrine and its origin in human phenomena continued as a typical purification by blood that was practised in the mysteries, either by baptism or sprinkling with blood, or drinking blood, or eating the "bloody wafer" of the Roman Eucharist. The natural blood sacrifice was feminine. The typical blood sacrifice was that of the red calf, the lamb, or the child. The lamb on the cross was the Christian victim until the eighth century A.D., at which time the man was permanently substituted for the lamb, and the blood sacrifice was thenceforth portrayed as human and historical. A doctrine of voluntary sacrifice was founded from the time when the human mother gave herself to be eaten with honour by her children in the most primitive form of the mortuary meal. She offered her flesh to be eaten and her blood to be drunk; she gave herself as a natural blood sacrifice on which the typical was founded when the female totem as a cow, a bear, or other animal was made a substitute for the human mother. Also, when the earth was looked upon as the mythical mother of food and drink who was a wet-nurse in the water, and who gave herself bodily to her children for food, the sacrifice was typically continued in totemism when the animal supplied the sacramental food. As before shown, the earliest form of voluntary sacrifice was female. The human mother as victim was repeated in the mythology as divine, the mother in elemental nature; she who gave her flesh and blood as life to her children was then continued as a type in the more mystical phase. Hence came salvation by the blood of Isis—that is, by the virgin blood in which Horus was incarnated and made flesh, as the saviour who thus came by blood.

A Spaniard, who was paying expensively to regain the lost favour of the Holy Virgin, on being told by his priest that Mary had not yet forgiven him, is said to have shaken his fist in the face of his fetish and to have reminded her that she need not be so proud in her present position, as he had known her ever since she was only a bit of green plum tree. The ancient Egyptians knew the natural origins of their symbols and dogmas. Christians have mistaken the bit of green plum tree for an historical virgin.

The earliest form of god the father who became a voluntary sacrifice in Egypt was Ptah in the character of Sekari, the silent sufferer, the coffined one, the deity that opened up the nether-world for the resurrection in the solar mythos. As solar god he went down into Amenta. There he died and rose again, and thus became the resurrection and the way into a future life as founder of Egyptian eschatology. Atum the son of Ptah likewise became the voluntary sacrifice as the source of life, but in another way and more apparent form. The mother human and divine had given life with her blood, and now the father, who was blended with the mother in Atum, is portrayed as creator of mankind by the shedding of his own blood.

In the cult of Ptah at Memphis and Atum at On there was a strenuous endeavour made to set creative source as male above the female. Hence it was said of the symbolic beetles that there was "no female race among them" (Hor-Apollo, B. I, 10). In cutting the member, Atum showed that he was the creator by the blood shed in a voluntary sacrifice. Male source is recognized, but according to what had preceded as the mother element, blood still remained a typical essence of creative life. And this is apparently illustrated by the rite of circumcision. The custom pertains, world over, to the swearing-in of the youths when they join the ranks of the fathers or begetters and follow the example of Atum as the father, Ra, who was previously Horus the son. Atum, like Ptah, was also the typical sacrifice in the earth of eternity, who gave his life as sun god and as the master of food that sprang up for the Manes in Amenta. Osiris follows. In him the human mother who first gave herself to be eaten, and the great mother Isis, who was the saviour by blood, were combined with god the father in a more complete and perfect sacrifice as mother and father of the race in one. Lastly, the son as Horus or as Iusa is made a vicarious sacrifice, not, however, as an atonement for sin, but as voluntary sufferer *instead* of his mother or his father. For in the Kamite scheme the mother never is omitted. Hence, when Horus comes in the character of the red god who orders the block of execution with the terrifying face of Har-Shefi, as the avenger of the afflictions suffered by his father (or by himself in his first advent), it is he "who lifteth up his father and who lifteth up his mother with his staff" (Rit., ch. 92, Renouf). Egypt, however, had anticipated Rome in attaining the "unbloody sacrifice" that was represented by the wafer, or loaf, of Horus as the bread of heaven, which took the place of flesh meat in the Eucharistic meal, whilst retaining the beer or wine, as substitute for blood, in representing the female element. Thus Horus was eaten as the bread of life, and his blood was drunk in the red ale, or wine, as the final form in Egypt of the sacrificial, voluntary, living victim that had been the human mother, the typical mother, the totemic animal, the cow of Hathor, the fish, the goose, the calf, the lamb, the victim in various forms, each one of which, down to the lentils and the corn, was figurative of the beneficent sacrifice that from the first was typical of a power in nature, call it mother or son, father, goddess or god, that provided food and drink, accompanied with an idea of sacrifice in the giving of life when blood was looked on as the life.

"How many sacraments hath Christ ordained in His Church?" is asked in the Prayer-book, and the answer is, "Two only as generally necessary to salvation—that is to say, baptism and the supper of the Lord." And both of these were Egyptian thousands of years earlier. The proof is preserved in that treasury of truth, the Ritual of the resurrection. In the first chapter of the Ritual (Turin Papyrus) it is said by the priest, "I lustrate with water in Tattu and anoint with oil, in Abydos." We might call the Egyptians very Particular Baptists for in the first ten gates of Elysium or entrances to the great dwelling of Osiris the deceased is purified at least ten times over in ten separate baptisms, and ten different waters in which the gods and goddesses had been washed to make the water holy (Ritual, ch. 145). The inundation was the water of renewal to the life of Egypt, and this natural fact was the course and origin of a doctrine of baptismal regeneration. The salvation that came to Egypt in the

Nile was continued in the Egyptian eschatology as salvation by water. "I give thee the liquid or humidity which ensures salvation," is said to the soul of the deceased (Rit., 155, 1). They did not think that souls were saved from perdition by a wash of water or a bath of blood, but bodily baptism was continued as a symbol of purification for the spirit. The deceased explains that he has been steeped in the waters of natron and nitre, or salt, and made pure—pure in heart, pure in his forepart, his posterior part, his middle, and pure all over, so that there is no part of him remaining soiled or stained. The pool of baptism is dual in Amenta. In one part it is the pool of natron, in the other the pool of salt. Both natron and salt were used in preparing the mummy of the deceased, and the same process is repeated in the purification of the soul to make it also permanent, which was a mode of salvation. The deceased says, "May I be fortified or protected by seventy purifications" (Mariette, *Mon. divers,* pl. 63, f), just as Christians at the present time speak of being "fortified by the sacraments of the Church." "I purify myself at the great stream (the galaxy), where all my ills are made to cease; that which is wrong in me is pardoned, and the spots which were upon my body upon earth are washed away" (Rit., ch. 86). "Lo, I come, that I may purify this soul of mine in the most high degree. Let me be purified in the lake of propitiation and of equipoise. Let me plunge into the divine pool beneath the two divine sycamores of heaven and earth" (ch. 97, Renouf). The pool of purification and healing that was figured in the northern heaven at the pole, and also reproduced in the paradise of Amenta, has been repeated in the Gospel according to John (ch. 5) as the Pool of Bethesda. In the Ritual (ch. 124, part 3) one of two waters is called the pool or tank of righteousness. In this pool the glorified elect receive their final purification and are healed. They are thus made pure for the presence of Osiris. The healing process was timed to take place at certain hours of the night or day. The Turin text gives the fourth hour of the night and the eighth hour of the day. But there are other readings. The Manes, as usual in the gospels, are represented by the "multitude of them that were sick, blind, halt, and withered," waiting to be healed. The elect or chosen ones are those who are first at the pool when the waters are troubled. Hence the story of the man who was non-elect.

It was a postulate of the Christians, maintained by Augustine and others, that infants who died unbaptized were damned eternally. This doctrine also had its rootage in the mysteries of Amenta. The roots have hitherto been hidden in the earth of eternity which has been mistaken for our earth of time. We are now enabled to exhibit them above ground and hold both root and product up to the light like the bulb of a hyacinth suspended in a glass water-bottle. These can now be studied, roots and all. The flesh that is formed of the mother's blood was held to share in the impurity of the female nature. It was in this sense solely that woman was the author of evil. The Child-Horus born of flesh and blood was the prototype of the unbaptized child—that is, the child unpurified by baptism. Without baptismal regeneration in Tattu there was no blending of the elder Horus with the soul or spirit of Horus divinized. According to the Egyptian doctrine, the development would be arrested and the soul from the earthly body might remain a wretched shade that was doomed to extinction, or, in the Christian perversion, was damned eternally. It was in Amenta that the dead were raised to inherit the second life. The resurrection had no other meaning for the Egyptians. And in the resurrection the Osiris is thus greeted: "Hail, Osiris! thou art born twice! The gods say to thee: 'Come! come forth; come see what belongs to thee in thy house of eternity'" (ch. 170). It is then that he is changed and renewed in an instant.

In blending the two halves of a soul that was dual in sex, dual also in matter and spirit, into one, according to the mystery of Tattu, there was a return to the type beyond sex from which the two had bifurcated in the human creation. This one enduring soul was typical of the eternal soul which included motherhood and fatherhood in one personality like that of the multimammalian Osiris which the Child-Horus could only represent in some form of duality that imaged both sexes in one, as do the deities who are figured with one female bosom as a mode of en-onement. Female mummies have been exhumed that were made up wearing the beard of a male. This was another figure of the soul completed by uniting the two halves of sex in one figure, the type affected by the Queen Hatshepsu when she clothed herself in masculine attire and reigned as Mistress Aten. It was the same with the Pharaohs who wore the tail of the cow or lioness. They also included both halves of the perfect soul, as a likeness of the biune being divinized in heaven which they represented on the earth. The doctrine was brought on in the iconography of the gnostic artists when Jesus is figured as a woman with a beard, who is designated the Christ as Saint Sophia (or Charis) (Didron, fig. 50), and also when Jesus is depicted in the Book of Revelation as a being of both sexes, a youth with female paps; in the likeness of Osiris, whose male body is half covered with female mammæ, and who is Osiris in the upper and Isis in the lower part of the same mummy. Not only was it necessary to be regenerated and reborn in the likeness of god the father; the Manes could only enter the kingdom of heaven as a being of both sexes or of neither. The two halves of the soul that were established for ever in Tattu were male and female; the soul of Shu was male, the soul of Tefnut female. When these were united in one to form a completed Manes and a perfect spirit the result was a typical creation from both sexes in which there was neither male nor female. This oneness, in the Horus who was divinized, is the oneness in Christ described by Paul: "As many of you as were baptized into Christ, did put on Christ. There can be no male nor female, for ye are all one in Christ Jesus." One of the fragments preserved by Clement Alexander and Clement of Rome from the lost "gospel of the Egyptians," which is more than fully recoverable in the Ritual, will show the continuity of the doctrine as Egyptian in a gospel that was designated "Egyptian." The Lord having been asked by Salome when his kingdom would come, replied, "when you shall have trampled under foot the garment of shame; When two shall be one, when that which is without shall be like that which is within, and when the male with the female shall be neither male nor female." The "garment of shame" was feminine, being as it was of the flesh. On this the Ritual has a word to say. The impurity of matter which came to be ascribed to the mother of all flesh, or female nature, is symbolically shown in the chapters for arranging the funeral bed (Rit., chs. 170-171). This is exemplified by means of the feminine garment—the apron—which is here considered to be a sign of all that was wrong in the deceased; the wrong that was derived from the mother, as elsewhere described in the Ritual, because it is the garb of impurity called "the garment of shame" in the Egyptian gospel, which was to be trampled under foot when the male and female were to be made one in spirit, or as spirit. In the ceremony of "wrapping up the deceased in a pure garment," the impure one being now discarded is alluded to in ch. 172. When the deceased was stretched upon the funeral bed the body was *divested of the apron* and clothed in the pure garment of the khus or spirits, "the pure garment allotted to him for ever" (Rit., ch. 171). But the feminine garment is still worn without shame by the masquerading male as the bishop's apron, which can be traced back as feminine to the loin-cloth and apron first worn by the sex for the most primitive and pitiful of human needs at the time of puberty. The bishop in his apron, like the priest in his petticoat and the clergyman in his surplice, is a likeness of the biune being who united both sexes in one; the modern Protestant equivalent for the Pharaoh with the cow's tail, and Venus with a beard, the mutilated eunuch, or any other dual type of hermaphrodital deity. Men who masquerade in women's clothing are commonly prosecuted, but the bishop carries on his mummery without even being suspected. He walks about as ignorant of his vestmental origins as any of the passers by. Usually the custom of men dressing in women's clothing is limited to our Easter pastimes, but the bishops still carry it on all through the year.

The Christians prattle about the divine "sonship of humanity," manifested in the historical Jesus. But they have no divine daughtership, no origin for the soul as female and no female soul. The Jews did all they could to get rid of the female part of the divine nature, and the exigency of the Christian history has suppressed the feminine element altogether in the human type that represented both sexes in humanity as it was set forth by the Egyptians in the mysteries. Finally, it has been frequently asserted that only through the Gospel Jesus has a god of the poor man ever been revealed—a statement most profoundly false. A god of the poor and suffering was personified in Horus the elder. But there is a corollary to the character. He is likewise an avenger of the sufferings. Horus at Edfu is said to protect the needy against the powerful. Also, in the great Judgment Hall the Osiris deceased upon his trial says, "I have not been a land-grabber. I have not exacted more than should be done for me as the first fruits of each day's work" (Rit. ch. 125). Various other statements tend to show that the unjust capitalists of those times had a mortal dread of facing Osiris the divinized judge, who was likewise god of the poor and needy. In an Egyptian hymn the one god, Atum the maker of men, is described as "lying awake while all men lie asleep, to seek out the good of his creatures" (line 12), "listening to the *poor* in their distress, gentle of heart when one cries to him. Deliverer of the timid man from the violent, lord of mercy most loving, judging the poor, the poor and the oppressed" (Hymn to Amen-Ra, *Records,* vol. ii., p. 129). Taht was the recorder in the Judgment Hall. At the weighing of hearts he portrayed the character of the deceased, and in one of the texts it is said that when he placed the heart in the scales against Maati, the goddess of justice, he leaned to the side of mercy, that the judgment might be favourably inclined, as though he exerted a little pressure on the human side of the balance.

It has also been said that the historic Jesus came to glorify the lot of labour, which antiquity despised, whereas the Egyptian paradise was the reward of labour, and Horus the husbandman in the harvest-field of the Aarru is the worker personified. No one attained the Egyptian heaven but the worker, who reaped solely in proportion as he had sown. The portion of land allotted to the Manes for cultivation in Amenta was enlarged only for those who had been good labourers on earth. The Shebti figures in the tombs are equipped for labour with the plough or hoe in their hands. As agriculturists they put their hands to the plough. There was no unearned increment for loafers in the earth of eternity. A flash of revelation lightens from the cloud of Egypt's past when we learn from the Ritual that a part of the work to be performed in the Aarru paradise or field of harvest in Amenta was to clear away the life-choking sand. These fighters and conquerors of the much-detested desert still retain that image of the earliest cultivators, the makers of the soil which they enclosed and first protected from the drifting, sterilizing sand. The Manes, addressing the Shebti figures, says to them, "O typical ones! If I should be judged worthy of doing the work that has to be done in Amenta, bear witness for me that I am worthy to fertilize the fields, to flush the streams, and transport the sand from west to east" (Rit., ch. 6). He became one of the glorified elect in being judged worthy of the work. This will show that in making the primeval paradise they were still the cultivators who had conquered on earth by their long wrestle with the powers of dearth in the desert when they made their passage through the wilderness of sand and held on to the skirts of Mother Nile, who led them to a land which she herself had made for them to turn into an oasis and a paradise of plenty with her waters for assistance in the war against Apap, or Sut, the Sebau, and the burning Sahara. It may also explain why the Pharaohs from the time of the eleventh dynasty were officially entitled "Masters of the Oasis," the oasis, that is, which had been created in Egypt by human labour to be localized in Amenta as the promised land that was to be attained at last among the never-setting stars in the oasis of eternity.

The prototypes of hell and purgatory and the earthly paradise are all to be found in the Egyptian Amenta. There is, says the Christian rhymer, Dr. Watts:

"There is a dreadful hell
  And everlasting pains,
Where sinners must with devils dwell
  In darkness, fire, and chains."

The darkness, fire, and chains, as well as the brimstone, which was the stone of Sut, and other paraphernalia of the Christian hell, are also Egyptian. But the chains were employed for the fettering of Sut, the Apap, and the Sebau, the evil adversaries of Osiris, the good or perfect being, not for the torturing of souls that once were human. The Egyptian hell was not a place of everlasting pain, but of extinction for those who were wicked irretrievably. It must be admitted, to the honour and glory of the Christian deity, that a god of eternal torment is an ideal distinctly Christian, to which the Egyptians never did attain. Theirs was the all-parental god, Father and Mother in one whose heart was thought to bleed in every wound of suffering humanity, and whose son was represented in the character of the Comforter.

Also the hell-fire of Christian theology, the hell-fire that is unquenchable (Mark ix. 43, 44), is a survival of the representation made in the Egyptian mysteries. The Osiris in Amenta passes through this hell of fire in which those who are condemned suffer their annihilation. He says, "I enter in and I come forth from the tank (or lake) of flame on the day when the adversaries are annihilated at Sekhem" (Rit., ch. 1). When the glorified deceased had made his voyage in heaven "over the leg of Ptah," and reached the mount of glory, he exclaims, "I have come from the lake of flame, from the lake of fire and from the field of flame." He has made his escape from destruction, and attained the eternal city at the pole of heaven. This lake of fire that is never quenched was derived from the solar force in the mythology on which the eschatology was based. Hence the locality was in the east, at the place of sunrise. The wicked were consumed by fire at the place where the righteous entered the solar bark to sail the heavenly waters called the Kabhu, or the cool, and voyage westward toward the heaven of the setting stars. The lake of flame was in the east, the lake of outer darkness in the west. For when the bark of Ra or the boat of souls had reached the west at sunset there was a great gulf fixed between the mount called Manu in the west and the starry vault of night, the gulf of Putrata (Rit., ch. 44), where the dead fell into darkness unless supported by Apuat the star-god, by Horus in the moon, and by Ra the solar deity, the visible representatives of superhuman powers in the astronomical mythology.

At the "last judgment" in the mysteries those who had failed to make the word of Osiris truth against his enemies, as the formula runs, were doomed to die a second death. The first was in the body on the earth, the second in the spirit. The enemies of justice, law, truth, and right were doomed to be destroyed for ever in the lake of fire or tank of flame. They were annihilated once for all (Rit., ch. 1). The doctrine crops up in the Pauline Epistles and in Revelation, where the end of all is with a destruction in the lake of fire. In the Epistle to the Hebrews the destruction of lost souls is compared with that of vegetable matter being consumed by fire. The doctrine, like so many others, was Egyptian, upon which the haze of ignorance settled down, to cause confusion ever since. Take away the Kamite devil, and the Christian world would suffer sad bereavement. The devil was of Egyptian origin, both as "that old serpent" the Apap reptile, the devil with a long tail, and as Sut, who was Satan in an anthropomorphic guise. Sut, the power of drought and darkness in physical phenomena, becomes the dark-hearted evil one, and is then described as causing storms and tempests, going round the horizon of heaven "like one whose heart is veiled" (Rit., ch. 39, Renouf), as the adversary of Osiris the Good Being. The darkness, fire, and chains are all Egyptian. Darkness was mythically represented by the Apap dragon, also as the domain of Sut in the later theology. Darkness in the nether world is identical with the tunnels of Sut in Amenta. The chains are likewise Egyptian, but not for human wear. Apap and the Sebau, Sut and the Sami are bound in chains. It is said to the pre-anthropomorphic devil, "Chains are cast upon thee by the scorpion goddess" (Rit., ch. 39). Sut is also imprisoned with a chain upon his neck (ch. 108). As already explained, the Sebau and the Sami represent the physical forces in external nature that made for evil and were for ever opposed to the Good Being and to the peace of the world. These were always rising in impotent revolt as the hosts of darkness and spawn of Apap, headed by the evil-hearted Sut. They had to be kept under; hence the necessity for prisons, bonds, and chains. The mythical imagery has been continued in the Christian eschatology, and the sinners put in the place of the Sebau, whereas in the Egyptian teaching the sinners, once human, who were irretrievably bad, were put an end to once for all, at the time of the second death, in the region of annihilation (Rit., ch. 18). Coming to an end for ever was, to the Egyptian mind, a prospect worse than everlasting pains, so profound was their appreciation of life, so powerful their will to persist. They represented evil as negation. Apap is evil and a type of negation in the natural phenomena that were opposed to good. In the eschatology Sut represents negation as non-existence. Evil culminated in annihilation and non-being for the Manes, and the negation of being, of life, of good, was the ultimate form of evil. The Egyptian purgatory, called the Meskat, is a place of purgation where the primitive mode of purifying may be compared with that of Fulling. It is effected by beating. Hence the Meskat is the place of scourging. The Manes pleads that he may not fall under the knives of the executioners in the place of extermination, as he has "*passed* through the place of purification in the middle of the Meskat." In chapter 72 the Manes prays that he may "not be stopped at the Meskat," or in purgatory, but may pass on to the divine dwelling-place prepared for him by Tum "above the earth," where he can "join his two hands together," and eat the bread and drink the beer upon the table of Osiris. The same plea, "Let me not be stopped at the Meskat," or kept in purgatory, is also uttered by the speaker in chapter 99. The enemies of the Good Being were likewise pilloried. Hence the Manes says, "Deliver me from the gods of the pillory, who fasten (the guilty) to their posts" (ch. 180).

A late attempt has been made on behalf of the Roman Catholic religion to lure people into Hades by showing that it is only a mitigated mourning department; that the devil himself is not so black as hitherto painted; and that there is really a tolerable amount of happiness to be obtained in hell. But this is only looking a little closer into the traditions of Amenta which survived in Rome. They belong to the same original source as that from which the Church derived its doctrines of purgatory, the second death, and other dogmas not to be found in the Gospels. There is no everlasting bonfire of eternal torture in the Egyptian hells, of which there are ten, known as the ten circles of the condemned, in the inferno or divine nether region. The utterly worthless suffer a second death upon the highways of the damned, and are spoken of as those who are no more. The Roman Church continued the dogma of a second death, and then somewhat nullified it by adding punishment of an infinite duration, as being more coercive to all who did or did not zealously believe. There was no other identifiable source for the Christian eschatology than the Egyptian wisdom. The Roman Church was founded on the Ritual. Possibly a version of the original may one day be found preserved in the secret archives of Rome, the text of which would explain numerous pictures in the Catacombs and other works of the gnostic artists who were the actual authors of the Egypto-Christian iconography, not the "few poor fishermen." The Roman Church will yet find that she is at root Egyptian, and will then seek to slough off the spurious history which by that time will be looked upon as solely incremental.

The Egyptians were the greatest realists that ever lived. For thousands and thousands of years it was their obvious endeavour at full stretch to reach the ultimate reality of eternal truth. Their interrogation of nature was like the questioning of children, very much in earnest: "But is it really true?" The real was the quest of their unceasing inquiry. To be real was the end and aim; that was living in truth. The only one god was the real god. Horus in spirit was the real Horus. Reality was royalty. In the time of the fifth dynasty a certain Tep-en-ankh claims to be "the *real* judge and scribe," the *"real* nearest friend of the king." For them eternal life was the ultimate reality. The Egyptian was pre-eminently a manly religion, and therefore calculated to develop manhood. In the hall of the last judgment the deceased expects justice and equity. His god is a just and righteous judge. He does not pray for mercy or writhe in the dust to seek a sentimental forgiveness for sins, or sue for clemency. His was not a creed of that nature. He knows it is the life, the character, the conduct that will count in the scales of Maati for the life hereafter. The human Horus put in no plea for sinners on account of his sufferings. Divine Horus throws no make-weight into the scale. The deceased is judged by what he has done and by what he has not done in the life on earth. He must be sound at heart. He must have spoken and acted the truth. The word of god must have been made truth by him to be of any avail at the bar of judgment. That was the object of all the teaching in all the mysteries and writings which were held to be divine. The standard of law without and within was set up under the name of Maati or Maat, a name denoting the fixed, undeviating law and eternal rule of right. Hence the same word signifies law, truth, justice, rightfulness, and the later righteousness. The foremost and the final article of the Egyptian creed was to fulfil Maati. This is the beginning, the middle, and the end of the moral law. The deity enthroned by them for worship was the god of Maati, the name, which has the fourfold meaning of law, justice, truth, and right, which are one as well as synonymous. Judgment with justice was their aim, their alpha and omega, in administering the law which their religious sense had divinized for human use; and its supreme type, erected at the pole, in the equinox, or the Hall of Judgment, was the pair of scales at perfect equipoise, for with them the equilibrium of the universe was dependent on eternal equity.

It may look like taking a flying leap in the dark to pass from the Egyptian Book of the Dead to Bunyan's *Pilgrim's Progress,* but whencesoever Bunyan derived the tradition, the *Pilgrim's Progress* contains an outline of the matter in the Egyptian Ritual. Christian personates the Manes on his journey through the nether earth, with the roll in his hand containing the word of life. The escape from the City of Destruction may be seen in the escape of the deceased from the destruction threatened in Amenta, when he exclaims, "I come from the lake of flame, from the lake of fire and from the field of flame" (ch. 98). The wicket-gate corresponds to the secret doorway of the mysteries; the "Slough of Despond" to the marshes in the mythos; the "Hill of Difficulty" to the Mount of Ascent up which the Osiris climbs with "his staff in his hand." The Manes forgets his name; Christian forgets his roll, the roll that was his guide book for the journey and his passport to the celestial city. The prototypal valley of the shadow of death is the Aar-en-tet in Amenta. This is the valley of darkness and death (Rit., ch. 19; 130, 6). The Ritual says, "Let not the Osiris advance into the valley of darkness" where the twice-dead were buried for ever by the great annihilator Seb. The monster Apap is the original Apollyon. The equipment of Christian in his armour for his conflict with Apollyon in the Valley of Humiliation is one with the equipment of the Osiris, who enters the valley "glorious and well equipped" for the battle with his adversary the dragon. The fight of Christian and Apollyon is identical with the contest between Ra and Apap. All the time of his struggle Apollyon fought with yells and hideous roarings; Apap with "the voice of strong bellowings" (Rit., ch. 39). Christian passes by the mouth of hell; the Osiris passes by the ten hells, with all of them, as it were, making mouths at him for their prey. There are two lions at the gate of the Palace Beautiful, and in the Ritual the two lions crouch at the beautiful gate of exit from Amenta (Vig. to ch. 18). The waters of the river of life, the green meadows, the delectable mountains, the land of Beulah, the paradise of peace, the celestial city on the summit, all belong to the mythology of Hetep or the Mount of Glory—a bare outline, the mere skeleton of which has been clothed at different times in various forms, including this of the *Pilgrim's Progress.* Possibly Bunyan the tinker derived the tradition from those travelling tinkers the gipsies. However this may be, the Egyptian Ritual is the verifiable source of Bunyan's *Pilgrim's Progress.*

Many illustrations might also be given to show that the mysteries of Amenta, which were finally summed up as "Osirian," have been carried to the other side of the world. In the mythology of the aborigines of New Holland, "Grogoragally, the divine son, is the active agent of his father, who *immovably* presides over all nature (like Osiris, the mummy god of the motionless heart). The son watches the actions of men, and quickens the dead immediately upon their earthly interment. He acts as mediator for the souls to the great god, to whom the good and bad actions of all are known. His office is chiefly to bring at the close of every day the spirits of the dead from all parts of the world to the judgment-seat of his father, where alone there is eternal light. There he acts as intercessor for those who have only spent some portion of their lives in wickedness. Bayma, listening to the mediation of his son, allows Grogoragally to admit some such into Ballima," or heaven (Manning, *Notes on the Aborigines of New Holland,* Sydney, 1883, copy from the author). Grogoragally is one with the hawk-headed Horus, the paraclete or advocate who pleads for the Manes before the judgment-seat of his father. Again, the aborigines of the McDonnell Ranges have a tradition that the sky was at one time inhabited by three persons. One of these was a woman, one was a child who always remained a child and never developed beyond childhood; the third was a man of gigantic stature called Ulthaana—that is a spirit. He had an enormous foot shaped like that of an emu. When a native dies he is said to ascend to the home of Ulthaana the spirit (Gillen, *Notes, Horn Expedition,* vol. iv, p. 183). This is a far-off folk tale that may be traced back home to the Egyptian myth. In this Child-Horus never developed beyond childhood, and so remained the eternal child. This was Horus of the incarnation who made his transformation into the Horus that rose again as the adult, the great man, Horus in spirit, the prototype of "Ulthaana." The bird type is repeated. Horus has the head of the hawk, as a figure of the man in spirit; Ulthaana, as a spirit, has the foot of an enormous emu.

The Arunta also have a kind of Amenta or world of spirits under ground. About fourteen miles to the south of Alice Springs there is a cave in a range of hills which rises to the north. This cave, like all others in the range, is supposed to be occupied by the Iruntarinia or spirit individuals, each one of whom is in reality the double of one of the ancestors of the tribe who lived in the Alcheringa. The individual spirits are supposed to live within the cave in perpetual sunshine and among streams of running water, as in the Egyptian meadows of Aarru. Here, as in Amenta, the reconstitution of the deceased takes place. Within the cave the Iruntarinia remove all the internal organs, and provide the man with a completely new set, after which operation has been successfully performed he presently comes to life again, but in a condition of insanity. This, however, is of short duration, and the coming round is equivalent to the recovery of memory by the Manes in the Ritual, when he remembers his name and who he is in the great house of the other world (Spencer and Gillen, p. 525). There are bird-souls also in this nether earth, which are favoured with unlimited supplies of down or undattha, with which they are fond of decorating their bodies as spirits. The mysteries of Amenta are more or less extant in the totemic ceremonies of the Central Australians at a more rudimentary stage of development, which means, according to the present reading of the data, that the same primitive wisdom was carried out from the same central birthplace in Africa to the islands of the Southern Sea, and there fossilized during long ages of isolation, which had been carried down the Nile to take living root and grow and flourish as the mythology and eschatology of ancient Egypt.

In the mysteries of Amenta the deceased is reconstructed from seven constituent parts or souls in seven stages of development. Corresponding to these in the Arunta mysteries, seven "status-terms are applied to the initiate." (1) He is called Ambaquerka up to the time of his being tossed in the air. (2) He is Ulpmerka until taken to the circumcision ground. (3) He is the Wurtja during the time betwixt being painted for it and the actual performance of the ceremony. (4) He is Arakurta betwixt the operations of circumcision and sub-incision. (5) He is Ertwa-kurka after circumcision until he passes through the ordeal by fire. (6) Following this he is called Illpongwura, and (7) after passing through the engwura he is designated Urliara. (Spencer and Gillen, *N.T.*, p. 638.) In the mysteries of Amenta the mouth of the resuscitated spirit is opened and the silence of death is broken when the lips are touched by the sacred implement in the hands of Ptah. It is said in the "ceremony of opening the mouth," "Let my mouth be opened by Ptah with the instrument of ba-metal with which he openeth the mouths of the gods" (ch. 23). The Arunta also perform the ceremony of opening the mouth by touching it with a sacred object when the initiates are released from the ban of silence (Spencer and Gillen, pp. 382, 385). A mystery of the resurrection is acted by the Arunta in the *quabarra ingwurninga inkinja,* or corroborree of the arisen bones, which bones imaged the dead body, whilst the performers represented the Ulthaana or spirits of the dead (p. 473). The bones were sacredly preserved by those who were as yet unable to make the mummy as a type of permanence.

Messrs. Spencer and Gillen tell us that every Australian native has to pass through certain ceremonies before he is admitted to the secrets of the tribe. The first takes place at about the age of ten or twelve years, whilst the final and most impressive one is not passed through until probably *the native has reached the age of at least twenty-five, or it may be thirty years*" (*N.T.*, pp. 212, 213). These two initiations correspond to those in the mysteries of the double Horus. At twelve years of age the Child-Horus makes his transformation into the adult in his baptism or other kindred mysteries. Horus as the man of thirty years is initiated in the final mystery of the resurrection. So was it with the gnostic Jesus. The long lock of Horus, the sign of childhood, was worn by him until he attained the age of twelve years, when he was changed into a man. With the southern Arunta tribe the hair of the body is for the first time tied up at the commencement of the opening ceremony of the series by which he is made a man. His long hair is the equivalent of the Horus lock. The first act of initiation in the Arunta mysteries is that of throwing the boy up into the air—a ceremony that still survives with us in the tossing of the new-comer in a blanket! This was a primitive mode of dedication to the ancestral spirit of the totem or the tribe, whose voice is heard in the sound of the churinga or bull-roarer whirling round. It is said by the natives that the voice of the great spirit was heard when the resounding bull-roarer spoke. The great spirit was supposed to descend and enter the body of the boy and to make him a man, just as in the mystery of Tattu the soul of Horus the adult descends upon and unites with the soul of Horus the child, or the soul of Ra the holy spirit descends upon Osiris to quicken and transform and re-erect the mummy. Where risen Horus becomes bird-headed as the adult in spirit the Arunta youth is given the appearance of flight to signify the change resulting from the descent of the spirit as the cause of transformation. When one becomes a soul in the mysteries of the Ritual by assuming the form or image of Ra, the initiate exclaims "Let me wheel round in *whirls,* let me *revolve* like the *turning one*" (ch. 83). The "turning one" is the sun god Chepera (Kheper), whose name is identical with that of an Australian tribe. Kheper is the soul of "self-originating force" that was imaged under one type by the bennu, a bird that ascends the air and flies to a great height whilst circling round and round in spiral wheels (Rit., ch. 85). Whether this be the churinga, the bribbun, turndun, or whirler in a glorified form or not, the doctrine of soul-making at puberty is the same in the Australian as in the Egyptian mysteries.

In the Egyptian mythology Horus is the blind man, or rather he is the child born blind, called Horus in the dark. He is also described as the blind Horus in the city of the blind. In his blindness he is typical of the emasculated sun in winter and of the human soul in death. At the place of his resurrection or rebirth there stands a tree up which he climbs to enter spirit life. And we are told that "near to Charlotte Waters is the tree that rose to mark the spot where a blind man died." This tree is called the *apera okilchya*—that is, the blind man's tree, and the place where it stands was the camp of the blind, the city of the blind, the world of the dead, in which the tree of life or dawn was rooted (*N.T.*, p. 552). Should the tree be cut down the men where it grows will become blind. They would be like Horus in the dark, this being the tree of light or the dawn of eternal day. In one of their ceremonies the Arunta perform the mystery of the oruncha which existed in the Alcheringa. These were evil spirits or "devil-devil men," malevolent and murderous to human beings, especially to the women after dark (*N.T.*, p. 329, 331, 390-1). In this performance they are portrayed as prowling round, crawling, peering about, and seeking whom they may devour. They run backwards and forwards on all fours as beasts of prey, growling and pretending to frighten each other. The oruncha are the creatures of the dark, with horns like the mediæval devil, and they correspond to the Sebau fiends or evil spirits of the Egyptian mythos who are the enemies of the good Osiris in Amenta. These devil-devil men made war upon the lizard men, the men of the lizard totem, but there were two brothers who rushed upon them as avengers, and slew the whole of the oruncha. The evil powers were the creatures of chaos, the spawn of darkness, the devils of drought, with whom there was no law or order. The two brothers = brotherhoods belonged to the lizard totem, together with their wives. This was the earliest totem of the Arunta.

In the last of the initiation ceremonies the Arunta raise a special mound, called the parra, on the engwura ground, where the final rites are performed and full initiation is attained. Here the nurtunga was raised, and the parra mound was, so to say, erected at the pole. Messrs. Spencer and Gillen tell us they were unable to learn the meaning of the word parra. But, as the comparison is not simply verbal, we note that para is an ancient Egyptian name for Annu, the place of the column, the mount of the pole, and of the balance in the Maat. The Chepara tribe of Southern Queensland also throw up the circular mound for their greater mystery of the kuringal, in which may be identified the baptism and rebirth by fire (Howitt, *Australian Ceremonies of the Initiation*). Amongst the initiatory rites of the Arunta mysteries is the purification by fire. When the initiate has passed through this trial he becomes a perfectly developed member of the tribe, and is called an urliara, or one who has been proved by fire (*N.T.*, p. 271). The natives say that the ceremony has the effect of strengthening the character of all who pass through it. This is one of the most obvious survivals. A fire ceremony is described in the Ritual as an exceeding great mystery and a type of the hidden things in the under world. It is an application of the fires by means of which power and might are conferred upon the spirits (khu) among the stars which never set. These fires, it is said in the rubric (ch. 137, A), shall make the spirit as vigorous as divine Osiris. It is a great ordeal, and so secret is the mystery that it is only to be seen by the males. "Thou shalt not perform this ceremony before any human being, except thine own self or thy father or thy son." Amongst other things, the fire is good for destroying evil influences and for giving power to Horus in his war with darkness. It is of interest to note the part played by the females in the ordeals by fire. In one of these the fire is prepared by the women, and when the youth squats upon the fire they place their hands upon his shoulder and gently press him down upon the smoking fuel (*N.T.*, p. 259). Now in the Egyptian mysteries of Amenta the punishers or purifiers in the hells or furnaces are women or goddesses, and it looks as if this character had survived in the mysteries of the Arunta. When the elders shout through the darkness to the women across the river, "What are you doing?" the reply is, "We are making a fire." "What are you going to do with the fire?" is asked, and the women shout, "We are going to burn the men." This occurs during a pause by night in the ceremonies of initiation, which terminate with the ordeal by fire. (Spencer and Gillen.) The concluding ordeals by fire and the "final washing" in the Australian ceremonies can be paralleled in the Ritual. "Lo, I come," says the speaker, "that I may purify this soul of mine in the most high degree" (ch. 97); and again, "I come from the lake of flame, from the lake of fire and from the field of flame, and I live." He is now a spirit sufficiently advanced to join the ancient never-setting ones and become a fellow-citizen with them in the eternal city (ch. 98). The initiate in the Australian mysteries having passed through the initiatory ceremonies, joins the elders as a fully-developed member of his tribe.

The most sacred ceremonial object of the Arunta is called the *kauaua*. This is erected at the close of the engwura mysteries. A young gum-tree, 20 feet in height, is cut down, stripped of its branches and its bark, to be erected in the middle of the sacred ground. The decoration at the top was "just that of a human head." It was covered all over with human blood, unless red ochre had been substituted. The exact significance of the kauaua is not known to the natives, but, as the writers affirm, it has some relation to a human being, and is regarded as common to the members of all the totems (p. 630). Its mystery is made known at the conclusion of the engwura, a series of ceremonies, the last of the initiatory rites through which the native must pass to become a fully-developed member who is admitted to all the secrets of the tribe, of which this is apparently final and supreme. All things considered, we think the sacred kauaua is a form of the Egyptian ka-statue, which is a type of eternal duration as an image of the highest soul. To make the kauaua, so to say, the pole is humanized. It is painted with human blood, and ornamented like the human head. It has but one form, and is common to all the totems. So is it with the Egyptian ka, the eidōlon of the enduring soul. The name of the kauaua answers to a long-drawn-out form of the word "kā," as kā-ā-ā. The mysteries of the Arunta, which sometimes take four months together for a complete performance, constitute their religious ceremonies, their means of instruction, their books, their arts of statuary, painting, and Sign-language, their modes of preserving the past, whether lived on earth, or, as they have it, in the Alcheringa, during the times of the mythical ancestors beyond which tradition does not penetrate. The main difference betwixt the Australian and the Egyptian mysteries is that the one are performed on this earth in the totemic stage of sociology, the other in the earth of Amenta in the phase of eschatology. Also the Egyptians continued growing all the time that the Australians were standing still or retrograding. Lastly, we may be sure that such mysteries as these did not spring from a hundred different origins and come together by fortuitous concourse from the ends of the earth, to be finally formulated as the Egyptian mysteries of Amenta.

THE SIGN-LANGUAGE OF ASTRONOMICAL MYTHOLOGY

Book V

(The Primitive African Paradise.)

It may be said that the dawn of African civilization came full circle in Egypt, but that the earliest glimmer of the light which turned the darkness into day for all the earth first issued from the inner land. The veriest beginning must have been coeval with the creature that first developed a thumb to wield a weapon or to shape an implement for human use, when in the far-off past but little difference could have been detected twixt the monkey and the Pygmy race of human aborigines. It is improbable that we shall get back any nearer to a beginning for the human being among the types extant than with those forest dwarfs, of whom a recent traveller says: "They have no records or traditions of the past, no regard for time, nor any fetish rites; they do not seek to know the future by occult means, as do their neighbours; in short, they are, to my thinking, the closest link with the original Darwinian anthropoid apes extant." These little folk of the forest are still upon the lowest step in the ascent of man. Not because they have retrograded, but because they have never grown. So far as is known, the Pygmies have *no verbal language of their own,* whatsoever words they may have gathered from outsiders. Otherwise, language with them is the same as it was in the beginning, with a few animal sounds and gesture-signs. They have no totems, no signs of tattu scored upon their bodies, no rites of puberty, no eating of the parent in honour for the primitive sacrament. Judging from specimens of the Pygmies that have been brought to England from the Ituri Forest, the foundation of the Negroid features, the thick lips and large, spreading nostrils, was laid in the Pygmean phase of development, but up to the present time the Pygmy has only reached the "peppercorn" stage of hair, and has not yet attained the "kinky" locks of the full-blooded Negro.

A German traveller lately claimed to have discovered a people in the forests of Borneo who show some vestige of the ancestral tail. He saw the tail on a child about six years old belonging to the Pœnan tribe. There was the appendage, sure enough—not very long, but plainly visible, hairless, and about the thickness of a man's little finger (*Daily Chronicle,* August 10th, 1904). Also the persistent rumour that some remains of a semi-simian race are yet extant among the hidden secrets of the old dark land is not incredible to the evolutionist. According to Lady Lugard, there is a tribe in Nigeria who are reputed not to have lost their tails (*Daily Mail,* March 2nd, 1904). The African Pygmies, however, have not publicly proclaimed the tail.

The one sole race that can be traced among the aborigines all over the earth, above ground or below, is the dark race of a dwarf negrito type, and the only one possible motherland on earth for these preliminary people is Africa. No other country possesses the necessary background as a basis for the human beginnings. And so closely were the facts of nature observed and registered by the Egyptians that the earliest divine men in their mythology are portrayed as Pygmies. Following the zoötypes, the primitive human form of Elder Horus was that of Bes, the dancing dwarf. Bes is a figure of Child-Horus in the likeness of a Negroid Pygmy. He comes capering into Egypt along with the Great Mother, Apt, from Puanta in the far-off south. In reality, Bes-Horus is the earliest form of the Pygmy Ptah. In both the dwarf is the type of man in his most primitive shape. The seven powers that co-operate with Ptah are also represented as seven Pygmies. Thus the anthropomorphic type comes into view as a Pygmy! Moreover, Ptah, the divine dwarf, is the imperfect progenitor of the perfect man in his son Atum. In this way the Egyptian wisdom registers the fact that the Pygmy was the earliest human figure known, and that this was brought into Egypt from the forests of Inner Africa and the record made in the mythology. In this mode of registering the natural fact the Egyptians trace their descent from the folk who were the first in human form—that is, from the Pygmies.

We have now to summarize a few of the pre-Egyptian evidences for the Inner African beginnings.

In one of the later chapters of the Book of the Dead (no. 164)—later, that is, in position—there are some ancient mystical names which are said to have been uttered in the language of the Nahsi (the Negroes), the Anti, and the people of Ta-Kenset, or Nubia. Dr. Birch thought this and other chapters were modern because of the presence of Amen-Ra. But the later insertion of a divine name or title does not prove the fundamental matter of the chapter to be late. In this the Great Mother is saluted as the Supreme Being, "the Only One," by the name of Sekhet-Bast, the goddess of sexual passion and strong drink, who is the mistress of the gods, not as wife, but as the promiscuous concubine—she who was "uncreated by the gods," and who is "mightier than the gods." To her the eight gods offer words of adoration. Therefore they were not then merged in the Put-circle of the nine. It is noticeable too that Sekhet is not saluted as the consort of Ptah. Sekhet was undoubtedly far more ancient than Ptah. But the point is that the outlandish names applied to her in this chapter are quoted from the language of the Negroes, therefore parts of the Ritual had been composed in those languages; and if in the languages, then in the lands where these languages were spoken, including the country of the Nahsi, who were so despised by the dynastic Egyptians. This we claim as a partial recognition of the southern origin of the Egyptian mythology. In agreement with this, the Great Mother may be identified in chapter 143 as Apt of Nubia, who had a shrine at Nepata on her way to Egypt, Khept, or Khebt. In a text upon a stele among the Egyptian monuments at Dorpat it is said to the worshipper, "Make adoration to Apt of the dum-palms, to the lady of the two lands" (*Proc. Soc. Bib. Arch.*, March 6th, 1894, p. 152). In this text the old first mother Apt appears as goddess of the mama-tree, that is the dum-palm, which in Egypt is a native of the south. This points to the farther south as the primeval home and habitat of the most ancient hippopotamus goddess, she who thus preceded Hathor in the southern sycamore as Mother-earth or Lady of the Tree, and who in the dum-palm was the "mama" or mother of the Inner Africans.

The King of Egypt as the Suten dates from Sut. The dignity is so ancient that the insignia of the Pharaohs evidently belong to a time when the Egyptians wore nothing but the girdle of the negro, and when it was considered a special distinction that the King should complete this girdle with a piece of skin in front and adorn it with the tail of a lioness behind. The oldest and most primitive form of the sacred house in Egypt known from inscriptions of the ancient empire is a hovel dedicated to Sut for a temple. It looks like a hut of wattle-work without dab, and is a prehistoric type of building in the Nile valley, belonging to a civilization immeasurably lower than that of Egypt. (Erman, p. 280.) Sut the son of Apt was the deity of the first Egpytian nome. Sut is synonymous with the south from which he came with Horus-Behutet, who halted by the way as deity of the second nome. Milne-Edwards has shown the African origin of the ass, and this was preserved by the Egyptians in its pristine purity of form. The serpents of equatorial Africa have their likeness in the huge reptiles portrayed in pictures of the Egyptian under-world. The sycamore fig of Hathor and the palm tree of Taht were imported into Egypt from Central Africa. The burying-places of Abydos, especially the most ancient, have furnished millions of shells, pierced and threaded as necklaces, all of which belong to the species of cowries used as money in Africa at the present day (Maspero, *Dawn of Civilization,* Eng. trans., p. 57). The hoes and wooden stands for head-rests used by the Egyptians have their prototypes among the East Central African tribes (Duff Macdonald). Dr. Peters found various customs among the Wakintu in Uganda which made him think the people were connected with the ancient Egyptians. One of these was the practice of embalming the dead and of excavating the rocks. Also their burial mounds are conical, he says, and look like pyramids.

One might fill a volume with figures from Inner Africa that were developed and made permanent in the symbolism of Egypt.

"My lord the lion" is an African expression used by the Kaffirs and others in speaking of the lordly animal, also of the chief as lion-lord. So likewise in Egypt Osiris as king of the gods was "my lord the crocodile," and King Assa is also called "my lord the king," as a crocodile. (Rit., ch., 142, line 17, Prisse. Pap. 41.) Again, the lion of Motoko is a totem with the Kaffirs in the neighbourhood of Fort Salisbury, Mashonaland. They have a priest of the lion-god called the Mondoro, who is venerated as a sort of spirit in lion shape.

Sacrifices are offered annually to the lion-god at the Zimbabwe of Mashonaland; and it is held by the natives that all true men pass into the lion form at death, precisely the same as it is with the Manes in the Egyptian Ritual, who exclaims, on living a second time, "I am the lord in lion form" (ch. 4), and who rises again when divinized in that image of superhuman power. Such types were Inner African when totemic, and, as the lion of Motoko shows, they were also venerated as representatives of spiritual or superhuman powers which were deified in Egypt as the crocodile divinities Apt, Neith, and Sebek, and the lion-gods Shu, Tefnut, Sekhet, Horus, and Atum-Ra.

In the Egyptian judgment scenes the baboon or Cynocephalus sits upon the scales as the tongue of the balance and a primitive determinative of even-handed justice. This was an Inner African type, now continued in Egypt as an image of the judge. In a Namaqualand fable the baboon sits in judgment on the other animals. The mouse had torn the tailor's clothes and laid it to the cat, the cat lays it to the dog, the dog to the wood, the wood to the fire, the fire to the water, the water to the elephant, and the elephant to the ant; whereupon the wise judge orders the ant to bite the elephant, the elephant to drink the water, the water to quench the fire, the fire to burn the wood, the wood to beat the dog, the dog to bite the cat, and the cat to bite the mouse; and thus the tailor gets satisfaction from the judgment of the wise baboon, whose name is Yan in Namaqua, whilst that of the Cynocephalus is Aan in Egyptian. This in the European folk-tales is the well-known nursery legend of "the pig that wouldn't go." How then did this Bushman or Hottentot fable get into the lowermost stratum of the folk-tales in England? We answer, the same way that "Tom Thumb" did, and "Jack the Giant-killer," the "House that Jack Built," and many more which are the poor relations reduced from the mythology of Egypt to become the märchen of the world. Again, the youthful hero who is Horus in Egypt, Heitsi Eibib among the Hottentots, and the redoubtable little Jack in Britain, is also an Inner African figure under the name of Kalikalange. The missionary Macdonald says, "We know a boy who assumed, much at his own instance, the name of Kalikalange, the hero about whom there are so many native tales, reminding one of the class of tales to which Jack the Giant-killer belongs" (*Africana,* vol. i, p. 115). This is the hero who slays the giant or dragon of drought and darkness, or cuts open the monster that swallowed him; who rescues the lunar lady from her imprisonment, and who makes the ascent to heaven by means of a tree, a stalk, or, as in the case of Child-Horus, *a papyrus reed*. In his *Uganda Protectorate* (vol. ii, p. 700) Sir H. Johnston has reproduced a local legend of creation derived from the natives, which contains certain constituent elements of the nursery tale of Jack the Giant-killer. Kintu was the first man. When he came from the unknown he found nothing in Uganda—no food, no water, no animals, nothing but a blank. He had a cow with him, and on this he lived. The cow represented the earth as giver of food. Kintu is a form of the universal hero, the hero to whom the tests are applied for discovering whether or no he is the real heir. Kintu eats or disposes of 10,000 carcasses of roasted cows, and thus proves himself to be the man indeed, as does Jack who outwits the giant in a similar manner. The story includes the beanstalk (or the bean), with other fragments found in the European märchen, including the bringing of death into the world through the disobedience of Kintu, the first man, or by his violating the law of tabu. The Wakintu of Uganda or Rhodesia derive their name from Kintu, the first man of the Central African legends.

In a Zulu legend the under-world is the land of cannibals. Here dwells the devourer from whom the youthful hero makes his escape, together with his sister, by climbing up a tree into the sky country, just as Horus climbs the tree of dawn in coming forth from the under-world. We read in the Ritual of a golden god-headed ape which is "three palms in height, without legs or arms." The speaker in this character says, "My course is the course of the golden cynocephalus, three palms in height, without legs or arms, in the temple of Ptah" (Rit. ch. 42, Renouf). What this means no mortal knows. It is known, however, that the dog-headed ape as Ani the saluter was emblematic of the moon. Now, in the Kaffir story of Simbukumbukwana there is a child born without legs or arms, who obviously represents the moon in its changes. He began to speak on the day of his birth. "The girl that was first born, who grew up in the valley and lived in the hole of an ant-heap," is called his sister. She has the power to give him legs and arms by repeating his name and saying, "Have legs and arms!" and to deprive him of them by saying "Shrink, legs and arms!" This, as a figure of waning and waxing, helps us to understand the dog-headed ape of gold as an image of the moon in the waxing and waning halves of the lunation. In "the story of the glutton" the conquerors of the swallower are the mother and her twins. These, in an Egyptian form of the mythos, are Sut and Horus, the twin brethren, who war against the monster as two lions, the Rehu, on behalf of their mother, who is the lady of light in the moon (Rit., ch. 80). In this way we can trace some of the oldest of the folk-tales concerning the deluge and the lost paradise, the hero as the wonder-working child who climbs a tree or stalk and slays the monster of the dark, to Inner Africa, and follow these and others in the mythology of the Egyptians on their way to becoming the universal legends of the human race.

The mythology, religious rites, totemic customs, and primitive symbolism of Egypt are crowded with survivals from identifiable Inner African origins. The Egyptian ka or image of a spiritual self was preceded by various rude but representative images of the dead. Livingstone tells us that the natives about Lake Moere make little idols of a deceased father or mother. To these they present beer, flour, and bhang; they light a fire for the spirits to sit round and smoke in concert with their living relatives. The Ewe-speaking natives of the Gold Coast also have their kra or eidōlon, which existed from before the birth of a child and is exactly identical with the Egyptian kra (Ellis, A. B., *Ewe-speaking Peoples,* p. 13). It is a common practice with the Bantu tribes described by the author of *The Uganda Protectorate* for the relatives of deceased persons to carve crude little images as likenesses of the dead, and set them up for worship or propitiation. Offerings are made to these in place of the later ka of the Egyptians. The earlier type of the departed was a bodily portrait. Hence the mummy. The ka is a later spirit likeness. But both imply the same recognition of the ancestral spirits that live on after death. The spirit huts provided for the honoured dead in the dense forests of Central Africa, as by the Wanyamwezi for their Musimo, by the Congo Pygmies (Geal), and by the Nilotic negroes, which the Portuguese called devil houses, are prototypes of the ka-chambers in Egyptian tombs. Erecting a little hut for the spirits is a recognized mode of propitiation. Lionel Décle, as we have seen, describes his Wanyamwezi as making little huts of grass or of green boughs even when on the march, and offering them to the Musimo or spirits of their ancestors (*Three Years in Savage Africa*, pp. 343-6).

One of the funeral offerings found in Theban tombs is a loaf of bread in the shape of a cone (our pastille), or a model in burnt terracotta that images the loaf. Why the offering should be conical is admittedly unknown. This typical cone is Inner African, and in a most peculiar way. The Yao people have the custom of making an offering to the dead in a conical form. They do not know how to make bread, but their offering to the spirits consists of a little flour. This they let fall slowly from the fingers on the ground, so that it may form a pile in the shape of a sugar-loaf. If the cone should shape perfectly it is an omen that the offering is acceptable to the spirits. It may be suggested in passing that the conical shape of the pile in flour and the funerary loaf was derived from that of the grave-mound of earth or stones dropped over the buried corpse as the still earlier tribute offered to the dead. British peasants give the name of "fairy loaves" to the fossil echini or sea-urchins found in Neolithic graves. Obviously these loaves were representative of funerary food that was likewise offered to the dead. The skeleton of a young woman clasping a child in her arms was discovered in a round barrow on Dunstable Downs, the burial mound being edged round with these fairy loaves.

Again, in the mysteries of the Yao people the young girls are initiated by a female who is called "the cook," "the cook of the mystery" (mtelesi wa unyago). This is the instructress who *makes* the mystery or is the "cook" that prepares it, and who is mistress of the ceremony. She is the wise woman who initiates the girls, and anoints their bodies with an oil containing various magical ingredients. She clothes them in their earliest garment, the primitive loin-cloth, that was first assumed at puberty with proud pleasure, and afterwards looked upon askance as the sign of civilized woman's shame. Now this primitive personage has been divinized as the Cook in the Kamite pantheon. In Egyptian, *tait* signifies to cook, and this is the name of a goddess Tait who is the cook in paradise and the preparer of the deceased in the greater mysteries of the Ritual, where she is the cook of the mystery more obviously than a cook as preparer of food. The deceased, in speaking of his investiture for the garden of Aarru, cries, "Let my vesture be girt on me by Tait!"

—that is, by the goddess who is the divine cook by name, and who clothes the initiate in the garment or girdle that here takes the place of the loin-cloth in the more primitive mysteries of Inner Africa (Duff Macdonald, *Africana,* vol. I, pp. 123-126; Rit., ch. 82, Renouf).

The Egyptian record when correctly read will tell us plainly that the human birthplace was a land of the papyrus reed, the crocodile, and hippopotamus; a land of the great lakes in Karua, the Koloë of Ptolemy, or in Apta at the horn point of the earth—that is, in Equatoria, from whence the sacred river ran to brim the valley of the Nile with plenty. The track of civilization with cities springing in its footprints is seaward from the south, not upward from Lower Egypt, which was a swamp when Upper Egypt was already the African home of civilization. The Egyptians always gave priority to the south over the delta in the north. Also the south was and is the natural habitat of the oldest fauna and most peculiar of the sacred zoötypes. It is in vain we judge of the race by the figures and faces of the rulers portrayed in monumental times. Primary data must be sought for amongst the Fellaheen and corroborated by the skulls. Captain Burton wrote to me in 1883, saying, *"You are quite right about the African origin of the Egyptians, and I have sent home a hundred skulls to prove it."* (Does anyone know what became of these skulls?)

The African legends tell us that the Egyptians, Zulus, and others looked backward to a land of the papyrus reed as the primeval country of the human race, and that on this, as we shall see, the Egyptians founded their circumpolar paradise in the astronomical mythology. There is a widespread African tradition, especially preserved by the Kaffir tribes, that the primeval birthplace was a land of reeds. The Zulus told the missionary Callaway that men originally "came out of a bed of reeds." This birthplace in the reeds was called "Uthlanga," named from the reed. No one knew where it was, but all insisted that the natal reed-bed of the race was still extant. It was a sign of lofty lineage for the native aristocracy to claim descent from ancient Uthlanga, the primeval land of birth. The Basutos identify Uthlanga the human birthplace with a cavern in the earth that was surrounded by a morass of reeds. They also cling so affectionately to the typical reed that when a child is born they suspend a reed above the hut to announce the birth of the babe, thus showing in the language of signs that the papyrus reed is still a type of the primitive birthplace in which Child-Horus was cradled on the flower of the papyrus plant or reed. The Zulu birthplace in the bed of reeds was repeated and continued in the nest of reeds and the morass that were mythically represented as the birthplace of the child, which was constellated as the uranograph of Horus springing from the reed. What indeed is the typical reed of Egypt, first in the upper, next in the lower land, but a symbol of the birthplace in the African bed of reeds? Lower Egypt, called Uat in the hieroglyphics, has the same name as the papyrus reed. Also Uati is a title of the great mother Isis who brought forth Child-Horus on her lap of the papyrus flower. Uat in Egyptian is the name of Lower Egypt; Uat is the oasis, Uat is the water, Uat is wet, fresh, evergreen. Uat is the reed of Egypt, the papyrus reed, and a name of the most ancient mother in the Kamite mythology.

Seb, the father of food, is clothed with papyrus reeds. The Mount of Earth was imaged as a papyrus-plant in the water of space. Lastly, the Mount of Amenta in the Ritual rises from a bed of papyrus reeds.

Hor-Apollo says of the Egyptians, "To denote ancient descent they depict a roll of papyrus, and by this they signify *primeval* food" (B. 1, 30). This is the same as with the Zulus. The papyrus reed, Uat, was turned into a symbol of most ancient descent precisely because it had been the primeval food of the most ancient people, a totem of the most ancient mother of the race when called Uati in Egypt, and a type of the African paradise. As the symbolism shows, people were sometimes derived from and represented by the food on which they lived. Thus the papyrus reed that symbolizes ancient food and long descent would be the sign of the people who once lived on or who ate the shoots of the water plant. The Egyptians continued to be eaters of the lotus and papyrus shoots. Theirs was the land of the reed, and they, like the Zulus or the Japanese or the Pueblos, were the reed people in accordance with the primitive mode of heraldry, just as with the Arunta tribes the witchetty-grub people are those who live on the witchetty-grub as their special totemic food. In later times the papyrus plant was eaten by the Egyptians as a delicacy. Its shoots were gathered for that purpose annually. Bread made from the roots and the seed of the lotus was the gourmand's delight. Lily loaves are mentioned in the Papyrus Anastasi. It is said in the Hymn to the Nile that when food is abundant the poor man disdains to eat the lotus or papyrus plant, which shows that it had been his diet when other food was scarce. The lotus and the papyrus are the two water plants worn as a headdress by the two figures that represent the Nile south and north, and who are often seen binding the flowers to the Sam symbol of Upper and Lower Egypt, as if joining the two countries together as the one land of the reed. Uthlanga is not irrecoverable. We glean from other Zulu legends that this was the African birthplace in the bed of reeds, where the two children, black and white, were born of dark and day, and where the race of the reed people broke off in the beginning. This cradle of creation is repeated mythically with Child-Horus in his nest of reeds or bed of the papyrus plant, when the field of reeds was figured in the heavens as the primitive paradise of food and drink.

In the so-called "cosmogony" of the Japanese it is set forth that the first thing in which life appeared on earth at the beginning was the reed, and the earliest land or "country-place stand" (Kunitoko tachi) was *the land of the reed.* Japan was named as the central land of the reed expanse from the fields of reed, whether geographical on the earth or astronomical in the fields of heaven. The "great reed" of the Japanese mythos is identical with the papyrus reed that represented the Mount of Earth in Egypt or the lotus of Meru in India. Any country figured as being atop of the reed would be the midland of the world, as Japan is said to be, and the Kamite reed will explain why the land of the Kami should be called Ashi-hara, the plain of reeds, when the reed is identified with the papyrus plant. *Ashi-hara no naka tsu Kuni,* "the Middle Kingdom of the Reed Plain," which lies upon the summit of the globe, is an ancient name for Japan. This, if mundane, corresponds to the land of the papyrus reed in equatorial Africa, the summit of our earth; or, if only mythical, *i.e.*, astronomical, to the reed field of the Aarru paradise upon the summit of the mount in heaven. Again, the great reed standing up out of the water is identical with the typical mount of earth in the Navajo mythology. As the mount grew higher, higher grew the reed. At the time of the deluge all that lived took refuge there, and were rescued from the drowning waters by the reed. This is the papyrus reed which cradled Horus amid the waters, like the infant Moses in the ark of bulrush, applied in a folk-tale on a larger scale (Matthews).

It is now proposed to seek for the birthplace of the beginnings in Central Africa, the land of the papyrus reed, around the equatorial lakes, by the aid of the Egyptian astronomical mythology and the legendary lore. In the first place, the Kami of Egypt, like the Kami of Japan, identify themselves by name as the reed-people. And the goddess Uati is the African great mother in the bed of reeds. For it was thence, in the region of the two lakes and in the land of the papyrus reed, that souls in the germ first emanated as the soul of life from water. The Kaffir tradition thus appears to preserve the natural fact which the Egyptians rendered mythically by means of the reed plant as a symbol of the primeval birthplace on earth with Horus issuing from the waters on the reed, which became the lap of life, the cradle and the ark of the eternal child, who is also called the shoot of the papyrus, the primitive Natzer.

A spring of water welling from abysmal depths of earth, that furnished food in the papyrus reed and other edible plants, is the earliest form in which the source of life was figured by the Kamite mystery teachers. This is recorded in the Ritual (ch. 172). It was in the birthplace of the reeds and of the reed people in the region of the reeds that light first broke out of darkness in the beginning in the domain of Sut, and where the twin children of darkness and of light were born. The Mother-earth as womb of universal life was the producer of food in various kinds, and the food was represented as her offspring. Horus on his papyrus imaged food in the water plant as well as in the later lentils, the branch of the tree, or in general vegetation. The stands of the offerings presented to the gods in the Ritual are commonly crowned with papyrus plants, which commemorate the food that was primeval. Thus the doctrine of life issuing in and from the papyrus reed was Egyptian as well as Japanese. Naturally the earliest life thus emanating from the water was not human life, but this would be included sooner or later in the mythical representation. Hence the legend of the first man, or person who issued from a reed in the water of the deluge. In this American Indian version the reed is a figure of the birthplace instead of the Zulu bed of reeds, or Uthlanga, the land of reeds, but the typical origin is the same; and as Egyptian the mythos is to be explained.

The origin of a saviour in the guise of a little child is traceable to Child-Horus, who brought new life to Egypt every year as the Messu of the inundation. This was Horus in his pre-solar and pre-human characters of the fish, the shoot of the papyrus, or the branch of endless years. In a later stage the image of Horus on his papyrus represented the young god as solar cause in creation. But in the primitive phase it was a soul of life or of food ascending from the water in vegetation, as he who climbs the stalk, ranging from Child-Horus to the Polynesian hero, and to Jack ascending heavenward by means of his bean-stalk. Now, of all the lands on earth there is no reed land to be compared with the land of the reeds round the equatorial lakes, where the papyrus grows about the waters in jungles and forests so dense that a charging herd of hippopotami could hardly penetrate the bush, which stands out of the water full fifteen feet in height (Johnston, H. H.), and there if anywhere upon this earth Uthlanga, the original reed land or birth land in the reeds, will yet be found. That is the natural fact which underlies the mythical representation when the Egyptians show us Horus "on his papyrus" rising from his natal bed of the papyrus plant. Child-Horus on his papyrus is the reed-born in mythology who reflects the natural fact of the human birthplace in the field, the bed, or nest of reeds on earth or in heaven—that is, the African oasis of the beginning, whether the offspring represents food or other elemental force. Now the Egyptian Aarru or paradise, established by Ra, was *"a field of reeds"* in seven divisions, and these were papyrus reeds which sprang up from the marshes. Thus the Kamite paradise was a land of the papyrus plant repeated on the summit of the mount in heaven at the north celestial pole (Naville, *Destruction of Mankind*). According to their way of registering a knowledge of the beginnings, the Egyptians were well acquainted with the equatorial regions, which they designated "Apta," the uppermost point, the mount, or literally the "horn-point" of the earth. This was afterwards reproduced at the highest point above, when the primeval birth land was repeated as the land of rebirth for spirits in heaven.

It has now to be shown that much of the sign-language of astronomy which still survives on the celestial globe is interpretable on the ground and for the reason that the fundamental data of the underlying mythos was Egyptian, although the commencement in Africa may have been indefinitely earlier than the fulfillment in Egypt. From the beginning certain types evolved in the Egyptian mythology have been configured in the planisphere, many of which remain extant on the celestial globe to-day. As a concept of primitive thought life came into the world by water. Hence in the mysteries of Osiris water is the throne of the eternal. Earth itself was the producer or the mother of the element, the wet-nurse in mythology, and water was her child by whom an ever-renewing source was imaged as a type in Child-Horus, the eternal child. Water, we shall see, was self-delineated as very heaven. Drought was self-delineated as a huge black reptile coiling round the mount of earth night after night and drinking up the water of light day after day. Darkness and light were self-delineated as two immense, wide-winged birds, one black and one white, which overspread the earth. The great squat-headed evil Apap in the Egyptian drawings is probably a water reptile, and possibly represents the mysterious monster of the lakes in the legends of Central Africa. But, wheresoever its habitat in nature, it supplied one of the types that were depicted in the astronomical ceiling of Kam—the types that have now to be followed by means of the mythography in the Sign-language of the starry sphere, amongst which Apap, the "hellish snake" of drought and dearth and darkness, still survives as our own constellation "Hydra," the enormous reptile imaged in the celestial waters of the southern heaven. The hero of light that pierced the serpent of drought or the dragon of darkness was also represented as the golden hawk (later eagle), and at Hermopolis the Egyptians showed the figure of a hippopotamus upon which a hawk stood fighting with a serpent (Plutarch, *On I. and O.,* p. 50). Now, as the hippopotamus was a zoötype of the Mother-earth in the water of space, the hawk and serpent fighting on her back portrayed the war of light and darkness which had been fought from the beginning, the war that was a primary subject figured in the astronomical mythology. The hawk represented Horus, who was the bruiser of the serpent's head. Thus the same conflict that was portrayed at Hermopolis may be seen in the constellation of Serpentarius as a uranograph depicted in the planisphere.

The Egyptians called the equator Ap-ta, as the highest land or summit of the earth. This, the earthly Apta in the equatorial regions, was then rendered mythically as the Apta or highest point of the northern heavens in the astronomical representation. And naturally the chief facts of the earthly paradise were repeated for a purpose in the circumpolar highland. Hence the Aarru paradise, *as a field of papyrus reeds* oozing with the water of life that supplied the world, from the two great lakes into which the element divided at the head of the celestial river or the White Nile of the "Milky Way." In coming down the Nile from Karua, the lake country, the migrants had to pass through parching desert sands, which made the south a synonym for Sut, as it is in Egyptian. Their future heaven was in the north, whence came the blessed breezes with the breath of healing from the very land of life. And all the time ahead of them was that fixed polar star in the north—fixed, that is, as a centre of rest and peace amidst the starry revolutions of the heavens. Emerging from the wilderness, they saw in Egypt an oasis watered by the river Nile. Cooler breezes brought the breath of life to meet them on the way, and plenty of sweet, fresh water realized the heaven of the African. The Kami found their old lost paradise in "Uat," the name signifying green, fresh, well-watered. Uat was literally the land of wet as water. Here then was heaven in the north, heaven as the north, heaven in the water and the breezes of the north. And on this they founded a celestial garden or enclosure, which was configurated by them in the northern heaven as the primitive paradise of edible plants and plenty of water. The river Nile was traced back by the Egyptians to a double source. This in later times was localized at Elephantine, but not originally. The Nile was known to issue from the two great lakes which were the southern source of the river according to the Ritual. A tablet discovered at Gebel Silsileh refers to two of the ancient festivals of the Nile which had fallen into disuse in the time of Rameses II. In this it is said, "I know what is written in the book-store kept in the library, that whenever the Nile cometh forth from the two fountains, the offerings of the gods are to be plenty" (*Records of the Past,* vol. x, 41). The river was timed to come forth from its double welling-place on the 15th of Epiphi, and the inundation to reach Gebel Silsileh, or Khennut, on the 15th of Taht. The first of these dates corresponds to our May the 31st; the second to August the 4th. This allows two months and three days for the inundation to travel from its swollen and overflowing double-breasted source, wheresoever that was localized, to Gebel Silsileh. The length of the river from the Victoria Nyanza to the sea is now estimated at 3,370 miles. It is less than 3,000 to Silsileh, and water flowing at the rate of only two miles an hour would make 3,120 miles in sixty-five days. This seems to afford good evidence that the two fountains were identified with the two lakes, and that the double source was afterwards repeated locally lower down at Elephantine. The Egyptians had tracked the river to its sources "in the recesses," called *"the Tuat of the south,"* and the inundation to the bursting forth and overflowing of the southern lakes at high flood (Hymn to the Nile; also Ritual, ch. 149).

The mother of water in the northern heaven was imaged as the water-cow. Another type of the birthplace was the thigh or haunch of the cow, and one of the two lakes at the head of the Milky Way in the region of the northern pole was called the "lake of the thigh." The Osiris (ch. 149), on attaining the divine regions of water, air, and food, or, as we say, *heaven,* exultingly exclaims, "I alight at 'the thigh of the lake.'" This was the thigh of the cow that was constellated in heaven at least twice over, as a sign of the birthplace, when the birth was water, or Horus, the child of the inundation. Now the name of Tanganyika, from the African "tanga" for "the thigh" and "nyika" for the water, signifies the lake of the thigh or haunch. But the thigh is only a symbol which in Sign-language denotes the birthplace that was imaged more completely by the Cow itself; the water-cow of Apt, in Apta, which represented earth as the great mother and giver of the water that, according to the legend, burst forth from the abyss in the deluge of the inundation when the lake was formed at first. The lake of the thigh = Tanganyika was constellated in the northern heaven by name as a uranograph, and this lake of the thigh or haunch was the lake of the water-cow. Hence we find the cow and the haunch are blended together in one group of stars that is labelled the "Meskhen," as the womb or birthplace at the summit of the pole. P. 289. And, although this lake in Africa is a little over the line to the south, it is near enough to have been reckoned on it, and therefore to have been the earthly prototype of the great lake at the horn-point of the northern pole which the Ritual denominates the "lake of *equipoise*" as well as the lake of the thigh. Amongst the other signs that were configurated at the summit of the northern heaven as object-pictures of the old primeval homeland were the fields of the papyrus reed, the waters welling from unfathomable depths, the ancient mother as the water-cow of Apt, who was the living image of Apta as the birthplace in the reeds. Thus, with the aid of their uranographs the Egyptian mystery teachers showed the birthplace in the fields of the papyrus plant; the reed bed in Uthlanga, where the black and white twins of darkness and day were born; the birthplace of the water flowing from its secret source in the land of the two lakes called "the lake of equipoise" and "the lake of the thigh," or Tanga, whence the name Tanganyika. There was the water that for ever flowed in fields for ever fresh and green, which figured now the water of life that has no limit, and the food that is eternal in the Kamite eschatology. In the astronomy Apta was the mount of earth as a figure of the equator, whereas the summit of the circumpolar paradise was the mount of heaven as a figure of the pole. In the final picture to the Ritual (ch. 186) the mount of Amenta stands in a morass of the papyrus reed. The cow that represented the great mother is portrayed in the two forms of Apt the water-cow and Hathor the milch-cow, as the typical mother amongst the reeds in the place of birth on the earth and thence of rebirth in heaven. Thus, as we interpret it, the imagery of equatoria was commemorated in the uranographic representation or Sign-language of the astronomical mythology.

Sir Harry Johnston sees traces of the Egyptian or Hamitic influence amongst the more primitive dwarfs and Negroes of the equatorial regions, but this he speaks of as the result of *a returning wave* from the Nilotic races. Assuredly the Kamite race of migratory colonizers on the lower Nile did return in later times in search of the old home. Their voyages by water and travels by land had become the subject of popular tales. But this was as travellers, adventurers, naturalists, and miners who explored their hinterland, dug for metals or gems, imported strange animals, and transplanted precious trees to furnish incense for the goddesses and gods. It was not the grown-up, civilized Ruti of Egypt, who called themselves "the men" *par excellence,* that went back to beget the ape-like race of negroid dwarfs in the central regions of Africa, or to people the impenetrable forests with non-civilized, ignorant, undeveloped manikins. That was not the route of evolution.

It is an ancient and world-travelling tradition that heaven and earth were close together in the beginning. Now the heaven signified in the oldest of all mythologies, the Kamite, was the starry heaven of night upraised by Shu as he stood upon the mount of earth. This was the heaven in which the stars of our two Bears revolved about the pole. The writer of the present work has seen in equatorial regions how the Southern Cross arises and the Bears go down for those who are going south. The northern pole-star dips and disappears, and with it sinks the primal paradise of mythology in general that was configurated in the stars about the pole. On coming north again, the old lost paradise arose once more as paradise regained. At a certain point, in regions of no latitude, the pole-star rests for ever on the horizon in the north, or, as the Egyptians figured it, upon the mount of earth in Apta. The heaven of the ancient legends and of the equatorial astronomers was close to the earth, because the pole-star rested on the summit of the mount like Anup on his mountain. Such traditions were deposited as the mythical mode of representing natural fact, however much the fact may be obscured. Now, the ordinary heaven of night and day could not supply the natural fact. Heaven is no farther off from earth than ever. Yet there is a starting point in the various mythologies that is equivalent to this beginning, at which time heaven rested on the earth, and was afterwards separated from it by the mythical uplifter of the sky. The name of heaven denotes the up-heaven. Nut or Nu, the Egyptian name for heaven, has the meaning and the sign of uplifted. And there was but one starting point at which the heaven could be said to rest upon the earth. This was in the regions of no latitude, where the pole-stars were to be seen upon the two horizons. As the nomads travelled towards the north, this heaven of the pole, which touched the earth in equatoria, naturally rose up from the mount, or, as mythically rendered, it was raised by Shu, who stood upon the steps of Am-Khemen to reach the height, and push the two apart with his huge staff that was the giant's figure of the north celestial pole. There were no solstices in Apta. Time, if any, was always equinoctial there. And on this equal measure of day and dark the first division of the circle, the *sep* or turn-round of the sphere, was founded. When Shu upraised the sky it was equally divided between Sut and Horus, the portion of each being half of the water, half of the mount, or half of the twenty-four hours. And this was the time made permanent in Amenta, where the later register for all such simple mysteries was kept. There are twelve hours light and twelve hours dark in this nether-world, the same as in the equatorial regions. It is the equinoctial time of Shu and Maati. The earth was *not* an upright pillar in Apta, with the starry sphere revolving round it on a horizontal plane. The risings and settings of the stars were vertical, and the two fixed centres of the poles were on the two horizons, or, in accordance with the Egyptian expression, on the northern and the southern sides of the mount of earth. The sky, as the celestial water, was also divided into two great lakes, one to the north and one to the south of the mount. These survive in the Ritual as the Lake of Kharu and the Lake of Ru to the south and the north of the Bakhu hill "on which heaven resteth" (chs. 108 and 109). The system of dividing the celestial water was apparently founded on the two great equatorial lakes at the head of the Nile, which were repeated in the two lakes of Amenta and in the other pictures of the double source of the great stream now figured in heaven at the head of the Milky Way as "the stream without end."

The Egyptians also preserved traditions of Ta-nuter, the holy land that was known by the name of Punt or Puanta. Maspero spells the name Puanit. The present writer has rendered it Puanta. One meaning of *anta,* in Egyptian, is yellow or golden. Hence Puanta the golden. The name is applied in the Ritual (ch. 15) to the land of dawn, or anta, as the golden = the land of gold. This was the mythical or divine Anta in Amenta where the tree of golden Hathor grew. In that case, Puanta or Punt is identical with the orient in the mythos . But the land of Puanta is also geographical, and there was an Egyptian tradition that this divine country could be reached by ascending the river Nile (Maspero, *Histoire Ancienne*, p. 5). It was reported that in a remote region south you came to an unknown great water which bathed Puanta or the holy land, Ta-nuter. This, we suggest, was that nearest and largest of all the African lakes, now called the Victoria Nyanza, from which the river Nile debouches on its journey north. We gather from the inscriptions of Der-el-Bahari that the inhabitants of that Puanta for which the expedition of Queen Hatshepsu sailed were lake-dwellers. The houses, built on piles, were reached by means of ladders, and pile-dwellings imply that the people of Puanta were dwellers on the lake. Further, it is recorded on the monuments that two naval expeditions were made by the Egyptians to the land of Puanta. The first occurred in the reign of Sankh-Ka-Ra, the last king of the eleventh dynasty, long before the expedition to Puanta was made in the time of Queen Hatshepsu (eighteenth dynasty). The leader of this earlier expedition was a nobleman named Hannu, who describes his passage inland through the desert and the cultivated land. On his return to Egypt from the gold land, he speaks of coming back from the land of Seba, and thus far identifies the one with the other. He says: "When I returned from Seba, or Sebœa, I had executed the king's command, for I brought him back all kinds of presents which I had met with in the ports of Puanta, and I came back by the road of Uak and of Hannu" (Inscription, Rohan). In the story of the shipwrecked sailor the speaker says of his voyage: "I was going to the mines of Pharaoh, in a ship that was 150 cubits long and 40 cubits wide, with 150 of the best sailors in Egypt." He was shipwrecked on an island, which turned out to be in the land of Puanta. The serpent ruler of the island says to the sailor: "I am prince of the land of Puanta." It is not said that this was the land of the mines, but he was sailing to the mines when he reached the land of Puanta (Petrie, *Egyptian Tales*, pp. 82, 90). An inscription found in the tomb of Iua and Thua (of the eighteenth dynasty), which tomb was rich in gold, informs us that the gold had been brought from "the lands of the south." Also the Mazai tribes are known to have had relations with the people of Puanta. Puanta, as a geographical locality, is said to lie next to the spirit world, or the land of the shades, which is spoken of as being in the south, but as far away as sailors could go up-stream; in fact, it was where the celestial waters came from heaven at the sources of the Nile. This surely means that Puanta, the gold land, was at the summit of this world, and therefore closest to the next, where there was nothing but the firmamental water betwixt them and the islands of the blessed.

If Mashonaland should prove to be the gold land of Puanta, this would be the geographical Puanta, not Arabia, from which the golden Hathor and the hawk of gold originally came. The symbolism of the ruined cities of Mashonaland, discovered by the explorer Bent, suffices at least to show that the Egyptians of a very remote age had worked the gold mines in that country. Horus on his pedestal or papyrus is a figure not to be mistaken, whether the bird is a hawk or a vulture, for there was also a very ancient Horus of the vulture that was the bird of Neith. The hawk or vulture on the pedestal or papyrus (Uat) was indefinitely older than the human type of Horus the child in Egypt. Horus as the hawk or vulture, standing on the column within the necklace zone or cestus, was the child of Hathor; and these two, Hathor and Horus, were the divine mother and child. The gold hawk of Horus is connected with the Egyptian mines, whilst precious metals and stones, especially the turquoise, were expressly sacred to the goddess Hathor. The Egyptian goddess Hathor, as a form of the Earth-mother, was the mistress of the mines, and of precious stones and metals, called mafkat. It was here she gave birth to the blue-eyed golden Horus as her child, her golden calf or hawk of gold. The

Egyptian labourers who worked the mines of the turquoise country in the Sinaitic peninsula were worshippers of this golden Hathor and the golden Horus. These two are the divinities most frequently invoked in the religious worship of the Egyptian officers and miners residing in the neighbourhood of the mafkat mines. Also the name for a mine in Egyptian is ba or ba-t, and baba, or babait, is a plural for mines, likewise for caverns, grottoes, and lairs underground. Moreover, this district of the Sinaitic mines was designated Baba or Babait by the Egyptian miners. And this name of Baba or Babait, with the plural terminal for the mines, would seem to have been preserved and repeated for the Zimbabwe mines in Rhodesia, the Egyptian word being left there by the Egyptian workers. Lastly, as Mafekh or Mafkhet is a title of Hathor, as mafekh is an Egyptian name for the turquoise, for copper and other treasures of the mines, as well as of Hathor, one wonders whether the name of Mafeking was not also derived from the Egyptian word "mafekh." The earliest Ta-Neter or holy land of the Egyptians, then, was Puanta in the south, which was sacred on account of its being the primeval home. But in the mythos the place of coming forth had been given to the sun god in the east, and this became the holy land in the solar mythology which has been too hastily identified by certain Egyptologists with Arabia as the eastern land.

At present we are more concerned with the original race and its primitive achievement than with the return wave from Egypt in the later ages of the Pharaohs. The oasis in Africa was a heaven on earth, a paradise in nature ready-made in the vast expanse of papyrus reed. Egypt from the beginning was based on the oasis, Uat. We might trace a form of the heptanomis with which Egypt began in the seven oases: the great oasis of Abydos, called Uaht, the great Theban oasis, the oasis of the Natron Lakes, the oasis of El-Kargeh, the oasis of Sinai, the oasis of Dakhel, and the oasis of Bahnesa.

Maspero says the Great Oasis had been at first considered as a sort of mysterious paradise to which the dead went in their search of peace and happiness. It was called Uit or Uat. As late as the Persian epoch the ancient tradition found its echo in the name of the "Isles of the Blessed" (Herod., III, 26), which was given to the Great Oasis. "So soon as the deceased was properly equipped with his amulets and formulas, he set forth to seek 'the field of reeds'" (*D. of C.*, Eng. trans., p. 183). The "field of reeds" was the field of Uat, the papyrus reed, which had been repeated in the heavens, from the Uat of Egypt; the Uat of the oasis, the Uat of the reed land that was in the beginning. For those who lived on the papyrus shoots, when this was a primeval food, there was a world of plenty in the region of the lakes, which would be looked back to as a very paradise by those who wandered forth into the waterless deserts and suffered cruelly from thirst and hunger midst the arid wastes of burning sand. In seeking "the field of reeds" the deceased was going back in spirit to Uthlanga, the cradle in the reeds, or to Karua, the land of the lakes; to Apta, the starting-point; to Puanta, the ever-golden; to Merta, the land of the two eyes, or some other form of the primitive paradise, where, as the Ritual has it, he would drink the waters of the sacred river at the sources of the Nile. This was the land where food and water had been abundant enough to furnish a type of everlasting plenty for the land of promise in the astronomical mythology and the eschatology.

It is necessary to postulate a commencement in equatorial regions, in order that we may explain certain primeval representations in the land of Egypt. We see a deluge legend originating in the woman's failing to keep the secret of the water source, which was followed by an overwhelming, devastating flood. We see that a legend of the first man—he who brought death into the world by disobeying the law of tabu—is indigenous to the natives of Uganda. A primitive picture of "the beginning" is also presented in an African story which was told to Stanley by a native of the Bashko on the Aruwimi River, and called "The Creation of Man." It is related that "In the old, old time all this land, and indeed the whole earth, was covered with sweet water. Then the water dried up or disappeared. No living thing was moving on the earth, until one day a large toad squatted by one of the pools. How long it had lived or how it came into existence was not known, but it was suspected that the water must have brought it forth from some virtue of its own. On the whole earth there was but this one toad"—which in relation to water was the frog. Then follows the legend of "creation." The toad becomes the maker of the primal human pair which came into being in the shape of twins (like Sut and Horus, or the Zulu black and white twins in the bed of reeds), and these are said to be "the first like our kind that ever trod the earth." (Stanley, H. M., *My Dark Companions and their Strange Stories,* pp. 5-30.) The legend we judge to be an African original relating to the primordial water in which the earth was figured as a "large toad," or frog, at the time when no other living thing moved on the earth, and there was no human creature known. The frog floating on the water in the act of breathing out of it was an arresting object to primitive man, and this became a type of earth emerging from the water of space. The constellation of *Piscis Australis* was known to the Arab astronomers as the frog. Indeed, the two fish, the southern fish and the whale, were named by them as the two frogs (Higgins, W. H., *Names of the Stars and Constellations*). But, whichever type was first, a monstrous frog or huge fish, a turtle or the water-cow, it was a figure of the earth amidst the firmamental water, in the lower part of which was the abyss. And here the primal pair are also born as twins, like Sut and Horus. In Egypt the north celestial pole was variously imaged as a mountain-summit, an island in the deep, a mound of earth, a papyrus plant or lotus in the waters of immensity, a tree, a stake, a pole, a pillar, a pyramid, and other types of the apex in heaven.

In Equatoria there was neither pole nor pole-star fixed *on high* in the celestial north. On the other hand, there were two pole-stars visible upon the two horizons, north and south. These, according to the imagery, might be represented by two jackals, two lions, two giraffes, mountains—the mount and horizon being synonymous—two trees, two pillars of the firmament, or by the two eyes of two watchers. "Heaven's-Eye Mountain" is a Chinese title for the Mount of the Pole (De Groot, *Fêtes d'Emoui,* I, 74). This would apply when only one pole-star was visible. But in Equatoria there were two poles or mountains with the eyes of two non-setting stars upon the summits, the only two fixed stars in all the firmament. These we hold to be the "pair of eyes" or merti that were also a pair of jackals in the Kamite astronomical mythology. But first of the two poles as pillars.

Josephus has preserved a tradition concerning two pillars that were erected in the land of Siriad. He tells us that the children of Seth (Egyptian, Set) were the inventors of astronomy, and in order that their inventions might not be lost, and acting "upon Adam's prediction that the world was to be destroyed at one time by the force of fire, and at another time by the violence and quantity of waters, they made two pillars, the one of brick, the other of stone; they inscribed their discoveries upon them both, that in case the pillar of brick should be destroyed by the flood, the pillar of stone might remain and exhibit those discoveries to mankind, and also inform them that *there was another pillar of brick erected by them. Now this remains in the Land of Siriad to this day.*" (*Ant.*, B. i. ch. 2.) Plato likewise speaks of these two columns in the opening of Timæus. The place where the two pillars, or one of them, traditionally stood was in the land of Siriad. Where that is no mortal knows, but Seri in Egyptian is a name for the south. Seri is also the mount that is figured as the twofold rock which is equivalent to the pillars of the two horizons, south and north. Seri is also the name of the giraffe, a zoötype of Sut, the overseer. Siriad, then, we take to be the land of the south where the pillar "remains to this day." According to John Greaves, the old Oxford astronomer, "these pillars of Seth were in the very same place where Manetho placed the pillars of Taht, called Seiread" (*English Weights and Measures*).

It is possible to identify the missing pillar of the two, the pillar of Sut in the south. There was a southern Annu and a northern Annu in Egypt, and possibly a relic of the two poles may be recognized in the two Annus, viz., Hermonthes, the Annu of the south, and Heliopolis, the Annu of the north. The original meaning of Annu appears to have been the place of the pillar, or stone, that marked the foundation which preceded the ⊕-sign of station or dwelling-place. There was an Egyptian tradition which connected Sut, the inventor of astronomy, with Annu, as the original founder of the pillar, which makes him the primary establisher of the pole. As an astronomical character Sut was earlier than Shu. The Arabs also have a tradition that one of the pyramids was the burial-place of Sut. The pillar of brick, being less permanent, went down as predicted in the deluge as a figure of the southern pole, whereas the pillar of stone remained for ever as an image of the north celestial pole, or of Annu, the site of the pillar, in the astronomical mythology. It is reported by Diodorus that Annu (Heliopolis in the solar mythos) was accounted by its inhabitants to be the oldest city in Egypt. Which may have been mystically meant, as Annu was also a city or station of the pole, the most ancient foundation in the northern heaven, described in the eschatology as the place of a thousand fortresses provisioned for eternity.

The two pillars of Sut and Horus were primal as pillars of the two poles thus figured in the equatorial regions as the two supports of heaven when it was first divided in two portions, south and north; and the pillar or mount of the south was given to Sut, the pillar or mount of the north to Horus. The typical two pillars are identified with and *as* Sut and Horus in the inscription of Shabaka from Memphis, in which it is said, *"The two pillars of the gateway of the house of Ptah are Horus and Sut."* The present interpretation is that the typical two pillars or props originated as figures of the two poles, the single pillar being an ideograph of Sut, that these were established in the two domains of Sut and Horus to the south and north of the land in which the veriest dawn of astronomy first occurred, and that the types were preserved and re-erected in the earth of eternity as the two supports of the heaven suspended by Ptah for the Manes in Amenta, even as the sky of earth had been uplifted and sustained by the two poles of the south and north in Equatoria. Sut and Horus, then, were the twin props of support twice over, once in Equatoria as the two poles, once in Amenta as the two tats of Ptah. Further, two brothers, Sut and Horus, as the founders of the two poles in building the heavens for the ancient mother, may explain the American story of the two brothers who planted each a cane in the house of their grandmother when they started on their perilous journey to the land of Kibalba. The old mother was to know how they fared by the flourishing or withering of the tree or cane, and whether they were alive or dead. Grimm traced the same legend in the story of the two gold children who wished to leave their home and go forth to see the world. At parting they say, "We leave you the two golden lilies: from these you can see how we fare. If they are fresh we are well; if they fade we are ill; if they fall we are dead." Now the reason why this story is told in Central America, in India, and in Europe we hold to be because it was first told in Africa and rendered mythically in Egypt.

It appears quite possible that a form of the two typical pillars which were visible at the equator also survives in the two sacred poles of the Arunta natives in Central Australia. These people "down under" have no northern pole or pole-star of the north, but they carry two symbolic poles about with them, which they erect wherever they go as signs of locality or encampment, both of which are limited to the south and the north. One is called the nurtunja. This, so to say, is the north pole of the two, and is never met with in the south. The other, called a waninga, is always limited to the south. The nurtunja is typical of the northern and the waninga of the southern part of the Arunta tribe. Each of these, like the Egyptian tat-pillar, is a sign of establishing or founding, as is shown from its use in the ceremony of young man making. In Greek myth the temple of heaven was raised on high by two brothers, who in one version are Trophonios and Agamedes, the builders of the temple of Apollo. The sinking of Trophonios into the cave also corresponds to the engulfing of Sut in his going down south with the disappearing pole.

One of the two legendary pillars of Seth disappeared, the other remained. And when the nomads of the equatorial regions had begun the movement northward on the way that led them down the

Nile, they would gradually lose sight of the southern pole-star, and whatsoever else had been configurated with it in the nightly heaven would sink below the horizon south, like a subsidence of land in the celestial waters. Thus in astronomical mythology a fall from heaven, a sinking down in the waters called a deluge, and a lost primeval home were natural occurrences as certain stars or constellations disappeared from sight for those who travelled northward from the equatorial plain. And these celestial events would be told of as mundane in the later legends of the "Fall" and "Flood" and man's lost paradise of everlasting peace and plenty. It is enough, however, for the present purpose that a star or constellation first assigned to Sut sank down into the dark abysm south, and disappeared from the ken of the observers who were on their journey of three thousand miles down into the valley of the Nile. It is certain that Sut went down south to some sort of nether-world, and so became the power of darkness in Amenta, when our earth had been completely hollowed out by Ptah, and Amenta below became the south to the circumpolar paradise in the celestial north. The ancient Egyptians had no antipodes on the outside of the earth. Amenta in the nether-world was their antipodes. Their two poles were celestial and sub-terrestrial. The north pole was at the summit of the mount. The south pole was in the root-land of the earth below. The Ritual describes the ways of darkness in the entrance to the Tuat as the tunnels of Sut, which tends to show that a way to the nether-world was made by Sut when his star and standing-ground went under in the abyss of the beginning in the south, where the Egyptians localized the Tuat or entrance to the under-world, which was the place of egress for the life that came into the world by water from "the recesses of the south."

Without doubt the contention of Sut and Horus began with the conflict of darkness and light or drought and water when these were elemental powers, and the birthplace of the twin brothers, one black, one white, was in the bed of reeds. This phase was continued by the twins that likewise struggled for supremacy in the dark and light halves of the moon, which imaged the light eye of Horus and the dark eye of Sut. But the war extended to the whole of nature, that was divided in halves betwixt the Sut and Horus twins, who were the first-born of the ancient mother in two of her several characters. In Central Africa the year is divided into two seasons of rain and drought. These are equivalent to the two opposite domains of Horus and Sut as powers of good and evil. The winds of the north and south follow suit. The wind from the north in the rainy season is warm and wet and beneficent; on the other hand, the wind that comes up from the South Pole is witheringly dry, the wind therefore of Sut, the power inimical to man and animal in physical nature. (Johnston, *Brit. Centr. Africa*, p. 42.) The desert drought, like darkness, was an element assigned to Sut. As this was the region of drought and sterility and Typhonian sands, and Sut the tawny-complexioned was the force that dominated in the south under the same name, we may see how and where he first acquired his character in Egyptian mythology as representative of the arid desert opposed to water, fertility, and food. Thus Sut versus Horus imaged the south versus north. Sut was deadly as the drought; Horus was "right as rain." This contention of the combatants and of the south versus the north was continued in the stellar mythos until their reconciliation was effected by some other god, such as Shu, Taht, or Seb. When Sut, or his star, went down from the horizon, mount or pole in the south, he gradually sank to the lowermost parts of the abyss which in the eschatology was called the secret earth of Amenta. Here his character as the opener of roads or ways in the astronomy was continued into the Egyptian eschatology by Ap-Uat or the jackal as the conductor of souls. He was the deity of the dark. In the oblong zodiac of Denderah the two jackals of the south and north, continued in the solar mythos, are figured opposite to each other. These represent the two forms of Ap-Uat, the opener of ways, who was imaged as a jackal, the seer in the dark. One jackal was known as guide of the southern ways, the other as opener of the northern ways. No Egyptologist has gone further than to suggest that this north and south may have been in Amenta—as they also were. But no one has dared to dream of a beginning with the primitive paradise in Equatoria.

Egyptian Wisdom.

> Deluded visionaries, lift your eyes,
> Behold the truths from which your fables rise!
> These were realities of heavenly birth,
> And ye pursue their shadows on the earth.

"The wisdom of the Egyptians," said Augustine, "what was it but astronomy?" (*City of God*, B. 18, ch. 39.) The answer is that it was not simply the science of astronomy in the modern sense, but astronomical mythology was the subject of subjects with the ancient "mystery-teachers of the heaven," as the Egyptian Urshi or astronomers were self-designated. The most puerile report of all which has played false with us so long is the exoteric tradition in the Hebrew Pentateuch.

Professor Sayce has asserted that "Babylonia was really the cradle of astronomical observation" (*Hibbert Lect.*, p. 397). To which one might reply with the wise Egyptian, "Do you really know that, or is it that you only pretend to know?" The author of *Researches into the Origin of the Constellations* of the Greeks, Phœnicians, and Babylonians also claims a Euphratean origin for these, whilst admitting that *"Egypt was not indebted to any foreign region for her original scheme of constellations, which are entirely or almost entirely distinct"* (Robert Brown, Jun.). But it is useless or puerile to discuss the genesis of astronomical mythology with the African originals omitted, and without allowing for the alterations that were made by Greeks and Euphrateans in the course of transmitting a celestial chart. To omit the Kamite "wisdom" from the reckoning is to dispense with evolution and leave no ground for a beginning—no gauge of time nor data of development. Moreover, the primary question of the origins is not astronomical but mythological. The types of this Sign-language had been founded in totemism. These were first employed for distinguishing the human motherhood and brotherhoods. They were reapplied to the elemental powers in mythology, and afterwards repeated in the constellation figures as a mode of record in the heavens which can still be read by aid of the Egyptian wisdom, but not by means of the Semitic legendary lore. The primitive constellations might be described as Egyptian ideographs configurated in groups of stars, with the view of determining time and season and of registering the prehistoric human past.

The principle of representation was similar to that of the modern teachers who draw their diagrams upon the blackboard. In like manner the mystery teachers of the heavens approximately shaped the constellation figures on the background of the dark, to be seen at night and to be expounded in the mysteries. For example, if they were desirous of memorizing some likeness of the old primeval home in Apta at the horn-point of the earth, this would naturally be done by repeating the especial imagery of the equatorial regions at the highest point of beginning in the northern heaven as seen in Egypt. Or, if they wished to show that the river of the inundation issued from an abyss of water in the remotest south, this could be accomplished by constellating the course of the stream in heaven on its long and winding way from the star Achernar to the star Rigel at the foot of Orion. Hence the water of the inundation was depicted in and as the river Eridanus. The contest between Horus the lord of light and the serpent of the dark was made uranographic in the "Serpent-Holder." The conflict betwixt Horus who came by water and the dragon of drought was exhibited by the Apap-reptile being drowned in the inundation as the monster "Hydra." The scene configurated in the southern heaven where the conqueror Orion rose to bruise the serpent's head or crush the dragon under foot is also represented in the Ritual when Apap is once more put in bonds, cut up piecemeal, and submerged in the green lake of heaven (ch. 39). Other imagery in the planisphere bears witness to the drowning of the dragon Apap in the waters of the inundation. The monster imaged in "Hydra" is treated as carrion by the crow that is perched upon it, pecking at its dead body. Or, if we suppose the mystery teachers of the heavens wished to constellate a figure of the *mount of earth* amidst the waters of surrounding space, and that this was in the time of the most primitive mound-builders, when no conical pillar could as yet be carved in wood or stone, how would they figure the object-picture forth as a uranograph? The earth was thought of as a mount amid the firmamental water, and to image this they would naturally raise a mound of earth. At the same time the heap of earth had acquired a sacred character in relation to the dead, and had become a kind of altar mound piled up with offerings of food. And such a figure we find in Ara, the southern altar or the altar mound. The earliest altar raised had been the mound of earth, and this was used to typify the mount of earth. Aratos, speaking of "the southern altar's sacred seat," calls this constellation "a mighty sign." Manilius says of the constellation, *"Ara mundi templum est"* (Astron., I, 427). It is traditionally connected with the war of the earth-born giants or elemental powers which were succeeded by the glorious ones or khuti in the astral mythos. The Mesopotamian mound-builders likewise show us that the most primitive type of foundation was the mound, that the earth-mound passed into the foundation of brickwork as the pillar, and the pillar culminating in the Ziggurat. So in Egypt the earth-mound led up to the pyramid with steps, that culminated in the altar-mound of stone. The Chinese still call the altar a mound. Because of its being a figure of the earth amidst the Nun, the altar-mound was raised immediately after the deluge in the Semitic mythos. In this way the teachers who first glorified the storied windows of the heavens, like some cathedral of immensity, with their pictures of the past, are demonstrably Egyptian, because the Sign-language, the mythos, the legends, and the eschatology involved are wholly Egyptian, and entirely independent of all who came after them. The so-called "wisdom of the ancients" was Egyptian when the elemental powers were represented first as characters in mythology. It was Egyptian when that primeval mythology was rendered astronomically. It is also Egyptian in the phase of eschatology. Speaking generally, and it would be difficult to speak too generally from the present standpoint, the Egyptian mythology is the source of the märchen, the legends, and the folk-lore of the world, whilst the eschatology is the fountain-head of all the religious mysteries that lie betwixt the earliest totemic and the latest Osirian, that were ultimately continued in the religion of ancient Rome. The mysteries were a dramatic mode of communicating the secrets of primitive knowledge in Sign-language when this had been extended to the astronomical mythology. Hence, we repeat, the Egyptian Urshi or astronomers were known by the title of "mystery teachers of the heavens," because they explained the mysteries of primitive astronomy.

For one thing, a later theology has wrought havoc with the beginnings previously evolved and naturally rendered. And we have consequently been egregiously misled and systematically duped by the Semitic perversions of the ancient "wisdom." There was indeed "a fall" from the foothold first attained by the Egyptians to the dismal swamp of the Assyrian and Hebrew legends. In Egyptian mythology compared with the Babylonian the same types that represent evil in the one had represented good in the other. The old Great Mother of Evil, called the Dragon-horse in the Assyrian version, was neither the source nor the product of evil in the original. The serpent-goddess Rannut, as renewer of the fruits of earth in the soil or on the tree, is not a representative of evil. We hold that moral evil in the mythical domain is an abortion of theology which was mainly Semitic in its birth. The Kamite beginning with the Great Mother and the elemental powers which are definite and identifiable enough in the Egyptian wisdom became confused and chimerical in Babylonian and Hebrew versions of the same Sign-language; the dark of a benighted heaven followed day. Elemental evils were converted into moral evil. The types of good and ill were indiscriminately mixed, pre-eminently so in the reproduction of the old Great Mother as Tiamat. Originally she was a form of the Mother-earth, the womb of life, the suckler, the universal mother in an elemental phase. But the types of good and evil were confounded in the later rendering. The creation of evil as a miscreation of theology is plainly traceable in the Akkadian, Babylonian, Assyrian, and Hebrew remains. The Great Mother, variously named Tiamat, Zikum, Nin-Ki-Gal, or Nana, was not originally evil. She represented source in perfect correspondence to Apt, Ta-Urt, or Rannut in the Egyptian representation of the Great Mother, who, howsoever hideous, was not bad or inimical to man; the "mother and nurse of all," the "mother of gods and men," who was the renewer and bringer forth of life in earth and water. Nor were the elemental offspring evil, although imaged in the shape of monsters or of zoötypes. As Egyptian, the seven Anunnaki were spirits of earth, born of the Earth-mother in the earth, but they were not wicked spirits. The elements are not immoral. These are a primitive form of the seven great gods who sit on golden thrones in Hades as lords of life and masters of the under-world. Moreover, the seven *Nunu* or Anunas can be traced to their Egyptian origin.

In the Cuthean legend of creation we are told that the great gods created "warriors with the body of a bird" and "men with the faces of ravens." "Tiamat gave them suck." "Their progeny the mistress of the gods created." "*In the midst of the* (celestial) *mountains they grew up and became heroes*" and increased in number. "Seven kings, brethren, appeared as begetters"—who are given names as signs of personality (*Babylonian Story of Creation: Records of the Past*, N.S., vol. i. p. 149). Now the seven children of the great Mother as Egyptian were produced as two plus five. The Sut and Horus twins were born warriors or fighters. They are portrayed as two birds, the black vulture or raven of Sut and the gold hawk of Horus. These, the first two children imaged as two birds, one of which is black, will or may account for the two bird races, one of which had the face of a raven and were a black race, or were the "black-heads" in Akkad. The Sut and Horus twins were succeeded by five other powers, so that there were seven altogether, all brothers, *all males or begetters*—the seven which constituted a primary order of gods, as *fellow-males* who were the "Nunu" of Egypt, which became the Anunas or primordial male deities of ancient Babylonia. But the seven nature powers evolved in the Egyptian mythos were the offspring of the great Earth-mother, not the progeny of Apap. They were native to the nether earth, but were not wicked spirits. They are spoken of in the Ritual (ch. 83) as "those seven Uræus-deities who are born in Amenta." The serpent type is employed to denote the power, but it is the good serpent, the Uræus-serpent of life and of renewal, not the evil reptile Apap. These the Euphrateans changed into the seven evil spirits or devils of their theology. The spawn of Apap in Egypt are the Sebau, which were numberless in physical phenomena and never were portrayed as seven in number. The Euphrateans turned the evil serpent Apap into Tiamat, the old Great Mother in the abyss of birth, where she has been supposed to have brought forth the seven powers of evil and to have been herself the old serpent with seven heads. In Egypt, happily, we get beyond the rootage of mythology in Babylonia and Akkad. The goddess Rannut was a form of the Earth-goddess as the serpent-mother. The serpent brood or dragon progeny of Rannut are mentioned in the Ritual, where they have become a subject of ancient knowledge in the mysteries (ch. 125). Elsewhere they are called the seven divine Uræi or serpents of life. There are no seven serpents of death, no seven evil serpents, in the Kamite representation. The seven Uræi, though elemental, born of matter, and of the earth earthy, like their mother, are not evil powers; neither are they in the same category with the Sebau of Apap or the Sami-fiends of Sut; whereas in the Euphratean version these have become seven wicked spirits as the evil brood of the Great Mother Tiamat. They are also portrayed as the seven heads or potencies of an infernal snake, which had been Egyptian, but without the seven heads, the types of good and evil being mixed up together as Euphratean. The Kamite elemental powers were just the powers of the elements represented by zoötypes. They might be sometimes fearsome, but they were not baneful. The inimical forces of external nature, the evil spawn of drought, plagues, dearth, and darkness, called the Sebau or the Sami, had preceded these, whereas in Babylonia the two categories are confused and the seven have been reproduced as altogether evil. They are sevenfold in all things evil: seven evil demons, seven serpents of death, seven evil winds, seven wicked spirits; seven in the hollows of the earth, seven evil monsters in the watery abyss; seven evil incubi, seven plagues. But even these seven baleful and injurious spirits of Babylonia originated as powers of the elements, no matter where. Hence the first is a scorpion of rain (cf. the *curse* of rain); the second is a monster with unbridled mouth (thunder); the third is the lightning-flash; the fourth is a serpent; the fifth is a raging dog; the sixth is a tempest; the seventh is the evil wind. Here the whole scheme of evil is meteorological, and is based upon bad northern weather (Sayce, *Magical Texts*, H. L., p. 463). The theological perversion and the degradation of the type are traceable in Babylonia. The seven serpent powers were originally the same. In Egypt they are the seven spirits of the earth. And of the seven in Babylonia it is said in the magical text from Eridu: "those seven in the earth were born. Those seven in the earth grew up. Those seven from the earth have issued forth" (Sayce, H. L., pp. 463-469). Only in Babylonia the Great Mother as the crocodile type of water has been confounded with the Apap-reptile of evil, and made to spawn the evil powers in the darkness of later ignorance. We can watch the change in a Babylonian version of the mythos. The seven nature forces here originated as seven evil powers; they were "rebellious spirits" and "workers of calamity" that were "born in the lower part of heaven," or the firmamental deep. (*War of the Seven Evil Spirits: Records*, vol. v; also vol. ix, 143.) They are called "the forces of the deep," for ever rising in rebellion. In short, they are one with the Sebau of the Ritual, who were the progeny of Apap, which have been confounded with the "seven" elemental spirits who were not originally evil. The beneficent great Mother-earth who had been imaged by the sloughing serpent as a type of renewal and rejuvenescence was transmogrified into the serpent of theology, the very devil in a female guise, the author of evil that was ultimately represented as a woman who became the mother of the human race, and who doomed her offspring to eternal torment ere she gave them birth in time. The Hebrews follow the

Babylonians in confusing the Uræus-serpent of life with the serpent of death. The primal curse was brought into the world by Apap the reptile of drought, dearth, and darkness, plague and disease, but the evil serpent began and ended in physical phenomena. Apap never was a spiritual type, and was never divinized, not even as a devil. The beneficent serpent Rannut represents the mother of life, the giver of food in fruits of the earth or the tree. She is portrayed as the mother both in the form of a serpent and also as the human mother. But good and evil have been badly mixed together in the Hebrew version of the Babylonian perversion of the Egyptian wisdom.

The way in which the Kamite mythos was converted into Semitic legendary lore and finally into Biblical history is palpably apparent in the story of the fall. The woman offering fruit as temptress in the tree was previously represented in Sign-language as the serpent which was the symbol of renewal in the tree, as is shown when the reptile offers the fruit to the man. Thence came the serpent-woman, who was a compound of the zoötype and the anthrotype, and who was damned as Mother Eve, and deified as Rannut, the giver of the fruits of earth. Conclusive evidence of the way that changes were made in the appropriation of the prototypes and their readaptation to the change of fauna, and likewise of later theology, can be shown in relation to the primordial great mother who is Tiamat in Babylonia. One of her typical titles is the "dragon-horse," and as the Egyptians had no horse, it might be fancied at first sight that such a compound type as the dragon-horse, which also figures in Chinese mythology, was not Egyptian. The ancient Egyptians had no horse, and their dragon was a crocodile. The hippopotamus was their first water-horse as male—that is, the water-bull. As female it was the water-cow. Now, the old first genetrix Apt (Khept, or Ta-Urt), when represented as a compound figure is a hippopotamus, that is the water-horse, in front, and a crocodile, that is the dragon, behind. The dual type of Tiamat the dragon-horse is based on the crocodile and hippopotamus, which are to be seen combined in the twofold character of the great Mother Apt, and *these two animals were unknown to the fauna of Akkad and Babylonia.* Thus as Babylonian they are not derived directly from nature, but from the mythology and the zoötypes that were already extant in Egypt as African.

Horus, as Sebek, was the great fish of the inundation, typical of food and water. This great fish is the crocodile, which was applied to Horus as a figure of force in his capacity of solar god, the crocodile in Egypt being a prototype of the mythical dragon—not the evil dragon, but the solar dragon, which was known in relation to Sebek and to Saturn as the dragon of life. In one of the Greco-Egyptian planispheres this dragon keeps its original form and remains a crocodile. It is portrayed as a constellation of enormous magnitude, and is truly the great fish of Horus-Sebek that was first of all a figure of the inundation constellated in the stellar mythos and reapplied to the power that crossed the waters as the solar Horus of the double horizon (Drummond, Œd. Jud., pl. 2). The only form of evil to be found in the abyss was the dark and deadly power of drought, that, as feared, might drink or dry up all the water. This was figured as the Apap-reptile or some other form of the monster Hydra, the prototypal serpent of the sea. The mother of life in the abyss was the giver of water as the wet-nurse of the world, not the destroyer of the water.

In Babylonia the tree of life was changed into a tree of death. The serpent in the tree that offers fruit for food, as Rannut, the giver of food and representative of Mother-earth, was transformed into the evil serpent that "brought death into the world and all our woe," but which had originated as a beneficent figure in the Kamite representation of external nature. The transmogrifying of Tiamat, the mother of all and suckler of the seven elemental powers, into the dragon of evil might be followed on other lines of descent, as in the conflict of Bel-Merodach and the dragon. In the Egyptian representation Apap the dragon of drought is drowned in the water by Horus of the inundation, whose weapon therefore is the water flood. Now in warring with Tiamat the deluge is the "mighty weapon" wielded by Bel. "Bel (launched) the deluge, his mighty weapon, against Tiamat, inundating her covering," or drowning the dragon of drought. Thus Tiamat is destroyed by Bel with the deluge, where Apap was drowned by Horus in the inundation. This again shows that the great Mother Tiamat, the suckler, as the giver of water, had been converted into the evil dragon of drought. The good crocodile has also been transmuted into the evil dragon and portrayed as falling down head foremost from the starry summit of heaven to be trodden under foot and crushed beneath the heel of Horus, who is Herakles in Greece, Krishna in India, Merodach in Assyria. It was the same with other fauna. The pregnant hippopotamus was changed for the always female bear or the pregnant woman. The two dogs have been substituted for the two jackals of the south and north, the first two openers of the roads in heaven. The eagle of Zeus takes the place of the hawk of Ra, and the raven, the black Neh of Sut; the legend follows, and the conflict betwixt the eagle and the serpent is substituted for that of the warring hawk and serpent in the Egyptian mythos. The huge Apap-reptile of drought and darkness has been supplanted by the chimerical monster that is slain by Gilgames the solar god. And when the totemic matriarchate has been followed by the patriarchate, and the goddess of the "living word" in heaven has been changed in the Euphratean system for the lord who is "the voice of the firmament"; when the waterman has replaced the multimammalian wateress, the cow or sow of an earlier system of signs; when the heroes, or mighty ones, have been superseded by simple shepherds of the heavenly flocks—it becomes a question of very minor import who made the changes and forged the counterfeits, or whether the originals were deliberately disguised by the Akkadians or Babylonians, Phœnicians or Greeks.

In the course of the present inquiry we shall learn that the creation exoterically described in the Semitic legends of the beginning was not cosmogonical. Neither was it what one writer has called it, "the cosmography of appearances" (Schiaparelli, *Astronomy in the Old Testament*). It was Uranography, not cosmography, and uranography is Sign-language constellated in the stars. That which has been called "chaos" in the "legends of creation" was a condition in which there was neither law nor order, time nor name, nor means of representing natural phenomena. But it does not mean there were no natural phenomena because there had been no mode of expression. "Things" existed even when they had no name or record in the Babylonian mythology. It was never pretended in the Egyptian wisdom that there was any creation of the elements. Ground to stand on, food to eat, water to drink, air to breathe, had always been, and were in no wise dependent upon any mode of representation; whereas the mythical representation *did* depend upon the elements or nature-forces being already extant to be named or to be constellated and become pictorial for the purpose of the mystery teachers. In no land or literature has the mythical mode of representation been perverted and reduced to drivelling foolishness more fatally than in some of the Hebrew legends, such as that of Jonah and the great fish, which is connected with the origin of the fish-man in mythology who was born of a fish mother whom we shall identify with the constellation of the southern fish, and Horus of the inundation. The most ancient type of the fish was female, as a representative of the great Mother-earth in the water. This as Egyptian was the crocodile. She was the suckler of crocodiles in the inundation. She was the bringer forth as the great fish or crocodile in the astronomical mythology. One of her children was the crocodile-headed Sebek, who made the passage of the Nun by night as sun god in the solar mythos. The fish-man was at first the crocodile of Egypt, next the crocodile-headed figure of Horus who is called "the crocodile god in the form of a man" (Rit., ch. 88). The deceased assumes this form to cross the waters in the nether-world, because it had been a figure of the solar god in the mythology. The conversion of the crocodile god in the Nun to the fish-man of Babylonia is thus made plausible. Jonah is a form of the fish-man in the Biblical story (which is neither mythology nor eschatology), and therefore a figure of the solar god who made the passage of the waters as Horus the crocodile or as Ea the fish-man of Nineveh. As usual in later legend, the anthropomorphic rendering refaces and thus defaces the type. It was the fish itself that swam the waters of the inundation. It was the typical fish that swam the nocturnal waters, or the sun god represented by the mighty fish, whereas, this being "history," Jonah is made mere man, and therefore needed the great fish to carry him across the Nun or to land him at Nineveh. Birth, or rebirth, from the great fish in the Lower Nun is one of the oldest traditions of the race. It was represented in the mysteries and constellated in the heavens as a means of memorial. The great fish that landed Jonah on dry ground may still be seen as "Ketos" with its enormous mouth wide open at the point of emanation from the Nun, just where the landing-place on earth is represented in the equatorial regions on the celestial chart.

Naturally there would be some changes in the constellations with the change of fauna as the primitive wisdom passed from land to land, but that is a different matter from working the oracle of the celestial orrery on behalf of false and therefore all the more virulent theology. It can be demonstrated that the astronomical mythology of Egypt passed into Akkad and Babylonia, with the race of the Cushite "black-heads," to become the wisdom of the "Chaldees" and the Persian magi in after ages, including such primary types as the abyss of the beginning in the lower firmament, the Great Mother as a fish or dragon = crocodile in the abyss, and the fish-man born of the fish-mother from the abyss.

According to the legend related by Berosos, a divine fish-man, Oannes, or Oan, who had his dwelling in the Persian Gulf or Erythrean Sea, came forth from thence to teach the Chaldeans all they ever knew, when, as it is said in the native tradition, the people wisely "repeated his wisdom" (*W. A. I.,* ii. 16, 37-71). In all probability the instructor as a fish-man in Babylonia was represented by Ea, whose consort was Davki or Davkina, the Earth-mother corresponding to the Egyptian Great Mother, one of whose names was Tef. "Among the chief deities reverenced by the rulers of Telloh was one whose name is expressed by the ideographs of a 'fish' and an 'enclosure,' which served in later days to denote the name of Nina or Nineveh" (Sayce, *Hib. Lectures,* p. 281). The same sign, *i.e.,* of a fish, and enclosure in the Egyptian hieroglyphics, signifies An, to appeal, to show, to teach, as did the fish-man. An in Egyptian is a name of the teacher, the scribe, the priest. An was the fish in Egypt. An, with the fish for ideograph, is an ancient throne name that was found by Lepsius among the monumental titles on a tomb near the Pyramids of Gizeh (Bunsen, *Egypt's Place,* vol. ii, p. 77). This An, to show, to reveal, An, the fish of the enclosure, An, the teacher, as the fish, is the likeliest original of the Oan or Oannes who issued from the waters to show the Babylonians how to live, as the mythos was reflected in the later legend. Horus-Sebek was the earliest fish-man known to mythology. He calls himself the fish in the form of a man. Yet he issued from the female fish as a fish, the crocodile as son from the crocodile as Apt the mother and not as a man ejected from the mouth of a fish, as the legend reads when ignorantly literalized. The fish-mother also survived in the divine lady Nina, who was represented by the ideograph of a fish enclosed in a basin of water (Sayce, *Hib. L.,* p. 37), which has the same significance as the fish-mother in the lake at Ascalon.

But to reach the beginning the bottom must be plumbed in the abyss or nether parts of the firmamental Nun upon the outside of the mount by means of which the earth was imaged in the astronomical mythology. The abyss was known by various names in different versions of the mythos. It is the Phœnician baev or deep. It is the bau of the Hebrew Genesis. It is the bau or bahu as Egyptian. The word bahu is also a name for the god of the inundation called *the power of the southern lakes.* "I am Bahu the Great" is said four times over (in the Magic Papyrus) at the breaking forth of the water power from its southern source in the abyss of the dragon, the crocodile, or the Southern Fish (*Records,* vol. x. p. 149). The Egyptian also has an earlier form of the word bahu in "bab," for the well or whirlpool as a welling source of water. Another term for this outrance from the Nun is the tepht, which signifies the abyss, the source, the outlet. The Tiavat or Thavath of Berosos is a form of the Great Mother as a type of the watery abyss which is the Egyptian tepht, the abyss, the source, the well, the hole from whence the water issues, the dwelling underground where the dragon-horse gave suck to her brood of monsters in the earth. Tepht or Tept is also an Egyptian name for the old first Great Mother as a figure of source. This likewise had been applied to the place of emanation for the waters of the Nile which issued from the well of source, the bahu, tepht, or tuat. But the tepht of source, the lair of the dragon, the "hole of the snake" had been the outrance of the Nile from the abyss before there was a goddess Thavath or Tiamat in Assyria. So was it with the bau, bahu, or bab. These names had been applied to the source of the inundation itself and localized in Egypt before they were repeated in the astronomical mythology to become a subject of Semitic legendary lore. The bau, the bahu, or bab is Egyptian. The tepht and tuat are likewise Egyptian; and these names had been (already) applied to the source of the inundation and to the facts of earth that formed the mould of the astronomical mythology.

In the later Semitic legend it was said the earth was founded on the flood, as if it were afloat upon the water of the abyss. But according to the primary expression the earth stood on its own bottom in the water, at the fixed centre, with the tree upon the summit as a figure of food and water in vegetation. The mythical abyss of the beginning was the welling-place of water underground where life was brought to birth by the Great Mother from the womb of the Abyss. In the Ritual this is described as the Tuat, a place of entrance to and egress from the lower earth of Amenta. It is a secret Deep that nobody can fathom, which sends out light in the dark, and "its offerings are eatable plants." It is the birthplace of water and vegetation, and therefore, more abstractly, of life. The bottomless pit is a figure that was derived from this unplumbed deep inside the earth itself. From this abyss the Mother-earth (as womb of life) had brought forth her elemental progeny as the perennial renewers of food to eat, water to drink, and air to breathe.

The Tuat in the recesses of the south is likewise identified in the hymns as the secret source of the river Nile, which is thus traced to the abyss. Such was the birthplace of the beginning, the birthplace of water in the beginning from which the papyrus plants arose as the primeval food, and as the fact is registered in the Ritual. In the Magic Papyrus the abyss is comprehensively spoken of as "the water's well." It is the habitat of the dragon called "the crocodile coming out of the abyss." It is also the lair of the Apap-monster, of whom it is said by Shu, "If he who is in the water opens his mouth, I will let the earth fall into the water's well," being the "south made north, or the earth turned upside down" (*Records,* vol. x.). Here the two dragons can be identified together as the crocodile-dragon of water and the Apap-dragon of drought, that were at war from the beginning as antagonists in the abyss. The strife in the abyss was betwixt the crocodile of water and the fiery dragon of drought, the two dragons of good and evil, Sebek-Horus and the dragon or reptile of Apap. Both were born of the abyss; hence the Scholia on ch. 17 of the Ritual add, "The devourer comes from the lake of Puanta," or the water of the abyss which the Egyptians traced to the "recesses" in the south. The beginning in heaven, as on earth, was with water. Water was the first thing rendered uranographically, not created, in the southern hemisphere. This when "gathered into one place" was localized as *"the water."* The

Egyptians had a huge southern constellation dedicated to Menat the wet-nurse, called *"the Stars of the Water"* (Egyptian Calendar of Astronomical Observations). The "Southern Fish" and "Ketos" are both depicted in this water of the south or the abyss. Aratos, speaking of the stars in the neighbourhood of these great fishes or monsters of the deep, says "they are all of them called 'the water'" (Aratos, line 399, Brown). Earth, the Great Mother, was imaged as the breeder of life and the bringer forth from this abyssal water in the south. She was represented in two mythical characters. In one she is the mother who brought forth on dry ground, as the hippopotamus (or its equivalent type); in the other she was the mother of life in water who is figured as the Southern Fish low down in the deep of the southern heaven.

In mythology that which has been called "creation" begins with duplicating by dividing: darkness was divided from light, dry land as breathing-place was divided from water; the north was divided from the south, and earth was divided from heaven, as in the Japanese creation. So the power of the two monsters (in the Book of Enoch) "became separated on the same day, one being in the depths of the sea and one in the desert"—that is, one in the water, as Leviathan (the crocodile or dragon), and one as the hippopotamus on dry ground. Enoch asks the angel to show him "the power of those monsters and how they became *separated* on the same day of creation, one in the depths of the sea, above the springs of waters, and one in the dry desert." It is said of the two monsters that they had been prepared by the people of God to *become food*. In this there is a broken ray of the refracted mythos. The two monsters had represented food and drink from the first, one as the mother of life in the earth, the other in the waters. These two monsters were prepared for food in the garden or enclosure of the beginning. The name of one is Behemoth, the name of the other Leviathan. Behemoth is the Egyptian Bekhamut, the female hippopotamus, and Leviathan answers to the crocodile or dragon of the deep. The rabbis repeated a true tradition when they rendered the Biblical "Behemoth" not as a plural of majesty, but as a pair of beasts. They were a pair of beasts in the mythology of Egypt. The female Behemoth was the original Great Mother Kep, or Apt; the male was her son. The crocodile also, as zoötype, was both male and female. For his purpose, however, Enoch makes Leviathan a male monster and Behemoth female. Of course the type is or may be differentiated by the sex. The two monsters in the Egyptian starry scheme are both female as two forms of the Great Mother, who was the hippopotamus in her fore-part and the crocodile behind, or the crocodile in the south and the hippopotamus in the north. Thus the hippopotamus and crocodile which were natural in the Nile had become two huge, indefinite monsters of legendary lore in the Book of Enoch, and the two survived as the types of dry and wet, for land and water. The suggestion now to be made is that the two monsters of dry and wet, or earth and water, were constellated as the Southern Fish and Ketos, or the whale, but that the whale has been substituted for the hippopotamus by the Euphrateans or the Greeks.

The Southern Fish on the celestial globe is portrayed in the act of emaning a stream of water from its mouth, whereas the monster Ketos is depicted as the breather out of the water, the two being representative of the earth as the mother of life in the water called the abyss. In the Sut and Horus mythos the first two children of the ancient mother represent the conditions of dry and wet. They were born twins because the conditions were co-extant in earth and water. In the course of time everything that was dry, desiccative, or of the desert was ascribed to Sut, whereas the products of water were assigned to Horus. Hence the two monsters were continued as types of the twins. The hippopotamus of earth as male was given to Sut. The crocodile of water was given to Horus, to typify the fish as food of the inundation.

The "abyss of waters" is described by Berosos as the habitat of most hideous beings, which had been produced by a "twofold principle" that was as yet undiscreted into wet and dry. "The person who was said to have presided over them was a female named Omoroca." Then came Belos "and cut the woman asunder, and of one half formed the earth, and of the other half the heaven or firmament." This is a mode of discreting the twofold principle of the dry earth and the celestial water. The story told by Berosos is a later legendary form of the mythos. The duplication of the motherhood is the same, but with a change of type. The later woman has taken the place of the cow that was cut in two, divided, or made twain as the water-cow of earth and the milch-cow of heaven. Omoroca is the Great Mother who was *one* as the representative of earth, and was then divided to become the representative of earth and water. The formation of earth and heaven out of the halves is identical with separating earth and water and distinguishing wet from dry.

The "creation" with which we are now concerned is uranographic as a mode of fashioning and giving names to the earliest constellation figures, those that were truly primitive. Thus in the beginning of the astronomical mythology there is a figure of uncreated ground that stands in space or amidst the firmamental water.

If we use the word "creation," which has been so ignorantly abused, the first creation figured in the astronomical mythology was the birth of water or, more abstractly, of life from the water, the source whence came the inundation with its blessings to the rainless land of Egypt. As Plutarch reports, the Egyptians held that water was "the beginning and origin of all things"—that was, as an element of life. Hence in the Osirian mysteries the throne of the Eternal rested on the element of water, and Horus the child-saviour, the Messu or Messiah, came by water in the power of the southern lakes. So in the building of the heavens the beginning was with water, or the firmament imaged in its aerial likeness. Thus it might be said the heaven was made from water, as it is said in the Babylonian "legends of creation," the water based on being the abyss of source. According to the present reading of the data, water had been recognized as the first and most vital element of life. Hence the beginning of all recorded human thought with water. Water in Africa was life indeed, where drought was very death. Horus on his papyrus as lord of water was the lord of life. One Egyptian name for heaven is kabhu, derived from water, or the inundation, as "the cool," and that which makes cool. Paradise was where water was plenteous. Hence water was divinized as heaven, and heaven is figured in the hieroglyphics as water suspended overhead, the firmament being held aloft on four sustaining props as water lifted up. There was no such crying want of water in Babylonia, no such devouring dragon of drought in Akkad, therefore no such *raison d'être* for the origin from water as in Africa.

The birth of water from the abyss of earth is figured in the "Southern Fish." The star Fomalhaut at the mouth of the Fish denotes the point of emergence whence the stream is seen ascending from its source beneath the constellation Aquarius. A soul of life from the element of water was manifested by the fish as Horus the crocodile, also by Horus cradled on the water-plant. Thus the water element was fundamental in the making of the heavens. This was as the firmamental water. Earth as the mother of life and giver of water was portrayed in the abyss as a great fish emaning water from its mouth, which represents the fact that the earth in the abyss had been already recognized as giver of life because it was the source of water, the primary wateress or the wet-nurse of mythology. She, the Great Mother, as we read the heavenly story-book, was next constellated in the Southern Fish as the producer of life and sustenance from water in the unfathomable abyss.

In various legends there is a beginning with a world all water. This is one with the Egyptian Nu or Nun. In the beginning was the Nun. Thus saith the primordial word. Not in the beginning of the heavens and earth, but in the beginning of the uranographic representation or entification in the astronomical mythology. The Nun is a name in Egyptian for the firmament when imaged in the similitude of water, the world that was all water at the intellectual starting-point. There is a relic of the ancient wisdom on one of the Assyrian tablets, the gnosis of which we hold to be Egyptian, and that as such it can be unriddled and read. As it is said, "the heaven was created from the waters." The earth was pre-existent. This is called the work of "Ansar and Kisar," who "created the earth," *i.e.,* when "creation" had been rendered cosmogonically. But "the heaven was created from the waters" which were firmamental and uranographic. The non-Semitic legend of Cutha describes the beginning with a condition of non-entity or pre-entity; there was nothing but an amorphous world of water. As it is said, "the whole of the lands were sea"; "the abyss had not been made" below, nor was there any seat of the gods above. There was no field of reeds; no tree of life had been planted in the midst of an enclosure. There flowed no stream from the abyss "within the sea" of the celestial water (Pinches, T. G., *Records of the Past,* 2nd Series, vol. vi. p. 107; Sayce, *Assyrian Story of Creation,* New Series, vol. i. pp. 133-153). This, when bottomed, means that configuration of the signs in the astronomical mythology had not as yet begun. But as space the firmamental water was extant, and dry earth itself had stood for ever in the midst thereof; earth and water were the uncreated substance which had no beginning, any more than they had in the Egyptian Nun. The monsters born of Tiamat had their home in the ground of earth. It was there she suckled them. Earth as the natural fact preceded the abyss in the astronomy. As Professor Sayce observes, somewhat naïvely, "There was already an earth by the side of the deep" (*H. L.*, p. 377). No. Earth was the ground to go upon in the deep, and this was the Mother-earth which brought forth in and from the deep that was depicted as the abyss, or as the Great Fish in "the water" of the southern heaven. It was in the extreme south that the Babylonians also placed their entrance to the under-world or the abyss. That is where the Egyptians had already localized the *outrance* from this mysterious region whence the inundation came. Here was the "Ununait" or place of springing up that was first applied to water in the pre-solar mythos, the water that was pictured in its rising from the fish's mouth.

The abyss or great deep of the beginning was represented in the mysteries as the Lake of the Great Fish. It was related by Ktêsias of Knidos that the sacred lake was seen at Bambŷkê or Hierapolis. It was also said that in this lake the life of Derketô, daughter of Aphrodite, was saved by the fish. And as the great fish of Kam was the crocodile, the likelihood is that the Lake Moeris, sacred to the crocodiles in Egypt, was also a form of the lake which represented the place of birth that was commemorated in the mysteries and told of in the legends as the abyss of the beginning, the birthplace or fontal source of water=life. A figure of the "abyss" or "deep" survives still in the "basin." Large ewers filled with water were used for purificatory rites in the Babylonian temples. These were called apsu, for "deeps" or "abysses." Tanks were used by the Egyptians for their baptistries. The baptismal font still images the fount of source. As a mythical or celestial locality the Gulf of Eridu is a mundane form of the abyss that was in the beginning. This was the birthplace where the Earth-mother brought forth as a dragon or great fish, the mistress in the abode of the fish. Hence it was the place from whence not only the fish-man Oannes, but the seven fish-like men or annedoti, ascended before the time of the Assyrian deluge. The source of water underground most naturally suggested the idea of a primordial deep, an unfathomable gulf, a bottomless pit. This was then applied to the point of beginning in the lower Nun or firmamental water where the abyss was figured in the uranographic representation.

If, as we suggest, the story of the heavens was written by the race here generalized as "the Egyptians," and if that race descended from the equatorial regions like the great river flowing from its source, it is to the southern hemisphere we must look for the imagery which first reflects the mythology. The southern constellations are comparatively few, but their character in relation to the Egyptian wisdom is unmistakable. Besides which, these uranographs of the beginning, or the first time, could not all have originated as Euphratean, because so many of the stars were too far south to be seen or constellated in Akkad or Babylonia.

The Southern Fish is figured as the bringer forth of water—that is, of life or of Horus the fish from the abyss. Ketos the monster represents the mother in another character. This, as we suggest, is the mother in the water emaning life upon dry land as did the water-cow. The head of the monster is half out of the deep, with jaws agape and gasping like a fish on dry ground, sufficient to show that these are a fish-form of the dual motherhood that was imaged as a crocodile and water-cow, as two cows, as two women, or as the woman Omoroca, who was cut in halves by Belos. If the sphere is carefully examined it will be seen that a stream of water is gushing upwards from the fish's mouth and apparently ascending towards the figure of Aquarius on the ecliptic. Hitherto it has been assumed that water in heaven always ran downwards from the northern pole into the abyss of the south; that the water from the urn of Aquarius was being poured into the mouth of the Southern Fish, and the river Eridanus started from the star Rigel at the foot of Orion and came to an end at the star Achernar, its course being from north to south, or from right to left of the sphere. But this reckoning has now to be reversed.

On the celestial globe, then, the life of the world that was born of water and imaged as Ichthus the fish is represented still as issuing from the mouth of "the Southern Fish." The word that issued from the fish's mouth is mentioned by the writer of a hymn to Merodach, in which it is said, "The holy writing of the mouth of the deep is thine" (Sayce, *Hib. Lectures,* p. 99). If this is rightly rendered, the word of Ichthus had then become the *written* word. Still, it issued from the mouth of the deep, which was that of the fish-mother, or the fish's mouth. Now, the mystical emblem known by name as the *vesica piscis* is still a form ⬭ of the fish's mouth, or *outrance* into life. The present writer once thought the *vesica* was uterine. And it is such as a co-type, but not in its origin, because the child first born of it was *not the human child!* It is the emaning mouth of that fish which gave birth to water as the life of the world and to the saviour who came to Egypt by water as the fish of the inundation. In the language of obstetrics, the *outrance* of birth is called the *os tincæ* or tench's mouth. That is the mouth of the fish, not because the origin in this instance was uterine, but because the fish's mouth was first, and this has been continued as a symbol of the birthplace when that which was pre-human was reapplied to the human organ. In the course of doctrinal development geometrical and anatomical figures are blended in the *vesica* as a symbol of the womb. It was not so when the great mother (of life in water) was imaged in the Southern Fish. It becomes so, to all appearance, when the door of life is figured in the shape of a *vesica* at the feminine (or western) end of a Christian church. The fish's mouth was figured in the heavens as the primordial door of *outrance* into life when the soul of life came to the world by water. And although the true meaning may have been suppressed by *overlaying* the doctrine, enough survives in the symbols to show that the child Christ in the Virgin's arms encircled by the *vesica piscis* has the same significance as had the figure in the planisphere where the water of life is issuing from the fish's mouth, and the star of annunciation is the star Fomalhaut. Only the water of life, still represented by Ichthus the fish, is personalized in later iconography by the human child as the type of eternal rejuvenescence. The oval being a co-type with the fish's mouth, the Virgin and her child are a later equivalent for the divine mother bringing forth her fish in the lake, piscina, basin, or other water type of the primordial abyss, as in the astronomical mythology. The *vesica* survives in Freemasonry as well as in the

Christian Church, which was founded on the fish and font in Rome. It represented an archetypal and ineffable mystery as a geometrical symbol, not one that was simply anatomical. Speaking of the *vesica,* Dr. Oliver says this mysterious figure *Vesica Piscis* possessed an unbounded influence on the details of sacred architecture, and it constituted the great and enduring secret of our ancient brethren. The plans of religious buildings are determined by its use, and the proportions of length and height were dependent on it alone (Oliver, *Descrip.,* p. 109).

The springs of water issuing forth as from the breast of the Mother-earth made her the wet-nurse to her children. As Apt she nursed her hippopotami; as Rerik she gave milk to her young swine; as Neith she was the suckler of her crocodiles; as Hathor, the cow-headed, she was the milch-mother who was said to give the white liquor that the glorified ones love. In each of these forms she was a type of Mother-earth, as we learn from the mythology.

The mundane source of water touches the origin of what has been designated the "worship" of wells and springs, which was at first a propitiation of the superhuman power of Mother-earth by those who needed water, and who, like the Egyptians, sought to be nursed at the dugs of the cow when reborn above as the glorified. In Ireland there could be no religious place without a holy well. St. Columbkille is said to have "sained three hundred well-springs that were swift [running]" (Whitley Stokes, *Three Middle Irish Homilies*). "Well worship," so called, is propitiation of the power in the well. This was the spirit of running water, which as an element had the credit of giving life and the power of purifying. The doctrine is extant as Osirian in the Ritual (ch. 17), where the water is a lake of healing at which all defects are washed away and all stains obliterated. The speaker says, "I am purified at the two great lakes" (the lake of natron and the lake of salt) which purify (or sain) the offerings that living men (on earth) present to the great god who is there—that is, Osiris, who had taken the place of the mother as the source of life in water. The point is that the water purified or sained the offerings that were made to the power in the lake or well or living spring. But the Great Mother was the first to be solicited for water—she who was the wateress in the abyss, the primary Great Mother in mythology, the water-cow as Apt in Egypt, the water-horse as Tiamat in Babylonia.

The primordial abyss had originated as the source of water in the earth. The well-spring underground was the fact in nature upon which the fabled fount of immortality and the subterranean lake of the waters of life were founded in the divine nether-earth. Water generated by the earth was that which came from very source itself thus visualized as wet-nurse of the world. Every spring or bubbling fount of liquid life that issued from this source below was suggestive of a deep without a bottom; the tepht, the bab, or bau of source that was afterwards represented in the astronomical mythology and constellated at the very foundation of the southern heaven as the mystical abyss. The first abyss was in the earth. The abyss of firmamental water is outside the earth; it is figurative because celestial. The Nun was heaven entified as water. But there had been two waters actual in external nature, as the waters that rose up in the fountains, wells, and springs of earth, and the water that fell in dew and rain from heaven. This was portrayed as falling from the tree of wet, which is the Egyptian tree of Nut or of heaven as water. Thence water from the well was the water of earth, and water from the tree was the water of heaven. These two water sources in earth and heaven were figured as the abyss or well below and the tree of rain above, with Apt or Hathor the Mother-earth in the abyss, and Nut the heavenly mother in the tree of wet above. And these two types seen in the well and tree are universal signs of so-called "water worship" with the oldest races in the world. The holy Well or water-hole is commonly found beneath the sacred moisture-dropping tree. The stone erected as an altar underneath the tree is almost as common. This was a place of propitiation and appeal to the elemental power. Libations of blood were poured out on the stone. Offerings were suspended on the tree; gifts were cast into the well and magical invocations made. The well suffices to establish the fact that the primitive want was water. But the source was dual in the water of earth and the water of heaven. The source in earth was imaged in the well as a form of the abyss. The water that fell from heaven was imaged by the tree of Nut. The altar-stone is representative of earth. Thus it is a meeting-point for the sycamore of Nut (the tree of celestial water, as Egyptian), the altar of earth, and the abyss of water under the earth. The object of the rite is the spirit or power that sends the water from its "double source" in earth and heaven, with the stone as altar for the sacrificial offering. The Egyptian old first mother, who is a hippopotamus in front and crocodile behind, and who is repeated in the Babylonian dragon-horse Tiamat, still survives in British tradition as the water-horse or kelpie, and also as the dragon. The river Yore near Middleham is held to be haunted by a water-horse (Longstaffe, *Richmondshire*, p. 96). The River Auld Grandt, that springs from Loch Glaish in Ross-shire, is dreaded as the abode of the water-horse. Sometimes the presiding power of the water in the well is indicated by the fish, sometimes by the frog. Once the dragon of drought left his co-type in a northern holy well. At the Devil's Causeway between Ruckley and Acton there is a well in which the animal type is the frog, and the largest of these, which naturally enough appears but seldom, represents the devil Apap. In one instance two old women are said to keep the secret of the water. These are equivalent to the two fish, the two cows, and the woman who was cut in two.

The double source of water having been identified as the water of earth and the water of heaven, the type of duality was applied to the firmamental water in the astronomical mythology, and heaven, as water, was divided into the two waters of the lower and upper firmament, the typical being founded as a figure of the actual. These two waters are also constellated in the two celestial rivers of Eridanus and the Milky Way. The one reflects the river of the inundation, therefore the water of earth below, emaning from the lower Nun or the mythical abyss. The other is the "great stream" of the *Via Lactea*. The inundation rose up in the south. Its ebullient superhuman forces in the Ritual are called *the powers of the south*. These powers of the south are in attendance "at the moment when the lord of his flood is carried forth and brings to its fulness the force that is hidden within him" (ch. 64). And when once we know which way the river runs in heaven, Achernar in Eridanus becomes our guide star from the south. From that the river travels northward to Orion's foot, or rather to the point at which Orion rises up as Horus of the inundation. Otherwise, Horus is brought to birth on his papyrus, as depicted in the Egyptian drawings.

The two waters of earth and heaven are both recognizable in the double source assigned to the river Nile. In some of the traditions it is described as emanating from the abyss of earth, in others as falling from the skies. Both origins are mentioned in the Hymn to the Nile. In the first stanza the water is said to descend from heaven. In line thirteen we are told that "the Nile has made its retreat in Southern Egypt. Its name is not known beyond the Tuat." Thus the retreat of the Nile in the south is identifiable with the abyss as the earthly source of the inundation, and its name is not known beyond the boundary of that other world from whence it issues. In Inner Africa the rains came from the cool heaven (Kabhu) of the north, and therefore in that quarter (or half) was the creatory and source of the celestial waters, as the fact was figured for ever in the constellation of the Water-Cow. In the hymns of adoration to the Nile the river is addressed as coming forth and bringing all good things to Egypt from the north, whereas the geographical Nile came with the inundation from the south. The Nile that issued from the two lakes of a double source was celestial in the north. The Nile that "made its retreats in Southern Egypt" (hymn 13) was the mundane Nile which came from the north to the south above, and from the south to the north below. As Hor-Apollo shows, two of the Egyptian vases denoted water from a double source, one being the earth as generator of water, the other heaven when the rains fell in the southern parts of Athiopæia (B. I, 21). The urn was a figure of the inundation. Aquarius was called the constellation of the Urn by the Arab astronomers. We shall understand the sign of "Krater" better if we take it as an extra-zodiacal image of the urn, which not only represented the inundation and its bounty, but also the abyss of source from which the welling waters came. The two urns are followed by the two vases at a later stage. Howsoever poured out, water was the primary means of fertilization. When the goddess pours out a libation from her vase—or two divine personages from two vases—on the water plant or shoot of palm, the signification is the same as when the wet-nurse Hathor suckles Horus as a child or Neith the crocodile as a calf. According to the most primitive imagery in Egypt, the waters of the inundation issued from the Mother-earth as the water-cow, the wateress in the primordial abyss or water source. But when the sky was looked to as a source of water, heaven was represented as the milch-cow, and the river flowing from the highest source was imaged as the Milky Way. Thenceforth there were two cows. The cow of earth was the water-cow, and the milch-cow was the cow of heaven. The water-cow of earth was constellated in the stars of the Great Bear, the milch-cow of heaven in the group now known as Cassiopœia, or the Lady in the Chair, which was the earlier constellation of the Haunch or Meskhen as a figure of the birthplace when the birth was typical of life in water (see fragment from a Theban Tomb, p. 289).

THE DROWNING OF THE DRAGON

The "mystery of evil," about which theologians ignorantly prate, was very simple in its origin. Water, food, and light were naturally good. Their opposites—thirst, hunger, darkness, and disease—were as naturally bad. In this way the origin of evil had its rootage in the conditions of external nature for which man could nowise be held responsible. The rest is mainly the result of a primitive doctrine being developed in the domain of theology. For example, Sut, the anthropomorphic devil of the later Egyptian religion, was previously the pre-anthropomorphic representative of drought, dearth, and darkness long before the type of evil had been personalized in the figure of a satanic Mephistopheles as the tempter of womankind. Thus the *representative* of evil, "that old serpent" in mythology, became the *author* of evil in theology, and the devil was evolved in the moral domain according to the eschatology.

At the commencement of mythical representation in Africa we meet the adversary of man in the shape of a monstrous serpent or devouring dragon. This in Egypt is the Apap-reptile, the dragon of drought or the serpent of darkness. In one phase Apap is the devourer of the moon in her eclipse, in another it is the destroyer of vegetable life, and in a third it drinks or dries up all the water, or there is a mortal fear lest the monster should do so. This was the primal adversary or prototypal Satan. There is a saying that "the devil is known by his long tail," and the long tail of Satan may be seen as the appendage of Apap the serpent of evil in the southern constellation Hydra. The Egyptians also have a class of evil beings called the Sebau. These were the spawn of the reptile Apap, born of darkness, drought, and other malefic influences in physical phenomena that were found to be inimical to man. The type of Apap, a flat-headed Inner African snake, is universal. It is the Bushman all-devourer *Kwai Hemm,* who swallows the mantis-deity at night and brings him forth again alive by day; it is the Norse dragon or worm, the Greek python, the throttling ahi or vrittra of the Vedas. With the Indians of Brazil it is still "the great serpent who is the owner of night." It is the snake, toad, or frog (in the legends) that swallows all the water in the world. Possibly the Apap-monster of Africa may be recognized even by name in Australia. In the centre of the continent whirlwinds occur that lift up columns of dust two or three hundred feet in height. The Arunta call them *Apapa*. The Warramunga say an unfriendly spirit, an Orantja, travels about in these on the look-out to kill black-fellows. Whether this be the old dragon of the desert or not, it is noticeable that the name of the Apap in Egyptian signifies to mount on high, become tall, vast, gigantic, like the swirling dust and darkness of the sand-storm (S. and G., *N. Tribes,* p. 632). Here begins the war betwixt the evil serpent and the woman, who is the Great Mother in mythology. It was the Apap-reptile who brought darkness, drought, and death into the world. The mother was the earliest slayer of the dragon, and the son of the woman followed as her helper. She may be seen as Isis, a form of the lunar goddess, spearing the head of Apap in the dark waters of night (Wilkinson). She may also be heard in this character as the Lady of Light, who exclaims, "I lighten up the darkness and overthrow the devouring monster" (Rit., ch. 80). In the Kaffir folk-tales we find the original mythos of the monster in three of its phases. In the story of "The Great Chief of the Animals" (Theal, p. 163) the victim swallowed by "the terrible monster" is the moon-mother. She tears her way out of the monster as the deliverer of herself, and sets free all her children whom the devourer as dragon of darkness had previously swallowed. The bows and arrows with which the twin brothers kill the monster tend to identify their weapon with the lunar bow that was periodically drawn and nightly employed to overcome the power of darkness. There is perhaps a further hint that the mother represents the moon, inasmuch as the children of the woman had been left for safety in charge of the hare, which is a lunar zoötype. In another Kaffir tale the woman is mother of the twins who correspond to Sut and Horus as the twin powers of light and darkness brought forth by the mother-moon in her dual lunation. In a third the swallower, called "the Inabulele" (Theal, p. 79), is slain by the hero Sikulum, who answers to Horus as slayer of the Apap-dragon.

Propitiation of a superhuman nature power for food and drink was the most primitive form of the appeal that ultimately culminated, as we know, in worship. The gods of Egypt from the beginning represented food and drink, not only as givers of sustenance—they *were* the sustenance in food and liquid. The Great Mother was the suckler or wet-nurse. Hathor offered food in the sycamore-fig and Isis in the persea tree of life. Child-Horus was the shoot, the branch, the calf, lamb, or fish. Seb, god of earth, was the father of aliment. Plenty of food and water first made heaven palpable to primitive or archaic men on earth. Hence the primitive paradise was imaged as a field of food. At one stage seven cows were configurated as the type of plenty that was eternal in the heavens. The tree of life was planted in the midst of the celestial oasis. Upon this grew the fruit as food on which the gods and the glorified were fed. The mother of food in the oasis of the papyrus plant, Uat, was divinized in the goddess Uati, as a mother of all things fresh, flourishing, and evergreen. The deity Atum-Ra, who first attained the status of "holy spirit" in the eschatology, says of himself, "I am the food which never perishes" (Rit., ch. 85). Horus of the inundation was constellated on his papyrus as the ever-coming shoot (Plan. of Denderah); he was also the giver of food as the fish, the calf, and the lamb, that were made celestial types in the astral mythology. An infinitude of water was an African ideal of the divine. A spring of water welling from the bosom of the earth made her the mother of life, and life that came by water was then divinized in Horus on his papyrus plant as the food-bringer. Thence came a saviour to the land of Egypt as Horus of the inundation; Horus the shoot or natzer, Horus as Ichthus the fish, Horus the mother's child who came by water. It is possible to show that Horus on his papyrus or lotus was the African original of Jack who climbed the bean-stalk. It may be premised that the stalk up which the spirit of vegetation climbs to furnish food was an earlier type than the tree of life, and that the fact was preserved in the Egyptian mythos. Also the tree of Tammuz in Eridu was "a stalk." Now the lotus in Egypt was literally a bean-stalk. Its large seed was known as the bean of Egypt. Thus when the lotus = papyrus was employed for the figure of food, and Horus, as the elemental spirit of vegetation, ascended the stalk to take his seat upon "the flower," he was the youth who climbed the "bean-stalk" to slay the giant Apap at first in nature, next in the mythos, and lastly in the legends. When water was the life, and Mother-earth was the source, she was imaged as the great fish, and her young one was the lord of life as the food-bringer in the inundation. Horus of the inundation was a real, ever-coming saviour of the world as periodic bringer of water and the food of life, who came in several characters. In one of which he was the fish. In one he climbed the stalk of the papyrus plant as the soul of vegetation. As the young hero it was he who fought and overcame the dragon of drought at one season and the serpent of darkness at another. A power of perennial renewal was perceived in nature. This was manifested by successive births. Hence the child-god of Egypt became a type of the eternal, ever-coming by rebirth in time and season and the elements of life and light, which in the character of Horus was at first by food and water. This was the eternal, ever-coming, ever-renewing spirit of youth. In the illustration from a Theban tomb the Great Mother,

The Meshken, or Birthplace.

who in one form is a crocodile, has just given birth to her child, Horus, Har-Ur, as the young crocodile poised on end in front of her. It is a picture of the young child that was brought forth annually from the water by the mother, who was constellated as the Crocodile or Hippopotamus at the northern centre of the planisphere. The history of Horus is depicted in the heavens as if upon the walls and windows of some vast cathedral of immensity. This was the subject of subjects in the astronomical mythology. He was conceived of a virgin mother in the sign of Virgo. His birth or advent was announced by the star Phact in the constellation Columbia. The earliest mother who conceived as a virgin in mythology was represented by the sacred heifer of the immaculate Isis. Also by the white vulture in the cult of the Virgin Neith. She was the dove of Hathor in the worship of Iusāas, the mother of Iusa. The human only comes in as a challenging element when the mythos is related as history. When the woman took the place of the heifer, the vulture, the dove, or other zoötype of virginity—that is, when the type was humanized and Horus imaged as a child—the doctrine of incarnation, or the incorporation of a spirit of life in matter, had entered into the human sphere. Thus the mystical virgin and child in human guise, whether in Egypt or in any other land, was a result of doctrinal development, and the doctrine itself could not be understood without a knowledge of the earlier phase. When the type of the Great Mother and her youngling had been changed from the totemic zoötype to the anthrotype, and the goddess was imaged as a woman, a child became the figure of a superhuman power that was ever-coming, ever-renewing, ever-repeating, ever-incorporating or incarnating, ever-manifesting in phenomena. Then the youthful god was naturally born as a child. This was Har-Ur, the child of Isis or the Virgin Neith. Horus the child or shoot, on the papyrus or on his mother's lap, is representative of the resurrection and renewal of life for another year. Horus came to Egypt as saviour of the people from the dreaded drought. He came, invested with "the power of the southern lakes," to drown the dragon in the inundation. In one he phase Horus is the saviour as the bringer of the water. In another he is the child of light. In both he comes to wrestle with the enemy of man in various natural phenomena on earth, and likewise in the internecine struggle which is represented by the astronomical mythology as the war in heaven, and which may be summed up as the war of Horus and the dragon. Horus brings the water of the inundation which is the source of life to Egypt. The little one is cradled on the Nile in his ark of the papyrus reed. He is assailed by Apap, the dragon of drought, who lies in wait to destroy the young deliverer when he is born. As bringer of the waters Horus slays the dragon of drought, which would otherwise have drunk the inundation dry. He also treads the serpent of darkness under foot as the renewer of light. Under the name of Iu-em-hetep, Horus came as the proverbial "prince of peace." The word *hetep* denotes peace or rest, plenty of food, and also good luck. His coming in this character had a very tangible significance, for the inundation brought the season of rest to Egypt, which was celebrated by the Uaka festival, when the prince came out of Ethiopia as the giver of rest to the weary, bread to the hungry, water to the thirsty, and wine for the periodic wassail. In the solar mythos Horus became the lord of light, but food and drink were first, according to the human needs.

The fabled "war in heaven" began with the contending elements that strove with each other for supremacy, whether as light and darkness, water and drought, or food and famine. Thus Horus of the inundation came by water as the deliverer when the land was suffering from the dragon of drought. The picture was then constellated in the southern heaven. Horus the victor was represented by Orion rising from the river and wielding the insignia of his sovereignty. His weapon is the club of Herakles in Greece; it was the whip of ruling power as the Egyptian khu. He rises from Eridanus as conqueror of the hydra-dragon that is overwhelmed beneath the waters when the drought was put an end to by the lord of life with the water for his weapon. Here is a motive for the war betwixt the dragon and the infant that was born to universal rule or predestined to be king. Horus also came as conqueror of the dragon of darkness. But it is of more importance to know that the evil reptile Apap represented drought and famine, disease and death. This was the mortal enemy of man that drank up all the water in the world; hence the battle for the water. All the earth round the warfare of the hero with the monster is for water as well as for light, because the monster is representative of drought as well as darkness. At first it is the water-reptile in the African lake; then the "hellish snake Apap" drinks up the water of the Nile. In Australia it is the monstrous frog that drinks up all the water. It is also the chimerical, malignant wild beast that is slain by Gilgames. This struggle, as some of the drawings show, is literally *over the water*. Lastly, it becomes the sea-monster of the Greek mythology, whereas the original conflict was for drinking water.

When Horus came by water as Ichthus the fish who gave himself for food, he swam the deluge of the inundation when there was no boat or ark to breast the waters. But when the bark was built Argo is constellated as the ark of Horus. This is figured in the planisphere with the child on board and the devouring Apap coiling round it seeking to destroy the babe, the infant saviour of the world, who brings the food and water as the lord of life.

Now Sothis in its heliacal rising was not the only star of annunciation at the birth of Horus the child. Farther south, the Dove, or rather the star Phact, was also a harbinger of the inundation. Still farther was the glorious star Canopus, the pilot of the Argo at the starting-point of the journey by water, which was the river Nile as the terrestrial water imaged uranographically. The Egyptians commemorated the birthday of the world—that is, of the age, the cycle, the beginning of time, as the day when Horus rose up on the lotus, or papyrus, from the waters of the Nun. Otherwise stated, this was the natal day of Horus in the inundation, which was afterwards applied to Atum by the priests of On or Annu in the eschatology. Thus the birthday of the inundation was the birthday of a primordial year, or the birthday of the world. The constellation Hydra represents the Apap-reptile of the Egyptian mythos. This is a monster extending over some one hundred degrees in the planisphere. From lack of better knowledge, this type of evil has been called the "water-serpent," which gives no clue to its character. It is figured in the water of the southern heaven, and is that fearsome monster which in various legends drinks up all the water. In the later solar mythos Apap, the enemy of Ra, is the blind devourer darkness. But as the adversary of the elder Horus—he of the inundation—Apap or Hydra is the dragon of drought. Drought in the old dark land was veritably "the curse," and the evil dragon as its deadly image was the primitive type of physical, not of moral evil. The inundation was the source of life to Egypt. It was her annual salvation, and Horus, or Sebek the fish-man, was her saviour. The earliest saviour ever known was the giver of food and drink to those who were famishing. This is the origin of a saviour as the shoot of a water-plant, the branch of a tree, or a great fish—the bigger the better, as a sign of abundance. This was how a saviour could be represented as Ichthus the fish. This was how a saviour could come by water to the world; hence the subject of subjects was the war of elements, of darkness in conflict with the light, of drought with the waters, of sterility with fertility, of dearth with plenty.

The powers of good and evil, represented in the mythos, were also figured in the stars and portrayed in the religious drama as the eternal conflict of the twins Sut and Horus, of Shu and the impious rebels, of Ra and the Apap-reptile. In the earliest mythos Horus precedes Ra as the eternal antagonist of the dragon or serpent. This is the first Horus who was the seed of the Great Mother, whom the Semites call "the woman." He bruised or pierced the serpent's head at one season, and was bitten by the serpent in the heel at another. One was the season of renewal for the waters, for food, for the growing light, and for the breezes of the north. The other was the season of drought, of sterility, of darkness, and for the withering blast of the desert. "In Upper Egypt," says Maspero, "there is a wide-spread belief in the existence of a monstrous serpent that dwells at the bottom of the river Nile" (*Dawn of Civilization,* Eng. trans., p. 90). This is the Apap-dragon of evil, especially of drought. Hence the crumbling of the banks and the falls of earth in the dry season are attributed to the great serpent which lies at the bottom of the river, where it was drowned by the inundation with great rejoicings of the people every year. It is as the fiery dragon of drought that the Apap is spoken of in an inscription of Amenhetep III. In this, vengeance is threatened on those royal secretaries who neglect their duties to the Theban god Amen-Ra, and it is said, "*They shall become like the hellish snake Apap on the morning of the new year; they shall be overwhelmed in the great flood*" (Brugsch, *Egypt,* p. 210, Eng. trans. in one vol.). The morning of the new year was at that time determined by the heliacal rising of Sothis as announcer of the inundation in which the Apap-dragon of drought was drowned. This picture is to be seen in the planisphere with the figure of the fiery Hydra overwhelmed in the water of the inundation. It was represented in the mythology that when Horus had conquered Apap in one of his great battles the reptile sank, pierced with wounds, into the depths of the waters, and this event was said to have occurred at the very moment of the new year (cited by Maspero from Birch and Chabas, *The Dawn of Civilization,* Eng. trans., p. 159). This is the exact position of Hydra in the waters of the south, as still shown on the celestial globe. Thus Hydra, as the drowned, dead reptile, forms a fellow picture in the planisphere to that of Apap drowned in the lake of heaven, according to the description in the Ritual (ch. 39).

That Apap was cut up and drowned in the waters of the inundation is likewise shown by the constellation Corvus, or the Crow. The bird stands on the body of the monster, and, as Aratos remarks (line 449) "seems to peck the folds" of its prey. Corvus thus plays its part as scavenger of the inundation, and at the same time demonstrates that Hydra is drowned and dead. Thus far we see that certain natural facts were given a celestial setting as object-pictures in the stars. The abyss of the beginning was constellated as "the water" low down in the south. The birth of water from the Mother-earth was figured in the Southern Fish. Horus, the young deliverer who came by water periodically as the bringer of food, was shown in the shoot of the papyrus plant; he also figures as Ichthus the fish. The river of the water of life was represented by Eridanus, which can be traced back to its birthplace in the abyss, with the inundation rushing from the southern lakes. Various herald-stars of Horus and the waters, like Fomalhaut, Achernar, Canopus, and Phact, can also be identified according to their rising at different stages of the progress made by Horus down into the valley of the Nile.

We will now take a turn round the zodiac, with a view of briefly identifying its signs with the seasons of Egypt and the characters in the mythology, the first and foremost being that of Horus, the eternal, ever-coming child. As represented in the zodiac, Horus of the inundation was conceived by his virgin mother in the sign of Virgo. This was the promised prince of peace who came to rest the weary from their work and to labour for them while they rested, listening to the waters and the welcome word the inundation brought. Then was the message of good tidings sent as if from heaven itself, which was made known by the mother of the babe. She first sang the song of invitation, "Come unto me, all ye that labour and are heavy laden, and I will give you rest." The mother of life was now descending with the waters, or with Horus *in utero,* as the most blessed among women the virgin brooding over her conception and inwardly working out the mystery of fertilization and fulfilment. In the mythical rendering of natural fact a child or youngling had been made prime mover of the universe. "I have set myself in motion," says Child-Horus (Rit., ch. 42). "I am the heir, the primary power of motion and of rest" (Rit., ch. 63A). The doctrine is repeated when the Greeks maintained that Eros was the primal cause of all things (Hesiod, *Theogony*). Babe-Horus in his coming forth is compared with the lotus or papyrus issuing from the great stream.

The birthplace of water (and of food) in the abyss of source became the birthplace of Horus in the inundation. This was represented in the later mythos by the swamps and marshes in which Isis hid herself with her babe and suckled Horus in a secret place. The water in which Horus came to Egypt was the inundation of the Nile that burst up from the abyss—the bau, the tepht of source in the recesses of the south. And as we read the signs, the river Nile was constellated in Eridanus as the river of the inundation. The name of Eridanus, like the celestial river itself, is very sure to have had an Egyptian origin. Eri, later Uri, was an Egyptian name of the inundation, meaning the great, the mighty; whilst tun or tanu signifies that which rises up in revolt, the bursting forth from the gulf or well of the south. Thus rendered, Eri-tana or Iarutana would be the mighty river rising up in the inundation and bursting forth from out the birthplace in the abyss, as is depicted in the Ritual. If we glance at the river constellated on the celestial globe, we see that Eridanus runs one way, from the foot of Orion to the star Achernar, which has been called "the end of the river." But, if looked at the other way, Achernar marks the point of departure from the south towards the north. And if this river represents the earthly Nile, the replica would naturally run the way of the original. That alone will explain the course of the water and its ending at the foot of Orion, who rises from the river as did Horus of the inundation coming "out of Æthiopia" (or Equatoria), or from that ancient south in which the tepht of source was localized at first as *"the water,"* and afterwards configurated in the stars that indicate the river of the inundation winding on its northward way. Other stars announced the coming of the Nile, or the birth of Horus in the water of the inundation. The star Phact, says Lockyer, "so little familiar to us northerners, is one of the most conspicuous stars in the southern portion of the heavens, and its heliacal rising heralded the solstice and the rise of the Nile before the heliacal rising of Sirius was useful for the purpose. In Phact we have the star symbolized by the ancient Egyptians under the name of the goddess Tekhi, whose figure leads the procession of the months" (*Dawn of Astronomy,* p. 224). In the Arabic names of the stars the star Phact is named from a word that signifies "the thigh," and the thigh was an Egyptian type of the birthplace, as we shall find it also figured in Egypt as well as in the northern heaven. Here it denotes a place of birth and a goddess in the southern heaven. Now, the so-called sacred year of the Egyptians opened at a certain starting-point on the first of the month Taht, or Tehuti, equivalent to our 20th of July. But this month in an earlier star calendar is called the month of the goddess Tekhi. Tekh or tekhi is an Egyptian word for liquid, to supply with drink, and Tekhi is the month of the inundation. But the month Tekhi, or Taht, was not named from the first beginning of the inundation. The previous month, the last of the twelve in the sacred year, was named Mesore, or Mesuri, from mes, for birth, and uri, later eri, the inundation. Thus the actual birth of the river (in one place or other) is marked in the last month of the Egyptian year instead of the first, the question being, *At what point of the course did the actual birth take place?* The birth of water, of Horus as Ichthus, had been indicated by the star Fomalhaut at the Fish's mouth; the star Phact was a herald of Horus in the inundation; Canopus, the pilot of *Argo Navis,* showed that Horus was on board the ark, or on his cradle of the papyrus plant; and the dog-star Sothis was the later guide to the watchers of the heavens in Egypt. If the arrival of the inundation at some particular point is dated by the heliacal rising of the dog-star in the month of Tekhi or Taht (July), the name of the previous month shows the birth of the waters was reckoned to be earlier. This is the month Mesore or Mesuri, and Mesore answers roughly to the month of June. In the sacred year the 1st of Mesore corresponds to our June 15th and to July 25th in the Alexandrian year. Obviously the name of Mesore refers to the birth of the waters *farther south,* which was announced by the herald star Fomalhaut, Achernar, Canopus, or Phact, according to their position and to the stage of high water at the different times along the route.

The seasons in Egypt have been previously compared with the imagery in the planisphere (*Nat. Genesis*), but might have been more closely verified. There were but two in the beginning with the Great Mother and her Sut and Horus twins. These were the seasons of the summer waters and the winter drought. The season of the waters and of rest is as plainly pictured in the southern heaven as ever it was actual in the valley of the Nile. That quarter on the celestial globe is full of the inundation and its signs, as it will be for all time. The inundation was not only pictured in the southern heaven rising from its most secret source in the abyss "down south," which was figured with the mouth of the Fish, and continued running northward in the river named Eridanus; it was also constellated in the zodiac, and can be traced there in accordance with the seasons of the year. The earliest hint of the inundation is given zodiacally in the month Mesore. In the Greco-Egyptian planisphere according to Kircher, Horus is figured in the decans of the Twins, at death-grips with the Apap-reptile which the inundation comes to drown. Thus the battle is portrayed twice over, once as the struggle of Horus (or Ra) and the serpent constellated *in the decans of the Gemini,* and once on the ecliptic as the contest of the Sut and Horus twins.

Amongst the harbingers of the inundation were the beetles that rolled up their seed in little balls of dung and buried them upon the river bank for safety against the coming flood. The Nile-beetle was figured where the Crab is constellated now. Here begins the imagery of the inundation in the zodiac, with the month Mesore. The beetle, busy on the banks of the Nile, was set above as a uranograph which showed the beginning or the birth of the new inundation *at some well-known point* in time and locality. The figure of the beetle rolling up its seed with its tentacles is apparently repeated in the Akkadian name of this same month, which is *Su Kulna, the seizer of seed,* with Cancer (or the beetle) for its zodiacal sign. An earlier type of Sirius than the dog was the bennu or nictorax. This was a beautiful water-bird that came to Egypt as a herald of the inundation, and was given the most glorious of extra-zodiacal signs. The bennu was the prototype of the mythical phœnix. The ibis as a bird of passage also came to fish the waters of the inundation. This too was constellated for a symbol. We find it figured in a zodiac attributed to the second Hermes—that is, Taht, the lunar deity (*Nat. Gen. plate*). In this the sign of Cancer is the ibis-headed god. The ibis was a typical fisher, and therefore a sign of coming plenty to the fishers waiting for the waters, and their wealth of food. The lion in the hieroglyphics is a figure of great force, and when the sun had reached the lion sign the rushing waters had attained their fullest volume. As Hor-Apollo tells us, the Egyptians portray a lion as a sign of the inundation, "because when the sun is in Leo it augments the rising of the Nile." Indeed, he says it happens at times that one half of the new water is supplied to Egypt while the sun remaineth in that sign (B. I, 21). At the same time of year the lion was a figure of the solar force at furnace heat, an image therefore of a double force. In the next sign is the Virgin who conceived the child that represented the food which was dependent on the waters of the inundation. This was indicated by the later ear of corn, the green wheat ear of the mysteries, which is held in the hand of Neith or Isis in Virgo, and still survives in the star Spica of this constellation.

The elder Horus came not only in the water. He was also the Kamite prototype of Bacchus as the lord of wine. When Horus came the grapes were ripe in Egypt and ready to be converted into wine. The season of grapes is dated July 13th in the Egyptian calendar. There is but little left upon the modern globe of the ancient constellation of the Vine, but the star Epsilon, called Vindemiatrix is still the sign of grape-gathering, and as we read in the calendar—"July the 9th: the Nile begins to rise abundantly. July 28th: abundance of grapes" (Egyptian Calendar, A.D. 1878, p. 19). Vindemiatrix, the sign of grapes being ripe, is described by Aratos as being so large in size and bright in splendour as to rival the stars in the Great Bear's tail, whereas at present it is but a star of the third magnitude (lines 130-140). The grape-gathering in Egypt is depicted in or near the signs of Virgo and the Vine. It is said of Horus at Edfu, "Thou didst put grapes into the water which cometh forth from Edfu." From that day forth the water of Edfu was called the water of grapes—that is, wine. So anciently was the metaphor of the gospel miracle founded on the natural fact. Uaka is a name of the inundation, and also of the festival at which the deluge of drink was symbolically celebrated by the libation that was correspondingly colossal. The vine was not only set in heaven to denote the vindemia or time for gathering the grapes, the overflow was also figured in the constellation Crater, or the Goblet, as a sign of the "uaka" that was held in Egypt when the land was full of water and the folks were full of wine. When the constellation Crater rose it showed that the urn or vase, an artificial type of the inundation, was overflowing with the waters that restored the drooping life of Egypt. At that time the Egyptians celebrated a feast in honour of Hathor, at which a deluge of drink flowed freely. It is frankly described in the inscriptions as "the festival of intoxication," and was commemorated at Denderah in the month of Taht, the month of the year that opened with the inundation and the helical rising of Sothis. Various other fruits were ripe, including dates. Also water-melons were abundant. But Horus is the vine, whose advent was celebrated at the uaka festival with prodigious rejoicings and a deluge of drink of which the vine and cup, or mixing-bowl, were constellated as celestial symbols. The juice of the grape was the blood of Horus or Osiris in the Kamite Eucharist. Hence the sacramental cup was figured in the constellation "Crater," the Goblet, or it may be the jar, from the Egyptian karau, a jar, the cup having two characters, one in the mythology and one in the eschatology.

In an ancient planisphere reproduced by Dupuis (*Planches de l'Origine de Tous les Cultes,* no. 10) the swallow appears in close proximity to Isis the virgin of the zodiac. In the Egyptian mythos the swallow represented Isis in her character of the widow, when she was wandering like the bird of passage from one land to another seeking for her lost Osiris. Thus Isis in her two characters of the virgin and the widow was figured in the zodiac and in the decans of Virgo, which two characters are only to be found in Egyptian mythology.

Libra, or the Scales, was at one time a figure of the equinox, but its more probable origin is in relation to the supremely important waters of the inundation. The four months of the water-season, the first of the three tetramenes, began with the lion, and ended with the scorpion. The inundation reached its point of equipoise coincidently with the entrance of the sun into the sign that was figured as the Balance or the Scales. The tortoise or abtu of the Nile had been an earlier zodiacal sign than that of the Scales, by which it was superseded. When the Nile-tortoise climbed the banks of the river to give itself for food, it naturally became a self-constituted sign of the inundation to be figured in a group of stars. Thus the tortoise = Libra would denote the point at which the earth was emerging like a tortoise or a turtle from the deluge of the waters which periodically overspread the land.

The scorpion was not a type of evil in the zodiac. It represented Isis-Serkh who fought for Horus when the birthplace was in Scorpio. A fragment of the myth survives in the Ritual. It is the merest allusion, but suffices to show that in the wars of the solar god (Horus or Ra) with the enemy Apap, Isis-Serkh joined in the battle and was wounded. The passage is confused but, as rendered by Renouf, it runs: "Apap falleth; Apap goeth down. And more grave for thee is the taste (tepit) than that sweet proof through the scorpion-goddess (Isis-Serkh) which she practised for thee, in the pain that she suffered." When the summer solstice was in the sign of Leo the autumn equinox occurred in Scorpio, and it would be then and there the scorpion-goddess gave proof of her sympathy and suffering on behalf of Horus or of Ra in the latter mythos. It is evident that Scorpio was the sign at one of the cardinal points, for it is said of Apap in this battle, "Apap is in bonds." "The gods of the south, the north, the west and the east have bound him." These include the goddesses as helpers. Hence it is said to Apap: "Thy whole heart is torn out by the lynx-goddess. Chains are flung upon thee by the scorpion-goddess. Slaughter is dealt upon thee by Maati." (Rit., ch. 39.) About the time of the autumn equinox the water of the inundation began to subside. At this point the power of Horus in the light was on the wane, and both were represented now by him who was born to die down in the dwindling water and the lessening light. The word Serkhu, which is the name of Isis as the scorpion-goddess, signifies to breathe, and to supply breath. Thus Scorpio is the sign of a breathing-space which followed the water-season. Whilst the sun was in the constellation Libra (or the tortoise) the waters had attained their height and were resting at the equipoise. Then it entered the sign of Scorpio. The scorpion lived in dry earth, and was only to be seen when the waters had subsided.

In some Egyptian zodiacs (zodiac of Esné) the Sagittarius, or Archer, is the compound figure of a centaur based on the lion instead of the horse, with the human face of Shu in front and the face of Tefnut the lioness behind. Shu was the elemental power of breathing force, and his twin-sister represents moisture. Her name Tef-nut signifies the dew of heaven, and the dew of heaven was now the water of earth in Egypt, the breath of Shu and moisture of Tefnut being imaged as the power of the twin brother and sister. Tefnut, the sister of Shu, was joined with him in his battles on behalf of Horus. "She is like fire against the wicked ones—" the Sami and the Sebau, "thundering against those who are to be annihilated for ever," as it is said in the magical texts. When the sun entered this sign the Nile was failing, the day grew shorter than the night; and Horus needed all the help that could be given. Hence Shu the fighting force was configurated as the Archer. Shu, the power of the Air, had been divinized as the warrior-god who fought for Horus as leader of the war against the rebel powers of darkness and of drought now mustering their forces in the nether-world for renewing the assault.

Nowhere is it more necessary to compare the face of the underlying fact with the mask of the mythos to see how closely the mould was fitted to the features of nature by the Egyptians. In Egypt, and in that country only, can the time of drought be absolutely identified with winter. Now the Apap-dragon in Egyptian mythology is the dragon of drought, and the dragon of drought is the fiery dragon. Hence Apap in the form of Hydra is cut in pieces to be drowned in the water of the inundation. In Egypt only did the figure correspond to fact as the image of drought in winter caused by the dragon of darkness. And it is this correspondence of natural fact to the symbolical figure which will account for the fire-breathing dragon of winter in Europe which *survives where it does not apply* from lack of the necessary climatic conditions. The Norse mythology preserves the fiery dragon as a representative of winter in countries where it cannot be correlated with heat or drought. It survives with us in the pastime of snap-dragon sacred to the winter season at Christmas. Here the dragon keeps its character as the representative of drought in relation to the proper season of drought in Egypt as the fire-breathing dragon. Moreover, the dragon of drought and of darkness are one and the same in winter; on that account only did the dragon of darkness apply at winter-time in Europe, and *not as the dragon of drought.*

Yet, the drowning of the dragon of drought became a European pastime in many lands where there were seldom any lack of water, and never any want of it in winter. According to the seasons of Egypt, at the time when the sun had reached the sign of the sea-goat not only had the fresh water of the inundation ceased to flow, the water from the Mediterranean travelling upwards from the sea was now the stronger current, bitter and brackish and detestable. The sea-goat is a compound type of goat and fish. The fish signifies water; the water was now coming from the sea, and the sea-water was naturally imaged by the sea-goat. Further, it is possible that the salt nature of the water at this point was indicated by the goat, seeing that a young goat is an Egyptian ideograph of the word Ab for thirst; or it may be the offensiveness of the goat represented the repellent nature of "Salt Typhon's foam."

When the sun was in the sign of Aquarius the moon at full had taken up the leadership by night in heaven, as the mother-moon. This was she who fetched the water of life from the lower regions and gave re-birth to vegetation in the upper-world. The great goddess that renewed the light above was also the renewer of the waters from the springs of source in the abyss below. In one legend which, like several others, is common to Egypt and Babylonia, the Great Mother, as Isis, also as Ishtar, descends into the under-world in search of the water of life, otherwise represented as her child, who was Horus or Tammuz according to the cult. The "Descent of Ishtar" is dated in the Aramaic-Akkadian calendar by the month *Ki-Gingir-na,* "the errand of Ishtar," which was dedicated to the goddess with "Virgo" as its zodiacal sign. This descent in search of the vanished water, the lost light, the disappearing child, was obviously made by the goddess in her lunar character. It was as the moon that Ishtar passed through the seven gates on her downward way when she was stripped of all her glory. (Talbot, *The Legend of Ishtar; Records of the Past,* vol. i.) This search for the water of life occurs some five months earlier in the Babylonian calendar than in the Egyptian year. Plutarch, in speaking of the mysteries, tells us that "on the eve of the winter solstice" the Egyptians "carry the cow seven times round the Temple," which is called "the seeking for Osiris." (Isis and Osiris, 52.) This in the pre-Osirian mythos was the elder Horus as the mother's child. Plutarch adds that the goddess who in one character is the earth-mother was in great distress from want of water in the winter-time. The lost Osiris of the legend was not only signified by the loss of solar potency that Isis went to seek for, it was also the renewal of water that she sighed for and wept in the first drops of the new inundation. The disappearance of the water in Egypt was coincident with the shrinking of the sun in the winter solstice; both were commemorated in the mourning of Isis. The journey of Isis in search of the water of life was about the time of the winter solstice, when the water disappeared from Egypt and the coming time of drought began. The season coincided with the sun in the sign of Aquarius when the lost Osiris or Child-Horus was re-discovered by the weeping mother seeking for the water in the nether-world. The same errand is ascribed to Ishtar in the Babylonian version of the mythos. But in the re-adjustment to the change of season in the Akkadian calendar, the search is given to the month *Ki-Gingir-na* when the sun was in the sign of Virgo.

The renewer of the water from the beginning was female. At first it was Apt the water-cow. Then Hathor or Nut the milch-cow, then Isis as the weeping-mother who had lost her child. In the legend of *Leylet en-Nuktah,* or "Night of the Drop," a miraculous tear was supposed to fall from Heaven on to the Nile, and, according to Pausanias, it was taught that the rise of the river was dependent on the drops that fell from the eyes of Isis. In the Coptic calendar the "Night of the Drop" is dated Baouneh 11th = June 17th, by means of which the first drops of the inundation could be traced to the Great Mother weeping for the lost Osiris, or the earlier Horus of the inundation. Now, when the tail of the Great Bear pointed northward and the sun coincided with the sign of Aquarius there was a re-birth of water from the abyss that issued from the mouth of *Piscis Australis.* The picture of source in the abyss was now repeated, and the wet-nurse or wateress was constellated in the zodiac as the multimammalian Menat, who was a later form of Apt the water-cow.

The imagery shows the perennial source of water in the under-world, and that which proceeded from the mouth of the fish now emanates from the numerous mammæ of the wet-nurse on the ecliptic. Thus the birth and re-birth of water are represented six months apart with the Great Bear presiding over both. In other words the water (or Child-Horus) that was lost to Egypt in the upper world was now re-found by the Great Mother seeking in the abyss of source from whence she drew the water of renewal for another year. The abyss was founded in the south. Aquarius is a southern sign, and it took six months altogether to bring the water from the abyss to its fulfilment in the inundation. The sun had reached its "Utat" at the point of *southing* for the region where the Urn of the waters was to be refilled; the Nile replenished from the abyss of source configurated as the fish's mouth. When the winter-sun was low down in the solstice it was southing slowly through the deep outside the earth. The hidden source of water was the same, when represented by the wet-nurse in the zodiac, as that from which the inundation issued in the south. There was but one abyss, whether this was indicated by the fish's mouth, the dugs of Apt, the female breast of Hapi-Mu, or the multi-mammæ of the suckler Menat. At the time when the inundation had run dry in Egypt the February rains were re-commencing in the equatorial regions. The lakes began to swell and the waters of the White Nile to rise and rush forth on their joyful journey towards the north. The new flood only reached the Delta just in time to save the country from drought and sterility. "Krater" was the urn or waterpot of the inundation. This in the south was brimming full. But when the sun had reached Aquarius, behold! the urn was empty. Hence the reversal of the vessel in his hands. The inundation was poured out. The urn needed to be replenished anew from the well of secret source, or the mouth of the abyss. Hitherto it has been conjectured that water from the urn was pouring *downward toward the mouth of the abyss*. But this would have no meaning in the mythos by which the imagery has to be interpreted. The water comes up from that welling-source depicted low down in the south now looked to for the future inundation. When the uranograph of Aquarius is rightly read, we see the last of the inundation in Egypt. The water poured out from the urn has come to an end. The urn, or bucket, being at times reversed, is consequently empty. Also the mode of replenishment from the tepht of source, or well of the deep, is indicated in the planisphere. On studying the figure of the "southern fish" we see a stream of water springing up from its mouth in the direction of Aquarius. And this is met by Aquarius with his empty urn held in position to receive the water of the new inundation from the welling-source in the abyss.

In the Osirian mythos Isis, or the cow-headed Hesi, had become the wateress or wet-nurse to the world in place of Apt the water-cow and Hathor the milch-cow; and now the New Nile was attributed to the tears which Isis shed for the lost Osiris or the earlier Child-Horus, when he vanished with the sinking water in the under-world.

It is possible to take one step further round the zodiac and thus include the sign of the fishes. But it has to be explained that Horus in the zodiac was not simply the lord of life, as the bringer of food and water in the inundation. Horus in the zodiac was also the solar god, who was the child conceived in Virgo, as Horus of the inundation, who was Horus of the resurrection, lord of the harvest, in the sign of Pisces. In the Greco-Kamite zodiacs the fish-mother gives re-birth to her child as a fish in the constellation of the fishes. (*Book of the Beginnings,* Plate.) Also in other monuments, the mother, as Hathor-Isis, bears the fish upon her head. Thus the fish-man or fish-god was re-born of the fish-mother in the abode of the abyss or the house of the fish, and the point of emergence for the sun-god in the zodiac was indicated by the sign of the fish or fishes at the time when the crocodile was the fish of Neith as Sebek-Horus. No representation of the inundation or the drought is directly apparent in the sign of Aries and Taurus. But the drama was not limited to the zodiac. The rising Pleiads and the "rainy Hyades" have ever been the harbingers of water or of spring. One name of the Hyades in Greek is Hues, the Sows or Suculæ, and in Egypt, Rerit the Sow was a figure of the Great Mother as the wetnurse or suckler, who was represented at one time by the seven sows, at another by the seven cows, at another by the many-breasted Menat as the typical provider of plenty.

In certain old Egyptian calendars, the periodic triumph of Horus over the plagues of drought and darkness was commemorated by a festival called *"the wounding of Sut."* The event is referred to as occurring on the first of the month, Epiphi—May 16th in the sacred year; June 25th in the Alexandrian year. This was exactly one month previous to the birth of the new inundation dated July 25th. And as the month Mesore agrees with the sun in the sign of Cancer or the beetles, so the month Epiphi coincided with the sun in the sign of the Gemini, who were Sut and Horus as the twins contending for supremacy in the equinox or on the mount. At this point Sut was mortally wounded, and the victory of Horus, the bringer of water and food and the renewer of light, was perfectly complete. (*Festival Calendars of Esné and Edfû.*) Now the worst was over. The long holiday celebrated by the Uaka festival had come at last with its relief. And here the Egyptian holiday was one with a holy day as the time of rest from labour, and the great feast of eating and drinking was a mode of giving thanks as well as of making merry. The fulfiller in the water and the grapes was welcomed in the drink he brought, with the drinking and the eating, at the festival of intoxication, dedicated to the goddess Hathor. The history of Horus the child-hero, the eternal Messu who became incarnate as a typical saviour of the world, was thus portrayed and could be repeated by all who understood the mythos which was depicted in the book above. His birth from the water was imaged by the figure of Horus on his papyrus, which is represented astronomically in a scene from the rectangular zodiac of Denderah. Horus in this is represented by the hawk on the papyrus-plant emerging from the water. By means of this we can identify the birth of the babe who was born "from between the knees of Sothis" (Rit., ch. 65) as Horus of the inundation.

The walls and windows of the house on high have been emblazoned like all Italy with pictures of the Virgin Mother and her child; the

Virgin Mother in one character who conceived, and the Great Mother as bringer-forth in the character of gestator. The planisphere contains a whole pantheon of Egyptian deities. They are the gods and goddesses of Egypt, the mythological personages and zoötypes that make up the vast procession which moves on for ever round and round according to the revolutions of the earth or the apparent revolution of the sphere. Taking the same order in which the sings on the ecliptic are read to-day when Aries has become Princeps Zodiaci, we can identify at least a dozen deities of Egypt with the twelve signs. (1) The ram-headed Amen with the constellation Aries; (2) Osiris, the Bull of Eternity, with the sign of Taurus; (3) the Sut-Horus Twins with the Gemini; (4) the beetle-headed Kheper-Ptah with the sign of the Beetle, later Crab; (5) the lion-faced Atum with the sign of Leo; (6) the Virgin Neith with the constellation Virgo; (7) Har-Makhu of the Scales with the sign of Libra; (8) Isis-Serkh, the scorpion goddess, with the sign of Scorpio; (9) Shu and Tefnut figured as the Archer with the sign of Sagittarius; (10) Num, the goat-headed, who presided over the abyss with the sign of Capricornus; (11) Menat, the divine wet-nurse, with the sign of Aquarius; (12) Horus of the two crocodiles with the sign of Pisces. Enough to show that the zodiac was a lower gallery in the pantheon of the Egyptian planisphere. And it is not humanly conceivable that all these gods and goddesses and nature powers of Egypt were constellated as figures in the starry vast by any other than the Egyptian "mystery teachers" of the heavens.

There may have been some kind of stellar enclosure round the pole of Sut in the south before a circumpolar paradise could have been configurated in the northern heaven by the Astronomers in the land of Kamit. But, even so, it is not necessary to assume a knowledge of Precession to explain the sinking of the pole and its accompanying stars that went down in the southern Deep. To those who travelled northward from the equatorial regions heading for the valley of the Nile there was an actual subsidence and submergence of a human fore-world in the south. This was a matter of latitude determinable by the stars that sank into the abyss, the natural fact that preceded the figure in mythology. The abyss became the grave as it were of some lost world which had once been real on the earth. But the imagery of this far country has been preserved twice over, and is still extant; once in the constellation figures and once in the double earth of Ptah's Amenta. That fore-world of the south was reproduced by the Egyptians of the north when they raised their circumpolar paradise to picture for all time some features of the old primeval home. The southern pole star sank into the blind abyss together with the little bit of foothold that was first established. This, in later legend, would become a fall from heaven, or submergence in a deluge, as the fact was figured in the astronomical mythology. Hence we find the legends of the lost paradise: the primal pair as man and cow, the twin brothers, the fall from heaven, the deluge, and other stories *as indigenous products at the centre of the old dark land.*

But the grand scheme of uranographic representation was completed in the valley of the Nile where the north celestial pole had become the central summit of the starry system. The south was the scene of so-called "creation." The creation which as Egyptian literally signifies "of the first time." And as we learn from the inscription of Tahtmes on the stele of the Sphinx, the first time goes back to the days and domain of Sut; Sut who is traditionally "the inventor of astronomy," and who as such had erected the pillar of the pole star. The domain of Sut was in the south. And it is shown by the ancient legends and the primitive constellations that the beginnings of the astral mythos were in equatoria looking south. The abyss of water was figured in the south. The earth-mother in the abyss is in the south. The monsters representative of her hugeness were constellated in the south. The tree first planted in the abyss was in the south. The fore-world that sank down beneath the waters of the deluge was in the south, and according to the legend lies to-day beneath the waters of Tanga, or the Thigh, in the lake of the birthplace, Tanganyika. Egypt was set in heaven as the upper land, and lower Egypt was repeated in Amenta. The name of Egypt is at root Egyptian. It is derivable from Kep, later Kheb, whence Khept, or Khepti, is a plural for the double land. Kep-Kep, another dual form, had been a name of Nubia. Kep, or Kheb, signifies the chamber, the womb, the birthplace. It is likewise a name of the water-cow that was configurated as a type of Egypt in the planisphere. The hieroglyphic "Khept" is a symbol of the birthplace. This is the Thigh, the Haunch, or Meskhen of the Mother Khept (or Apt). Thus the Egyptian Nome of the "haunch" was the Nome of the birthplace in Khept, Khebt, or Egypt. When the anthrotype had succeeded the zoötype we find that Egypt was figured as a female lying on her back with feet to the northward pointing in the direction of the Great Bear constellation. This was the motherland in the likeness of the human mother who had taken the place and position of the African water-cow, an image of the birthplace and abode being thus palpably continued (Stoboeus, *Ecl. Eth.*, p. 992, from a fragment of Hermes) as a figure of Egypt thus identified by nature and by name as the birthplace and bringer-forth. The "haunch" or thigh is an ideographic sign that was constellated in the northern heaven as a figure of the birthplace, and if so in the celestial chart, assuredly it had the same significance for a birthplace on the Libyan bank of the river Nile, hence its elevation to the sphere as a uranographic symbol of locality. A place of settlement is still called the seat, and the "haunch" in sign-language was the seat. Primordially it was the natural seat of the squatters who sat with heel to haunch. And the same symbol was figured in the northern heaven to denote the astronome of the "haunch" as a seat or birthplace above, whatsoever the birth and whosoever was the divinized Nomarch. We may be certain it was not without intention that the great pyramid of Gizeh was founded by King Kufu in the nome of the "haunch," the seat of the Great Mother, Khebt, or Egypt. The inhabitants of lower Egypt also remained faithful to the Tree as a twofold sign which is the sycamore of Hathor in the south, and the sycamore of Nut in the north. There was a territory of the upper and lower Oleander, also of the upper and lower Terebin tree. As Maspero remarks, "the principality of the Terebin (tree) occupied the very heart of Egypt, a country well suited to be the cradle of an infant civilization" (*Dawn of Civilization*, p. 71, Eng.

tr.). "The district of the white wall, marched with that of the haunch" alongside of each other on the Nile, as they were likewise constellated in the northern heaven.

Am-Khemen, the paradise of the eight great gods in the mythology, had its likeness in the nome of the hare, the chief town of which was Khemenu, the present Ashmunein, the town of Taht, who was an eighth to the seven gods in the lunar mythos. It was upon the steps of the mound in Khemenu that Shu stood as elevator of the cow of Nut = heaven of the eight great gods, which shows the priority of the nome in Egypt as the prototype of the astronome that was constellated in the northern stars. Kenset is an Egyptian name for Nubia, and according to the pyramid texts there was a celestial locality of the same name in the astronomical mythology which holds the mirror aloft to reflect the Kenset that was prototypal on the earth, as it likewise reflected the nomes of the haunch, the tree, the pillar, or others localized at first below.

Another Egyptian nome was called the Serpent-mountain, which was also repeated above with the great serpent winding round the tree or mountain of the north celestial pole. Thus the beginnings of the race and the environment were depicted for a purpose in the heaven of the north, and the field of the papyrus-reed that furnished the primeval food in the southern birthplace was set in Heaven, as the Aarru-field of peace and everlasting plenty on the summit of Mount Hetep at the pole.

In the Ritual (ch. 109) the paradise of plenty, first denoted by the water plants, has become the harvest-field which is surrounded and protected by a wall of steel. The wheat in this divine domain grew seven cubits high and was two cubits long in the ear. The barley, from which beer was brewed, was four cubits in the ear, but the original paradise, the Aarru or Allu, from which the Greeks derived their Elysian fields, was constellated as the land of the papyrus reed, the shoots of which were eaten as the primitive food that grew in the greatest abundance in the region of the two great lakes. The most primitive ideal of paradise was that of an ever-green oasis, in the midst of the African desert, welling with life-giving water, and with the large-leaved sycamore fig tree or dom-palm or the papyrus plant at the centre as a figure of food. Inner Africa contains the prototype of the Egyptian paradise in a land of welling waters where the food came of itself and was perpetually renewed, and there was little need for labour. And when the outward movements of the wandering nomads began, and thirst and hunger were to be faced in waterless wastes of rootless desert sand, there would be yearnings of regret for the old lost home and birth-land left behind, now glorified by distance and the glamour of tradition. And so the universal legend grew which was not absolutely baseless. The felicity enjoyed in this primeval land of legendary lore is such as was possessed at one time on the earth, the upper paradise being a sublimated replica of a lower or terrestrial paradise. Thus, the primitive paradise of the Egyptians, as a land from which the human race had come, was constellated in the northern heaven as the top of attainment in a world to which they were going for an everlasting home, and in a clime where food and air and water never failed.

In the North, an Egypt of the heavens was figured first within the circle of the Greater Bear. This was the land of Khept, as a celestial locality. The circle was then divided into south and north, as double Egypt, upper and lower, and the two halves were described as the domains of Sut and Horus, who were the first two children of the ancient Genetrix, the mother of seven offspring altogether.

Thus, according to the present reading of the astronomical mythology, the imagery configurated in the stars was African in origin, and the teachers of its primitive mysteries were Egyptian. The seven astronomes in the celestial heptanomis of the seven Egyptian nomes, we hold to have been figured first on earth, and subsequently imaged in the heavens. Following the totemic sept of the sevens Egypt appears to have been mapped out first in seven nomes, and this heptanomis below to have been repeated in the planisphere. Seven nomes are said to have been, according to a later transliteration of names, those of the Memphites, Heracleopolites, Crocodileopolites, Aphroditopolites, Oxyrhynchites, Cynopolites, and Hermopolites. The great and lesser oases were considered to be parts of the heptanomis (Budge, E. A. W., *The Mummy*, p. 8). The goddess of the Great Bear, Khebt or Apt, was mother of the fields of heaven when they consisted of the seven astronomes. Those fields of the papyrus reed were figured within the circle made by the annual turn round of the seven stars about the north celestial pole. This, in the mythos, formed the enclosure of the typical tree, which was planted in the midst of the garden—the tree of life or food in the celestial waters, otherwise the tree of the pole in the astronomical mythology. The constellation of the female hippopotamus (or Great Bear) was the mother of the time-circles. It was a clock or horologe, on account of its wheeling round the pole once every four and twenty hours. This, or the "haunch," is obscurely referred to in the text from the Temple of Denderah, as the clock or instrument by which the moon-god, Tehuti, measured the hours. Hence, the hippopotamus remained a hieroglyphic sign for the hour (*Hor-Apollo*, B. 2, 20). The Great Bear was also a clock of the four quarters in the circle of the year, as is witnessed by the saying of the Chinese: when the tail of the Great Bear points to the east it is spring; when it points to the south it is summer; when it points to the west it is autumn; when it points to the north it is winter. In Egypt, when the Great Bear pointed to the south, or, astronomically, when the constellation had attained its southernmost elongation, it was the time of the inundation, the birthday of the year, which was also called the birthday of the world. Now, this is the particular point at which apparently the planisphere, or orrery, was set at starting, whether two thousand or twenty-eight thousand years ago. As the celestial globe has come to us it looks as if a starting-point in time might still be made out in the year of the Great Bear and the inundation with the tail-stars of the Bear as pointers to the birthplace of the waters, coming from the south with their salvation, and with Horus in the ark as the deliverer from the dragon of drought and thence doctrinally as the saviour of the world. It is a common assumption that the earliest Egyptian year was a year of 360 days based upon twelve moons of thirty days each. There was such a reckoning, and no doubt its origin was lunar. This would be attributed to the moon-god, Tehuti (Taht), who was the measurer, although not only as the reckoner of lunar time; hence he became the opener of the year, beginning with the first month assigned to Taht. But, in an older table of the months found at the Ramesseum and at Edfu, the goddess Tekhi is the opener of the year, and not the moon-god, Taht. Here the first month has the name of Tekhi *versus* Taht. The word Tekhi signifies a supply of liquid, to supply with drink, and the goddess Tekhi is the opener of the year with the inundation. We regard this year of the Great Bear and the inundation (that of Apt, Menat or Tekhi) as primary. Next comes the year of 360 days, to which the five days were added by Taht; this was lunar, or luni-stellar. The inundation was a primary factor in the establishment of time in Egypt and the foundation of the year. The fact is recognized in the "Hymn to the Nile" when it is said "Stable are thy decrees for Egypt," that is, in the fixed periodic return of the waters. Also, as the teacher of time, the Nile is said to be the inspirer of Taht, who was the measurer of time by means of the Great Bear, the moon, and the inundation. Under the name of Tekhi, the Old Great Mother was the giver of liquid and supplier of drink; as Apt or Khept she was the water-cow with a woman's breasts; as Neith she was the suckler of crocodiles; as Rerit she was the suckler in the form of the many-teated sow; as Hesi (Greek Isis) she was the milch-cow, and as Menat she was the wet-nurse. Under all these types she was primordially the Mother-earth, and fundamentally related to the water-source, or in Egypt to the inundation. This is the Old First Mother who was given the Great Bear as her constellation in the northern heaven where she became the maker of the starry revolutions or cycles, and thence the mother of the earliest year in time. It was a year dependent on the inundation and determined by the birth of Horus as the crocodile-headed Sebek who, like Arthur, was the son of the Great Bear, otherwise the crocodile of the inundation. The birth is represented in the astronomical fragment from a Theban tomb. In this the Old First Mother has just given birth to her young crocodile and dropped it in front of her. Thus we behold the birth of Sebek, which according to the sign-language is equally the birth of another year, at the moment when the Great Bear's tail is pointing to the birthplace (see fig., p. 289).

One of the old Egyptian legends, briefly repeated by Plutarch, may afford us a hint concerning this beginning of the year with the annual revolution of the Great Mother in Ursa Major as the hippopotamus or crocodile. According to this the solar god discovered that the Great Mother, Rhea, had been cohabiting secretly with Saturn. He consequently laid a spell upon her that she should not bring forth a child in either a month or a year. Then Hermes being likewise in love with the goddess copulated with her, and afterwards playing counters with the female moon he won from her the seventieth part of each one of her lights. Out of the whole he composed five days, and added these to the three hundred and sixty, which days the Egyptians call the additional days. Who then were the Kamite originals of the Greek Rhea, Saturn and Hermes? Rhea, like Apt, or Nut, was the mother of the gods.

Saturn the dragon was a form of Sebek, the crocodile-headed Horus, the prototype of the good dragon; and Hermes is the Egyptian Tehuti, the moon-god. The secret connection of the Great Mother with Saturn agrees with the connection between the goddess of the Great Bear and Sebek, who was married to his mother. The year of the Great Bear and the inundation, or of Apt and Sebek, was found to be wrong, and this was righted when Taht-Hermes, the measurer of time by the Great Bear and the moon, had added the five additional days to the earlier year, and thus established the truer cycle of 365 days to the year, by means of his co-operation with the moon. Thus the mother of the revolutions established the earliest cycle of time in the circle of the year which ended when the Bear was pointing to the birthplace of the water in the south, and the festival of "the Tail" was celebrated for the coming of the inundation. The tail of the Great Bear, as pointer or indicator on the face of the celestial horologe, was obviously still employed and reckoned with for the Set-Heb festival, which was celebrated by the Egyptians every thirty years. This feast, or a section of it, was known by name as "the Festival of the Tail." It was the anniversary of some very special year of years. There was a lord of the thirty-year festival, who was at one period Ptah, at another Horus. The birthplace of the inundation when the Great Bear pointed to it in the southern quarter was a point for ever fixed in the region of the waters, let us say (for the moment) coincident with the sign of Leo. That point did not retrocede. But when the place of birth, as solar, was shifted to the vernal equinox and the equinox receded, the birthplace went with it from zodiacal sign to sign. The time of the sun parted company with the time of the Great Bear and the inundation, for a cycle of 26,000 years. A great change was made when the time of the inundation was supplemented by the time of the sun. The birthplace of Horus (of the waters) had been in the south at the season of the year when the tail of the Bear denoted the birthplace in that quarter of the heavens and the Great Mother presided over the birth of the child, the crocodile or the papyrus shoot. The birthplace in the solar mythos was shifted, and the point was determined by the position of the vernal equinox as it travelled from sign to sign in the great circuit of precession: from Virgo to Leo, from Cancer to the Twins, from the Bull to the Ram, from the Fishes to the Waterer. Whether in the pre-solar or the solar mythos, whether as Apt, Tekhi or Hathor, the old Genetrix presided over the birth of Horus, on this great birthday that was commemorated in Egypt as the birthday of creation. It was an unparalleled meeting-point. The star Phact, in the constellation Columbia, far south, announced the inundation. Canopus showed the babe on board the bark, ascending from the south. Heralded by Sothis, his dog, Orion rose up from the river, at the north end of Eridanus, the stellar representative of him who came as Horus of the inundation. This advent is depicted in the monuments (Maspero, *D. of C.*, Eng. tr., p. 97).

Thus the Egyptian sacred year is that of the Inundation and the Bear. Its opening coincided roughly with the summer solstice—when the solstices had at length been recognized—with the sun in the lion-sign. And of course when the solstice, or the sun, was in that sign, the vernal equinox was passing through the sign of Taurus. Now, the earliest year we read of in Babylonia is that which opened with the vernal equinox in the sign of the "directing bull." This was the same year or cycle, sign for sign, as the Egyptian sacred year with the solstice in Leo, but with a different point of commencement, the Egyptian starting from the solstice; or rather from what had ever been the fixed point of the inundation; the Babylonian from the vernal equinox. Khebt, the goddess of the Great Bear, was said to "preside over the birth of the Sun." In the stellar mythos she had presided over the birth of Horus in the inundation. But when solar time was established the child was solar too, and the sun-god Horus Har-Makhu superseded Sebek of the inundation. His place of birth was shifted to the vernal equinox, and the birth itself was thenceforth timed no longer to the inundation. Horus, the Child or Messu of the inundation, on his papyrus, was now brought forth by Hathor, with Sothis as the Star of Annunciation. The birth took place in "Sothis," the birthday being determined by the heliacal rising of the star, as well as by the Tail of Ursa Major. Khebt, or Apt, the Old First Mother, still presided, as great correlator over all, as if she were the midwife or meskhenat in attendance at the birth when Hathor had become the mother. The goddess Hathor was termed the mistress of the beginning of the year in relation to the rising of Sothis; and Hathor was a form of the hippopotamus-headed mother of the beginnings in the Great Bear, with the milch-cow substituted for the water-cow; both being types of the wet-nurse and giver of the precious liquid of life. And when the celestial figures of the astral Mythology were constellated in the *northern heaven* the ancient Genetrix had been portrayed already in the three characters of mother-earth, the mother of water, and the mother of breath. But before we have done with the Great Bear Constellation in the northern heaven we have to point out a primitive symbol of her who was figured as the mother of beginnings by nature and by name.

A magical implement commonly called the "bull-roarer" is found in divers parts of the world. It is one of the simplest things that ever acquired a primitive sacredness from being made use of as a means of invocation in the religious mysteries and totemic ceremonies of the past; an implement that is dying out in England to-day as a toy now called the "fun of the fair." The Arunta Churinga shows that the "whirler," "roarer" or thun-thunie, originally represented the female. Hence it has the phallic emblem of the vulva figured on it as a device in the language of signs. (N. T., p. 150.) Others of the churinga are womb-shaped. The ornament of others also indicates the human birthplace. Moreover, life is portrayed in the act of issuing from the wood, as tree-frogs issued from the tree. Enough to show the primitive nature of the symbol. It is used in the mysteries as a means of calling the initiates who are about to be made into men. The special dance of the nude young women, their exhibition of the embellished organ and peculiar appeal to the youngsters, demonstrates that the call is made by female nature at the time for that fulfilment of the male which was the object of the ceremony. These women were making the visible call that was audible in the sound of the bull-roarer. In the course of time the implements had changed hands as the mysteries became more and more masculine and the women were excluded from the ceremonies. But the Kurnai have two kinds of "Roarer," one of which represents the inspiring spirit as female; this was primary. At first the "whirler" used in the mysteries to call the initiates for young-man-making was the voice of the female calling on the male, to become a man; to be brave in fulfilling the laws of Tabu and rules of personal conduct; to be true to the brotherhood, and "not to eat the forbidden food." The forms of the magical instrument differ, but all are used for whirling round to make the call. Now Khebt, the Old First Mother in Egyptian mythology, who was constellated in the Great Bear, is portrayed with the "bull-roarer" held in front of her womb. The name of the Egyptian instrument is *"menait,"* which literally signifies the whirler, from *men* to rotate, to whirl round. Thus the symbol of the whirling round can be traced to *the mother of the revolutions as a figure in the astronomical mythology of Egypt.* The Great Bear goddess was portrayed in this position as the "mother of the revolutions" and the *maker of motion in a circle.* Hers was the primary power that drew or turned, hurled or whirled the starry system round about the pole, as the mighty hippopotamus in the celestial waters. Her names of Rerit and Menait both indicate the character of rotator, which is signified by the menait in her hands. The goddess of the Great Bear (hippopotamus) was adored at Ombos as the "living word." She is configurated in the planisphere with huge jaws wide open in the act of uttering the word, or of roaring. The Egyptian wisdom implies that the menait held in front of the First Mother signified the female emblem, the original instrument of magical power. With the roar of Rerit the water-cow called to her young bulls, and her roar would be imitated by the bull-roarer, menait or turndun, in calling them, and as the voice of the female calling on the males it was continued in the ceremony of young-man making, in the totemic mysteries. Thus we find the goddess Apt, or Khebt the roarer, as a hippopotamus, the Great Bear, "rurring" or whirling round, with the "bull-roarer" as her sign and symbol, at the centre of the northern heaven (see fig., p. 124, also p. 311).

There is a remarkable survival of what may be tentatively termed the cult of the Great Bear amongst the Mandaites or Sabeans of Mesopotamia, who are worshippers of the "living word." In the performance of their worship the eyes are fixed upon the pointers of the Great Bear. They celebrate a kind of feast of tabernacles annually, for which they erect a tabernacle called the Mishkena or Meskhen. Lastly, the primordial star-cult of the Great Bear is also British. In the ancient Welsh mythology the Great Mother Arth is the goddess of the Great Bear, and Arthur = Horus is her solar son who makes his celestial voyage with the seven in the ark.

Hitherto Egyptologists have been inclined to regard the female hippopotamus (our Great Bear) and the "haunch" as one and the same constellation. This premature guess is erroneous. They were both signs of the Great Mother, but in two separate constellations which represented two different characters. In the Egyptian planisphere, as at Denderah, the female hippopotamus answers to our Great Bear, whereas the sign of the "haunch" is on the far side of the Lesser Bear, in the position of Cassiopoea, the lady in the chair. If we take the tail-star of the Bear as guide, the constellation Cassiopoea is almost exactly opposite. Thus when the tail of the bear is pointing north in winter, Cassiopoea is at its southern elongation. These are two different types of the Great Mother, who was Apt the Earth-Mother in one character, as the water-cow, and Nut the Mother Heaven in the other, as the milch-cow. Also in the illustration on a Theban tomb the constellation of the "haunch" is widely distinct from the hippopotamus. And it is this constellation that is distinguished by name as the "meskhen" with the hieroglyphics written on it which read, 𓏠𓊃𓐍𓈖, Mes-khe-n, the womb as place or chamber of birth depicted in the constellation of the "haunch" or "thigh." It is noticeable that the head of the milch-cow is portrayed upon the "haunch." This distinguishes the one cow from the other, the milch-cow of Nut from the water-cow of Khebt or Apt, or our Great Bear. It also shows that the "thigh" or "haunch" belonged to the milch-cow, and represented the same celestial "seat" and place of origin as the later lady in the chair. But, whether it is figured as the cow or Meskhen, the "thigh," "haunch," or leg of the cow, it signified the birthplace of the celestial waters in the mythos, and the place of re-birth for souls in the heaven of eternity. Then follows the tampering and retouching process of the Euphrateans, Greeks, or other modern claimants to the ancient wisdom. The place of the "seat" or "thigh" was given to a woman sitting in a chair, and the lady of the chair usurps the throne of Isis with her seat and the pre-anthropomorphic type that was constellated ages on ages earlier in Egypt as the cow of Nut or heaven. The "thigh" in sign-language is a type of birth and thence of the birthplace, when the birth was water, as we find it constellated in the northern heaven. The star "Phact" (in Arabic, the thigh) shows us that this birthplace *had been* constellated in the southern hemisphere as the sign of Tekhi the giver of water in the inundation. Thus the "thigh" was figured both in the south and in the north to signify the birthplace and the birth of water. In the south the water was the river Nile, and in the north it is the river of the Milky Way. These are the two waters of earth and heaven proceeding from the cow that was the water-cow of Apt or Tekhi in the earth, and the milch-cow of Nut in heaven. As before said, one of the two great lakes at the celestial pole is the Lake of the "Thigh" or "Haunch," which is mentioned by name in the Ritual (ch. 149). It is also called the Thigh of Khar-aba, at the head of the canal, or Milky Way. The Lake of the Thigh was the birthplace of the waters above, where the milch-cow or her "haunch" was a constellated figure of source whence flowed the great white river of the *Via Lactea*. The leg (thigh, seat, womb, or haunch) of Nut, the celestial cow, once stood where the lady in the chair is seated now. Nut, or the milch-cow, was the bringer to re-birth in this region of the pole. The Seven Powers brought to their re-birth in Seven Great Spirits were constellated as her children in the Lesser Bear, as seven stars that never set, but were fixtures for eternity. The two constellations of the hippopotamus and the "haunch," or Meskhen, are also found in the rectangular zodiac that was carved upon the ceiling of the Great Temple at Denderah.

As may be observed, the two figures of the hippopotamus and the "haunch" (or milch-cow) are yoked together by a chain, one end of which is held by Apt, and the other is made fast to the "haunch" or cow. This is in the position of the pole which was the yoke or bond of heaven, and which was known in Babylonia as "the yoke of the enclosure." The chain shows that the Great Bear was made fast to the pole for security in its swing round. It also shows that the pole was once imaged either in or by the constellation of the "haunch," the seat, or milch-cow in that region. The leg or thigh was an Egyptian figure of the pole, as we find it in "the leg of Ptah," a constellation

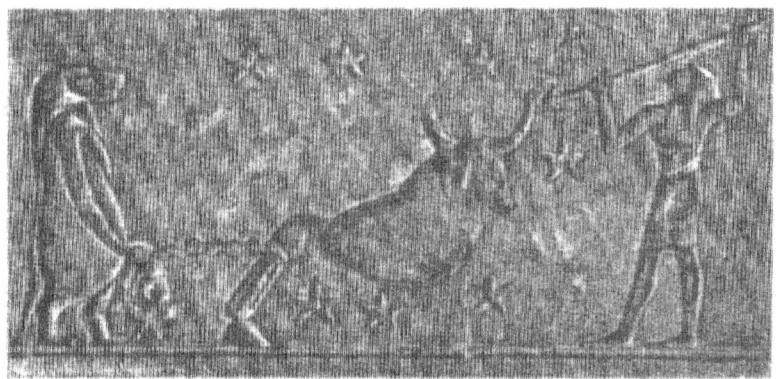

Hippopotamus and Haunch.

which has been identified with the lady of the seat. Hence, "above the leg" is equivalent to "over the pole" (Ritual, ch. 7, 74, and 98, Renouf).

Heaven as a source of liquid life that dropped in dew and rain upon the earth was likened to a cow, or, in sign-language, was *the cow.* Apt is the cow of earth and Nut the cow of heaven. Apparently the cow of heaven, or Nut, supplied the earliest foundation for the pole which, as the figure of the cow dislimned, was represented by the leg of Nut (otherwise called the "thigh," the "haunch" or "seat") as the central figure of support in heaven. The cow being primary, it follows that the "leg of Nut" was an earlier image of the pole than the "leg of Ptah," the staff of Anup, or the backbone of Osiris—which were also figures of fixity whether at or as the pole of Heaven. The leg or haunch of the cow was then left standing in the midst of the Milky Way. The speaker in the Ritual thus addresses it, "Oh, thou leg in the northern sky, and in that most conspicuous but inaccessible stream," which is elsewhere termed the canal. In the pyramid texts it is called *"the leg (Uarit) of the Akhemu-Seku,"* the stars that never set—the eternals, as a type of stability (Pepi I, 411). Cassiopoea, the lady in the chair, also sits in the midst of the Milky Way. Thus the "seat" remains, if only as a chair; the white river flows, with nothing to account for it; and the lake of milk, the cow, the haunch, thigh or leg of Nut are all dislimned or have passed away.

The Great Bear made her circuit on the outside of the never-setting stars, whereas the "leg" or "haunch" was a constellation in the circle of perpetual apparition. It never set below the horizon, nor did any of its stars go down through all the period of the long great year. Thus the bit of foothold in the watery vast of space was figured as the "seat," the Meskhen, womb, or re-birth-place in the heaven of eternity. The deceased, when speaking of his going forth from the tomb, identifies this constellation with the place of re-birth above, saying, "I shall shine above the 'haunch' as I come forth in heaven" (Rit., ch. 74). That is, at the point where the "leg" was constellated to show the upward way upon the starry map to him who lay looking heavenward "with a corpse-like face." Deceased in Amenta pleads for his re-birth above betwixt the thighs of the divine cow as a type of heaven (Rit., ch. 148). The Old Great Mother, as the hippopotamus, we repeat, was not within the circle of the never-setting stars, in the circumpolar Paradise. It was the milch-cow Hesit, not the water-cow, that "gave the white liquor which the glorified ones love"; the milk that flowed from the cow, whether she was divinized as Nut, or Mehurit the Heaven, or Hathor, or Isis the cow-headed goddesses. The cow Hesit was designated "the Divine Mother and fair nurse" as giver of the liquid of life when this was represented in heaven by the milk of the celestial cow.

This identification of the "thigh" as a totally different constellation from the Greater Bear will alter the reading of certain inscriptions in which the "thigh" and "Bear" have been mixed up together. For example, when the alignment was made for the Temple of Hathor to be rebuilt at Denderah, in the time of Augustus, the King tells us that he oriented the corners and established the temple as *"it took place before,"* whilst looking to the sky and directing his gaze to the Ak of the "thigh" constellation. Here the "Ak" denotes a central point, the axis or middle of the starry group. Also when the temple at Edfu was refounded (about 257-37 B.C.) the King who "stretches the measuring-cord" and lays the foundation-stone is represented as saying, that when doing this his eye was fixed upon the Meskhet or Meskhen, which has been supposed to be in the Great Bear. This also was in the constellation of the "haunch," as may be seen by the fragment from a Theban tomb (p. 289) where *the "haunch" is labelled the "Meskhen"* or chamber of birth which the constellation indicated; the birth chamber of the cow above, that was copied in the temple of the cow-goddess below (Lockyer, *The Dawn of Astronomy*, p. 172).

The cow of heaven as the milch-cow was portrayed standing or resting on the summit of the mount which was "connected with the sky," as portrayed in the monuments. This, in the Persian rendering, was the cow upon the summit of Mount Alborz. In the Norse mythology it is the cow Audhumla. As the *Prose Edda* describes it, "immediately after the gelid vapours had been resolved into drops, there was formed out of them the cow named Audhumla. Four streams of milk ran from her teats, and thus she fed Ymir" (*Prose Edda* 6), just as the cow of heaven suckled Horus. Heaven, as the cow, is called the spouse upon the mountain. She is the mother of the solar bull, and, as goddess, is described as suckling her child Horus, and as having "drooping dugs" (Renouf, *B. of D.*, ch. 62, note 1). The Milky Way was pictured as the celestial water, now called milk, that flowed from the cow of heaven couched upon the summit of the mount, the apex of which was at the celestial pole; whether the cow was called Nut or Hesit, the Arg Roud, Audhumla, or the good lady. Now if we take the lady on the seat and the "haunch" or "thigh" as a figure of the cow, the position on the globe is this: the lady of heaven = the cow, or the mistress of the mount, is constellated in the middle of the Milky Way, which runs in two directions downwards from the summit of the pole. If we restore the figure of the cow or its co-type the "haunch," this is the exact spot at which the river of milk once issued from the cow of heaven that gave her white liquid to Horus and the glorified; or water to the world in dew and rain. The Milky Way has been disfigured sadly by the Greeks, but still runs visibly as the river of the Nun or great deep, the white river that engirdles all the earth. The river Ganges, issuing from the mouth of the cow, retains the primitive type of a celestial source for the water that fell from heaven, as it was seen by night descending in the river of the Milky Way, or in four streams that issued from the udder of the cow, which supplied a figure of four quarters to the mount. The cow of heaven, or Nut, as giver of liquid life, was the earliest mistress of the mountain, or divine lady of the mound. Then the type of the good nurse, the suckler, was made anthropomorphic and the udder of the cow was superseded by the mammæ of the human mother. But it was a long way from the African cow or sow, as the suckler, to the wet-nurse divinized in human form.

Lastly, the cow of earth was the mother of salt water as well as fresh; both fresh and salt water being found in the African lakes. The Albert Nyanza, for instance, is a salt-water lake, and one of the two lakes of the cow or "haunch" at the pole was evidently a salt-water lake, as the primitive lake of purifying and healing. One of these, repeated in Amenta, is called the salt-water lake (Rit., ch. 17). The Zulu form of this celestial "source" is a young woman who makes the water. "Leave it to me" says Lu, the Samoan Nut, when there was no water, and she makes the water, which was salt (Turner, *Samoa*, p. 12). This may account for the origin of salt water in heaven. To very primitive folk urine was the first salt water used for cleansing, purifying, and healing. The earliest soap was made from the alkali in urine mixed with oil from the human skin. The Inoit, amongst others, still wash themselves with urine. The Banians of Momba wash in cow's urine, because, as they say, the cow is their mother. An early type of the mother as wateress in heaven was the cow, and first of all it was the water-cow. Urine was a very primitive form of holy water as a means of purifying. At the present time holy water is yet *sained* and made sacred by adding the ingredient of salt to water that is fresh. Urine is also a means of purifying when the English schoolboy, about to bathe in the stream, will micturate down his left leg as a protective charm against the raw-head-and-bloody-bones, our form of the Apap monster, lurking at the bottom of the water. Thus, as the pitiful human need was primitively reflected in the African heaven, the earliest water of purification, the salt water, the source of the lake of purification, was made by the cow. And so unbreakable is the chain with which the human race, its customs, its theology, and religious symbolism are bound together from the beginning that we may be absolutely certain that this is why salt is put into the baptismal font to make the water holy. This, we think, also touches the origin of the "salt woman" in the Navajo legend who is described as resting at the top of the reed mountain which rose up beyond the reach of the deluge. When the anthropomorphic type had been adopted the woman that made the water on the summit of the mount took the place of the cow. In such ways the matter of mythology was continued in the heavens on the grand scale of uranographic representation. In this celestial sign-language, the oldest book of wisdom in the world was written by the mystery teachers and can still be read upon the starry scroll of ancient night.

The "upliftings of Shu," are spoken of and portrayed in the Egyptian Ritual. The first of these is said in ancient legends to have taken place at Hermopolis, where Shu stood on the mound to raise the firmament. This was the mound by which the mount of earth was imaged in Egypt as the altar of the mound-builders, constellated in Ara. At least two of Shu's upliftings can be identified. In his *rôle* of An-hur, Shu was the uplifter of heaven, or Nut, by name. He is portrayed upon the mount or mound in the at of raising up the cow of Nut with his two hands, or pushing up the heaven assisted by his support-gods. And Kepheus standing on the mount with the rod in his uplifted hand remains a representative of Shu, who stood upon the mound to raise the firmament of Am-Khemen. In his character of An-hur, he was the uplifter of the sky or firmament in the pre-solar mythos. In the solar mythos he becomes auxiliary to Ra, and is called his son, Shu-Si-Ra. He is now the supporter of the sun-god who uplifts the solar orb upon the mount of dawn, or, as it is also phrased, he brings the eye of light to Ra. In doing this he kneels upon the horizon as the uplifter. He is the helper of the solar god (Horus or Ra) upon the horizon when the great battle was waged against the Apap of darkness, who fought so long and fiercely that the god came staggering upwards fainting from his wounds. (Rit., ch. 39.)

It has been said that all tradition respecting the personage known as "the kneeler" has been lost. Aratos knew nothing of the character. (Brown, *Phainomena of Aratos,* Introd., p. 5.) But in the Egyptian astronomical mythology the god Shu IS "the kneeler" personified. In this form he is portrayed upon the horizon or mount of dawn stooping on bended knee to uplift the solar disk, or to bear it on his head. He who had uplifted the starry firmament with his two hands, or with the forked stick called his rod, now represented the force that heaved up the sun in the position of "the kneeler." In the "Phainomena" Aratos describes "the kneeler" in an attitude of worship with arms upraised "from both his shoulders each stretching on its side about a full arm's length." (Brown, lines 66, 69.) This is the attitude of Shu, but with the solar disk omitted. "The kneeler," then, who is Al Jatha in Arabic and Engonansin in Greek, we identify with Shu, the deity who kneels upon the horizon to support his father Ra, the solar god, in his battle with the hosts of darkness. He also passed into the

Eschatology as the typical kneeler; thence the keeper of the door in the hall of judgment is named after Shu, "the kneeler." The keeper says to the initiate in the mysteries, "I open not to thee, I allow thee not to pass by me, unless thou tellest my name." The password, given in reply, is "the knee of Shu," which he hath lent for the support of Osiris, is the name, that is as the supporter of the sun-god in the character of "the kneeler." (Rit., ch. 125.) Shu-Anhur, in his twofold *rôle* may still be recognized on the celestial chart in the constellations of Kepheus and Leo, partly by means of the double Regulus. As An-hur in Kepheus he stands upon the mount to lift up heaven with his rod or staff, and as Shu or Regulus in Leo he is the supporter and uplifter of the solar orb on the horizon as "the kneeler."

Shu the Kneeler.

A picture in the constellation Lyra has survived to show us how the stories of the solar god were given a starry setting on the background of the dark. If we refer to this group upon the celestial globe we find a figure of the winged Disk or Hut which still identifies the constellation with Horus of Edfu, who is now called Horus-Behutet. What then was the story told of Horus in the stars by night which could be read in Lyra when conjoined and illustrated with the winged Solar Disk? We are shown a picture of Horus with his lyre, the prototype of Apollo with his lyre, and Orpheus with his lute. Horus with the lyre or harp of seven strings was the sevenfold one as a divine type of attainment, the octave and the height in music as well as in the building of the heavens. This Horus was the first form of the All-One, or Pan, in whom the Seven Powers were unified in perfect harmony, or in the music of the spheres. It was Horus who tore out the sinews of Sut and by depriving him of power turned the discord of the universe to harmony. He was consequently depicted in the constellation Lyra as the maker of music that was played on the harp, the lute, the lyre, or the sevenfold pipes of Pan as a figure of the All-One.

The Serpentarius, or "Ophinchus huge" was constellated in the Decans of Scorpio as a figure of Horus wrestling with the serpent of darkness. At this stage in the periodical display of the celestial pictures the sun was about to descend into Amenta from the point (say) of the Autumn Equinox in Scorpio, to grapple with the powers of darkness, decay, and dearth now rising in rebellion and gathering together for the annual assault. The drama could not be rendered in imagery directly solar; hence the representation figured as an object picture in the rising stars that showed the Lord of Light at death-grips with the serpent of the dark, in that sign where Horus or Osiris received his mortal wound. Thus, all along, *the Gnosis was pictorially portrayed in heaven.* Hence when the Osiris obtains command over the celestial water he says, "Collector of souls is the name of my Bark. *The picture of it is the representation of my glorious journey upon the canal.*" The bark of salvation in which the souls of the glorified were gathered, we repeat, was solar, whilst the picture shown by night was stellar. The canal is the name of the Milky Way, and on this the glorious voyage was made by the Manes "to the abode of those who had found their faces as the glorified." In another illustration the great ship of heaven, in the solar mythos, is the Ark of Ra. When seen by day, the solar orb is carried on board together with the solar god and the spirits perfected. But the literature of the subject, so to say, was represented, and the story was repeated, nightly in the stars.

The blind god "hungering for the morn" is a Greek figure of Orion, which explains nothing of itself. But Orion is the stellar representative by night of Horus the solar god in the darkness of Amenta who is An-ar-ef the sightless Horus, or Horus as the blind god whose sight was restored to him at dawn. Several constellations, Orion the hunter, Herakles, Serpentarius, Boötes, are portraits of Horus configurated in his various characters both mythical and eschatological. Amsu-Horus was the husbandman twice over as Egyptian; once in the mythology which sets forth the natural facts according to the seasons in Egypt; and once in the eschatology which figured the same facts typically in relation to the harvest in the after-life. Amsu, we consider, was the original of Boötes. On the celestial globe, high over Spica, Boötes rises with the sickle in his right hand as a symbol of the husbandman. Amsu issues from the tomb as the divine harvester, with the flail in his right hand. He is also the good herdsman, as is shown by the crook, whether as goat-herd or shepherd, and this character of the husbandman as guardian is repeated by Boötes in the character of Bearward.

Some Egyptologists have conjectured that the wars of Horus in the Astronomical mythology were historical in Egypt. But this is to follow the will-o'-the-wisp of a popular delusion. The mass of primitive "history" in many lands has been derived from nursery legends and as folk-tale versions of the Egyptian wisdom. The lords of light and life that overcame the powers of drought and darkness were converted into ethnical personages and glorified as natural heroes. We are told by Diodorus of Sicily that the Egyptians looked upon the Greeks as impostors who reissued the ancient mythology as their own history; in this they were not alone. But the wars of Horus were fought in heaven and Amenta against the Sebau, the Dragon, the Serpent, with Orion for one of his great stellar figures. If there is any one figure constellated in heaven as the hero *par excellence,* in various characters, it is pre-eminently that of Orion. This, as Egyptian, is Horus or Heru. The word Heru signifies the chief; the one who is the over-lord, the ruler, the mighty one, the hero. This hero as Horus of the inundation was pre-solar. He was the annual bringer of food and drink before there was a sun-god, when the stars were the annunciators of the coming times and seasons to the waiting, watching world. Then the character was made solar, and lastly eschatological. Horus the mighty conqueror, the Nimrod, the slayer of the gigantic Apap, is

The Sign-Language of Astronomical Mythology 317

the giant-killer of all later lore, not only as the solar god but also as the earlier elemental power, and the various legends are the reliquary remains of his several characters.

They have to go a long way round to work who would understand the scientific grouping of the stars according to the principles of astro-mythology. For instance, Orion as the hunter and Lupus the hare are two southern constellations. But Orion does not mean that a scriptural character was taken out of the Bible and constellated as a typical sportsman, and the mighty hunter of a miserable hare. It is an almost universal representation that the sun or solar god pursues the moon for ever daily and nightly in a never-ceasing chase. This is how the story was configurated by the mystery teachers of the heavens in the grouping of the stars. Such a chase implies the character of the hunter, and Orion, as representative of the solar Horus, is the hunter. The pursuit of the moon is signified by the stellar symbol of the hare. In sign-language, and in many lands, the hare has been a lunar zoötype as the wide-eyed leaper that was followed night by night, day after day, by the solar hunter in his perpetual round. Thus the hare, known as a symbol of the moon over half the world, is shown to have been a totemic type of the nome, and a figure of the lunar deity in Egypt. The hare was imaged as a primitive constellation at the feet of Orion, who in one character was the mighty hunter. But he is not the hunter of so insignificant an animal as the hare. Neither was Orion the hunter only a figure of the sun pursuing the moon, or the hare. He was the mythical hunter in other characters. In the stellar mythos he was the hunter of the powers of darkness with the dogs of Horus, Kyon and Prokyon. On coming forth from the darkness of Amenta in the resurrection, the Osiris says: "I come forth as a Bennu (a type of Sothis) at dawn." "I urge on the hounds of Horus" (Rit., ch. 13). He was the hunter of the powers of darkness on behalf of Horus in the solar mythos, and likewise in the phase of eschatology as Sahu-Orion, or Orion as the Sahu, that is Horus in his glorious body. We may look on Horus, the original of Herakles, as the earliest child that ever strangled serpents. He is portrayed in this character as the child standing upon two crocodiles and crushing the

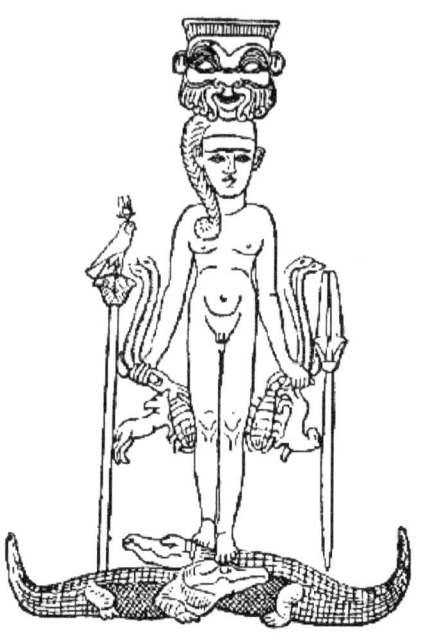

Horus strangling Serpents.

serpents with both hands. In later legends told of Herakles the Greeks have added the cradle as a further illustration of the children's story. But, ages earlier, before the figures were humanized, Horus pierced the serpent of evil when he was represented in the form of a hawk fighting with a serpent on the back of a hippopotamus at Hermopolis (Plutarch, I. and O., p. 50). He also fought the serpent as an ichneumon or mongoose, and as a cat, each of which preceded the anthropomorphic type of an infant in the cradle. The wars of Apap and Horus, or Ra, also of Sut and Osiris in the eschatology, were thus dramatically rendered in the astronomical mythology. The grapple first began with Horus and the reptile Apap. This is repeated by Horus the little hero crushing the serpent in the constellation of "Ophiuchus," that is by Horus in the character of conqueror who triumphed over drought, darkness, decay, and finally of death. In a scene copied by Maspero from the zodiac of Denderah, Horus, on his papyrus, rises from the waters, and is preceded by Orion in his papyrus bark. Orion was a figure of the stellar Horus, or Horus of the inundation. But Horus represented by the sparrow-hawk has become the solar god now born of Hathor the milch-cow. All three appear together in this scene (*Dawn of Civilization,* Eng. tr., p. 97). Now if we turn to the celestial globe we find Orion standing club in hand as the mighty warrior with one foot on the waters of the river Eridanus = Horus of the inundation invested with the majesty and power of the solar god. In the Egyptian drawing the two characters are distinct, but in the Greek compound these are blended in the one hero known as Herakles the slayer of serpents as an infant in his cradle.

In very old Egyptian traditions Sahu-Orion was represented as the wild hunter who traversed the nether world by night and hunted there whilst it was day on earth. The powers of darkness, the Sebau and the Sami, were the objects of pursuit. They are hunted for food; and the chase, the capture, killing, and cutting up of the carcases are described in the terminology of cannibals—so ancient is the legend of the wild hunter, a form of whom may probably survive with us as Herne = Orion the hunter. In the solar mythos the lord of light was Horus, or, later, Ra or Osiris, waging war upon the evil powers in the under-world, and hunting them to death by night and devouring them as the mode of destruction; the drama being represented in the stellar phase with the figure of Orion as the lord of light made visible by night. The cannibalism of the past becomes present in the language of the inscriptions. Eating and drinking were the primary modes of assimilating strength and sustenance. The idea still lives in partaking of the Eucharistic meal in which the god is supposed to be assimilated by the eating and drinking of the elements. It is said in the Book of the Dead (ch. 149) that the great spirits, the khus, or glorious ones, "live on the shades of the motionless." They eat the souls of the undeveloped dead; eating being applied to spirit as well as matter.

It is probable that the giant as the eater of the Shades, the as yet unquickened souls of the buried dead, was figured in heaven as the ghoul. The star Beta in the group of Perseus, the hero with Medusa's head, is called Al-Ghul, the ghoul, in the Arabic names of the stars (Higgins, *The Names of the Stars and Constellations,* p. 27). In Amenta the ghoul was the eater of the Shades; and like many mythical characters is the denizen of another earth than ours. "O eater of the Manes," says the Osiris, "I am not a thief." (125. 17.) This is one of those who prey upon the dead; one of the forty-two types of terror which the guilty had to face in the great judgment hall. Thus, the ghoul or vampire of another earth that survives as eater of the dead in this world was also figured in the planisphere as a type of terror to evil-doers. Indeed, Amenta is a museum full of such prototypes, and the ghoul secured a starry setting with the rest, though the figure is not extant on our celestial globe. A striking instance of the use of the planisphere in conveying the teaching of the mysteries may be seen in the Ritual. In some *recensions* of the first chapter, when the Manes enters the Amenta, one of the first things he asks is to see the starry ship or floating ark of the holy Sahus making its voyage by night in heaven. He exclaims, "Let me see the Sekhet-Nut of the holy Sahus (the ship of heaven) traversing the sky." He was in the paths of darkness and desirous of seeing the nocturnal sky with its old familiar stars by which he sought to make out his way to the place of re-birth and the region of Maati upon the mount of glory, from this valley of the shadow of death. The constellation of Horus as Orion was the ship of the Sahu, and ark of salvation configurated in the celestial waters as a boat that saved the soul's from an eternal shipwreck. This was the sign of spiritual resurrection for the completed Manes. In another text the speaker prays that his soul may shine as a Sahu in the stars of Orion or Horus. It is said of Horus in the "hymn to Osiris" the whole earth glorifies him, when his holiness proceeds (on the vault of the sky) "he is a Sahu illustrious amongst the Sahus," that is among the spirits glorified. The Sahu is a glorified form in which the soul of the deceased is re-incorporated for the life hereafter; this was represented by Orion the conqueror of death and darkness in the phase of eschatology. Now one frequently finds that this secondary stage had been attained by the Egyptian mythos before it went out of Egypt into other lands as the lesser and the greater mysteries. For instance, there is a constellation called the Sah or Sahu in the Babylonian astronomy. This is identical by name with the Egyptian Orion, that is Horus in his resurrection as the Sahu or glorified likeness of the risen god or soul; the Sahu in the planisphere who represents the Manes rising from Amenta to the enclosure on the summit which was paradise above.

The descent of Herakles into Hades to grapple with the triple-headed Kerberus was preceded by the descent of Horus into Amenta, where the devourer is triple-bodied if not three-headed. The speaker in this character (Rit., ch. 136B) says, "Grant that I may come and bring (to Osiris) the two jaws of Rusta," the outrance from Amenta. Herakles in the lion's skin is identical with Horus in the lion-sign, and his fight with the Lernean hydra of the Hesperides and the great wild boar is a repetition of the battles that were fought by Horus with the Apap hydra and the black boar Sut. The same speaker at the same time says, "I have repulsed the Apap reptile and healed the wounds he made," which is equivalent to the struggle of Horus with the monster hydra. The twelve legends of the solar hero Gilgames relating to the twelve signs and the twelve labours of Herakles are, of course, comparatively late, as they are based upon the zodiac of twelve signs which belongs to the final formation of the heaven that was preceded by the heaven in ten divisions, and earlier still by the heptanomis in seven. But the twelve labours of Herakles are zodiacal, and the first of these was at a point of commencement in the lion-sign. The Greeks with their accustomed indifference to the facts, and their fondness for figures and fancies, played many pranks with the astronomical mythology. It was fabled by them that "an enormous crab came to the assistance of Hydra and bit the foot of Herakles" when he was doing battle with the dragon of drought (*Apollodorus* 2, v. 2). By re-translating Greek fable into astronomical fact, this statement can be read, only the Greeks have placed the crab on the side of the evil power, which it was not, any more than the beetle. The retouching by the Greeks, like that of the Semites, tended to efface the figures or falsify the meaning of the mythos; and the astronomical facts are of a thousandfold more importance than all the pretty embellishments of irresponsible fancy. The forms and pictures figured in the planisphere are not merely mythical, they are also celestial illustrations for the eschatology of the Egyptian Ritual and the oldest religion in the world. Perhaps the worst perversion of the true mythos made by the Greeks was in their treatment of the polar dragon. This, as already shown, was founded on the crocodile, not on the Apap reptile. The crocodile was the good dragon, the solar dragon, the dragon of life, represented by the stellar Draconis. Apap is the dragon of evil, of negation, and of death. It is not easy to uncoil the dragon, or rather the two dragons, the dragon of light and the reptile of darkness, on Greek ground. The evil dragon was imaged once for all below the ecliptic in the constellation Hydra. But it was the good dragon, not hydra, that coiled by night about the pole of heaven to protect the golden fruitage on the tree of life, the Chinese peach-tree of the pole. So far from Herakles being called upon to make war upon the good dragon, or crocodile, it was a starry image of Horus (Sebek) himself, who is the prototype of Herakles.

Naturally there must have been some mutilation and disfigurement on the palimpsest of the starry heavens, but this has not effaced the African imagery of the celestial signs, which proves the ground-plan of the structure to have been Egyptian. The present purpose is to trace the *raison d'être* and meaning of the constellation-figures as types of characters that were pre-existent in the mythology of Egypt. For, as herein maintained, it was Egypt that peopled the planisphere and for ever occupies the celestial globe. The heavens are telling nightly of her glory and her workmanship on high, which is more marvellous even than any that she left upon the surface of the earth. The vast revolving sphere unfolds a panorama of her prehistorical past. The constellatos form a long procession of her seasons, her goddesses and gods for ever circling round about a wondering world that sees but cannot read the primitive uranographic signs.

THE SIGN-LANGUAGE OF ASTRONOMICAL MYTHOLOGY (PART II)

Book VI

THE ancient Apt, the first great mother who was the bringer-forth in Apta, as the womb of life, was elevated to the planisphere as bringer-forth in heaven. She was constellated in the Hippopotamus or Greater Bear, and called "the mother of the fields of heaven"; "the mother of beginnings"; "the mother of movement in a circle"; "the mother of the starry revolutions," or the cycles of time. As such, Apt was the builder of a heaven that was founded on the seven pillars of the Heptanomis. Now the most primitive Egyptian type of building is a figure of *turning* round, as might be in making pottery. The conical pillar, pile, or mound of earth was also a type of this turning round. Thus the Heptanomis was built on seven pillars, and the mother of the revolutions was the founder of the heptanomis. How this was built has yet to be explained according to *"The Mystery of the Seven Stars."* The Heptanomis of the old Great Mother and her seven sons was followed by the Octonary of Am-Khemen, the park or paradise of the eight great gods. This, as we reckon, is the circumpolar enclosure which was founded when Anup, the power of Polaris North, was added to the primordial rulers, or Nomarchs, and whose animal-type, the jackal, remained as guide star in the Lesser Bear (planisphere of Denderah, plate in *Book of Beginnings*). The octonary was one of the "upliftings of Shu" which are alluded to in the Ritual. The heaven, that is also called the mansion of his stars, which was again and again renewed (ch. 110). Shu had been one of the sustaining powers of the firmament who were known as the seven giants. He then became the elevator of the heaven that was imaged as the cow of Nut; and lastly his was the sustaining power with Atum-Horus in the double equinox. Apparently this change from the Heptanomis of the ancient mother and her seven sons to the heaven of the eight great gods upraised by Shu is indicated in the Magic Papyrus. In this the giant of seven cubits is addressed. A divine command is given to him: "Get made for me a shrine of eight cubits! And as thou hast been (or wast) a giant of seven cubits, I have said to thee, thou canst not enter this shrine of eight cubits. And, as (or although) thou wast a giant of seven cubits, thou hast entered and reposed in it." The "giant of seven cubits" in the shrine of seven cubits now gives place to one who "has the face of a Kafi ape, with the head of hair of a monkey Aani." The type, that is, of the moon-god, Tehuti-Aani, in the shrine of eight cubits, or the heaven of the eight great gods in the enclosure of Am-Khemen, the Octonary of Taht, upraised by Shu (Magic Papyrus, *Records of the Past,* vol. x, pp. 151-154). Aani, the Kafi ape, was Taht's own especial monkey of the moon, and is a sign that the shrine of eight cubits was the octagonal heaven or Octonary of Taht, the lunar god which tends to identify this with the enclosure of Am-Khemen that was upraised by Shu. In all likelihood the giant thus addressed is Shu, the lion of the uplifting force.

It is related in very old Egyptian legends that when Shu-Anhur lifted up the paradise or park of Am-Khemen he was compelled to make use of a mound or staircase with steps to it in order that he might reach the height. This mound, says Maspero, was famous throughout all Egypt. The event (as supposed history) took place at Hermopolis, the city of which Taht was lord; therefore we may look to the lunar deity for the origin of the step-mound. A figure of this mound may be seen in vignettes to the Ritual as a pyramid with *seven* steps called the ladder or staircase of Shu. How then did the steps or stairs of the mound originate as a lunar type of the ascent? and why should the steps be seven in number? The answer is because they were lunar. The moon fulfilled its four quarters in twenty-eight steps; fourteen up and fourteen down. For this reason, Osiris in the moon was represented by an eye at the top of fourteen steps. The moon in its first quarter took seven steps upward from the underworld to the summit, which in the annual reckoning was the equinoctial mount. In other words Shu now made use of a lunar reckoning previously established by the moon-god Taht, when the ark of seven cubits was superseded by Am-Khemen. There are two sets of names in the Ritual given to the seven primordial powers in two of their astronomical characters. The first seven are called (1) An-ar-ef the great. (2) Kat-Kat. (3) The Bull who liveth in his fire. (4) The Red-eyed One in the House of Gauze. (5) Fiery face which turneth backwards. (6) Dark face in its hour, and (7) Seer in the night. The second seven are (1) Amsta. (2) Hapi. (3) Tuamutef. (4) Kabhsenuf. (5) Maa-tef-f. (6) Karbek-f. (7) Har-Khent-an-maa-ti. The first four of the latter seven are the gods of the four quarters, who stand on the papyrus of earth and who became the children of Horus in a later creation.

In this new heaven raised by Shu another god was born as eighth one to the seven. This was Anup (a form of Sut), as a deity of the north celestial pole. The Egyptian eight great gods consist of 7+1. The Phœnician Kabiri were 7+1. The Japanese Kami are 7+1. In the Vâyu-Purana the group of Rishis, who are usually reckoned as seven, are spoken of as eight in number, and are therefore another group of the 7+1. The company of eight British gods were seven with Arthur as the eighth. The seven powers *plus* one are also to be seen in the seven sleepers of Ephesus and their dog. Moreover, the dog can be identified with Anup as the golden dog or jackal at the pole. When the god of the polestar was appointed in the north it was as an eighth to the seven, and he who was the eighth became the supreme one, the head over all, like the occiput at the top of the seven vertebral joints in the back-bone of Anup, Ptah or Osiris (which was a figure of the pole). The head or headland in Egyptian is Ap (or Tep), and the same word signifies the chief, the first, and also the number eight or the eighth. Anup was distinguished from the seven earth-born powers. He is expressly called "the son of the cow." That is the son of Nut the cow of heaven; the heaven that was lifted up by Shu in the shape of the cow which brought forth Anup at the pole. Ap-ta-Urt, the cow of earth, had been the mother of the seven, who were reproduced by Nut as the Khuti or glorious ones who are eight with Anup added as the power of Polaris. Anup the highest power at the pole, then becomes arranger of the stars in this new heaven of the eight great gods, that was upraised by Shu the giant, who had been one of the primary seven powers. Anup, the eighth, is said to fix the places of the seven glorious ones, who follow after the coffin of Osiris, on the day of "Come thou hither"; which was the first day of some new creation in the Astronomical Mythology. (Rit., ch. 17.) In the solar mythos the sun-god took the place of Sut-Anup, who was the earlier maintainer of the equipoise and equilibrium in the revolving system of the heavens. The speaker in the Ritual (ch. 54) says,—"I am the god who keepeth opposition in equipoise, as the egg which circles round." The egg is the sun. But he continues—"For me there dawneth the moment of the most mighty one Sut" (or Sut-Anup), who was the most mighty one as prevailer on the side of order at the pole before the equilibrium of forces was known to depend upon the power of gravitation and the revolution of the sun. What the sun is at the centre of the solar system, the pole-star had been at the centre of the stellar universe in the most ancient astronomy. In place of gravitation the force that swung the system round was represented by a cord or chain attached to the pole as its symbol of controlling power. This eighth one added to the seven primary powers came at times to be designated father of the seven. Thus the eighth was raised to the headship over the seven Japanese Kami. Anup, as representative of the polar star, is lord over the seven Akhemu or non-setting stars. The Phœnician Sydik is father to the seven Kabiri, and he is the just, the righteous one. Which means that he also was a representative of the pole, identical with Anup, who is the judge. The character is the same in relation to the seven earlier powers now called the sons, as the just one, or the judge. "King of the seven sons of earth" is a title of Anu. Reference is also made to the king of the seven Lu-Masi. (Maspero, *Dawn of Civilisation,* p. 631, note 1, Eng. Tr.) This was the god who, as eighth to the seven and the highest of all, was the chief, the Suten or King, that is, Sut-Anup, chief to the Kamite seven in the circumpolar heaven of the eight great gods. The Assyrian seven are likewise designated the sons of Bel as the seven Anunnaki or earthly Anunas. Anup the jackal-headed was the primordial judge, but so anciently that he had been superseded by Atum and Osiris in that character. The pictures to the Ritual show him in the judgment-hall reduced to the position of inspector of weights and measures in the presence of Osiris, who has now become the great judge in Amenta. But allusions to the earlier status still remain. As it is said in the inscription of Khnumhetep "all the festivals on earth terminate on the hill" or over the hill of Anup. That is in the eternal feast upon Mount Hetep, the mount of glory in the polar paradise. (Inscription. Line 96, Records, v. 12, p. 71.) In the Rig-Veda (x. 82.2) the habitation of the one god is placed in the highest north "beyond the seven Rishis." These are often supposed to be represented by the seven stars in the Great Bear, but erroneously so. The seven Rishis, Urshi or divine watchers were grouped in the Lesser Bear, *the stars of which constellation never set*. These were the chief of the Akhemu under Anup, god of the pole-star. The Subbas or Mandozo, the "Ancients" of Mesopotamia, are what is called worshippers of the pole-star. To this they turn their faces in prayer, and in going to sleep. The reason assigned is that when Hivel Zivo the Subban creator assumed the government of the worlds which he had formed, he placed himself at the limits of the seven Matarathos, at the extreme point of the universe where the pole-star was then created to cover him. (Siouffi. *La Relig. des Soubbas.* Paris 1880.) The original old man of the mountain was unquestionably the ancient deity of the pole-star. Hence the group of seven stars which accompany the head of the "Old Man" on the Gnostic stones showing that he was the head over the seven glorious ones. (King, *Gnostic Remains.*) The old man of the mountain then, is Anup, who arranged the stations of the seven on the day of "Come thou to me" (Rit., ch. 17). It is just possible that we may now discover the origin of the mystical eight-rayed star in the numerical symbol of the eight great gods, who consisted of the seven, with Anup, on his mountain, as the eighth and highest in the stellar mythos. In this way: there is a Gnostic gem of loadstone figured in King's Book on which Anup is portrayed like Horus holding two monstrous scorpions in his hands. He is accompanied by the sun, as a winged scarab, the crescent moon and a star with eight rays. (Second Ed., pl. G.) This emblem was given to the solar god in Egypt, Assyria, India and in Rome, but here it is assigned to Anup the supreme one of the eight great gods, and the first who was the eighth to the seven in the Octonary of Taht or the ark of eight measures that was lifted up by Shu in the paradise of Am-Khemen.

As the pictures show, the zodiac was founded on the inundation. The mother of water figured in the southern fish, as the womb of source itself, was afterwards repeated on the ecliptic, as the wateress (later Aquarius) with all her myriad mammæ streaming from the fount of liquid life, in the abyss, the Tepht, or Tuat, that was localized in the recesses of the south from whence the inundation came, and from which it was perennially renewed. When the zodiac was established, she who had been the mother of water in the south would naturally be given a foremost place. The waterer was now repeated as the multimammalian wet-nurse in the sign of Aquarius; the same in character, whether as the southern fish, the water-cow, or the suckler divinized. However represented, earth as the giver of water was the type, and in Egypt the water was the inundation. The first two children of the great mother came into existence as the twin brothers, who contended with each other in the opposite elements of drought and water, or darkness and light, and in other phenomena. These twin powers were constellated in the sign of the Twins at the station where the two combatants were first reconciled, that was at the equinoctial level. These then, we reckon, were amongst the earliest founders of the zodiac on some old common meeting-ground of night and day, or drought and inundation which is yet visible for us in the sign of the Gemini. Moreover it is related in the ancient legends and folk-tales that once upon a time there was a pair of brothers who were twins, and these twin brethren were the builders of a city. A typical illustration may be cited in Romulus and Remus as the mythical twins who are the reputed founders of the city of Rome. In Egypt the brother builders are the Sut and Horus twins. The city which they built was in the heavens, not on earth, and this, the Gemini remained to show, was in the circle of the ecliptic. Thus Sut and Horus, following the great mother, are also founders of the zodiac. The first pair of twins were male. These were followed by a pair in Shu and Tefnut, that were male and female, called the brother and sister. These were twinned, back to back, Shu in front, Tefnut behind, to form the figure of Sagittarius on the other side of the zodiac exactly opposite the Gemini (oblong zodiac of Denderah).

We reckon Shu, the lion of breathing force and uplifter of the firmament, to be third of the elemental powers born of the ancient Genetrix. Shu upraised the heaven of day in one character and the heaven of night in the other. He is a pillar of support to the firmament as founder of the double equinox. He sustains the heaven with his two-pronged stick, his two arms, or with the two lions of force which represent himself and his sister Tefnut the lioness. It was at the equinoctial level that the quarrel of Sut and Horus was settled for the time being by Shu. Shu thus stands for the equinox as the link of connection betwixt Sut and Horus in the north and south. The heaven in two parts, south and north, as the domains of Sut and Horus was now followed by the heaven in three divisions that was upraised by Shu as establisher of the equinox in the more northern latitudes. And this heaven in three divisions was the heaven of the Triangle which preceded the one built on the square, by Ptah. Horus and Sut had been the twin builders and the founders south and north. Shu followed with the new foundation in the equinox, which was double, east and west. Sut, Horus, and Shu then, aided by his sister Tefnut, founded the heaven of the triangle based upon the twofold horizon and the crossing. Shu as the equinoctial power is the third to Sut and Horus of the south and north. With him a triad was completed and the two pillars with a line across would form the figure of the triangle ▽. Thus, the twins in Gemini and Shu in Sagittarius, being the three first of the seven powers, point at least to the equinoctial line being laid in those two signs of the zodiac. More particularly as his sister Tefnut, a form of the great mother, is joined with Shu in constituting the sign of Sagittarius. Thus the three brothers, Sut, Horus and Shu with one female (as the mother or sister) are found together in these two fundamental signs of the zodiac. A third power born of the great mother in heaven was now added to the other two. Another of her seven sons was born, or the lion of force (Shu) joined the crocodile (Sebek-Horus) and the hippopotamus Sut, in a trinity of powers that sustained the firmament.

As elemental forces Sut and Horus had been ever lawless combatants and claimants, always fighting for supremacy. When Shu had lifted up the heaven of Am-Khemen as the paradise of peace upon Mount Hetep, "he reconciled the two warrior gods with each other" and "with those who had charge of the beautiful creation which he raiseth up." Law and order were established by putting "bounds to the contentions of the powers" and by dividing the whole universe from Zenith to Nadir into the two domains called the portion of Sut and the portion of Horus. The contention betwixt Sut and Horus had originated ages before the satanic character of the Evil One in his anthropomorphic guise had been assigned to Sut. The twin opponents had been on a footing of equality in the stellar, lunar, and solar mythos. But there always was a question of boundaries to be settled. Shu is the arbitrator in the stellar phase. (Rit., ch. 110.) In the lunar stage Taht the moon god was the judge and reconciler of the warring twins. And in the solar mythos Seb, the god of earth, adjudicates—as shown in the mythological text from Memphis (*Proceedings Society of Bib. Archy.*, v. 23, parts 4 and 5). When Ptah had built his mansion in the double earth the two horizons were united, or, as it is said, the double earth became united, "the union is in the house of Ptah," and "*the two pillars of the gateway in the house of Ptah are Horus and Sut.* The united ones made peace; they fraternized completely. They made a treaty." Seb says to Horus and Sut, "there shall be an arbitration between you." Seb said to Horus, "come from the place where thy father was submerged," that is in the north. Seb said to Sut, "come from the place where thou wast born," that was in the south. "A mountain in the midst of the earth unites the portion of Horus to the portion of Sut, at the division of the earth." This, in the solar mythos, was the mount of the equinox. Now Horus and Sut each stood upon a hillock; they made peace saying "the two earths meet in Annu for it is the march (border) of the two earths." In this legend there is a shifting of boundaries from south and north to east and west in the union that is now contracted in the house of Ptah, "in the house of his two earths in which is the boundary of south and north" that was drawn from east to west by the equinoctial line. "Here the united ones fraternized completely. They made a treaty"; which was sustained by Seb. And henceforth the twin powers, Sut and Horus, now called Horus and Sut, who had stood as the two pillars, south and north, for the two poles in Apta, are now "the two pillars of the gateway to the house of Ptah"; which two pillars are afterwards portrayed as the double Tat of eternal stability in the making of Amenta (*Text from Memphis*).

In this phase the quarrel of Sut and Horus represents the difference betwixt darkness and light in the length of night and day which went on round the year and was rectified at the point or on the Mount of Equinox. Before the solar god attained his supremacy as the determiner of time Shu was the readjuster of the power of the equinox. Hence Shu is said to have kept the contention of these warring powers within bounds and brought about their reconcilement (Rit., ch. 110). Thus the "reckonings of Shu" involved the readjustment of the equinoctial point and re-establishing the equilibrium of the equinoxes in the different reckonings of time. Taht the lunar time-keeper does the same thing when he "balances the divine pair," and puts a stop to their strife in the circuit of precession (Rit., ch. 123). All the year round, except at this point of place, it was one scale up and the other down in the contention of Sut and Horus for the mastery. But at the vernal equinox the scales were at the perfect level and the twins were exactly equal in power for the time, with Horus the fulfiller about to rise in the ascendant. Horus was the bringer of the golden age to earth. This in Egypt was the time of the inundation; in other lands and later days it is the spring-time of the year. The Saturnalia was a mode of celebrating this equality at the time of the equinoctial level, by means of various kinds of levelling customs. Slaves were equal with their masters and mistresses. Women were equal to men, the sexes changed clothing with each other, on the natural ground of equality. This Saturnalia survived as a relic of the Golden Age called Saturnian by the Greeks and Romans.

In Egypt Sut and Horus changed positions and were figured as Har-Suti, with the hawk of Horus in front and the black Neh or Typhonian animal of Sut behind. This reversal represented the change of seasons in relation to the north and south. In Equatoria the desert and the drought were given to the south, which was the domain of Sut. Refreshing rain and cooling breezes came from the domain of Horus in the life-giving north. In Egypt the water and the food of life were brought by Horus of the inundation *from the south*. Whereas the north in winter was the realm of darkness and of drought, and therefore the domain of Sut became that of the evil elemental power of the twins. The three powers of earth, water, and breath, or Sut, Horus, and Shu, were given stations in the zodiac; the twins, Sut and Horus, in the sign of Gemini, and Shu, as the Archer, in the sign of Sagittarius. The heaven founded on the south and north by Sut and Horus, the Twin Builders, was now followed by the heaven that Shu uplifted in the equinox as the lion of sustaining power, or rather as the dual lion of Shu and Tefnut, his sister, who is seen to be conjoined with him in Sagittarius. Thus far the zodiac was founded on the Great Mother with two pairs of twins; Sut and Horus as the Rehiu lions, with Shu and Tefnut as the Ruti or lions of the double horizon, one at each end of the equinoctial line or level where the lost balance of the contending Twins was periodically restored by the reconciler Shu.

In one character Horus is designated "Horus of the Triangle," and a theory has been put forward in Germany to the effect that the figure represents the pillar or cone of the zodiacal light. But the unexplained peculiarity of Horus of the Triangle is that *his* triangle is figured in a reversed position with the apex downwards and the base above, ∇. Whereas the pillar of zodiacal light was never seen bottom-upwards in that way, and never could have been so represented. On the other hand, the triangle which was constellated in "Triangula," is, we hold, *the figure of a tripartite division of the ecliptic, and the triple seasons of the Egyptian year.* The water-season being represented by Horus; the season of wind, or breathing life, and of the equinoctial gales by Shu; and the season of dryness, or drought, by Sut. These were called the water season, the green season, and the dry season. The three signs of which are (1) "water," (2) "growing plants," and (3) a barn or storehouse, which showed the crops were harvested. Four months for the water season gives the correct length of the inundation. The Egyptian harvest occurred in the eighth month of the year. Then followed a season of drought and dearth, which came to be assigned to the destroyer Sut. These three seasons can be traced as a basis for the zodiac that was afterwards extended to one of four quarters and twelve signs. Horus of the inundation was given the Lion as a solar zoötype. The Archer, four signs further round, was assigned to Shu, the god of breathing force, and four signs are the correct measure of one season, or a tetramene. The Lion and Archer, or Horus and Shu, represent the two seasons of the inundation and of breathing life. The name of the Archer in the Hermean Zodiac is Nephte, and Neft signifies the soul or breath. Sut was continued in conflict with Horus in the constellation of the Twins, the power of drought that was opposed to the water of life. Shu was the reconciler of these two continually warring powers, and in the zodiac he represents the green season of vegetation and breathing life that came betwixt the two seasons of water and of drought. This was fundamental, the rest is filling in. The three seasons of four months each would naturally lead to the circle of the ecliptic being measured and divided into three parts, which tripartite division was followed, at a distance, by the Babylonians in their mapping out of the sphere, and continued by them in a far later calendar of twelve signs. The Egyptian month was divided into three weeks of ten days each, which obviously corresponded to the heaven of the triangle, the tripartite ecliptic, and the three seasons in Egypt. Then followed a heaven of four quarters or sides, in which may be traced the houses of Sut, Horus, Shu and Taht; but the division of the month or moon and the ecliptic in three parts equated with the three seasons in a circle or zodiac that was measured monthly by the lunar god with his $3 \times 10 = 30$ days. The two roads of heaven had been divided between the twin brothers Sut and Horus. The three roads were next divided between Sut, Horus, and Shu in the heaven of the triangle that stood as it were upon a tripod, = three roads of the south, north, and equinox.

Type after type, the mythical Great Mother and her children passed into the legendary lore of the whole world. The mother and her twins were followed by the mother in the character of sister, who is the companion of three brothers, our Sut, Horus, and Shu in the triangular heaven or triple division, the uranographic symbol of which was constellated in "Triangula," composed of three stars held in the hand of Horus (Drummond, *Œd. Jud.*, pl. 3). Three brothers with one female, then, as an Egyptian group, are representatives of the

Great Mother and her first three sons or elemental powers; the powers represented in her portrait by the water-cow, the crocodile, and lioness. The mother being indicated by the pregnant womb. The same group is also Japanese, consisting of the three (out of seven, or the eight) Kami, with their sister Izanami. The three Kami, called the "All-alone-born Kami," our stellar Trinity, were gods of the beginning, and are connected with the sister in the raising up of heaven (Satow, *Pure Shinto,* p. 67; Chamberlain, *Kojiki,* p. 19). And when the Christian divinity of a triune nature is portrayed with a triangular aureole upon his head, that figure relates the deity once more to the phenomena in which a god of the Triangle had originated. The god of the Triangle was of a threefold nature in the trinity of Sut, Horus, and Shu, which three were one with the mother in the heaven of the Triangle, the mount with the triple peaks, the Ecliptic in three divisions, the year in the three seasons, the month in three weeks. The Triangle, like the Oval, is a figure of the female, as it was on the Goddess Nana in Babylonia. The trinity of three males associated with one female, who was originally the Great Mother, survives in two ways still, for whilst they are performing in church four more primitive representatives of the same *dramatis personæ* still keep it up in the pantomime, as in the dumb show of the more ancient mysteries, in the characters of columbine, clown, harlequin, and pantaloon. Harlequin is Har (or Horus) the transformer. We might say the double Horus, one with and one without the mask. The clown is Sut, the sly and cunning one, whose zoötype was the jackal. Pantaloon and his crutch are the remains of Shu and his celestial prop of the pole. Columbine corresponds to Tefnut, the sister of Shu, which explains her peculiar relationship to pantaloon, whom she rejects in favour of harlequin. Now these four appear upon Mount Hetep when the later heaven is portrayed in the ten divisions that preceded the final twelve as a trinity of primeval powers united with the Great Mother, who was the abode as Triangle when the heaven was not yet builded on the square (Rit., ch. 110). The other four brothers who make up the group of seven great gods (at least in one form) are Amsta, Hapi, Tuamutef, and Kabhsenuf, who stand on the lotus or papyrus, and are the four gods, paddles or eyes of the four quarters. Thus, the seven are (1) Sebek-Horus, the crocodile; (2) Sut, the water-bull; (3) Shu, the lion; (4) Hapi, the ape; (5) Tuamutef, the jackal; (6) Kabhsenuf, the hawk; (7) Amsta, the man, who, together with the Great Mother, were the founders of the zodiac—three in the Triangle and four in the Square.

Whatsoever the seven Khuti were *as individual stars,* they were also configurated as a group in Ursa Minor and called the followers of the coffin of Osiris, which was imaged in the Greater Bear. The seven in the stellar mythos had become the lords of rule, devoid of wrong, and living for eternity. This was as spirits perfected under the type of stars that never set (Rit., ch. 72). And here it may be explained that we have all been persistently wrong about the seven glorious ones, the seven Rishis, the seven Lu-Masi, the seven Elohim or the seven Kabiri, the "Seven Sleepers" being the seven stars in the Great Bear. For this reason, in all the starry vast there is but one group of seven non-setting stars, and these are in the Lesser, not in the Greater Bear. Polaris was at one time chief of all the heavenly host, on account of its being fixed at the centre as a type of stability and uprightness. The characteristics and qualities assigned to the divinity were first seen in the steadfastness of the pole. The stars in Ursa Minor were circumpolar. These showed the seven in a group who never could be drowned by the deluge of darkness. The waters did not reach them. Not so the seven in the Greater Bear, the seven that were not circumpolar stars. About 5,000 years before the present era there was but one, the star Dubhe in Ursa Major that was circumpolar or non-setting (Lockyer, *Dawn of Astronomy,* p. 152). These, therefore, could not have been the seven never setting stars, who were the watchers and the rulers in the great year of the world; the starry type of the eternal powers. The typical seven were grouped in the Lesser Bear as an object picture of something out of sight, with Anup as El-Elyon at the pole. In all the mythologies the Pole-star is an emblem of stability, a seat or throne of the power who is the highest god *pro tem.,* as was Anup in Egypt, Sydik in Phœnicia, Anu in Babylonia, Tai-Yih (the arch-first) in China, Avather, or Zivo, in Mesopotamia, and others. It was not the seat that was worshipped, but the power; the sustainer and the judge that was enthroned upon the stellar Mount of Glory as the god.

The Pole-star was a type of the eternal, because apparently beyond the region of time and change. It was the earliest type of a supreme intelligence which gave the law in heaven that was unerring, just and true; if only as the law of equipoise or, as we should now say, of gravitation. This was the sole point at which there seemed to be any certainty of foothold in that moving ocean of the starry infinite. And this became a standpoint in the heavens for the mind of man to rest on at the centre and radiate to the circumference. The summit was well-named the Mount of Glory. Around this island-mount the hosts of heaven appeared to wheel by night in one vast, glorious, never-ceasing "march past" in the presence of the "Royal Arch" or, more religiously regarded, the Most High God. The earliest law in heaven was given on the mount because the mount was an image of the pole. It was administered by the judge, whether as Anup, in the north, or Sut as jackal of the south, because the jackal in Egypt was a zoötype of the judge. It is not the mount, then, that was the divinity, but the power that dwelt upon it, as the deity called by the Japanese "the *God Eternal-Stand* of the heavens" (Ame-no-Foko-Tachi Kami). The power of stability fixed as the centre of the universe was the typical eternal. This was represented by the jackal, which is to be seen at the centre of the Denderah planisphere. The jackal also is a type, not a divinity, and a type may be variously applied. The jackal itself is "Ap-Uat," the opener or guide of roads; probably as the seer and crier in the dark and leader of the pack. But it was the dog of Sut and of Sothis as well as of Anup. Thus the type in Sign-language may not always determine the nature of the deity. But, as *Hor-Apollo* rightly says, the jackal denotes the judge (B. i., p. 39). The governor at an early period was the judge, with the jackal as his sign. There were several kinds of judges in Egypt, and the "totem" of each is the sab or sapient jackal. Hence the jackal, representative of Polaris, was placed above the seven as the judge of heaven because he had imaged the judge on earth. Naturally the type was not always repeated; other countries, other fauna. Besides which, the anthropomorphic succeeded the zoömorphic in an indefinitely later time; and the Semitic, Hindaic, Greek, and various other renderings are mainly anthropomorphic. But the judge *quâ* judge thus set in heaven by the Egyptians at the polar centre, with his seat upon the summit underneath the tree, was repeated and continued in other mythologies upon the stellar mount. Anup became the great judge in heaven, and the seven are his ministers, as executioners, upon the judgment-day. They are termed the seven "arms of the balance on the night when the eye is fixed"; that is the eye of the judge, who saw through the dark (Rit., ch. 71). The Eye of Heaven that Judges the Wicked is the name of a Chinese constellation; and the god Anup was the judge whose eye was the Pole-star in the north. He was the seer in the dark, therefore the jackal was his zoötype; and the jackal was followed by the later dog as a symbol of Polaris.

The lunar mythos succeeded the stellar, but the moon-god Taht was not reckoned as the ninth one. Neither was Horus. The eighth was the highest power till the time of Ptah and the Put-cycle of the nine. The group of seven remained intact. Anup, as the eighth, was the highest in the stellar mythos; Taht-Khemen (later Smen) was highest in the lunar mythos; and Horus was the highest in the solar mythos, the highest being worshipped as the "Only One." Anup and Tehuti then became two witnesses to the supremacy of Horus, the one as the eighth, who in turn became the witness for his father, Ra-Unnefer. The deity of the Pole-star was known to the Chinese as the supreme god in nature, who has his abode on the Great Peak of Perfect Harmony. When Dr. Edkins asked a schoolmaster at Chapoo who was the lord of heaven and earth, the reply of the Chinaman was that he knew of none but Tien-hwang Ta-ti, god of the Pole-star. (*Religion in China,* p. 109.) Shang-ti, the supreme ruler, was the highest object of worship. His heavenly abode, Tsze-wei, is "a celestial space round the north pole" (Legge, *Chinese Classics,* v. iii., pt. i., p. 34) and his throne was indicated by the polar star (*Chinese Repository,* v. iv, p. 194). This is the most sacred as well as most ancient form of Chinese worship. A round hillock is the altar on which sacrifice was offered to him. It is said in the archaic Chow Ritual (Li) that when the sovereign worshipped Shang-ti he offered up on a round hillock a first-born male, as a whole burnt sacrifice (Douglas, *Confucianism and Taouism,* pp. 82-87). Both the mount and the first-born male are typical. Sut was the first-born male, and, as Sut-Anup, he was the first male ancestor. The hillock is an image of the mount. This deity was also known to the Chinese as the "Divine Prince of *the Great Northern Equilibrium,*" who promulgated "the laws of the silent wheels of the heavens palace," or the cycles of time determined by the revolutions of the stars (De Groot, *Fêtes d'Emoui,* v. I, pp. 77, 80).

HORUS OF THE DOUBLE HORIZON.

One of the profoundest secrets in the Egyptian astronomical mythology was the mystery of the twofold horizon, or, more exactly, the mystery of the double equinox, and one of the earliest forms of the solar god in the zodiac was Horus of the double equinox, when this had been established by the sky-uplifter Shu, with the aid of his sister Tefnut.

Until the time of Har-Makhu the fatherhood of god had not been individualised in Ra. Har-Makhu was the mother's child when she was a virgin, represented by the white vulture of Neith, or the sacred heifer of Isis. The child could be self-generated as the spirit of life in vegetation, or in light, the phenomena being pre-human from the first. Child-Horus in the solar mythos was the little autumn sun conceived upon the western mount as the calf or child. Adultship was attained upon the horizon east with what was termed the double force. The cult was that of Hathor and Horus, the mother and the child, who was the calf on one horizon and the bull of the cow upon the other. In these two characters he was the double Horus, or the "double Harmachis," the solar god of both horizons, and fulfiller annually in the double equinox. The power of evolution was portrayed in Kheper, the transformer. Kheper showed the old beetle changing into the young; the tadpole transfiguring into the frog; the human embryo developing in utero; the enduring spirit emanating from the mortal mummy. Kheper was a form of Har-Makhu, as we learn from the inscription of the Sphinx. From Har-Makhu, the father-god, Ra-Har-Machis was developed in the mythology which preceded the Egyptian eschatology. Atum was Ra in his primordial sovereignty. The divine fatherhood was developed from Har-Makhu, who became the great god Ra in his primordial sovereignty. Har-Ur, the elder, first-born Horus in the mythos, was the child of the mother when she had no husband, and he had no father; hence she was the virgin mother who conceived but did not bring forth. There was nothing human in the transaction except the terminology. Horus in the eschatology was he who died and was buried, and who rose again in spirit at his second advent. This time he was imaged in the likeness of the father as the beloved only begotten Son of God, who manifested as the fulfiller of his word and doer of his will. Two types in this way were deposited and made permanent in Horus, the child of twelve years, and Amsu-Horus, the man of thirty years. Both characters were united and made one as solar in Horus of the double horizon. This character of Horus, as Repa or Heir-Apparent, may be traced historically at a later time as that assigned to a Pharaoh of the 12th dynasty, who represents the double Harmachis, the sun-god of the twofold horizon. He claims a divine origin as the virgin's child that was not begotten by God the Father. As an infant "in the egg," he was exalted to be "the Lord of both parts," or both horizons, like Har-Sam-Taui. Speaking of the god he says "he anointed my forehead as Lord of men, creating me as chief of mortals. He placed me in the palace as a youth not yet come forth from my mother's womb." He was born in the likeness of elder Horus to be king, or to become the royal Horus in the horizon of the vernal equinox, where the two parts were united as east and west in the solar mythos, which followed the stellar Peseshti, or two halves, that were the south and north of Sut and Horus (*Records,* v. 12, pp. 53, 54).

Without a fundamental knowledge of the mythology as framework it is impossible to comprehend the doctrines of the Egyptian religion. Horus of the double horizon, or the double equinox, was the solar prototype of the double Horus in the eschatology. As sun-god on the western horizon in the autumn equinox Har-Makhu was born, conceived or incorporated as the virgin's child. It was at this point, that Horus entered earth or the matrix of the mother in the mount, and thus became the child of Seb and Isis by adoption, though not by begettal. In the eastern equinox he rose again as Horus of the double force and master of the double feather, or the later double crown. When the sun set at night, or in the autumn season, it sank down into the waters of the abyss below the horizon, which Horus-Sebek swam as the fish. The crocodile, then, expressed the unparalleled power by which the sun-god crossed the waters and rose again. The crossing was from equinox to equinox, from the western to the eastern side of the mount, let us say from the sign of Virgo in the autumn to the sign of Pisces in the vernal equinox.

Neith, the suckler of crocodiles, was an earlier form of the Virgin Mother than Isis, and by her aid we may obtain a foothold in the zodiac, like that of Horus resting on the mystical two crocodiles, which became the two fishes in the sign of Pisces. When the autumn equinox occurred in Virgo that was the place of conception for Sebek, the fish of the inundation. Six months later the sun rose in the sign of Pisces, and in the eastern equinox, where the fish, as child and consort, or as the two crocodiles, became the two fishes with Neith as the mother on one horizon and Sekhet on the other. Thus as we read the signs, the virgin Neith conceived her child as Sebek-Horus, the fish of the inundation, which was duplicated to express the adultship, and there were two typical fishes. A well-known picture of Child-Horus shows the youthful sun-god standing on two crocodiles, which we take to express the power of the double, or, more exactly, the *doubled* Horus. In this representation Har-Ur is described as the old child who becomes young. That is the elder who transforms into the younger Horus on the Mount of Glory in the vernal equinox. Standing on the two crocodiles Har-Ur has now acquired the double power—the power, for example, to take up serpents and other poisonous reptiles in his hands without receiving any hurt.[1] Thus, the crocodile-headed Sebek as the child attributed to Neith in Virgo, crosses the gulf of darkness or the abyss of waters to rise up in the east as Horus of the twofold horizon which he had united in the double equinox as Horus of the doubled power. The doubled power of the sun or god in symbolism was expressed by duplication of the type. For example, it was in the autumn equinox, or, as more primitively imaged, on the western mount—the mount of the cow which was covered with crosses indicating the equinox (Wilkinson)—that Child-Horus was conceived in the mythology or incarnated in the eschatology. In the first he was the little suffering sun of the crossing, or the cross, who went down into the underworld to die

[1] See fig. of Horus, p. 317.

and be buried; to transform and to rise again. In the zodiac of Denderah, the sign of the "Scales" contains a portrait of Har-pi-Khart, or Horus the child, who was conceived or incorporated in that sign as Horus of the double equinox called Har-Makhu. The name identifies Child-Horus with the sign. The word for the scales or balance in Egyptian is Makhu. Further, the scales denote the equinox, as the point of equipoise. The Greek name of Harmachis is derived from the Egyptian word Makhu, for the balance or scales, and thence for the level of the equinox, where the balance was erected on the day of weighing words and of reckoning the years. The Horus of the double equinox was also termed "the double Harmakhu" (*Records*, v. 12, p. 53), and this duality was also imaged in the twofoldness of the Sphinx, with its tail to the west and its head to the east, pointing to the equinox each way. But how was the crossing from west to east effected at the time when no Amenta had as yet been opened in the under world?

The passage of the sun-god *through* the mountain had been imaged as a passage through the cow of earth. We have a perfect survival of the mythos in the Märchen of Tom Thumb or Little Tom, whom we claim as a British form of the solar Tum (or Nefer-Atum). In the Egyptian mythos Tum makes his passage through the mount by means of the cow, and is reborn as Little Tum = Tom Thumb, from the Khepsh of the cow Meh-ur. It is said of him in setting from the western horizon, "*Earth stretches her arms to receive thee.*" He is embraced by the mother, whose womb is the Meskhen of rebirth (*Magic Papyrus,* p. 6, lines 3 and 4). And, again, at his going forth to the eastern horizon, it is said, "Thou hast rested in the cow; thou hast been immerged in the cow Meh-ur" (*Inscription of Darius,* lines 27, 28). Sebek-Horus swam the water as a crocodile. The eel of Atum made the crossing through the mud of the morass. Kheper the beetle bored his passage through the earth; Behutet rode upon the vulture's wings; Horus made the aerial voyage as a hawk, and Har-Makhu crossed from one horizon to the other *through the hollow body of the Sphinx.* These were modes of making a passage when the nether earth had not been opened up by Ptah, and the Sekru-sledge, which preceded the boat, had not been laid upon the stocks as the means of travelling by land which was illustrated in the mysteries of Memphis. But, however represented, the Horus who crossed the abyss was named Har-Makhu, the god of the double horizon, or the double equinox. The principle of this duplication on the horizon of the East can be established by means of the two lions, which express the double glory of the double Horus, who was lord of the solar force that was double in the vernal equinox. Horus of the double horizon was also Horus of the two lions. In the Ritual Horus rises again saying, "I am the twin lions, the heir of Ra" (ch. 38, 1). He is Horus rising in the strength of the two lions as the "lion of the luminous course." Again, he says: "I am the twin lions" (62, 2). "I am the double lion" (72, 9). "I go out from the dwelling of the two lions to the house of Isis the divine" (which was in Sothis), "I complete the greatness of Shu the lion" (78, 22, 24). In a vignette to the Ritual the sun of to-day rises betwixt two lions, which represent Safre the sun of yesterday and Tua the sun of to-morrow. This is the Horus-sun, and the two lions image the double strength or glory of Horus in the sign of Leo.

One title of Har-Makhu, or Horus of the double horizon, is Har-Khuti-Khepera, the Horus who made his transformation as the beetle-headed Khepera. The astronomical locality for this particular transformation would naturally be in the sign of Cancer, which the Egyptians sometimes represented by two beetles, at other times by one. Either way, the beetle was the sign of Khepera as Horus of the two horizons. Thus, two beetles mark another station in which the Horus of the double horizon manifests, as the solar deity, with reduplicated power; just as he emerges on the double horizon from betwixt the two lions or Kherufu, in the sign of Leo, as the lion of the double force. Under one of his zoötypes, child-Horus was "the lamb, son of a sheep;" and the lamb on the western horizon or mount attained the double power of the adult, *as a ram in the opposite sign of Aries on the eastern mount*. Indeed, Pisces is the first of six signs in all of which this duplication of the solar power was represented in the zodiac. In the sign of Aries, Horus was the lamb upon the western mount who became a ram upon the horizon east, as the adult figure of reduplicated power. In the sign of Taurus he was the calf which became a bull. A vignette to ch. 109 of the Ritual shows the "Horus of the solar mount" as the calf in presence of the god, and of the morning star upon the western mount. Hathor, the divine cow, is also present with the calf upon the mount. This is the calf that is to become a bull, "the bull of the mother" on the Mount of Glory in the double equinox, where Horus, the fulfiller, attained the double power. Now, if we suppose the autumn equinox to coincide at the time with the sign of Scorpio, the vernal equinox would then occur in Taurus, and in that sign the Horus calf would become a bull as symbol of the solar power that was doubled in the vernal equinox. When the autumn equinox coincided with the sign of Virgo the place of double glory was in the sign of Pisces on the opposite horizon. The god was conceived as the child, calf, or youngling, in the west. As Sebek, his image was the crocodile of Neith, the virgin in the sign of Virgo. The crocodile in the Ritual is the Kamite "great fish." Two crocodiles are therefore the two fishes. These are exactly opposite the sign of "Virgo," and the two fishes = two crocodiles are the dual sign of Horus in his double glory, as the expression of his double power in Pisces, like the two lions in the sign of Leo. *This principle of duplication may be traced in six of the solar signs:* There are two lions as supporters of the sun-god in the sign of Leo; two beetles in the sign of Cancer; two twins in the sign of Gemini. Further, Horus was the calf on the western horizon, who became the bull on the horizon east; also the lamb on one side and the ram upon the other. Thus the duplication extends from the sign of Leo to the sign of Pisces inclusive, which represents the sun-god as Horus the child and Horus the adult, whose double power or glory was expressed by two lions, two crocodiles, and other types of twinship, in addition to the twins or Gemini who were figured in the human form.

Or if we read the signs the forward way, the two fishes correspond to the two crocodiles of Horus. The sun in Aries answers for the ram and lamb; in Taurus for the bull and calf. In the sign of the

Gemini there is a pair of twins. The sign of Cancer or the Crab was represented by two beetles in Egyptian planispheres. In the lion sign two lions, called the Kherefu, supported the young solar god in his resurrection on the horizon in Leo. Thus, when Horus of the double horizon was conceived with the autumn equinox in the sign of Virgo, he was twinned and brought forth with the vernal equinox in Pisces, where two fishes = two crocodiles, mark the birthplace. The lamb and ram are twinned in Aries; the calf and bull in Taurus. If we take these six signs in the circle of precession the two lions correspond to the duality of Atum-Horus; the two beetles to Kheper-Ptah; the two Gemini to Sut and Horus; the bull and calf to Osiris and Horus; the ram and lamb to Ammon-Ra and Khunsu, and the two fishes to the twin crocodiles, as six different illustrations of the sun of the two horizons at six different landing-stages on the other side of the celestial deep. Thus, the double Harmakhis includes two characters corresponding to the two equinoxes on the double horizon. In one he is the concept of a virgin, in the other he is brought forth by the parturient mother. In one he was the calf in time, in the other he is the bull of eternity. In the one he is Horus in matter, in the other he is Horus in spirit. In the one he is the child of twelve years; in the other he is the adult of thirty years. The first was the founder, the second is the fulfiller. The first was Horus of the incarnation, the second is Horus of the resurrection. Horus of the resurrection in the solar mythos was the prototype of Amsu in the eschatology, who rose up in spirit from the inert condition of the mummy, as conqueror of death and all the banded powers of evil. In both phases of character this is Horus of the double force, the double crown, the double feather, the double Uræi, the double life, or other types of duplication, including the double equinox.

Thus the doctrine of a twofold advent for an ever-coming child, born of a virgin mother, can be traced in the solar mythos to a beginning with Horus of the double horizon. Whatsoever the point in precession, the horizon of the resurrection or the mount of glory coincided with the vernal equinox. The little sun, the calf, or the child Horus entered the mount at the beautiful gate of entrance in the West, for breeding purposes, and rose again as the great sun, the bull, the lion, the adult Horus, that went forth at the beautiful gate of exit in the East to become the bull of the mother when the godhood consisted of the mother, the child, and the divine adult.

The mystery of the double horizon was indeed a riddle of the Sphinx. The great Sphinx of Gizeh is traditionally reputed to symbolize the river Nile at its rising, when the sun coincided with the signs of Leo or Virgo in the water-season of the year. It is now known, however, to be a representative image of the god Har-Makhu. *The Sphinx itself has spoken once.* On the stele of Tahtmes IV. it is called "the Sphinx of Khepera, the very mighty, the greatest of the Spirits and the most august." Now Kheper, the son of Ptah is, as already said, a form of Tum-Harmakhis who was not simply a solar god of the double horizon. In the eschatology he became the god in spirit, the one god living in truth, the sole power that was worshipped as eternal. This is the "greatest of spirits" represented by the Sphinx of Khepera.

There had been a sort of hollow under-world made out before Amenta was established as "the earth of eternity" by the opener Ptah. This was the Akar, Khar, or Kar, over which the Sphinx presided brooding in her mysteries of birth—the birth of light, of water, of food, of the young solar god, and, lastly, of an ever-living soul. We learn from the Ritual that the mystery of the Sphinx originated with the mount of earth as the place of passage, of burial, and re-birth for the solar god. An ancient Egyptian name for the Sphinx is Akar. This also was a name for the hollow of the under-world. The speaker, in the character of the newly-risen solar god, exclaims, "I am the offspring of yesterday. The tunnels of the earth have given me birth, and I am revealed at my appointed time" in the coming forth to day (ch. 64, Renouf). It is said that the very bones of the deities quake as the stars go on their triumphant courses through the tunnels of the Akar (Pyramid Texts, *Teta,* 319). It is demonstrable that a passage through the mount of earth, the same that was made through the Cow, was followed by the passage through Akar, the Sphinx, which was built for the god Har-Makhu, the Horus-sun that was immeasurably earlier than Ra. The speaker is in Akar, which is represented by the goddess Akerit because it was the place of burial and re-birth. The tunnel through the mount of the Sphinx is oblong; and it is noticeable that the oldest known pyramid in Egypt, that of Medum, is neither conical nor quadrangular, but oblong. To understand the nature of the Akar, says Renouf, we have to imagine a tunnel starting from the spot where the sun sets and extending through the earth as far as where the sun rises. Each end of the tunnel has a sphinx-like form. A human-headed lion couches at the entrance and also at the end. It is through the paws of this double sphinx that the galley of the sun-god enters on the western horizon and comes out on the eastern mount. In the picture, Plate 14, taken from the tomb of Rameses IV. "Fair entrance" (Aka Nefer) is written at one end of the tunnel, "Fair exit" (Par Nefer) at the other (*Proceedings, Society of Biblical Archy.,* vol. xv. Pt. 8, p. 385). These two gates of entrance and exit on the horizon were called the gates of Akar, and sometimes the gates of Seb, the god of earth. They were the two gates of earth for the sun in the mythology, and the two gates of Akar for the manes in the eschatology. Thus the twofold horizon was imaged for Har-Makhu in the figure of the double Sphinx. The traditions lead one to think that profound secrets were buried in the building of the Sphinx, as was the way with these builders, who put all they knew into all they did. We gather from the stele of Tahtmes that the monument was built to commemorate the sacred place of creation, or, literally, "*of the first time,*" an Egyptian expression generally used for the creation or "in the beginning." This sacred site is said to go back to the days of the masters of Kher or Kar, which as a divine locality was the Neter-Kar of the under-world or the abyss. Kher is likewise an ancient name of the Egyptian Babylon, old Cairo. Like Babylon, this was the gate or pathway of the gods—the place of exit, as we read it, for the seven elemental powers who issued from Amenta, as the uræus-deities, or seven spirits of earth. (Rit., ch. 83.)

In the beginning was the Mother-earth as the womb of universal life; vegetable, animal, reptile, fish, bird, and human life. The uterine figure was repeated in the making of Amenta as "the Tuat" for the birthplace of water and for edible plants, or, more generally, the elements of life. Thirdly, this type was imaged as the abyss of the beginning in the uranographic representation of the southern heaven. Earth was the womb of life when life was born of water. The birth-place was imaged by the abyss of the Tuat, the well, the gorge, or other type of utterance, from the secret source in the sacred place of creation, the creatory of the Mother-earth. The water of life became a type of the eternal, the fabled fount of immortality that was so preciously preserved in the divine under-world; the living water that was sought for by the mother when she periodically lost her child, who was the same to her as the water of life, and who was found in the abyss, which was indeed the place of its rebirth. The generation of life by water, the birth of Horus by water and in food, was the profoundest of mysteries. This was the way that life actually came into the world, before the subject was made doctrinal. This was a life which did save the world when Horus the Messu was the saviour who naturally gave fulfilment periodically to the promise that he made. In various legends the secret of this water of life that wells up in the subterranean region is jealously guarded by dragons, crocodiles, or other monsters of the deep. In the Chaldean versions the seven anunnaki or spirits of earth are the guardians appointed to keep the secret of the waters of life in this under-world to which the dead descended and from which the elemental powers first ascended to the surface of the upper earth. There is warrant for assuming that the mystery of the beginning from the abyss was also one of the great secrets that was guarded by the Sphinx at Gizeh. The final fact is that the Sphinx was carved out of the rock at the exact centre of the earth to commemorate "that sacred place of the creation" or beginning which goes back to the domain of Sut, and to "the days of the masters of Kher." That is the beginning in and with the primordial mundane abyss from which life emanated and from which the elemental powers or seven uræus-deities were born of Mother-earth. The Sphinx, then, like the cow of earth, or the hollow mount, was a means of crossing the abyss in which human handiwork had succeeded to the natural type as the figure of a passage. It was made as the means of crossing for Horus of the two horizons or the double equinox. Thus, the Sphinx is a monument that commemorates the founding of the equinox in the double horizon, and as this was assigned to Atum Harmachis, it may account for the Hebrew tradition which associated Adam with the equinox, Adam being a Jewish form of the Egyptian Atum. Harmachis entered the Sphinx at sunset in the west or hinder part, and was reborn in the east as Horus of the fore part, lion-faced. The means of crossing the dark gulf in the solar mythos was now the bridge in death and the mode of uniting the two worlds in one, when the re-arising of the sun was succeeded by the resurrection of the soul, the lion having been adopted for the Sphinx upon the horizon east as an emblem of the double power which made the passage for the sun-god or the soul. The Sphinx is male in front and female in the hinder part. It is a compound image of the Mother-earth and the young god whom she brought forth upon the horizon of the resurrection. Without the mother there was no rebirth. Where the earth opens for the sunrise it was called the *unnu* or outrance of Neith. As the Sphinx appears to us it has the human face. But the god Tum-Harmachis was the lion of the solar glory, and his bringer-forth as Sekhet was the lioness. The perfect type was dual as the lion and the lioness combined, only the forepart has been rendered anthropomorphically in the likeness of the Pharaoh who was the lion-ruler at the time. The great Sphinx as keeper of these secrets was couched in mountainous repose upon the horizon in the eastern equinox, when the gate of "fair exit" was in the lion-sign and the gate of "fair entrance" was in Aquarius, the water-sign that is figured over the abyss of source on the celestial globe. The Sphinx then is a figure of the double horizon and the duality of Har-Makhu when the place of conjunction was at the point of precession in the lion-sign. And if, as is the Egyptian way, the fact was registered forthwith, we may date the Sphinx as a monument which was reared by these great builders and thinkers, who lived so largely out of themselves, some thirteen thousand years ago.

The "Aten" of the so-called disk-worship was an ancient form of Har-Makhu, god of the double horizon. This, however, was not a worship of the solar disk. The disk was but an emblem of the circle made by Aten as the god of both horizons. His was a compound type of godhood, in which the mother was dual with the son who was her child on one horizon and her bull or fecundator on the other. The word Aten, from At, was an ancient name for the child. Horus-Behutet, god of the hut or winged disk, we take to have been the earliest form of Aten. This is the solar god who crossed from the horizon west to the horizon east upon the vulture's wings, which were an emblem of the motherhood. The "hut" was a dual emblem of the divine infant and the mother as bearer of the child. As the bird she carried him over the intervening void of darkness where the Apap lay in wait. Thus the godhood of Aten consisted of the mother, her child, and the adult male or bull of the mother, in a cult which preceded that of the fatherhood of Atum-Ra. The glory of Aten as the power that is doubled on the horizon of the Resurrection was the object of regard in this religion, not the disk.

This cult of the mother and the child who was worshipped in Egypt as Har-Makhu, the child commonly called Horus on the horizon, had an unsuspected development amongst the Mediterranean races. *The Mycenæan Tree and Pillar Cult* is the title of a somewhat recent work by Arthur J. Evans (London, 1901). The title implies the common notion that trees and pillars, "stocks and stones" were directly worshipped instead of the power that was represented by them in sign-language. But a volume of evidence might be collected showing that the supreme object of worship in this cult was the deity of the double equinox, the youthful solar god who in Egypt was called "the double Har-Makhu." Both tree and pillar had been figures of the pole before they were erected in the equinox. The tree was planted in the abyss as a figure of the southern pole, the "tall sycamore of Sut" or tree of the south. The column of stone was raised in Annu, as the pillar of the northern pole. When the equinoxes were established, tree and pillar both were continued and often blended at the point of equipoise as figures of the birthplace that was shifted to the zodiac in the solar mythos. The Mithraic monuments show us that the tree was a figure of the equinox, and that two trees represented the double equinox when this was resting in the signs of Scorpio and Taurus (Drummond, pl. 13). Both tree and pillar had been types of Hathor as the abode of Horus. In the Egyptian Ritual the tree marks the place of coming forth and point of emergence from Amenta in the equinox. "I am the babe," says Horus four times. "I am the god within the ash tree." "I am the link which connecteth the solar orb with yesterday"—and also with to-morrow, as is shown by the two lions (ch. 18). This connecting link is Horus of the two horizons, who is here brought forth from the ash tree. When columns could be carved, the raising of the stone pillar took the place of planting the tree, or was added to it as a co-type of station. In the twelfth dynasty the foundation of a solar temple is described. Amenemha and his son Usertsen I. were on the throne conjointly as representatives of the solar god of both horizons. The King says, "Henceforth I will make monuments and erect carved columns to *the double Harmachis.*" (*Records of the Past,* vol. xii., p. 53.) That is, to the sun-god of the two horizons or the double equinox, who was here represented by the Pharaoh and his son.

The Mycenæan symbolism of the two lions with the central tree or pillar can be read if followed as Egyptian, but not otherwise. The tree, the pillar, or the mount was female as a figure of the birthplace, the place of exit for the babe born from the mount, the meskhen, or its equivalent (in wood or stone). For example, a birthplace in the stellar mythos was in Sothis, the star that showed the birthplace of the babe. Both child and mother met in Sothis as Hathor and her infant Horus. She was the house of Horus. The house was imaged as a cone or a tree. This will explain why the Mycenæan figure accompanying the tree-pillar is at times a woman and at other times a child. They are the goddess and her babe, identical with Hathor and Child-Horus in the place of birth. In the gold shrine found at Mycenæa (Evans, fig. 65) the figures on each side are two doves. Now the dove in Egypt was the very ancient bird of Hathor, and the two doves are a figure equivalent to the mother and the child that was born within her shrine, her house, her pillar, or her tree, as her dove of the generative spirit, or the later Holy Spirit. The cult of the mother and child is also illustrated on the impression of a gem from Knossos. A sheep represents the mother as suckler of the child beneath her—that is, her lamb, as Horus was called when this type had taken the place of the calf (Evans, fig. 17). In two of the Mycenæan pictures the goddess in person is placed betwixt the two lions (Evans, figs. 44 and 45). This is she who was the tree or pillar, shrine or birthplace, whether as Hathor-Sothis or as bringer forth of the deity of the double horizon in the vernal equinox. Hathor was continued as the Venus of the Mediterranean races. What then was the object of the supposed "worship"? Was it the tree, the pillar, or both? or was it the goddess who was represented by the tree and pillar? or was it the child who was re-born from the birth-place in the tree or rock or shrine? The solar birthplace on the horizon had long been represented by the tree, the mount, the cone, shrine, gate, portal, the *unnu* or other forms of the opening which was always female, and a figure of childbirth in the mythos, when the mother was the earth. As Egyptian the goddess herself is sometimes portrayed; sometimes the child, and sometimes both the mother and the child, are imaged inside the pillar or cone which stands for the place of birth (Schiaparelli, *Piramidi Egiziane,* plates). The cult, then, whether as Egyptian or Mycenæan, was a worship of the mother and child, the divine duad that was so prevalent amongst the Mediterranean races, and not a tree-and-pillar cult, not a worship of "stocks and stones."

The double axe of what has been called "the Mycenæan tree-and-pillar cult" is an emblem of the doubled power, and the so-called god of the double axe is consequently a god of the double equinox, who was Har-Makhu, the Horus who passed into Atum-Ra as the Egyptian Zeus. The sun that made its way through the earth or the abyss was known as the divider, or the cleaver. This was the solar power which clove its way from west to east and from horizon to horizon as Har-Makhu, god of the double horizon or double equinox in the annual round. He was the cleaver of the earth, who was represented by the cleaver as an axe which, we take it, was a sign of Horus, the cleaver of the way. The god of the double equinox who completed the course from horizon to horizon was Horus of the double force, which doubled force was variously imaged by the double crown, the double uræi, the double feather, the two lions, the two crocodiles, and other dual types. Hence the god himself is called "the *double* Harmachis." He was cleaver of the way, whose double power was likewise imaged by the two-headed weapon which has been termed the "divine double axe" of the Mycenæan cult. The type itself may have been derived from the Egyptian nuter-sign of divinity, or power divinized, which was the stone axe of the palæolithic age; and a double axe would be the visible symbol of the power that was doubled in the vernal equinox. On a Mycenæan vase from Old Salamis the double axe is figured between two bull's heads, each of which supports a double axe. If we take the double axe as a sign of the power that was doubled in the equinox, it seems to follow that this representation indicates an equinox in the sign of Taurus; and as the bull's head and the axe are both dual, this will be the equinox that was double at the time of celebration, therefore the double equinox determined by the two bull's heads and the double axe as signs of the solar power that was doubled in the vernal equinox.

The reader has but to take up Count d'Alviella's book on the *Migration of Symbols* to see how widely spread this equinoctial imagery became. In this we find:—

Fig. 58. The tree standing betwixt two lions (from the Cathedral of Torcello).
Fig. H, Pl. 4. The tree betwixt two lions (from a bas-relief of Bharhut).
Fig. 35. Gilgames flanked by two lions, which he holds at arm's length.
Fig. 65. The tree between two goats (Assyrian cylinder).
Fig. A, pl. 4. Tree between two cherubs (Chaldean art).
Tree betwixt two winged unicorns (bas-relief of Nineveh).
Fig. B, pl. 4. Tree between two cherubs (from a Phœnician bowl).
Fig. D, pl. 4. Tree between two rams (from a bowl).

Fig. 67. Tree betwixt two giraffes (vase from Curium).

Fig. 71. Tree or stalk and winged solar disk betwixt two hare-headed looking animals (Khetan cylinder).

Two figures guarding the tree upon a Syrian amulet (fig. 110). The tree here is shaped like the ankh-cross, thus showing it to be the tree of life upon Egyptian ground.

The Assyrian combination of the sacred tree and winged solar disk unites the tree of dawn with the rising sun, and the symbol has the same significance no matter whether the sun-god climbs the tree or the disk is borne on wings above its branches. The tree of dawn stands in the solar birthplace. This is in the vernal equinox as birthplace of the annual sun. That which brings forth is the female, and the feminine nature of the type explains the fecundation of the tree by the two acolytes or geni who take the place of the two lions, crocodiles, dragons, beetles, cherubs, birds, and other types of the supporting pair. Amongst the co-types of the tree may be reckoned the figure of a god or child, a cone or a cross, a pillar, papyrus-reed, a lotus or a vase, the unnu or opening, the meskhen or birthplace, whence issued the youthful solar deity now fulfilled of his duplicated power. The two confronted lions are common on the Mycenæan gems as two heraldic supports of the central figure. This in one instance is the radiating solar orb itself (fig. 41, Evans). In another a male divinity stands betwixt the two lions (fig. 43, Evans). In others the figure standing or seated between the two lions is the divine mother who brought forth in the equinox. On two different glass plaques from Mycenæa (Evans, figs. 13 and 14) the supports on either side of the tree-pillar are two lions. Amongst other figures may be seen:—

Two lions with the sun rising from between them, the same as in the Egyptian representation. (Evans, fig. 42, A and B., Ritual, vignette, ch. 18.)

Two lions supporting a tat or tree-pillar. (Evans, fig. 35.)

Two lions back to back with the tree-pillar between. (Evans, fig. 39.)

Two lions with the tree-pillar. (Evans, figs. 40.)

Two lions pouring out libations on the pillar. (Evans, figs. 12, 13, 14.)

Two lions with the god in person between them in place of the tree or pillar. (Evans, fig. 43.)

Two lions, with the goddess in person between them in place of the symbols. This is she who *was* the tree, the shrine, pillar, or birthplace. (Evans, fig. 44.)

Two lions with the goddess seated between them. (Evans, fig. 45.)

Other pictures show the mount of the equinox, the tree at the meeting point of sun and moon in the equinox (Evans, fig. 4), the equinox as mount betwixt two bulls (Evans, fig. 3). In another scene two bulls support a tree-pillar (Evans, fig. 34). In one instance two sphinxes support the tree-pillar (Evans, fig. 33). The solution now to be propounded is that the mount or pillar—the shrine or the tree—determines the point of equinox; that the dual nature of the symbol shows it to be the double equinox as place of re-birth for the god of the double horizon, and that the two lions, two sphinxes, two beetles, two bulls, rams, or goats denote the particular sign of the zodiac in which the vernal equinox and the re-birth of Har-Makhu occurred at the time that is thus visibly portrayed.

The mystery of Har-Makhu and the double equinox was known to Paul, who was a master of the secret wisdom. The doctrine concerning Tum-Harmachis is well stated by him, only it has been rendered Hebraistically. The two Atums, or Atum and Nefer-Atum, are replaced by the first and second Adam as the man of earth and the man from heaven. The second Atum was "he who is our peace" with the title of Iu-em-hetep. This, as the second Horus, was "he who made both one" and "broke down the middle wall of partition," "that he might create in himself of the twain one new man." "The middle wall of partition" is a figure in the eschatology of that which was a fact in the equinoctial mythos (Eph. ii. 14, 15).

Whatsoever the type, the double equinox was indicated by the twofold figure. Thus, if a tree were the symbol, then two trees were the sign of the double equinox, and when Horus of the resurrection rises, let us say, as the good shepherd betwixt two trees, it is, as now suggested, a portrait of Har-Makhu, the connecting link between the two horizons or two lives. Now, one of the commonest scenes in the Roman catacombs is this of the two trees betwixt which rises the so-called Good Shepherd, who is sometimes a goatherd. There is a scene from the Roman catacombs in which the good shepherd is the central figure betwixt the two trees, two birds, and also the lamb and ram, by which the resurrection is to be identified with the vernal equinox in the sign of Aries (Lundy, fig. 76). In another of the pictures from the catacombs the good shepherd is accompanied by both the lamb and the ram, which are at least equivalent to the dual type of the equinox in Aries. He carries the lamb upon his shoulders, whilst the ram is resting at his feet (Lundy). Horus was the lamb upon the western and the ram upon the eastern horizon, both being united in a figure of the double power. A kindred representation is portrayed upon a gnostic stone now in the British Museum. This *is* Horus the Gnostic Jesus as Ichthus the fish. That the scene occurs in the sign of Pisces is shown by the two fishes, one of which is over the head of Horus, the other under his feet. The latter also repeats the ancient type of the crocodile on which the divine child was supported in the Cippi of Horus. There is also an image of the Palmyrene at Rome which has the image of the solar god on one side, and on the

Horus in Pisces.

other a conical cypress tree, the foliage of which exhibits *a child carrying a ram upon its shoulder* (d'Alviella, *Mig. of Symbols*), which shows a singular reversal in the position of the child and adult. But it was the child = the lamb that issued from the maternal tree, to be followed by the adult as the ram. When Horus rises from the dead in the Egyptian tombs it is as the good shepherd. The crook and whip (or flail) of rule are the insignia of his sovereignty. According to the Ritual (ch. 109), he rises up between two trees called the "two sycamores of emerald." Thus he is the perfect prototype of the good shepherd in the Roman catacombs. The god who rises in this character is Horus of the double equinox in the mythology, and Horus in spirit in the eschatology, who by his resurrection joined the two lives together and the two worlds in one. The good shepherd in the catacombs is self-identified by the cloak he wears, which is the cloak of royalty, as a figure of the royal Horus, the child who was born and predestined to be king.

The doctrines of the incarnation and the resurrection had already been established in the cult of Har-Makhu, the Horus of the double equinox. Horus the child in one equinox, who was Horus the adult in the other, constituted the double Harmachis, one as the founder and one as the fulfiller—one as Horus of the incarnation, the other as Horus of the resurrection. The doctrine was at first solar, and next eschatological. In both phases it was earlier than the fatherhood of Ra. The incarnation was at least as ancient as the virgin in the zodiac, who conceived in Virgo, and the mother whou brought forth in Pisces, which we calculate may have been some six-and-twenty thousand years ago. The solar god who united the two horizons was the fulfiller of the annual circle, and came to reign as the king of one year, first in the inundaiton, then in the zodiac. He also came in the characte of the great judge to see that justice should be periodically administered. In the stellar mythos Anup had been the judge, with the seat of judgement at the place of equipoise, which was then at the celestial pole. In the solar mythos this was shifted to the vernal equinox, and the mount of glory to the east. An ideal of justice, truth, and righteousness, imaged by the balance or scales, was postulated as established and central in the heavens as the reign of law, and there was an annual attempt to make that justice visible and veritable on earth. Har-Makhu came as the great judge, accompanied by the seven great spirits who were his executioners, called "the seven arms of the balance." The balance was erected as a figure of the equinoctial level, for the weighing of hearts and of words. The unjust were punished, wrongs were righted, restitution was enforced. The judgement day in the Easter equinox was similar in point of time to what we in Europe call the "March Assizes." This was represented as the judgement in Amenta.

The Making of Amenta

The puzzle-picture of the astronomical mythology had to be collected from its many scattered parts and put together piecemeal, and the method of presentment is panoramic. It was not practicable to tell the story straight through with chronological sequence. For instance, in portraying the eschatology of the Ritual, in the fourth book, the existence of Amenta had to be taken for granted, before the making of this under-world had been described as the excavation made by Ptah the opener and his seven Ali or co-workers. As a group, the eight great gods of Am-Khemen were followed by the Put-cycle or Ennead of the Nine. The word Put, whence the name of Putah or Ptah, denotes the number nine, and the Put-cycle was formed when Ptah was added to the earlier eight great gods. Neither Anup nor Taht was now the highest one. The groups of seven and eight, however, were not submerged. The group of seven survived as the seven Knemmu, moulders or metallurgists who assisted Ptah the divine craftsman, and the group of eight to which he was the ninth god are sometimes described as the children of Ptah. In an inscription at Edfu they are called "the most great of the first time; the august who were earlier than the gods, children of Ptah, who issued forth from him, engendered to take the north and the south, to create in Thebes and in Memphis; the creators of all creation," according to the later, *i.e.*, solar mythology. The earliest form of a divine fatherhood was outlined though not perfected in the pygmy Ptah; hence one of his titles is "the Father of the Fathers," which indicates the fatherhood that was founded on the eldest brother. Ptah was a solar god who did not attain the status of Ra.

Now, until the time of Ptah, Amenta was not founded as the earth of eternity in the subterranean regions, nor excavated from one horizon to the other as a pathway for the nocturnal sun and the Manes. Sebek, the crocodile-headed god, swam in the water round about the earth from west to east upon the outside of the mount. Horus crossed the waters on the wings of the hawk. Behutet or Aten of the disk rode on the wings of the vulture, Tum-Horus was the calf that issued from the cow of earth, and Har-Makhu passed from one side of the mount to the other through the body of the Sphinx. The Amenta had not then been hollowed out. The passage through the mount from west to east was tunnelled now by Ptah and his co-workers, who in this character might be called his seven navvies. When Ptah, the supreme craftsman of the gods, constructed his terrestrial and subterranean house of the double earth he built it on the earlier foundations, such as the Akar and Tuat of the abyss that were previously extant. The two pillars of the south and north were likewise utilized. As it is said in the mythological text from Memphis, "the two pillars of the gateway of the house of Ptah are Horus and Sut," which had previously represented the two poles of Sut and Horus, the twin founders, as we show, in the beginning.

An inscription found both at Edfu and Esné mentions the "festival of the suspension of the sky" by Ptah, which was connected with a celebration of the winter solstice. It has been suggested by Krall that this had descended from the time when "the winter solstice marked the beginning of the year and also of the creation" (cited by Lockyer, *Dawn of Astronomy*, p. 284). Under another figure this suspension of the sky by Ptah in Amenta was celebrated in the mysteries of Memphis by the erection of the double Tat-pillar which supported the sky and was originally a twofold figure founded on the pole, but the sky now suspended in the double earth of Ptah was not the sky of day. It is the firmament of the nocturnal sun through which it passed at night when in the nether world which is for the first time fully opened up by Ptah the great architect of the universe, who followed the earlier sky-supporters, Sut, Horus, and Shu.

The Kamite Amenta is "the grave of man's lost world," where his legendary garden of the beginning may be rediscovered. In this subterranean country will be found a copy of the primary paradise of all mythology, which can be restored from the Ritual and the imagery set in the stars of heaven, and proved to be the work of ancient

Egypt's wisdom. The most primitive imagery was sacredly preserved in Amenta, which makes the Book of the Dead an eschatological record of the beginnings in mythology that is unparalleled, and not until we have mastered the wisdom of Egypt as recorded in Amenta shall we be enabled to read it on the surface of the earth. First comes the natural fact, next the mythical representation, and lastly the eschatological application of the type, be it the mount, or tree, the Deluge, the ark, the evil serpent, or the victorious young hero. All three phases have to be studied, collated, and compared; and for this purpose the Egyptian Books of the Dead and of Amenta are worth all other sacred writings in the world. The primal paradise of universal legend was above the earth upon the summit of the mount, up which the spirits climbed to reach the region of eternal rest among the stars that never set. It was configurated round about the pole of heaven. This has yet to be depicted as the mount of glory. The later paradise was sub-terrestrial, the earthly paradise of legendary lore. The first was stellar, the last is solar, and it is this last that was founded on the subterranean path of the nocturnal sun first opened up by Ptah. The duplicating of paradise was partly a result of repeating the imagery of the stellar representation in the solar mythos. The mount of glory in the east was added to the mount of glory in the north, with the wide water of the heavens flowing round between the terrestrial and celestial paradise. Kosmas Indikopleustis (A.D. 535) tells us that beyond the ocean in every direction there exists another continent which cannot be reached by man, but of which one part was inhabited by him before the Deluge. To the east, just as in other maps of the world and in later systems, he placed the terrestrial paradise and the four rivers that watered Eden which came by subterranean channels to water the post-diluvian earth (Blake, *Astronomical Myths,* pp. 266-7). This can be followed by means of the upper paradise of Am-Khemen, that was raised by Shu, and the lower one now configurated by the opener Ptah, who suspended a sky overhead in Amenta.

In the mythology, Amenta is the subterranean country of the sun by night. The dawn and sunset were its gates of glory. It is called the beautiful Amenta, the earth of eternity. It was the passage of the sun that made the pathway of the solar circle which was completed in the eastern equinox. Hence it is said of the sun-god, "The junction of the double earth is the head of the coffin of Osiris, the beneficent soul in Sutenkhen, who hath determined the paths of eternity," that is in completing a circle by making the passage through Amenta (Rit., ch. 17, Renouf). The road to heaven for the manes *now* began with a pathway through the nether earth, from the place of sunset to the gate of sunrise. Previously the way to heaven was up the mount which was a figure of the north celestial pole. There was no solar passage through the nether regions in the stellar mythos; the sun went round the mount of earth, not through it. Ptah the opener added earth to earth and heaven to heaven, the solar mythos to the stellar. The sky upraised by him is indicated by the figure of heaven reversed. It is called the firmament of Ptah. Hence it is said by the Osiris in Amenta, "Mine is the radiance in which Ptah floateth over his firmament" (Rit., ch. 64), his firmament being that of the nocturnal sun in the under-world. There was now a firmament above and one below the earth. The firmament uplifted first by Sut, Horus, and Shu was supplemented by a nether sky upraised and suspended by the opener Ptah. The nnu, nun, or heaven is the celestial water, and this, as sky, was both above and below the earth. Now, the account of creation in the book of Genesis, with its waters above the firmament and its waters below the firmament, could not have been written until the division of these waters of heaven above the earth and of Amenta below the earth was effected when Ptah created the firmament of the nether-earth and raised another heaven in Amenta. In many places the name of Nut has the sign of heaven ▬ in the reversed position, thus ▬. Renouf asks, is this one more proof that the Egyptians believed in a sky below the horizon? (*Book of the Dead*, ch. 15, note 7). This, however, does not touch bottom. The Egyptian wise men did not *believe* in this nether sky; they created it as a figure in sign-language. Thus in the making of Amenta there was a sky above the under-world as well as over the upper earth; this is the nether sky that was suspended overhead by Ptah and memorized in the mysteries.

When the sun-god Atum-Ra mounts into heaven from the garden of Aarru it is from the lower Aarru in the secret earth of Amenta. Hence it is said at the same time he "goeth to the field of Aarru, approaching to the land of spirits in heaven" (Rit., ch. 17, Renouf), *i.e.*, to the upper Aarru, which was in the heaven of eternity, not in the nether-land of the double earth, called the earth of eternity. This duality has to be completely comprehended before the Ritual can be read, or its traditions followed round the world, as for example, in the Hebrew Genesis and the Assyrian legends of creation.

Paradise in Amenta is said by the deceased to be the "beautiful earth of eternity." But the deceased does not stay in it as his place of repose. It is not the eternal dwelling. In passing through Amenta he is bound for the heaven of eternity above. This below is but the earthly paradise, and there is an upper paradise to be attained across the celestial waters by those who can secure a seat in the boat of Ra. The typical mount was doubled; a mountain east was added to the most ancient mount of the north, which sometimes makes it look as if the site of the primitive paradise had been shifted and slewed round from the north to the east. The mistake hitherto made regarding the mount is in supposing the mount of earth, or Amenta, to be identical with the mount of the north, whereas the two belong to two distinct systems of the mythos, stellar and solar. The mount of heaven was stellar in the north; the mount of earth is solar in the east. The mount of heaven had its summit at the north celestial pole; the mount of Amenta was level with the sky-line on the horizon. There is also a double judgment seat, and a twofold judgment. One great hall was in Amenta. The other was at the apex of the hill of heaven, the maat of the final judgment that was given on the last great day. When the two are sundered, we sometimes find the judgment seat is imaged at the north celestial pole; at others, the great judge is seated as the Rhat-Amenta or Rhadamanthus, in the maat of the nether-earth. This double maat or seat of judgment can be explained by the Egyptian wisdom. It was the individual judgment that now took place in the maat of Amenta. This was the first judgment of two; the second is the last great judgment in the maat above. The first is beneath the tree of dawn, the second is under the tree of the pole. Those who were condemned as guilty in the primary trial of the dead suffered the second death in Amenta. They went no farther, but were extinguished in the tank of flame or annihilated on the highways of the damned. Thus the two different resurrections are differentiated the one from the other, in the Gospel according to John, when it is said the dead are to come forth; they that have done evil to "the resurrection of judgment," and they that have done good unto "the resurrection of life." Both resurrections occur in the Ritual; one for the judgment in Amenta, the other on the mount for the last judgment and the resurrection to eternal life.

The garden of Aarru or paradise of the eight great gods, whom we identify as a group with the seven in the Lesser Bear, *plus* the deity of the pole-star, was in the north. Not on the horizon north, but at the celestial pole that was figured as the summit of a very lofty mount, the mythical mountain of the north, diamond-pointed at the apex with the polar star, whereas the Semitic Eden is the garden eastward. This is relatively late, because it belongs to the solar and not to the stellar mythos. It is not the circumpolar paradise of earlier tradition. That may be the reason why the mount is omitted from the book of Genesis. It is not Am-Khemen, the paradise of the eight great gods. It is the enclosure of the pair who in the solar mythos were Atum = Adam and the Great Mother Kefa = Chavah.

The earth itself was figured as a mount; its highest point was in Apta, at the equator. When tunnelled for a passage through it, this became the mountain of Amenta, also the funeral mount. The place of entrance for the sun or the manes of the dead was in the west, or, as it was termed, the western hill. The mount of earth is the mount of birth for Horus in the solar mythology. The mount of heaven is the mount of rebirth for souls in the eschatology. Both have been linked together but not blended in the Egyptian representation, when the Osiris makes his journey from the base of the mount in Amenta, to the summit of the heavenly hill, the topmost peak of which is at the pole. In this ascent from the root-land of the mount of earth, or of Amenta, to the summit of Mount Hetep it may look as if the mount were all in one, but it is not so. There was a double mount; the mount of earth which was solar, and the mount of heaven which was stellar. In the Ritual (ch. 108) the mount of earth is said to be "the hill on which heaven resteth." This is called the hill Bakhu, the solar mount. Its dimensions in length and breadth are given in some of the early papyri. In the Papyrus of Nebseni the hill is 300 cubits in breadth. In the Turin Ritual it is 140 cubits in breadth. Now it happens that in the Mexican mythology there is a "mountain of the locust" or the mount of Capultepec, and the ideographic signs of this mountain include the following numerical figures: ∩∩∩∩ ∩∩∩∩ ∩∩∩∩

These figures are Egyptian. The sign ∩ is a figure of ten, which goes back to the origin in digital reckoning, as it is derived from the two hands clasped and cut off at the wrists. The Mexican figures therefore repeat the Egyptian at the value of 10 × 14 = 140, whatsoever the numbers may mean (Kingsborough, 1, pt. 3, p. 10, fig. 218).

The Japanese also have the double Mount Kagu; one is on the earth, or rather *it is the earth;* the other is in Ame or heaven, the divine mount, that *is the heaven,* which had the North Pole for its highest peak (*Trans. As. Soc. Jap.,* VII, p. 431). The Japanese likewise have the eight great gods of the mount, who are said to have been produced by Kagutsuchi, which we take to be a form of the original eight Kami that correspond to the Kamite Khemenu, the eight great gods in Am-Khemen, the heaven upraised by Shu. The same duality of the mount is illustrated in the two Chinese Kwenluns. Here the terrestrial paradise is described as being at the centre of the earth. The Queen-Mother dwells there alone in its midst. At the summit there is a resplendent azure hall, with lakes enclosed by precious gems. Above the clear ether rules the ever-fixed, the polar star (*Chinese Recorder,* vol. IV, p. 95). This is the Egyptian mount of Amenta in which Hathor was queen. The "azure hall" is the empyrean over the summit of the mundane mount, which is here identified as the mother-mount. The other mount is celestial; on its summit at the north star is the heavenly palace of Shang-ti at the centre of the circumpolar paradise, with its circle of thirty-six gods or rulers, which answer to the thirty-six decans of the zodiac.

The Todas also have the twofold mount. Their mountain of the world is the Makurti, or navel of the earth, the pillar of the firmament. It is a towering rock, upon the table-land of which the souls of the dead assemble for the leap into the abyss of waters that lies betwixt them and the mount of heaven. Either they, in common with some other races, have lost, or never had, the solar boat of the Egyptian eschatology, by which the base of one mount was reached from the summit of the other. But, sink or swim, the journey is the same. So is the celestial chart. Hence the Todas can see the cows that grace the fields of heaven in the nebulæ of the Milky Way. These correspond to the Kamite cows, the givers of plenty in the meadows of Aarru, that rest by the still waters at the head of the river of light and the twin lakes in the region of the north celestial pole.

This stellar mountain in the northern heaven and solar mountain in the east will likewise account for the twofold mount of the Babylonians. Lenormant describes the two somewhat confusingly, but no explanation of their duality has ever been given. He says, "Above the earth extended the sky, and revolving round the mountain of the east, the column which joined the heavens and the earth and served as an axis to the celestial vault. The culminating point of the heavens, the zenith (Nuzku) was not this axis or pole. On the contrary, that was situated immediately above the country of Akkadia (in the north), and was regarded as the centre of the inhabited lands, whilst the mountain which acted as a pivot to the starry system was to the north-east of this country. Beyond the mountain, and also the north-east, extended the land of Aralli, which was rich in gold, and was inhabited by the gods and blessed spirits." (Lenormant, *Chaldean*

Magic and Sorcery, Eng. tr., pp. 151, 152.) The mount of earth and mount of heaven become the double mount in the Babylonian version. As it is said of Gilgames, "To the mountains whose name is double, to the twin mountains in his course he came." The mount of earth or Amenta below was entered in the west. The upper mount was also entered at the west in the heaven of the setting stars. There is probably an astronomical datum in the Babylonian legend. The scorpion-men are said to keep the gate and guard the sun. "Over them rising was the threshold of heaven. Below them the tomb sank down." The tomb is Aralli (or Amenta) in the mount. The threshold of heaven was at the summit of the mount. We take the scorpion-men to denote the western equinox in the sign of Scorpio when that was the gate to the twin mountains, otherwise the mount of earth and heaven, the mount whose summit was the rise in Hetep at the pole. In Pahlavi the two mountains of heaven and earth are known as Mount Taêra, the centre of the universe, and Kakad-i-Dâîtîk, the centre of the earth (*West. Pahlavi Texts,* I, pp. 22, 36). Here the earth centre is distinct from the centre of the universe or mount of heaven which preceded the mount of earth, and the two different centres correspond to the two different forms of the mount of earth and the mount of heaven.

The heaven of the beatified had been apparently shifted from the north to the east when certain chapters of the Ritual were written, which is the same as saying the solar had then succeeded and to a great extent superseded the stellar mythos. The sun in its supremacy obscured the stars. Anup was merged in Osiris; the seven glorious ones became the servants of Horus and subsidiary souls of Ra. The place of sunrise in the east was figured as the mount of glory in relation to Amenta instead of the mount in the celestial north; otherwise said, it was interpolated in the solar mythos. Paradise now was both terrestrial (or sub-terrestrial) and celestial; in the east as well as on the northern summit, because it was solar as well as stellar. Not that the upper paradise was obliterated or really lost. That only happened in the absence of the gnosis. Am-Khemen remained aloft, and the upper paradise of two was still led up to by the mount, the tree, the way of souls, or the river of the Milky Way.

One form of this duality was represented in the Ritual by the mythical two houses, the great house and the house of flame. The speaker says, "Let my name be given to me in the great house. Let me remember my name in the house of flame on the night when the years are counted and the months are reckoned one by one" (ch. 25). The great house was stellar in the heaven at the celestial north; the house of flame (Pa-Nasrut) was solar in the east. Egyptian temples were built upon this dual plan, and each had its great house and its house of flame. The great house was central, like the lady-chapel in European churches, and the house of flame was on one side of it. The great house in a central position corresponds to the mount of heaven with its spire at the celestial pole. The house of flame was a kind of side entrance to the mount in the east, which is equivalent to the gate of sunrise. The church to-day remains a dual figure of this double house when both are blended together in one building. The nave with its doorway to the east corresponds to the mount of earth, and the spire is a figure of the pole or mount of heaven. One of the most perfect ways of illustrating this duality is shown by the mode of burying the dead in the Pyramid of Medum. Prof. Petrie says the bodies were laid on their left side with the head to the north and the face turned to the east (*Medum,* pp. 17, 21). This position of the dead is also indicated by the prayer of the manes that he may "feed on the food of Osiris, on the eastern side of the mead of amaranthine flowers" (the kaiu of the oasis) (Rit., ch. 26, Renouf). The face is here turned after death to the eastward side of the paradise that was primarily figured in the northern heaven.

When it was discovered that the earth rotated on its axis and was afloat in space, it was known to revolve on the double poles, and what we call the two poles of the earth were signified by the twofold tat-pillar of Ptah. The tat is a type of stability. The double tat is the sign of tattu as the place of establishing for eternity, and tattu, like other mythical localities, was doubled when Amenta was founded. It is noticeable that when Queen Hatshepsu had erected her two pillars she says she has made two obelisks for him who is the lord of the thrones of the two worlds, or, as we should say, of earth and heaven (*Records,* vol. II, p. 132; 2, *Pap. of Ani,* Pl.). This touches the origin of the well-known double pillar, the significance of which is not known. The double obelisk is a co-type with the twofold mount, and the two pillars of Tattu, the place where it was shown that earth was fixed and heaven made stable for ever, on the two pillars of Sut and Horus, which had been the two poles in Equatoria. The two obelisks then, imaged the thrones of two worlds, the double earth, or earth and heaven; and in Amenta the two pillars form the doorway from the one world to the other. So in the Japanese mythology the divine pillar of earth, Kuni-no-mi-Hashira, was added to the divine pillar of the heavens, Ame-no-mi-Hashira (*Kojiki,* Chamberlain's Version, p. 19). How it was added can be explained by the Egyptian wisdom. The pillar of heaven was first erected. Shu-Anhur lifted up the heaven from the earth with that which constituted the divine support as prop, pillar, or lion-like strength in sustaining the paradise above.

The pillar of heaven naturally stood upon the earth to support the heavens; but when the earth was hollowed out by Ptah, the excavator, there was another earth below in which the pillar had to be re-erected, and this pillar of the double mount was represented by the double Tat of Ptah as the backbone of that god, or later of Osiris. The Japanese also have the two pillars called the awful pillar of heaven, the pillar being a co-type with the mount. "Heaven's one pillar" was an ancient name for the Japanese island of Ski (Chamberlain, *Kojiki,* p. 23). The Japanese have also a pillar whose foundation is at the centre of the world, where stands the tat or pole of Ptah supporting the nether sky. In Chinese legendary lore there is a pillar that sustains the earth. They also have a pillar which sustains the heaven. These two correspond to the pillar of Shu that supports the firmament above and the tat-pillar of Ptah which supports the earth in Amenta below. These are distinct from each other; they belong to two entirely different mythical creations, and cannot be resolved into one single pillar derived from the mount of earth as axis-pillar of the heavens. Heaven had rested on the pillar of the earth or the pillars raised upon the mundane mount by Shu. But the tat-pillar of Ptah was erected in the nether earth of two. Consequently our earth was then supported on the pillar of Ptah. This will explain the tradition of the Chinese, the Thlinkeet Indians, and others, that the earth rests upon a pillar. Thus, as Egyptian, there are two divine pillars answering to the double mount, which we call the pillar of Shu and the tat-pillar of Ptah. One is the sustainer of the firmament above the earth, the other is the support of the firmament below the earth. The two together are the double pillars of earth and heaven. This will enable us to read one of the many Greek märchen, which reflect and refract the Egyptian mythos.

There is a legend of Herakles relieving Atlas as sustainer of the heavens, or, in the original, the ceilings of the double earth. Atlas is the Egyptian Shu-Anhur, the elevator of the sky. And the relief of Atlas by Herakles is equivalent to the relief of Shu by the sun-god Ptah as sustainer of all things in Amenta, when the pillar of earth or tat of Amenta was added to the pillar of heaven. When the earth was doubled and the nocturnal sun god passed through Amenta as Ptah or Sekari with his tat, he was the sustainer in the nether earth who might be said to relieve Shu of his burden in the upper earth. Horus is the prototype of Herakles, and Horus or Ptah in Amenta is the mighty Herakles of this Greek fancy which so often takes the place of fundamental fact. There is no trusting the märchen in their Greek or Hindu, Hebrew or Christian guise, without comparing them with the originals. Greek legends also assert that Herakles *separated two mountains* to form the two columns or pillars which were a dual figure of the twofold mundane and celestial mount. This helps to identify the double columns with the mount of earth and the mount of heaven. Many illustrations could be cited of these two pillars erected at the entrance to the temple or house of a god. Herakles, says Herodotus, was worshipped in a temple at Tyre, and in the temple "were two pillars, one of *fine gold,* the other of *emerald stone,* both shining exceedingly at night" (Bk. II, 44). These are, to say the least, somewhat suggestive of the green mount of earth, the Egyptian mount of emerald, and the golden mount of heaven, which survive as the "green hill" far away and "Jerusalem the golden" in the Christian hymns.

The backbone was a figure of the pole: it is at one time the backbone of Sut, at another the backbone of Anup, at another of Ptah or Osiris—the backbone being a natural type of sustaining power. This at first was single as a figure of the pole. It was duplicated in Amenta, the same as was the pillar of support and other figures of sustaining power. The power of Ptah in Amenta is not simply that of the pillar or backbone. These are doubled in the earth of eternity to express his power as sustainer of the universe. The figure is referred to in the magic papyrus as the long backbone of Ptah, the Nemma. "O Nemma of the great face, of the long backbone, of the deformed legs! O long column which commences in (both) the upper and the lower heaven. O lord of the great body which reposes in Annu," the place of the column or pole, now doubled in Amenta (*Magic Papyrus, Records,* vol. X, p. 152). There was a tendency to blend the twofold mount in one as in the double Mount

Meru, which is sometimes denominated the North Pole, but was primarily a figure on earth of the pole in heaven, like the mound of earth and the cone or pillar. But Meru was doubled or divided into upper and lower, called Su-Meru and Ku-Meru, when it imaged the mount that was opened for the passage of the heavenly bodies through the nether earth. One mountain standing in the east and one in the north were not vertically blended in one. They were symbolical of the double mount of earth and heaven as a figure, but this was in the end, not at the starting-point.

The Kamite teachers also imaged the two poles as the two trees called the two sycamores of the south and north. The later tree in Eridu, as well as the Norse tree Yggdrasil, was compounded of the two as the tree which had its roots down south or in the under-world, and its branches high up in the northern heaven; a two-fold tree that corresponded to the double mount. Again, the rock is a co-type with the mount, and the double rock is equivalent to the twofold mount. These two were also blended in one as in the rock that "begat" the Israelites. The rock and the double rock are both mentioned in the Ritual (ch. 134). Taht the moon-god is said to be the "son of the rock proceeding from the place of the two rocks" in Anruti (Renouf, ch. 134). The name of Anruti identifies the double rock with the double horizon, which was also called the double mount, ᗑ. The son of the rock who proceeds from the two rocks is the moon-god as the son of earth and heaven, or son of the double mount of earth and heaven, the two rocks having been blended in one as a typical figure of Osiris, the rock of eternity, imaged as the pole of heaven. The twofold origin of the mythical mount is now sufficiently established in relation to identifiable natural facts which alone can furnish the proof that the mount, the pole, the tree, the paradise, pillar, column, or backbone were single in the stellar and are duplicated in the solar mythos, and that this duplication followed on the making of Amenta.

The Rig-Veda speaks of "him who, as the collective pillar of heaven, sustains the sky" (Wilson, 3, 143, 144). This collective pillar was the dual type of the twofold mount of earth and of heaven imaged in one figure of support. The Hebrew pillar of the lower and upper paradise that is called "the strength of the hill Zion" was another form of the collective pillar. As Egyptian, this collective pillar was the double tat of Ptah erected in Amenta. The tat-pillar of Ptah and Osiris was continued in the ancient Germanic Irmin pillars, which were mostly made of wood. The mythical pillar Irminsul was that which joined together earth and heaven, like the mount of Amenta and the tat-support of the gods. The Irmin-pillars were a form of the Hermae in Greece that were set up as boundary signs at cross roads and street corners to mark the extent of certain lands. This points to an origin for their name. In Egyptian the word remen or ermen denotes the extent as far as the limit or boundary. Rema or erma is a measure of land. The deity Irmin, like Hermes of the pillar, was a god of boundaries.

If the mount or the pillar had been single and not double, there would have been no voyage *across the water* that flowed between the mount of earth and the mount of heaven; no need of boat or bridge or place of "jumping off" from one side to the other. If the mythical mount had simply been a single figure of the universe axis (as O'Neil describes it), the climbers would have gone straight up to heaven, whereas the solar mount of glory in the east did not and could not blend vertically with the stellar mount of glory in the north. The mount was dual; the water ran betwixt the two, and that necessitated the means of crossing from one to the other. Nothing could make the universe axis twofold, in keeping with the double mount of earth and heaven. And this duality alone will explain why one type should be considered female, the other male. The mount or pillar of earth was an image of the Great Mother as bringer-forth, and the mount or pillar of heaven was typical of the fatherhood, the "rock that begat," or rather of two sexes in one nature as they were blended in the deity Ptah, Atum, Osiris, Ihuh, and Brahma. The type of this duality is to be seen in the navel, the umbilicus, and the nabhiyoni united and imaged in one as a figure of the birthplace and prototype of the navel mounds; the pit below and the pile of stones above, the well and pyramid, the church and steeple, the grave and monument.

When the solar mythos had been added to the stellar, the pathway to paradise was through the nether-world. The road of the sun in the mythos now became the road of souls in the eschatology. The entrance to the under-world was consequently in the west. The maker of the road was the nocturnal sun as the bull or god of the west. One name of the western hill is Manu. It is said to Ra when setting, "Wake up from thy rest; thine abode is in Manu" (Rit., ch. 15). This apparently survives in the Samoan Mane. At death, the soul went to a paradise in the western horizon called Mane = Manu. "The dying," says the missionary Turner, "were urgent in begging those around them to see and make the tapunea or pessomancy go all right, and so secure an entrance to the Mane paradise" (*Samoa*, p. 294). If the pebbles used for divination turned out odd instead of even it was thought that the soul would be caught and crushed between *two great stones* at the entrance to the mount. The "hollow pit" was a name of the Samoan Hades. At the bottom there was a running stream which floated the spirits away to the Hades of Polotu. They were but little more than alive and only half conscious until they reached Polotu, where there was a bathing-place called Vaiola or "the water of life." In this water all infirmities were washed away and the aged recovered their lost youth. Their new bodies were singularly volatile, like the Egyptian sahu. They could ascend to earth at night, become luminous sparks or vapour, revisit their old homes and retire at early dawn to the bush or to Polotu (Turner, *Samoa*, pp. 258, 259). The subterranean world of the Lapps is identical with the Amenta of the Egyptians. Jabma-Aimo is the house of the dead in the nether-earth, which is a place of transition for those who have their bodies renewed, who pass on and are taken up to heaven. Their home of the gods, Taivo Aimo, also answers to the upper Aarru-paradise of the Ritual. The jackal or dog is the guide of the dead through the paths of darkness in the nether-earth, and the Inoit dead are said to descend by the "dog's path" into their under-world. This is a most obscure road, answering to the path of darkness in Amenta. The subterranean region described at times as being submarine is the common sub-terrestrial paradise of the Inoit people generally.

When the nether-world had been completely excavated by Ptah, Amenta was established as the lower story of two in the mount of earth which henceforth becomes the mount of Amenta. The name denotes the hidden or secret (Amen) earth (ta). It is also called the earth of eternity, the land of the living; for the Egyptians call those the living whom the less spiritualistic moderns designate the dead. The mount of earth became the mount of Amenta because Amenta had been tunnelled through the lower earth. It became the funereal mount because Amenta was the earth of the manes. In the Egyptian chart the west is the beautiful gate of entrance to this divine nether-world, otherwise called the land of life. It is not paradise itself, but the way to it through purgatory. The beautiful gate of exit was at the place of sunrise, not sunset, in the garden eastward, and this was the locality of the terrestrial paradise, which was a copy of the garden of Aarru first configurated in the circumpolar heaven of the stellar mythology. The dead in Egypt were called "the westerners." On the way to the place of burial the mourners sang the funeral song "To the west, to the west, to the west!" The mummy was ferried over the water to the western mount, where Hathor-Isis or the cow waited to receive the solar god, and in his track the souls of the departed. The entrance to the mount was shown as the mouth of the cow, or cleft in the rock, such as was seen in the immediate neighbourhood of Abydos, which was reached through a narrow gorge in the Libyan range, whose "mouth" opened in front of the temple of Osiris-Khentamenta a little to the north-west of the city (Maspero, *Dawn of Civilization,* Eng. Tr., p. 197). Here the souls of the departed were supposed to enter and descend into the nether-world. The sun-god is described in his passage to the western horizon (or mount), whilst earth, as the mother, stretches her arms out to receive him. "In rapture is thy mother, the goddess Meru, as thou dost emit the irradiation of light till thou reachest that mountain which is in Akar," *i.e.,* till sunset, when he will enter the female receptacle for his new birth. Taking this to be imaged by Isis as the sacred heifer, the place of entrance is her mouth, and the place of exit was uterine, to the east of the mount (Magic Papyrus, p. 5, *Records,* vol. x, 145.)

The entrance into the mount of earth which was personified as the old first mother is one of the exploits of Maui in the märchen of the Maori. Maui, at the end of his victorious career, that is at sunset, comes back to the country of his father and the land of his great ancestress Hine-neu-te-Po, the great woman of the under-world, who is to be seen in the horizon, "flashing, and, as it were, opening and shutting." So Apt the hippopotamus and Hathor the cow may be seen in the cleft of the mount that opened at sunset for the passage of the solar god, the mouth of the cow being equivalent to the cleft in the mount. Maui came to where the ancient giantess lay sleeping, with the object of passing through her without waking her. He entered her body, but when he was half in and half out, a little bird, the Tiwakawaka, laughed aloud to see the sight, and woke the sleeper, who closed her thighs on Maui and crushed him so that he died, and thus brought death into the world; otherwise, it was fabled that the solar hero died to rise again in passing through the nether-world of darkness, and this was a primitive mode of portrayal. In the Kamite mythos he passes through the female hippopotamus or cow, or the sphinx, all of which were figures of the mother in the mount, otherwise the ancient Mother-earth. It is common for a cavern or entrance in the west to be pointed out as the way into spirit-world that leads to the fields of paradise. This is found in the Aztec Mictlan or land of the dead. The Fijian descent into the underworld is exactly the same as the Egyptian. The dead go down in the west on their way to the judgment seat of Ndengei (Williams, *Fiji*, vol. i, p. 239), just as the Egyptian dead embark in the west for the judgment seat of Osiris. The nether-earth, Ngamat, of the Australian Woiworun also corresponds to the Kamite Amenta. It is the receptacle of the sun beyond the western edge of the earth, and likewise an abode for the departed, who do not remain there permanently, but come back to our earth at times as the ngamaget, like the manes in the Ritual. (Howitt on Australian medicine-men.)

In various märchen and other irresponsible legends derived from mythology we hear of heaven being situated in the west—that is, as the place of sunset. The Buddhists have their western paradise. The paradise of the Ottomacks of Guiana and of the Araucanians is in the west. The heaven of the Todas, the Kalmucks, the Samoans, and others was localized in the west. The Iroquois and Ojibwas describe the souls of their dead as travelling westward till they come to the plains of paradise. The Sekhet Hetep or the fields of rest in Aarru are represented in the noble island of Flath Innis, the place of rest from storm and strife to which the Keltic heroes went in death, as a paradise in the western ocean. The elysian fields and golden isles of the Greeks were in the west. But that is only because *the entrance to the earthly paradise was in the west,* according to the solar mythos. At Samoa, says Gill, a spirit leaving the dead body at the most easterly island of the group would be compelled to traverse the entire series of islands, passing the channels between at given points, ere it could descend to the subterranean spirit-world at the most westerly point of Savaiki (p. 160), which rightly identifies the west with *the gate of entrance* to the earth of eternity.

In the wisdom of "Manihiki" it is related as another of the exploits of Maui that he found out the way to the nether-world. He had watched and seen his father go according to his wont to the main pillar of his dwelling and say "O pillar! open, open up, that Manuahifare may enter and descend to the nether-world," which was the Heptanomis or seven sunken islands of Avaiki. The pillar immediately opened, and Manuahifare descended. Maui repeated the magic words of his father, and to his great joy the pillar obediently opened, and he boldly made his descent into the lower regions. Whilst exploring this subterranean spirit-world, Maui fell in with a blind old woman, who turned out to be his own grandmother. Here also was the paradise in which the tree of healing grew, and with the fruit of which Maui restored sight to the eyes of Ina-the-blind. (Gill, *Myths and Songs,* pp. 64-66.) The incident of a rock or door that opens when the magic formula is uttered, and in no other way, is well-nigh universal. It may be termed the "open sesame" legend. In a Chinese version Chang discovers the entrance to the under-world by finding out the secret of the stone door in the cave of Kwang-siu-fu in Kiang-si. "One day he overheard a genie saying, "Stone door, open! Mr. Kwei-ku is coming." Thereupon the door opened and the genie went in. When he came out he said, "Stone door, shut! Mr. Kwei-ku is going." Chang tried the charm, and found a vast paradise within, and there he lost his old grandmother. (Denny's *Folk-lore of China*, p. 134.) In a Zulu tale the word is "Rock of two holes, open for me, that I may enter" (Callaway, *Tales*, pp. 140-142). In a Samoan rendering it is "Rock, divide! I am Talanga: I have come to work" (Turner, *Nineteen Years in Polynesia*, p. 252). The sacred hole-stone, the needle's eye, the chimney, or the cow, and other apertures through which the twice-born was passed as an initiate in the mysteries derive their symbolical significance from this passage through the rock or mount of earth. It was the same with the human soul in the eschatology as it had been with the soul of the sun in the mythology. Sometimes the hole in the dolmen or other stone that people wriggled through was very small. This increased the difficulty, and was a practical illustration of the trials in the passage of Amenta. There was one near the summit of a rocky mountain island in Ireland called the "eye of the needle," which is described as "a narrow opening like a chimney." To understand the custom we must read the Ritual.

The sun-god made his passage through the mount of earth, or the sphinx, for his rebirth and resurrection on the eastern side, and the opening in the rock was at the end or at the summit, in the Tser hill, the rock of the horizon. In the Russian märchen Prince Ivan = Horus the prince, climbs up the magical ladder to get into the "great house" of the "tremendously high steep mountain." His sister = the princess, or lunar lady, calls to him from the balcony. "See, there is a chink in the enclosure. Touch it with your little finger and it will become a door!" This he does, and obtains entrance into the mountain of Amenta. (Ralston, *Russian Folk-tales*, 102.)

The cleft or opening in the mount was also termed the grotto. And it is possible that this survives in the "grotto" that is exhibited in England, and is made of oyster-shells at the time when oysters are supposed to be *first opened* on one particular day of the year. This illustrates an ancient custom but not a legal enactment respecting oysters. The opening of the oyster = the annual opening of the earth in the equinox. The grotto is an interior or shrine, and the light which is kindled within it points rather to the sun than to the lamp in any Christian sanctuary. The day and the ceremony have been assigned to St. James, but that is only one more item in the total system of falsification designated Christian. Osiris also had his shrine "which standeth in the centre of the earth." (Rit., ch. 64, Renouf, and Book of Hades.) The under-world of the Karens of Burmah is the Egyptian Amenta. They also have the double mount into which the sun enters at sunset (or in the equinox). The mount consists of two great strata of rock, one lower and one upper, which continually open and shut as with an upper and a lower jaw, but the

Karens have no idea how the upper stratum is supported. At their departure from earth the Manes are thus addressed: "Thou goest unto Thama. Thou goest through the crevices of rocks. At the opening and shutting of the western gates of rock, thou goest in between. Thou goest below the earth where the sun travels." (Mason, "Karens," *Journal of the Asiatic Soc.*, Bengal, pt. 2, pp. 233-4, 1865.) The dead descend to Khu-the and appear before Thama the great judge in Hades, who may be identified with the Egyptian Tumu or Atum, the great judge in the Kamite Amenta, who is the representative of the setting sun as Atum-Ra and of the rising sun as Atum-Horus (Nefer-Atum).

The difficulty of obtaining entrance to the mount was insuperable to mortals. Hence the need of divine assistance. The sun-god as opener in the mythology led up to the god as opener for souls in the eschatology. In this character Horus became the door and the way of life to the manes, who followed in his wake of glory through the dark of death. The principle subject of the inscriptions written on the sarcophagus of Seti I., now in the Soane Museum, is the nocturnal passage of the sun or the sun-god through the nether-earth by night, having the blessed on his right hand, the damned upon his left. There are twelve divisions to the passage, which correspond to the twelve hours of the night. But the first of these divisions, that of entrance, is without a door, whereas the last of the twelve, that of exit, has a double door. Here the entrance to Amenta consists of a blind doorway or a door which neither mortal nor manes could know the secret of, and none but the god, primarily solar, could open. Hence the need of a deity as the opener, or a god who is the door and the way on grounds as tangible as those of the door in the mythology of Amenta. (The Book of Hades, *Records of the Past,* vol. x., p. 81.) When the god comes to illuminate the valley of darkness the doors open one after the other and he enters with his followers—those who were equipped or, as the legend of the Ten Virgins has it, whose lamps were already trimmed. The door then closes, "and they who are left behind in their porch cry out when they hear it shut." Thus we attain a natural origin for the mythos, the eschatology, and the folk-tales told concerning the hidden door that was sometimes represented by a revolving stone, and the secret password or "Open sesame!" that was communicated to the initiates in the mysteries. If properly equipped, the Osiris is in possession of the magical words of power that secure the opening of every gate, including this hidden entrance to Amenta. These words he carries in his hand, in death, as his papyrus roll; or, better still, he knows them by heart, and has made them truth in his own life and death. He exclaims, "I am accoutred and equipped with thy words of power, O Ra," the god, that is, who says of himself, "I am he who closeth and he who openeth, and I am but one" (Rit., ch. 17, Renouf).

In the lower paradise was the land of gold, not as metal, but as the glory of the sun by night. The sun god rising from this land that was yellow with gold is thus addressed, "Adoration to thee, who arisest out of the golden and givest light to the earth" (Rit., ch. 15, Renouf). Still, mining for metals had commenced when Ptah and his pygmy workers hollowed out the under-world. Amenta was based upon the mine. It was the secret earth in which the treasures were concealed. These were guarded by the dragon, but they were likewise known to the dwarfs, the wee folk, the fairies, the Tuatha de Danan. Amenta was the land of precious metals and the furnace of the solar fire. Hence Ptah, the miner, became the blacksmith of the gods, the Kamite Vulcan. Some missing details respecting the work of Ptah the metallurgist may be found in the Greek rendering of this god as Hephaistos. Ptah, working in concert with the goddess Maati, built the great double hall of Truth and Justice, which was gilded and glorified with his precious metal. Hephaistos is the architect of the house of the gods. As a proof that his place and work are in the nether earth, Hephaistos does not know what occurs until he learns it from the coming sun.

Following the burial on earth, the deceased enters as a manes into Amenta, the land of the living. He seeks to get on board the boat of souls. The priest says, "O ye seamen of Ra, at the closing of day let the Osiris live after death as Ra does daily." Here the helmsman: "As Ra is born from yesterday, so he too is born from yesterday, and as every god exults in life so shall the Osiris exult even as they exult in life." (Ch. 3, Renouf.)

A subterranean pleasaunce opened to the eastward of the mount of earth called now, the earth of eternity. This is a paradise to which the manes look forward on their path of progress. It was the field in which they had to till and grow the divine harvest as the food of the gods. For Aarru was apportioned on the small allotment system. Each one had a share of arable land to cultivate, and by the fruit was known and judged at the great harvest-home as a true worker or a lazy one; and by their labour in this spirit-world Egyptians earned their living for the life hereafter. The lower Aarru, the garden eastward in Amenta, is that earthly paradise of legendary lore in search of which so many heroes sailed. In the Erik Saga, Erik sets out in search of Odainsakr, a form of the Norse paradise, which is said to be encircled by a wall of fire. He enters a dark forest-land in which the stars are seen by day. A dragon bars his way across the river—the Apap of darkness in the valley of darkness (Rit., ch. 7). He rushes into the monster's mouth and passes through its body—a common way with the solar hero. Erik emerges with his companions in the land of light, the lower paradise of the mythos. After awhile they come to a tower that is suspended in the air without any visible supports; access to it was obtained by means of a ladder that enabled the seekers to reach the top of the tower, which had neither foundations nor pillars. They had now attained Odainsakr, the earth of living men, the Egyptian land of the living, but not the upper paradise, the place of spirits perfected, which is said to be so glorious that Odainsakr in comparison was but a desert. Erik's is but the journey of the nocturnal sun or the annual sun in the inferior hemisphere represented in the primitive form of a passage through the nether-earth.

The aim and end of the Osiris on the journey by water or by land is to reach the circumpolar paradise and secure a place among the stars that never set, the glorious ones that "beacon from the abodes where the eternals are." The mount of earth was the point of emergence in the mythology. It was the place of birth for the sun upon the mount to the east where the temple of Sebek-Horus stood. In the eschatology it was the place of rebirth for the souls or manes who ascended by the mount or by the tree of dawn to the summit from which they entered the bark of the sun to make the voyage over the waters round to Manu in the region of the west. This underworld, with its mount of birth as a point of departure for the sun and manes in the east, became the traditional birthplace and point of departure in the legends of various supposed ethnical migrations of a similar nature to that of the Jews in the exodus from Egypt.

The passage from the mount or island of earth to the mount of the upper paradise across the water was already mapped out in the time of Pepi I., as the following extract from his pyramid shows: "Hail thou who (at thy will) makest to pass over to the field Aarru the soul that is right and true, or dost make shipwreck of it (if wrong). Pepi is right and true in respect of the island of the earth, whither he swimmeth and where he ariseth." (Budge.)

This is not very clear, but the island of the earth is the mount on the eastern summit of which the manes joined the solar bark to make the voyage from Mount Bakhu east to Mount Manu in the west on their way to the mount of glory at the north celestial pole. Thus the pathway for the dead from this life to the upper paradise was laid down by the Egyptians. It was they who tunnelled the mount of earth and hollowed out Amenta with its places of purgatory, its hells, its paradise of plenty in the Aarru meadows; its means of ascent for the Manes by the mount or up the tree; its solar bark and boat of souls that voyaged over the waters of the Nun from east to west; its steps or ladder that was raised at the landing-place by night for the ascent to heaven in the upper Aarru paradise. This pathway of the dead is well-nigh universal in mythology, and it can be traced from beginning to end by means of the Egyptian mythology and the eschatology. Led by the jackal Anup as guide through all the ways of darkness, and lighted by Taht, the lunar god, who carries in his hand the lamp of light and eye of Horus as the moon of Amenta shining through the night, we emerge at length from underneath the upper earth. We are now outside the mount of earth, which stands upon a vast illimitable plain of the nether-world. We thus retain our foothold in the Nun where upper earth comes to an end. We follow the track of the sun and therefore issue on the eastern side of the mountain, which the solar god ascends at sunrise when seen by the dwellers on the upper earth. Now we are facing the solar east and the garden eastward, which originated in the oasis of Inner Africa.

The Book of the Dead is primarily based on the Amenta and the journey through its under-world. The track of the all-conquering sun is followed by the soul of the deceased. He enters the mount in the west by the opening in the rock, or at a later stage is carried on the boat. He is accompanied by those who have gone before as guides. He does battle with the adversary, and is victorious in the character of Horus. He opens all the paths and gates with his words of magic power and spells of might. He cleaves open the earth for the resurrection. He is delivered from the devouring demon who lurks invisibly in the lake of fire and feeds upon the damned (ch. 17). The caverns of Putrata, where the dead fall into darkness, are opened for him. He is supported by the eye of Horus or lighted by the moon. Apuat, the opener of roads, raises him up and acts the part of the giant Christopher in carrying him across the waters (ch. 44). He wanders in the wilderness where nothing grows. He obtains command of the water in the nether-world and prevails over the deluge. He escapes the second death (ch. 58). The double doors of heaven are opened for his coming forth (ch. 68). Still following the course of the sun, the passage of Amenta endeth with the garden eastward and the ascent by which the Manes enter the bark of Ra. "O great one in thy bark," says the suppliant, "let me be lifted into the bark," "let me make head for thy staircase" (ch. 102). Deceased has here attained the summit of the solar mount of glory on his way to the circumpolar heaven and the stars that do not set. There is a voyage now in heaven from east to west, and as the sun was lifted up to enter the maatit bark at dawn, so is it in the eschatological rendering. The souls of the departed who were pure enough in the presence of the sun now entered the maatit bark to continue the voyage round the mountain to the region of Manu. They were now the westerners in another sense which was eschatological. All day the manes make their voyage in the solar bark, and come at sunset to the land of the west about which the song was sung in the funeral procession, "To the west! To the west!" At this landing-stage they leave the maatit for the sektit bark. The sun goes down to Amenta in the west each night, but their sun sets no more. They have done with the mount of earth in the mythology, and come to the mount belonging to the heavens. But there is a great gulf fixed between the mount of Amenta and the stellar mount of glory. This is the lake of darkness and the lair of the Apap-dragon. The void is spoken of as the cavern of Putrata, where the dead fall into darkness. It is also called the void of Apap. In strict accordance with natural phenomena, the gulf or void of Putrata lay betwixt the place of sunset on the western side of the mount of earth and the heaven of the setting stars. It is the prototype of the abyss or lake of outer darkness, the pit, in the Christian version of the legend; the great gulf that was fixed betwixt those who remained in the lower Amenta and those who had attained the bosom of Ra, an Egyptian expression for the boat. On the other side of the water "Shu standeth erect, and the non-setting stars are instantly active in raising the ladder" by which the sinking souls or setting stars are saved from destruction in the lake of outer darkness. These steps are carried round from east to west for that purpose on board the solar bark. (Vignettes to Ritual.)

With the change of boat another voyage begins by night, along the great stream of the Milky Way. This is described as "that most conspicuous but inaccessible stream" when contemplated from the earth. (Rit., ch. 98.) When the departed reach the starry shore, the seven steps or ladder for ascending the mount of heaven is now erected in the boat. This ladder, as Egyptian, was double in the time of King Pepi. It is called the ladder of Sut for the ascent from

Amenta, and the ladder of Horus for the ascent to heaven. A bark that can *ascend the stream* awaits the voyagers. This picture of the bark that made its glorious journey upward to the circumpolar paradise was obviously constellated as the *Argo Navis,* which is figured in the position of ascending backwards on the white waters of the Milky Way. The cavern and gulf of Putrata no doubt existed when there was as yet no boat or bride extant. Hence in various legends the manes have to spring from one side of the chasm to the other. The "jumping-off place" for departed spirits is known in several legends of the aboriginal races, and this was the rock on the western side of the mount. There is a stone at the west end of Upolu called "the leaping-stone," from which departed spirits in their course leaped into the sea, swam to Manono, sprang from another stone on that island, crossed to Savaii and went overland to the Fafā, at Falealupo, as the western entrance to their other world is called. (Turner, *Samoa,* p. 257.) With the Greeks, "to leap from the Leucadian Rock" was a proverbial equivalent for death. In the Khond representation, the souls of the dead "have to jump across the black unfathomable gulf to gain a footing on the slippery leaping rock, where Dinga Pennu, the judge of the dead, sits writing his register of all men's daily lives and actions." The Guinea negroes tell of a divine judge whose judgment seat was on the other side of the water that spirits crossed in death, analogous to the Egyptian maat in the circumpolar region. Those who had religiously kept the laws of tabu were conducted into paradise, whereas those who had not were sunk headlong in the waters like the damned that went down headlong in the waters of Putrata. (*Bosman,* Pinkerton, vol. xvi, p. 401; Rit., ch. 44.)

The souls that ascended from the mount of Amenta by the Milky Way, the path of spirits, were hawk-headed like the Horus-soul, and with the Lithuanians this way of souls was called the "road of birds," along which the departed went like birds, or AS birds in the Kamite representation, to the regions of eternal rest. As Egyptian, this road was a great stream, because with them the water was their earliest way (ch. 86). Another Egyptian name for the heaven as water is urnas or uranus. This we claim to be the Kamite original of the Greek uranus. Dr. Birch renders it in his dictionary "Urnas, Ouranos, the celestial water." The Egyptians did not personalize it under that name; still, the urnas is the celestial water, and urnas = uranos. The okeanus that flows around the world was neither a fabulous sea nor a stream of water, but the firmament itself, that was figured as the celestial water surrounding the mount of earth. Through this ocean ran the great stream of the white water or the Milky Way. Thus we have the okeanos and the ocean stream of Homer for the first time separately identified. Again, the water appeared divided into two lakes at the head of the celestial river united to form one stream in the Via Lactea. The system of the waters in the Bundahish is identical with the Egyptian. It is said that all the waters in heaven and earth had their origin in the heavenly mount of Ardvi Sura at the summit of Alborz upon which the red cow rested. There is but one source and only place of discharge for all the rivers in the world. This was the river of the Milky Way, which the Egyptians figured as descending from the celestial lakes to be continued in the lakes and in the Nile below. In China the Yellow River is looked upon as a continuation of the Tien Ho, or Milky Way, the river of heaven continued as the river of earth (Mayers' *Manual,* p. 98).

The Osirian looking heavenward in death exclaims, "O very high mountain! I hold myself in thy enclosure" (Rit., 149, 14). He also says, "A divine domain hath been constructed for me. I know the name of it; the name of it is the garden of Aarru." (Rit., ch. 109, Renouf.) But the enclosure at the summit of the mount was not only figured as a paradise of plenty. It was a dwelling-place which had expanded to a city; the city of the blessed, the holy city, the city of the great king, the heavenly city, the eternal city, that was the model of Memphis and Annu, Thebes and Abydos, Eridu and Babylon, Rome, Jerusalem, and other sacred cities of the world. On approaching this, the Osirian says, "I stand erect in the bark which the god is piloting, at the head of Aarru, and the non-setting stars open to receive me, and my fellow-citizens present to me the sacred cakes with flesh" (ch. 98, Renouf). In an earlier chapter he had said, "I arrive at my own city" (ch. 17). On the Stele of Beka the speaker says, "I reach the city of those who are in eternity." That is the eternal city. When the Osiris has attained the land of eternity he says his future is in Annu. That is Annu as a celestial locality, Annu as the eternal city, not Heliopolis in Egypt. (Rit., ch. 133.) Annu, like Tattu, was a form of the celestial city at the pole. An is a name of the mount and the column, the pole, and in Annu was the pillar, fortress, or rock of eternity.

In one form the polar mount was called the white mountain. It was Mont Blanc in heaven. The Koreans term it "mount everwhite." As a house it was the white house. As a city it was the city of the white wall. As the seat it was the great white throne of the eternal. As a country it is the land of the silver sky. It is also known as the mountain of white limestone, the stone of Sut. The house constructed by Ptah was double-storied, a house of the lower and upper paradise combined in one. Finally, the heaven of astronomical mythology was figured as the great house of Osiris. This included all the previous formations: the circle of the Bear; the heaven of Sut and Horus, south and north; the triangular heaven of the ecliptic; the heaven built on the square; the double house of Amenta below the earth, and the eternal dwelling-place above, whence the house of Osiris at Abydos, called the mansion of Seb and Nu, or earth and heaven, was built in two stories. (*Magical Texts,* p. 6; *Records,* vol. vi., p. 118.) "In the year 22 of the reign of King Aahmes, his majesty gave the order to open the rock-chambers anew, and to cut out thence the best white stone (limestone) of the hill-country (called) Annu, for the houses of the gods," including the house of Ptah at Memphis (Brugsch, *Egypt under the Pharaohs,* Eng. trans. in one vol., p. 130). The mountain of white limestone was an actual fact on earth to the Egyptians. It was in a spur of the Arabian range which projected in a straight line towards the Nile as far as the village of Troiu, and contained an inexhaustible supply of the finest and whitest limestone. The Egyptians had quarried the white limestone mountain from the earliest ages to obtain materials for their pyramids. (Maspero, *Dawn of Civilization,* Eng. trans., p. 383.) It furnished the limestone for building the city of the white wall, which represented the celestial city on the summit of the mount in heaven. The name of Troiu, modern Turah, is suggestive of the Greek city of Troy, which in its mythical aspect was another form of the city on the mount. The deceased are lifted up in the white house or within the circle of the white wall by Sekhet the lioness-consort of Ptah (Rit., chs. 42 and 106), which was an astronomical foundation that followed the heaven of the eight great gods. The Osiris says, "May Sekhet the divine one lift me up, so that I may arise in heaven and deliver my behest in Memphis" (Rit., ch. 26, Renouf). With the Chinese Taoists the city on the summit of the mount is "the metropolis of pearl mountain." (Edkins, *Religion in China,* p. 151, 2nd. ed.) This corresponds to the Kamite city of the white wall, the celestial Ha-Ptah-Ka. To the dweller in Annu the eternal city was Annu on the summit of the celestial mount. To the dweller in Thebes the eternal city was Thebes on high. To the dweller in Jerusalem the eternal city was Jerusalem above. Only once was there a mundane original for the paradise or later city set in heaven at the pole. That is demonstrably derived from the land, the river, the Annu, the Troy or Teriu of Egypt. The Egyptians set "the pattern in the mount," and from this the later builders of the sacred cities, the ark cities, on the mount of heaven, derived the plan. The city of Troy on earth was a type of the eternal Troy upon the summit of the mount. Both city and name are demonstrably Egyptian, as Troy = Terui. Terui denotes the circumference or enclosure, and this was a name of Sesennu, and consequently of Am-Khemen—the paradise of the eight, the enclosure on the mount of heaven which afterwards supplied a name for the city of Troy in Greece. The "Tale of Troy" is based on the downfall of the great city on the summit, which was the lofty dwelling-place of those whom we may term the people of the pole. The Greeks are solarites, with the sun-god Achilles as their leader. This fall occurred when the stellar representation was followed by the luni-solar mythos. The fall of Babylon in the book of Revelation is another form of the tale of Troy; and both were representations of the one great original in the astronomical mythos. The Semites would have had no heaven on the summit of the mount to go to if the Egyptians had not enclosed it and planted it, and showed the way in their astronomy. They would have had no Sheol if the Egyptians had not excavated the Amenta for the passage of the sun in their mythology and for the souls in the eschatology. And it is by means of the Egyptian imagery that we shall be able to restore something of the lapsed sense to the Hebrew writings.

Entrance into the eternal city was preceded by baptism, with Anup, father of the inundation, as the baptiser and sprinkler both in one. On approaching the two lakes the speaker says, "Lo, I come that I may purify this soul of mine in the most high degree. Let me be purified in the lake of propitiation and equipoise. Let me plunge into the divine pool beneath the two divine sycamores of heaven and earth." (Rit., ch. 97, Renouf.) This precedes the sacrament or eating of the sacrifice consisting of bread, beer, and meat. He also says, "Give me bread and beer. Let me be made pure by the sacrificial joint, together with the white bread," that is, by partaking of the sacrament. (Rit., ch. 106, Renouf.)

Heaven as a house had been founded by Sesheta or Sefekh, a form of the old First Mother as co-worker with Taht in the lunar mythos. Atum-Ra was also a builder of the house in the solar mythos. His son Iu-em-hetep, the Egyptian Solomon, was the builder or designer of the temple to whom *The Book of the Model of the Temple* is ascribed (Dümichen, *Temple Inschriften,* vol. I, pl. 97). It was the temple in heaven that was built without the sound of workmen's tools; "there was neither hammer nor axe nor any tool of iron heard in the house while it was building" (I Kings vi. 7). This only applies to the mythical building, which was astronomical, and which is still continued in esoteric Masonry. When such language is applied to building on earth it has no direct meaning. The eternal city was preceded by the place of assembly. Before the time of building on the mount there was a gathering-place under the tree that represented the roof of heaven. This was the Egyptian maat or judgment seat when it consisted of a stone beneath a tree. The seat of assembly, the seat of judgment on the summit of the mount, was continued as a sacred tradition by races who never saw the pole star of the northern heaven. The Australian blacks have no north pole to look to for their paradise. It sank out of sight for them long ages since, when they were emigrants from the old world, nor have they replaced it with the southern pole. But they still turn to a mount of the north as the gathering place for the souls of the departed. The Tundi, a judicial assembly of the tribe, is there—an equivalent in its way for the Egyptian maat. When an old Australian aborigine was dying he pointed upward and said, "My Tundi is up there!" (Taplin, *Native Races of South Australia,* p. 36). The great pyramid was built as a replica of this eternal home. One name of this is khut, a word which does not merely signify "light," or the horizon. It was the mount of glory permanently fixed in stone; a type of heaven perfected which included all the mansions in the great house of Osiris. Earth being figured as a mount or island in the abyssal water, it seems probable that the island in the water mentioned by Herodotus (B. ii. 127), where they say "the body of Cheops is laid," was imaged in the subterranean chamber of the great pyramid. And if so, it follows that the pyramid itself is a figure of the mount that stood amidst the water of surrounding space. For example, the "Queen's Chamber" is seven-sided, and therefore a figure of the Heptanomis. Of the "King's Chamber" Sandys says, "The stones are so great that eight floor it, eight flag each end, and sixteen the sides." It is therefore a figure of the lunar octonary, or the heaven of Am-Khemen. The Amenta of Ptah was imaged below as the abyss or well of the nether world. The steps or pathway to heaven were figured in the passage looking upward to the pole. In such monuments the architecture of the heavens found its supreme expression on the earth. He whom Herodotus calls "the priest of Vulcan" is obviously the deity Ptah. The Greek writer speaks of the temple of Vulcan at Memphis (ii. 153), when he means the temple of Ptah. Thus the reign of the priest of Vulcan refers to the dynasty of Ptah. Herodotus says, "The Egyptians having become free, after the reign of the priest of Vulcan—for they were at no time able to live without a king—established twelve kings, having divided all Egypt into twelve parts" (B. ii. 147). This was in the Egypt of the heavens. The divisions were zodiacal. The twelve kings are those that rowed the solar bark around the twelve signs now established in the circle of the ecliptic. "The twelve kings," continues Herodotus, "determined to leave in common a memorial of themselves, and having so determined, they built a labyrinth, a little above the lake of Mœris." This labyrinth "surpasses even the pyramid." It has twelve courts enclosed with walls, with doors opposite each other, six facing the north and six the south," which points to a building that represented the heaven of the twelve kings and twelve zodiacal signs, that is, the heaven of Atum-Ra the son of Ptah. The starry roof was taken, so to say, indoors, to glorify the temples of the gods, and was reproduced more or less as in the ceiling of Denderah. This has been shallowly described as Greek, because Greek artists were employed in the workmanship when the chart was last repeated, "as it had been before," according to the text. But the types in this planisphere are Egyptian, not Greek. To mention only a few: At the centre is the old first mother of all, the pregnant hippopotamus, Apt or Khebt, with the jackal Ap-Uat, the guide of ways in heaven; and the haunch or leg of Nut the celestial cow. Anup and Tehuti are figured back to back on the equinoctial colure; Shu and his sister Tefnut, back to back, constitute the sign of Sagittarius. Child-Horus is enthroned on his papyrus plant; he is also portrayed as Har-Makhu in the sign of the Scales. Khunsu-Horus offers up the black boar of Sut as a sacrifice in the disk of the full moon. Enough remains intact to show the origin of the constellation figures and to prove their derivation from the astronomical mythology of the Egyptians, by means of which they can be read to-day and for ever, but not as Greek or Euphratean (*Book of the Beginnings, Planisphere*).

THE IRISH AMENTA

Anyone who cares to become familiarly acquainted with the Kamite mythology and the scenery of Amenta can have little difficulty in recognizing the source of the ancient British and Irish legendary lore. Arthur, who owes his birth to what has been termed the shape-shifting of his father, is identical with Horus, who owes his birth to the transformation of Osiris, his father. Finn the posthumous child, who is reared in the woods to become the avenger of his father, is one with Horus born in the reeds to become the avenger of Osiris. Gawain as the child "born to be king" is brought up in the forest to which his mother had fled for concealment, as Isis fled to hide herself and bring forth Horus the heir-apparent in the marshes of Amenta. The battle of the brothers Sut and Horus is paralleled in the fight between Gawain and his brother Gareth. The "loathly lady" who transforms from a reptile at Gawain's kiss answers to the frog-headed Hekat, who represents the moon that changes into Sati at the sun-god's kiss.

In an Irish legend the heroes Diarmait and Finn Mac-Camail set out on a voyage in search of the men that had been carried off by a wizard chief or a giant called the Gruagach. The Gruagach is a Keltic ogre, or giant, who disappears at dusk into the well. The fight is the same as the conflict long continued betwixt Horus, lord of light, and the Apap-dragon of darkness in the land where the dead have "gone to the dragon." Also when the conflict ceases for a time the beaten Gruagach sinks down into the well, just as Apap sinks into the gulf or void and is drowned in the lake of darkness. (Joyce, *Old Celtic Romances,* "Pursuit of the Gilla Dacker," ch. 4.) Assuredly the dragon of drought survived as British in the dragon of Wantley, who is reputed to have been "*a formidable drinker.*" He was slain by "More, of More Hall," who hid himself in the well of the under-world where the dragon came to drink. (Percy, *Relics of Ancient Poetry.*) Entrance to Amenta was opposed by the giant lurking in the "gulf of Apap" (ch. 7). Immediately after entering the valley of darkness Horus, the solar conqueror in the mythology or the soul that followed him in the eschatology, had to contend with the black monster and pass through him one way or the other. The hero is depicted in the act of piercing the Apap's head (Naville, *Todt,* vol. I, kap. 7, vignette). This monster of drought and darkness becomes the huge black giant in the legends which are related of Kynon and of Cuchulain the victorious invader of the black fellow's domain.

The lady of the tree that stands in the pool of the persea-tree of life, who is Hathor in Egyptian mythos and Nut in eschatology, is one with the lady of the fountain in the Welsh Mabinogei, who was won by Owen when he slew the black knight of the fountain and performed the same deed as Horus who rescued Hathor from her devourer, the dragon of darkness, otherwise the black giant. Horus enters Amenta by the blind door of death and darkness as the deliverer of the manes who are held captive by the powers of evil, Apap the giant, Sut the black man, and their confederates. To effect the rescue he, like Diarmait, goes down to the "land beneath the billow" in the lower parts of the Nun. This liberation of the captives in Amenta is common in the British legends. The Aarru-paradise is the land of promise in a lake-country. This lakeland is Lochlan of the Welsh version, "a mysterious country in the lochs" or waters beneath the earth. In this realm of faerie Finn and Diarmait found their lost friends all safe upon the island that was known as the Promised Land, which is identical with the Land of Promise that was sought for by the Jews, and by all who ever set out for the terrestrial or sub-terrestrial paradise, which never was and never could be found outside the Egyptian earth of eternity; and finally in the upper paradise or heaven of eternity on the other side of the celestial water. There is also a numerical note in the statement that those who succeed in snatching some of the fruit from the tree of life in the under-world returned forthwith to the typical age of thirty years, even though they had completed their hundredth year: and in the Egyptian representation Amsu the victor of Amenta, the conqueror of the black fellow, is the Horus of thirty years, the divine *homme fait,* that anointed son of god who is always thirty years of age.

When going over the ground previously the present writer was not sufficiently versed in the mysteries of Amenta, and Akar had not yielded up its secret treasures.

Application of the comparative method to the voyages of Maelduin and Bran will show that one of the most satisfactory survivals of the Kamite wisdom is to be met with in the Irish mythology and märchen. The voyage of Horus and his companions in the solar bark that makes a circle is repeated in the Imram or "rowing about" of the Irish heroes and their associates in the boat, or of British Arthur with the seven in the ark. The voyage of Maelduin is undertaken by him in search of his father's murderers. This is the object of Horus or the deceased in the Egyptian Ritual. They sailed together over the waters to the west until they came to a cliff so steep and high it seemed to touch the clouds. Diarmait undertook to climb the cliff and search for the missing men. He looked inland and saw a lovely country. He sets out to walk across the plain; he sees a great tree laden with fruit. This is surrounded by a stone enclosure, a circle of pillar-stones, with a large round pool of water clear as crystal in the midst which bubbled up at the centre and flowed away to nourish all the land. The story need not be followed any farther as a story, but now for the interpretation. The missing men who were spirited away denote the manes. The way across the water to the west was the road of souls along the solar track. The steep and very lofty cliff was the mountain of Amenta, which is said to reach the sky. The lovely country or the plain was the field of Aarru in the Egyptian lower paradise, with the enclosure that protected it from Apap; its well of water as the living source of all supply; its tree of life that bore the *unforbidden* fruit, and other features of the mythos are all identifiably Egyptian.

In the opening of the Ritual (chs. 3 and 4) the hero enters the vessel of the Kamite Charon and addresses the helmsman and sailors. He is in search of his father, Osiris, who has been murdered by Sut, and says: "I am the beloved son. I have come to see my father, Osiris, to pierce the heart of Sut," and to slay the conspirators (Rit., ch. 9, Renouf), Horus being, like Maelduin, the avenger of his father (Rit., chs. 1, 17, 92, Renouf). Amenta is the land of life (ch. 15); the sun sets into the land of life; it is the land of the tree of life and the water of life, in which the dead become the living, resting in the land of life. The mount in the west is called Mount Ankhu, the mountain of life. One name for the mount (otherwise the horizon) in Egyptian is Sut or Set, ⌒ ᨈ or ⌒ ▽, the rock, hill, or mount, which agrees with the Irish Síd for the hillock and the mound of the unseen world. The mounds were made as dwellings for the dead, and in the Irish legends the people of the other earth, the *Tuatha de Danan,* the wee folk and fairies, are dwellers in a world that is represented by the hillock or mound. "'Tis a large Síd in which the *Aes Síde* dwell," therefore equivalent to the mount, and their hollow in the mount is one with the Kamite Amenta. There is no consciousness of time in this happy other-world. Those who have dwelt there for centuries seem to have been there no time. This is one way of identifying the land with the earth of eternity. The Irish nether-world is the land of the ever-living ones; as an irresistible lure to men it is set forth as the land of ever-living, ever-lovely women.

In the Egyptian Ritual Anup, the jackal-god, the swift runner, who as the earliest form of Mercury preceded Taht-Hermes, is the guide of ways in the astral mythology and the conductor of souls in the eschatology. Anup was not only the guide through Amenta; he is also god of the pole-star and therefore lord of the polar paradise, before he fell from heaven and his station was assigned to Asar in the later solar cult. In our British and Irish mythology, Manannan, the son of Lir, is a form of Mercury. And in the legend of "Cormac and Faery" he is lord of the promised land. He also acts as guide to Cormac, and says to him, "I am Manannan, son of Lir, lord of the land of promise, and I brought you here that you might see the fashion of the land." This is the guide of ways, Ap-Uat, whom Cæsar calls the "patron of roads and journeys," who was worshipped by the Gauls above all other gods.

The great adversary of the solar god whom Horus went forth to slay is the Apap-serpent or dragon of darkness, a huge water reptile lying at the bottom of the abyss. We get a glimpse of this monster in the following description. In the Tale of Laegaire the land of heart's delight is described as being under the waters instead of across them, or in the hollow of the mount. This, however, involves no discrepancy. The nether-world of Ptah-Tanen was below the waves. When the sun entered the mount it descended into the hollow earth toward the bottom of the mount, which stood on its own fixed base in the abyss or surrounding waters of the Nun. The title of Ptah-Tanen indicates the land (ta) in the Nun or Nnu which engirdled the earth outside. Thus the outer world was below the level of the waters at the same time that it was in the nethermost parts of the mount of Amenta. This necessitated the rampart that was erected by the builder Ptah against the deluge and other incursions of Apap the destroyer. The mythical water round about the earth is described with exquisite delicacy of touch in the Voyage of Maelduin: "It seemed like a clear thin cloud, and it was so transparent, and appeared so light, that they thought at first it would not bear up the weight of the curragh" (ch. 23, Joyce). Looking down through this water of aerial tenuity, they saw a beautiful country, and in one place "a single tree," and on its branches "they beheld an animal fierce and terrible to look upon," and whilst they looked they saw the monster stretch forth his neck, and, darting his head downward, he plunged his fangs into the back of the largest ox of a whole herd. This he lifted off the ground into the tree, where he "swallowed him down in the twinkling of an eye." When Maelduin and his people saw this from the boat they were in fear lest they "should not be able to cross the sea over the monster on account of the extreme mist-like thinness of the water; but after much difficulty and danger they got across it safely" (Joyce, ch. 23). This lovely country seen beneath the waters, the sunken city of so many märchen, is the "beautiful Amenta" of the Ritual. The tree is the tree of life in Amenta, and the monster is the Apap-reptile. The ox as victim represents the bull of Amenta, a title of Osiris. The herd here answers to the herd of cows to which the bull is lord. There is also a man on guard at the tree with shield and spear and sword, who corresponds to Ra, the guardian who defends the persea tree (Rit., ch. 17) against the devouring monster Apap. The passage over the pellucid water with the monster lurking darkly down below is described in the Ritual. "O thou who sailest the ship of heaven over the gulf which is void, let me come to see my father, Osiris" (Rit., chs. 44 and 99). Horus and his companions had to cross the abyss of Apap, and the insubstantial element of the Irish version answers to the hollow void of the original.

When the deceased is making his way through Amenta, Hathor the goddess of love and loveliness = the amorous queen, emerges from the tree and offers him a dish of the fruit which she has gathered to woo him with. By accepting this he is bound to remain the guest of the goddess and return no more to the world of the living, unless by her permission. Hathor is identical with the amorous queen of the Keltic legends. Seventeen grown-up girls attend on her and prepare her bath. These in the original mythos are the seven Hathors, and it looks as if the seven had been changed to seventeen, which is a number otherwise unknown to the original mythos. Hathor is the goddess in the tree who furnishes the fruit on which the souls are fed. The amorous queen gives the magical fruit from her apple-tree to visitors from the human world. The queen of Love was called the Golden Hathor, and in the Tale of Teague the gracious queen is "draped in vesture of a golden colour." Hathor was the goddess of music, and the approach of the amorous queen of faerie is announced by music magically sweet. Hathor was the goddess who drew men with the golden cords of a love that was irresistible. This is naïvely rendered in the Irish märchen. When Maelduin and his men have stayed for three months with the amorous queen and enter their boat to sail away, she rides after them and "flings a clew" which the hero catches. It clings to his hand, and he is drawn back again to the queen by the magical clew that represents the cord of love. Hathor the queen of love is the provider of food and drink for the manes in Amenta, who have, or who pray to have, whatsoever heart can wish. So the amorous queen provides food and drink for the wanderers, which has every savour that each one may desire. Hathor was the goddess of beauty, to whom the mafkat and other precious stones were sacred. The necklace was her typical ornament, the predecessor of the cestus of Venus. And it is noticeable that the treasure snatched at by the foster-brother of Maelduin, which cost him his life, was the magical necklace that was in every sense irresistible. The lower paradise in which the tree of Hathor grows is in Amen-Ta. Ta is the earth or land. Amen signifies the secret or hidden. May not this be represented by Emain the *nomen regionis* in the voyage of Bran? From Emain comes the branch of the apple-tree, or fruit-tree that may have been a fig-tree, which would correspond more closely to the sycamore-fig of Hathor.

There is unlimited love-making in the land of the amorous queen, who is the Irish Aphrodité. She is a direct survival from the time when the divine female was the ruler of men and the object of their kneeling adoration. She is the queen of faerie, who was once the queen of love. Hathor in the Ritual is especially the sovereign. The speaker says, "Let me eat under the sycamore of Hathor the sovereign (ch. 52), among those who rest there." It is promised to the mortal who attains the elysium with the amorous queen that he shall enjoy the delights of love "without labour." Even in the Egyptian Ritual the speaker pleads that he may have the investiture of the garden, that he may be glorified there, eat and drink, and have his fill of sexual intercourse. The text in the Nebseni papyrus reads *nahap am,* not mere love "in the abstract," for nahap signifies coition. This is in agreement with the unlimited love-making in the land of women which was the primal paradise. The Kelt remains to-day a true child of the matriarchate that was piously transferred from earth to heaven. In this religion the mother with the child is the object of supreme desire, the religion that began as and still continues to be uterine. This divine ideal has fired the imagination of the Kelt as whisky fires the blood and brain. It was this that ultimately made him so devout a Roman Catholic with Mary for a portrait of the earlier amorous fairy queen. The Keltic land of promise is a land in which deep-bosomed, ever-living, glorious women dwell and make it worth while for men to strive and reach that heaven in the land of heart's desire.

In the Ritual, ch. 17, the nocturnal sun is represented as a cat, the seer in the dark who keeps the watch by night in Amenta. The cat especially protects the tree of life and its food and drink from the assaults of the serpent Apap and the encroachments of those prowling thieves the Sebau. The cat is said to "govern the Sebau, and regulate that which they do." The tree, be it remembered, is Hathor's in the Ritual, and she is the queen of love who reappears in Irish legends as the amorous queen. Now in the voyage of Maelduin they come to the "island of the amorous queen." They also come to a fort which is encompassed by "a great white rampart" wherein there is nothing to be seen but a cat that keeps on leaping from one to another of "four stone pillars." The fort itself is full of food and drink and shining raiment. As the voyagers are leaving, one of them tries to steal a necklace, whereupon the protecting cat "leaps through him like a fiery arrow, burns him up so that he becomes ashes," and then the cat "goes back to its pillar." This description indicates the nature of the type. As in the Ritual, the cat represents the protecting solar god. The cat in Amenta is going round the night-side of the solar circle. The four pillars were the supports at the four corners called the four pillars of Shu. The solar god as watchful cat consumes the thief (one of the Sebau) to ashes, and "goes back to his pillar" or goes on his way.

It is the zoötypes that tell the nature of the origins in sign-language and identify them as Egyptian. Two or three of these may be dwelt on for a moment. The cat as a protector of the "property" in Amenta; the ancient bird that renews its youth, not as the phœnix of fire, but by bathing in the lake of the water of life; the seven cows that give their milk in sufficient abundance to feed the whole inhabitants of the land of promise; the Apap-monster, the youthful solar hero, the mount of Amenta, and lastly the tree of life in the garden eastward of the mount. "When Maelduin was on his voyage he came to an island on which there stood at the centre of it —a single apple tree, very tall and slender. Its branches were likewise slender and exceeding long, so long that they grew up over the circular high hill and down to the sea that bounded the island." (Joyce, *Celtic Romances,* "Voyage of Maelduin," ch. 8.) So long were the branches that for three days and nights, whilst the ship was coasting the island, Maelduin held a branch all the time, letting it slide through his fingers, till, on the third day, he came to a cluster of apples at the very end. This was the fruit of the tree of life.

Alfred Nutt remarks on the gigantic stature of the people who are met with by Finn and his men in the land of marvels, but does not think the trait has any traditional significance (Bebind Story). But the giants of the promised land are identical with those in the Hebrew märchen, and the prototypes of both are to be found in the Kamite mythos. One origin will account for all. There are two classes of giants in the Ritual, the glorified and the wretched giant shades. The glorified ones are those who reap the fields of divine harvest in the lower Aarru and in presence of the powers of the east. These are said to be each nine cubits in height, *i.e.,* fifteen or sixteen feet. The giants of the fore-world were not magnified men, but representatives of the elemental powers, like the gigantic Apap of darkness, the hippopotamus of Sut, the crocodile of Horus, the giant ape of Hapi, the lion of Shu, in the pre-anthropomorphic phase. This was the race of giants that preceded the pygmies of Ptah in the Egyptian mythology. So in the Irish legends the Brobdingnagian race of the Fena, the mighty heroes of enormous stature, passed away and were followed by the little men who were Lilliputians in comparison; there are also dwarfs as denizens of the land beneath the waters. (Joyce, *Old Celtic Romances,* "The Last of the Fena.")

Africa, the home of the pygmies, is presumably the birthplace of the dwarf races now represented by the diminutive wee folk of the Dark Continent. The earliest emigrants who made their way out of that land and wandered over Europe would be akin to these in stature, like the Lapps who follow them at a short distance. These were the wee folk in human form. But there is another factor to be taken into account before we can ascertain the origin of the wee folk as spirits in a tiny fairy shape. These do not simply represent the pygmy race of human beings, but are the same primitive people translated into spirit-world, from the time when the race was of the pygmy stature. We gather from the secret wisdom that the earliest beings who entered the nether earth were dwarfs or dwarfish people. The god Ptah, who opened the under-world by tunnelling the mount of Amenta, is himself a dwarf. The seven Knemmu that assisted him were pygmies. First come the African pygmies. Second, the mythical pygmies of Ptah. Third, the human souls that are the same in stature. Fourth, the wee folk of the legends, who inhabit the mounds, who work the mines, who dwell beneath the sea, the natural, the mythical, and spiritualistic dwarfs being somewhat mixed up together. The märchen or folk-tales of the Asiatic and European races are the *débris* of Egyptian mythos. Fairyland is no conception of the Kelt, nor original product of the Aryan imagination; it is *the Kamite earth of eternity in the lower world of the mount of earth which was excavated by the pygmies of the opener Ptah.* From no other land or literature than the Egyptian can we explain the wee folk in the fairy mound or Síd. (Síd, pronounced shee. Cf. the Egyptian she or shu, for the hollow, the void, and sheta, the sarcophagus.)

Various episodes of the passage through the nether earth and over the waters to the upper paradise that were represented in the drama of the mysteries and detailed in the mythos have been reduced to mere allusions in the Ritual. For example, there is a land of weeping, a dwelling-place of the god Rem-Rem, or Remi the Weeper. (Rit., ch. 75, and Litany of Ra, line 21.) The manes on his way to Annu says, "I have come out of the Tuat. I am come from the ends of the earth. I pass through the noble dwellings of those who are coffined. I open the dwelling of Rem-Rem, that is *the place of weeping.* (Rit., ch.75, Renouf.) In the Irish legendary "Yarn" the voyagers come to the Island of Weeping. This island is large and "full of human beings black in body and raiment, and resting not from wailing and weeping. Whosoever lands in this place falls a-weeping." This lot happens to one of Maelduin's foster-brothers and others of the wanderers who are sent to bring him off. The coffined ones in the Ritual, chief of whom was Osiris in his coffin, offer a *raison d'être* for the weeping in Rem-Rem (as a place).

In their thirty-first adventure Maelduin and his companions come to an island of which it is said, "Around the island was a fiery rampart, and it was wont ever to turn around and about it." This was evidently the revolving sphere. "Now, in the side of that rampart was an open door, and as it came opposite them in its turning course, they beheld through it the island and all therein, and its indwellers, even human beings, beautiful, numerous, wearing garments richly dight, and feasting with golden vessels in their hands. The wanderers heard their ale-music, and for long did they gaze upon the marvel, delightful as it seemed to them." This is a glimpse of the pleasant plain, the promised land, the land of heart's delight and ever-living women, with their lure of love—in short, the Aarru-paradise. There was a protecting rampart reared around this garden, the lower paradise in the earth of eternity. "A divine domain hath been constructed for me; the name of it is the garden of Aarru. I know the garden of Aarru; the wall of it is steel" or the bright shining ba-metal. (Rit., ch. 109.) Inside the rampart were the glorified ones, "each of whom is nine cubits in height." Also the manes were there as workers in the human form, who cultivated each their field of corn and fed upon the food and drank the beer that were made from it and divinized as sustenance for souls.

The twofold paradise, terrestrial and celestial, is also extant in Irish legendary lore. Not as an Irish conception, pagan or Christian, not as a "vision of the great young godland-haunted Irish imagination," but as a survival from the Kamite source that once supplied the world with a system of representation, mythical and eschatological, which remains almost intact as Egyptian, whilst it has gone to wreck and sea-drift elsewhere on other shores. The typical mount of earth with its hollow of the under-world has its representative in the Irish mound of the Síd, and the elysium across the sea is one with the paradise of Hetep over the celestial water.

Alfred Nutt points out the difference betwixt the Irish paradise in the hollow hill and their paradise that is over-sea. "In the hollow hill type (The Wooing of Etain) the wonderland is not figured as lying across the sea, but rather . . . . within the Síd or fairy hills. No special insistence is laid upon the immortality of its inhabitants," nor is there any portion of this land in which the amorous women dwell alone, as in the elysium over sea. (Nutt, *The Voyage of Bran. The Happy Otherworld,* ch. 9.) This is exactly as it would be if derived from the Kamite original. The lower paradise of two is in the mount of earth, also called the funeral mount of Amenta. The departed are not born immortals in that land; immortality is conditional. They have to fight and strive and wrestle with the powers of evil to compass it. These, like the Irish manes dwelling in the Síd or hollow hill, were the "folk of the goddess," who was Hathor in the mount; whereas the spirits made perfect in the upper paradise are more expressly children of the supreme god, who was Horus, or Ra, or Osiris, according to the cult. We can trace the voyagers on the water way to this *upper paradise.* When Horus, or Ra, and his companions have conquered Apap, the Sebau, and other monstrous progeny of darkness, the solar bark emerges from the under-world upon the horizon of the orient heaven, and enters the water of dawn which is designated the "lake of emerald." The speaker says, "O ye gods in your divine cycles who travel round the lake of emerald, come and defend the great one who is in the shrine from which all the divine cycle proceedeth"—that is, the god on board the solar bark. So in the voyage of Maelduin, after passing the islands of monstrous animals, the giants and devourers, the companions come to a sea of green crystal sparkling in the sunlight, and so transparent that they could see the sand quite clearly at the bottom. In this water they saw neither monsters nor any ugly animals. In like manner the crystal water is described in the Ritual as having neither fishes nor snakes in it. (Rit., ch. 110; *Voyage of Maelduin,* ch. 22, Joyce.)

The "Isle of Truth" is a name of the divine land across the waters, "Whosoever set foot on it was unable to tell a lie." A naif way of indicating its truth-compelling influence. Surely this must be the Egyptian Maat, the land of truth. In starting on his voyage over sea it is the desire of the speaker to "attain the region of Maat" (Rit., ch. 1), which may be the region of truth, law, or righteousness. The celestial bridge betwixt the two is described in the *Voyage of Maelduin* as a bridge of crystal leading to a palace (ch. 18, Joyce). It also appears in the form of a solid arch of water which spans the elysian island from side to side. Under this the travellers walked without ever getting wet. (ch. 25, Joyce.) This in heaven is the archway of the galaxy that was represented as the river overhead. It is related that when the voyagers came at last in sight of land it was a little island with a large palace on it. Around the palace was a wall white all over without stain or flaw, as if it had been carved out of one unbroken rock of chalk, and it was so lofty that it seemed almost to reach the clouds. "A number of fine houses, all snowy white, were ranged round the inside, enclosing a level court in the middle on which all the houses opened." (Joyce, *Old Celtic Romances,* pp. 131-133.) This in the Egyptian is the city of the white wall of the celestial Memphis that was seen in the northern heaven at the summit of the mount. The Osiris looking up to this, his journey's end, exclaims "May Sekhet the divine one (consort of Ptah) uplift me so that I may arise in heaven and issue my behests in Memphis, the city of the white wall." (Rit., ch. 26.)

The mount or rock of Anup, also called his cliff (Rit., ch. 31), survives as the rock or fortress of Manannan in the land of promise. One title of the Irish mount is "the hill of two wheels in the pleasant plain of the Land of Promise." (*Clidna Dinnshenchas,* Nutt, *Voyage of Bran,* p. 197.) This promises to shed light on a crux in the Ritual. In the description of the mount and the two portions of Sut and Horus the sign O is employed ambiguously. (See Book of the Dead, Renouf, pp. 193-199.) But if the halves of night and day were figured as two cycles or circles of time the reading would be perfected, and the mount of Hetep would also be the hill of two wheels in the pleasant plain. It is said in the Rig-Veda (ch. 3, p. 6), "the two adorable Krishnas successively revolve." It is also said, "the dark day and the light day revolve alternate." The table-land which is called the plain of joy, the great plain, is one with Hetep, the table of the mount, in the Kamite paradise. The bathing on the great table-land in the island of the amorous queen is particularly noticeable. All who reach that summit bathe. Cormac was bathed, "though there were none to bathe him." This answers to the place of final baptism in the lake of propitiation and of *equipoise,* where souls are purified "in the most high degree" (Rit., ch. 97). The tree of food in the midst of the garden of Hetep grows the fruit on which the gods and the assembled multitude of the manes feed and live. This, as aforementioned, is repeated in the Tale of Teigue as a "thickly-spreading apple-tree bearing fruit and ripe blossom alike." This tree is to "serve the congregation that is to be in the mansion." It also bore a fruit for the gods and spirits. Beer is the divine drink of the beatified, not only in Amenta, but also in the upper paradise. Osiris in the mythical Memphis, Hat-Ptah-Ka, says "O thou God of nutriment, O Great One who presidest over the mansions on high, give me bread and beer" (Rit., ch. 106). And beer was supplied in overflowing abundance. In the Wooing of Etain, Mider the lover sings of beer as the divine drink in the earthly paradise. "Heady to you the ale of Erin, but headier is the ale of the Green Land." "When thou comest, Woman, to my strong folk, fresh swine's flesh and beer shall be given thee by me, O white-skinned Woman." It is also said of this wonderland, "When it rains, 'tis beer that falls." Now, the beer that rained in the Irish paradise is identical with that which came down from the Egyptian heaven.

Notwithstanding the difference betwixt the number of attendants on the amorous queen and the number of Hathors, the seven have been correctly preserved in their primitive shape and character as the seven cows in the Irish paradise, the same as in the meadows of the Egyptian Aarru. In the adventures of Cormac in Faëry, the old wife tells the true tale of her seven cows, the milk of which is plentiful enough to supply all the inhabitants of the land of promise with nutriment. These are the cows of the Elysian Fields in the Ritual who are called the seven cows, providers of plenty. They are portrayed along with the bull who is personified as the hero in the folktales (*Papyrus of Ani.*, pl. 35; Rit., ch. 148), and are invoked by the spirit of the Osiris to give him food and drink and sustenance for ever. Thus the "Irish version of the happy otherworld" becomes a dim-eyed memory of the old Egyptian astronomical mythology and eschatology. And as it is in Ireland so was it in Babylonia, India, China, Greece, Britain, and other lands that were lighted by the rays of Egypt's wisdom that went down as the sunset of an ancient world, and rose again unrecognized by name as dayspring of the new. And thus the nearness to nature in its tenderest traits, the nobility of manners, the serene placidity, to be found in the Welsh and Irish fragments of the antique lore, were not necessarily native to the soil, but may have belonged to the higher civilization that was elsewhere developed, as now we know it to have flourished in the valley of the Nile. Neither was the painted Pict or woad-stained Briton the source of all this gentilesse and chivalry imported in the mythos and replanted in the islands by the "men of peace." Such characters as Arthur and his twelve knights were not the products of men who dwelt in caves and wore the skins of animals. His mother Arth was goddess of the Great Bear—she who was Ta-Urt, the oldest form of the Great Mother in the astronomical mythology of Egypt. And as the characters were imported in the mythology, so likewise were the traits of character, and therefore these would not be indigenous to the islands of the north.

The Upper Mount of Glory.

Whatsoever shape was taken by the eternal dwelling-place on high, it was only attainable at the summit of the mount that reached up to the never-setting stars. And there is a consensus of widely-scattered evidence to show that the paradise of peace and plenty, of reunion and rejoicing, which is the object in view of "the Osiris" all through his journey outlined in the Ritual, is the upper paradise of a legend that is universal, the origin of which can be discovered in the astronomical mythology of Egypt. The general tradition is that this paradise was a primæval place of birth, and that it was in the north, upon the summit of a mount now inaccessible to the living anywhere on earth. This circumpolar paradise is known to the oldest races in the world as an initial starting-point for gods and men.

We have sought to trace an origin for the primitive paradise of this universal legend to the human birthplace on *the mount of earth,* or Apta, with the beginning in the time and the domain of Sut, which was commemorated as a secret of the Sphinx. This place of birth, as we suggest, was thus repeated as a place of rebirth by the Egyptian mystery-teachers in the astronomical mythology, from which the universal legend spread around the world.

The Namoi, Barwan, and other tribes on the Darling River, in Australia, point out a paradise up the Milky Way to which the spirits of the righteous are welcomed by Baiame, who corresponds to the Kamite god of the polar paradise. He is called "the great master" and is the maker. It is he who sends the rain; and it was he who initiated the black-fellows into their mysteries (Brough Smyth, vol. ii. p. 285). The aborigines of New Holland describe the dwelling-place of "Bayma" as a paradise to the north-east in a beautiful heaven. His throne is a crystal mountain of vast magnitude, the base of which is fixed in the great water, and its stupendous summit rises to the stars. In addition to this upper paradise upon the mount they also have an earthly paradise below. Moodgeegally, the first man, who lives in this nether paradise, is alone immortal; the same as human Horus in the lower paradise of Amenta. He has the power and privilege of visiting the upper heaven of Ballima, which is a three days' journey from the happy land below. He climbs up to the heaven north-east by a lofty and precipitous mountain covered with beautiful trees. His ascent on foot is made easier by a path winding round the mountain which he ascends. A ladder or flight of steps erected at top of this mountain, leads up to heaven itself. Ballima, where the sun shines by night beneath our earth, is the Egyptian Hades. The exceeding high mountain is the mount of Amenta, and the great water out of which it rises with the steps up to heaven is the Egyptian Nun. But neither the aborigines of New Holland, nor the missionaries, nor Mr. Manning knew anything of the Egyptian Book of the Dead, or of the Nun, or the mount of Amenta, or the Aarru-fields, the double paradise, or the steps that led up to the solar boat. Yet these and other features of the Kamite mythos are all identifiable in the version here recovered from the aborigines of New Holland. (Notes on the Aborigines of New Holland made by James Manning in 1844-5. Copy presented by the author.)

The mount of the gods and the glorified is common in Africa, where, as we hold, the foundations of Egyptian mythology were laid; and there, as in other lands, it is a point of departure in the beginning for the race. Duff Macdonald says of the Yao tribes: "Some distinctly localize Mtanga as the god of Mangochi, the great hill that the Yao people left. I regret much that I did not see this hill before leaving Africa, as I have heard so much of it . To these people it is all that the many-ridged Olympus was to the Greek. The voice of Mtanga, some hold, is still audible on Mangochi. Others say that Mtanga never was a man, and that Mtanga is another word for Mulungu (god or spirit). He was concerned in the first introduction of men into the world, and he is intimately associated with a year of plenty." Thus we find the main features of the mythical mount extant in Inner Africa, which culminated in Mount Hetep as Egyptian. It is the seat of the gods and the glorified. It is the primæval birthplace. It is the land of promise, of peace and rest, of water and eternal plenty, the scene of the Golden Age. It is the primitive paradise of the aborigines (*Africana,* I, 71). The god whose seat or station was the pole is the power that gives the water of heaven to our world. Anup in Egypt is the master of the inundation (Rit., ch. 97). The pole was imaged by the mount, the cone, the round hillock, the artificial mound. Now the Gold Coast Africans worship a deity or nature-power named Bobowissi, whose seat or stool is the conical hill near Winnebah known as the Devil's Hill, a title given by the Portuguese. He is the maker and sender of rain, which descends in a devastating deluge when he is provoked to anger by those who break his law. Bobowissi also appoints the local deities, even as Anup assigned their places to the seven on the opening day of creation in the Egyptian solar mythos (Rit., ch. 17; Ellis, *The Tshi-speaking People*, p. 22).

The heaven of the western Inoits, in which good spirits dwell, is a paradise above the firmament. This revolves about a mountain of prodigious magnitude and majesty, a Meru that is situated in the remotest part of the polar regions. Here, as in the Egyptian circumpolar paradise, the spirits whose innate excellence has been proved by an extraordinary activity for good go to mingle with the never-setting stars. Various other features of this heaven are Egyptian. Mount Hetep as the land that is blest with water and the breezes of the north is an African, but not an Esquimaux, ideal. The god, as Num, is the breath of those who are in the firmament. The Inoit supreme being Torngarsuk, the Great Spirit, is the "lord of the breezes." Still more remarkable is the fact that the souls of the Inoit are drawn from *an atmospheric reservoir of soul*, to which in death the spirits of the just return. This is identical with the Egyptian lake of Sa, one of the two lakes in the polar paradise, which is the source of spirit-life and of life to the gods and the glorified. They also have the earthly and celestial paradise, one at the root of the mount, the other at the summit; the same as the Egyptian Aarru in Amenta below, and Aarru in the polar paradise of the northern heaven (Réclus, *Primitive Folk*, Eng. Trans., p. 106). This upper world of the Esquimaux, says Dr. Rink, may be considered identical with the mountain about the summit of which the vaulted sky for ever circled round. This is the celestial mountain as a figure of the pole. It was their mount of glory lighted with the aurora borealis.

The Egyptian Ta-Nuter or divine land of the gods is usually described as being in the Orient. But there was also a Ta-Nuter Meh-ti, which is rendered by Brugsch, "das nördliche Gottesland" (Brugsch, *Astron. and Astrol. Inscript.*, p. 179). This was the land of the gods in the north—that is, the polar paradise in heaven, not an elevated part of our earth. The breeze of the north was the breath of life to the Egyptians. It is synonymous with blessedness. The paradise of Hetep is the garden blessed with breezes. The breeze of the north, however, would not represent heaven to the dwellers in the northern quarter of the world. But the paradise was figured in the north originally, and there it remained in every land to which the wisdom of Old Egypt went. This will explain the paradise of Airyana Vaêjô described in the Avesta. Ahura-Mazda tells Zarathustra that he has created a delectable spot which was previously unapproachable or nowhere habitable. But in this first of regions and best of countries there was *winter during ten months of the year*. "Ten months of winter are there, two of summer, and these (latter) are cold as to water, cold as to earth, cold as to plants; then as the snow falls around there is the direst disaster" (Vendidad, Fargard i.). The good god made the good creation, and Angro-Mainyus, the dark and deadly, is said to have formed a mighty serpent and brought on the frost that was created by the Dævas, who correspond to the Sebau in the Ritual as agents of evil in physical phenomena. It is also said in the Minokhird (p. 322, ff.) the Dev of winter is most vehement in Airyana Vaêjô. Which does not mean that the primal paradise was created at the northern pole of the earth, to be overtaken by the glacial period. The true interpretation is that the legendary paradise was astronomical, and that it was an enclosure at the north celestial pole, and not in the northern regions of the earth. In the Vendidad version it has been made geographical and rendered according to climate in some northern region of the earth; the evils of a winter world being then attributed to the devil, or the opposition of the black mind, Angro-Mainyus. There was no frost or winter in the circumpolar paradise, nor in the African birthplace of the legend in the oasis, whereas frost and winter were both met with in the highlands of the north, whether in Asia or in Europe, and this leads to a paradise in which there are ten months of bitter winter weather, which is the result of rendering the celestial by the terrestrial north. In a supplement to the first Fargard of the Vendidad the time has been changed to suit a milder climate: "Seven months of summer are there; five months of winter were there," which is in direct contradiction to the original text, and also opposed to the prototypal paradise with the life-giving breeze of the north in Africa, but is suitable to a milder climate, although one that is still in the cold north. The Chinese paradise, like the Egyptian, is at the north pole, the apex of the celestial mount. The summit is the seat of the gods. Heaven divided into the ten regions of space is identical with the Kamite heaven at the summit of Mount Hetep, that was divided into ten divine domains (Rit., ch. 110) which followed the celestial heptanomis and the enclosure of Am-Khemen, and preceded the zodiac with twelve signs. In no country is the mount of the north more sacred than in China. For thousands of years the Chinese emperors have ascended the holy mountain T'ai to offer sacrifice to heaven. This mount is designated "Lord of the World." To the north there is nothing but hills upon hills. It has 6,000 steps of hewn stone, each fifteen feet in length, leading upward like a staircase to the skies, exactly the same as the throne of Osiris, who "sits at the head of the staircase."

The pole-star determined the one visible fixed centre of the starry universe, and the name of the Ainu as Ai-no-Ko is said to signify the "offspring of the centre." That centre was the circumpolar paradise. The Japanese god of the pole-star, Ame-no-mi-naka-nushi-no-Kami, is likewise "the lord of the centre of heaven." The tradition of the Ainu is that they came from the northern summit of the world. So high and inaccessible are those lofty tablelands that none of the living can attain them now. But the ancestral spirits go back to them after death. This, of course, identifies the circumpolar paradise of all the legends that had but one and the same origin—in the astronomical mythology. The region is identified still further by the bears. The ancestors of the Ainu are said to have married the bears of the mountains in this high homeland of the north (Griffis, *The Mikado's Empire,* pp. 27-29). We have the bears to-day, seven in the lesser and seven in the larger constellation, still revolving round the stellar mount of glory.

The Koreans possess the same tradition of the human birthplace in the circumpolar paradise. Their first man, as ruler of Korea, descended from the great white mountain Tê Pek San. This also was the point of migration or beginning for the race, as it is in various other versions of the primeval tradition (Lowell, Percival, *Choison,* p. 209). The Badagas say that in the north arises Mount Kaylasa, their Meru. In the north infinity opens on the kingdom of the shades. If four men be dispatched to the four cardinal points, three will return, but never will he who has walked beneath the rays of the polar star. He makes the ascent of the north, which is not a quarter, but the summit to a mountain, as in Egypt. All that is great and powerful comes from the north. The mother of the cow-goddesses dwelt on the Amnor, and the ancestors of the Badagas followed the cow. They came from the paradise of the north. Between the invisible mountains of Kaylasa and Kanagiri flows the dread river that divides the world of the living from the world of the dead. That is the celestial water, the river of souls, which runs betwixt Mount Manu and Mount Hetep on the Egyptian map of heaven. This is not the north of the geographers. At the top of Mount Kaylasa is the palace of souls, the home of the blessed, in which their efforts are crowned with final success. This palace of souls answers to the royal palace referred to in the Ritual, where the speaker says, "I have made my way into the royal palace, and it was the bird-fly (or Abait) who brought me hither" (Rit., ch. 76, Renouf).

Montezuma the elder, in repeating an ancient tradition to Cortez, said, "Our fathers dwelt in that happy and prosperous place which they called Atzlan (a word that signifies whiteness). In this place there is a great mountain in the middle of the water which is called Culhuacan, because it has the peak turned somewhat over toward the bottom; and for this cause it is called Culhuacan, which means 'crooked mountain.'" The rest of the description of this delightful country shows that it was the circumpolar paradise upon the summit of the mount. And when it is identified with the mount of Hetep we may surmise that it became the mountain with its apex leaning over because it imaged the pole; so that when the pole-star changed, the bent posture of the summit would become the curved figure by which Culhuacan was portrayed. In an Assyrian prayer this celestial mount is called the silver mountain. It is said, "Grant ye to the king, my lord, who has given such gifts to his gods, that he may attain to grey hairs and old age! And after the life of these days, in the feasts of the silver mountain (at the white summit of the pole), the heavenly courts, the abode of blessedness; and in the light of the happy fields may he dwell and live a life eternal, in the presence of the gods" (*Records,* vol. iii. pp. 133-4). Gwynnwesi, the blissful white abode of the Welsh, is another form of the paradise on the summit of the celestial mount in the north, which answers to the white mountain of the Koreans, the city of the white wall, the peak of pearl, and the Assyrian land of the silver sky. Another form is Gwasgwyn, the white mansion, which is the happy abode of the beatified dead. The imagery survives in the legends of Merlin, where we meet with the glass house, the bower of crystal; the tower without any wall, or without any "closure"; the transparent prison that was aerial as "a smoke of mist in the air." Also the typical tree appears as a noble whitethorn, all in bloom—a figure, as we take it, of the starry pole.

When Merlin died he is said to have taken with him the thirteen treasures of Britain, as he passed into the house of glass (Guest, *Mab.*, II, p. 354). The ancient British Avalon was represented as an island in the north on which the "Loadstone Castle" stood. This identifies the island with the celestial mount and the magnetic pole of the north. Another local figure of the same significance is the Monte Calamitico, a magnetic mountain in the sea to the north of Greenland (Humboldt, *Cosmos,* vol. ii. p. 659, Bohn's Ed.). In the Apocalypse of Zosimas the Hermit there is a description of the paradise in which the blessed dwell. The seer was conveyed across the water that divides our earth from heaven by means of *two trees* which bent down and lifted him over in their arms (James, *The Revelation of Peter,* p. 69). The two trees are Egyptian, but as usual in Christian documents, the miracle has been added. "Lo, I come," says the seer in the Ritual. "Let me plunge into the divine pool beneath the two divine sycamores of heaven and earth," when he is about to ascend that "most conspicuous but inaccessible stream," the Milky Way (chs. 97, 98).

One ideograph of Hetep, the mount of glory, is a table heaped with provisions as the sign of plenty. In the mythical rendering it is a table-mountain. This will explain the round table of King Arthur and that table of the sun which was said to exist among the Ethiopians as described by Herodotus. "There is a meadow in the suburbs," he says, furnished with the cooked flesh of all sorts of quadrupeds. It is filled with meat at night, "and in the day time whosoever chooses comes and feasts upon it. The inhabitants say that the earth itself from time to time produces these things." Such is the description given of what is called the table of the sun. (Book iii. 17, 18.) This table of the sun is referred to in the Ritual (rubric to chs. 1 and 72). If the deceased has kept the commandments, it is said that there shall be given to him bread and beer and flesh upon the table of Ra—that is, the table of the solar god, which was the table-land upon the summit of Mount Hetep, the mount of peace and plenty, where the followers of Horus as the spirits of the just made perfect gathered together at the table of the Lord for their eternal feast. When the beatified spirit attains the meadow of Aarru and the "table of the sun," he says, *"I rest at the table of my father Osiris"* (Rit., ch. 70). The deceased asks that he may be made strong with the "thousands of loaves, beer, beef and fowl, and the flesh of the oxen and various kinds of birds upon the table of his father" (ch. 69). Thus, as the Egyptian Ritual of the Resurrection shows, "the Lord's table" was an institution in the Osirian mysteries which did not wait to be founded at the beginning of the present era. It has, of course, been remarked that the fellowship of Jesus with the twelve in the Gospels is a table-fellowship, and that he uses the image of a supper to symbolize the meeting in his father's kingdom. The gorging in a paradise of plenty described by later legends is indicated in the Pyramid Texts (Pepi I, 432; Merira, 618). When the deceased is on his way to the mount of glory, he is borne to a region where he is filled with food by being fed from evening until daybreak, and then he is said to seize upon the god Hu, the god of aliment, of corn, of food—in short, the bread of life in a spiritual sense. The gorging and guzzling which are customary accompaniments of the Christmas festival in the north are a survival from the time when the primitive paradise was portrayed as a place of the grossest plenty. Even the more refined Egyptian gloried in the prospect of the earthly abundance being repeated for ever in heaven. This is what he says on sitting down at *the table of the Lord*: "I sit down in the midst of all the great gods of heaven. The fields lie before me; the produce is before me; I eat of it. I wax radiant upon it, I am saturated with it to my heart's content." (Rit., ch. 77.)

The mount or altar in Hetep which is imaged as a pile of plenty, a table of offerings, a mountainous heap of food, is the prototype of those artificial mountains exhibited, for example, in Naples at the public festivals, from which all kinds of eatables are distributed in the wildest profusion among the people, whilst the goddess Tait, who is the cook of divine dainties in that land of Brobdingnagian abundance, will account for the paradise of cooks and cookery which survives in various versions of Le Pays de Cocagne, where the most delicious food already cooked is spontaneously produced like fruit upon the tree of life. A version of this promised land is current in the Southern States of America, amongst the Negroes, who preserve the tradition of a tree of life, on the branches of which hot buck-wheat cakes hang over a lake of molasses that takes the place of the Kamite lake of the waters of life. This land of the goddess Tait, the cook of the cakes and joints of meat already cooked, is the Kamite original of Cockaigne, the land of laziness and luxury, in which the streets were paved with pastry. The name is probably derived from the cookery: *coquo,* in Latin, to cook; *Kuchou,* in German, for a cake; and *cocaigne* in Old French, signifying abundance. The witches' Sabbath, however degraded, was a mode of celebrating this great festival according to the most primitive ideal of a paradise which overflowed with food and drink, and the glory of the sex was celebrated with Titanic women, fierce as Sekhet, in evoking and matching the animal passion of primitive men. Even in the Rig Veda (ch. x. p. 154) it is said of the man who wins this heaven of blessedness, "Non urit ignis membrum virile nec arripit deus Yama semen ejus" (much womankind shall be his in heaven). The witches' festival was held on the hill-top or high place, which is Mount Hetep in miniature. Each one brought an offering of food and drink to the feast, and Mount Hetep is an altar, heaped with oblations and offerings for a feast that was to last for ever. The food was brought in raw for this celestial banquet. The speaker says, "I net the ducks and I eat the dainties. I take care to catch the reptiles." With these we may compare the reptiles in the witches' cauldron. There is also a gruesome witch-like Kamite goddess Tseret, with long, flowing red hair, who is armed with horns. The divine drink that was brewed in Hetep as beer is imitated by the witches as a product of the magic cauldron, the cauldron of Keridwen in the ancient British mysteries, which survived to some extent in the witches' Sabbath.

The milk of seven rich-uddered cows was typical of eternal plenty in the green pastures of this African paradise; or, in the later anthropomorphic imagery, seven women, young and beautiful as Hathor the goddess of love and loveliness, of music and dancing and sexual delight, were the figure of infinite felicity in this heaven which Mohammed so successfully adopted for the Turks. In both phases the seven were seen as the seven great stars of Ursa Major that were in attendance on "the bull of the seven cows," or the spirit of the glorified deceased who had risen to heaven in the image of Amsu-Horus. The Hebrew paradise upon the summit of the mount in the promised land is the same ideal of primitive blessedness. "In this mountain," says the prophet Isaiah, "shall the Lord of Hosts make unto the people a feast of fat things, a feast of wines on the lees, of fat things full of marrow; of wines on the lees well refined" (Is. 25, 6). Papias, that ignoramus of a primitive Christian, also recounts how "the elders who saw John, the disciple of the Lord, related that they had heard from him how the Lord used to teach in regard to these times, and say: *The days will come, in which vines shall grow, each having ten thousand branches, and in each branch ten thousand twigs and in each true twig ten thousand shoots, and in each one of the shoots ten thousand clusters, and on every one of the clusters ten thousand grapes, and every grape when pressed will give five and twenty metretes of wine. And when any one of the saints shall lay hold of a cluster another shall cry out, 'I am a better cluster; take me: bless the Lord through me.'* In like manner (the Lord declared) *'a grain of wheat would produce ten thousand ears, and that every ear should have ten thousand grains, and every grain would yield ten pounds* (quinque bilibres) *of clear, pure, fine flour; and that all other fruit-bearing trees, and seeds and grass, would produce in similar proportions* (secundum congruentiam iis consequentem). *And these things are borne witness to in writing by Papias, the hearer of John, and a companion of Polycarp, in his fourth book, for there were five books compiled* (syntetagmena) *by him. And he says in addition, 'Now these things are credible to believers.'*" (Irenæus, B. 5, ch. 33, 3-4, Ante-Nicene Library.)

The Kamite paradise was the place of plenty and of strong drink. The Indian's idea of future felicity, which consisted in being eternally intoxicated, is but an extension from this primary basis. The "cauldron of regeneration for spirits" was derived from the brewing-vat. Also it is noticeable that the Egyptian garden of Aarru or Allu, in the Ritual, has the same name as the grape, the vine-branch, and the wine. Hetep was the land that flowed with milk and honey, and the imagery is demonstrably Egyptian. It flowed with honey because the flowers were always in bloom. A curious illustration of this land of honey and its Egyptian origin may be drawn from the Ritual. There is a typical conductor that leads the spirits to their home in the Egyptian fields, called the abait or bird-fly, which in one form is the praying-mantis and in another the honey-bee. This divine guide is called in ancient texts the tiller of the rudder of the neshemit ship of Osiris in which the spirits made their voyage across the waters to the land of honey, guided by the bee (Rit., chs. 76 and 104). The land flowing with milk is indicated by the seven cows of plenty, whilst the heavenly Nile would represent the honey, as it was the water that was likened to honey for sweetness. Indeed, there is a tradition that in the time of Nefer-Ka-Ra the Nile ran with honey or the taste of it for eleven days. (Brugsch, *Egypt under the Pharaohs,* Eng. trans. in one volume, p. 30.) The Egyptian paradise of Hetep is mapped out in ten divine domains which correspond to a heaven in ten divisions. These ten divisions were lost, or superseded, like the ten islands of the lost Atlantis, when the zodiac of twelve signs was finally established. And naturally there would be ten populations lost, as in the Assyrian deluge. It follows that the ten tribes of Israel, who preceded the twelve, were lost at the same time and in the same way, the legend being one as astronomical, wheresoever met with in the märchen. There is a tradition that they will be found again in the Aarru-Hetep or Jerusalem above, the promised land which they attained at last. In the Æthiopic "Conflict of Matthew" it is said that the ten tribes "feed on honey and drink of the dew." "The water we drink is not from springs, but from the leaves of trees growing in the gardens" (James, *Texts and Studies,* 70). These were they who passed in death like all the rest across the waters "into a farther country where mankind never dwelt," because it was in the spirit-world. (2 Esdras xiii. 40-42.)

The 110th chapter of the Ritual suffices of itself to prove the Kamite origin of the mount of glory and the circumpolar paradise. This is the chapter of coming forth from the nether-world by day, or with the sun, and arriving in the garden of Aarru, on the mount of resurrection in Hetep, and at "the grand domain, blest with the breezes." This was the heaven lifted up by Shu of old as the summit of attainment. It is called "the beautiful creation which he raiseth up," the mansion of his stars which had been again and again renewed in the heaven of astronomy. In the eschatology it was the heaven of reconciliation, reunion, and of rest. It had been the heaven of Abydos, of Annu, Thebes, Memphis, Hermopolis, and other cities on earth, and now it was the heaven of eternity, the heaven of spirits perfected; also the heaven of Chaldean, Hebrew, Hindu, Japanese, Greek, and all the others who repeated the astronomical imagery and founded their religious teaching on the wisdom of ancient Egypt. The summit of Hetep was the seat of Hathor, queen of heaven and mother of fair love on earth. She who had drawn the world in offering her full breast as nurse to Horus now offered it upon the mount of glory to the weary spirits whom she gathered in her motherly embrace. She was also represented by those seven cows or meris, as the giver of plenty in the meadows of Aarru, so abundantly that the river called the Milky Way was as the overflowing plenitude from this perpetual source. On a tablet in the Louvre (ch. 14) this divine mother of gods and men is asked for "the white liquor that the glorified ones love." This is distinctly called milk upon a Florentine tablet (2567), and vases of her milk are mentioned in the inscriptions of Denderah (Rit., ch. 110, note 9, Renouf). Hesit the cow is identified with Hathor the divine mother, the fair nurse, the mistress of heaven and sovereign of the gods. She was the cow-mother, and her child was the calf who became her bull as fertilizer. Hence the deceased as Horus in Hetep exclaims, "I am the bull, raised on high in the blue, lord of the bull's field" (Rit., ch. 110, Renouf), whose cow or nourisher is Hesit. (Dümichen,

Resultate, 27, 6.) In this way the cow of heaven supplied not only milk for the infant Horus, but for all who were reborn as babes in the new life, and the heaven of plenty and of rest was tenderly pictured in the welling bosom of the motherhood, thus divinized upon the mount. When the departed have reached the summit of life upon the mount of spirits perfected, they emerge in the garden of Hetep or paradise of Aarru. Here they attain the land of promise in the highest sense of spiritual fulfilment. They eat of the fruit of the tree and drink the water of life, or the milk of the old First Great Mother, who yields it in the form of Hesit the cow: the ancient mother of gods and men to whom the Egyptians assigned a foremost station in the starry heavens. Here the beatified spirits who sat upon their thrones of ba-metal, "raised on high in the blue," among the never-setting stars, extended the hand of welcome to the coming generations of human beings. Three classes of human beings are recognized in the past, present, and future of existence: the *Pait* are those of the past, the *Rekhit* are the living, and the *Hamemet* are the future generations. In one of her inscriptions Queen Hatshepsu appeals to these latter as future witnesses to the glory of her present work. She says, "I make this known to the Hamemet, who will live in times to come." (*Records,* vol. xii. pp. 131-136.) The name denotes the unembodied, or, more literally, the un-mummied, from *Ha,* before, and *mem* or *mum,* the mummy. These are the future beings to whom the glorified spirits extend their welcome in the garden of beginning and rebirth; and it is in this enclosure or paradise that we shall at last discover the garden on the summit of the mount in the north that has become a traditional cradle and creatory of life itself as the rebirthplace of the glorified. It is said to Ra, who had become the highest god, "Glory to thee upon the mount of glory. Hail to thee who purifiest and *preparest the generations yet unborn,* and to whom this great quarter of heaven offereth homage." (Rit., ch. 130.) This great quarter was the northern summit in the region of the two lakes of Sa and of Purification. The divine rebirthplace of the soul constellated in the meskhen was converted by the later races, Asiatic, European, American, Polynesian, into the primeval place of human birth, from whence the successive migrations were supposed to have issued forth, because the localities and the scenery of earth had been substituted for those of the divine or mythical world of the Egyptian eschatology. The "original Aryan home," the Iranian paradise, the Semitic garden of Eden, the Greek elysian fields are each derived from the Egyptian Sekhet-Hetep, the fields of peace and plenty, or the Sekhet Aarru, where amid the still waters are portrayed the islands of the blessed, the amaranthine meads and pastures ever green. When Assyriologists speak of Urdu the mountain of the world as the primitive cradle of the human race (*Trans. Soc. Bib. Arch.,* vol. vi. p. 535), they are oblivious of the fact that there are fifty or a hundred such cradles of the race. Hence over eighty different sites have been assigned to the garden of the beginning, called Edin or Eden by the Semites. The Akkadian Urdhu is one with or corresponds to the Egyptian Urtu, a name both for the ascent or mount and the thigh or haunch, as a figure of the birthplace, human or divine. The emigrants from Urdhu, like the Meropes, were the people of the thigh. The Hyperboreans were reputed to dwell above the north wind, as Festus says, "supra aquilonis flatum," which gives us an astronomical hint. Apparently the bird aquila represents the Egyptian vulture mut, which is described in the Ritual (ch. 149) as being on or above the leg constellation: "I am the divine vulture who is on the uarit." But whether it does or does not, the Hyperboreans are localized above Aquila in the northern heaven in the celestial pole-land, where dwelt the ancestors of the Ainu, and the Hamemet of the Egyptian theology. Again, the constellation of the thigh, as sign of the meskhen, womb, or birthplace, will show us the origin of the Meropes. The word μέροπες (or people of the thigh) was a sacred expression used by the Greeks to denote mankind. It is said of the Hyperboreans by Hellanikos (fragment 96) that they dwelt beyond the Ripaian mountains, and were the teachers of justice, and ate the fruit of trees. This identifies them with the glorified spirits in the polar paradise by two unmistakable determinatives of locality. One is the tree, or wood, of life, on the fruit of which the gods and glorified were fed; the other is the maat or judgment seat upon the summit of the mount, where sat the great judge as Anup, or Atum, or Osiris, in succession according to the reigning dynasty of gods, that were stellar, lunar, or solar.

Mythical monsters like the Cyclops have descended from this birthplace of the beginning. According to Hesiod, the Cyclops were Titans, and the Titans are the giants who were properly a group of seven in later tradition. They were the assistants of Haphæstus, the worker in fire, who was the Greek Vulcan. This tends to identify them with the seven Knemmu, who were the assistants of Ptah, the metallurgist; the seven who were the giants of an earlier time as turners of the sphere in huge and monstrous form. Homer calls Mycenæ, the ark-city on the summit, the altar of the Cyclops; and the altar is a final form of the mount which was figured in the constellation "Ara." In one character the seven powers that were grouped in the Lesser Bear were the giants, and the giants as Cyclops had but one eye between them. Naturally Polaris as the one eye to the seven was said to be the one eye of the seven, and the giants were then said to have been one-eyed. This would account for the Arimaspoi and other one-eyed people as dwellers in the uttermost vertical north. All was golden in the primal paradise, and according to Hesiod there was a "golden race of men." These were they who came the first. This race was stellar, like the gold that made the circumpolar heaven golden. They were the glorious ones, the never-setting ones, the born immortals in the everlasting "golden-hued region whose food never fails," described in the Vendidad (Fargard ii. line 103).

Now, the question for those who looked up longingly to this paradise of peace and plenty as the summit of attainment for another life was how to reach that landing-place of souls and haven of supreme desire. There was heaven, but by what means could the height be climbed or the water crossed when as yet there were no boats or bridges built? Clearly there was nothing for it, from the first, but to leap or swim the waters flowing twixt the mount that was mundane and the mount of glory. Hence the Great Mother Apt and Sut her son were figured as totemic hippopotami, and Sebek as the crocodile, for the passage of the water. This was in a mythical representation of natural phenomena, the same mode of progression being continued in the eschatology. When the deceased is about to cross the water betwixt the two worlds he says, "It is I who traverse the heavens. May I have command of the water." (Rit., ch. 62.) But, previous to being self-invested with the necessary power, he prayed to be carried across by the Great Mother, who was imaged as the pregnant hippopotamus in the constellation of the bear, or as the milch-cow in the meskhen, or the moon. For this reason the Great Bear was also called the coffin of Osiris, as the typical place of rebirth. She is the ark of souls who saved them from the waters in the cabin which was uterine. The mother of life as Apt the water-cow was followed by Hesit the milch-cow, and in a later though very ancient representation it is the domesticated cow that carries the dead across the waters to the summit of the mount. But the earliest carrier of souls across the waters in death is Apt, the most ancient mother of life. In the astronomical phase she is the goddess of the seven stars in Ursa Major and mother of the seven typical eternals who were safe for ever from the deluge in the never-setting stars (Rit., ch. 17). In lands of lower latitude than ours the Great Bear, *i.e.*, the female hippopotamus, set at times beneath the horizon or was hidden behind the mount of earth, to rise again as the bringer-forth of life from the waters, because the reproducer of souls for a future life. It is as the bringer of human souls to their rebirth that she, the hippopotamus, is portrayed as human in her abundant breasts and procreant womb. In that guise she was the womb of life, great with the souls she carried across the waters on their way to the upper paradise, when there was neither boat nor bride extant. This is generally represented by the mummy being borne upon the back of the cow that carries it off full speed by land or water till the islands of the blessed are in view. In these scenes the dead are carried outside the cow, whereas with Apt the souls were carried in the uterus or meskhen. In the mysteries of the Ritual (ch. 64) when the Osiris (deceased) is crossing the waters that have burst forth in a deluge, he exclaims, "Anup is my bearer." In this instance the jackal is the carrier, the psychopompus, because it represents the power of the pole as the support of the soul in death. In consequence of being raised up by Anup, the guide of roads (Ap-Uat), the deceased also exclaims, "I hide myself among you, O ye stars that never set." Which shows that he was raised to the region of the eternals, the Akhemu-Seku, or non-setting stars (ch. 33) whose position was fixed for ever as the most ancient lords of eternity, with Anup at their head. When the concept of an atmosphere succeeded the likeness of water, the birds of air could be employed as types. The sun was represented by the golden hawk, the moon by the black and white ibis; the stars, that did not set, as beautiful white birds a-floating on the lake in the paradise of Aarru on the summit of the mount. The deceased also exclaims, "I am the swallow! I am the swallow!" as one particular form of a bird of passage, on his way to the celestial country (ch. 86). Or he assumes the power of the bennu-bird, or the shen-shen, both of which ascend the air to a great height in spiral whirls. The deceased in this character prays that he may "wheel round in whirls" and circle heavenward with the spiral motion of the bennu, *i.e.*, the typical phœnix (ch. 83). It was in this guise the soul of Osiris rose again to ascend the tree of life or of dawn, hence the soul of *the* Osiris does the same. The moon was imaged also as the ibis on whose wings the orb made its celestial ascent. The Osiris pleads that he may ascend to heaven in the disc of the moon, or in the power of Taht, the lunar god who showed the way by night. The ibis now bears off the deceased across the water on its wings, and does battle with Sut, the power of darkness, for a passage.

The natives of Torres Straits Islands have a tradition that at death the spirits of their departed wing their northward way in the shape of flying-foxes to the polar paradise of all the aboriginal races. The power of wings is thus added to the spirit as the superhuman mode of flight. Swimming and flying are the two modes of locomotion here illustrated, until we come to the tree as means of climbing. The natural human way of ascent is climbing. But by no direct means could the helpless watchers climb the heavens with their hands and feet, and they had no wings of their own. As they were frugivorous, they could climb the tree, and the tree supplied a mental means of ascent for those who climbed the heavens as the souls of the departed. Dawn on the summit was imaged as a great green tree upon the mount. Thus the ascent was represented by both the mountain and the tree. Both were means of the ascent at the coming forth by climbing from the dark land of Amenta. It may be premised that the papyrus-reed which rose from out the water was an earlier type of climbing heavenward than the tree. Child-Horus on his papyrus was a figure of this ascent by means of the plant or stalk. When the Messu came by water it was by climbing up the stalk like little Jack. The pedestal of Horus, made of stone, was based on the papyrus-plant emerging from the water, and when this was buried with the mummy it was a type of the ascent to heaven. The ascent emerging from the deep, as Mount Meru in India, was called "the lotus (= papyrus) of immensity," which also shows the water-plant to be a co-type with the mount or tree as the figure of the ascent. The tree is portrayed as a means of salvation amid the overwhelming waters which had to be crossed by the manes in the Ritual. The tree, then, like the mount and steps, was a typical means of ascent to heaven by which spirits attained the polar paradise. It was a natural ladder. There is no race so primitive but has a tree-type of the ascent to heaven. With the Mbocobis of Paraguay the souls of the dead ascend the llagdigua tree, which is a connecting link betwixt their earth and heaven (Humboldt). The same water and tree occur in the Rig-Veda (II, 66 and 183), when Bhuggu, son of Tugra, has to cross the great waters and is "cast headlong into the deep and plunged into inextricable darkness." He likewise clings for support to the tree "stationed in the midst of the ocean." The Australian natives make use of the tree as a mode of ascent to heaven for the spirits of the departed. The wizards also profess that they go up to consult the spirits of the dead by ascending a tree. Some of them make a pathway for the spirits to ascend and descend the tree of earth and heaven by cutting out a strip of bark, taken spirally from the top of a large tree down to the ground. (Howitt, *On some Australian Ceremonies of Initiation*.) The tree or pole as means of climbing is variously illustrated. The Yao-Miao people bind their dead with withies to a tree for the soul to make the ascent. At other times the branch of a tree or bamboo pole is stuck in the grave for the soul of deceased to climb by (Colquhoun, A. R., *Across Chrysê*, vol. ii. p. 369). The Guarinis of Brazil were the worshippers of the god Tamoi who ascended the tree of dawn, like Tum his Egyptian prototype. Up this the spirits were to follow in his wake, and he would welcome them to paradise when they attained the summit of the tree. The Polynesians tell of the tree that reached up to the moon. When the deluge of Raitea occurred and the world of the seven divisions was submerged the survivors were saved by the tree that reached up to the moon or on an island (the mount) named Toa-marama, the moon-tree or the tree reaching to the moon (Ellis, *Polynesian Researches*, vol. ii. p. 58). So that both the mount and tree are here described together under one name. The Samoans have various legends of the way to heaven. One of these describes it as a mount, the summit of which reached up to the skies. Another tells of the tree that measured sixty miles in height. According to one account, when the topmost branches of the tree were reached the climbers had to wait for a high wind which swayed them to and fro for a while and all of a sudden slung them into paradise. The Samoans also had a tree with steps that formed a sort of ladder up to heaven. Thus the mount, tree, and ladder were all extant in one group amongst the people of the Pacific islands (Turner, *Samoa*, pp. 199, 200). Both the mount and tree were modes of ascent in thought, and physical means of reaching a little higher towards heaven in making offerings to the powers. In Africa the prayer-tree is a common institution. The Yao people lay their offering of first-fruits at the root of the prayer-tree before they themselves begin to eat the new crop of maize or pumpkins. In another widespread custom the offerings were hung upon the branches of the tree. The Molucca Islanders have the typical tree of ascent to heaven. This tree stood at the place of sacrifice where the offerings were made. Thus with them, as with various other primitive races, the tree was the first natural altar and stairs that figured the way and means of ascent to heaven. The Kasia of Bengal hold the opinion that the stars are souls which once were men who climbed up to heaven by means of the tree, and were left aloft in the branches when the trunk was severed below. In the Huron version given by Brebeuf, the tree of ascent to the upper world has passed into the trunk of a tree that enables the departed to cross the water of death. Here, too, we find the guide of roads for the spirits as the dog that is both the guardian and the guide of souls. In the Choctaw rendering the tree has become a log of pine stripped of its bark—that is, a kind of slippery pole by which men cross or climb to paradise or else fall off into the chasm that awaits the wicked down below.

Then the tree type passes into the pole and staff. But the most tangible figure for mental foothold in climbing based on natural fact was the mount. In almost every land there is a mountain known as the mount by which the souls of the dead ascend to the paradise first mapped out astronomically at the celestial pole. This in mythology is the mount of the north, the mount of the cow, of the haunch, the navel, the womb, the leg, the meskhen and other images of the birth-place on earth applied to the place of rebirth in heaven. In Borneo the native guides pointed to the summit of Mount Kina-Balu as the landing-place of the ancestral souls. They showed the meat on which the spirits fed, but did not dare to pass the night in this abode of the re-arisen dead, or rather the local likeness of the celestial mount. In the Rocky Mountains, near Denver, is the "Garden of the Gods" and the mount of ascent up which the manes climb to attain the summit of life and happiness. So is it in West Java, where the mountain Gunung Danka is described as being the site of paradise, which means, here as elsewhere, that the paradisaical mountain was the earthly local representative of the celestial mount of glory.

"The Path of the Shades," by Basil Thomson, in the *New Review*, April, 1896, p. 417, contains an account of the Fijian sacred mountain Nakauvandra, together with the motive for rearing it. According to local tradition, the ghosts of the dead were great disturbers of the living. They were willing to leave this earth if they could but make their way to the sacred mountain by which the heaven of rest was reached. The tribes then banded together to make a road for the ghosts to travel over on their last journey, so that they might trouble the living no more. In the year 1892 a surveyor employed to traverse the boundaries of native lands in Fiji re-discovered this most ancient Via Sacra, or pathway of the shades. He was taken by his guides along the crest of a high ridge, the water-shed between the Rewa river and the eastern coast of the island of Vitilevu. Cutting a way through the undergrowth, he found that the path on which he walked was level, and was seldom more than two feet wide; that hill top was joined to hill top by a razor-edged embankment. He reflected that nature never works in straight lines with so soft a material as earth: that natural banks of earth are always washed into deep depressions by the rains until they become mere rounded uneven slopes. And when his guides had cleared away a patch of the undergrowth, he came upon unmistakable proof that the embankment on which he stood was artificial. The little glens had been bridged with causeways, thirty or forty feet in height in the deepest parts, tapering to a feather-edge at the top, so as to form a winding path along the line of the hill tops that extended, so the natives said, clear to Nakauvandra, the sacred mountain, forty miles away. For a people without spades or picks, the piling of this embankment must have been a gigantic task. Every pound of earth must have been carried up laboriously in little cocoanut-leaf baskets, and paid for in daily feasts to the workers. And all to represent the road to heaven.

Whatsoever the means of ascent, the toil of climbing up to heaven was stupendous. The Mexican Mount Culhuacan, for instance, is a Hill Difficulty indeed. The upper part is formed of sand so fine that it offers no foothold for any mortal tread. This is a mode of showing, not merely saying, how hard it is to climb, and none but righteous spirits could attain the paradise upon the summit.

Naturally the staircase, as the work of human hands, is comparatively late. But it follows, as the pathway from the tomb. At

Abydos, the seat of Osiris as god in the highest is at the head of the staircase, when he was the power presiding over the pole of heaven (Rit., chs. 7 and 22). Thebes was another city in which the celestial staircase was imaged. As it is said in the inscription of Queen Hatshepsu, "Thebes is a heaven upon earth. It is the august staircase of the beginning of time. It is the Utat of the universal Lord, his heart's throne, which sustains his glories and holds within it all who accompany him" in the circle of Osiris, who presided at the top of the steps above the pole of heaven. (Rit., ch. 7; *Records,* vol. xii. p. 133.) The mound or stairway with the seven steps was permanently figured in the seven-stepped pyramid of Sakkarah as an image of the mount with steps that showed the way to heaven in the astronomical mythology. The ambition of the Babel-builders, described in the book of Genesis, is to erect "a tower whose top may reach to heaven" (Gen. xi. 4). Here the tower with seven tiers takes the place of the mount with seven steps or tree of seven branches, or the ladder, as a mode of reaching the summit of attainment.

The pillar follows the mount as a co-type of the pole, first as a pillar of wood, then as a pillar of stone, or metal, or of glass. In various legends the celestial pole is imaged as a pillar of glass or other slippery substance, which also indicates the difficulty of getting to heaven. This is the pillar by which the manes make their ascent every Sabbath day from the lower to the upper paradise; and having got a glimpse of all the glory, they slide down again into the subterranean world (Yalkut Kadash, f. 57. c. 2, Stehelin, vol. ii. p. 25).

It is related in a Taoist work that once upon a time a Chinese king endeavoured to climb up to heaven by a pillar of enormous height, but it was so slippery that he always slid back again to the ground (*Chinese Repository,* vol. vii. p. 519). And without doubt this slippery pillar still survives as the greasy pole of the British pastimes, which are not continued for their grossness, but because they once had a sacred significance. In this, the heaven of eternal plenty on the mount is represented by the leg of mutton at the top of the pole.

The slippery pole or pillar of glass can be paralleled in the Odyssey. "One rock reaches with sharp peak up to the wide heaven, and a dark cloud encompasses it. No mortal man may scale it or set foot thereon, for the rock is sheer and smooth as if it were polished."

This is not the mundane mount where mortals find their foothold, but the celestial mount, which none but spirits ever scaled in any form of the mythology. When glass began to be manufactured it would supply the material for a very perfect likeness to the aërial mount of heaven. The tower of glass would succeed the tower of brick and the mound of earth. There is a story told by Nennius in his *Historia Britannium* of "Nimeth the second who came to Erin," and who, in sailing the ocean with his thirty vessels (luni-solar month), sees a glass tower in the midst of the waters, with men on it who give no answer when they are addressed. This seems to have been because of its height. So in Taliessin's account of the glass fort of Arthur, "three score hundreds stood upon the wall; it was hard to converse with the watchmen." Nimeth attacks the tower, and all his thirty vessels are sunk or wrecked. (Rhys, *Hibbert Lectures,* pp. 263-264; Skene,

Book of Taliessin, vol. ii. 155.) Taliessin the Bard professes to have been in the tower of glass as well as in Amenta or Hades. This juxtaposition of the tower with the nether-world shows that the dome of glass was a form of the celestial summit. There is a glass hill in the Norse folk-tales. The princess is only to be won by the youth who can ride up the hill of glass. The ash-lad, a male counterpart of Cinderella, is the only one who at all succeeds. At the first trial he rides a third of the way up, and the king's daughter rolls a golden apple down to him. On the second day he rides two-thirds of the way up, and wins a second golden apple. On the third day he ascends to the top of the hill, and takes the third apple from the lap of the princess. Of course he wins the daughter of the king and half the kingdom besides. In this version the glass hill is the mount of the pole. The king in these märchen is Ra in the Egyptian mythos. The princess was Hathor, goddess of love. The kingdom in two halves was the double earth. Horus wins the second half, and unites the two into one kingdom by climbing the hill of glass and winning the princess as his wife. The tree on which the golden apples grew is the tree of dawn, the tree of Hathor the princess. The hero, who is the king's son, sometimes lives as a kitchen-lad beneath the stairs; and in the mythos the staircase is a co-type with the mount or hill of glass. This shows that the stairs stand in the lower world, where the fire of old suns and moons will explain the ashes in which the cinder-girl or ash-lad proverbially sit in their poor and lowly estate when the moon and sun are in the nether earth.

One typical mode of rising to heaven was by means of a dense column of smoke! This was acted by kindling a fire on the grave of the deceased, so that the spirit might ascend as it were in a chariot of cloud. (*Samoa,* Turner, pp. 199 and 335.) The Samoans explained that this was done to save the soul from sinking into the pit. The same type was obviously continued in the smoke of incense rising from the altar. Other illustrations might be cited to show that the ladder by which the wizard, witch, or conjurer sought to reach the land of spirits was imaged by means of something drawn out of or in some way emitted from his mouth, a mere thread, a film, a substance like gossamer, which probably represents the spirit in a filamental form, when the soul was identified with the breath or under the same name as it is in the Egyptian word "nef" for breath and spirit. Thus the substance drawn from the mouth of the wonder-worker represented a kind of ladder as the visible mode of ascent for the soul exhibited in primitive mysteries. The mystery is still extant and still performed to a gaping crowd in the English market-place, when the conjurer, who is now an acrobat, draws from his mouth a ladder or spiral pole made of shavings, or shall we call it the cone of the pole, which was once a figure of the ascent to heaven, that was followed by the ladder and the steps, the pyramid, the Babel-tower, the minaret and spire, until its final form upon the lowermost line of descent became the pinnacle made in spiral coils of shavings proceeding upward from the conjurer's mouth by dexterous sleight of hand, as the great mount of god, the staircase of Osiris, the figure of the pole at its final vanishing point. Thus the conjurer's twist of shavings drawn from his mouth may illustrate a mode of the mysteries when it was taught that the soul of breath came forth from the mouth as its own ladder or means of ascent to the upper world.

Another illustration of the difficulty in climbing up to heaven may be seen in the ladder formed of knives which is made use of by the Taoist jugglers in China. This is constructed of two upright bamboos, with knives or sword-blades set between, edge uppermost, for steps. The ladder was a co-type with the mount and steps of ascent. The Japanese have a mythical mountain called Kurahashi, the dark ladder. The speaker, in a passage quoted by O'Neil, says he climbs this vertical ladder by the aid of his sister. "Steep though Kurahashi be, steep it is not when I climb it with my sister" (*The Night of the Gods,* vol. II, p. 1015). The sister is a goddess whom we look upon as lunar. There was also a ladder-mount near Ptolemais which is mentioned by Josephus (*Jew. War,* II, 70). Certain sacred hills in England, called the "Step Hills," repeat the ladder of ascent to heaven. There is one near Ivinghoe (Bucks) which is evidently an artificial formation. Cader Idris is reputed to have had 365 steps from bottom to summit. The Egyptians solemnized a feast of the dead or festival of the steps, by which they celebrated the ascent of the manes from the valley of Amenta to the summit of the mount.

When bridges were built, a bridge supplied the typical means of crossing the celestial waters. The earliest figure of a bridge in heaven was probably the rainbow. This was the Norse bridge made by the gods that reached from earth to the height of heaven and down again to the earth, and was therefore a visualized way for the coming and going of souls. In the *Prose Edda,* Gangler asks, "Which is the path leading from earth to heaven?" The answer of Har is, "Hast thou not been told that the gods made a bridge from earth to heaven and called it Bifrost? But perhaps thou callest it the rainbow." (*Prose Edda,* 13.) The name of Bifrost denotes the evanescent aërial bridge. The rainbow is certainly a form of the celestial bridge, though possibly the type may not have been Egyptian. It is a pathway for spirits to the Brahmanic Svarga. It is the snake-bridge that crosses the river of the dead to the dwelling beyond in a North American Indian version of the mythos. Also, the souls of Maori chieftains are supposed to mount heavenward by means of the rainbow. The Samoans called the rainbow Laa Maomao, the great step or the long step of the god (Turner, *Samoa,* p. 35). Wang-liang, or the king's bridge, is a constellation in the Chinese planisphere which is described as the bridge that spans the moat of the ruler's castle. This is crossed by kings and chieftains when they go to pay their homage to the monarch. The moat was also crossed by boat. This moat corresponds to the waterway of the Egyptians, and to the "way which is above the earth"; in short, the galaxy on which the souls of the dead were carried in the bark of Ra (Rit., ch. 4). The bridge, boat, and water, together with the tree of life, and other symbols of the garden of peace, including the kissing doves, may be seen portrayed upon the ordinary willow-pattern china plate. The bridge survives in some old British ballads as the "Brig o' Dread." One of these is called "a lyke-wake dirge," in which the journey of the dead is described. In "Lady Culross's Dream" it is "a narrow bridge of tree" suspended over an unfathomable gulf. But, as Scott points out, the most minute description of "the Brig o' Dread" occurs in the legend of Sir Owain, who, after many frightful adventures in St. Patrick's purgatory = Amenta, arrives at the bridge which, in the legend, is placed between purgatory and paradise.

> " Lo! Sir Knight, see'st thou this?
> This is the Bridge of paradis.
> Here over thou must go.
> Whoso falleth off the Brigge adown,
> For him is no redemption."

He falls into the void of Apap, or the lake of outer darkness. The moral of the dirge is that whatsoever good works have been done on earth will be waiting at the bridge and help the deceased to cross the gulf. (Scott, *The Minstrelsy of the Scottish Border*.)

The pyramid is an artificial figure of the mount as means of the ascent to heaven. And now, if we place ourselves with the mummy at the bottom of the Well, we shall see that the tubular shaft of the great pyramid at Gizeh represented the way to heaven as it was imaged to Egyptian thought. The Pharaoh resting at the foot might scan not merely the starry vast, but could fix his gaze in death upon the heaven of spirits at the summit of the mount, the paradise of peace, the enclosure that was finally configurated in the circle of the seven pole-stars that crossed his telescope (the passage pointing northward) one by one in the circuit of precession, or the heaven of eternity. The pole-star, *a Draconis*, was not the only one that would come within range of that great tube. The great pyramid was founded on the Egyptian astronomy, but was not built simply to register the fact that *a Draconis* was the fixed point and polar pivot of all the stellar motion during some 3,700 years in the vast circuit of precession. The ceilings of the pyramid chambers were sprinkled over with stars to resemble the face of the sky by night. Astronomical tables gave the aspect of the heavens *tenat* by *tenat* throughout the year. So that the manes "had but to lift their eyes" and see in what part of the firmament the course lay night after night. Thus, lying in his sarcophagus, the dead man found his future destinies depicted thereon, and learned to understand the blessedness of the gods. (Maspero, *Egyptian Archy.*, Eng. trans., pp. 158-160.) The chief course was mapped out along the river of the Milky Way, as is shown in the Ritual, by the boat of souls ascending to the polar paradise. The deceased, who is about to rise again and set his legs in motion, prays that he may "go up to Sekhet-Aarru, and arrive in Sekhet-Hetep." Lying as the mummy in Amenta, he says "I shine above the leg as I come forth in heaven, but (here, meantime) I lie helpless with a corpse-like face. I faint. I faint before the teeth of those whose mouth raveneth in the nether-world." (ch. 74, Renouf.) The cynosure of the watcher is a point above the constellation called "the leg" by the Egyptian astronomers. This was a constellation in the northern sky which has been identified by Renouf with the group of Cassiopeia, and which the Egyptians named the meskhen or creatory of the cow. The earliest figure of an ark in heaven, or on the waters of the Nun, was that of Horus on his papyrus-reed, who issued as the soul of life in vegetation from the abyss. As the sacred bark borne heavenward in the mysteries shows, this was a figure of the papyrus-flower which had been the cradle of Child-Horus previous to its being imaged in the eschatology or astronomy. When the boat was built the souls of the deceased were ferried over the waters in the mythical bark which was at first stellar, next lunar, and lastly solar. There is a bark that voyaged round the pole as Ursa Minor, with seven souls or glorious ones on board, seen in the seven stars that never set, a primary type of the eternals. In another text we find a prayer for the deceased, "that he may reach the horizon with his father the sun, in the solar bark; that his soul may rise to heaven in the disc of the moon; that his Sahu (or celestial body) may shine in the stars of Orion, on the bosom of heaven" (*Book of Sen-Sen, Records,* vol. iv. p. 121). Here are three forms of the boat of souls, one in the stellar, one in the lunar, and one in the solar representation, at three different stages of the mythos. Modern astronomy speaks of the starry vast as a revolving sphere, where the ancient wisdom called it the ship of heaven or the bark of eternity. At first the superhuman force that hauled the system round was thought of as a mighty monster swimming the celestial lake—a hippopotamus or a crocodile, or a compound of both. This was the Great Mother of the revolutions, who was constellated as the *primum mobile,* the goddess Apt depicted in the Great Bear as the procreant womb of life, the mother and nurse of universal life. Seven powers were born of her, and represented under different types as hippopotami, crocodiles, jackals, apes or uas-eared animals. Seven such were figured as the pullers round the pivot of the pole. When the boat was launched the seven were grouped as seven kabbirs or sailors in the Lesser Bear that made the voyage nightly, annually, and for ever round the mount. They were likewise portrayed as seven tow-men of the starry vast, and *haulers* of the solar boat, the bark of millions of years, the vessel that was rowed by the twelve kings or twelve great gods around the final zodiac. We learn from the solar mythos that the rope of the towers was made fast to the star Ak, which is to be identified with the pole. The tow-men say, "The rope is with Ak." "Ra calls it, and the rope puts itself in its place." Ra is then in Amenta, and the rope of the towers is fastened at the upper end to the pole. Ra says, "Power to you, towers. Tow me to the dwelling of stable things. Free yourselves on this mysterious mountain of the horizon." This towing upward of the solar bark is one of the great mysteries of Amenta. (*Book of Hades,* vi. pp. 8-32.) The "navigators for this great god" who tow the boat are also said to take their oars and row for Ra. Ra says to them, "Take your oars, unite yourselves to your stars." "O my pilots, you shall not perish, gods of the never-setting stars" (Akhemu-Seku). Thus the solar boat or ship of heaven was navigated by the gods of the non-setting stars who voyaged round about the pole; who did not sink below the horizon, but became the lords of eternity.

A Chinese constellation in the Milky Way is called "the ship of heaven," and the "ship of Nu" as Egyptian IS the ship of heaven by name. It is sailed over the void of the Apap-reptile or dragon of darkness, also called the lake of Putrata, into which the souls fall headlong who do not secure salvation on board the bark, and have no other means of attaining the "tip of heaven" in the Aarru-paradise

(Rit., ch. 99). The ship Argo Navis, as a constellation, is a reduced form of "the ark of heaven" which is described in the Ritual (ch. 99). Four parts of the ship of Nu remain in the Arabic figure of Argo Navis, viz., the "poop," the "keel," the "mast," and the "sail." In the Ritual the "ship of Nu" is described in all its parts. "Backbone of Apuat" is the name of the keel. Akar (in Amenta) is the name of the hold. "Leg of Hathor" is the name of the hull. The "two columns of the nether-world" is the name of the stem and stern posts, or masts. "Amsta, Hapi, Tuamutef, and Kabhsenuf" are the names of the ribs; "Nut" is the name of the sail. "Bearer of the great one whilst she passeth" is the name of the mast. "Lord of the double earth in the shrine" is the name of the mooring-post. The foundation was laid on, or in, the backbone of Anup, which was once the type of stability as a figure of the pole, the earliest fixed foundation laid in the building of the heavens. Akar is another name for Amenta, the hollow nether-world of three, this ship being a three-decker. Amsta, Hapi, Tuamutef, and Kabhsenuf are the supports of the sky at the four corners or sides of the vessel. They are also the four oars of the vessel. The mooring-post was an image of the pole, to which the stellar ark or solar bark was fastened by the cable, as it made the voyage round the starry mount. The ship of heaven, then, is a figure of the nether-world in its hold and of the four quarters in its ribs, which are also represented as the four paddles, one at each of the cardinal points. This was constellated in the heavens as an ark that made the voyage up the Milky Way to the tip of heaven and the place of coming forth upon the mount of glory. The ship of heaven was an ark of salvation for souls. Those who did not find safety on board are described as falling headlong into the gulf of Putrata where the dragon Apap lurked to devour them. Now, in the planisphere the constellation Hydra is next to the ship Argo, and Hydra the water-snake is identical in character and position with the Apap-reptile who devoured those that fell into the void, otherwise the bottomless pit of the abyss. A knowledge of this ship and its constituent parts, together with the course of its journey through the heavens, was necessary to the initiate in making his passage to the paradise of the pole. The Osiris was not allowed to pass on board unless he could answer every question put and tell the name of every part of the vessel. The names given show that the different parts of the vessel were configurated in the stars according to the mythical types, and that the mystery was astronomical. Finally, the great bark of salvation was solar, with Horus at the outlook. The deceased prays to the god who is on board, "O Ra, in that thy name of Ra, since thou passest through those who perish headlong: do thou keep me standing on my feet." "Are you coming into the bark?" says the great god Atum-Ra, with a naïve familiar invitation that reminds us somewhat of the invitation "come with us" of more recent salvationists. "The bark advanceth. Acclamation cometh from the mount of glory and greeting from the lines of measurement." These are the cheers with which the boat is hailed and welcomed by the inhabitants of the upper paradise. "Lo, the lamp is lifted up in Annu" as a light by night to lead them on the way when they come to the heaven of the stars that set, and they have to steer by the pole-star as their guide of ways. While the Osiris passes over the waters to the west the Khabsu gods get ready for lighting up the heavens with their starry lamps, to greet the passengers approaching in the bark with acclamations of great joy. "All right is the Osiris; his future is in Annu," the eternal city at the pole. The glorified deceased sails in the great bark on the stream of the god Hetep, the White Way, until he comes to the ten divisions of the circumpolar paradise. These he enters to take possession of them one by one. As an astronomical foundation, the upper paradise of all mythology upon the mount of glory was dependent on establishing the celestial pole for a fixture in the waters of surrounding space, or, as the Ritual phrases it, "a mooring-post" for the ship of souls. Here was the rock of safety and the tree to which the sinking spirits clung for their salvation. Here the mariner says, "I make myself fast to the block of moorage on the heavenly stream." That is, to the pole which was figured as the final mooring-post upon the landing-stage of an eternal shore.

The Kamite paradise, as an enclosure of the water and the tree of life upon the summit of the mount, is traceable in four different forms. At first it was the primitive paradise of the Oasis in the south. Next it is the circumpolar paradise of Am-Khemen, upraised by Anhur in the north. The third one is the paradise of Atum in the garden of Amenta. The final paradise was founded on the mount of glory for the spirits of the just made perfect in the heaven of eternity. Thus there are four types of paradise. And these apparently are enumerated and described in Irish legendary lore when Cesair, "the first woman who landed in Ireland before the Flood," says of her great knowledge, "Truly I am well versed in the world's history, for *Inis Patmos* is precisely *the earth's fourth paradise,* the others being (1) *Inis Daleb* in the world's *southern,* (2) *Inis Escandra* in its *boreal part,* and (3) Adam's paradise." The fourth paradise is that in which the righteous dwell who have attained to everlasting life (*Adventures of Teigue, Son of Cian,* Nutt, *The Happy Otherworld,* p. 203). In such ways relics of the astronomical mythology remain unrecognized in many scattered fragments of the ancient wisdom.

EGYPTIAN WISDOM AND THE HEBREW GENESIS

Book VII

THE Egyptian system of uranographic representation has been outlined and many of its details have been identified in the chapters on the astronomical mythology. It has now to be shown that the so-called "legends of creation" chiefly known as Semitic are the detritus of the Egyptian wisdom. These legends did not wait for their beginning until the Mosaic Pentateuch had been carried round the wide circumference of the world either by the scattered Jewish people or the Christian missionaries. As we have seen, the Semitic theologians did not know enough of the ancient sign-language to distinguish the evil serpent from the good, the great Earth-mother from the chimerical dragon of the deep, or the beneficent spirits of elemental nature from the Sebau, the Sami or fiendish forces of external phenomena. The Semitic versions of the legends, Babylonian, Assyrian, or Hebrew, mainly reproduce the *débris* of the astronomical mythology, which has so often been reduced to the status of the nursery-tale. It is their fatal defect that they are not the original documents, and have no firsthand authority. In these the primitive wisdom of old Egypt has been perverted, and the mythical beginnings, which had their own meaning, have been transmogrified into what is herein termed a cosmogonical creation. For example, the mythical abyss or deep was not the mother of all things. That was the Mother-earth in the abyss, the nun, or firmamental water. As the Mother-earth she brought forth her elemental progeny in and from the abyss. Hence she was the wateress, or wet-nurse who suckled her young within the earth, as it is said of the monster Tiamat, because, as primordial bringer-forth, she was the Mother-earth. In the Babylonian legends of creation the seven associate-gods, who are the creators in the Egyptian mythos, have been converted into the seven evil spirits of a later theology. And on one of the tablets (W.A.I.4.I.1.36, 37) it is said of these seven evil spirits, "The woman from the loins of the man they bring forth." Thus the creation of woman is made to be the work of seven evil spirits, who, as the Kamite wisdom witnesses, *did not originate* as wicked spirits or as powers of evil. (Sayce, H. L., p. 395.) The legends of creation are known, more or less, as Hebrew, Phœnician, Babylonian, and Assyrian, but as Kamite they have not been known. And when the mythical representations of natural phenomena first portrayed by the Egyptians were turned into cosmographical creations by the Semites, they had no verifiable meaning either as history or mythology. Even Lenormant held that the Chaldaic and Hebrew versions had one common origin and were not derived from each other, but he made no attempt to trace that origin to the Egyptian astronomical mythology, which was to him a sealed and secret book. Egypt's knowledge of beginnings was laboriously derived by the long, unceasing verification of scientific naturalists. Their ancient wisdom did not fall from heaven ready-made, nor had it any claims to a miraculous birth. It was dug for and quarried out from the rock of reality. It was smelted, shaped, stamped, and warranted for current coin as perpetual symbol of the truth, however primitive. It was and is, to-day and for ever, a coinage genuinely golden, though the figures on it may be sometimes difficult to decipher. The ancient wisdom in the Hebrew books has been converted into a spurious specie, and passed off on the ignorant and unsuspecting as a brand-new issue from the mint of God. According to Egyptian thought, "creation" was mainly limited to the bringing forth of life—the life of water, fish and fowl, animal, reptile, and other forms from the meskhen or creatory of earth, when this was represented by the womb of Apt the pregnant water-cow. This idea of birth from the womb is portrayed in Apt the first Great Mother (fig., p. 124). Next the idea of birth from the womb is repeated in the making of Amenta with the Tuat as the creatory or the place of rebirth for the manes. And thirdly, in the astronomical mythology the meskhen, womb or place of birth, was constellated in the "thigh" of the cow as the sign of rebirth in the celestial rebirthplace. We have now to formulate the Egyptian origins of the creation legends that have come to us in a Semitic guise or disguise.

In their account of "the beginnings" the Egyptians make no pretence of knowing anything about a *cosmical creation*. Theirs is the natural genesis. A common Egyptian phrase for creation was "of the first time," and the expression is well represented in the opening words of the Hebrew book of Genesis, which are rendered "in the beginning" (Stele of the Sphinx, "Of the first time"). This beginning was "in the domain of Sut," "that sacred place of the first time." This first time, says the inscription, goes back to the domain of Sut and to the days of the masters of Khar, the later Akar and Neter-kar of the under-world. Darkness was the domain of Sut, as a condition of commencement, and the birthplace was where light broke forth from out the darkness. It was the African birthplace of the black and white twins of night and day. Otherwise the beginning in "the first time" described by the Ritual was with birth from the abyss, which was the birthplace of water within the earth. It is portrayed as "the Tuat which nobody can fathom," the place that "sent out light in the dark night," which was the birthplace of water and of eatable plants (Rit., ch. 172). Thus we have the Deep, the darkness on the face of the deep, the light breaking out of the darkness; the waters and the life springing forth from the waters in eatable plants, grouped together in Amenta the earth of eternity. Water had revealed the secret of creation in the life which came as food by water from the Mother-earth in the unfathomable deep. The secret of water as the source of life was the primal mystery to the Egyptians, as is shown by Kep (or Apt), the ancient mother of mystery, when the mystery was that of fertilization by means of water, as in the inundation of Egypt by the river Nile.

That secret of the precious water-source, the divulgence of which was the cause of the deluge at Lake Tanganyika, the secret that is so persistently preserved as a matter of life or death by the Bushmen amongst other African races, had been entrusted with occult significance to the keeping of the Sphinx. The Sphinx was a figure of the primitive abyss called Akar, the unfathomable deep of earth or womb of life, and it is a monument that marked the sacred place of creation or "the first time." As the inscription says, "The Sphinx reposes in this very place"—the place, that is, where life came into the world by water with food from the unfathomable abyss and light from the primeval darkness. This was also the sacred way by which the elemental powers or gods came into being, who originated as the masters of the nether earth. The number is not given, but these are known under several types and names as the primordial seven powers, the seven spirits of earth, or seven Uræus divinities, who were born in the lower earth before this had been hollowed out by Ptah in the making of Amenta.

In the several Semitic accounts of the first time, or in the beginning, more especially that of the Hebrew Genesis, the astro-mythological representation has been merged in a material creation, as the result of a later and more literal rendering of the subject matter; the later the version, the more exoteric the rendering. In the Assyrian epic the upper and lower firmaments, called "Ansar and Kisar," are described as a cosmogonical creation. "Ansar and Kisar were created." This is identical with the creation of the upper and lower firmament in the Hebrew Genesis. But in the Egyptian wisdom only can we make out what "creation" means *as a mode of representation* in the ancient sign-language. There are some remains, however, of the astronomical mythology in the Babylonian and Assyrian legends. One of these is the beginning with a world all water as an image of the firmament, or, when otherwise expressed, with the lands that were wholly sea. This is followed by the stream that divided the celestial Okeanos, and the consequent formation of a firmamental abyss, where the lower waters were gathered together into one place. In the Babylonian account of creation there was a time when the upper region was not yet called heaven; the lower region was not yet called earth, and the abyss was not yet formed. So, in the "non-Semitic" version the abyss had not been fashioned, the waters had not been gathered into one place; the whole of the lands were sea, and there was no stream yet configurated in the celestial ocean (Talbot, *Records of the Past,* vol. ix.; Pinches, *Records of the Past,* 2nd series, vol. vi.). Beginning in the heavens was with the uncreated Nun. When this was divided into an upper and lower firmament so-called "creation" had commenced. When the waters were gathered into one place the firmamental abyss had been opened, and a basis laid for the astronomical mythology or uranographic representation. The same beginning with the uncreated undivided Nun, as in the Egyptian myth and Babylonian legend, is apparent in the book of Genesis. The Nun, or Nnu, was the firmamental water. This is *"the water"* of the Hebrew version; the water on which darkness brooded and from which the spirit of the Elohim emerged; the water that was divided into the upper and lower firmaments, as an act of so-called "creation." The Nun was likewise the celestial water of the Akkadians and Babylonians, as well as the Egyptians. When Nuna or Anuna signifies the sky that is as the primordial water, the same as in the Kamite Nnu or Nun. The Irish firmament or celestial water is also called the Nion, an equivalent for the Kamite Nun.

The first three of the seven powers born of the Kamite mother of the elements were represented by Sut the power of darkness, Horus the power of light, and Shu the power of the air or breathing force. These three Ali or Elohim appear in the opening statement of Genesis. Though unpersonified, they are present as the primary elemental powers. In the Hebrew beginning, darkness brooded on the face of the deep, and the spirit of the Elohim moved upon the waters. The beginning, therefore, is with night or darkness. The spirit of Elohim was the breathing force of Shu or the breeze of dawn. The name of Tefnut, who was born twin with him, denotes the dews of dawn. Thus the powers or elements of dawn emerged from out the darkness of the firmamental deep with Shu and Tefnut as the elemental powers of breath and liquid life. The next two offspring of Neb-er-ter, the All-one in the Egyptian account of creation, are Seb and Nut, or earth and heaven. These were unformulated by night, but the two were separated by Shu at dawn when Nut was lifted up from Seb, and heaven and earth were thus created or distinguished in the only possible way. It is this "beginning" that was followed in the book of Genesis and in what has been made to look like a cosmical creation of the physical universe.

This creation is a representation of natural phenomena which might have been seen any day and night. But the gods of Egypt have been defeatured and dislimned and resolved into their elements of darkness and the firmamental deep, the breeze of Shu, the moisture of Tefnut; and the earth of Seb distinguished from the heaven of Nut. The action of the spirit moving on the waters had been perfectly expressed in the Egyptian version, when Neb-er-ter says that he created by means of divine soul, and that in founding a place where he could obtain foothold, he "worked with the spirit which was in his breast." This, according to Egyptian thought, was *the breathing spirit* first divinized in Shu as the power of the air or animistic soul of life. In the Hebrew version the elements of earth, heaven, darkness, light, water, spirit (or breathing force) are directly called into being, whereas in the Egyptian, four of these come into existence or are made apparent by means of divine types. Shu was the figure of breathing force with which the darkness was dispersed at dawn. This likewise was the breathing spirit with which Neb-er-ter created. In a vignette copied by Maspero (*Dawn of Civilization,* p. 169) Shu is accompanied by a group of gods in lifting up the firmament. There are seven altogether, chief of whom is Shu himself standing underneath the upraised heaven. These seven as the Ali who are co-workers with Shu are equivalent to the Elohim in the Hebrew book. Shu is called the separator of heaven from the earth, the elevator of heaven for millions of years above the earth. He is the conqueror of chaos and the progeny of darkness. Instead of the Elohim saying, "Let there be light" with this uplifting of the firmament, the Egyptian version represents Shu first as raising the firmament and next as bringing Ra his eyes to see with after the nocturnal heaven had been raised. In a Japanese account of creation the starting-point is also with the uplifting of the heaven from the earth. In the preface to the Japanese Kojiki this beginning with the separation of heaven and earth is described by Yasumaro, the editor: "Heaven and earth first parted, and *the three Kami* performed the commencement of creation. The passive and active essences then developed, and the two spirits became the ancestors of all things." These two are identified with Izanagi and Izanami in the Japanese system, and with the Yin and Yang in the Chinese. The three Kami called the *"alone born Kami,* who hid their beings," are one with Sut, Horus, and Shu, whilst the twin brother and sister are identical with Shu and Tefnut, who represented breathing power, or air, and moisture, as the two halves of a soul of life—Shu of breathing, Tefnut of liquid life, the active and passive essences which blended and became the creative spirit moving on the face of the firmament. In Genesis the powers of darkness and light are present when the drama opens, not as powers personified, but as elements. "Darkness was upon the face of the deep," and the Elohim said, "Let there be light." These, as Sut and Horus, were the first of the primordial powers in an elemental phase, the black Neh being the bird of night or Sut, and the solar hawk of Horus the bird of day. There was Sut the power of darkness on the one hand, and on the other Horus the hawk of light; these are equivalent to "there was evening and there was morning one day." It is noticeable, too, that the Hebrew word for evening, ערב , is also the name for the raven, the black bird of Sut. It is said in later texts that these nature-powers were derived from the primeval stuff or matter of the Nun, which means that they originated in and were embodied from the physical elements, such as Sut from darkness, Horus from light, Shu from air, Hapi from water, Kabhsenuf from the solar fire, Tuamutef from earth, Amsta from the mother-blood.

Certain matters of mythology were differently manipulated in various versions of the mythos. The process had already begun in Egypt. In the creation performed by Kheper-Neb-er-ter the first two powers produced as breathing force and moisture, or wind and water, are divinized in Shu and Tefnut. The next two are Seb the god of earth and Nut the goddess of heaven. These are now portrayed in the after-thought as having been emaned or emitted from the body of the one Supreme Being who had now become the Lord over all, whereas in an earlier myth the earth and heaven came into existence or were discreted when Shu upraised the heaven, or Nut, and separated her from Seb the god of earth. The coming into being of these four, Shu and Tefnut, Seb and Nut, is traceable in the Hebrew Genesis, but in a different mode and order of setting forth. "In the beginning Elohim created the heaven and the earth." These in the original are Nut and Seb, who were divided from each other (not created) and permanently propped apart by Shu and the supporting powers or Elohim. But, instead of a cosmogonical creation, the Egyptian wisdom shows that the making of heaven and earth was a mode of representation in the astronomical mythology. Some hints of this natural origin may be gathered from the Babylonian fragments of legendary lore. In the first tablet of the Chaldean account of creation, rendered by Talbot, the process is partially described (*Records of the Past*, vol. ix. 117). It is said of the Creator, "He fixed up constellations, whose figures were like animals." It is also said on the seventh tablet, "At that time the gods in their assembly created (the beasts). They made perfect the mighty (monsters)." These, as is shown by the context, were figures of the constellations. But in the Hebrew rendering the living creatures of the water, air, earth, or other element have been literalized, whereas they were as much figures in the astronomical mythology as were the two firmaments, the abyss, or the constellated lights of heaven. The Chaldean account of creation also describes the construction of "dwellings for the great gods." These were celestial habitations, as we say "houses" of the sun and moon. In the Kamite creation by Ptah they are called the shrines of the gods. "He formed the gods, he made the towns, he designed the nomes, he placed the gods in their shrines which he had prepared for them" (*Inscription of Shabaka*, lines 6, 7). Thus "creation" in this phase was a mode of representation in the heavens. It began with the abyss and the water, the creatures of the abyss, such as the southern fish and ketos, the water-serpent, and other "constellations whose figures were in the likeness of animals": and the habitations of the gods that were built upon "a glorious foundation." When the abyss had not been made, and Eridu had not yet been constructed, it is said that the whole of the lands were water. But when a stream was figured within the firmamental sea, "in that day Eridu was made; E-Sagila was constructed which the god Lugal-Du-Azaga had founded within the abyss." Two earthly cities were built upon a heavenly model, and the earthly Eridu corresponded to a celestial or divine original. Thus the earliest seats of civilization founded in Babylonia were modelled on cities that were already celestial and therefore considered to be of divine origin; the seats in heaven that were founded first in the astronomical mythology, as we hold, of Egypt.

But it was not the genesis of the universe that is imaged in astronomical mythology. The firmament was there, already waiting to be distinguished as upper and lower, and divided into the domains of night and day, or Sut and Horus, or Ansar and Kisar. The constellations were not created from nothing when they were figured out of stars. The firmamental water was not *created* by being divided into upper and lower. The earth was not *created* because distinguished from water as ground to go upon. Darkness was not *created* when it was portrayed as a devouring dragon. The pole of heaven was not *created* in being represented by a tree or mount or altar-mound. Heaven and earth existed when these were nameless, and did not come into existence on account of being named. Things were not created when images were assigned to them, nor because names were conferred upon them. The confusion of names and things is modern, not ancient; Aryan, not African.

The starting-point of a beginning was from the Nun, the firmamental water, which encircled all the world with the aërial ocean of surrounding space. This was the world all water. The earth was imaged mentally, thence figured mythically, as a fixed and solid substance in the waters of the Nun. These have been mixed up together by recent writers in a watery mass or mush of primordial matter, from which the cosmos is assumed to have been solidified or created out of chaos. But that is an exoteric misinterpretation of the ancient wisdom. There was no such creation. The earth stood on its own foundation in the lower Nun. The name of earth or land in Egyptian is Ta. Hence, land or earth in the Nun is "Ta-nen," which is the name of the earth in the waters of the Nun, the lower earth of the Egyptian Tanen. Tanen as a locality was earlier than Amenta, and the name was continued in the title of Ptah-Tanen, the opener of the earth, which had been founded in the Nun by the order of gods or powers called the "Nunu," as fellow-males, and a form of the first company, who were seven in number. In the Hebrew account of creation, the earth and firmament were already extant, but "the earth was waste and void; and darkness was on the face of the deep." Therefore the beginning is with the formlessness of the unfeatured Nun. Darkness existed. Light came forth. The light was then divided from the darkness as a mode of differentiating and describing day and night. Next, the upper firmament was separated from the lower, or, as it is otherwise stated, the waters above were divided from the waters below; whereas in the genuine mythos the upper and lower waters were the upper and lower firmament because the water was a figure of the firmament. Then follows the formation of the abyss, the waters "under heaven" being gathered together unto one "place"—the same as in the Chaldean account of creation (first tablet, line 5). The dry land is made to appear. "And the Elohim called the dry land, earth, and the gathering together of the waters they called seas."

In the beginning, then, was the unformed firmament or uncreated Nun. This was the universal, undivided water of the mythos and the legends. Creation, as uranographic formation, followed in the astronomical sign-language. A stream was seen and figured in the atmospheric ocean as a dividing line. The firmament was discreted into upper and lower. In the lower the celestial abyss was formed. This was figured, as the Chaldean and Semitic legends tell us, when the waters were gathered into one place and were given the constellation of *The Water* as their uranographic sign in astronomical mythology. According to Esdras (2 Es. vi. 41-2), the waters were "gathered in the seventh part of the earth." In this seventh part, "where the waters were gathered together," the two monsters of the deep were figured, which are here called "Enoch and Leviathan," who represent the water and dry land, as do Leviathan and Behemoth in the book of Enoch, and whose images, as we have suggested, still survive in "the southern fish" and the monster "Ketos." Taking the foothold of earth as a basis of beginning, there was nought around it but the firmamental water of space. This was without form or void throughout pre-constellational time. In an Aztec version of the beginning earth is separated from the waters in the form or under the type of shell-fish emerging from the deep. In other legends, one of which is Japanese, this shell-fish was the earth-tortoise amidst the waters. The earth emerging from the waters under the fish-type is constellated, as we show, in the gasping "Ketos," or it was represented by the hippopotamus which came up from the water to bring forth its young upon dry ground.

The firmament at first was thought of as water raised on high. In the Hebrew Genesis the water is one with the firmament. This celestial water was figured by the Egyptians as a lake, the largest water known to Inner Africa. In Greece the firmamental water became the Okeanos of Homer, flowing round the earth. It is the water that was first divided in twain. If we call the one water a lake, we find the one was divided into two lakes, one to the south and one to the north of the circumpolar enclosure. The Okeanos was divided by a river that encircled all the earth. This is visible in the river of the Milky Way. In the Ritual it is called "the stream which has no end." It is also described as *"the stream of the lake in Sekhet-Hetep"* or paradise (ch. 149). Further, the two lakes are portrayed as "the lake of Sa and the lake of the northern sky (Rit., ch. 153, A). It was observed that a stream came forth from the great lake in a white river that divided the one water into two great lakes. In this we see "the stream of the lake in the Sekhet-Hetep," just as "the river went out of Eden to water the garden."

As previously said, the Babylonian accounts of the so-called creation did not *begin* as cosmogonical. They are legends of the first time, when as yet the heavens were not mapped out to illustrate the mythology. There were no types yet constellated in the firmament. The glorious dwelling of the gods was not yet built. The abyss was not yet formed; the waters were not yet gathered into one place. They were universal. The whole of the lands were sea, or the celestial water of the Nun. There was no stream or Via Lactea limned in the aërial vast. The upper region was not yet called heaven; the lower region was not yet called earth. Then the dwellings were constructed (in heaven) for the great gods. *Constellations were fixed up whose figures were like animals.* One of the figures constellated is that of the Great Mother, Tiamat. As it is said in the Assyrian story, "Then the Lord measured the offspring of the deep (Tiamat); the chief prophet *made of her image the house of the firmament."* So in the Egyptian mythos the house of the firmament had been made in the image of Nut, the cow of heaven, or previously of Apt, the water-cow. In the Egyptian documents creation generally is attributed to Ptah, the first form of the god who was lord of all; one of whose zoötypes was the beetle, as a figure of the former or the moulder of matter, which preceded the anthropomorphic image of the potter. Kheper was a title of Ptah as the former. The Egyptian word Kheper signifies formation, causing to assume a shape, as when the potter moulds his clay or the beetle rolls its eggs up in a ball of earth. Ptah is portrayed as a beetle in the matrix of matter shaping the product. At this stage the seven elemental forces enter his service as the moulders who are called his seven assistants or associate-gods, the Ali = Elohim. In one of the hymns it is said to Ptah, as Tanen, "There was given to thee a power over the things of earth that were in a state of inertness, and thou didst gather them together after thou didst exist in thy form of

Ta-tanen, in becoming the uniter of the double earth, which thy word of mouth begot and which thy hands have fashioned." This was in making the lower earth of the Nun as the ground floor of Amenta, when the command to "let the earth come into being" was uttered by the God. It is also said, "When the heaven and earth were not as yet created, and when the waters had not yet come forth, thou didst knit together the earth; thou didst find thyself in the condition of the one who made his seat and who fashioned, or moulded, the two earths" (Budge, *Gods of the Egyptians,* vol. I, pp. 509-10) or who duplicated the earth.

In the Egyptian mythos Ptah was the great architect of the universe. But not the universe as a cosmological creation. The building, so to call it, was begun when the two pillars of the south and north were raised up by Sut and Horus, in that creation "of the first time" which is ascribed to Sut on the stele of the Sphinx, and in the creations that were indicated by the "upliftings of Shu" or the uniting of the double horizon by Har-Makhu. Various structures and structural alterations preceded the work of Ptah, the architect of the double earth and finisher of the building on a new foundation perfected for all eternity. Creation in the book of Genesis is described as an event, or a series of events, occurring once upon a time and once for all, whereas the genuine mythos represents the natural phenomena as constantly recurring. The earth was seen emerging every morning from the firmamental water, but not once for all. Darkness was seen rising up and coiling like some black reptile round about the earth at night, but not once for all. When Shu divided heaven and earth, or Nut from Seb at morning, this went on for ever: Nut descended on a visit to her lover every night. There was a first time to the uranographic representation of the myth as Egyptian, but not to the phenomena in external nature. In a sense there was no Horus or Orion in the heavens either figured or named until the type was constellated by the mystery-teachers, but the group of stars was always there ready to be called into being by name in what is termed "creation," or the astronomical mythology. As Egyptian, then, the only creation of the heavens and the earth was mythical, not cosmological. It was uranographic formation, not the making of matter. But to show how the mythical creation was rendered cosmogonically we have only to take the title of Kheper-Ptah in his character of "Let-the-earth-be," or let the hidden earth come into being. This in the Genesis becomes "Let the dry land appear (i. 9, 10), and the Elohim called the dry land earth."

There is an Egyptian account of "creation" to be found in the Papyrus of Nes-Amsu (British Museum, No. 10, 188), which was written for a priest of Panopolis in the thirteenth year of "Alexander the son of Alexander," or about B.C. 312. It is called "The Book of Knowing the Evolutions of Ra, and the Overthrowal of Apap." It purports to contain the words that were spoken by Neb-er-ter, a title of Osiris, the entire or all-one-god, as lord over all. There are two versions of the legend. In the first the creator-god is Kheper-Ptah. In the second he is Osiris; the same legend being applied in two different cults, at Memphis and Abydos. In the second version Osiris-Neb-er-ter is the speaker as creator. He says, "I produced myself from primeval matter. Osiris is my name. There existed no created things in this land." A land is here described in which the plants and creeping things of earth had no existence. Neb-er-ter was alone by himself in that land, and there was no other being who worked with him in that land. This was in Tanen, the nether earth of Ptah. The beetle-headed Ptah was the Egyptian creator in his primary form, the so-called maker of the heaven and the earth, but in a creation that was not cosmogonical. These, then, are the words that were also spoken in the first version by Kheper-Ptah, who formed the earth of eternity and discreted the two earths in the making of Amenta, on his coming into existence, when, according to the current phraseology, neither heaven nor earth was yet extant, and when the soil of earth, the plants and creeping things of earth, had not yet been created in *that land*. Kheper-Ptah then found a co-worker in the goddess Mā, the Egyptian Wisdom, whom the present writer had previously identified with the Hebrew Kochmah in "A Book of the Beginnings." Working with Mā denotes creation according to eternal law or undeviating rule.

Evidence for the non-cosmogonical nature of Kheper-Ptah's creation may be gathered from the fact that the celestial bodies, sun, moon, and stars, were not among the things that were called into being by him. The sun as "the eye of Nu," the Nun or firmament, and the primeval matter of the paut were pre-extant. Nor does either of the two versions mention the creation of birds, or beasts, or cattle. Moreover, a male-god who existed alone in the Nun as Kheper the begetter or father-god is impossible on the face of the inscription, because Nu the god of the celestial water was already extant in the character of a begetter. Kheper calls him "my father Nu," and the solar orb is also called "the eye of Nu." Besides which Kheper-Ptah was preceded by several dynasties of deities, lunar, stellar, or elemental. The Put-company of the nine gods was preceded by that of the eight; the eight by that of the seven Ali, or associates; the seven Uræus-divinities; the seven Khuti; and these by the mothers Apt, Neith, Tefnut, and the seven cows or Hathors.

The foundation of monotheism was laid when the various powers were combined in a single deity to be worshipped as the one true eternal spirit. These were primarily the Great Mother and her seven elemental powers. And when the goddess was superseded by the god Ptah, both sexes were included in the one Supreme Being who was now the Lord over all. It was the same with Osiris, as the pictures show. Asar was the mother and child (Hes-Ar) in one, and the perfect triune type was completed in God the father. There was no God the father without God the mother and God the child. In the mythological text from Memphis we read of Ptah in his divine forms. In one of these he is designated "Ptah of the earth." "The *Mother* giving birth to Atum and his associate-gods" (line 14). Ptah of the earth was then "in the great resting-place" as the maker of Amenta. This was the place of that new creation and rearrangement of the things that were pre-extant before the time of Ptah the opener, and this one god who was latest is now considered to be the source of all the gods and goddesses who had preceded him. Ptah became the god who was born of his own becoming, or of his own self-originating force, and who came into existence in the person of his own son—as a mode of representing the eternal manifesting in the sphere of time. According to the school of thought, the male had been substituted for the mother as the begetter in matter. Hence the beetle of Kheper was solely male, that is, as the type of a divine parent; and the female now became subsidiary to the male. Illustrations of Kheper in this phase of male-creator can be seen in the great French work on Egypt, a copy of which may be consulted in the British Museum. In these pictures, as in the legend of creation translated by Dr. Budge, the imagery shows with sufficient plainness how creative source was figured in the likeness of male nature. This has been rendered with all its naked crudity, but needs the gnosis for an explanation. By the gnosis here is meant that science of Egyptian symbolism which alone enables us to read the palimpsest of the past that was scribbled over and over again by the teachers of the ancient wisdom. For example, Kheper in the pictures is the male, as beetle, who emanes the matter of creation from his own body, as does the spider or the silkworm. In the later legend of Ra and Apap the anthropomorphic type replaced the beetle; Kheper has been imaged in the likeness of a masturbating male, and then the act has been attributed in reality to the black-skinned race (Budge, *Gods of the Egyptians,* vol. i. p. 304.) But as the beetle was a pre-anthropomorphic type of Kheper, we might ask if that also was a masturbating male, as the producer of matter from itself? So necessary is the gnosis of the primitive sign-language for the reading of these remains, to prevent debasement of the type and perversion of the meaning.

After coming into being himself Kheper-Ptah is called the creator of all things that came into being. And here, if anywhere, we may identify the Word that was in the beginning, and was God. For Kheper says he brought his name into his own mouth; he uttered it as the word that was in the beginning. Other things were spoken or called into being by the word of his mouth. Of these things he says, "I raised them up from out of the Nun (or Nu) and from a state of inertia." He had found no place where he could stand. But he laid a foundation with Mā, who, as we know, became the co-worker with Ptah the divine artificer. In version B. of the Egyptian document the creator, as Kheper, says, "I made what I made by means of divine soul; I worked with the spirit," which is the action assigned to the Elohim, however differently stated. Soul, it is said in one of the texts, is "the breath of the gods" (Budge, *Gods of the Egyptians,* vol. i. ch. 8). Creation by means of the word was the work of Ptah in his character of "Let the earth exist." Stated in modern language, he might be said to have called his creations into being by word of mouth in uttering the word to his co-workers. This word, as Egyptian, was the well-known Hekau or great magical word of power, which was female before it was assigned to the deity as male; the living word of Apt; the great magic power of Isis or of Mâ, before it was ascribed to Ptah in the monotheism of Memphis. Creation by the word is calling into being things which did not pre-exist or were not previously entified, figured, or known by name. In the Ritual the word of power becomes a ceremonial act, and, as a mode of sign-language, to be said or uttered magically, is to be performed. Creation by the word is expressed in the character of Ptah by his title of "Let-the-earth-be." This is the creation by fiat, or the word, in the book of Genesis, when the Elohim say, "Let there be light" —"Let there be a firmament"—"Let the dry land appear"—"Let the earth put forth grass"—"Let the earth bring forth"—"Let us make man in our image"—and it was so. The word and act were one. And this was the Kamite creation by the word that was in the beginning; the word of Kheper-Ptah, who said, "Let the earth come into existence"—that is, the lower of the two, called Amenta, the secret earth. This mode of calling and coming into being by means of the word explains how the god could issue forth from silence as a word, how created things or beings could be said to have emanated from the mouth of the god, and how the divine wisdom, whether as Mā or Kochmah, could be said to come out of the mouth of the most high. It is known that the name was often held to be an equivalent for the thing, the act, or person, and in the text from Memphis the creation by Ptah is in a measure resolved into a process of naming. In this it is said, "Now the creation of all the gods (that is to say, of Atum and his associate-gods) was when proclamation was made of all the divine names in his wisdom"—the wisdom of Ptah. Thus things, in this case gods, or powers, were created when names were given to them. The principle is applied in the book of Genesis, when it is said that "out of the ground Iahu-Elohim formed every beast of the field and every fowl of the air, and brought them to the man to see what he would call them. And the man gave names to all cattle, and to the fowl of the air, and to every beast of the field" (ch. ii. 19-20). In these and other texts creation is reduced to a process of naming as a mode of representation, and in this way the uranographic mythology was founded on the figuring and naming of the constellations.

When the Supreme Being had been imaged or personified, the powers previously extant were represented as his offspring, his names, or members of his body. Hence the seven associate-gods, the Ali or Elohim, are now called the limbs, joints, the hands, the fingers, the lips, the teeth, the breath of the god, or, reversely stated, these parts of the one god *become* the associate gods, as a sevenfold emanation from Kheper-Ptah. "Now Ptah was satisfied after his making of all things, and conferring all the divine names. He formed the gods, he made the towns, he designed the nomes, he placed the gods in their shrines. He made their company flourish." "All the limbs moved when he uttered the word of wisdom which came forth from the tongue and worked a blessing upon all things." The word (lit. *speech*) became *the making of men* and the creation of gods for Ptah-Tatanen-Sepu.

"Let-the-earth-be" is one of the titles of Ptah as the god who calls the earth into existence. Which looks, at first sight, like a cosmographical creation. But *the earth* which was evolved by Ptah and his associate-gods, the Ali, Phœnician Elohim, is not this world, not our earth. If it were, it would not be the double earth, the earth that was duplicated in the making of Amenta. In the text from Memphis (line 6) it is said that "Ptah was satisfied after making all things, all the divine names." He saw that it was good, and this satisfaction of the creator in his work is repeated in the book of Genesis. Seven times over Elohim saw that the work was good, and like Ptah, or the Put-company of gods, he or they were satisfied. But the making of Amenta by Ptah and the great paut of gods or Ali was an actual creation of imagination, not a mere "calling" of things into existence by naming them. It was also the creation of an earth, but not of the earth on which we stand. It was known as Ta-nen, the earth in the Nun; also as the lower earth distinguished from the upper earth, to which it was added when the earth was duplicated as the work of Ptah and the associate-gods. The firmament of upper earth was raised aloft by Shu, when establishing the pole of Am Khemen. The firmament of the nether earth was lifted up by Ptah. This was celebrated as his suspension of the sky. But the lower firmament is the sky that was raised up by him in Amenta, the earth of eternity, not in the upper earth of time.

Thus, the creation of Amenta was not the commencement of the external universe, although another heaven and earth were then called into being. At first there was no heaven and no earth in this unformulated realm of desert darkness. Or, as the Hebrew version has it, "the *earth* was waste and void." There was no light of day or lamp of night, as neither sun nor moon could pass that way until the earth was hollowed out and a sky suspended overhead by Ptah the opener and his Ali, or companions, who were afterwards repeated in the Elohim of the Hebrew Genesis. So in the enclosure of Yima there was at first no light of stars, or moon, or sun. This was the condition of primeval darkness in which the Elohim said, "Let there be light, and there was light." The question being where and how? In the making of Amenta Ptah was the uplifter of the lower firmament, with which he roofed the under-world within the earth. This is recognized in the Ritual (ch. 64), when the speaker down in Amenta says, "Mine is the radiance in which Ptah floateth over his firmament"—that is, the light of this new heaven and earth, which were solely *a creation of astronomical mythology*. In another text we read, "Hail to thee, Ptah-Tanen. The heaven was yet uncreated, uncreated was the earth, the water flowed not; *thou hast put together the earth,* thou hast united thy limbs, thou hast reckoned thy members; what thou hast found apart, thou hast put into its place. O let us give glory to the god who hath raised up the sky, and who causeth his disk to float over the bosom of Nut, who hath made the gods and men and all their generations, who hath made all lands and countries, and the great sea, in his name of *Let-the-earth-be*" (cited by Renouf, *Hibbert Lectures,* pp. 222-3). This, being late, has the look of cosmology. But the sky raised up by Ptah was over the earth in Amenta; the sky that was imaged by the sign of heaven reversed. When Ra is being exalted above all previous gods in the glosses to the seventeenth chapter of the Ritual it is said that he had exercised his sovereignty as Unen the opener when there was as yet no firmament. That is before Ptah had created the firmament below the earth, which is called the "lower firmament" in the Babylonian legends of creation. This beginning with the raising of the firmament is alluded to in the name of the gate-keeper to the second hall in the House of Osiris, who is designated "Him who raised up or created the beginning" (Rit., 147, 7). But, as before shown, there were two upliftings of the firmament, one above the earth and one below.

There is hieroglyphic evidence that the Egyptian creation of the earth by Ptah was not cosmical but a mode of hollowing out Amenta in the lower earth, and of tunnelling the mount to make a passage through. The sign for Ta, the earth, is a hollow tube, a pipe, a reed, or the *tibia* (leg-bone). Thus, a passage hollowed out is an ideograph of the earth that was formed by Ptah and his Knemmu, the moulders. It was the tunnel of Ptah with its gates of entrance and exit that first gave significance to the expression, "the ends of the earth." The manes in the Ritual who has passed through exclaims, "I have come out of the Tuat: I am come from the ends of the earth" (ch. 75, 1). The opening of Amenta was a primitive mode of *thinking through the ground of solid earth,* as it stood in the waters of the Nun, and of making out a pathway for the sun or solar god to travel by in passing through from one horizon to the other. Thus, the making of Amenta was a work of imagination based upon a ground of natural fact. Before the earth was known to float and revolve in space, it was thought of as a fixture like a mountain or an island, a tree or a stalk of papyrus standing in the firmamental water. Then it was made out, as mythically rendered, that somehow the sun passed through the under-world of earth by night. This was portrayed in several ways. In one, a tortoise was the type. With Kheper-Ptah, the beetle was the burrower in and through the hidden earth. Ptah, as the divine worker, shaper, or creator in this subterranean world, was also imaged by an embryo-in-utero as way-maker in the womb of matter, or the earth. Fire was another solar type. Hence Ptah was the worker with that element, and his associate-gods became the blacksmiths and metallurgists, who *blazed* their way below from west to east through Tanen, earlier Tanun, termed the earth of Ptah. Then followed Ra in his primordial sovereignty as Atum, son of Ptah. He crosses (later) in the solar bark that sailed the Urnas water by night. But first of all he had to wriggle through the mud of the abyss in the likeness of an eel.

Before Amenta had been moulded by the Put-cycle of powers there was a secret and infertile earth conceived of in the Nun, where nothing grew and nought was cultivated, as no soil or *sata* had been yet prepared, and no light had then appeared. But this earth of eternity was *not the world of human life,* and consequently no human beings were created in Amenta. Atum, though a man in form, was not a human being. This will explain why neither man nor woman was created or formed by Kheper-Ptah, in the Book of Knowing the Evolutions of Ra. There was no man or woman in the genuine mythos. These only came into existence when the gods and manes had been euhemerized and creation was set forth as cosmogonical through literalization of the astronomical mythology and adulteration of the ancient wisdom.

It has been assumed by some Egyptologists that the two earths, or *the double earth,* were limited to the division of space into south and north by the passage of the sun from east to west. But in the making of Amenta the one earth was divided into upper and lower, with a firmament or sky to each, and thus the earth was duplicated;

hence the making of Amenta was *the creation of a double earth* or an earth that was doubled. An apt illustration of this double earth may be seen in the vignettes to the papyrus of Ani, where scenes in the upper-earth life are portrayed at the head of the page, with scenes in the life of Amenta underneath. Thus on pages 5 and 6 the funeral procession of Ani is to be seen wending its way to the sepulchre, carrying the laid-out mummy, whilst Ani as the manes is to be seen on his journey through the nether earth accompanied by Tutu, his wife in spirit-world.

The nether earth, when not yet excavated, was a world of solid darkness, because unvisited by sun or moon. When Amenta was hollowed out by Ptah it was for his son Atum, who is Ra at his first appearance in Amenta as the solar god, the first to pass through this realm of subterranean night. Naturally when the sun appeared "there was light," and darkness with its host of evil powers fled, as related in the legendary lore. It is to this old netherland of darkness, with no outlet, that the goddess Ishtar descended in search of the water of life. It was a land without an exit, through which no passage had been made; from whose visitants, the dead, the light was shut out. "The light they behold not, in darkness they dwell." "Dust is their bread; their food is mud." Still the secret source of water, and thence of life, was hidden in that land. This was the world of the gnomes, the goblins, and other elemental sprites, which, as Egyptian, are summed up, under the serpent-type, as seven Uræus-powers born in the nether earth (Rit., ch. 83). As Babylonian they were the seven "spirits of earth," or anunnaki. The beginning in this region was with the abyss inside the earth from whence the water welled that was to be most sacredly preserved as very source itself. This subterranean realm had somewhat the character of a mine with the water welling upward from the unplumbed depths below. It was a mine of hidden treasure, one form of which was gold. But first of all the treasure was water, the primary element of life. Hence a fount of the water of life was localized in the well of this under-world which the Egyptians divinized as the Neter-Kar because it was the sourse of water and the way by which life came into the world. Here the spirits of earth, the powers of Khar, the Assyrian anunnaki, were portrayed as watchers over the water of life and protectors of the hidden treasures underground. It was these spirits of earth that peopled our mines and became the jealous guardians of their metals. These were the elemental spirits, not the spirits of the dead who were worshipped as the human ancestors; the gods, not the glorified. It is distinctly stated in the great Harris papyrus (plate 44, lines 4 and 6) that Ptah the opener "formed the hollow of the under-world, *so that the sun could pass through as revivifier of the dead;* and that he also encircled the earth with the firmamental water on which the solar bark might ride all round." The sun-god here was Atum in his eschatological character. Also, in a hymn to the earlier elemental powers found upon the walls of the temple in the oasis of El-Khargeh, it is said to Ptah, "Thou hast made the double earth. Thou hast placed thy throne in the life of the double earth. Thy soul is the four-fold pillar and the ark of the *two heavens.*" Ptah the excavator of the nether earth is now the builder of the ark in which the dead are borne across the waters of Amenta to the other world. The speaker in this character (Rit., ch. 1) says, "I am the arch-craftsman on the day in which the ship of Sekari, or the coffined one (whether as Ptah or Osiris), is laid upon the stocks." This was represented in a ceremony at Memphis, where the coffin, ark, or shrine of the god was placed upon a sledge and drawn in a procession round and round the great sanctuary when the drama of the resurrection was performed.

It was as the maker of Amenta that Ptah became the architect of the universe. When completed, the Egyptian universe consisted of heaven, earth, and the under-world, but it was not finished until he had formed the under-world or made the nether earth and heaven. Then Ptah, as the maker of Amenta, was called the architect of the universe. The tat-symbol, which was erected in Amenta as a type of eternal stability, was the backbone of Ptah as a figure of the god who was now the vertebral column and sustaining power, under, as well as over, all. The tat was also duplicated to form the gateway of eternity in the region of Tattu, when the double tats took the place of the two pillars of Sut and Horus in the house of Ptah. Ptah is described as the former of the egg of the sun and the moon. He is depicted in one of the representations, at Philæ, sitting at the potter's wheel in the act of giving shape to an egg (Rosellini, *Mon. del Culto,* 21). But this is not to be taken literally. The representation is symbolical. Ptah was the creator of the circle in which the sun and moon revolved, when the passage through the under-world was finished; and the egg is a hieroglyphic sign of the circle, which circle was also a figure of the eternal pathway. This solar pathway made by Ptah reminds one of Vaughan's magnificent image:

"I saw eternity the other night,
Like a vast ring of pure and endless light."

Now, no Egyptologist whose work is known to the present writer has ever discriminated betwixt the "making of Amenta" and the cosmological creation in the Hebrew book of Genesis, which is a chief object of the present section. In his work on *The Dawn of Civilization* (Eng. Tr., pp. 16-19) M. Maspero has given a version of what he supposes the Egyptians thought of *the earth*. He tells us "they imagined the whole universe to be a large box, nearly rectangular in form, whose greatest diameter was from south to north, and its least from east to west. The earth with its alternate continents and seas formed the bottom of the box; it was a narrow, oblong, and slightly concave floor, with Egypt in its centre." M. Maspero's oblong box, which is longest from the south to the north, is just a figure of the Nile valley, reproduced in the nether earth of Amenta as a mythical locality, not as a picture of the universe. He has taken the cover off Amenta and exposed its depths to the stars of heaven, as if it were the cavity of an immeasurable crater, and has left no ceiling to the lower earth, no nether sky of Nut for the sun to traverse when it was day in the under-world; consequently he has failed to reproduce the double earth that was the creation of Ptah and his co-workers.

The creation of Amenta by Ptah the opener was the cutting, carving, and hollowing out of the earth as tunnel for the heavenly bodies and the manes, which were now to make the passage *through* instead of *round the mount*. This for the first time renders the fundamental meaning of the Hebrew Bara (ב ר א) to create, as when it is said (Gen. i. 1) that the Elohim created the heaven and the earth. Bara, applied to the creation of the world by the Elohim, signifies to cut, carve, fashion, and, in the form of Bari, to divide. The Elohim are the Ali or companions who, as the Knemmu or moulders with Ptah the opener, were the cutters, carvers, or potters, as fashioners of Amenta in the work of dividing the upper from the lower earth. The divine creation of the world resolves itself into the creation attributed to Ptah the opener and his co-workers the Ali, who divided the earth into upper and lower, and thus created, shaped, or moulded a nether world as the secret earth of eternity, the next world made tangible for foothold in spirit life. There was no use for one firmament above and one below until the double earth was created by the opener Ptah, and it was in the making of Amenta that the firmament was duplicated.

It was on account of this new arrangement when the double earth was formed or the house of the two earths was built by Ptah that the fresh treaty was made by Seb betwixt the two opponents Sut and Horus. Seb, as arbitrator, calls on Sut and Horus to come from where they were born in the south and north, their original stations, to the mountain in the middle of the earth, which joined the portion of Sut to the portion of Horus in the equinox. This was the solar mount in Annu or Heliopolis. "The two earths meet in Annu, for it is the march or border-land of the two earths." Peace was there proclaimed betwixt the warring twins. "This union is in the house of Ptah"; "the house of his two earths" in which is the boundary of south and north, and also the meeting-point of the two earths, lower and upper, as well as the junction of the domains of the north and south in the earlier division of the whole. When Amenta was made out the east and west were added to the south and north, and the heaven of four quarters was thus established on the solstices and equinoxes as the house of Ptah. The two earths are the upper earth of Seb and the lower earth of Ptah-Tatanen, lord of eternity. "Now Seb gave the inheritance (of his earth) to Horus." "So Horus became the chief of the land," which henceforth consisted of the two earths. Horus wears the double diadem as ruler of the double earth. He is now called "the traverser of the two earths," and is no longer merely the uniter of both horizons. In the preface to the inscription from Memphis he is hailed thus, "Live Horus, the traverser of the two earths; the conquering Horus, the traverser of the two earths" (*Stele of Shabaka*). On this the English translators of the text remark, "We are not aware that this epithet occurs elsewhere than in the titles of Shabaka." It could only apply to the solar god who shone upon the earth of time by day and on the earth of eternity in Amenta by night. The title was dependent on the creation of the twofold earth by Ptah. Broken as is the inscription, it is evident that the Osirian mythos has been tacked on partially to an earlier version relating to Ptah, his son Atum-Horus, and the Ali or associate gods of the Put-cycle. Thus Horus, the son of Osiris, takes the place of Atum-Horus, the son of Ptah, who was the earliest traverser of the two earths.

Amenta was not entirely "the happy other-world"; it was a world of various states and many parts. These included an upper and lower Egypt, the seven nomes of the Heptanomis, also the fourteen domains that were based upon the lower half of the lunar circle, and the fifteen domains that belonged to the solar reckoning (Rit., ch. 142). The inferno, the purgatory, and the paradise of Dante Alighieri are extant recognizably in the Book of the Dead as domains of Amenta. The manes had to go through the purgatory and pass by, if not through, the hells before they came to the outlet from the mount of earth in Amenta. This outlet was to the east; and here the Aarru field was planted to produce the harvest of eternity. In this field, which the garden followed as a type of tillage, stood the sycamore-tree of wisdom. We also meet with the two sycamores of the north and south that correspond to the tree of knowledge and the tree of life in the Garden of Eden. The tree of dawn was figured rising up above the horizon of earth with its rootage in the secret earth of Amenta. Here also rose the mount of rebirth, and either by climbing the mount or the tree in the wake of the sun-god the manes made their ascent to the upper paradise of Aarru in the fields of heaven. When Horus, or Iu, the Egyptian Jesus, came up from Amenta for his manifestation in the vernal equinox, it was from the terrestrial paradise of the lower Aarru.

If we would get a glimpse of the old lost earthly paradise we must descend in thought with the sun or manes in the west and traverse the subterranean passage to the east. There we emerge in the Aarru-fields to find ourselves in the Eden of Egypt glorified as the nether land of dawn. The great tree that towers evergreen above the horizon has its rootage here, and underneath this tree the blessed find rest and drink of the divine life-giving liquor which was afterwards called the homa, the soma, nepenthe, nectar, or other name for the drink which made immortal. In the mythology it was Hathor the goddess of dawn who gave the dew of the tree for drink and the fruit of the tree for food; which tree in Egypt was the sycamore fig. In the eschatology it is the heaven-mother Nut who pours out the liquid of life from the tree. The evidence for the Egyptian origin is fourfold. First, the green dawn is African, without parallel. Next, the tree is the sycamore fig, the tree of knowledge and of life in one. Thirdly, the imagery belongs to the mythical representation of the beginning; and lastly, it is repeated for a religious purpose in the eschatology. It is a common charge brought against the paradise of theology that it does not provide for progress and development in the life hereafter. But the Egyptian paradise in Amenta was not a place of unchanging bliss considered to be a kind of unearned increment. For them the world to come in Amenta was what they made it here. And the world to be in the upper paradise was what they made it by hard labour and by purification in Amenta. The sub-terrestrial paradise was mapped out for the manes to work in and work out their salvation from the ills of the flesh and blemishes of the life on earth. This was the promised land depicted at the end of the journey through the nether-world, whether as a garden, a vineyard, a harvest-field, or a table-mountain piled with food and drink. Every purpose of the primitive paradise had been summed up in the promise of everlasting plenty, but in the Egyptian Aarru the plenty was the reward of industry. This was the field of divine harvest, no mere pleasure ground, where abundance was the result of toil. The soil was apportioned by the Lord of Eternity, and each one had to cultivate his share, no one lived upon another's labour (164, 13). Indeed, the allotment in this life was cultivated magically whilst the workers were yet upon the upper earth. The Egyptians had outgrown the African custom of killing slaves for the purpose of sending their spirits as *avant courriers* to prepare the way for the potentate in spirit-world, but the *modus operandi* was symbolically practised.

Amenta may be said to open with the funeral valley in the west, and to end with the mount of resurrection in the east. In the Osirian mythos when the sun god enters the under-world it is as the mummy or the "coffined one" upon his way to the great resting-place.

Except when lighted by the sun of night. Amenta was a land of darkness and a valley of the shadow of death. It remained thus, as it was at first, to those who could not escape from the custody of Seb, the god of earth, "the great annihilator who resideth in the valley" (Rit., ch. 19). The resurrection in this nether region was the issuing forth to day which followed the burial on earth.

As it comes to us, the Ritual is comparatively late. The pre-Osirian mythos—solar, lunar, and stellar—is obscured by the Osirian eschatology. It lives on, however, in the Litanies and other fragments, which show that Atum-Horus, the son of Ptah, was the earliest representative of the nocturnal sun that made the passage of Amenta and rose again upon the horizon of the resurrection as the master, and, as was also said, the maker of eternity, by perfecting the circle through and round the double earth. Amenta, in the solar mythos, was looked on as the graveyard of the buried sun that died or became inert upon his journey through the under world. In the eschatology it was also depicted as a sort of cemetery or burial-place. Hence the chapter of "introducing the mummy into the Tuat on the day of burial" (Naville, *Todt.,* kap. I. B)—not the earthly mummy, but the mummy of the dramatic mystery as a figure of the living personality. In the book of knowing that which is in Amenta there is a description of the sandy realm of Sekari and of those who are resting on their sand. This points to the sandy district as a primitive burial-place in which the bodies of the dead were first preserved from corruption and decay. Before the mummies could have been embalmed in Egypt, the dead were buried in the sand for preservation of the body; and the burial-place in a sandy district was repeated in Amenta as the sandy realm of Sekari, the silent or the coffined one, who was Ptah-Sekari in the pre-Osirian religion.

It is the creation of Amenta, then, not of the universe, that is the subject of the mythos which was made cosmical in the Hebrew book of Genesis. The speaker is the god who came into being in the form of Kheper the creator or maker of all things that came into existence after he came into being. He was in Ta-nen, the earth of the Nun, the abyss within the upper earth. This was a land of darkness, the place where nothing grew, a type of which was preserved in the region of Anrutef. In this land there was no heaven, no sun or moon overhead, nor earth beneath the feet. Or, as the text has it, there was nothing *to stand on*. And as there was no earth, there were no plants nor creeping things of earth. No created things yet existed in this land, this lower earth that was waste and void; and there was only darkness on the face of the deep. There was nothing but the primeval matter for Kheper-Ptah and his assistants to mould into shape for the making of the secondary earth in Amenta. Whilst the under-world was yet the primordial abyss, it was the void of Apap, the dwelling-place of the things of darkness; but now it was the work of Atum as the master of Amenta to make war on Apap; to protect the tree or plants and the water of life; to bruise the serpent's head or slay the dragon of drought and the destroyer of vegetation.

Now according to a very ancient myth, there had been war in heaven from the time when the slayer of the dragon was female, and the Great Mother protected her child from the devouring reptile of the dark with her arrow or lance of light in the moon. This is seen when Isis pierces the head of Apap in the firmamental water. Also when Hemt-Nu, the lady of heaven, lightens up the firmament by overthrowing the devouring monster of the dark (Rit., ch. 80). The two opponents Sut and Horus also fought their battle in heaven when an eclipse befell the moon, and when Sut flung his filth upon the face of Horus, and Horus seized the genitals of Sut with his own fingers to emasculate him (Rit., ch. 17). But when Amenta was formed the scene of strife was shifted to the new earth that was shaped by Ptah the divine artificer. As it is said in the Book of the Dead (ch. 17), when Amenta was created, and Ra assumed the sovereignty, Amenta also became "the scene of strife among the gods." The speaker, who is Atum-Ra, says, "I am Ra at his first appearance. I am the great god self-produced. A scene of strife arose among the gods when I assumed command" (ch. 17). The great cause of strife in Amenta is depicted as the Apap-reptile, of whom it is said, "Eternal devourer is his name." It is the serpent of darkness, the fiery dragon of drought, the destroyer of vegetable life. Night by night the evil reptile attacks the tree of life in the midst of the garden, as shown in the vignettes to the Ritual. This, in the eschatology, is the adversary of Osiris and the enemy of souls. The nocturnal sun as seer in the darkness of Amenta is depicted as the great cat in conflict with the evil serpent. Ra says, "I am the great cat who frequenteth the persea-tree (of life) in Annu, on the night of battle when the defeat of the Sebau is effected and the adversaries of the inviolate god (Osiris) are exterminated." On the night of conflict occurs the defeat of the children of failure. And it is added, "There was conflict in the whole universe, in heaven and upon the earth." The conflict betwixt Ra and the Apap is identified as being fought for the water as well as for the light; the mortal enemy of man being drought as well as darkness. The strife in heaven, earth, and Amenta was the *raison d'être* of his coming who is called the prince of peace, and, who, as Iu-em-hetep, is the bringer of peace because he came to stop the war that was elemental, not tribal or racial, but the war of darkness against light, the war of drought against water, the war of famine against fertility, or, as mythically rendered, the war of Apap against Ra, the Sebau against Un-Nefer, Sut against Horus, or the serpent against the seed of the woman. The types had been evolved in the mythology which were continued in theology. Horus of the inundation had come as the prince of peace who slew the dragon of drought; as the young solar god he pierced the serpent of darkness. As prince of peace he passed into the eschatology. This is he who in his incarnation says, "I am the lord on high, and I descend to the earth of Seb that I may put a stop to evil. I come that I may overthrow my adversaries upon the earth, though my dead body may be buried" (Rit., ch. 85). Iu-em-hetep, as is indicated by the name, comes to bring peace and goodwill to earth as conqueror of drought, and dearth, and darkness. He grapples with the dragon in the constellation Hydra, and vanquishes it with the water of the inundation. He bruises the serpent of darkness as "Ophiucus"; he wrestles with the evil Sut and overcomes him in the constellation of the Twins.

The first chapter of the Book of the Dead was repeated on the day when the Osiris N. was buried. His entrance into the under-world as a manes corresponds to that of Osiris the mummy of Amenta, who represents the inert or breathless god, and who also enters the place of burial called the Kâsu. In the absence of the sun there would be nought but darkness visible, in this the land of the dead, but for the presence of Taht the moon-god. In this character the manes greets Osiris, saying, "O bull of Amenta, it is Taht the everlasting king who is here!"—as the night-light of the sufferer dying in the dark. "I am the great god in the bark who have fought for thee"—that is, against Apap and all the powers of evil. Apuat is also present to uplift and save the manes who might otherwise fall headlong into the lake of Putrata, where the monster lies in wait to devour its prey. (Rit., ch. 44.) It was as the moon in Amenta that Ra is said to have created That—a far older god—as a beautiful light to show the face of Apap, his evil enemy. But this was not the moon that was made and hung up in the Hebrew Genesis as a creation of four-and-twenty hours. Taht carried the lunar lamp called "the eye of Horus" in the darkness of the nether earth, to show the hidden lurking-place of the adversary. Thus, in the opening chapter of the Ritual the manes rises in Amenta after death on earth in the character of Taht the god who is the lunar light as representative of the supreme god in the dark of death and in the ways of darkness in the under-world, which means that the Osiris N. deceased enters the nether earth, in the likeness of Taht, to make war upon the dragon on behalf of the sun-god struggling with the monster coiling round him in the darkness of Amenta. In this way the war that is fought out in the night of the nether earth was dramatized in the Book of the Dead, where the souls of the deceased carry on the battle on behalf of the good Unnefer, whether as Horus or Osiris-Ra.

After the making of Amenta there followed a re-division of the earth betwixt the two contending twins, which, as herein maintained, was now the double earth of day and night, of Seb and Ptah, of time and eternity. The war that broke out in Amenta, when Atum took possession of this nether earth that was prepared for him by Ptah, includes the conflict of Ra and the Apap-reptile which is portrayed in the vignettes to the Ritual, and the battles of the twin-brothers Sut and Horus for possession of the Aarru-garden, the same that they had fought in external nature.

In a document translated by Chabas there is an account of the agreement between Horus and Sut. This is a calendar of lucky and unlucky days with mythological allusions. Under the date of Athyr 27th, it is said that Kamit, the cultivated land, was given to Horus as his domain; and the Tesherit, the red land or desert, was given to Sut as his domain (Papyrus Sallier, IV., Chabas, *Le Calendrier des jours fastes*). The black land of rich fertile loam, and the red land, or desert, thus divided were a form of the double earth as the upper and lower land which followed on the founding of Amenta; the division being no longer limited to south and north, or to the two halves of the lunation. The upper and lower crowns, white and red, were also brought to bear as symbols of the upper and lower earth. Hence we are told in this papyrus that on the 29th of Athyr the white crown was given to Horus and the red crown to Sut, as the rulers of the two territories here assigned to the two opponents warring for supremacy in the Egypt of Amenta. The red and white crowns had been previously given to Sut and Horus as the rulers of the south and north; Sut being Suten in the south, and Horus king of the north. But in the Sallier Papyrus a change is made in the disposition of the two crowns. The white crown was now given to Horus and the red crown to Sut, as the symbols of the upper and lower lands, the desert of Sut and the fertile land of Horus, or the wilderness of Anrutef and the paradise of plenty in the Sekhet-Aarru. In one of his battles with Sut, Horus, having got the better of him, takes possession of both the upper and lower land. He says, "I am Horus, the lord of Kamit (the black land) and the heir of Tesherit (the red land), which I have also seized. I who am the invincible one" (Rit., ch. 138). It is also said to Horus in "the crown of triumph" (Rit., ch. 19), "Thy father Seb hath decreed that thou shouldst be his heir. He hath decreed for thee the *two earths,* absolutely and without condition." Horus thus becomes the ruler of the double earth and the wearer of the double diadem, who united the white and the red crown of the upper and lower earths, not merely as the two crowns of the north and south in the earlier mythos.

A new type of deity had been evolved in Atum-Horus, the son of Ptah. As solar god, he was the first that went both under and over in making the eternal round of night and day. "It is thou who hast created eternity," is said to Atum-Ra, the divider and traverser of the double earth. This is the god "who goeth round in his orb, and giveth light to the whole circumference which the solar orb enlighteneth." He who had been Horus of the two horizons and also Kheper the self-originating force was now the traverser and enlightener of the double earth with his rays (Rit., ch. 15). After being concealed from men by night he presents himself each day at dawn; his glories are too great to be told as he "arises out of the golden." "The land of the gods, the colours of Puanta are seen in them, that men may form an estimate of that which is hidden from their faces" (ch. 15, Renouf). He divides the earths by his passage through. He lights up the tuat with his glories and wakens the manes in their hidden abodes by shining into their sepulchres and coffins. He opens the tuat and disposes of all its doors in the under-world. The Litany of Ra is described as being the book of the worship of Ra and the worship of

Tum, that is Atum-Ra, in Amenta. He is worshipped as the master of the hidden spheres who himself is invisible in darkness and who causes the principles (of life) to arise. He is the only one that unites the generative substances. His body is so great that it conceals his shape. He is born of his own becoming and manifests as his own son. In the adoration of Ra it is said to Atum as he entereth Amenta or "setteth in the land of life," "All the gods of Amenta are in exultation at thy glory. They of the hidden abodes adore thee, and the great ones make offerings to thee, who have created for thee the soil or ground of earth." That was in the making of the double earth, not in the making of the earth itself as a cosmogonical creation. In short, it was not earth-making, but the framing of the double earth, with Amenta as the pathway of eternity.

With the opening of Amenta, not only was a new world established in the double earth of Ptah—a new dynasty of deities was also founded. This was the Osirian group of five, consisting of Osiris, Isis and Nephthys, sightless Horus and Sut, who were called the children of Seb. Here, again, the twin opponents, Sut and Horus, were far older than Osiris, but were brought on with the great gods, the Great Mother, and the two sisters, in this newer combination of the powers effected in the under-world, the nether portion of the double earth.

Amenta in one aspect was the world of the dead, the Kâsu or burial-place in the Osirian cult. In this it was claimed to be "the great resting-place" of Osiris the mummy-god, which it became. But it had been created by Ptah for his son Atum before the Osirian dynasty was founded at Abydos. It was the way of the Egyptians to put all they knew into all they did in bringing on and aggregating their wisdom of the past. Thus the circumpolar paradise is repeated in the earthly paradise of Amenta. The stellar mount of glory in the north was reproduced as solar in the east. The Heptanomis with its seven entrances; the twenty-eight lunar stations, fourteen in the upper and fourteen in the lower hemisphere; the house of Osiris with its thirty-six gates. Various stars and constellations known on high, such as Orion, Sothis, and Polaris, were repeated as the guiding stars in this firmament of the lower earth to which the looks of the manes were directed in death. Amongst other reproductions in Amenta we find the Aarru garden; the abyss of the Nun as the womb of earth; the tree or edible plants in the water of the abyss; the dragon of drought or the serpent of darkness; the old first mother; the warring twins, Sut and Horus; the company of seven elemental powers; the lower firmament; the two pillars of Sut and Horus erected in Tattu, the house of eternity; Taht, the bearer of the lunar light; the Sebau, or powers of darkness, fog, mist, cloud, plague, storm, and eclipse—all of which were pre-extant before Amenta had been made by Ptah. The primary group of seven elemental powers was succeeded by the eight great gods, and the eight by the Put-circle of nine. Ptah was then considered to be the one supreme god, begotten by his own becoming, the maker of all things, who himself was not made. The eight were looked upon as his children. The nine formed the Put-circle or cycle of Ptah, who are equivalent to the Elohim of Genesis. In this connection we may note that No. 9 was the full Egyptian plural. The word for nine is Put, and Putah (or Ptah) is of a ninefold nature. Ptah was indeed the full Egyptian plural as a group or Put of powers that were combined in a supreme self-originating force whose mode of becoming was by transforming from the elemental power or powers through the human into the divine. As "creators," Ptah and his company of artizans did not originate in that which had no previous existence. They were the transformers of that which had always been as elemental in matter. The element of earth was pre-extant, likewise the power that brought forth life from the earth in water. This power operated by transformation, and one of its types was the serpent of Rannut (a form of the Mother-earth), which was a type of transformation because it periodically sloughed its skin and renewed itself. The element of water was pre-extant, also the power that transformed in the water to bring forth life in food. This transforming power in the water was objectified by the tadpole visibly turning into the frog. It was the same all nature through. The "creators" were the formers and transformers as unseen forces operating in the physical domain, with each one traceable to an elemental origin. First the elements themselves. Next the elemental forces or self-originators in two categories, the baleful and the beneficent. Then the goddesses and gods that were portrayed totemically, and afterwards personalized as divinities in the human likeness.

Ptah was the divine artizan. In his time the masons, builders, potters, blacksmiths were at work, each in their companionship, or brotherhood, as they are seen, hard at it, when the workers in the valley of the Nile come into view. He is especially called the father of beginnings. He was the former in the likeness of the scarabæus, the transformer in the image of a frog, and as the embryo in utero Ptah exhibits the earliest attempt at imposing the human likeness upon the shaping power that was previously imaged by means of the typical insect, or symbolical animal, as in totemism. There is a group of primeval powers described in later times who are said to be "the first company of the gods of Aarru," or the fields of heaven. They are addressed as the mighty ones, the beneficent ones, the divine ones, who test by their level the words of men as the lords of law, justice, and right; or as the lords of Maat. They are saluted in these words, "Hail to you, ye gods, ye associate-gods, who are *without body,* ye who rule that which is born from the earth, and that which is produced in the house of your cradles. Ye prototypes of the image of all that exists; ye forms, ye great ones, ye mighty ones, first company of the gods of Aarru, who *generated men* and shaped the type of every form, ye lords of all things. Hail to you, ye lords of everlasting" (Louvre Papyrus, 3283; Renouf, *Hib. Lectures,* pp. 208-209). In this text the Aarru is celestial, not the Aarru in Amenta, but the Aarru of the fields above, of which the goddess Apt is said to have been the mother as the bringer-forth of the seven primeval powers in their stellar character. As lords of Maat they are identical with the seven lords of rule or divine governors who are called "the arms of the balance on the night when the eye is fixed" (Rit., ch. 71). This first company of the gods in the fields of heaven were the Ali or Ari (as in the seven Kab-ari) by name, and the Ali are a group of companions who are herein set forth as co-creators of all that exists in heaven or in earth. The primordial nature-powers are mentioned under several types and names. They are the seven Uræus-gods, born of Mother-earth as non-sentient elemental powers (Rit., ch. 83). They are the seven Khus or glorious ones whose place in heaven was appointed by Anup on the day of "come thou to me" (Rit., ch. 17). They are the seven who assist the great judge in the Maat at the pole on the night of the judgment day, called "the seven arms of the balance," as executioners of the guilty, who accomplish the slaughter in the tank of flame when the condemned are exterminated (ch. 71, 7). They are the seven wise masters of arts and sciences who assisted Taht in his measurements of earth and heaven. In the solar mythos they are to be seen in several characters with Horus, Ptah, and Ra. They were portrayed as the seven with Horus, in the eight great stars of Orion. They are the seven souls of Ra, also the seven divine ancestors in the boat of the sun, the seven who support Osiris in Amenta. In whichever phase of phenomena, they are a group, a brotherhood, a companionship of powers originally seven in number. It is now proposed to identify this "first company" of creators who passed through these several phases in the Egyptian mythos as seven elementals, seven with the ancient Genetrix, seven with Anup, seven with Taht, seven with Horus, seven with Ptah, as the group of companions called the Elohim in the Hebrew Genesis, who were known to the Gnostics and Kabalists as seven in number, with Ialdabaoth, a form of Sut, at their head.

The word Elohim in Hebrew is employed both as a singular and a plural noun for god and gods, or spirits, with no known origin in phenomena by which the plurality could be explained. For this we must consult the Egyptian wisdom in the mythos which preceded the eschatology. In the "Dispatches from Palestine" there is a perfect parallel to the twofold use of Elohim in the plural and singular forms employed in the Hebrew book. The scribe addressing the Egyptian Pharaoh says, "To the king, my lord, *my gods,* my sun-god." (*Records of the Past,* vol. ii., p. 62, 2nd series.) Here the gods were the powers gathered into the one god as supreme. These when sevenfold were called the souls of Ra. They become the eight in the paradise of Am-Khemen. They are nine in the Put-cycle of Ptah, they were ten as the Sephiroth of the Kabalists, they are twelve in the final heaven of Atum-Ra. In a word, they are the Elohim as a form of the Egyptian Ali or Ari, a companionship of workers, and later creators. "In the beginning Elohim created the heaven and the earth." The astronomical mythology of Egypt, from the time of Sut to that of Ptah, is involved in that brief statement. There are at least three different groups of the Elohim—that is, the Ali or Ili—with the plural ending of the name as Semitic. The first group of these creators was seven in number, with Sut at their head. The second was that of the eight in Am-Khemen, with Anup added to the seven. The third is the company of Ptah, who formed the Put-circle of the nine. These preceded Atum, who was Ra in his first sovereignty. And to show how the past of Egypt opens into immensity, Ptah is credited with being the supreme ruler for 9,000 years. Still earlier the followers of Horus reigned for 14,000 years; and, as the astronomical legends show, the primary seven creators had previously marked out one great year in the circle of precession before they could become those lords of eternity at the north celestial pole, which were represented by a group of seven stars that never set. Under the title of Elohim, both the one god and the company of gods are present, though concealed, just as Ptah and his associates the Ali were included in the Put-cycle, as Ptah the god, Iu the son of god, and the paut as the group of gods. And if the Put-cycle of the Ali, as now maintained, are the originals of the Phœnician and Hebrew Elohim, it follows that the deity Ptah is *the one god of the group* in the Genesis as well as in the original mythos. Although the name of Ptah may not be given, yet the creator as the worker in earth, the potter, the moulder or carver, is plainly apparent in the Hebrew Genesis. Also it may be parenthetically remarked that the Hebrew word פת, puth, or peth, for the opening, is identical with Put, in Egyptian, to open; and that Ptah or (Putah) was named from this root as the opener, whether as opener of the nether earth for the sun to pass through, or for the resurrection of the manes from Amenta in the coming forth to day. Moreover, there is a biblical name, that of Puthahiah (פתחיה), which apparently proclaims the fact that Iah is the opener, or that he is identical with Ptah (1 Chron. xxiv. 16; Ezra x. 23; Neh. ix. 5 and xi. 24). The same root enters into the name of Pethuel, which is equivalent to Ptah-El or the divine opener, who was the Egyptian god Ptah (Joel i. 1).

In the Egyptian divine dynasties Ptah is god the father in one character and Iu the son in the other. In the person of Iu he is the youthful deity who rises from the dead both as the sun-god and as the soul which was imaged for the resurrection in the form of a sahu-mummy risen with the solar hawk for its head, as symbol of the soul issuing from the body of Kheper-Ptah. Iu, in the character of the son, is also representative of the Put-cycle, that is of the Elohim or company of the creators. Thus the Elohim are represented in the first creation of man by the maker = Ptah, and in the second by Iu the son of Ptah; and Iu the son of Ptah is equivalent to Iahu-Elohim, who becomes the creator of the second Adam in the second chapter of the Hebrew Genesis. In the first of two creations Ptah and the Ali who are his associate-gods, the Ali or Elohim, are the creators of Atum, the Hebrew Adam, who in the first phase was created male and female, man and woman in one. The associate-gods or Elohim are said to become the lips, the teeth, the joints, the hands, of Atum the son of Ptah. In another version they are the seven souls of man. In the second creation it is Atum and his associate-gods who are the creators of man, the same as Iahu-Elohim in the Genesis. The parallel is perfect; only in the Hebrew rendering the gnosis is omitted. Still there are two Adams, man the mortal on earth, and man the manes in Amenta. It is the present writer's contention that the Elohim in the plural are the Ali or associate-gods of Ptah, and that Iahu-Elohim is the deity Iu, who was a form of Ptah as god the son, and who afterwards became the father god in Israel under the name of Ihuh or Jehovah. Iu or Iu-em-hetep, he who comes with peace, is the Kamite original of the promised prince of peace, whose coming was periodic and æonian for ever and ever, or from generation to generation. The writer further maintains that the creation in the first chapter answers to the creation of Kheper-Ptah and his Ali, that the creation of Iahu in the second chapter is identical with that of Iu or Atum and his associate-gods, and that the garden in Eden is the Aarru garden which Ptah and his Ali or Elohim created for Atum the son to cultivate as the earthly paradise in Amenta.

Thus, the two different creations in the first two chapters of Genesis are in their proper order. In the first "the heaven and the earth were finished, and all the host of them." Man, or Adam, also was made. All through this chapter the creators are the associate-gods, the Egyptian Ali, the Phœnician Elohim. In the second chapter, one of the Elohim is individualized by name as Iahu or Iahu-Elohim, translated "the Lord God," which might be rendered the god Iahu = Iu-em-hetep. After the Elohim had finished their work, it is said in the second chapter of Genesis that Iahu-Elohim now made the earth and heaven which had *already been assigned to the Elohim as makers in the previous chapter.* This also may be explained by the Egyptian mythos. Ptah the creator and father of the Ali, or Elohim, was one with Iu in the person of the son. Ptah, the speaker for the group in the first chapter, is the father, and Iahu in the second chapter is the same one god continued as the son, Iu, Iusa, or Iu-em-hetep. Thus the dual character of Ptah-Iu was continued in Atum-Iu as the divine father and son. Also, there are two Atums, corresponding to the two types of Adam, one human, one divine. One was the Atum who died=the Adam in whom all men die, as Paul expresses the doctrine; the other is the second Atum called Nefer-Atum, or Iu the son, who rose again to change the earthly into the heavenly man, in whom the dead were to be made alive again in Amenta, as it was taught in Egypt some ten thousand years ago. In the Hebrew version Atum-Iu has been divided and brought on in two characters which really correspond to the two Adams, human and divine, the first Adam or man, who was of the earth earthly, the second Adam or man, who is of heaven heavenly, the "life-giving spirit," who became Atum-Ra the "holy spirit" in the Kamite eschatology. More of the Genesis survived amongst the Kabalists.

Atum at Annu, like Ptah at Memphis, was the one god in the two characters of father and son; the eternal father who was personalized in time as the ever-coming son. The birth was periodic in phenomena. Horus of the inundation on his papyrus came as the shoot; Iu as the fish. Thus to have any meaning the coming son was the ever-coming one as a type of the eternal. The title of Ptah as Kheper has the meaning of becoming. The name of the son Iu signifies the coming one. This was he who came for ever, first as manifestor for the mother, "the seed of the woman," and then as the representative of the father. In the cult of Ptah both characters of the father and son were combined in one god, and both were continued in Atum. Iu the bringer of peace was god the coming son in both religions. The coming son, we repeat, was the *ever-coming* one. There was no advent once for all. Food and vegetation, water and light, depended on continual repetition and renewal. This was a subject of the astronomical mythology, in which the "coming" according to time and season had perennial fulfilment. The war of Horus the son with the serpent of darkness was fought out nightly. His conflict with the dragon of drought was repeated annually. But in the Hebrew version the "coming" has been relegated to the domain of prophecy. The saviour or deliverer is to come to bruise the serpent's head once for all; and in this passing of mythology into the later eschatology the ever-coming was changed into the long-expected and, as it turns out, *never-coming* son of the Holy Spirit and a mother who was ever-virgin. It was not the object of the adapters to be more explicit, but to all intents and purposes the two characters of Atum the father-god, who was designated "the father of mankind," and of Iu the son have been reproduced in Genesis as Adam the human father and Iahu-Elohim as the god.

It is the making of Amenta by Ptah and his associate gods that has been converted into a creation of the heaven and the earth in the book of Genesis. This is shown by the firmament that was suspended in the midst of the waters which were under the firmament and separated from the waters which were over the firmament. This is the firmament that was made by Ptah when he divided the heaven of Nut below from the heaven of Nut on high, and thus suspended a lower sky above the nether earth. But when the heaven and the earth were made and the work was finished, the result was a world so unfurnished and unfit to live in that "no plant of the field was yet in the earth, and no herb of the field had yet sprung up": no rain had fallen, and "there was not a man to till the ground" (ch. ii. 5). This was in Amenta, the hidden earth that was opened by Ptah for Tum (Atum) and his associate gods to cultivate. Now the impossibility of the Hebrew creation being cosmical is fixed for ever, inasmuch as the heaven and earth are *made twice over. In the second chapter there is a second creation of heaven and earth, and the first creation is followed by the making of a second man.* The creation of the garden, in the Egyptian mythos, is a separate and subsequent creation from the calling of a nether earth into existence. Amenta was first made, and then the Aarru-garden was planted in Amenta. This twofold creation will account for the two Adams, the man of earth and the man from heaven, or man the mortal and man the manes. In the mythology the first Atum was solar. In the eschatology the second Atum is spiritual. The garden was made for the manes to cultivate, and the manes represents the second Adam, who as Egyptian is Nefer-Atum, or Atum in sprit—otherwise man the manes in the garden of Amenta.

In the book of Genesis there are six creations or acts of creation, set forth as the work of six days or periods. (1) The light was divided from the darkness, and there was evening and morning—one day. (2) The firmamental water was divided into upper and lower, and there was a second day. (3) The waters were gathered into one place for the dry land to appear; the earth put forth grass and herbs and trees, and there was a third day. (4) The lights were set in the firmament for signs and seasons, and there was a fourth day. (5) The creatures of the waters were brought forth and the fowls of the air, and there was a fifth day. (6) The earth brought forth the living creatures after their kind, including man, and there was a sixth day. Then in the moralizing of the mythos the work of creation being ended on the sixth day, the seventh is to be solemnized as a day of rest. In the course of literalizing the pre-extant mythos it is said that when Elohim finished his work he rested on the seventh day from all the work which he had made. "And Elohim blessed the seventh day and hallowed it, because that in it he rested from all his work which Elohim had created and made" (ch. ii. 2, 3). So in the book of Amenta it is said that the nether earth was created by the solar god, who rested in that which he had made, just as Ptah was satisfied after making all things, and all the divine names, when like the Elohim he had finished the work and saw that it was good.

There is no great difficulty in discovering the origin of the day of rest which has been ascribed to the Elohim upon the seventh day of creation. Amenta was created as the place of rest for the sleeping dead, and also for the god of the resting heart. It had been the work of Ptah and his associate gods to create the great resting-place in the under-world. And consequently this character of Ptah, as the maker of Amenta, is determined by his designation of "Ptah in the great resting-place" (Stele of Shabaka, line 16). The great resting-place was created for the god who rested there, as did Atum and later Osiris of the resting heart. This was the work which the creator or craftsman Ptah completed in seven stages or periods that were ultimately reduced to seven days. The mount called Hetep in the earthly paradise is named as the mount of rest. It was a kind of "rest-and-be-thankful" half-way up the ascent from the world of the dead to the summit on the mount of glory. The word Hetep has the various meanings of rest, peace, plenty, all of which were to be realized in Hetep, the garden of the blessed dead. The great object is "to take possession there." The manes says, "I am united there with the god of rest"—that is, with Osiris, god of the resting heart. "I take my rest in the divine domain. There is given to me the plenty which belongeth to the kau and the glorified." "Rise in Hetep (the mount) blest with the breezes, I arrive in thee, my head is uncovered. I am in my own domain." One of the blissful islands of this earthly paradise is expressly called the isle of rest or Hetep. The voyager makes fast his bark to "the block of moorage on the stream," and utters his praises to the gods who are in the garden of rest. The garden of Amenta was a place of rest in the refreshing shade of Hathor's tree. It was called the garden of Hetep. The word Hetep is also spelt Hept. In fact, to judge from the hieroglyphical inscriptions in the Pyramid of Medum, it seems that this was the earliest spelling of the word. Thus Amenhetep would be Amenhept. Now Hept (Gr. Επτα) in Egyptian also signifies the number seven. This may be related to the work of creation in seven days, which according to the non-biblical Jewish legends represented the earthly paradise in seven divisions as a figure of the celestial heptanomis, the work in seven parts being computed as a work of seven days, and Hept the place of rest transformed into the seventh day of rest. In the later Semitic märchen, Assyrian and Hebrew, a division in time has been substituted for the division in space—that is, the seven divisions of the astronomical heptanomis have been converted into a creation of seven days, and a great day of rest has been substituted for the great resting-place. We can perceive the Semitic Sabbath in the making and also where it was made. In the elder version of the Assyrian legend of creation there was no Sabbath. The seventh day is a day of labour, not a day of rest. But whatsoever was signified by the seven successive divisions, acts, stages, or periods of creation that were ultimately commemorated by the festival of the seventh day, the Semitic Sabbath belongs to the superstructure, not to the foundation, and is not original, either as Hebrew or Assyrian. Time did not begin with Sunday, either as the first or the seventh day of the week. The week was preceded by the month or a moon, and a moon by the year of the inundation that was commemorated by the festival of the Great Bear's tail. In the Chaldean account of creation there is a hint of the solar origin of the Sabbath. In this it is said of the creator, "On the seventh day he appointed a holy day. And to cease from all business he commanded. Then arose the sun on the horizon of heaven." (Lines 17, 18, 19.) The day dedicated to the sun was Sunday, but the solar calendar was the latest. An indefinitely more ancient version than anything Semitic has been preserved in the Hawaiian legend of creation. This is said to have begun on the 26th day of the month, on the day of Kane, and continued during the days named Lono, Manli, Maku, Hilo, and Hoaka. In six days the creation was completed, and the seventh day, the day of Ku, became the first holy day. The first and sixth of these seven days have been kept sacred ever since by all generations of Hawaiians. Yet the Polynesians generally did not solemnize a weekly Sabbath, and had no week of seven days. (Fornander, vol. i. p. 121; *Natural Genesis,* vol. ii. p. 56.) More than once we meet with a sixth-day Sabbath in Africa. Dos Santos described this sixth day of rest as being observed in the ploughing season by the Monomatapa, which, according to Bent (p. 341), is continued among them to-day. "At Mangwedis during the ploughing season they only work for five consecutive days. They observe the sixth and call it Muali's day, and rest in their huts and drink beer. These days are feasts of the ancestral spirits or muzimos, called "the days of the holy ones who are already dead."

A week of seven days concluding with the Sabbath, which was at first a festival, is more expressly Semitic. Not that the Egyptians had no seven-day period in their reckonings of time. The *tenait* was a period of seven days, as well as of fourteen days or a half-moon; but a cycle of seven days as the measure of a cosmogonical creation had no meaning. The seven periods of creation did not originate with seven days of twenty-hours each. As will be seen, when all is put together, the Egyptians reckoned time upon a scale so vast that it included the great year of the world. That is, the heptanomis founded upon seven astronomes had been repeated in the great year with its seven periods in precession which were represented by the seven changing pole-stars before the backward movement could have been calculated by the position of the equinoctial colure. The reduced scale of the Semitic seven days is but a one-inch-to-the-mile sort of rendering of the seven stages in precession which have yet to be explained.

The traditions show that one type of the under-world was the heptanomis, which had been mundane in Egypt and was made celestial in the astronomical mythology. This was likewise reproduced in the making of Amenta. Ptah is said to have designed the Nomes (Text of Shabaka, line 6). The Nomes were seven in number. The Knemmu who assisted Ptah were seven. The creations that culminated in man the speaker were seven. Also in one of the Rabbinical traditions concerning the lower and upper, or the earthly and heavenly, paradise, it is said that before his fall Adam was the heavenly dweller in a habitation which contained seven palaces or mansions. These, according to the Sohar, were afterwards *rearranged* to become the abodes of the blessed. This contains a fragment of the genuine legend when rightly interpreted. Adam is here considered to have been a dweller in the paradise of the celestial heptanomis. This was repeated in Amenta when the lower paradise of the solar mythos was mapped out in seven domains for Atum = Adam, as the land of promise destined for the glorified elect. It is related by Rabbi Manasseh Ben-Israel that the souls of men were created during the six days of the beginning, independently of bodies, like the first company of the Kamite gods. These were the spirits derived from the external elements that preceded the embodiment of a special soul in human form. (*Nat. Genesis,* vol. ii. p. 282.) "True Israelites believe," says the Rabbi, "that all the souls which have existed from the first time, and which shall be to the end of the world, were generated in six days of creation." These are the six souls of the fish, the fowl, the beast, the reptile, and other forms of life which preceded the seventh soul of the speaker, man, or Atum = Adam. The seventh of the elemental powers, in the human shape, is described in the gnostic systems of the Ophites and Sethians when they teach that Ialdabaoth called upon the rest of the Elohim, saying, "Come, let us make man after our own image." They also relate that Ialdabaoth in the character of elder brother as the would-be father created six sons, he himself being the first person in the group. They further declare that these are the seven mundane demons who always oppose and resist the human race, because it was on their account that their father (Ialdabaoth) was cast down to this lower world. (Irenaeus, Bk. I, ch. 30, 8.)

It is also represented in the Rabbinical writings that the souls of the Israelites had a higher origin than the souls of the Gentiles. The souls of the Goim, they say, have their origin from the external powers, the power of klippoth or the demons, whereas the souls of the Israelites are derived from the Holy Spirit. The first originated from the elemental powers that were imaged by the zoötypes, and were denounced as evil spirits by the later theology. As for Atum-Ra, the father of Iu, he was the Kamite holy spirit. The souls of the idolaters were not called men, because they were born in the totemic stage of sociology and were derived from the spirits of the elements which had been imaged by the zoötypes. More simply stated, they were not men only because the mode of representation was pre-anthropomorphic, and the soul of blood was not yet traced to the maternal source, or the spirit of man to the father. In the Babylonian legends the totemic zoötypes, which preceded the man derived from the soul of blood, have been confused with the beings born of the abyss as the creatures of darkness. "Then Belos the sun-god came, and the animals died, as they were not able to bear the light. Belos seeing a vast space unoccupied, though by nature fruitful, commanded one of the gods to cut off his head and to mix the blood with the earth, and from thence to form other men and animals which should be capable of bearing the light." (Eusebius, *Chron.*, i. 4) This in its way is a mythical creation of the man who was made from the soul of blood. In another legend a great destruction follows a rebellion called "the revolt in heaven," which is only mentioned here for the sake of citing the statement that when the rebels were destroyed or driven out by the supreme god, "in their room he created mankind." As we understand the gnosis, a group of six totemic powers was extant before the seventh, the soul of man, was specialized as a human soul that was incarnated in the blood of the motherhood, the first soul, so to say, that could talk. This group of six zoötypes with no human figure included is widely extended over the world. As the Arunta tell us, in the Alcheringa, or Auld Lang Syne, there were no men or women, only pre-human creatures designated the Inapertwa. In the Egyptian mythos the six zoötypes of Sut, Horus, Shu, Hapi, Tuamutef, and Kabhsenuf are followed and completed by the human figure in Amsta the man or Horus the child. The Arunta version comes fresh from an almost unknown world. It may have been carried there from Africa, but it is certain that the Egyptians did not derive their mysteries, mythical legends, and sign-language from the natives of Central Australia. The tradition of the Inapertwa only applied to certain totems, six in number (this will bear repeating). The preliminary pre-human creatures who were made into men and women by the Ungambikula belonged to the six following totems: Akakia, or plum tree; Inguitchika, or grass-seed; Echunpa, or large lizard; Erliwatchera, or little lizard; Atninpirichina, or Alexandra parakeet; and the Untaina, or small rat. Here are six totemic types of creatures that preceded the human voice and image. There were six groupings of elemental spirits based upon six elemental powers that were imaged by means of zoötypes before ever an elemental power was imaged in the human likeness, or, as it was rendered at a later time, before the creation of man, who was seventh in a series of seven, or as the earliest *human* soul. Miss Kingsley gives it as the opinion of Dr. Nassau of Gaboon that the nature-spirits commonly affecting human affairs, which are believed in by the natives on the West Coast, can be classified "fairly completely" in *six orders* (Kingsley, M. H., *Travels in West Africa*). The Damaras derive from six pre-human powers by means of six descents or eundas. Six descents from superhuman powers would naturally follow for those who derived their descent from the powers, gods, or spirits that might be represented by six totemic zoötypes such as the serpent, crocodile, hippopotamus, lion, hawk, and other figures of the elemental forces that preceded the human image as a primitive type of power. Afterwards the six powers would account for six different classes of spirits recognized in the animistic interpretation of external nature according to religion in the fetishtic phase. In India there was a first form of the Aditya, six in number, who preceded the groups of seven and eight. There was also an Egyptian "mystery of the six" which has not been unveiled. The seventh of the series is the soul that was first considered to be human because it was the soul of man, the speaker, which in this phase was discreted from the totemic souls by means of language. No distinction could have been more natural.

As we have previously seen in Book IV., the Osiris deceased is reconstituted for the life hereafter by the blending of his seven souls, which correspond to the seven souls of Ra. And when he has become a spirit by the seven being put together at last in the likeness of the ka, it is said to him, *"Thy perfect soul, O Nefer-Uben-f, triumphant, hath the power of speech"* (Rit., ch. 149, 15). Speech was the property of the perfect soul—that is, the highest of the seven souls—which was consequently human. The Chinese also have the very ancient "six honoured ones," or six Tsung. The Zuni Indians adored the six powers that preceded the seventh in the likeness of man. In "The Wisdom of Jesus" or the book of Ecclesiasticus there is a description of the creation of man. It is said that men "received the use of the five operations of the Lord, and in the sixth place he imparted to them understanding, and in the seventh speech" (Eccles. xvii. 5). This contains a fragment of the Egyptian wisdom. The creation of man from seven souls takes place in Amenta for the next life, with speech as the seventh constituent. In the mythological text from Memphis there is an account of Ptah's creation, in which it is said that all the limbs moved (*i.e.*, as parts of the pauti or company of the gods) when he *uttered the word of wisdom* which came forth from the tongue and worked a blessing upon all things. *Speech caused (or literally became) the making of men and the creation of the gods for Ptah* (Proc. Soc. Bib. Arch., vol. XXIII, pts. 4 and 5, pp. 173-4). Thus the making of man *qua* man is attributed to speech in this Kamite creation of man as the speaker, the same as in "The Wisdom of Jesus." This may account for the custom, or religious rite, performed by the Hindu father, who puts his lips to the right ear of the new-born babe and mutters three times, "Speech! Speech! Speech!" This gives it a name. The previous souls were only known by totemic types and semi-human souls, not by proper names. (Kelly, *Indo-European Folk-Lore*, pp. 145-6.)

Hindu sages tell us that six of the seven primordial souls were born twins; the seventh alone came into existence as a single soul. This too can be read by means of the gnosis. The six souls were pre-human. That is, they were totemic souls. Now, the totemic zoötype was the representative of both sexes; the male stood for the men, the female for the women. "Of those that are born together, sages have called the seventh single-born, for six are twins" (Rig-Veda, Wilson, ii. 131, 132). Totemic man was born twin as represented by the zoötype of both sexes. Six of these preceded the human figure, which as *homo* or man was born single and had to be divided into man and woman according to the mythical representation of the cutting out in the second creation by Iahu-Elohim.

(Gen. ii.). The twin-soul was what the Egyptian Ritual describes as the one soul in two bodies (ch. 17). One of these was male as Shu, the other female as Tefnut. This was the man or Adam of the first creation in Genesis, who was figured as both male and female (Gen. i. 27). Shu and Tefnut were born twins, he as brother, she as sister, and both under one type, that of the lion. In the same way the crocodile was female as Apt and male as Sebek. Thus a single totemic type denoted a soul that was born twin when souls were prehuman. It is the same doctrine when the Kabalists assert that in the beginning of the world souls were created by God in pairs consisting of a male and female. The twin-soul here is a product of the primary creation; the single soul belongs to the second creation. The doctrine is apparent in the first chapter of Genesis, when Adam was created in the likeness of the Elohim, and was both male and female. Whereas in the second creation (ch. ii.) man, or Adam, is not a twin soul; he is fashioned singly, and the woman is taken from the body of the man to form a consort for him. When the supreme power of seven was imaged in the human likeness this constituted a mythical man as the seventh in a series of seven prototypes. Thus Enoch, the seventh from Adam, is pre-eminently the man. Also, when the group of manes travel round the zodiac, in the Hindu astronomy, the seventh is a divine man or a Buddha. The seventh Buddha is always the man who is held to be divine. The seven Buddhas are often portrayed in the temples and monasteries of Tibet, where they are better known as the seven Sang-gye, meaning increase of purity, who are named: (1) He who saw through and through, (2) he who had a crest of fire, (3) the preserver of all, (4) the dissolver of the round of life, (5) golden might, (6) the guardian of light, (7) *the mighty* Shakya. The seventh is that pre-eminent personage known as Sakya-Muni or Gautama, whose life and history were evolved from the pre-extant mythos, like those of the Christ in the gospels—the true Buddha, who could no more become historical than the Christ of the gnosis. If Buddhism could but explicate its own origins it would become apparent that it is both natural and scientific. But the blind attempt to make the Buddha historical in one personality will place it ultimately on the same level with historical Christianity at the bottom of the ditch. The seventh Buddha that comes once in a phœnix-cycle of 500 years is the divine man, who can only be repeated as an astronomical figure—a measurer for the eternal in the cycles of time. But the manifestation of the seventh, the man of the group, has been made exoteric as an incarnation of the seventh Buddha in the human form on earth. The divine man as the seventh of a series is yet extant and operative in British folk-lore when the seventh son of a seventh son is always the great healer. The totemic soul was twin. The human soul was singly born as the soul of the man or woman. It was not as the Hebrew Adam that man was made, but as the Egyptian Atum, earlier Tum; and Tum in Egyptian means "*created man.*" Adam is a later rendering of the name. And this "created man" was made as Atum son of Ptah with the aid of his Ali or co-creators. It was they who created the senses of man, the breathing of the nostrils, the sight of the eyes, the hearing of the ears, the thought of the heart, and utterance by the tongue.

Man was made according to the outline of Child-Horus sketched by Ptah; the anthrotype that was to supersede the zoötype. Man that is composed of seven souls, according to the doctrine, was the product of seven elements. These were recognized at first as nature-powers that were ultimately divinized as makers or creators. They had been divinized as the first company of the associate-gods before the time of Ptah, and when Kheper-Ptah, Neb-er-ter, became supreme, the seven Ali were associated with him in the work of creation, the evolution of man, and the making of the garden in Amenta. Thus man in the Egyptian mythos was a late creation, which is in agreement with the legends of the aborigines. Man was also made twice over, once as mortal on the earth, and once as the spirit-man or manes in Amenta. Hence the first and second Adam or Atum, the man of earth and the man from heaven. These will also explain the two forms of Adam in the book of Genesis (i. 27 and ii. 7). The seventh of the elemental powers was the soul of blood. This was represented in the elder Horus as the soul of matter by a child that was unseeing, inarticulate, and altogether imperfect. The soul of blood as paternal source was added to the rest when Atum cut himself to produce his offspring Hu and Sau (Rit., ch. 17). In the Assyrian legend, when the head of Belos is taken off the blood that gushes out is mingled with the soil of earth or matter. *"Thence men were formed.* On this account it is that men are rational, and partake of divine knowledge." That is as human beings born of the soul of blood, which in this later creation was added to the six pre-human souls of Mother-earth, when the human origin was recognized as higher than the earlier and pre-human source of soul, such as air, water, and earth. The blood now mixed with the soil of earth is the soul of blood united with the earth or matter in the märchen. The highest of the seven was but a soul descended from the mother-blood, with no immortal spark of spirit that was afterwards derived from God the Father who is Atum-Ra; but it was reckoned the superior of any soul that was previously derived from the external elements. The seventh alone was consequently given the human likeness in Child-Horus, or in Atum.

Man is created twice over in the book of Genesis. The first Adam is formed in the image of the Elohim or elemental powers. The Elohim said, "Let us make man in our image, after our likeness" (ch. i. 26). In the second creation man is formed by Iahu-Elohim, who "breathed the breath of life into his nostrils and man became a living soul" (ch. ii. 7). These are the first and second Adams of Paul's doctrine. "The first man Adam became a living soul, the last Adam a life-giving spirit. The first man is of the earth, earthy; the second man is of heaven" (1 Cor. xv. 45-8). These two as Egyptian are Atum-Horus and Atum-Ra, who are identical in nature with the first and second Horus—the soul in matter and in spirit. The first man was a failure. In a gnostic version man was formed, but could not stand erect, because the seven workmen, the Ali or Elohim, were unable to inspire him with an enduring soul. He writhed and wriggled like a worm upon the ground. Then the "power above" took pity on him, seeing the creature had been fashioned in his likeness, and shot forth a spark of life which enabled him to rise erect and live. (*Nat. Genesis,* vol. ii, p. 39.)

The seventh power in the human image can be traced in

legendary lore. For example, Apollodorus the Athenian grammarian relates that there was at one time a tradition current in heaven that the giants or Titans could only be conquered by the aid of a man; and as he wrote his work on mythology before the era called Christian, this has been taken as pointing to the incarnation of a Jewish Jesus. It was a floating fragment of old Egypt's wisdom. In the battle with the Sebau or the rebels, and the Sut-Typhonians, the powers of evil are conquered by Horus, who was incarnated in the human form on earth as son of the woman, and who is victor in Amenta over death and darkness and typical rebels, in the person of Amsu-Horus the man in spirit—son of the god in human form. Thus the Titans or rebels, called the children of defeat, had already been conquered by the god, who became incarnate *not as a man* but *in the form of man,* from the time when Atum-Horus first assumed the human type as vehicle of the divine.

In the Egyptian mythology the great change in the mode of becoming and of representing was effected in the cult of Ptah—the change, that is, in the genesis of souls from the incorporation of totemic souls by the elemental powers to the creation of souls in the human image by the one god, Neb-er-ter. This change, which runs through all later mythology, is traceable in Egypt. Ptah is the link betwixt the elemental powers and the spirit-ancestors; the link by means of which the zoötype passed into the anthrotype; the gods as Elohim into the one god, Atum, called the son of Ptah, or Iahu-Elohim in the book of Genesis. Ptah is the first one god of the Egyptian religion whose totality was compounded from the pre-existent powers. The Ali or associate-gods were now combined in him who was the one god and who comprised the group in one. The group were now the nine or the Put, and Ptah, as the all-one that was named from the Put. The Put-cycle of gods, which was summed up in Ptah the one god, as father, will explain why and how the Elohim are plural as a company called the Ali, and single as the one in whom the powers were unified called Ptah, who was the biune parent of Atum-Horus in Amenta, and the maker of man, or Atum, with the aid of the seven powers that were previously extant. The Elohim, then, we take to be a form of the Put-cycle of Ptah the opener of Amenta. As a company of associate-gods they originated in the primordial powers, which were seven in number; seven with the Great Mother; seven with Anup; seven with Taht; seven with Horus; seven with Ptah. When grouped in the Put-cycle, with Ptah and Atum-Horus added as father and son, the associate-gods are nine in number; sometimes called the ennead of Memphis, or of Annu. Thus Ptah and his Ali answer to the Phœnician Elohim, who were one as the highest El (in the singular) and plural in the group of the Elohim. Ptah was now portrayed as the author of becoming in the human form, and thence the mythical maker of man. He had been represented by the beetle and the frog as the transformer in matter. Afterwards he is imaged as the human *embryo in utero,* when he had become the creator of a human soul distinguished from the totemic or elemental soul, which had been common to man and beast.

Ptah is portrayed in the monuments as the creator of the seventh, or human soul. Wilkinson met with a very rare picture of the god who is *alone,* and who was engaged in sketching with a pen the figure of Child-Horus. In other words, he is outlining an image of the human soul that was incarnated in the mother-blood and personalized in Horus as the child of Isis, one form of whom was Tum or Atum-Horus.

Ptah is also portrayed in the image of a male-mother. He is the earliest type of the god with a womb in whom the male and female nature were united in a biune parent who was divinized as the all-one. We learn from Joseph Thomson's travels that when the Masai of Central Africa get married it is a native custom for the bridegroom to dress himself in women's clothes and wear them for a month after the marriage. He is assuming the phase of parentage in the guise of the mother, and literally following suit to the female, because the maternal type and imagery of parentage are still dominant, and thus the father comes into existence, so to say, as the male-mother. The significance is the same as in the custom of couvade. The father was assuming the parentage in the likeness of both sexes. Thus Ptah, or Atum, or Osiris, presents a form of the same duality as the Australian "man with a vulva," who in his primitive way was a two-fold figure of the all-one. To recapitulate: in the Egyptian Genesis "created man" is Tum, later Atum, the original of the first man Adam. Atum was the son of the creator Ptah, the earliest biune parent divinized. The seven primordial powers had been previously recognized in nature as the offspring of the mother. Six of these were pre-human powers or souls developed from the external elements. The seventh was the earliest human soul, born of the mother-blood. This was the blind imperfect soul in matter that was imaged in Child-Horus, An-ar-ef. The soul of all the seven was matriarchal; they were the children of the mother only. Two other powers were added to make up the total in the Put-cycle or ennead of Memphis. The "double primitive essence" had been assigned to Ptah. Doctrinally this was the soul of blood derived from the maternal source, in combination with the spirit of the male. Thence came the human soul that was constituted in two halves, the soul in matter and in spirit. This biunity was first personified in Ptah as the mother and father in one divinity, and, as the biune parent, Ptah gave birth to man, or created his son Atum. In the text from Memphis the god is called "Ptah of the earth. *The mother giving birth to Atum*" (line 14). Here Atum = Adam has a mother, an item which is omitted from the Hebrew version. Thus Atum-Horus is the product of this biune parent; and the seven powers that contributed the seven souls or constituent parts of created man with Ptah and Atum, and the seven associate-gods compose the cycle or ennead of Annu. In this way the Put-cycle of the nine gods consisted of Ptah and his eight sons; an eighth one being added to the primary seven as the highest because he was the son of god the father, not merely the product of the mother, like the seven Ali or Elohim. That son of Ptah was Tum or Atum, born as Child-Horus, and one of Atum's names or titles is Iu the coming son, or Iu-em-hetep, he who comes with peace. And in this Iu we propose to identify the Jewish divinity and also the name of Iah, or Iahu, distinguished from והוה (Ihuh). The compound title Iahu-Elohim shows that Iahu is one of the Elohistic group who was continued in a new *rôle* as the planter of the garden in the second of the two creations in the book of Genesis.

In the making of man by Ptah and the Ali or associate-gods, it may be said that man or Tum was created by their being converted into man, Tum, or Adam. It was they who made "the dexterity of the hands and the walking of the feet"; also they "created the sight of the eyes, the hearing of the ears, and the breathing of the nostrils." In other words, they contributed those faculties to the creation of the human being—such faculties as the sight of the hawk (Horus), the breathing force of the panting lion (Shu), the ears of the jackal (Anup), the nose or neb of the knowing ibis, the hand of the ape, and others which had been exalted as superhuman and were now made use of in the creation of man or Atum by the Kamite Elohim. These powers in themselves were indefinitely earlier than Ptah, but in the theology of Memphis they became auxiliaries to the supreme one god, and were then held to proceed from him and to become his members and his attributes. The change is indicated when it is said of Ptah, "His associate-gods in his presence are the teeth and lips, the joints and hands of Atum, for these *become* the associate gods" (line 10). The same doctrinal change is apparent in the Ritual (ch. 17, 4), when it is said of the supreme one god, "It is Ra creating his members, which became those gods who are with Ra."

Iu, the coming one, is the ever-coming son of the father who was re-born as his own son; and Iu (or Atum) with his associate-gods corresponds to Iahu-Elohim in the Hebrew Genesis, who follows the gods of the primary creation in the first chapter. Thus Ptah and his Ali are the prototypes or originals of the Elohim, in both the singular and the plural use of the word; whilst Iahu-Elohim answers to Iu and his associate-gods in the second creation. This development in the divine character may supply a rational explanation of the discrepancy concerning the name of Iahu in the first two books of the Pentateuch. It is related in Exodus (vi. 2, 3) that "Iahu spake unto Moses and said unto him, 'I am Iahu. I appeared unto Abraham, unto Isaac, and unto Jacob as El Shaddai, but by my name Iahu I was not made known to them.'" Whereas the *name* of Iahu had most certainly been known from the time of the second creation (Gen. ii.). This therefore must be a question of the nature, not merely of the name of the deity. If Iahu were one of the group of the Ali = Elohim he would be a son of the mother, one of the Baalim who preceded the fatherhood of Ihuh or Jehovah. The god who was known by the name of El was also one of the Baalim, Elohim, or Ali; the first company of the associate gods, who ruled under the matriarchate. Atum was born "Iu" as the son of Ptah at Memphis, and the same god became the father as Atum-Ra at On. The development is to be traced in the fact that the first Iu as Egyptian was only a form of god the mother's son, whereas the later Ihuh had attained the status of the maker, as god the father, who was Atum-Ra in Egypt.

Chapter v. announces that "this is the book of the generations of Adam." In this the previous "generation of the heaven and the earth" are represented as the generations of Adam, who meanwhile had been transformed from the divine Atum of Egypt into the human

Adam of the Jewish writings, and the genuine mythos transmogrified into a spurious history. The translators of the Memphian text point out the extreme likelihood that there were two "originally independent texts" which have been artificially blended to produce a deceptive appearance of unity. This agrees with the fundamental difference betwixt the Elohistic and Jehovistic versions in the book of Genesis, those of the Elohim and Iahu-Elohim, in which two accounts of the creation have been run into one. It is plainly apparent in the book of Genesis that two originally independent legends of creation have been imperfectly welded together to give an appearance of unity. This is proved by the two different beginnings in which the heaven and earth are formed, and man is made twice over. The first chapter contains the generations of the heaven and the earth when these were created *by the Elohim.* The second contains the generations of the heaven and the earth when they were created in the day that earth and heaven were made by Iahu-Elohim. As Egyptian, these were (1) the Ali, or associate-gods with Neb-er-ter or Kheper-Ptah; and (2) Iu the son of God, who became the one god of both the Egyptians and the Jews, who, as we shall show, were the worshippers of Iu = Iahu.

The man created by the Elohim, or Ali, was totemic man, like the legendary Adam with the tail of an ape, a lion, or other zoötype. It was thus the elemental powers were represented: Sut by the hippopotamus; Sebek by the crocodile; Atum by the lion; Iu by the ass; Seb by the goose; Taht by the Ibis; Anup by the jackal; Kabhsenuf by the hawk, in whose likenesses totemic men were imaged. This first man was the Adam, who failed and fell from lack of the vitalizing spark of the individual fatherhood; the man who was only born of the group in communal marriage under the matriarchate. These totemic forbears of man may also account for a Rabbinical tradition in which it is related that previous to the creation of Eve the man Adam entered into sexual intercourse with the animals. Which is doubtless an ignorant misinterpretation of the totemic status of man and animals made by theologians who were ignorant of totemic sign-language. Some of the Rabbins asserted that the first man, Adam, was created in the Garden of Eden with a tail like that of an ourang-outang. His tail was afterwards cut off to improve his appearance. The legend contains a fragment of the mythos which has been reduced to the status of Jewish märchen. This may furnish another link betwixt the Hebrew Adam and the Egyptian Atum, as the fiery-spirited ape was a type of Atum, the solar god of the garden in Amenta.

The pre-existent superhuman powers or associate-gods contributed all that they had previously attained for themselves to constitute the higher type of god as father. Atum was born as Horus or Iu, child of the mother, and afterwards developed into Atum-Ra as god the father. Hence he became the maker or creator of gods and men as the *begetter,* who succeeded the transformer Kheper-Ptah. The seven primordial powers had been recognized and divinized as offspring of the old First Mother. The Great Mother was combined with the male in Ptah. Atum, or "created man," was formed by Ptah as an evolution from the seven elemental powers. These became the seven souls of Atum-Ra, otherwise called the seven souls of man; the seven as elements or powers that went to the making of the manes in Amenta, or the human being when the rendering was literalized. Thus the evolution of man, according to the Egyptian wisdom, was from seven powers of the elements, on which a doctrine of the seven souls was founded. Six of these had been pre-human souls. The seventh alone attained the human type and status, whether as Child-Horus or the man as Atum the first father. These souls of life had been identified and divinized in the mythology: the soul of water as the fish of Sebek, the breathing force as the lion of Shu, the "creeping thing" of earth as the beetle of Kheper-Ptah. Such was the creation of man according to the Egyptian wisdom. The seven elemental powers then furnished his seven constituent parts, or seven souls, as co-workers with Ptah, and merged themselves in Atum or were absorbed in created man. In the second chapter of Genesis the god Iahu succeeds the Elohim. As an Egyptian deity Iu = Iahu was the son of Ptah. The oneness of the father and son, with the son as representative of the father, is a doctrine that was founded in the cult of Ptah at Memphis and perpetuated in the religion of Atum-Ra at Annu. It is Atum who says he is both the closer and the opener, and he is but one (Rit., ch. 17). And it is the father, whether as Ptah or Atum, who comes into being as his own son. Also, when Osiris has been mutilated by the murderer Sut he is reconstituted by Horus, and the father lives again in and as the son. It was by his ever-coming and continual rebirth that the son brought life and immortality or continuity to light as demonstrator in phenomena on behalf of god the father.

The earliest Egyptian type of a creator is the moulder or potter. The god Khnum, for example, is depicted as the potter in the act of forming man from the matter of earth. Ptah, sometimes called the son of Khnum, is likewise the divine potter. He is portrayed at Philæ in the act of heaping plastic clay upon the potter's table from which he is about to form the image of man, which he had sketched in the likeness of Child-Horus. Previously the goddesses and gods were shaped in the likenesses of zoötypes. Khnum himself was ram-headed; Kheper, the former, was beetle-headed. Up to the time of Ptah, or Bes, the Negroid pygmy, the human likeness was not given to any god; and his son Atum-Horus is the earliest divinity in *perfect* human form. Now, as Egyptian Atum is the original of the Hebrew Adam, it follows that we are witnessing the creation of Adam from the earth in a mythical representation, when Ptah, the potter, shapes the archetypal man as his son Atum from a lump of plastic clay.

We are also witnessing the creation of man, or of Tum, the son of Ptah, in the human likeness, when "the associate-gods as the Ali or Elohim created the sight of the eyes and the hearing of the ears, the breathing of the nostrils, and sent up that which gave pleasure to the father." That is to Ptah, who is the father of Tum in this creation of man by the Put-cycle of the primordial powers, which corresponds to the first creation of Adam by the Elohim in the first chapter of the Hebrew Genesis. "Then was ordained the utterance of every decision of the tongue, which repeats the deliberation of the heart."

"Now the creation of the gods," that is to say "of Tum and his associate-gods, was when proclamation was made of all the divine names in his wisdom." "The associate-gods in his presence are as the teeth and lips, the joints and hands of Tum, for these become the associate-gods," or *the associate-gods become the members and powers of Tum, Atum or Adam the created man,* who was formed in the likeness of Iahu-Elohim. We are told in the texts that "men are mortal since the time of Ra," that is since the time when a father in heaven or in Amenta was depicted in the image of man instead of being represented by some pre-human and totemic type. This was Atum. Atum in the solar mythos was Ra in his first sovereignty, and Atum = Hebrew Adam was primordial man. Otherwise stated, Atum was the first god delineated in the form of man. Hence men are mortal or human since the time of Atum-Ra (Rit., ch. 17). Previously they might be imaged as beetles and frogs in the time of Ptah, kaf-apes in the time of Taht, crocodiles in the time of Sebek, and hippopotami, giraffes, or black vultures in the time of Sut. This difference betwixt the animal and human types is also recognized in relation to Ra (Rit., ch. 153, A) when the first creatures or beings are called "the ancestors of Ra" and "the ancestors of Seb," and are designated "worms" to express their inferiority. They were mere reptiles in comparison with the human type. In the Hebrew Genesis, when the man as Adam was created (I. 26) he was to have dominion over all creatures of the water, air, and earth. And Atum, or Tum in the Ritual (ch. 79), is designated "the Lord of all creatures," that is when he makes his appearance in the figure of man, who is described as being "in the form of the Lord of all creatures" (Rit., ch. 82). Atum, whom comes as the unique one god in the form of man, is hailed in the Ritual as the lord of heaven who "issues forth from the earth and createth whatever is begotten," and "who giveth vigour to the men now living." "I am summed up as Atum," says the speaker (Rit., ch. 83). As Atum he exclaims, "I am a soul, and my soul is divine. It is the self-originating force." The speaker, in the character of Atum-Ra, who makes his advent as a man, explains that the seven Uræus-divinities formed his body, but his soul is divine. It is an image of the eternal. These Uræi were a type of the seven primordial powers that were grouped and unified in one, whether as god or man. They are companions, seven in number, who became the associate-gods of Ptah in his creative work, and who were afterwards absorbed in Atum as constituents of his body, or the means of his embodiment as man.

The ascent of soul through various elemental phases of existence is alluded to in one of the "sayings of Jesus" when it is said that the fowls of the air, the beasts of the earth, and the fishes of the sea all "draw us" to the kingdom. These led the way as elemental and pre-human souls. A soul of the air was imaged by the bird; a soul of earth was imaged by the beast, or reptile; a soul of water by the fish; a soul of vegetation by the shoot or branch; and so on through the series, all of which were offspring of the Great Mother. But the highest soul was now derived from god the father as an effluence of the holy spirit. Therefore it is said, "The kingdom of heaven is within you; and whosoever shall know himself shall find it." "Know yourselves (then), and you shall be aware that ye are sons of the Father." Horus in his resurrection, at his second advent, came to proclaim the father as the begetter of a spirit that should attain eternal life. He also came to personate that spirit in the likeness of the father to the manes in Amenta. Atum, the Egyptian holy spirit, was the author of that spirit by which totemic man became a living soul. With the Egyptians the soul was of both sexes. The divine being, as Ptah, Atum, or Osiris, was of a biune nature. Hence Ptah and Osiris are portrayed as the male and female in one image, and this one prototypal soul was discreted as human in the two sexes. In passing through Amenta the human soul is represented as the male accompanied by the female, the wife, sister, or some other female as supplemental to the male. This soul, divided in the two halves of sex, was united again in establishing an eternal soul. One form of the dual type is imaged by the twins, Shu and his sister Tefnut, who are blended in Tattu. They represent the soul that had been discreted in two sexes which is joined in one again to fulfil the likeness of the eternal spirit Atum-Ra, who was self-divided in creating the two sexes. Tefnut, the sister sould, was absorbed in Shu the brother who wears her emblem on his head, and who is the twofold type of a dual soul now unified in one. Thus the soul that lived for ever was held to be established for eternity by the female being blended with the male. Now amongst the primitive races, African, Melanesian and others, the women will volunteer to be strangled at the funeral, or buried alive in the graves of their husbands (or the chiefs), believing it to be solely in company with the male that they can reach the realms of bliss; and the favourite wife in the abode of the blessed is held to be the one who meets her death with the greatest fortitude. That is, by the female being blended with the male in death, as Tefnut was blended with, or absorbed in, Shu.

When the human soul had been derived from the essence of the male instead of the blood of the female, the woman was naturally derived from the man, as she is in the second of the Hebrew creations described in the book of Genesis. A soul derived from Atum was dual in sex. This soul was divided into Adam and Eve, the typical two sexes of the Hebrew legend. Adam was Atum in the original mythos, and the soul derived from Atum was discreted in Adam and Eve, as the two sexes derived from the one primordial soul, which was figured first as the soul of Shu and Tefnut in the Egyptian mythos. Tefnut was not cut out of the side of Shu, but she was depicted as the hinder half of the lion with Shu as the fore-part. Atum was the lion as representative of the soul or force, and the lion was severed in two parts, head and tail, as the dual type of Shu and Tefnut, which preceded the anthropomorphic representation in Adam and Eve. So late is the Hebrew rendering compared with the Egyptian. The "self-splitting" of Atum is shown in the mutilation of his members. Hence we have made the suggestion that in the rite of sub-incision practised by the most primitive of races, like the Australian Arunta, this "self-splitting" of the male denoted the claim of the man to being the potential source of both sexes, and that, whereas the male was derived from the female under the matriarchate, it was now asserted that the woman was made from the man in a process of self-splitting illustrated by the practice of sub-incision, and by the later creation of the female from the male in the mythology. Queen

Hatshepsu claimed that the true image of the creator was formed by a combination of the mother and the male in one, which image she personated under her title of Mat-Ka-Ra, the true image of Ra, but gave pre-eminence to female nature as the bringer-forth from the beginning. The picture of the male endeavouring to take the place of the female as producer of the child is at times exceedingly pathetic. He carved the likeness of the female member on his own, as do the Arunta in their rites to-day, and masqueraded as "the man with a vulva." He wore the woman's garb in marriage. In the custom of couvade he went to bed to become a mother like Ptah, and to nurse the new-born little one.

In the earliest mythology the woman was dominant. Men derived their descent from the mothers. This was in the time of the first creation. In the second, when the woman was derived from the man, (even by a surgical operation), the male comes uppermost, the matriarchal woman succumbs to patriarchal man. This is glanced at obliquely in the doom pronounced upon the woman by Iahu-Elohim for "plucking the forbidden fruit." "Unto the woman he said, I will greatly multiply thy sorrow and conception; in sorrow shalt thou bring forth children; and thy desire shall be to thy husband, and *he shall rule over thee.*" There is to be an end of matriarchal supremacy, and descent, as previously reckoned from the motherhood, is to be suppressed in this the second of two creations for the Adamic race. The two races of Adam are referred to by Esdras (II. vi. 55-56): "O Lord, thou madest the world for our sakes. As for the other people , which *also come of Adam,* thou hast said that they are nothing, but be like unto spittle." Both were Adamic, however, but the first came from the red earth or the mother-blood only; the second were derived from the fatherhood. In the Latin version of Esdras those who are nothing are the people of the first-born world, whereas those of the second creation are called the "only-begotten." In the mythical rendering of this twofoldness the first Horus was born but not begotten. He was the child of the mother only. The second Horus is the only begotten of the father, twice born and once begotten. In the primary phase he corresponds to the totemic people who were born under the matriarchate, those of the first-born world. In the second he is a representative of the people who are called the "only begotten" because they are the children of the fathers. The two primary castes or classes of Aryas in India, the sons of light and the children of darkness, were based upon the same original distinction betwixt those who were born of the matriarchate and those who are begotten under the divinized fatherhood. The Rabbins have retained some fragments of totemic tradition without the gnosis. It is said in the Targum of Palestine, "The Lord God created man in two formations." This dual formation, or creation, is common to the märchen, which we are tracing to the original mythos. The first men recognizable were made of red earth, which, when interpreted, means that flesh was shapen from the mother's blood. Then, say the Melbourne blacks, the god Pungel blew the spirit of life into the man at his navel (*Nat. Gen.,* vol. ii. pp. 34-40). The Arunta tribes likewise hold that the animistic spirit enters the navel to cause conception in their women. In the Egyptian texts it is also said of those who derive from the mother, the Amu, the Tamehu, and the Negroes, "Sekhet has created them and she creates their souls," the souls that were created under the matriarchate, and were only souls of blood, whereas the Ruti were derived from Ra the holy spirit. In a magical text supposed to be of Akkadian origin there is a version of the "cutting out" of the woman from the man which is a little nearer to nature than the creation of the female from a rib of the male in the Hebrew Genesis. It is said the woman was derived from the flank of the man. (Boscawen.) Scattered fragments of the ancient wisdom now identified as Kamite are often to be found in what the Christian writers ignorantly scout as the wild and foolish fables or the absurd fancies of egregious Talmudists. Here is an instance. It is related that the Lord caused a deep sleep to fall on Adam whilst he extracted something from his *members* which was dispersed over the globe so that the whole earth might be inhabited by his seed (*Endeckt. Judenthum*). This account is nearer to the original than the version given in Genesis. The creation of the human race by Atum is biological. The "double primitive essence" of life was first assigned to Ptah. This consisted of blood and protozoa, and the twin source was personalized in Atum, who as creator was an image of the male and female blended in one person. Atum is described as producing his children by spontaneous emission, and also by the drawing of blood from his members, which was a way of showing the duality of source that was made one in the primal parent thus personified in Atum or in Adam, and in the male with the image of the female cut twice over on his member, once in the ovoid figure and once in the opening by sub-incision.

According to the second Hebrew account of creation, "Iahu-Elohim formed man of the dust of the ground and breathed into his nostrils the breath of life" (Gen. ii. 7), which can have no direct relationship to aught that ever did occur in this our human world, nor had it any such signification in the esoteric version of the mystery teachers. But this can be followed in the mysteries of Amenta, in which Ptah was the vivifier of the manes for the afterlife. The process of vivification was by opening the mouth of the dead and *inspiring the breath of life into the nostrils*. In the chapter by which the mouth of a person is opened for him in the earth of Ptah the Osiris pleads, "Let my mouth be opened by Ptah, and let the muzzles which are on my mouth be loosed by the god of the domain. Let my mouth be opened by Ptah with that instrument of steel or ba-metal wherewith he openeth the mouths of the gods and the manes." (Renouf, Rit., ch. 23.) Breath was restored to those who had been deprived of it. In the chapter by which air is given in the nether-world it is said, "O Atum, let there come to me the air which is in thy nostrils" (chs. 54 and 56). Again, the Osiris says, *"My nostrils are opened in Tattu,"* the place of being permanently established; and by these ceremonies performed in mysteries man became a breathing soul after he had passed into the land of life. For it was the man who had died on earth to reappear as a sahu-mummy in Amenta whose mouth was opened and his nostrils inspired with the breath of second life derived from Atum-Iu = Iu-Elohim. Atum likewise is the giver of breath in the new life of

Amenta. He gives it to the spirit in the egg. This is a re-creation of Adam, or man, as manes in the earth of eternity, not the creation of a human being from the dust on the surface of our earth, as it has been misrendered in the Hebrew version.

The legend of the fall is not reproduced in the first account of the Hebrew creation. In this, *homo* had been created male and female in the likeness of the Elohim or the powers which were imaged by zoötypes. The first Adam was totemic man with a tail, who is said to have had connection with all or any of the animals. In the second chapter of Genesis the first formation by the Elohim is not recognized in the human figure as man. For it is said *"there was not a man* to till the ground." Now, the real man comes into being as "a living soul." Iahu-Elohim breathes into his nostrils the breath of life. Iahu-Elohim is the author of a new creation; and it is this second Adam for whom the garden eastward is planted in Eden. "And there he put the man whom he had formed," into the garden of Eden to cultivate it, or "to dress it and to keep it" (ii. 15). These two creations answer to the two creations in the Egyptian Genesis, which are the creation of Amenta by Ptah and his associate-gods the Ali = Elohim, and the creation of the garden for Atum and his associate-gods. In the Hebrew, Iahu and his Elohim take the secondary place of Tum and his associate-gods in the original. And however shadowy some of this may seem, the shadow is all there was to go upon so long as the substance was out of sight—the substance which is Egyptian.

The Litany of Ra describes itself as being "the book of the worship of Ra," and identifies Atum with Ra in Amenta. It is said that "when anyone reads this book, the porcelain figures are placed upon the ground at the hour of sunset—that is, of the triumph of Ra over his enemies in Amenta" (Litany of Ra). When he arrives in the Amenta at sunset, "his form is that of the old man"; in his resurrection his form is that of the lion. He sets as Ra; he rises again as Horus. Atum in Amenta is the hidden soul of life that was imaged by the nocturnal sun. He is the supreme power who dwells in darkness and causes the principles to arise. He is "the pillar of Amenta" like the Tat with which Ptah supported the sky. He is manifested or born as his own son; he who was Ra as father is Horus as the son—Atum in the western mount, and Horus in the east. He is worshipped as the supreme power in seventy-five characters, under the same number of names. Atum is the one god who is always depicted in the human form, and who therefore enters Amenta in the shape of man for the overthrowal of Apap the monster and all the powers of evil.

Atum not only passed into the Hebrew legends as the earthly father in the book of Genesis, but also as the Adam Kadmon (אדם־קדמון) of the Kabalah, who is the primordial, archetypal man, the heavenly man or man from heaven. The first Adam, like the first Horus, was finite and imperfect; the second was infinite and perfect. These are the first and second Adam according to the doctrine of Paul, who tells us that "the first man is of the earth, earthy; the second man is of heaven." The first man Adam became a living soul.

The last Adam became a life-giving spirit. Howbeit, that is not first which is spiritual, but that which is natural. Now, as Atum is the god who followed Ptah as a birth of the Put-cycle, he is the tenth, and the god of the ten circles of Ra (Rit., ch. 18) is now called the creator of the nine. This was done in the process of compounding and unifying the powers, and of exalting the latest in the development to the position of the first in status. The present point is that in an address to Amen, a form of Atum, it is said, "The gods proceeded from thee. Thou didst create the *nine gods* at the beginning of all things, and thou wast the lion-god of the twin lion-gods." (Budge, *The Gods of the Egyptians,* vol. ii. p. 88.) This was in the course of making the latest in development first in status, which was the common course in the evolution of Ra. Thus in the cycle of Ptah the gods were nine in number. With Atum added as Ra, the number is ten; and as Ptah was called the father of the eight, so Atum is the father of the nine. In the hymns to Amen-Ra he is adored as one and the same with Atum; hence we infer that "Amen" is a later title of Atum as the hidden god of Amenta, the secret earth, the garden in which was made for him by his father Ptah. The object of the present comparison is to suggest that these ten powers or potencies were the originals of the ten Sephiroth which constituted the heavenly Adam Kadmon of the Kabalists, and which, according to the metaphysical doctrine, were the means whereby the En-Soph, the infinite or boundless, manifested within bounds (Ginsburg, *The Kabalah*). Atum, as we reckon, was the builder of the heaven in ten divisions which preceded the final one in twelve.

There is no Garden of Eden created in the first chapter of Genesis. No tree of life or knowledge was planted, nor is there any prohibition against eating the fruit of the tree. On the contrary, the primal pair, the male and female, are told that every herb and *every* tree are given to them for food. The theology of the Elohim differs from that of Iahu-Elohim. This agrees with a *non-Semitic version* of the creation legend (*Records,* New Series, vol. vi.), in which there is no garden created, no mention of man being placed in the garden to tend it; no tree of life, nor tree of knowledge; and no temptation by the serpent, or story of the Fall. The primal paradise, that of Shu and the seven support-gods in Am-Khemen, is thus differentiated from the garden of Ptah in the secondary creation or representation. To reach the Kamite root of the matter we have to distinguish betwixt the making of Amenta and the planting of the garden eastward. When "the heaven and the earth were finished, and all the host of them," man was formed; then Iahu-Elohim planted a garden eastward, in Eden, and there he put the man whom he had formed, to dress it and to keep it. We have now to tell the story of Eden from the indefinitely older documents, legendary fragments of which have been mixed up together by the Elohistic and Jehovistic narratives in the book of Genesis.

Amenta and the garden of rest were not created for man the mortal, as mortal, on this earth. The man who was brought into being and placed in the garden to protect the tree of life and defend it from the depredations of the evil Apap, the serpent of darkness, the dragon of drought, the devouring reptile, was man in the likeness of Atum, or man the manes; the only man in the garden of Amenta, whether this is called the Aarru-Sekhet (field) or gan-Eden. The primal paradise was founded on the natural fact of the oasis. Following this, the fundamental idea of a paradise made by human workmanship is an enclosure in which there was a tree or plants for food and an unfathomable well-spring of water for drink. It was the oasis with some kind of fence about it, which survives in the "little garden walled around" that is sung of in a modern hymn. Now, when the nomads of the equatorial regions wandered northward they left their primal paradise behind them as a geographical locality. This suffered a subsidence, in common with the southern pole, and was hidden beneath the horizon to become the legendary paradise that sank down under the waters and was lost, as would be indicated by the disappearing guide-stars, to become a subject of the Egyptian astro-mythology.

The legend of a paradise, or state of supreme blessedness, that was lost through the eating of forbidden food, or in not keeping the law of tabu, is indigenous to Inner Africa. It is the story of the first man, Khentu, in Uganda, previously cited. Dr. Nassau offers evidence that the Bantu tribes (who extend over a quarter of the continent) have the legend of a great chief who always warned people not to eat the fruit of a certain tree, but who ate of it himself and died. In another native legend it was a woman who brought the fruit of a forbidden tree to her village. She swallowed it to hide it, and then became possessed of an evil spirit, which was the beginning of witchcraft. (Nassau, F., *Fetishism in West Africa,* p. 40.) It is an ancient tradition that the homeland of the human race was actual at the sources of the Nile. Milton alludes to and repeats it in his "Paradise under the Æthiop line by Nilus' head." The Rabbins likewise affirm that "Paradise is localized under the middle line of the world, where the days are always of equal length." That is in equatorial regions. Such a tradition, however true, could only come to us by means of mythology and the folk-tales. The Sekhet-Aarru or field of papyrus-reed was one name of this oasis on high, which was a heaven of boundless food and drink, and therefore a paradise of plenty. The point to be established now is that water and vegetable food were the primeval elements of life in equatorial Africa in such abundance as to constitute a permanent ideal; and these were constellated later in the northern heaven by the Egyptians as a picture of an earthly paradise that "once upon a time," somewhere or other, had been geographical. Now, this circumpolar paradise upraised by Shu in Am-Khemen was reproduced with improvements and additions in the earthly paradise or garden of Amenta, the stellar imagery being repeated *in the solar mythos.* The mount of glory, the tree on the summit, the source of the water of life, the Apap-reptile of drought, the youthful hero and other types established in the upper paradise, were duplicated in the paradise below—the garden enclosed by Ptah for Atum his son to cultivate. The upper was the circumpolar paradise upon the stellar mount of glory in the region of the stars that never set. At first there was the water only, called the celestial sea or lake. The pole was imaged by the stalk, the reed or papyrus that was planted in the waters as the sign of a fixed support in a double sense. This became the later tree in the midst of the garden or cultivated enclosure. In the Pyramid Texts it is called the khat-en-ankhu or tree of life, on the fruit of which the gods and the glorified were fed. When the garden in Amenta was created by Ptah this paradise of rest was repeated in the earth of eternity, to become the earthly paradise of the manes in the Book of the Dead.

As previously shown, the Jewish Kabalists preserve the tradition of an upper and a lower paradise. Manasseh Ben-Israel says, "Those who are learned in the Kabalah affirm that there is a paradise here on earth below." Between the two it is said there is a pillar fixed that joins the two together, which is called "the strength of the hill Zion" (*Nishmath Kajim,* ff. 25, 26; *Stehelin* vol. II, pp. 2-8), and which corresponds to the ladder and the mount in the Ritual. The upper paradise, he says, is called by seven names: (1) The bundle of life, (2) the tabernacle of the Lord, (3) the holy hill, (4) the courts of the Lord, (5) the house of the Lord, (6) the hill of the Lord, (7) the holy place. He likewise gives the seven appellations of the lower paradise: (1) The garden of Eden, (2) the palace of the Lord, (3) the land of the living, (4) the sanctuary of God, (5) the city of God, (6) the dwelling of the Lord, (7) the lands of the living. Notwithstanding the vagueness of a later generalization, we may see (1) the garden of Amenta in "the garden of Eden"; (2) the palace of the prince in "the palace of the Lord" (Rit., ch. 1); (3) the earth of the living in "the land of the living"; (4) the shrine in the midst of the earth in "the sanctuary of God." The ladder that is raised up in Amenta for the glorified to get a glimpse of the gods (Rit., ch. 149), when the manes says, "I raise my ladder up to the sky to see the gods," is repeated in the pillar that is the means of communication betwixt the lower and the upper paradise. By this (says the *Jalkut Kodash,* f. 57, c. 2) they are joined together, and it is called "the strength of the hill Zion," the hill which touches the sky being another Egyptian figure of the means of ascent. "By this pillar, on every Sabbath and festival, the righteous climb up, and refresh themselves with a glimpse of the divine majesty, till the end of the Sabbath or festival, when they slide down and return to the lower paradise." The heptanomis is repeated in the plan of both the lower and upper paradise. In both there are seven mansions or dwellings for the reward of the righteous. All the glory, the excellency, the delight which the righteous obtain in the upper paradise is prepared for them in the lower paradise. In the vignettes to the Ritual the ba-soul is seen ascending and descending the ladder to visit the mummy in the tomb. In like manner it is said in *Nishmath Kajim* (f. 28, c. 1) that every twelve months after leaving the body the deceased descend and visit it, because they cannot be absolutely separated from their mummies.

Like other mythical types, the twofold paradise passed on into the legendary lore of various lands. It is to be seen in the enclosure of Yima in the Avesta. In one form this is Eran Veg, the paradise that was in the beginning, or in the first time, the paradise upon the mount of glory answering to the Am-Khemen that was upraised by Shu. Amenta, the secret earth of eternity, is also identifiable when it is said the human race shall be *reconstituted* in Yima's enclosure; and for that reason it was made in a secret place = Amenta (Avesta).

It was in Amenta, the secret earth, that Osiris and the Osirified were reconstituted for the life hereafter. The Garden of Eden in the Hebrew Genesis is called the garden eastward. This is the position of the Aarru-garden in Amenta. It was on the eastern side of the mount of glory, in the very depths of dawn. According to the Ritual, life originated in the garden eastward. Hence it is there the man as manes inhales the breath of a new life (ch. 57), and drinks the water of life and plucks the fruit from the tree of life. An oasis is the figure that was followed by Ptah in making the garden of Aarru in Amenta. A mound or rampart is described as built around the water and the plants or tree at the centre, to protect them and to keep the Apap-serpent from the sacred precincts where Atum-Ra "frequenteth the persea tree of life." "I know this field of Aarru, with the ba-enclosure," says the Osiris in the Ritual (ch. 109, 4). The enclosing wall was made of ba, a word that meant earth at one time, then iron, and lastly steel, as the rampart was characterized according to the progress made in work from earth to iron and from one metal to another. This zeriba or barrier notwithstanding, the destroyer night by night and year after year was continually breaking into the beautiful garden of Aarru, to drink up the water and to wither the tree of life. The abyss within the earth from whence the water welled with life in the beginning, the abyss that is configurated in the southern heaven, was repeated in making the garden of Amenta. It is described in the Ritual as the Tuat "which nobody can fathom," which "sends forth light in the dark night," and "the offerings from which are eatable plants" (ch. 172). Also there are two lakes of water in Amenta, one of which is designated "the great *Deep*" (Rit., ch. 17). This agrees with the abyss which nobody can fathom (ch. 172). Thus the beginning with the abyss, the breaking forth of light, the water welling from the abyss, and the primeval food issuing from the water were repeated and preserved. The tree of life was planted in the water of life as the persea or ash, which is the tree of life by name in Egyptian, and which had taken the place of the papyrus-reed as the sign of vegetation.

When the Garden of Eden was created the tree of life is said to be in the midst of the garden, "and a river went out of Eden to water the garden, and from thence it was parted, and became four heads." We shall find the same water going forth from the Aarru-garden in Amenta. The original river that issued from the lake of the abyss at the centre of the garden is determined by the 150th chapter of the Ritual, in which it is said the fourteenth division is "the domain of Kher-aba; the deity in it is *the Nile*." The river that went forth from the circumpolar paradise represented the Milky Way, whereas the water that issued from the midst of the garden in Amenta is the divinized river Nile (Rit., ch. 149). Also in this form the celestial Nile is traced to its earthly source in the lakes and to the powers of the inundation or high flood in the south. Thus the Egyptian Ritual, which is not to be gainsaid, indubitably shows that the river which "went out of Eden to water the garden" in the original version of the mythos was the river Nile reproduced as the water-source of life in the garden of Amenta.

On entering the lower earth the departed spirit prays, "May there be given to me a homestead in the fields of Aarru" (Rit., ch. 15). And again, the speaker for the pair says, "Open ye to the gods (or divinized spirits) who *came to cultivate the soil* and grow the food" (in this earth of eternity). "Let the god Amsu, the divine husbandman, give me the ground to till. Let the god of green things open his arms to me," as giver of abundance. (124, 5.) In the Egyptian original this delightful garden is the place in which the spirit was refreshed "under any type it wished"—a mode of saying that it offered all that heart could desire, and to wish was to have. It was the typical land of grapes and peaches, where the plenty flowed in rivers of milk and honey according to the Hebrew report. But it was likewise a land of labour and industry—no lubber-land of lotus-eating laziness. In the true Egyptian representation worship is work, and in these fields of food

> "They suck no honeycomb of drowsy peace
> Because ennobling natural cares all cease;
> They live no life, as many dream, caressed
> By some vast tideless sea of endless rest;
> For there, as here, unbusy is unblest."

In proceeding to this elysium the Osiris takes the good path to the fields of flood. He says, "A divine domain hath been constructed for me: I know the name of it, the name of it is the garden of Aarru" = Eden (ch. 109). "I know the place where to plough the earth and mow the corn, to collect the harvest in it daily. I am in it, I prevail in it, I understand in it; food is in my hands from the lord of earth" (ch. 110). This agricultural mode of earning an eternal living was typified by every one of the shebti figures set up in the tombs with the hoe of the husbandman in their hands. It is said, "When thou hast mowed with the souls, having *kept* their *stride* to the closed gates, thou art acquitted, and approachest thy house after thy labours, to the delight of thy two souls."

The Aarru paradise in Amenta is also the garden of the two trees, the same as the Hebrew Garden of Eden. A form of Eden is undoubtedly Babylonian, even by name. According to the native tradition, the type was localized in Eridu, the place of the eternal tree or stalk at the centre of the circumpolar paradise, or of Eridu in the firmamental water termed "the abyss." In the mythos the Great Mother is called "the divine lady of Edin," and also "the goddess of the tree of life." As the tree she brings forth her child, the branch, the same as Hathor does in Egypt. The name of Hathor signifies the house of Horus, as the tree. So the Great Mother Zikum is the house of Tammuz, as the tree that grew in Eridu. But the Egyptian stalk of the uat or papyrus plant is indefinitely earlier than the typical tree. One fact of itself will serve to show that the biblical Eden was not derived from the Assyrian Edin, because in this garden there is but a single tree, which is apparently the tree of life. The divine lady of Edin is the goddess of the tree of life, and there is no mention of a tree of knowledge. Secondly, the serpent as a type of evil in the book of Genesis is not the Babylonian dragon Tiamat. The biblical dragon is of neither sex, whereas Tiamat is female. The Hebrew dragon or evil serpent is the Apap of Egypt from Genesis to Revelation. Apap is a water-reptile whose dwelling is at the bottom of the dark waters called the void of Apap, from which it rises in rebellion as the representative of drought. This is the serpent described by Amos: "Though they be hid from my sight in the bottom of the sea, thence will I command the serpent, and he shall bite them" (Amos ix. 3). Another reason. The Hebrew Eden is in a land that was watered by a mist that went up from the ground, and where no rain fell on the earth (Gen. ii. 5-6). That land above all earthly prototypes was Egypt, which assuredly did not suffer like Babylonia from the "curse of rain," from which the Akkadian month "As-an" was named. But there was a pre-solar paradise enclosure which had but one tree in it.

This as Egyptian is the paradise of Am-Khemen, which Shu uplifted with his two-pronged prop that images the pole, when he divided earth from heaven and raised the upper circumpolar paradise. Paradise, says Ibn Ezra, is the place of one tree. Mount Hetep in the northern heaven is a kind of typical one-tree-hill. In some of the Mexican drawings there is a point of departure by water from the mount which has a single tree upon its summit. This we look on as the tree which represents the pole, the "one-tree-hill" of a legend that is universal. This typical one-tree-hill is also to be found at Sakapu in Manchuria, where it is represented by a mountain designated "lone tree hill." The Norse tree Yggdrasil is single. Nor is there more than one tree or stalk in the garden of Eridu, where the Great Mother is the lady of the eternal tree. The eternal tree was certainly the pole. Its seven branches show it to have been a numerical type of the heptanomis. Hence we infer that in the circumpolar paradise there was but one tree as a figure of the northern pole of heaven. The Chinese Fu-tree, the self-supporting, is likewise a figure of the pole. Hence it is said to grow *on the summit of a mountain in mid-ocean at the north,* and it is 300 Chinese miles in height. (Schlegel, Prof. G., *Fou-Sang Kono.*) There is nothing gained by calling this the tree of the universe instead of the pole. That is only to lose in vagueness all that the astronomers had gained by their definiteness.

The two trees in the Garden of Eden can be accounted for upon Egyptian ground, but on no other; one being the tree of the pole in the stellar mythos, the other the tree of life or of dawn in the garden eastward. The two typical trees are recognizable as Egyptian in the Book of the Dead. In one chapter (97th) they are called the two divine sycamores of heaven and earth. The sycamore of heaven is identified as the tree of Nut. It stands in the "lake of equipoise," which is at the celestial pole. The tree of earth is the tree of Hathor and of dawn. Atum-Ra, the solar god, is also described as coming forth from betwixt the two trees. "I know those two sycamores of emerald, between which Ra cometh forth as he advances over the firmament" (ch. 109). The tree of earth, or Hathor, and the tree of heaven, or Nut, were brought on together and united in the tree of burial for the mummy. Wherever it was possible the Egyptian coffin was made from wood of the sycamore tree, the khat-en-ankhu, or tree of life, so that the dead might be taken in the embrace of the mother of life, who was represented by the tree. This was Hathor as bringer to birth in the mythology, and Nut the bringer of souls to their rebirth in the eschatology. The relative positions of these two goddesses with the tree were illustrated by the pictures painted on the coffin. Hathor as a form of the mother-earth, the tree-form, is portrayed inside the coffin on the board upon which the mummy rested, taking the dead to her embrace as the mother of life. Nut, the mother-heaven, was represented on the inner part of the coffin-lid arching over the mummy as bringer of the manes to new life above. It was burial in the tree when the tree had come to be elaborately carved in the shape of a coffin. This symbolized a resurrection of the spirit from the tree of life as Horus rose again from out the tree of dawn. Now when Amenta was planted by Ptah, the father of Atum, several features of the circumpolar paradise, as before said, were not only repeated, they were duplicated. One of these was the typical tree. The tree of the pole remained as the central support of the universe, the tree of the three worlds, *i.e.,* of Amenta, earth and heaven (Egyptian), Arali, earth and heaven (Babylonian), hell, mid-gard and heaven (Norse), and others that might be added. In Egypt this was almost superseded by the tat of Ptah, which is a pillar of the four corners based upon the tree as type of the pole when this was erected in Amenta. Thus, the primal paradise was the place of one tree. The paradise or garden in Amenta is the place of two trees—because the ground-rootage had been doubled in phenomena. These two trees appear in the Ritual as the tree of Hathor and the tree of Nut; the tree of earth and the tree of heaven; the tree of the north and the tree of the east.

The tree of Hathor was a tree of life in Egypt. It was the sycamore-fig tree, from the fruit of which a divine drink of the mysteries was made. Therefore it was a tree to make one wise, which became a tree of wisdom or abnormal knowledge. The tree of Nut was the tree of heaven and eternal life, hence it was designated the eternal tree. As herein suggested, the two trees originated as a dual symbol of the two poles in Equatoria. These were continued in two tree-pillars called Sut-and-Horus by Ptah in his making of Amenta. Again they are repeated in the garden or cultivated enclosure of Eden. Here they are called the tree of knowledge and the tree of life. As shown in the vignettes to the Book of the Dead, the tree or eatable plant and the water supplied the elements of life to the manes in the lower paradise. The goddess Nut pours out the water and offers the fruit of the tree to Ani and his wife, when he has reached the garden of Amenta (Pap. of Ani, plate 16). The pole had been the tree first planted in the astronomical mythology. It was the tree of Nut, or heaven, in the stellar phase, and being astronomical it was naturally the tree of knowledge. But in the making of the nether earth a second tree was planted in the garden eastward. The mythos now was solar, and this was the tree of dawn, the tree of wet or dew, which was a veritable tree of life in Egypt. It was the emerald sycamore of Hathor in her character of goddess of the leafy-green dawn. The first was the tree in the most ancient stellar mythos, the second was added as an equinoctial type, the sycamore of earth now rooted in the land of dawn. This is the tree in which Child-Horus, the young solar god, proclaims himself to be the new-born babe (Rit., ch. 42) at his coming forth as the sun of another day, or the offspring of Hathor. He comes forth from between the two sycamores just as the good shepherd or royal Horus issues from betwixt the two trees in the symbolism of the Roman catacombs (Bosio, *Rom. Sott.*, p. 311; Lundy, in *Mon Christy*.). It is related in a legend cited by M. de Gubernatis that the tree of Adam reaches to hell, Sheol, or Amenta with its roots, and to heaven with its branches, and that the infant Jesus lives in the top of the tree (*M. des Pl.*, vol. i. 18), like Horus, Unbu, and Bata. This, like a thousand other things related of the divine, that is mythical, child, would be extremely interesting if the legend had not been put forth under the false pretence of its being historical. The only infant in the tree, who finally supplied the subject of a nursery song, "Hush-a-by Baby on the Tree-Top," was the youthful god whose cradle was the tree of dawn, and who says in the Ritual (ch. 42), "I am the babe. I am the god within the tamarisk." The tree of Adam was the tree of Atum in the garden of the lower Aarru which Horus or Jesus (the Su of Atum) climbs when he goes upwards from the garden to the eastern heaven. The infant was also Horus on his uat-papyrus, a symbol of the earth amidst the waters of the Nun, and a co-type of the tree of dawn (Rit., ch. 17). In one representation, the child issues from the papyrus or lotus, in another from the tree. The sun as soul of life in the tree of dawn is probably the nature-type of the soul in the bush, the "bush-soul" of various African races, *i.e.*, the spirit of vegetation and food. The name of Heitsi-Eibib the Hottentot deity in his solar character signifies the one who appears in the tree, misrendered by Hahn as the "one who has the appearance of a tree." The god was not the tree itself but the power appearing in the tree as giver of food. This tree that springs up below the horizon on the eastward side of the earth may be meant by the bush of the Australian blacks who, on being asked by a missionary where the soul went when it left the body, said it went "behind the bush," the same bush that was signified in the custom of the Hottentots. Behind the bush was equivalent to our "beyond the veil." The typical two trees in the enclosure are both Egyptian, and both are represented in Amenta. The tree of earth is Hathor's, called the sycamore of the south. The tree of heaven is the sycamore of Nut, who pours the water from it for the revivification of the manes. Water, as the supreme element of life, retains its primacy of place in the Amenta in relation to the two waters of earth and heaven and the two goddesses Hathor and Nut. The sycamore of Hathor had been the discoverer of water with its deep rootage in the desert sand. The sycamore of Nut dropped down the liquid of life in dew and rain as water of heaven. These two are both represented by two lakes or pools of water welling in the garden of Amenta from the fount of source itself in the abyss. The tree of life is imaged standing in a pool of the water of life in the midst of the Aarru-garden and the goddess in the tree who gives the water also gives the fruit for food and sustenance to the Osirified deceased. The tree is thus portrayed with its roots in the water of earth and its branches dropping down with the life-giving dew or

Horus the Shoot of the Papyrus.

divine drink of heaven. In some of the Egyptian drawings the goddess Nut is represented in the tree of knowledge, gathering baskets-full of figs from the sycamore-fig tree, and presenting them to the souls of the departed. At other times she offers fruit directly from the tree itself. Nut in the tree offering its fruit to the pair in the garden, who are Ani (male) and Tutu his wife, in the papyrus of Ani (plate 16), are the nearest likeness to the woman tempting Adam to eat the fruit of the tree; and Nut is the goddess feeding souls with the fruit of the tree of life here figured as the sycamore-fig tree. No name of species is given to the tree of knowledge in the book of Genesis, but we assume it was the fig-tree that furnished the leaves from which the loin-girdles of the primal pair were made. And the fig-tree as now traced was the sycamore-fig of Egypt. This was the tree of Hathor in the Aarru-paradise. Moreover, the goddess Iusāas, the consort of Atum-Ra and mother of the coming son, Iusa, or Iu-em-hetep, was a form of the cow-headed or cow-eared Hathor, lady of the sycamore-tree in the temple of the sun at Annu.

Doubtless one cause of the curse pronounced upon the tree was on account of its being the tree of Hathor, the goddess of fecundity. No better or more beautiful description of Hathor in the tree could be found than the one in the "Wisdom of Jesus." This Jesus, as Iu the son of Atum, was brought forth by Hathor-Iusāas from the tree. As Wisdom, she identifies herself with the tree of knowledge. The pæan of her exultation might be called the hymn of Hathor. Hathor was the Egyptian goddess of love, though the love first personated by her was not the sexual passion. It was the love of the mother for her offspring; the love of the mother of life who fed the child in the womb and at the breast as the divine wet-nurse. In her pre-anthropomorphic form she is the mother imaged as the milch-cow (this being preceded by the water-cow) and therefore not a type of sexual human love. As the wet-nurse she was also depicted in the tree of life and the tree of dawn, which dropped the dew as very drink of life. Hathor is the habitation (from hat, the abode), one primitive form of which was the tree, and hence the tree of dawn was a typical abode of the young god born of her, or from her sycamore as the branch of endless years. "I was exalted like a cedar in Libanus, and as a cypress-tree upon the mountains of Hermon. I was exalted like a palm-tree in En-gaddi, and as a rose-plant in Jericho, as a fair olive-tree in a pleasant field, and grew up as a plane-tree by the water. As the vine brought I forth pleasant savour, and my flowers are the fruit of honour and riches. I am the mother of fair love, and fear, and knowledge, and holy hope; I therefore, being eternal, am given to all my children which are named of him. Come unto me, all ye that be desirous of me, and fill yourselves with my fruits. For my memorial is sweeter than honey, and mine inheritance than the honeycomb. They that eat me shall yet be hungry, and they that drink me shall yet be thirsty." ("The Wisdom of Jesus," ch. 24, 13-21, translated in the time of Euergetes.) The woman who offers the fruit of the tree of knowledge in this book of the secret doctrine is in one form the goddess Hathor, and if the Hebrew version of the tree of knowledge had been true, this would be the song of the siren tempting her lovers to perdition.

The tree of knowledge being the sycamore-fig tree of Hathor the goddess of love, we see in that fact the raison-d'être of its being degraded by the Semitic bigots and turned into the tree of temptation and the cause of the fabled fall. Very proper physiological knowledge was also taught by means of the fable, but the primary motive for the perversion of the tree was the religious hatred of the motherhood by those who exalted the fatherhood as unique and alone. Precisely the same spirit is shown in the cursing of the fig-tree, which is the sycamore-fig, in the Gospels. "If ye had faith as a grain of mustard-seed, ye would say unto this sycamore tree, Be thou rooted up, and be thou planted in the sea" (Luke xvii. 6). Cursing and casting out the sycamore-fig was damning the tree of the woman, the emerald sycamore of the lovely Hathor, and also the sycamore of Nut, whether in the Old Testament or the New. And this was a mode of destroying "the works of the female" (Gospel of the Egyptians).

The tree of the upper paradise was held to have been thornless. As it is said in the Persian Revelation, on the nature of plants and trees, "before the coming of the destroyer, vegetation had no thorn or bark about it. And afterwards when the destroyer came, it was coated with bark and grew thorny" (*Bundahish*, ch. 27, West). Thus the tree in the celestial paradise was differentiated from the tree in the earthly paradise, which became thorny as the result of Adam's fatal fall. Egypt is not a cloudy land, though there is sufficient morning-mist, however thin and filamental, for the golden rays of the sun to blend with the azure tints of upper heaven and produce a greenish colour from the mixture of the two. This was represented as the great green sycamore of dawn, of Hathor or Nut, which in Egypt was a tree of life that struck its roots down to the eternal springs and would find moisture even in a Sahara of desert sand. And from this tree of heaven the earth was watered with refreshing dew. This imagery of Egypt is virtually repeated in the book of Genesis (ii. 5, 6) when the writer tells us that "Iahu-Elohim had not caused it to rain upon the earth, but there went up a mist from the earth and watered the whole face of the ground." The sycamore of dawn is mentioned in the Ritual. It is also spoken of as the sycamore in the eastern sky (*Pyramid Texts*, Pepi, I, 174). Few things in literature are more lovely than the way in which the imagery of dawn was thus utilized as the road to travel by in attaining the other upper land of life. So far as the Babylonians and Assyrian versions of the mythos have been recovered we find no written account of the creation of man or the placing of the man in the Garden of Eden "to dress it and to keep it." But the garden is represented on one of the cylinders in what has been termed the scene of the temptation by those who read the subject backwards according to the Hebrew story of the fall. The tree in Eridu is called *the shrine of the two*, whom we understand to be the primeval mother and her son, who as Egyptian was called the bull of the mother. The pair are also described as "the lady of the eternal tree" and the great supreme bull, he who was both the child and consort of the mother. These two, we now suggest, are the male and female pair who are seated underneath the tree as the scene is pictured on the Assyrian cylinder. The bull of the mother is obviously represented by the pair of horns upon the figure of the male. A tree with seven branches is portrayed with the pair of male and female figures seated underneath, and the serpent erect at the back of the female, as if posed and holding forth in the character of the legendary tempter. The reptile corresponds to the flat-headed Apap of the Egyptian drawings, which signifies evil because it is the serpent of darkness, drought, dearth, and negation. One cannot resist the impression that this representation may be responsible for the legend of the serpent, the temptation and the fall that is found in the Hebrew book of Genesis. The Babylonians were such perverters of the Kamite mythology in relation to woman and the serpent. But instead of a human pair, the male and female seated under the tree are two divinities. The figure next the serpent is a form of the Great Mother. Thence we infer that the male is a form of the son, and that the pair are the well-known duad of mother and son, as in Ishtar and Dumuzi or Zikum and Tammuz, the genetrix with the son who became his own father, as did Sebek-Horus, the son who was the husband of his mother. Also, on the third tablet of the creation series there is a Babylonian prototype for the Hebrew legend of the fall that followed on the eating of forbidden fruit. In this it is said that "the command was established in the garden of the god." But, "in sin one with the other in compact joined." "The asnan fruit they ate, they broke in two; its stalk they destroyed. Great is their sin. Themselves they exalted. To Merodach, their redeemer, he (the god Sar) appointed their fate" (Boscawen). The doctrine of a fall and of a redemption therefrom is plainly apparent in this inscription which the Hebrew compilers apparently followed and in that way the later theological legend would get intermixed with the original mythos in a Semitic moralizing of the Kamite mythology.

Assyrian Cylinder.

Various vignettes to the Ritual show us Ani and his wife, the pair, as spirits, in the Aarru-garden eating the fruit of the tree and drinking the water of life, but with no relation to a fall from paradise through plucking the forbidden fruit. The pair of beings in the Semitic versions are supposed to have fallen from the garden of the beginning through eating the forbidden fruit of the *asnan* tree. And according to the rendering of the myth in Hebrew, the pair are driven forth lest they should also eat of the tree of life. "And Iahu-Elohim said, Behold, Adam is become as one of us, to know good and evil: and now lest he put forth his hand and take also of the tree of life, and eat and live for ever: therefore Iahu-Elohim sent him forth from the garden. So he drove out Adam." As there is no mention of the woman in this expulsion, the man must have gone alone upon his "solitary way," unless the woman is included in Adam-homo as in the first creation. "So he drove out Adam, and he placed at the east of the Garden of Eden the cherubim, and the flame of a sword which turned every way, to keep the way of the tree of life" (Gen. iii. 22-24). The tree of life, we repeat, was the tree of dawn with its rootage in the garden of Amenta. In the Hebrew Genesis, the tree is to be protected by the flame of a sword that turns in all directions, which conveys the idea of a swordsman dexterously making the moulinet figure of defence. Now let us turn to the great original symbolism which has been so mutilated. The tree of life, the emerald sycamore of dawn, stood with its roots below the horizon in the garden eastward. It needed protection by night from the insidious assaults of the Apap of darkness, drought, and dearth, as shown in the illustrations to the Book of the Dead. The precious water and tree of life were protected within the enclosure formed by Ptah that was raised against the incursions of Apap, the eternal devourer.

The prohibition against eating the fruit of the tree would have had no meaning for Ani and his wife. They were there to eat of it and live as spirits. For that purpose the water and fruit are being given to them by Nut or Hathor in the vignettes. The protector of the tree of life by night is Atum-Ra, the solar god, whose weapon is the flaming orb of the nocturnal sun (Rit., ch. 15). The sword that turned in every direction is depicted in the radiating disk which is set all round as it were with sword-blades of the solar flame. "Salutation to Ra radiating in his disk as the light that issues out of the horizon," is a greeting made by the worshipper (Rit., ch. 148). In the pictures to the Ritual the sun is imaged by a radiating disk that rises up from the tree of life, the emerald sycamore-fig or the fig-tree of the garden eastward, and this is described as being *a symbolical representation of Atum-Ra*. The radiating life-giving disk is a sworded flame which turns every way, seeing that it is rayed and darting fire all round. The way of the tree of life is towards the eastern horizon where the sun goes out of the garden eastward, and the sworded disk is not only in the way of the tree of life, it also rises out of the tree, and is described as turning round when it rises. The "flame of a sword which turns every way" is no doubt an adaptation of the radiating disk which is here portrayed at the summit of the tree of life. Ra "circulating in his disk" (15, 32-3), who "radiates in his disk: who fashions himself in his metal and *turns round so soon as Shu upraises him on the horizon*" (Rit., 17, 50). In one passage it is said that the flame of the solar disk emblematically designed saves the god Ra from Apap (Rit., ch. 149, 12, Pierret), which is the prototypal equivalent of the sworded flame that revolves to keep the way of the tree of life in the book of Genesis. The way of the tree of life that goes out of Eden can be identified with the way that goes out of the field of Aarru in Amenta. The speaker in the Ritual had travelled that way, as one of the manes, but NOT AS A MORTAL. He says (149, 5-9), "I know the way of the field Aarru by which Atum-Ra goes forth to the east of heaven" (or from the garden eastward). The "way of the tree of life" in Genesis is the "road of the disk" in the Ritual (ch. 129, 1). We learn from Origen that there was a certain diagram current amongst the gnostic Ophites, which contained the seven ruling dæmons. Amongst the other matters mentioned is the flaming sword that kept the tree of life at the gates of paradise. Of this he says the picture in the accursed diagram was impiously unlike the figure drawn in "Sacred Writ." "The flaming sword was depicted as the diameter of a flaming circle, and as if mounting guard over the tree of knowledge and of life" (B. 6, ch. 33). From this description of the figure we perceive that the gnostic diagram contained a copy of the Egyptian original.

The Flaming Sword which Guarded the Tree.

As first pointed out in the *Book of the Beginnings* (1881), the word cherub, or kerub, is Egyptian. It signifies a primary figure, a model form. The type may vary, but the word denotes primacy whatsoever the figure. The variant kherp means the first, chief, principal, forepart or foremost. Still more to the purpose the Kamite kherefu = kherebu are a pair of lion-gods joined back to back that keep the gates of dawn, or we might say, the way of the tree of life, which is the green sycamore of dawn. The Egyptian kherefu lift up the solar orb upon their backs; they form the primary figure of support for the god that preceded the ark or chariot, which consisted of an ark that rested on the boat. The twin lions or kherefu form the natural throne or seat of the solar deity "Atum-Iu" (Vig. to ch. 18, Rit.; Pap. Ani., Pl. 7).

According to Josephus (*Ant.* I, II, 6, 5), Moses had seen such things as the cherubs near the throne of Iahu; and here we find the kherefu, in the form of twin lions, are the throne of Atum in the Easter equinox when it coincided with the Lion sign. These things are not merely matters of philology. The kherub as a determinative type passes into the griffin. A pair of griffins still keep the gate or gateway of the avenue of trees that leads up to the great house. Also the crab and the scarab still represent the kherub both by name and type. In some of the ancient Egyptian zodiacs the scarabæus takes the place of the crab. In others the sign is represented by a pair of scarabs or beetles; and two scarabs are also equivalent to the two cherubs. Thus when the equinox had passed into the sign of Cancer the two kherefu or kherubs as lions were succeeded in the astronomical mythos by the two scarabs that now kept the way of the tree of life at the point in precession where the vernal equinox was stationed for the time being—namely, in the sign of the Crab or the beetles.

The mother of beginnings, the primordial parent in the abyss of earth and the height of heaven, was also reproduced as the Great Mother in Amenta. In the vignettes to the Ritual Apt is portrayed in both forms of the cow, the hippopotamus and the milch-cow, among the papyrus plants of the morass at the foot of the mount of Amenta, as the bringer to rebirth for the upper paradise (Papyrus of Ani, Pl. 37). The mother of life on earth was now made protector of the dead in Amenta, and she who was the kindler of the stellar sparks in heaven by night became the re-kindler of the sparks of life from the eclipse of death (Rit., ch. 137, B; Papyrus of Ani, Pap. Nebseni). Thus we can identify Eve, or Chavvah, as Kefa or Kep, the Great Mother, with Adam or Atum in the garden of Amenta. The name of Eve in Hebrew (hvx), Chavvah, signifies life or living, whence Eve is the mother of life. Life, however, is a somewhat abstract term. Still the mother of life, as Egyptian, was Khep, Kep, or Kefa = Chavvah by name. Kep signifies the ferment of life, the mystery of fertilisation, the enceinte mother; the Khep, Khev, or Kefa, as Egyptian, we hold to be the original of the Hebrew Chavvah. Kefa appears along with the great scarab in the thirteenth domain of Amenta (Renouf, Book of the Dead, ch. 149, pl. 52). Moreover, the lioness Kefa, or Kheft, is a form of Sekhet the solar goddess, who was the beloved consort of Ptah and the mother of Atum-Ra.

According to the Jewish legends Adam had two wives, one named Lilith, the other Chavvah, or in the English version, Eve. Atum also had two wives. These at Annu are Neb-hetep and Iusāas, the mother of the prince of peace, in her two characters of "lady of peace" and she who is great with Iu the coming son (or su), who was the prince of peace as conqueror of the serpent and all the evil powers in earth, in heaven, and in Amenta; otherwise in drought, in darkness, and in death. We can identify the wife of Adam with the old first genetrix of gods and men and mother of beginnings in at least three of her mythical characters. In one she was imaged as Rerit the sow. In another she is Kefa, or Kheft, the lioness. Lastly, she was portrayed as the mother of life in human form, the prototype of Eve. Now, as the mother of Atum was the lioness Sekhet, as the mother of "the princes of Israel" was a lioness (Ez. XIX. 2) who nourished young lions for her whelps, the inference is that Eve or Chavvah represents the lioness Kefa. In Rabbinical tradition Lilith is known as Adam's first wife, but only Chavvah has been brought on as Eve in the garden of the beginning. The Great Mother was single in herself, but may be dual or several in type. She remained single in the fields of heaven, the upper Aarru, where the Great Bear was her constellation, but she might be represented as Rerit the sow, or Kep the hippopotamus, or Kefa the lioness, according to phenomena. Father Atum is connected with the sow. He also has two wives. One of these, Iusāas, is a form of the goddess Hathor, and in one character Hathor was Shaat the sow. The sow was sacred in Israel because it had been a zoötype of the multimammalian Great Mother in Egypt. According to the totemic law of tabu, the eating of the sow as ordinary diet was prohibited because it was sacred to the periodic celebration which passed into the Eucharistic meal, at which it was religiously eaten once a year. For a long time the Jews remained faithful to the Great Mother in their sacramental eating of swine's flesh among the graves (Isaiah lxv. 4, and lxvi. 17). The graves identify the mortuary meal, and the swine's flesh will answer for the mother, who was imaged in one form as the many-teated sow, the flesh of which was prohibited in later ages because it was sacred and had originally represented the mother, who was at one time eaten with honour in *propria persona*. This also tends to identify Eve, or Chavvah, with Kep or Kefa, the first mother in the

Egyptian astronomical mythology. The story of Lilith, Adam's first wife, has been omitted from the book of Genesis. There are two wives involved, however, in the two different creations, although no name is given to the first. Man, as *homo,* was created "male and female" by the Elohim (ch. i. 27). The Rabbinical tradition relates that the woman was created out of the ground together with the man, and was named Lilith. She obviously represented the first Great Mother, one of whose Egyptian names was Rerit = Lilith, and whose zoötype was the sow as well as the hippopotamus. The submerged gnosis respecting the priority of the matriarchate comes to the surface in the story of the contention betwixt Lilith and Adam for marital supremacy. The two wives of Adam answer to the two consorts of Atum, who were Neb-hetep, the lady of peace, and Iusāas, she who was great with Iu-em-hetep, the bringer of peace, the Kamite Jesus, as Iu-sa the coming son.

In the Hebrew legend it is the woman Eve who offers the fruit of the tree of knowledge. In other versions, especially the Greek, the fruit is offered to the man by a serpent in the tree. Now the serpent was another type of the Great Mother, Kep, who was earlier than the serpent-woman, Rannut; and whether portrayed in the shape of a serpent or in the human form, she was the primordial giver of fruit from the tree. The serpent, the crocodile or dragon, the hippopotamus, the sow, the cow, the lioness and woman all meet as one in Kep, the earliest mother of life. The primal mother in the Kamite representation was the bringer-forth of Sut and Horus as her first two children, who were born twins. These, as the powers of darkness and light, or drought and fertility, were a pair of combatants who fought for the supremacy until one brother slew the other. This is one of those primary legends that became universal, but not because it had a hundred different origins at different times. Sut and Horus were indefinitely earlier than the solar Atum. But in the cult of Atum-Ra at On or Annu they were fathered on him and continued as his sons. Sut and Horus offer an instructive instance of evolution in mythology. They were born sons of the first Great Mother as two of the primordial powers, the twin powers of darkness and light. But in the re-cast of their theology the priests of Annu brought them on as the warring sons of Atum-Ra, who fought each other "up and down the garden" until, as here related, one of them was slain. In various inscriptions Sut and Horus are called the sons of Atum (Renouf, *Hib. Lectures,* p. 84). Otherwise stated, they became two of the associate-gods, the constituent parts and powers of Atum, as the sons of Ptah and members of the Put company of the Ali.

The battle in Amenta was not only fought betwixt the Apap of darkness and the sun-god Ra. When the two brothers Sut and Horus were repeated in the solar mythos, as the sons of Atum, the conflict was continued for possession of the garden. This was now the motive of the warfare. Previously it was for the water of the inundation or light in the moon. Now it was for the water and the tree of life in the Aarru-garden. In one version of the mythos, Sut is the murderer of the good brother as Osiris. In the other, Sut pierces and puts out the eye of Horus. This is represented as the contest between Cain and Abel, the two sons of Adam, in the book of Genesis. Sut and Horus represented two contending nature-powers. They fought each other as the two rehus or lions in the light and dark halves of the moon, with Taht as the adjudicator of the landmarks. They also fought as two dragons, or as the crocodile of water and the dragon of drought, both of which were rightly represented in the astronomical mythology. "Hydra" remains for all time as the "hellish Apap" who drank up the water. And "Draconis" is a figure of the good dragon or Horus-crocodile. Lastly, the two opponent powers were portrayed as twin-brothers, fighting for the birth-right, or seeking to overcome each other. Thus they contended for possession of the garden in Amenta, where they fought upon the mount of glory or were constellated as the Gemini contending in the zodiac. The conflict of the brothers was continued in the Garden of Eden, and Cain fulfils the character of the murderer Sut, the slayer of his brother. There is an attempt even to discriminate betwixt the two domains of Sut and Horus, when it is said that "Abel was a keeper of sheep, but Cain was a tiller of the ground" (Gen. iv. 2, 3).

The Aarru-garden, or paradise, planted in Amenta by Ptah for Atum his son, was founded on food and liquid, that is on the water, and the tree, or plant, as food of life. These, in the Hebrew version, are called "the trees in the midst of the garden," and "the river that went out of Eden to water the garden." They represent the mythical tree and the water of life, which had their beginning in actual food and drink, and were afterwards repeated, on earth, in heaven, and in the making of Amenta. The well or water-spring that was the source of life to primitive man was here continued as a basis for the re-beginning of life in the earth of eternity. In the Ritual the manes, or Osiris N., says, "I am he whose stream is secret." This was the hidden source of water in the earth itself that was repeated as divine source in Amenta. In some of the vignettes to the Ritual Osiris, god of Amenta, is portrayed upon his throne within a shrine that rests upon the water welling from the underworld. One of his titles was the water of renewal. So supreme an element of life was water, by the aid of which the Aarru-paradise was made. "I know the names of the streams within the garden," exclaims the manes; "I utter my praise to the gods who are in the garden" (Rit., ch. 110). The water issues now from underneath the throne of Osiris. But in the earlier cult the source of life as water was the secret of the great god Ptah. In a hymn on the walls of the temple at El-Khargeh, Ptah is saluted as the lord of all, from the very beginning. It is said, "Thou hast made the double earth." "Thou hast placed thy throne in the life of the double earth." It is also said of this one god, "Thy secret is in the depths (or the deep) of the secret waters and unknown" (Renouf, *Hibbert Lectures*, p. 231). This secret rests in the beginning with water. The source of water was the well within the earth, the well-spring of life in the Neter-Kar, the secret water emanating from the Nun, as if it broke up through the solid earth. It was the secret guarded by the Sphinx, by the seven spirits of the earth, the seven Anunnaki seated on their golden thrones. It was the water of the tuat in the Ritual called "the deep which no one can fathom" (Rit., ch. 172). This is the beginning of life with water and vegetation now repeated at the point of a new departure in the making of Amenta by

Ptah the planter of the Aarru-garden. The four waters into which heaven was divided are portrayed in the Sekhet-hetep or fields of peace. Cool water, eatable plants, and refreshing breezes constituted the Egyptian heaven as it had been from the first time in Inner Africa. And according to the pictures, paradise in Amenta is mapped out in four divisions of land amidst the cooling waters of the Aarru meadows or Elysian Fields, the Semitic Garden of Eden. The sign of heaven or the sky is to be seen above a vertical table which is divided into four parts. The garden is intersected by the four waters of the book of Genesis. The great water is the celestial Nile, called the father of the gods, the giver of plenty. The other three are designated the power of the water, innumerable waters, and great place of the water (Rit., ch. 110, and vignettes).

But the paradise depicted in the vignettes to the Ritual is sub-terrestrial, not celestial or circumpolar; it is the earthly paradise. This is the garden of the lower Aarru, not the garden on the summit of the stellar mount of glory. In that, the one water was divided into the two lakes with the river running down from the north to the south. The terrestrial paradise in Amenta is based upon the four quarters of the sky that was suspended by Ptah, and the four quarters are equivalent to the four waters or rivers in the vignettes to the Ritual. The four rivers of Eden belong to this later heaven that was divided into four parts and are a co-type with the four quarters. Hence they are portrayed as issuing from the four sides of the mythical mount in pictures of the garden. In a Buddhist legend, cited by Hardy, a tree takes the place of the mount and four great rivers flow unceasingly from the four boughs of this tree of immensity. The river names, in the biblical version, belong to a later geography, which has to be allowed for; they are a mixture of Egyptian and Assyrian. "A river went out of Eden to water the garden, and from thence it was parted and became four heads." The first is Pishon, the second is Gihon, the third is Hiddekel, the fourth is Euphrates. Of the water or fountain-head Pishon it is said, "That is it which compasseth the whole land of Havilah, where there is gold, and the gold of that land is good; there (also) is bdellium and the onyx stone" (Genesis ii. 11, 12). This land of the good gold corresponds to the Egyptian Puanta or Ta-Neter the divine land which is called "the golden" in the Ritual (ch. 15). But this land of gold was the land of the solar glory. Adorations are offered to Atum as he rises out of "the golden" or comes up from Puanta to illumine the earth.

Atum was the god in spirit, the one god in spirit and in truth; and Atum or Adam in the garden was the man in spirit striving as manes for assimilation to the god. The man of earth as the first Adam passes into the Amenta to become the second Adam in the garden as the heir of life eternal. Atum in Amenta represents generic man and individual manes. He is the god-man, both human and divine, the man in matter and the man in spirit. The French Egyptologist, M. Lefébure, who has lately identified Adam with the Egyptian Atum, as the present writer had done seven years earlier in *A Book of the Beginnings,* refers to a scene on the coffin of Penpii in the Louvre, which is similar to the history of Adam in the sub-terrestrial paradise, where a naked and ithyphallic personage called "the lord of food" (Neb-tefa) *is standing before a serpent with two legs and two arms,* and the reptile is offering him a red fruit, or at least a little round object painted red. The same scene is again found on the tomb of Rameses VI. And on a statue relatively recent in the museum at Turin it is to Atum = Adam that the serpent, as tempter, is offering the round object, or fruit of the tree. The same writer says, "The tree of life and knowledge was well known in Egypt." And "whether the scene of Neb-tefa can be identified with the history of Adam or not, we can see that the greater number of the peculiar features of this history existed in Egypt—the tree of life and knowledge, the serpent in paradise, Eve thinking of appropriating divinity to herself, and in short Adam himself, are all there" (*Trans. S. Bib. Arch.,* vol. ix., pt. i. p. 180).

The entrance to the hidden earth was in the western region, founded on the pathway of the sun. The garden of Aarru was the land of promise, peace, and plenty on the eastward side of the Amenta. The manes carries the title-deeds of his allotment with him. In later copies of the Book of the Dead some lines were added to ch. 109: "There are writings in thy possession for the grant of fields, of cornland in which there springeth corn from the effluxes or sap of Osiris." "Enter boldly at the mysterious portals, and be purified by those who are there." The promise is that when the purified deceased comes forth to the Sekhet-Aarru wheat and barley shall be given to him there, and he will sow and reap it with the glorified (Rit., rubric to ch. 72). In another chapter, when the speaker has arrived, he exclaims, "I am the great owner in the garden of Aarru. O this garden of Aarru, the walls of which are of steel (or ba-metal)." "I know the inner gate of the garden of Aarru, out of which cometh Ra, in the east of the sky." "I know those two sycamores of emerald, between which he cometh forth as he advanceth to the eastern gates of the sky, through which he proceedeth" (ch. 149). This is the garden to the eastward of Amenta, or of Eden in Genesis. The speaker also describes it as the garden which is a field of divine harvest. "I know this garden of Ra (Atum): the height of its wheat is seven cubits, the ears are two cubits, the stalks five cubits, the barley is seven cubits. It is the glorified ones, each of whom is nine cubits in height, who reap there in presence of the powers of the east" (ch. 149). Whether imaged as the garden or the harvest-field, this was the earthly paradise, the land of promise and of plenty, and Atum in the harvest-field or Aarru-garden represented not the man of earth, but the manes of Amenta, the man who died and was buried and who rose again in spirit to cultivate his plot of ground for edible plants, or the wheat that grew seven cubits high in this the earth of eternity. The manes makes his way towards those who have become the lords of eternity living for ever, the spirits made perfect, or the gods and the glorified. And it is probable that when he says, "Let me go up to the Sekhet-Aarru and arrive in Sekhet-hetep" (ch. 72), there is a reference to the ascent from the lower to the upper paradise by way of the mount, the tree, or ladder of Ra which reaches to the sky—that is, from the garden of the vine in Amenta to the field of rest in heaven. Hence the need of the ship.

The ship of Nu is thus addressed by the manes in chapter 106: "O thou ship of the garden of Aarru, let me be conveyed to that bread of thy canal like my father, the great one, who advanceth in the divine ship, because I know thee," as was shown from the examination of the initiate in chapter 99.

The garden was divided into fourteen portions called domains, a number which indicates a foundation in one half of the lunar circle. The first of these is entered by the manes in the character of Atum = Adam. He enters with the crown of Atum on his head. He says, "Doff your headdress in my presence. I am the great one; I am the lord among the gods." "Horus has crowned me with 'the diadem of Atum.'" The garden of Aarru itself is the second of the fourteen domains in Amenta. The manes in the character of Atum = Adam enters the second domain as the owner of it, saying, "I am the great proprietor in the garden of Aarru." This he goes on to describe. It is on the horizon of the east = *the garden eastward*. The god who is in the garden with the manes is Har-Makhu, that is Atum. And as Atum is the Kamite original of the Hebrew Adam so the garden of Atum is the Gan-Eden of Adam (ch. 149 and vignette). The third is the domain of "the glorious ones," the seven great companion-spirits who assisted Ptah as his craftsmen in the making of Amenta. In this, the third domain, the manes assumes the divinity of Atum himself, saying, "I am the lord of the red crown which is on the head of the shining one, he who *gives life to mankind with the breath of his mouth.*" It was Atum who gave life to mankind or the manes with the breath of his mouth. This is repeated (Gen. ii. 7) when Iahu-Elohim breathed into his nostrils the breath of life, and man became a living soul. In the fourth domain there is a great and lofty mountain of the nether world, the mountain of Amenta, three hundred measures in length and ten in width, the highest point of which ends with the sky. There is a serpent coiling on it seventy cubits in its windings. "He with sharp knives is his name," or, in a word, it is the "piercing" serpent. "He lives by slaughtering the glorious ones and the damned in the nether world." This is the Apap-reptile who may be seen in a vignette to the Ritual facing Sebek on the mount (ch. 108). The manes addresses the monster in the fourth domain, saying, "I see the way towards thee. I gather myself together. I am the man who put a veil upon thy head, without being injured. I am the great magician. Thine eyes have been given to me, and through them I am glorified. Who is he that goeth on his belly? Thy strength is on thy mountain; behold, I march toward it (the mountain), and thy strength is in my hand. I am he who takes possession of thy strength. I go round the sky; thou art in thy valley, as was ordered to thee before." He has deprived the serpent of his magical power and cast him down in the dust, or into the valley.

No sooner was Amenta made and the tree of life, which represented vegetation, planted in the water of life than the Apap-reptile, the serpent of darkness or the dragon of drought, broke into the enclosure. As the representative of drought, its fangs were fastened on the tree of food, of dew, of life. As the representative of darkness it warred against the light of Atum, Horus, Ra, and Taht. And, as the

Ritual has it (ch. 17), "There was conflict now in the entire universe," in heaven, upon earth, and in Amenta, inclusive of the garden. In the great battle betwixt Ra and Apap, described in chapter 39 of the Ritual, Atum as Horus the son fights for the father Ra. When the victory is won Atum says, "Lift up your countenance, ye soldiers of Ra!" The same part is taken by Atum in the garden of Aarru when he delivers Ra from Apap in the third domain. There is a scene in the vignette to ch. 17 (Pap. of Ani, plate 10), in which Atum Ra appears as god the father and Atum-Horus as god the son. The youthful solar god is imaged in the form of a cat, the seer in the dark, and is grappling with the serpent and cutting off or bruising its head. Ra the father is intently gazing at his son whilst the battle is raging. The group of gods looking on are watching the struggle betwixt the great cat and the serpent Apap. The god in conflict with the serpent is Iu the son of Atum, otherwise Atum in the person of the son. And here we have delved down to a tap-root of the Jesus legend. Iu-em-hetep in the cult of Atum-Ra is the coming son, the ever-coming su or son of the eternal; and Iu the su=Iusu, or Iusa the son of Iusāas, is the original of Iusu or Jesus. In one phase the battle was fought nightly betwixt Iu the son of Atum, or, in the Osirian version, betwixt Horus the son of Asar and the loathly reptile. In another phase of the mythos the great battle was fought annually between the saviour-son and the serpent in the garden of Aarru hard by the tree of life, as described and portrayed in the Ritual (ch. 17, 20-22). This war betwixt the serpent and the son who came to save went on for ever, every night, every year, and every other period of time; hence the bruiser of the serpent's head was the saviour who for ever came as the lord of light, the giver of life, protector of the tree of life at its rootage in Amenta.

Horus bruising the Serpent's Head.

There is another personification of the woman who wars against the serpent as Sekhet, otherwise Pasht. This goddess is sometimes depicted standing at the prow of the boat in the act of spearing the serpent as he raises his head and tries to hypnotise the passengers with his evil eyes (ch. 108, ll. 3, 4). It is Sekhet who is mistress of the water in which the Apap lurks by night (ch. 57, l. 1), because she was a lunar goddess, the seer by night, who was also imaged as the cat that killed the serpent or the rat abominated by the sun. Thus there are two versions, lunar and solar. In one the woman or goddess is the slayer of the serpent, in the other it is the son of the woman that bruises the reptile's head. The Romish Church has perpetuated the former; the latter survives in the Protestant world, and, as here shown, both are Egyptian. Moreover, Sekhet the cat-headed consort of Ptah was the mother of Atum-Ra. When we have identified the son in this disguise of a great cat killing a serpent as defender of his father, we may perhaps experience less surprise on learning that the cat was also continued in the Christian Church as a living type of the "historical Christ." At Aix, in Provence, the great cat was a representative of the newly-born Jesus. On the solemn festival of Corpus Christi the finest tom cat to be found in the canton was exhibited in this character. It was wrapt up like a child in swaddling-clothes and made a show of in a gorgeous shrine. Every knee was bowed in adoration to this effigy, who was Iu in Egypt, and Iahu, cat and all, in Christendom. (Hampson, *Medii Ævi Kalendarium;* Mill, *History of the Crusades.*)

In the pre-Osirian mysteries of Amenta Atum the father was re-born as his own son Iu, the bringer of peace and plenty and good luck, as manifestor for the eternal in time. The birth was periodic because the phenomena were first recurrent in external nature—in the renewal of the light, the return of the waters, the rebirth of vegetation. Hence the Messiah was known as "the king of one year." The son, as Horus, son of Isis, or Iu the su (son) of Atum, was incorporated or incarnated in matter as a spirit from heaven to become the second Atum, Iu-em-hetep, the ever-coming son, whom we identify as the original Iu-su, the Egyptian Jesus. His mission is sufficiently set forth in the texts and pictures of the Ritual, more expressly as the opponent and the conqueror of Apap, the evil serpent. The fight is several times alluded to in which Horus, or the deceased who impersonates him, defends the enclosure against the Apap-serpent. "He makes his way. He repulses the attack of Apap. He crosses the enclosure and repulses Apap" (Rit., 144, 20). "He puts an end to the rage of Apap and protecteth Ra against him daily" (ch. 130). Again, he says, "I have repulsed Apap, and healed the wounds he made" (ch. 136, 3). Ra is identical with Atum, but the character is duplicative. In one Atum-Ra is the father-god, in the other Atum-Horus, or Iu, is the son; and as the son he is the protector and deliverer of his father when he staggers forth upon the horizon from his conflict with the serpent, bleeding with many wounds (Rit., ch. 39).

There is hardly any more precious document on the face of the earth at the present moment than the Papyrus of Ani (published by the British Museum). In this the happy garden is portrayed with the pair of souls, once human, passing through the various scenes which are depicted in the Ritual. The soul, or manes, makes the journey through Amenta in the two halves of sex; "male and female created he them." Thus Ani is accompanied in the pictures by his wife Tutu, who had died eight years before him, and who comes to meet him at the entrance to Amenta, to protect him on the way she travelled first, and to scare away all evil spirits with the shaking of her sistrum as she guides him to the heaven of the glorified elect. As gods, the divine pair in the garden of this late beginning, called Gan-Eden, were Atum and Iusāas. As human, they may be any pair of manes, or translated mortals like Ani and his wife, to whom an allotment in the Sekhet Aarru was given for them to cultivate. In the Hebrew version the divine pair have been humanized in Adam and Eve, as beings *on* this earth, and thus the mystery of Amenta loses all the meaning, which has to be restored by reading the mythos once more in the original. The male and female pair are portrayed together in the vignettes to chapters 15, 15a, 2; 15a, 3; 15a, 4; 15b, 1; 15b, 2, all of which scenes belong to the earth of eternity. (Naville, *Das Ægypt., Todt.*, pp. 14, 15, 16, 17, 18, 19.) The primal pair of human beings, who are Adam and Eve in the Semitic version of the legend, had been represented in the Papyri as Ani and his wife Tutu, the man and woman that once were mortal on the earth, but have passed into the state of manes, who are on their way to or in the terrestrial paradise. They enter the Aarru-garden. They drink the water of life at its secret source in the Tuat. They eat the fruit of the tree of life, which is offered to Ani, the man, by the divine woman in the tree, who may be Nut or Hathor. If it be Hathor who offers the fruit of the tree, there is a possible link betwixt this scene and the story of Adam's temptation by the woman in the book of Genesis. Hathor's was the tree of earth, Nut's was the tree of heaven. The pair are pictured in the earthly paradise, and therefore in the place of Hathor's tree, the sycamore-fig tree. Now Iusāas, the wife of Atum=Adam and mother of Iu at Annu, was a form of Hathor. So that Hathor-Iusāas offering the fruit of the sycamore-fig to Atum in the Sekhet-Aarru is equivalent to Eve, who offers the fruit of the tree of knowledge to Adam in the Garden of Eden, which, as shown by the apron of fig-leaves, was a fig tree.

When Ani and his spirit-consort, who had been his wife on earth, appear together in the happy garden, they drink the water of life and eat the fruit of the tree, as spirits among spirits. They nestle in the green bower of Hathor the goddess of love, and the pleasures of the earthly paradise are denoted by their playing games of draughts together in the garden. In one scene the pair are portrayed hard by the tree of life, both of them drinking the water of life that flows from beneath the tree. In the next vignette the man is kneeling *alone* before the tree, which is a sycamore-fig tree. A woman in the tree is offering some of its fruit to Ani. This is the goddess Nut, the lady of heaven, who presents the fruit of the tree to the man in the garden of the earthly paradise (Pap. of Ani, pl. 16), and who has been converted into the woman that tempted Adam to eat of the tree as the cause of the fallacious fall. The biblical rendering of this representation is a blasphemy against the Ritual, against womankind, against nature, and against knowledge. The goddess Nut, who offers the fruit of the tree of knowledge to the kneeling man, is in shape a woman, and the meaning could be only too easily misread, as it has been in the legend of the first woman who tempted the first man to eat of the forbidden fruit and to cause the loss of paradise.

According to the Ritual the manes who receive food in the garden of Aarru (ch. 99, 32, 38) or who eat of the fruit of the sycamore-fig tree of Hathor (ch. 52) are empowered to make what transformation they please, and go out of it as spirits. They literally become spirits among spirits as a result of eating the fruit of the tree. The manes says, "Let me eat under the sycamore of Hathor! Let me see the forms of my father and mother" (ch. 52), as he would when the spirit sight was opened for him to perceive with the beatific vision. This is sufficient as a text for the serpent when it says, "Ye shall not surely die; for God doth know that in the day ye eat thereof, then your eyes shall be opened and ye shall be as gods, knowing good and evil" (Gen. iii. 4, 5). Instead of being damned eternally through eating the fruit of the tree, the manes in Amenta are divinized piecemeal as the result of eating it (82, 2, 5). In the rubrical directions at the end of chapter 99 we read, "This chapter being known, the deceased appears in the field (or cultivated enclosure) of Aarru. He receives food there, the produce of its fields. His members become like to those of the gods. He goes forth pure spirit." (Lines 32-34.) Instead of referring to the fall of man from the terrestrial paradise, this relates to the ascent of souls from a lower heaven won by hard labour in Amenta to an upper heaven attainable at last by spirits perfected. When the manes have literally done their digging in cultivating the fields of Aarru, they ascend the mount of re-birth in heaven to enter the ark or bark of souls, and sail or row themselves to the Hesperian isles.

It follows that the hiding of the guilty pair in the garden is derived from the manes being overshadowed and concealed by the foliage of the tree of Hathor under which they were refreshed. If these do not hide themselves, they make their refuge and secret resting place beneath the tree. "I embrace and *make my asylum* of the sycamore," says the speaker in the Ritual (64, 24).

In the book of Genesis the fruit of the tree is the means of knowing good from evil, and in the Ritual both the good and evil are determined by the nature of the food presented to the cultivators of the garden, or field of divine harvest, in Amenta as it was on earth. The speaker has a choice between the good and the evil—that is, betwixt the food offered by the Apap-serpent of evil, which is denounced as detestable, vile, excrementitious, and the fruit of the tree, upon which the gods and all good spirits feed. The speaker repudiates the typhonian diet. He only accepts that which is offered to him by a messenger who comes from the gods and not from the Apap-serpent. He subsists on the food which is the bread of Horus and Taht. "The Osiris feeds on *the fruit which is produced by the sycamore-fig tree of Hathor.*" On that he is nourished in his turn. In Egyptian the wise spirits are the akeru, which are the wise spirits of the instructed dead, and in eating the fruit of the tree the eaters are to become the wise as spirits. This therefore is the tree of wisdom, or of knowledge. In this way, eating of the tree is a part of the process by which the manes in the garden make their transformation into pure spirits. Certain of the baser sort of manes were represented as feeding in Amenta on the excremental foulnesses of human life. In chapter 32 the speaker exclaims, "Back, crocodile of the east, who livest upon *those that devour their own excrement!*" There is a Mangaian representation of some poor wretches in Savaiki who are doomed to endure the indignity of being befouled by the fæces that fall from the more fortunate spirits who are happy in their world of plenty overhead. (Gill, p. 164). The doctrine is native to the Book of the Dead. The Egyptians held that those who were foul and filthy in this life would be fed on excremental matter in the next. The dirty would be dirty still. The Catamite and Sodomite would devour the fæces that are probably denoted figuratively by the words *hesu* and *ushem*, which the deceased abominates when he asserts that he does not eat the dirt or drink the lye.

It is possible that hints for the story of eating that which was prohibited, and the becoming aware of their nakedness by the guilty pair, and their hiding under the trees, were taken from chapters 53 A, B and 124 of the Ritual. The speaker who has been constituted a soul by Osiris says, *"That which is forbidden I do not eat: I do not walk upon it with my sandals."* Here the forbidden thing is odious because it is evil, filthy, excremental. For those who abstain from such repulsive food, the object of unclean appetites, there are pure foods and proper nourishment provided. To these the manes, man and wife, the pair seen in the pictures, uplift their hands. The speaker for both says they eat under the trees and beautiful branches of the tree upon which the fruit grows within reach (124, 1, 4). The notion of a tree that grew forbidden fruit is probably of totemic origin, with a mystical application to sexual uncleanness. The people whose totem was a particular tree would be forbidden to eat of its fruit, or if it were eaten it must be sacramentally, because it was sacred to them. "Do not eat forbidden food," is a command sternly spoken to the young men in the initiation ceremonies of the Arunta tribes.

In one episode the guilty pair, having eaten of the tree that was to make them wise, perceive themselves to be naked in the garden, and are then clothed with skins by Iahu-Elohim. This also may be explicated by the gnosis. The manes in the Ritual consist of the clothed and the naked. Those who pass the judgment hall become the clothed. The beatified spirits are invested with the robe of the righteous, the stole of Ra, in the garden. There was a special investiture by the god in the garden of Aarru. This clothing in the garden is likewise a part of the process by which the manes pass into the state of spirits. The investiture in the garden of Hetep denotes a spirit made perfect in the likeness of the Lord. This is followed at a distance in the Hebrew Genesis. When the man and woman are invested in their coats of skin they also become spirits, if not as the spirits of the just made perfect. And Iahu-Elohim said, "Behold, the man is become *as one of us,* to know good from evil." The deceased pleads that he may attain the "investiture of the garden" (ch. 110). When clothed they issue in what is termed the "coming forth from the swathings in the garden of Aarru, and the coming forth in exultation" (Renouf, ch. 99). "I hasten to the land, and I fasten my stole upon me, that I may come forth and take possession of the wealth assigned to me" (ch. 110). "I range within the garden of Hetep; I fasten my stole upon me" (ch. 110). "I am the girdled one, coming forth in triumph" (ch. 117). Now in the judgment scenes there is a skin called the nem-skin suspended over a sign that represents the ba-soul (Hor-Apollo, I, 40). The word nem denotes another, a second, also to repeat. Thus the nem skin is a second skin, covering, or investiture. That which it hangs on in the vignette signifies a soul. So that the nem-skin means another garment for the soul. The lord of transformations is said to have numerous skins, as the rehabiliments of souls. A new skin was equivalent to a new lease of existence. It is this clothing of the manes in a coat of skin that is repeated in the book of Genesis.

Whatsoever astronomical data there may have been for the typical rendering of a fall in heaven, or from the Garden of Eden, *it is the Semites, not the Egyptians, who are responsible for introducing a fall into the moral domain and calling it the veritable fall of man in the beginning.*

The Babylonians handling of the Egyptian wisdom was begun by falsifying it on behalf of an indefinitely later system of theology, which was continued on the Hebrew line of descent in the book of Genesis. Besides which, if the fall of Adam from paradise is identifiable with the falling away of Atum in the astronomical mythology, it becomes at once apparent that the restoration from the effects of such a fall is equally astronomical and a matter of scientific verification. Atum, as father, sank down to Amenta every night, and every morning there was a restoration of the light made by the second Atum in his character of the youthful solar god. In the same way Atum, the closer of the year, was the autumn sun that went down in the winter solstice and rose again in the equinox as opener and restorer in the person of Nefer-Tum, the coming son, who was Iu-su = Jesus as Egyptian. So was it through all the cycles of time, including finally the cycle of the great year of the world. On the scale of precession he who made the lapse at first as Atum or Adam would naturally make the restoration as Iu at the end of 26,000 years for those who rightly kept the reckoning and did not mistake this great ending in time for an actual ending of the world. It was the subject of astronomical prophecy that Atum in person of the son (that is, the su or sa) would come again to restore that which was lost of old, when time had once more travelled to the place of the beginning in the Lion sign, the station of the sphinx in heaven, who kept the secret for the mystery teachers of the eternal, or in whichever sign the cycle was to be fulfilled, when paradise would be regained, and all would be once more as at the first; when, as Vergil sang of the great cyclical renewal, "There shall be another ark, steered by another pilot, bearing the chosen heroes" (the twelve kings or gods that voyaged in the solar bark), "and there shall be other wars, and great Achilles shall be sent once more to Troy" (Vergil, Eclogue iv). In other words, the wandering Iu or Horus, Prince of Eternity, would travel once more round the cycle of precession as divine manifestor and fulfiller in the great year of the world. The tree of life retained its place and prominence in the new heavens of Hebrew prophecy as in the old heaven of the astronomical mythology. "For unto you is paradise opened; the tree of life is planted, the time to come is prepared, plenteousness is made ready, a city is builded, and rest is allowed. Sorrows are passed, and in the end is shown the treasure of immortality" (2 Es. viii. 52-54). All of which had been realized for the Egyptians in the garden of Hetep, the Aarru-paradise upon the stellar mount of glory.

Apart from the astronomical allegory, the only fall of man was that of the Adam whom the seven Elohim tried to make out of the red earth, but failed from lack of the immortal spark of spirit, which was ascribed to the father in heaven when the human father had been individualized on earth. This was the man of flesh who was born, not begotten; the man who descended from the mother only—that is, totemic man, who was shaped by the apprentice hands of the seven powers, together with their mother, and who preceded the supreme being. The first-formed Adam was of the earth earthy, of the flesh fleshly, the man of matter = the mother. This was the origin of an opposition betwixt the flesh and spirit, the man of earth and the man from heaven, which led to a doctrine of natural depravity and pollution of the flesh when compared with the purity of spirit. The doctrine of natural depravity did not originate in the moral domain, it originated in matter considered to be at enmity with the spirit. The cause of this depravity in the flesh was ascribed to the woman after the soul or spirit had been assigned to the fatherhood. The mother was the maker of flesh from her own blood or the red earth, and in one particular phase the blood of the woman was held to be vile and filthy. Job asks, "How can man be clean that is born of a woman?" (xxv. 4). But this "depravity" was a result of confounding the blood as virgin source of life with the menstrualia. There is a hint of the doctrine in the Ritual. In the chapter "whereby one cometh forth to day from Amenta," the manes says, "Shine thou on me, O gracious power; as I draw nigh to the divine words which my ears shall hear in the Tuat, *let no pollution of my mother be upon me.*" The speaker is making his transformations into the glorious body of a manes who will be perfected in becoming pure spirit, which is the antithesis of the earthly body that was made flesh in the blood of the mother. "Let no pollution of my mother be upon me" is equivalent to saying, "Deliver me from all fleshliness of the old earth life." Here, however, the utterer of this prayer is one of the manes who has risen in the shape of the old body, but changed in texture, and who is desirous of being purified and perfected in the likeness of the holy spirit, which is personalized in Amenta as Horus, the anointed son of god the father. A hundred times over one sees how these utterances pertaining to Amenta have been perverted through being assigned to human beings in the life on earth.

The additional features added by the Semites to the original version of the mythos consist in the introduction of a primal pair of mortals eating the forbidden fruit; the temptation and seduction of the woman by the deceiving serpent; the turning of the woman into the tempter of the man; the criminality of the first parents, who lost the world and damned the race before a child was born; the creation of an original sin which was destined to overshadow the human family with an antenatal cloud of guilt and of hereditary depravity, and thus prepare the way and the need for the Christian scheme of redemption to regain a paradisaical condition which was never lost and never had existed. These were the crowning achievements of those who falsified the teachings of the Egyptians. Nothing could better illustrate the difference between the two versions than the opposite treatment of work. In the biblical travesty the curse is to come to the man in the shape of work and to the woman with the labour pangs of maternity. Whereas in the Ritual work is the blessing and the workers in Aarru are the blessed. They cultivate their own allotted portions in the field of divine harvest, and may be said to make their way and win their other world by work. For the Egyptian could find his heaven in the satisfaction of accomplished work. Again, if we take Ani and his wife, Tutu, as representatives of the pair, once human, and now manes, in the garden, we shall find that so far from the "woman" having been the cause of a fall in the Egyptian Genesis, so far from her having been an agent of the evil serpent, or of Satan, as the Christian fathers ignorantly alleged and brutally maintained, she, the only one who ever had been a woman in this or in other forms of the pair, is portrayed as defender of the man all through the trials and temptations that beset him in his passage through the nether world. She is his guide and protector. She propitiates the powers with offerings on his behalf. She makes his music and his magic all the way.

The pair in Eden or the earthly paradise fulfil two characters in the Kamite myth and eschatology. They are either two of the gods, as Atum and Kefa (Kep), or two of the glorified, as Ani and Tutu. But in neither are the male and female in the garden a pair of human beings; both as the gods and the glorified they are supra-mundane and *doubly non-human*. Finally, if the "fall" had ever been a veritable fact, the subsequent history of man might be summed up as one long, vast, unceasing, vain endeavour to remedy the disaster and the failure that befell the divine government of the universe in such a helpless way as would destroy all future trust. The vessel would have been lost in the act of being launched, and not a hand reached forth to save the victims until some nineteen centuries ago, when God himself is said to have come down in person for a long-belated rescue of shipwrecked humanity. But the Semitic story of the fall is false, and the scheme of redemption founded on it is consequently fraudulent. As it comes to us, the book of Genesis is based on misappropriated legends. It is responsible for an utterly erroneous account of creation and the origin of evil, and its damnation of the race through Adam's fall is the sole ground on which the Christian world can now find foothold for its coming Saviour. And, however long or however short a time the imposition lasts,

"The same old lie, for ever told anew,
Will never serve to make the falsehood true."

THE EGYPTIAN WISDOM IN OTHER JEWISH WRITINGS

Book VIII

THE Kamite mythos of the old lost garden may be seen transforming into Hebrew legendary lore when Ezekiel describes an Eden that was sunk and buried in the lowermost parts of the earth. "Thus saith the Lord . . . When I cast him (Pharaoh) down to Sheol with them that descend into the pit: and all the trees of Eden, . . . and all that drink water were comforted in the nether parts of the earth. . . ." "To whom art thou thus like in glory and in greatness among the trees of Eden? Yet shalt thou be brought down with the trees of Eden into the nether parts of the earth; thou shalt lie in the midst of the uncircumcised." (Ez. XXXI. 15, 16, 18.) This is the *garden of Eden in Sheol,* and Sheol is a Semitic version of the Egyptian Amenta. That is why the lost Gan-Eden is to be found in the nether parts of the earth as an outcast of the later theology.

When the word Sheol in the Old Testament is rendered in English by "the grave," it is inadequate times out of number. The Hebrew writers were not always speaking or thinking of the grave when they wrote of Sheol, which has to be bottomed in Amenta, the divine nether-earth, not simply in the tomb. The grave is not identical with hell, nor the pit-hole with the bottomless pit. The pangs and sorrows of Sheol, like the purging pangs of the Romish purgatory, have to be studied in the Egyptian Ritual. Many of the moanings and the groanings in the Psalms are the utterances of Osiris or the Osiris suffering in Amenta. They are the cries for assistance in Sheol. The appeals in the house of bondage for help from on high, and for deliverance from afflictions and maladies more than human, were uttered in Amenta before they were heard in Sheol, and the Psalmist who first wrote the supplications on behalf of the manes was known as the divine scribe Taht before the Psalms in Hebrew were ascribed to David. The speaker of Psalm xvi. is talking pure Egyptian doctrine in Amenta concerning his soul and body when he says, "My flesh shall dwell in safety, for thou wilt not leave my soul in Sheol; neither wilt thou suffer thy holy one to see corruption; thou wilt show me the path of life; in thy presence is the fulness of joy, in thy right hand there are pleasures for evermore." As we see from the Ritual, this is the manes expressing his confidence in the duration of his personality, the persistence of his sahu or mummy-soul in

Amenta, and his hope of being vivified for ever by the Holy Spirit and led along the pathway of eternal life by Horus the Redeemer to the right hand of his father, Atum-Ra. He is the sleeper in Amenta when he says, "I shall behold thy face in righteousness; I shall be satisfied with thy likeness when I awake" (Ps. xvii. 15). The Osiris woke in Sekhem, where he saw the likeness of his Lord who left his picture there; his true likeness as the risen one transformed, transfigured, and divinely glorified, that looked upon the manes, smiling sun-wise through the defecating mist of death, for the Osiris to come forth and follow him. The speaker was in Amenta as the land of bondage when the "cords of Sheol" were bound about him. He was assimilated to the suffering Horus, sitting blind and helpless in the utter darkness, pierced and torn and bleeding from the wounds inflicted on him by Sut, who had been his own familiar friend, his twin-brother, and who had turned against him and betrayed him to his death. The most memorable sayings in the Psalms, and the most misleading when misunderstood, are uttered in this character of Osiris, who was the typical victim in Amenta, where he was tormented by the followers of Sut, the forsaken sufferer who was piteously left to cry, "My God! My God! Why hast thou forsaken me? Why art thou so far from helping me?" The sufferer is in Sheol, the miry pit, when he says, "I sink in deep mire." "Deliver me out of the mire, and let not Sheol shut her mouth upon me" (Ps. lxix. 2, 14, 15).

Sheol, then, is one with Amenta, and the drama with its characters and teachings belongs to the mysteries of Amenta, which are attributed to Taht, the Egyptian psalmist, who is the great chief in Sekhem, the place where Horus suffered or Osiris died. Taht was the writer of the sayings attributed to Horus in his dual character of the human sufferer in Amenta and of Horus-Tema, the divine avenger of the sufferings that were inflicted on Osiris by the "wicked," the Sami, the co-conspirators with Sut, the Egyptian Judas. This will account for the non-natural imagery and hugely inhuman language ascribed to the supposed historic David, who as writer was primarily the psalmist Taht, and who called down the divine wrath upon the accursed Typhonians for what they had done in binding, torturing, and piercing Horus (or Osiris) and pursuing him to death. So far as the language of Taht remains in the Psalms of David, it is inhuman because the characters of the drama were originally non-human. This is one of the many misrenderings that have to be rectified by means of the Egyptian Ritual, when we have discriminated between the earth of time and the earth of eternity, between the denizens of Judea and the manes in Sheol, and learned that the Hebrew and Christian histories of these mystical matters have been compounded out of the Egyptian eschatology.

It is noteworthy that certain of the Psalms, in two different groups (xlii. to xlix. and lxxxiv. to lxxxviii.), are specialized as "Psalms of the Sons of Korah." These were the rebels, once upon a time, who, according to Hebrew tradition, disappeared when the earth opened and swallowed them up alive. This is a legend of Amenta. The only earth that ever swallowed human beings was the nether-earth of Sheol; and if we take our stand with the sons of Korah in Amenta we can read these Psalms and see how they should especially apply to those who were swallowed by Sheol in the nether-world. "One thing," says a commentator, "which added to this surprising occurrence, is that when Korah was swallowed in the earth his sons were preserved." They went down to the pit in death, but lived on as did the manes in Amenta. The sons of Korah are in Sheol. But, says the speaker, "God will redeem my soul from the power of Sheol" (Ps. xlix. 15). He exclaims, "Bring me unto thy holy hill and to thy tabernacles." Psalm xlv. is a Psalm addressed to the anointed son, the king = the royal Horus, who comes as a conqueror of death and Sheol. Psalm xlvii. is a song of the resurrection from Amenta. "God is gone up with a shout," to sit upon his holy throne, in the eternal city" on his holy mountain," which was the way up from the dark valley for those who, like "the sons of Korah," sank into the nether-earth, but who lived on to rise again and reach the summit of the sacred mount. The Kamite steps of ascent were buried as a fetish figure in the coffins with the dead for use, typically, when they woke to life in Amenta. It is said to the Osiris in the Ritual, "Osiris, thou hast received thy sceptre, thy pedestal, and the flight of stairs beneath thee"; this was in readiness for his resurrection. These images of the stand on which the gods were elevated, like Anup at the pole, the tat of stability, and the steps of ascent to heaven, were buried with the mummy as emblems of divine protection which are with him when he emerges from the comatose state of the dead. The steps thus buried stand for the mountain of ascent. We are reminded of this by the Psalmist when he sings, "O Lord, thou has brought up my soul from Sheol. Thou, Lord, of thy favour hadst *made my mountain* to stand strong" (Ps. xxx. 37)—the mountain that was imaged in the tomb by the steps with the aid of which the deceased makes the ascent from Amenta, and can say, "I am the lord of the stairs. I have made my nest on the horizon" (Rit., ch. 85). The Pharaoh Unas exults that the ladder or steps have been supplied to him by his father, Ra, as means of ascent to spirit world. When King Pepi makes his exodus from the lower earth to the elysian fields Sut sets up his maket, or ladder, in Amenta by which the manes reaches the horizon; and, secondly, Horus erects his ladder by which the spirit of Pepi reaches up to heaven. This divides the steps of ascent into halves of seven each as these are figured in the seven steps of the solar boat. Thus the total number is fourteen, as it was in the lunar mythos when the eye of the full moon was attained at the summit of fourteen steps or top of the staircase. The number, as may be explained, was fifteen in the soli-lunar reckoning of the month. Thus in one computation there were fifteen steps to the ladder of ascent from the depths of Amenta to the summit of the mount. Now, fifteen of the Psalms (cxx. to cxxxiv.) are termed "Psalms of degrees." In the Hebrew they are called "a Song of ascents." In the Chaldee they were designated "a song that was sung upon *the steps of the abyss.*" These are the steps from the abyss or depths of Sheol mentioned by the speaker, who says, "Thou shalt bring me up again from the depths of the earth" (Ps. lxxi. 20). "Out of the depths have I cried unto thee, O Lord" (Ps. cxxx. 1). Thus the steps constituted a means of ascent from Sheol or Amenta, and in the song of ascents we can identify the staircase of the great god by which the summit of the mount was attained. The speaker has dwelt long in the death-dark land. He will lift up his eyes to the mountains, or the mount: "Unto thee do I lift up mine eyes, O thou that sittest in the heavens." "The Lord hath chosen Zion: he hath desired it for his habitation"—as he had already done when his name was Khnum, or Osiris, the lord of Sheni (Rit., ch. 36). The celestial mountain is the place where the throne was prepared for the last judgment in the mysteries of Amenta, and figured in the maat upon the summit of the mount. It was there Osiris sat "in his throne judging righteously" "as king for ever." The mount was also called the staircase of the great god. Osiris is said to sit at the head of the staircase, surrounded by his circle of gods (Rit., ch. 22). In the pre-Osirian cult it was Atum-Ra who sat as the great judge in the maat, the hall of truth, law, and justice. As we have seen, the mount on high was also imaged by other types of the ascent to heaven.

The speaker in the song of ascents or the psalms of fifteen degrees is at the base of the mythical mount in Sheol = Amenta. The lord whom he addresses is upon the summit of his holy hill, just as Osiris, or Atum or Sebek, is the great god seated at the head of the staircase. In his distress he cries unto the Lord for deliverance from the enemy, who is Sut the liar and deceiver; "him that hateth peace." "My soul," he says, "hath long had her dwelling with him that hateth peace. I am for peace." "Woe is me!" he cries, "that I sojourn in Meshech" (Ps. cxx. 5). Meshech, or meska in the Egyptian, as a place-name signifies the place of scourging and purifying in Suten-Khen. It is the Kamite purgatory as a place of rebirth in Amenta (Rit., ch. 17) for the soul, on its resurrection from the dead prior to the ascent of the steps, the ladder, staircase, column, or mount. On passing through the sixth abode of Amenta (Rit., chs. 72 and 149) the speaker pleads, "Let me not be stopped at the meska; let not the wicked have mastery over me." "Let me join my two hands together in the divine dwelling which my father Atum hath given me, he who hath established an abode for me above the earth, wherein is wheat and barley of untold quantity, which the son of my own body offereth to me there as oblations upon my festivals." And when the manes has passed through the meska or place of purifying he prays to be delivered from the hells that await the damned. In Meshech or the meska the sufferer says he will lift up his eyes unto the mountains from whence his help shall come. The mount is pluralized, but it is the summit upon which stands the heavenly Jerusalem, "builded as a city that is compact together, whither the tribes go up, even the tribes of Ihuh, to give thanks unto the Lord." There were set "the thrones for judgment, the thrones of the house of David," which are the twelve thrones in heaven, as described in the book of Revelation. The single mount is Zion, the Egyptian shennu, or hetep, the mount of rest.

> "For the Lord hath chosen Zion,
> He hath desired it for His habitation;
> This is my *resting-place* for ever."—Ps. cxxxii.

On the last of the fifteen steps of ascent a call is made upon the starry luminaries to praise the Lord. "Bless ye the Lord, all ye servants of the Lord, which by night stand in the house of the Lord. Lift up your hands to the sanctuary, and bless ye the Lord. The Lord bless thee out of Zion" (Ps. cxxxiv). These are they who stand by night around the throne at the top of the steps, and this last finishing touch is very definitely astronomical. As Egyptian, there was an upper circle of the great spirits round the throne upon the summit of the mount, who were called the shennu, and the mount of the shennu = Mount Zion.

Under one of its Egyptian names the valley of Amenta or Sheol is called "Akar." This valley of Akar we identify with Achor, the valley of sorrow in the Hebrew. 'Achor's gloomy vale" is sung of in the Christian hymn, and this is the essential character of Akar. It has been observed by Renouf that the notion of obscurity is connected with Akar, whereas the notion of brightness is essentially associated with the mount (*Proc. Soc. Bib. Arch.*, March 7, 1893, p. 223). The two gates of Akar are mentioned in the pyramid texts of Pepi (line 72) as equivalent in sense to the two gates of Seb or the earth (Renouf, Rit., ch. 39, note). The difference lies betwixt the mythical and eschatological application. The gates of Seb refer to our earth, and the gates of Akar to Amenta, the land of shades in the earth of eternity. When the valley of Achor is to become a door of hope it is in the wake of the solar god who goes forth from the gate of Akar to the summit of the mount. Israel was to be judged and to make answer in the judgment hall (which stood at the place of exit in the topography of Amenta), "as in the day when she (previously) came up out of the land of Egypt," which was one and the same thing in the mythical representation of the Exodus (Hosea, ii. 15). In fact, the supposed history is identified with the mythos by Esdras, who portrays the last judgment, which is to be as it was in the time of Achan when he was doomed to die in the valley of Achor, the Egyptian valley of the shadow of Akar (2 Es. vii. 26-37). In this valley was the sepulchre of Osiris, betwixt the two mountains or horizons of the west and east. So the graves of the Hottentot deity Heitsi-Eibib were made in a valley or narrow pass between two mountains, and from these he, like Osiris, rose again and made his transformation in the tree of dawn.

The nature of Achor is indicated by Hosea when he says of Israel (ii. 14, 15), "I will allure her and bring her into the wilderness, and I will give her the valley of Achor for a door of hope, and she shall make answer in the judgment there." It was in Achor that the stoning of Achan occurred, in the valley of vengeance, and it is there that Israel was to answer for all her iniquities. Thus, whatsoever events had occurred in Achor's gloomy vale took place in the Akar or Aukerti of the nether-earth, which was a place of passage for the manes through Amenta. In the distance lay the Aarru-paradise with the seven cows called the providers of plenty resting in the green fields of peace and prosperity. The vale of Akar led to the Aarru-meadows, and out of these arose the mountain of the Lord, upon the summit of which was the place of rebirth in the upper paradise, the abode of the blessed. This is the imagery made use of by Isaiah (lxv. 9, 12): "Thus saith the Lord: I will bring forth a seed out of Jacob, and out of Judah an inheritor of my mountain; and my chosen shall inherit it, and my servants shall dwell there. And Sharon shall be a pasture for flocks, and the valley of Achor a place for herds to lie down in, for my people that have sought me. But ye that forsake the Lord, that forget my holy mountain, that prepare a table for fortune and that fill up mingled wine unto destiny, I will destine you to the sword." This is the mountain of Amenta. Fortune and Destiny are two Egyptian deities who are mentioned here by the name of Gad and Meni, but only mentioned to be abjured. As Egyptian the goddess of fortune was Rannut, who was also the giver of good fortune in the harvest. The god of destiny or fate was Shai, the apportioner of the lot. These are to be cast out and their worshippers destroyed, but the mould of the imagery remains in the valley of Achor. Indeed, the chart of Judea looks like a copy of the scenery in Amenta as it would be if the land had been originally mapped out by the emigrants from Egypt. Amenta and the Aarru-paradise, with its heaven on the summit of the mount, have been repeated at innumerable sacred places of the world, such as the Garden of the Gods and the holy mountain of Shasta in Colorado.

The first resurrection of two and the coming forth to day occur in the valley of Akar. The valley of passengers, the burial-place for Gog and his multitude; the valley of Elah, the valley of giants, the valley of the Rephaim, the valley of death, the valley of judgment, the valley of Siddim, the valley of Hinom—are all figures of Amenta in the nether-earth of the mythos and eschatology, and therefore of the Hebrew Sheol. The "valley of decision" (Joel iii. 14) is likewise the valley of Amenta associated with the mount of the Lord, the valley of the lower earth in which the great judgment was delivered at the end of the world, or age, or cycle of time, which was annual in the mysteries, as it still is in the Jewish ceremonies celebrated at the end of every year. The Lord is about to judge the whole world in the valley of judgment, here called Jehosaphat. "Multitudes, multitudes in the valley of decision, for the day of the Lord is near in the valley of decision. The sun and moon are darkened, and the stars withdraw their shining. And the Lord shall roar (as the god in lion form—Rit., 54, 1) from Zion, and utter his voice from Jerusalem; and the heavens shall shake; but the Lord will be a refuge unto his people, and a stronghold to the children of Israel. So shall ye know that I am the Lord your God dwelling in Zion my holy mountain. And it shall come to pass in that day that the mountain shall drop down sweet wine, and the hills shall flow with milk, and all the brooks of Judah shall run with waters, and a fountain shall come forth out of the house of the Lord and water the valley of the acacias." Every feature of this imagery is and ever had been Egyptian. The valley of decision is the Egyptian valley of judgment in which the great hall of mati, the house of the Lord in the solar mythos, was the judgment-seat. The lord who sat in judgment was Atum, in his lion form as lord of terrors. The lord enthroned upon his holy mountain was Atum-Ra upon the mountain of Amenta which the manes climbed for their rebirth in heaven. The mountain that souls are commanded to flee to for safety in the time of trouble and threatened destruction—which is repeated in the New Testament—is the mountain of the manes, who fled to its summit in the likeness of birds. This is expressed in Psalm xi. "In the Lord put I my trust. How say ye to my soul—flee as a bird (or birds) to your mountain. For lo, the wicked bend the bow; they make ready their arrow upon the string, that they may shoot in darkness at the upright of heart. The Lord is in his holy temple, the Lord, his throne is in heaven," on the summit of the solar mount to which the hawk-headed manes fled and were out of the reach of the rebels, the Sebau, the wicked, the Sut-Typhonians who pursued and shot at them in the darkness, and who were rained upon with fire and brimstone and the burning blast, or overwhelmed with the inundation in the Red Sea or lake of Putrata in Amenta. According to the ancient Osirian mythos, there was a cleft in the hill-side at Abydos, through which the manes passed as human-headed birds in the shape of hawks or herons. This was a prototypal representation of the souls fleeing for refuge to the mountain, that was afterwards repeated in Semitic legends, Hebrew and Arabic.

The typical valley, then, goes with the mythical mountain or mountains in the Hebrew writings. The valley of Amenta is the dwelling-place of the manes, which are represented as the rephaim who answer to the Egyptian repait. The repait, or pait, are the dead below the earth who are in the custody of Seb. The rephaim are the dead in the Hebrew Sheol. In the day of vengeance, says Isaiah, "it shall be as when the corn is reaped and the ears are gleaned in the valley of Rephaim." In the valley of Amenta was the field of divine harvest and the vintage of vengeance. In tracing the Israelites on their journey out of Lower Egypt we shall meet with the rephaim, who are the giants and at the same time shades of enormous stature. Meanwhile, whatsoever battles were fought or vast events occurred in the valley of the rephaim, they took place in the earth of the dead, and not upon the upper earth. The giant king of Bashan was one of the rephaim; Goliath, the colossus, was another of the rephaim; and these giants dwelt in the valley of the rephaim. Consequently, the conquerors of the rephaim, whether called Moses or Abraham, Joshua or David, who warred with the giants as shades of the dead in the valley of the rephaim, could no more be historical characters than were the rephaim themselves.

On entering the dark valley of Amenta the Egyptian manes most assiduously seeks for the place of refuge and safety provided by the great god, and for the entrance to the ark or tabernacle of Osiris-Ra. This is a secret covert in the midst of Akar. Osiris is denominated "lord of the shrine which standeth at the centre of the earth" (Rit., ch. 64). It is said by the speaker in the Litany of Ra, "Here is the Osiris; carry him into the hidden sanctuary of Osiris, lord of eternity, who is under the care of the two divine sisters that give protection in the tomb! Carry him into the hidden dwelling where Osiris resides, and which is in Amenta, the mysterious sanctuary of the god at rest. Bear him, open your arms to him, stretch out your hands to him, take off your veils before him, for he is the great essence whom the dead spirits do not know," but to whom they are indebted for the resurrection to new life. In the Psalms the tabernacle or sanctuary in Sheol takes the place of the ark or secret shrine of Osiris in Amenta. "Lord, who shall sojourn in thy Tabernacle?" (Ps. xv. 1). "In the court of his tabernacle shall he hide me" (Ps.

xxvii. 5). "In Salem is his tabernacle, and his dwelling-place in Zion" (Ps. lxxvi. 2). The resurrection of the manes took place in Sheol or Amenta. And it is as the risen manes in Sheol that the speaker seeks to dwell in the sanctuary of the Lord and to contemplate his temple. Hence he says, "In the covert of his tabernacle (or dwelling) shall he hide me. He shall lift me upon a rock. I will offer in his tabernacle sacrifices of joy" (Ps. xxvii). Such sacrifices or offerings are made to Osiris in his shrine of earth or tabernacle in Amenta, as shown by the vignettes to the Ritual. This was the "stronghold of salvation to his anointed" in the earth of eternity. This we take to be the tabernacle, sanctuary, or house of the lord in Sheol, of which it is said, "Who shall sojourn in the tabernacle?" "In the day of trouble he shall keep me secretly in his pavilion. In the covert of his tabernacle shall he hide me" (Ps. xxvii. 5, 6), "in the place where the divine glory dwelleth" (Ps. xxvi. 6).

The mummy-Osiris in Amenta is the figure of a sleeping deity. This, as the mummy-Ptah or Putah, we hold to have been the prototype of the sleeping Buddha. The mummy-image of divinity was continued in Osiris-Sekeri. He is the inert in matter, the sleeping or resting divinity, the breathless one; Urt-Hat, the god of the non-beating heart, the silent Sekari. Such also is the divine sleeper who is piteously appealed to by the human sufferer in Sheol, and who is identical with Osiris sleeping in Amenta. The speaker in the Psalms cries "unto the Lord with his voice," "Arise, O Lord! save me, O my God!" "Arise, O God, judge the earth. O God, keep not thou silence. Hold not thy peace, and be not still, O God" (Ps. lxxxii. 8, lxxxiii. 1). The waking preceded the great judgment. "Arise, O Lord, in thine anger; lift up thyself against the rage of mine adversaries, and awake for me. Thou hast commanded judgment" (Ps. vii. 6). "O Lord, when thou awakest thou shalt despise their image." "Awake; why sleepest thou, O Lord? Rise up for our help" (Ps. xliv. 23, 26). "Then the Lord awaked as one out of a sleep, and he smote his adversaries backward" (Ps. lxxviii. 65). This is the awaking of the god as Amsu, whip in hand, when he arises and asserts his sovereignty over all the opposing powers. The speaker is in the position of *the* Osiris, as the mummy sleeping in Amenta when he pleads with the protecting power, "Keep me as the apple of the eye. Hide me under the shadow of thy wings from the wicked that spoil me, my deadly enemies that compass me about." "As for me, I shall behold thy face in righteousness; I shall be satisfied with thy likeness when I awake" (Ps. xvii. 8-15). In these passages Osiris the mummy-god as sleeper in Amenta and the Osiris as a manes are both represented, and are both distinguishable each from the other. The speaker in Psalm xvii. is in Sheol waiting to awake in the living likeness of this redeemer from death, and he is surrounded by "the wicked," who are the "deadly enemies" that compass him about. He cries, "Deliver my soul from the wicked which is thy sword"—as power of punishment (xvii. 13). It is the wicked who come upon the sufferer "to eat up his flesh," not as cannibals on earth, but as evil spirit-powers of prey (Ps. xxvii. 2). The opponents of the sun and the manes appear in the Psalms as the adversary and the adversaries. The individual adversary is discriminated from the adversaries. Also the individual adversary is reproduced in the two characters of the Apap-dragon and of Sut or Satan, once the familiar friend or twin brother of the good Osiris, and afterwards his betrayer and inveterate personal enemy. Now, the adversaries of Osiris, or of souls in Amenta, include the Sebau, and these are the "wicked" by name, for the word in Egyptian signifies the profane, impious, blasphemous, culpable, or wicked. They rise up from Amenta as the powers of darkness in revolt, but are for ever driven back into their native night by Horus or Ra, Taht or Shu. These are the wicked of whom it is said in the Psalm, "They shall return or be driven back to Sheol" (Ps. IX. 17).

The comparative process shows that, like Taht, the Psalmist opens in Amenta, the place of the wicked who have no power to "stand in the judgment." The "wicked" in Amenta are the adversaries of the sun and the soul of man. These are the rebels who for ever rise in impotent revolt against the Lord and his anointed, Osiris-Ra and Horus in the Ritual, Ihuh the father-god and David the beloved in the Psalms. The "wicked" rage against the Lord and his anointed, saying, "Let us break their bands asunder and cast away their cords from us" (Ps. ii. 3). These are the "cords of death," the "cords of the wicked" (Ps. cxxix. 4), the cords with which the manes are fettered in the land of bondage and the depths of Sheol. The Lord that sitteth in the heavens has these children of failure in derision. He has set his son as king upon the holy hill of Zion, who is to break them with a rod of iron and dash them in pieces like a potter's vessel. These are they of whom it is said to the Lord, "Thou hast broken the teeth of the wicked." That is in defence of the sufferer in Sheol, who exclaims, "I cry unto the Lord with my voice, and he answereth me out of his holy hill. I laid me down in death and slept; I awaked, for the Lord sustaineth me" (Ps. iii. 4, 5). Osiris the typical sufferer in Amenta was imaged as the mummy bound up in the bandages of burial. As Osiris the mummy he was the Karest or prototypal Corpus Christi. As Osiris-Sekeri he was the coffined one. As Osiris-sahu he rose again in a spiritual body. As Osiris-tat he was a figure of eternal stability. For reasons now to be adduced, Osiris, or the Osiris, represents that typical sufferer whose cries and ejaculations are to be heard ascending from Amenta in the Egyptian Ritual and from Sheol in the Hebrew Psalms.

David pleading in the cave is equivalent to Osiris crying in the caverns of Sut in Amenta. He says, "I cry with my voice unto the Lord. With my voice unto the Lord do I make my supplications. I said, Thou art my refuge, my portion in the land of the living" (he being in Sheol, the land of the dead). "I am brought very low. Deliver me from my persecutors. Bring my soul out of prison" (Ps. cxlii.). The prison here is identical with the deep, the pit, the miry clay of Sheol, elsewhere specified. The sufferer in Amenta is Osiris or Horus in the Egyptian eschatology. He is also *the* Osiris as the suffering manes. Both have to be taken into account in tracing the sufferer in Sheol. He enters Amenta as a prison-house. He prays that it may be opened for him to come forth, so that he may be finally established with those who have secured a place among the stars that never set, and who are called the masters of eternity. He cries, "O Ra, open the earth! Traverse Amenta and sky! Dissipate our darkness! O Ra, come to us!" (Book of Hades, 4th div., tablets 2, 7, and 8). Amenta or Sheol was the prison-house of the soul in death, and the soul of the deceased is portrayed as a prisoner in the bandages of the mummy, like Osiris in the Kâsu. The Osiris says to the warders of the prisons, "May I not sit within your dungeons, may I not fall into your pits" (Rit., ch. 17). Horus, the deliverer of the "spirits in prison," comes to set the prisoners free from their sepulchres, to dissipate the darkness and open all the pathways to the land of light. In the chapter by which the prison-house of Amenta is opened to the soul and to the shade of the person, that he may come forth by day and have the mastery over his feet, the speaker prays that the eye of Horus may deliver his soul. He cries to the keepers, "Imprison not my soul, keep not in custody my shade. Let the path be open to my soul. Let it not be made captive by those who imprison the shades of the dead" (Rit., ch. 92). Horus is the Kamite prototype of the chosen one, called the servant by Isaiah, who came "for a light of the Gentiles, to open blind eyes, to bring out prisoners from the dungeon and them that sit in darkness out of the prison-house" (Is. xlii. 7). It is not pretended that mortal Horus was born on earth of a mother who was a human virgin in the house of bread at Annu, or that he lived as Unbu the branch at Nazareth or its Kamite equivalent. Such localities in the Ritual are in Amenta, and the transactions take place there, not on this earth. There was the prison-house of death, and from thence the resurrection to a future life by transformation of the human soul into an immortal spirit, as it was represented in the greater and most solemn mysteries.

When the mortal entered Amenta, it was in the likeness of Osiris, who had been bodily dismembered in his death, and who had to be reconstituted to rise again as the spirit that never died. The mortal on earth was made up of seven constituent parts. The Osiris in Amenta had seven souls, which were collected, put together, and unified to become the ever-living one. The deceased in the image of the ba-soul asks that he may be given his new heart to rest in him (Rit., ch. 26). He becomes a sahu, or glorified body (ch. 47). He pleads that the way may be made for his soul, his khu (glory), his shade, and his ka (chs. 91 and 92). These have to be united in the likeness of the typical divine soul which was personalized as Horus the son of Ra, in whose image the spirits of the just made perfect finally became the children of God. When the deceased enumerates his souls, he is a manes in Amenta, and it follows that when the speaker in the Psalms does the same, he is in Sheol, the Hebrew Amenta, not on earth, and therefore is neither a King David nor any other mortal. This identifies the doctrine as Egyptian.

As we have seen, man, formed in the image of God, had seven souls. Seven souls were assigned to Atum-Ra, and the human being who was made in his likeness had seven component parts. These were described as the ka, the I or ego; the ba, a human-headed soul; the hati, or breathing heart; the sahu, or spiritual body; the khu, or glory; the khabit, or shade; and finally, the perfect spirit. At least six of these can be identified in a passage of the sixteenth Psalm. "Because he (the Lord) is at my right hand, I shall not be moved. Therefore my *heart* is glad and my *glory* rejoiceth; my *flesh* (the mummy-form) also shall dwell in safety. For thou wilt not leave my *soul* in Sheol; neither wilt thou suffer thine *holy one* to see corruption. Thou wilt show me the path of life." In this passage we can perceive a reference to the hati or breathing heart, the khu or glory, the sahu or mummy-form, the ba-soul, the Horus-spirit, and the ka. If the khabit or shade had been mentioned, there would have been seven altogether, which constituted the totality of a future personality. The speaker in Psalm vii. had said, "Let the enemy pursue my soul" (or human-headed ba); "let him tread my life (ankhu) down to the earth, and lay my glory (khu) in the dust," but for all this he will be avenged upon his adversaries in the judgment. The khu is the particular soul of the seven that was known as the luminous one, or the glory—the soul that was brought up from Sheol or Amenta when it had attained the glory or become one of the glorified. At this stage the speaker in the Ritual says, "Here am I; I come, and am glorified and filled with soul and power" (ch. 94). He has attained the glory of the khu. In the book of Psalms the speaker, who has passed through Sheol, says, "Thou hast brought up my soul from Sheol." "Thou hast girded me with gladness, to the end that *my glory* may sing praise to thee" (Ps. xxx. 3, 11, 12). "Awake up, *my glory*" (Ps. lvii. 8). "I will sing praises with *my glory*" (Ps., cvii. 1). The language is akin to that of the manes in the Ritual, who says he may be buried in the deep, deep grave and be bowed down to the region of annihilation, yet he shall rise again and be glorified (ch. 30, A), or he will attain the glory of the venerable khu.

Sheol is a land of darkness and the shadow of death. So is Amenta, until lighted up with the presence of the sun by night in its nether firmament. Sheol is the place of the rephaim or shadows of the past. The rephaim are to be found in Amenta as giants, huge shades of enormous stature; types of terror, made more formidable by their exaggerated size. Sheol is the place of the shades, the under-world to which the souls of the departed went, and from which the dead were summoned by the consulters of *oboth* or familiar spirits. It includes purgatory and hell, the Ethiopic Siol and Assyrian Saul. There were deeper abysses in the abyss, and chambers of death in the house of death. "Tophet" is another Hebrew name for Sheol. "A Tophet is prepared of old . . . . deep and wide" (Is. xxx. 33), which may be traced to the Egyptian Tepht, a name of the abyss, the cavern of Apap or hole of the serpent. It was from Amenta, the hidden earth, that the ghosts of the dead were summoned by the magi, or rekhi-khet, not as evil demons, but as pure, wise spirits. It is from this nether earth of Amenta that the soul of Samuel is supposed to have ascended when invoked by the witch, pythoness, or Ἐγγαστρίμυθος of Endor. "And the woman said unto Saul, I see a god (or Elohim) coming up out of the earth," but which earth of the two is not stated in the Hebrew (I Samuel xxviii. 13). In several of the Psalms the singer utters the cries of a soul that suffers purgatorial pains in Sheol. As we have seen, the Egyptian purgatory is a domain in Amenta called the meska = meshek. It was a place of spiritual rebirth by purgation—a meaning that survives in the name of purgatory. This is described in the Ritual (ch. 17) as "the place of scourging and purifying." "Let not the Osiris advance into the valley of darkness." "Let not the Osiris enter into the dungeon of the captives." "Let him not fall among those who would drag him behind the slaughtering block of the executioner" are cries of the Manes.

Amenta is the land of monsters, chief of which in the mythos is the Apap-dragon, which has its lair in the lake of outer darkness. In Amenta the crocodiles have to be repelled (ch. 31). Also the serpent Seksek (ch. 35); Apshai, the devourer of the dead (ch. 36); the serpent Rekrek (ch. 39); the serpent Haiu (ch. 40); the serpent Abur (ch. 42); the crocodile-dragon in the land of bondage (ch. 72); the raging bull (ch. 78); the devouring monsters (ch. 80); the howling dogs (ch. 102); the piercing serpent (ch. 108); the black boar of Sut (ch. 112). Baba, the eternal devourer of the condemned, is the monster most eminent in the eschatology. "Deliver me from the crocodile (or devouring monster) of this land of bondage" (Rit., ch. 72). "Grant that I may come forth and have the mastery of my two feet. Let me advance to the goal of heaven." "Deliver me from Baba, who feeds upon the livers of princes, on the day of the great reckoning." These are also the cries of the manes.

The appeals for divine protection during the passage of Amenta and for deliverance from the pangs of purgatory and the terrors of the hells are echoed in the land of Sheol. "Many bulls have compassed me. Strong bulls of Bashan have beset me round. They gape upon me with their mouth" (Ps. xxii. 12, 21). "Thou hast sore broken us in the place of jackals, and covered us with the shadow of death" (Ps. xliv. 19). "My soul is among lions. I lie among them that are set on fire" (lvii. 4). "Deliver not the soul of thy turtle unto the wild beast" (lxxiv. 19). There is a description in the Ritual of the torn and mutilated Osiris encompassed by the howling dogs of Amenta. "Salutation to thee, Ur-ar-set, in that voyage of heaven and the disaster in Tennu, when those dogs were gathered together, not without giving voice." The dog is a prominent type of the devourer in Sheol. The sufferer exclaims, "Deliver my soul from the sword; my only one (or my soul) from the power of the dog" (Ps. xxii. 20). The dog in Amenta represents the devourer "who lives upon the damned. His face is that of a hound and his skin is that of a man. Eternal devourer is his name" (Rit., ch. 17). He seizes upon souls in the dark, and is therefore said to be invisible, as a type of very great terror. Osiris bound as a mummy in Amenta prays to be released by the god who had tied the cords about him in the earth. That is, by Seb, the god of earth, who was custodian of the mummies in the earth, whose hands and feet were bound up typically in Amenta in the likeness of the earthly mummy. The sufferer in Sheol cries, "My God! Why hast thou forsaken me? All they that see me laugh me to scorn. They shoot out the lip, they wag the head, saying, He trusted on the Lord that he would deliver him." "Thou hast brought me into the dust of death. For dogs have encompassed me. The assembly of evil-doers have enclosed me. They bound my hands and my feet. They look and stare upon me. They part my garments among them, and upon my vesture do they cast lots." "Yea, mine own familiar friend in whom I trusted, which did eat of my bread, hath lifted his heel against me." "I looked for some to take pity, but there was none; and for comforters, but I found none." They gave me also "gall for my meat; and in my thirst they gave me vinegar to drink." These are the pitiful cries and ejaculations of the suffering Osiris or Horus, the saviour in the Egyptian wisdom, and these scenes, circumstances, and sayings have been reproduced as the very foundations of the "history" in the Gospels. They were confessedly found among "the parables and dark sayings of old," which, as the scribe admits, "we have heard and known and our fathers have told us." That is, they were found in the writings of the divine scribe and psalmist Taht, which were preserved in the psalms of the Hebrew David. The matter of the mythology goes with the mythical characters, and this has been mistaken for prophecy that was to be fulfilled in some future human history.

There is a chapter in the Ritual on not letting the mummy decay—that is, the mummy as a type of the personality continued in a future life (ch. 154). In this the mummy-god Osiris is addressed as the father by the Osiris as the manes in Amenta. The speaker says, "Hail to thee, my father Osiris! Thy limbs are lasting, thou dost not know corruption." And as with the god so is it with the manes. In spite of death, he says, "I am, I am; I live, I live; I grow, I grow; and when I awake I shall awake, I shall awake in peace. I shall not see corruption. I shall not be destroyed in my bandages." "My limbs are lasting for ever. I do not rot. I do not putrefy. I do not turn to worms. My flesh is firm; it shall not be destroyed; it shall not perish in the earth for ever." (Ch. 154, Naville.) In the parallel passages of the Psalms the speaker says, "My heart is glad and my glory rejoiceth; my flesh shall dwell in safety (or confidently). For thou wilt not leave my soul to Sheol; neither wilt thou suffer thine holy one to see corruption. Thou wilt show me the path of life." "As for me, I shall behold thy face in righteousness. I shall be satisfied with thy likeness when I awake." (Ps. xvi and xvii.) The "flesh" in the Psalm takes the place of the mummy in the Ritual. The speaker in the Psalms "cries out" continually, and calls on the ka or image of the eternal, in the likeness of which he expects to rise again and live as Horus or as Jesus the beloved son.

Another type of the beloved son in Sheol is the turtle-dove. The speaker cries to the god of his salvation, "Oh, deliver not the soul of thy turtle-dove unto the wild beast. The dark places of the earth are full of the habitations of violence" (Ps. lxxiv. 19, 20). The soul of the turtle-dove is the dove that was a symbol of the soul. When the transformation from the mummy was made in Amenta the deceased became bird-headed as a soul, and thus assumed the likeness of Ra the holy spirit. This bird of soul in the later eschatology was the hawk, the sign of a soul that was considered to be male, the soul of god the father. The dove of Hathor was an earlier type of a soul derived from the mother. This is the turtle-dove of the Psalmist. In one of the Egyptian drawings the soul is portrayed in the process of issuing from the mummy in the shape of a dove, instead of the usual hawk.

Both are emblems of the risen soul, but the dove in monumental times was almost superseded by the hawk of Ra and Horus.

In the Ritual snares are set and a net is prepared to catch and destroy the manes. The deceased prays that he may not be taken like a foolish fish in the net. In the Psalms the speaker, who is David in the cave, exclaims, "They have prepared a net for my steps" (Ps. lvii). "Pluck me out of the net that they have privily laid for me" (Ps. xxxi. 4). These are the liers in wait (Ps. v. 8) who privily lurk to catch the passing souls. In vignettes to the Ritual the souls of the ignorant are shown in the guise of fishes being caught in the net by Cynocephali, who are allowed to capture them because of their ignorance.

The waters of the deep were in Amenta. The deep is identical with the pit, the pit with Sheol, and Sheol with Amenta. "Save me, O God; for the waters are come in unto my soul. I sink in deep mire, where there is no standing. I am come into deep waters where the floods overflow me." "Deliver me out of the mire, and let me not sink. Let me be delivered from them that hate me. Let not the water-flood overwhelm me, neither let the deep swallow me up." In the Psalms the Hebrew deity is he who sitteth on the waters. "The Lord sitteth on the flood; yea, the Lord sitteth as king for ever." "He hath founded the earth upon the waters and established it upon the floods" (Ps. xxiv. 2). "Even the Lord upon many waters." This is the picture of Osiris in Amenta sitting on his throne of the waters as lord of all the earth. The earth itself is imaged by the lotus rising from the water as the mount arose from out the Nun, and the water springs up and flows from underneath the seat which is the throne of the god. The representation in the great hall of judgment is precisely the same as that described in the book of Revelation: "And he showed me a river of water of life, bright as crystal, proceeding out of the throne of God" (Rev. xxii. 1). The action of the god throughout nature is imaged as a welling and a flowing forth of water from its secret source. Ihuh the Lord is described by Jeremiah as "the fountain of living waters" (ch. xvii. 13). When it is said that the Lord sitteth on the flood (Ps. xxix. 10, 11), or that "Ouranos (Οὐρανὸς) is the throne of God" (Matt. v. 34, 35), the imagery is Egyptian, with certain features defaced. The Ouranos is heaven as the celestial water, upon which the lord has been left sitting without the solar boat. The lord as Ihuh is one with Atum-Huhi or Ra, who is described as making his voyage nightly on the Urnas = Ouranos, leaving the trail of otherworld glory in the river of the Milky Way. It is the same solar deity that rode through the deserts of the under-world, but again the *modus operandi* is omitted. In this way the Egyptian imagery has been divorced from the natural phenomena which it was intended to portray. In the Ritual the waters are described as bursting forth in an overwhelming deluge. "Knowing the deep waters is my name," exclaims the sinking manes (ch. 64). "Do thou save me!" he cries to the Lord. Then he exults in not being one of those who drown. "Blessed are they that see the bourne. Beautiful is the god of the motionless heart (Asar), who causeth the stay of the overflowing waters. Behold! there cometh forth the lord of life, Osiris my support, who abideth day by day. I embrace the sycamore, I am united to the sycamore." The tree is a type of stability and safety in Amenta. In Sheol the refuge of the sinking soul is depicted amidst the waste of waters as the everlasting rock, but both have one and the same significance as the means of safety from the flood.

The mummy sleeping in Amenta as the god or as the manes waits the resurrection there. Horus wakes the manes in their coffins for the coming forth, when they are freed from the cerements, which he rends asunder. This resurrection is attained in Sheol when the speaker says, "I will extol thee, O Lord, for thou hast raised me up. Thou hast loosed my sackcloth and girded me with gladness, to the end that my glory (the khu) may sing praise to thee and not be silent" (Ps. xxx.). In the Kamite resurrection there was a change from the earthly body. The bandages of burial were cast aside and the sahu mummy was invested in the robe of immortality. In fact, to be invested thus was to become a spiritual being. The "glory," as one of the Egyptian seven souls called the khu, was now attained by the Osiris in the course of his being reconstituted. Salvation for the Egyptian was being saved from the fate of the irredeemably wicked, the doom of the second death, which was annihilation. Salvation was continuity of life hereafter, and this was only attainable by the righteous—those who did the right and acted justly, those who effected the truth of the word in their own life and pursued it through Amenta. They attained eternal life by personal, not by imputed, righteousness. Hence the deceased pleads his righteousness before the lord of righteousness in the great hall of righteousness. He pleads not what he believes, but what he has done. "I have done that which maat (the law) prescribeth, and that which pleases the gods. I have propitiated the god with that which he loveth. I have given bread to the hungry, water to the thirsty, clothes to the naked, a boat to the shipwrecked." "I am one of those to whom it is said, Come, come in peace, by those who look upon him"—that is, the divine company of the gods. He passes in peace, and is invested with the robe of the righteous on account of his own righteousness. This is the doctrine of the Ritual, and it is likewise the doctrine of the Psalms. "Answer me when I call, O God of my righteousness" (Ps. iv. 1). "Judge me, O Lord, according to my righteousness and to mine integrity" (Ps. vii. 8). "As for me, I shall behold thy face in righteousness" (Ps. xvii. 15). "The Lord rewardeth me according to my righteousness" (Ps. xviii. 20). This is not Christian doctrine, but it is Jewish, because it was Egyptian. Personal righteousness is pleaded in the Psalms, the same as in the Ritual. "Judge me, O Lord, according to my righteousness" (Ps. vii. 8). "The Lord rewarded me according to my righteousness" (Ps. xviii. 24). In the Kamite judgment hall the speaker says, "I have done the righteousness of a lord of righteousness. There is not a limb in me which is void of righteousness" (ch. 125). This, as we interpret the Hebrew version, is the position of the speaker in Sheol who is awaiting judgment amidst the trials and the terrors that beset the manes in the caverns of Sut, through which he has to grope his way. On arriving at the judgment hall the Osiris says, "Hail to thee, mighty god, lord of righteousness. I am come to thee, O my Lord; I have brought myself that I may look upon thy glory." He pleads in presence of those whose natural prey is the souls of the wicked, "devouring those who harbour mischief and swallowing their blood, upon the day of searching examination in presence of the good Osiris. Behold me; I am come to you void of wrong, without fraud; let me not be declared guilty; let not the issue be against me. I subsist upon righteousness. I sate myself with uprightness of heart. I have propitiated the god with that which he loveth. I am come, and am awaiting that inquisition be made of righteousness" (ch. 125). In the Psalms "God is the judge" (Ps. vii. 11). "Righteousness and judgment are the foundations of his throne" (Ps. xcvii. 2, xcviii. 2). "Thou sattest in thy throne judging righteously" (Ps., ix, 4). "The Lord sitteth as king for ever. He hath prepared his throne for judgment, and he shall judge the world in righteousness" (Ps. ix. 7, 8).

In one form of the mythos Sut and Osiris, in the other Sut and Horus, are born twin brothers. Sut becomes the adversary of Osiris, the Good Being. This conflict of the two opponent powers reappears in the Psalms as well as in the book of Job. "Yea, mine own familiar friend, in whom I trusted, which did eat my bread, hath lifted up his heel against me (Ps. xli. 9-11). But thou, O Lord, have mercy upon me, and raise me up, that I may requite them. By this I know that thou delightest in me, because mine enemy doth not triumph over me." "It was thou, a man mine equal, my companion and my familiar friend. We took sweet counsel together, we walked in the house of God with the throng." "He hath put forth his hands against such as were at peace with him; he hath profaned his covenant. His mouth was smooth as butter, but his heart was war; his words were softer than oil, yet were they drawn swords" (Ps. lv. 20, 21). Nothing could more aptly reproduce the figure of fact as a figure of speech than the quotation from the Psalmist to the effect that he, the intimate friend and very brother, had "lifted his heel against" the Christ, the Lord's anointed. In the double figure of Horus and Sut they are twinned together back to back and therefore heel to heel. David and the adversary are equivalent to Osiris and Sut, or to Horus and Sut in another phase of the mythos, the twin brothers being characters in both.

When Sut and the Sebau had compassed the death of Osiris, a day of dissolution followed the great disaster. There was an overthrowal of the pillars—the tat-pillar at the centre of all, and the four supports at the four corners. Then Horus came as the avenger of his father and as the judge of the wicked, who after trial were annihilated on the highways of the damned. The tat was re-erected, and the four pillars (posts or flagstaffs) were set up once more "on the night of setting up the pillars of Horus and of establishing him as heir of his father's property." This was at the time when Horus, as Har-Tema, came to judge the adversaries of his father Osiris (Rit., ch. 18). A fragment from this would seem to have strayed into the 75th Psalm, like many other wandering words that have lost their senses. "When I shall find the set time, I will judge uprightly. The earth and all the inhabitants thereof are dissolved. I have set up the pillars of it"—which looks as if the Osiris deceased in Sheol were speaking in the character of Horus who re-erected the pillars. In the Ritual the dissolution and re-establishing of the earth by setting up the pillars, immediately follows the battle with the Sebau, the Apap, and Sut; and in the preceding psalm (lxxiv.) the war with the dragon is described. "Thou breakest the heads of the dragons in the waters." "Thou breakest the heads of leviathan in pieces; thou gavest him to be meat to the people inhabiting the wilderness." The dragons in the psalm are the evil crocodiles in the Ritual.

A profound study of the Ritual reveals the fact that the wisdom of Egypt was the source and fountain-head of the books of wisdom assigned to Moses and David, to Solomon and Jesus; and also proves the personages or characters to have been Egyptian. It is chiefly the wisdom of Egypt that gives a value to the Hebrew writings, as will be indubitably demonstrated. In Psalm xxiv. there is a glorification of the coming king of glory:

> 7. Lift up your heads, O ye gates;
> And be ye lift up, ye everlasting doors;
> And the King of Glory shall come in.
> 8. Who is the King of Glory?
> The Lord strong and mighty,
> The Lord mighty in battle.
> 9. Lift up your heads, O ye gates;
> And the King of Glory shall come in.
> 10. Who is the King of Glory?
> The Lord of Hosts,
> He is the King of Glory.

This king of glory was the sun-god in the astronomical mythology. The Hebrew repeats the king of glory, the gates, and the doors, but omits the astronomical foundation; and in this way the wisdom of Taht was deprived of its scientific value. But who is this king of glory? and what are the gates that are called upon to open and let him in? As the "Lord of hosts" we know him for Iao-Sabaoth, lord of the seven great spirits; therefore he is the solar god; but we must turn to the Ritual to understand the nature of the gates. There are thirty-six altogether, corresponding to the thirty-six decans of the zodiac. At the same time the gates are thirty-six doors in the great house of Osiris. Chapter 145 is devoted to the passage of the sun-god through twenty-one of these celestial gates. The sun-god is the king of glory in the Ritual. In "the book that was made on the birthday of Osiris," in which "glory is given to the inviolate one," Taht, the Kamite psalmist, sings, "Opened be the gates of heaven! Opened be the gates of earth! Opened be the gates of the east! Opened be the gates of the west! Opened be the gates of the southern and of the northern sanctuaries! Opened be the gates and thrown wide open be the portals as Ra ariseth from the mount of glory, the swift of speed and beautiful in his rising, and almighty through what he hath done." "Glory to thee, O Ra, lord of the mount of glory." (Rit., ch. 129.) The gates and doors are those that open as the solar god comes forth at dawn. He is the king of glory; these are the gates of glory that were opened on the mount of glory "at the beautiful coming forth of his powers." "It is the gate and the two doors and openings through which Father Atum issueth on the eastern horizon (or mount) of heaven." (Rit., ch. 17.) That is Atum-Huhi = Ihuh. The mythology is absolutely necessary all through for us to understand the eschatology, whether in its Egyptian guise or Hebrew disguise.

When the Psalmist says, "The Lord is my shepherd," it has become a mere phrase. The Egyptians presented the portrait. Horus was the lord as leader of the flock and guardian of the fold, because he represented the first who rose again from the dead, though not at any particular historic date. Amsu-Horus, with his crook in hand, shepherded the flocks of Ra beyond the grave. After the resurrection in Amenta he says to his first four followers, who are called his children, "Now let my fold be fitted for me as one victorious against all those adversaries who would not that the right should be done to me, the only one" (Rit., ch. 97). He is the "master of the champaign" and "of the inundation," and therefore of the green pastures and the still waters of life. Horus, the son of god, came into the world as shepherd of his father's sheep, to lead them through the darkness of Amenta to the green pastures and still waters of the final paradise upon Mount Hetep in the heaven of eternity. It was not supposed that he came to secure the Jew his cent. per cent., or the Christian capitalist the power to rob the workers of the fruits of their labour, or the Boers and Belgians to eat up the aborigines and lie down as loafers in the still pastures of their stolen lands.

Psalm xxiii. contains a description of the green fields of pasture and the still waters that run through that paradise of plenty, peace, and rest:

> The Lord is my shepherd; I shall not want.
> He maketh me to lie down in green pastures:
> He leadeth me beside the still waters.
> He restoreth my soul:
> He leadeth me in the paths of righteousness for his name's sake.
> Yea, though I walk through the valley of the shadow of death (Amenta or Sheol),
> I will fear no evil: for thou art with me;
> Thy rod and thy staff, they comfort me.
> Thou preparest a table before me in the presence of mine enemies:
> Thou anointest my head with oil; my cup runneth over.
> Surely goodness and mercy shall follow me all the days of my life:
> And I will dwell in the house of the Lord for ever.

The staff of Amsu was a symbol of Osiris who rose again as Horus. It was buried with the deceased, and is found in the oldest coffins together with other weapons that were interred with the dead as types of a protecting power. "The Osiris receiveth the Amsu staff wherewith he goeth round the heaven" (Rit., ch. 130). This elsewhere is called the palm of Amsu. It was the support of the Osiris in life and in death. This psalm is one of those that have been least denuded of the original object-pictures. The valley of the shadow of death is the Ar-en-Tet or valley of the dead in the Ritual, where those who suffer the second death are buried for ever (Rit., ch. 19) by the great annihilator Seb. Horus in one character is the good shepherd, but the lord, as leader in the green pastures, is the bull of the seven cows, who are the providers of plenty. He is called the lord of the pastures, or fields of the bull, the green meadows of Aarru. He also says, "I am the bull, the lord of the gods." This answers to "The Lord is my shepherd; I shall not want." "He maketh me to lie down in green pastures," says the Psalmist. The speaker in the Ritual says, "I take my rest in the divine domain." "I sail upon its stream, and I range within its garden of peace." The speaker sings for joy, it may be, in the Psalms of Taht. He exclaims, "I utter my praise to the gods who are in the garden of peace." The "still waters" are in Hebrew the "waters of rest"; these, in the Egyptian, are the waters of Hetep = the waters of rest and peace. The departed rests beside these waters in the green fields where Hetep, as the god of peace, is "putting together the oblations" for the spirits of the just made perfect. "Thou preparest a table before me," says the Psalmist. The table likewise was prepared upon Mount Hetep, and piled with heaps of imperishable food. Hence the Osiris says, "I rest at the table of my father Osiris" (Rit., ch. 70). Mount Hetep was itself the tableland of the oblations. The "house of the lord" is designated by the speaker in the Ritual "the mansion where food is produced for me," the mansion that was lifted up by Shu, the paradise of Am-Khemen. Two paths led up to it, called the "double path." These are the "paths of righteousness." The deceased in the Ritual is seen ascending the mount with the supporting rod or staff in his hand. Where the Psalmist says, "He restoreth my soul," the speaker in the Ritual says rejoicingly, "My soul is with me." This in Egyptian is the ka, that was ultimately attained in the garden of peace. The ka is the final form of the soul restored to the departed when they are perfected in the assembly or congregation on the mount. The speaker in Hetep says, "There is given to me the abundance which belongeth to the ka and to the glorified." It was in Amenta that the lord's anointed was begotten: one mode was by the transformation of Horus the mortal into Horus the beloved son. In the Hebrew Psalms the same transaction is repeated in the place of the "wicked" who rebel and rage against the Lord and his anointed. The son begotten by the father is born to become the ruler over them, and to effect the triumph of the father over all his adversaries on the day of judgment, the same as in the Ritual (ch. 1). The Lord himself that sitteth in the heavens "shall have them in derision," yea, he has also set the son as king upon the holy hill of Zion, the mountain of the Lord. Here it may be remarked that the change from Horus the human youth with the side-lock to Horus the divine avenger would lend itself to the euhemerists for the conversion of David the shepherd boy into the solar hero who made war upon the giant and slew the Philistines.

The Jews, we are told, believe in a twofold kind of immortality, the one being in a state immediately following death, the other in the resurrection from Sheol at the judgment-day. These two aspects of continuity after death are to be explained by the Egyptian eschatology. The Hebrew Sheol is the Egyptian secret earth of eternity, the divine nether-world. In death the manes passed into the Amenta as a body-soul that survived the body and became a ghost or shade with power to reappear as an apparition on the earth. After passing through purgatory and all the other places and modes of purification, and making the necessary transformations as an Osiris, or human Horus, the manes rose from Amenta to the paradise of spirits perfected in the likeness of Horus the divine. The immortality that was previously potential for the human Horus or manes was established in Tattu and assured by the resurrection of the glorified spirit from the Akar (Rit., 30, A). The manes in the Ritual says of himself, "After being buried on earth I am not dead in Amenta." He is there "reunited to the earth on the western side of heaven," to become a "pure spirit for eternity" (ch. 30, A). This is the original doctrine of a body, soul, and spirit—a body on earth, a manes soul in Sheol, and an immortal spirit in the resurrection on high. Horus was incarnated in the human body on earth. He died and rose again in Amenta as a sahu or soul in a rarer but corporeal form. This was a resurrection from the first death. Then he made his transformation into Horus the pure spirit, and ascended to his father in heaven, hawk-headed or dove-headed, from the mount of Amenta or the double earth. These things were visibly portrayed upon the walls and in the papyri of Egypt, not to be lost sight of there; but, away from Egypt, the pictures were no longer present, and the Jews lost their living memory of Amenta. They had only words, without the means of verification in the representative signs which had given a palpable reality to the most ancient mysteries in the chambers of Egyptian imagery; and gradually Sheol dwindled to the dimensions of the grave, as we find it continued in the Old Testament. In the mythology the messianic resurrection from Sheol was the annual re-arising of the Horus-sun at Easter. In the eschatology it was the resurrection of Horus divinized as son of Ra the holy spirit who ascended with his followers to the fields of peace in the upper paradise of the celestial Aarru. And just as the colours in Egyptian tombs remain at times as fresh as if the paint had never dried, so do the pictures and portraits survive in the mythology and eschatology, unfading in colour and imperishable in form, after they had grown dim and dead for the Hebrews and Greeks, to be *counterfeited as historic* for the Christians, who had no means of detecting the imposition by any reference to the prototypes, that are as living to-day as the hues in which the imagery was painted by Egyptian scribes, whose drawing was a means of bringing on and on the most ancient wisdom down from the days of gesture-language, when there was as yet no possible registry in words, to the time of the Egypto-gnostics.

There is plenty of proof that the same fundamental matter belonging to the wisdom of Egypt, in which Osarsiph of On was an adept, appears thrice over in the Hebrew writings. It is mythological in the books of Genesis, Exodus, and Joshua. It is eschatological in the Psalms. And in the later books it is converted into matter of prophecy. All three phases were Egyptian. With this difference: the sole possible fulfilment of prophecy was astronomical, not humanly historical. To illustrate two of these phases: the land of bondage in the book of Exodus is the Amenta of the solar drama, the lower Egypt of the double earth, the scene of the never-ceasing battles between the powers of light and darkness, the sun-god and the Sebau, Ra and the dragon, or Horus and Sut; Amenta in the mythology becomes Sheol in the Hebrew eschatology. The land of bondage, then, is the place of suffering souls that seek deliverance from the desert of darkness, the prison-house of death and hell. It is the sufferer in Sheol, the Osiris of the Ritual, who says, "Thou wilt not leave my soul in Sheol; neither wilt thou suffer thy beloved to see corruption. Thou wilt show me the path of life" (Ps. xvi. 10, 11). "That thy beloved may be delivered, save with thy right hand and answer us" (Ps. lx. 5). There is the same assimilation of the manes to the suffering Horus, or Osiris, as in the Ritual. There is also the same mixture of the mythical and eschatological. This is especially marked in the 18th Psalm, which purports to contain the words that were spoken by David on the day the Lord delivered him from all his enemies.

According to the Egyptian wisdom, whoever the speaker may be in the Hebrew Sheol, it is the suffering Osiris or the Osiris in Amenta; and the god appealed to by him in his trouble is the god who was Ra the father in heaven as Atum-Huhi in the Egyptian and Ihuh in the Jewish cult. Also it is the solar god alone that will account for the imagery. Not only are the ground-plan and total scheme Egyptian, the mythology and eschatology can be followed in innumerable details. It looks at times as if the scribes were directly citing the earlier scriptures, from which the mythos is quoted and converted into prophecies, chiefly concerning the coming judge and avenger, who in the Egyptian original is the avenger of Osiris-Un-Nefer, and his followers, the chosen people, or the glorified elect, who suffer in Amenta from the persecution of Sut and the Sebau, his co-workers in iniquity.

Let the 34th and the 35th chapters of Isaiah be compared with the Hymn to Osiris. (There are two versions of this hymn in the *Records of the Past*, first series, vol. iv., and 2nd series, vol. iv., that by Mallet being much the closer rendering.) "Seek ye out the book of the Lord and read," exclaims Isaiah in his description of the coming one. The day of vengeance for long-suffering had obviously been foretold in this book. And at the advent of the Lord who was to bring deliverance to his people, it is said, "The wilderness and the solitary place shall be glad, and the desert shall rejoice and blossom as the rose." "They shall see the glory of the Lord, the excellency of our God." "Behold, your God will come with vengeance: he will come and save you. Then the eyes of the blind shall be opened, and the ears of the deaf shall be unstopped." The dumb are to break forth into singing, and the lame to leap for joy. Waters are to well forth in the wilderness, streams in the desert, and the mirage on the sands is to turn them to a pool. All this belongs to the mythical representation of the advent in the earth of eternity which was celebrated in the mysteries as occurring once a year. And it is this coming of Messiah as Horus the prince of peace on earth and the avenger who makes Osiris triumphant over his adversaries in Amenta or Sheol that is described in the Hymn to Osiris. When he has gone forth in peace by the command of Seb (that is, as the human Horus born of Seb, god of earth), the divine company of the gods adore him, the inhabitants of the Tuat prostrate themselves to the ground, the loftiest bow the head, the ancestral spirits are in prayer. When they behold him, the august dead (in the nether-world) submit to him. The two lands (of the double earth) unite in one to give him the glory, marching before his majesty: glorious, noble (or highest) among the sahus, from whom proceeds all dignity, who establishes supreme authority; excellent chief of the divine company of the gods, with beautiful aspect, beloved of him who has contemplated him, extending his terror through all countries that may proclaim this name before all others. The great prince, eldest of his brothers, the chiefs of the divine companies, who establishes the truth in the double land, who seats the son (himself) upon the throne of his father, the favourite of his father Seb, the beloved of his mother Nut (heaven, one of whose names is Meri). Very valiant, he overthrows the impious; strong of arm, he immolates his adversary (Sut = Satan); breathing terror upon his enemies, conquering the distant frontiers of the wicked. Firm of heart, his feet are vigilant. Flesh (or heir) of Seb! Royalty of the double earth! (Horus of the royal countenance). Seb contemplates his benefits (the benefits of his advent to the earth); he has ordered him to govern all countries to assure their prosperity. . . . The *desert carries its tribute* to the son of Nut; Egypt is happy when it sees him appear upon his father's throne. The author of evil (Sut) pronounces magical words and displays his power in his turn, but the son of Isis makes his way to him and avenges his father, sanctifying and honouring his name. The paths are cleared, the roads are opened, evil flees away. He has caused the authority of his father to be recognized in the great dwelling of Seb—that is, of earth. In this abstract the advent of Horus, which was annual in Egypt, whence he was the king of one year, is hymned in various phases of his pre-Christian character. He comes by order of Seb, the foster-father on earth, as his favourite of the brothers, who were five in number when Horus is counted as one. He comes in peace, but also brings the sword as a terror to the workers of iniquity and as the immolator of his adversary Sut. He comes also as Horus of the inundation; and thus the desert is made to blossom, and to carry its tribute to the son of Nut, who has conquered Sut, the cause of drought and sterility, in his contest with the devil in the wilderness in which Horus vanquishes his adversary and avenges his father.

Again, the following might have been designated a song of Har-Tema, who is Horus the fulfiller at his second advent. "The spirit of the Lord is upon me, because the Lord hath anointed me to preach good tidings unto the poor. He hath sent me to bind up the broken-hearted, to proclaim liberty to the captives and the opening of the eyes to them that are blind; to proclaim the acceptable year of the Lord's good pleasure and the day of vengeance of our God" (Is. lxi. 1, 2). Horus in his second advent came hawk-headed in the likeness of Ra as the anointed and beloved son. The divine hawk was his sign that the spirit of the Lord was upon him. He brought good tidings for the poor and comfort for the oppressed. He is Horus the compassionate. One of his titles is "the Comforter." In one passage of the Ritual he says, "I have been produced to repulse the evil powers"—literally those who grovel on their bellies. "I come as the forerunner or messenger of the Lord, as councillor of Osiris." He goes forth from the state of the disk to bring light and liberty to the manes who are darkling in their prison cells. He solaces those that mourn, he wipes away the tears from those who weep, and opens the eyes of those who are breathless, bound, and blind.

At the same time he was the stern avenger of injustice. The judgment day and dread assize were annual, in accordance with the natural fact, and there was a time of terrible vengeance once a year. The "acceptable year of the Lord" was based upon this judgment and readjustment, the setting of the captives free and punishing the guilty once a year; and both the first and second advents of Horus were of annual occurrence in the year of "the Lord's good pleasure."

The fundamental doctrines and the imagery of the book of Job are also Egyptian. These include the Amenta or secret earth of eternity (the hidden place) (xl. 13), which is the land of darkness and the shadow of death (x. 21). The sufferer in Amenta, the redeemer from the dust of earth, the resurrection of the righteous and annihilation of the wicked (xix. 25-26, xviii. 5) The house of the prince (Hat-Saru) (xxi. 28). Stretching out the heavens (ix. 8). The day-spring on high (xxxviii. 12). The group of the glorious ones, the sons of God, including Sut or Satan, the adversary (i. 6). The Lord as a lion in his terrible majesty (x. 16). The serpent pierced by the hand of God (xxvi. 13). The nest and the phœnix (xxix. 18). The papyrus plant (viii. 11). The pyramid tombs (iii. 14). Leviathan, the crocodile-dragon (xli. 1), and the rephaim beneath the waters. These are one and all Egyptian.

That which is non-human as matter of the mythos becomes inhuman when retailed as history, and it is inhuman in the one phase because it was not human in the other. This criterion is infallible. For example, the persecution of Job by Satan the adversary repeats the treatment of the good Osiris by the evil Sut. This of itself suffices to show that the drama was non-human in its oldest form. The Osirian drama unfolded in the mysteries of Amenta likewise furnished matter for the book of Job. The land of darkness described as Sheol by Job is one with Amenta in its secret unillumined parts. It is the land of darkness and the shadow of death, a land of thick darkness, as darkness itself, a land of the shadow of death (Job x. 21, 22). This is the Ar-en-Tet of the Ritual (ch. 19), the valley of darkness and death, whose unmitigable gloom conceals the secrets that are absolutely unknowable, and where those who died the second death were buried for ever in their mummied immobility. This is the condition threatened in the book of Job (xlix. 19) for the wicked: "He shall go to the generation of his fathers; they shall never see the light." This region of impenetrable darkness becomes the whole of Sheol, or Sualu, in this version of Amenta. Sheol is especially described as the land of shade, which suggests a Kamite origin for the name. As Egyptian, the root-word "shu" signifies shade, shadow, to be destitute, dark, void. Thence, *the* void, the hollow, the land of shade, is the land of Shual or Sheol as a Semitic place-name. The book of Job has been described as the most profound and wonderful drama of humanity ever written, yet those who so described it could not have told us what it is actually about. Fundamentally Egyptian, it has been re-adapted without the wisdom of Egypt. All has been changed by making the sufferer Job a human personage on this earth; and when we know the true nature of mythical characters like those of Job or Samson, David or Jonah, or Jack the Giant Killer, it lessens the interest we might otherwise take in them as human heroes. We must resort to the original. The drama of Job and Satan contains a euhemerized version of the ancient conflict betwixt the prince of darkness, Sut, and Osiris or Horus, who suffers from the adversary in Amenta. The Hebrew Satan was the Egyptian Sut, who became the evil one of the later theology as an anthropomorphic rendering of Apap the serpent of evil. Sut was one of the seven sons of the old First Mother, the goddess of the Great Bear in the astronomical mythology. He was not one of "the sons of god," as there was no god extant when he was born. Sut was brought forth twin with Horus, and first born as the adversary of his brother Osiris. In a truer version of the mythos the conflict was in phenomena that were physical, not moral. There are no morals in mythology, when the characters are non-human, and when the mythical heroes and monsters have been represented as human characters we need to know the mythology once more. The Bible is full of such characters, and Job is one of them. In the Ritual Sut is the adversary of Osiris, or, still earlier, the opponent of Horus. He undoes what the Good Being does. He is a malicious destroyer; the author of disease. He is permitted to persecute Horus and Osiris to the death. In his character of the adversary, the power of darkness, he says, "I am Sut, who causeth the storms and tempests, and who goeth round the horizon of heaven, like one whose heart is veiled" (Rit., ch. 39). Which is equivalent to saying, "I am black-hearted." Sut is here the prototype of Satan, who "goes to and fro in the earth," and of whom it is elsewhere said, "Your adversary the devil walketh about as a roaring lion seeking whom he may devour" (I Peter v. 8). So Satan the destroyer plays the devil with the person, the possessions, the belongings of Job, who answers to the suffering Osiris in this development of the ancient drama, in which Horus or Job was no more a human personage than is Sut or Satan. They can be studied in the Ritual without disguise or falsification of character, and without a long series of disputations, lamentations, and sermons taking the place of the primitive mystery. The "parable" taken up by Job is the battle of Sut and Osiris in the mythical representation. Job the afflicted one is the suffering Osiris who passed into Amenta as the victim of the power of darkness, Sut the tormentor, the tempter, the desolator, the destroyer. Amongst other devilries, Sut flung his ordure at Horus (Rit., ch. 17); he also pierced him in the eye; but, where Osiris suffered dumbly and opened not his mouth, Job laments his lot, and takes to cursing the day of his birth and wishing that he had been addled in the egg. The character of Job is fathomlessly inferior to that of the good Osiris, called the motionless of heart.

The suffering Horus transforms in "the west" and becomes the bennu Osiris or the phœnix. Job does the same, or expects to do so, when he says, "I shall die in my nest, and I shall multiply my days as the phœnix." The phœnix was the emblem of the solar god who died to resuscitate in the nest of Amenta. He enters the nest as a hawk and issues forth as a phœnix (Rit., 13, 1). When the battle with Sut is over and Horus rises again triumphant over all his trials that were inflicted on him by the adversary, his property is doubled; he is crowned with the double crown as conqueror and king of the double earth. This is puerilely represented by the Lord restoring to Job two-fold of all he had before and overwhelming him with material wealth.

The drama in the mysteries of Amenta was a stupendous representation, true to nature; but when the chief character has been turned into a human personage covered with putrefying sores, when the adversary is made equally personal, and the Lord commissions the Devil to try to torment and to tempt this poor human sufferer *because* he was a perfectly just, good, and upright man, the drama becomes a stupendous misrepresentation not only of divine justice, but of the original setting forth and rendering of the mythos. The name of Job is commonly taken to signify "the assailed one," which perfectly describes the type of the suffering Osiris. He is the assailed one, and Sut is the assailant. How the good Osiris was assailed by the evil Sut and his Sami, the Apap-dragon and the Sebau, may be seen through all the mysteries of Amenta or of Sheol.

Sut the prototypal adversary is the evil one personified in Amenta as opponent of the deliverer Horus; he is the keeper of the prison-house for death, to which Horus comes as lord of life and liberty. The speaker in the Ritual cries to Ra, "O deliver me from the god who seizes souls. The darkness in which Sekari dwells is terrifying to the weak." This god is Sut (the Hebrew Satan), and darkness is the breath of his domain. In this darkness the Osiris suffers, supplicating Ra for light. Job sitting in the ashes, covered with boils from head to foot, and scraping himself with a potsherd, is a gross physical rendering of the manes in Amenta, who is scraped to get rid of the impurities and uncleannesses with which the soul from this world finds itself afflicted in the other life. The querulous, complaining Job is but a poor portrait of the speaker in the Ritual, and the Egyptian wisdom has to be restored before the genesis of the drama can be understood.

Osiris was the great god in matter as source or well-spring of life. He rested as the perfect one in Amenta, without sign of breath or beat of heart, but as the fount of motion and the fulfiller of existence in the nether earth, where he suffered in his death and burial, though not directly. Deity could not die nor suffer in itself; and this part of the character was represented by the human Horus. He was the sufferer in various natural phenomena; and being portrayed in human guise as the mortal, this led the way to the later euhemerizing of the mythical representations and the reproducing of the drama as human history. It was the human Horus who was pierced and tortured by Sut in death when it was his time to triumph and he became the king and conqueror in his turn. The suffering Horus only conquered Sut when he transformed and became the god in his turn and made his resurrection from Amenta. Job is this fearfully afflicted Horus or Osiris, suffering every evil that could be let loose on him by his adversary. But the scene is in Sheol, not on earth. Job is the "servant," like the suffering Messiah described by Isaiah, and like the human Horus, who was maimed and deformed, dumb and blind, as An-ar-ef in the land of darkness. When Job "takes up his parable" he is the sufferer in Amenta, the Hebrew Sheol. He goes blackened where there is no sun. He is a brother to the jackals in the paths of darkness, and a companion to ostriches which furnish the feathers of Maati in the Egyptian judgment hall. He is cast into the mire of the pit. He exclaims, "Why do ye persecute me as a god, and are not satisfied with my flesh? And after my skin hath been thus destroyed, out of my flesh shall I see God" (Job xix. 22, 26). A skin for the body is an expression peculiarly Egyptian. The god who is called the divine soul in the Ritual (ch. 165, A) is addressed as the "concealer of skins"— that is, a hider of the body of those who rise again transformed in the divine likeness of a soul eternalized. In the judgment scenes a second skin = a second body is the sign of re-embodiment after death, as a sahu or divine mummy. That is the shape in which Amsu-Horus rises from the tomb as vindicator and avenger of Osiris and the buried dead, the naked who become the clothed in the new body. In the case of Job it seems that the Lord has taken the skin or body of flesh, but is not satisfied. Job is a manes in Sheol. Nevertheless his resurrection from the pit is assured. Hence his exclamation, "I know that my vindicator liveth, and that he shall stand up at the last upon the earth. And after my skin hath been thus destroyed, yet from (or without) my flesh shall I see God"—for himself, and not vicariously by means of another (Job xix. 25-27).

There is an imposing picture in the book of Job (ch. xxvi) which is purely Egyptian. "The dead tremble beneath the waters, and the inhabitants thereof in the presence of the deity. Sheol is naked before him, and Abaddon hath no covering. He stretcheth out the north over empty space and hangeth the earth upon nothing. He bindeth up the waters in his thick clouds, and the cloud is not rent under them. He closeth in the face of his throne and spreadeth his cloud upon it. He hath described a boundary upon the face of the waters unto the confines of light and darkness. The pillars of heaven tremble and are astonished at his rebuke. He stilleth the sea by his power, and by his understanding he smiteth Rahab. By his spirit the heavens are established. His hand hath pierced the fleeing serpent." The stretcher of heaven for covering was Atum-Iu (or Ra) when he attained the solar sovereignty. He is addressed in this character by the manes, who is in dread of the deluge: "O thou great coverer of heaven, in thy name of stretcher (of the sky) grant that I may have power over the water and not be drowned" (Rit., 57). The heaven thus stretched overhead was represented as water, hence the greatness of the power that held it aloft in safety. The deceased beneath the waters are the manes in Amenta, where the waters are an image of the lower Nun, the sky as water below the horizon. Abaddon or destruction lurked below in the shape of the Apap-reptile, the destroyer, the great serpent in the waters of darkness, who was pierced and smitten through and through when he rose up in rebellion against Ra or Horus or Atum-Iu = Iahu. Atum-Iu the Lord, whom we shall identify with Ihuh, was the architect who finished the building of the heavens; and in the book of Job it is Ihuh the Lord who claims to have laid the foundations of the earth and says, "Declare, if thou hast understanding, who determined the measures thereof, or who stretched the line upon it. Whereupon were the foundations thereof fastened, or who laid the corner-stone thereof when the morning stars sang and all the sons of God shouted for joy?" (Job xxxviii. 4, 7.) To "stretch the line" is an expression peculiarly Egyptian, used frequently as synonymous with laying the foundations of the temple. The last chapters of the book contain the chief zoötypes belonging to the Egyptian astronomy. "The Bear with her sons" (ch. 38, 32) is a picture of the ancient mother in the celestial heptanomis with her seven sons. The first and foremost of these was Behemoth, the hippopotamus of Sut (and his mother), who is described here as "the chief of the ways of god." His fellow was the crocodile of Sebek-Horus, which is here called Leviathan. The foundations of the heavens were certainly laid in or by the bear and her seven sons, the first two of which were the twins Sut and Horus, the hippopotamus and the crocodile; and it is equally certain that these foundations were laid in the Egyptian astronomy. This will show that the writer is employing the Egyptian wisdom, and therefore it may be that he refers to the course of precession, albeit vaguely, in the following allusion: "Hast thou commanded the morning since thy days began, and caused *the dayspring to know its place,* that it might take hold of the ends of the earth?" which looks like the equinox upon its travels, although treated as the "morning" and the visiting "dayspring" from on high that makes its all-embracing circuit in the great year of the world.

When Job "took up his parable" he found it in the Book of the Dead, and is himself the speaker as the manes in Amenta, where we obtain foothold once more in the phenomena of nature, which were represented sanely and scientifically by the Egyptian sages, who laid the ground so that the eschatological rendering could follow the earlier mythos. Names have been omitted, the prototypal figures effaced, wisdom turned into ignorance, and the remains of Egyptian mythology and eschatology have been foisted on the world as an original revelation given in the Hebrew tongue; whereas the fundamental subject-matter of the sacred writings and the very God himself who is supposed to have revealed the truth in them are non-original as biblical, and only recognizable as Egyptian. The prayer of Jonah in the belly of the fish shows him to be another form of the Afflicted One who is for three days and three nights in the lowermost depths at the time of the winter solstice. In this legend the belly of the fish is identical with the belly of Sheol, the womb of the under-world. In the ancient fragment quoted in the second chapter Jonah says, "I called out of mine affliction unto the Lord, and he answered me; out of *the belly of Sheol* cried I; thou heardest my voice. For thou didst cast me into the depth, in the heart of the seas, and the flood was round about me; all thy waves and thy billows passed over me. And I said, I am cast out from before thine eyes; yet I will look again towards thy holy temple (*i.e.,* on the mount). The waters compassed me about, even to the soul. The deep was round about me; the weeds were wrapped about my head. I went down to the bottoms of the mountains; earth with her bars (closed) upon me for ever; yet thou hast brought up my life *from the pit,* O Lord my God." There is nothing whatever about the fish in this fragment. On the contrary, the speaker is in the belly of Sheol, which is the Kamite Amenta. In this nether-world he is at the roots of the mount of earth which stands in the waters of the abyss. The womb of Sheol might be represented as it was by the water-cow or a great fish. A great fish in the form of a crocodile was one of the types of the ancient mother who brought forth Sebek-Horus from the Nun as her young crocodile, just as she

THE EGYPTIAN WISDOM IN OTHER JEWISH WRITINGS 497

brought forth Sut as her young hippopotamus. The sufferer in Sheol is the same here as in the Psalms and the book of Job, and both are identical with the suffering Osiris in the mysteries of Amenta. We have now to take a backward look in the course of establishing the links between the Egyptian wisdom and the Hebrew writings.

Religion in Egypt first began in worship or propitiation of the primal providence that was figured as the Great Mother who brought forth the seven elemental powers called her children. These powers in Egypt were the seven Ali. In Phœnicia they are the seven Elohim, in Assyria they are seven forms of the Ili, and in Israel the seven Elohim, Kabirim, or Baalim. Sut was one of these, and Sut upon his mountain at the pole became El-Shaddai in his Hebrew form of Seth. The company of seven (with the Great Mother) passed into the astronomical mythology as the seven great spirits which were divinized as star gods with Anup, a form of Sut, at the pole. Under the figure of Israel, the abandoned female, later writers in the Old Testament denounce the pre-monogamous Great Mother as the harlot of promiscuous sexual intercourse. Jeremiah rejoices furiously because "she that hath borne seven languisheth," ashamed and confounded, and "hath given up the ghost" (xv. 9). When the one god had been "lifted up" as Ra in the solar mythos and Huhi the eternal in the eschatology by both the Egyptians and the Jews, or by the Egyptian Jews, the previous divinities called the ancestors of Ra were superseded, or their powers were absorbed in or blended with the one great power, who was now the all-one as Neb-er-ter.

"When the children of Israel did that which was evil in the sight of the Lord" (Ihuh), and served the Baalim and Ashtoreth (Judges ii. 11, 14), they were returning to the worship of the most ancient Great Mother and her sons the Ali, the companions, the brothers in the first circle of the gods; the Baalim being one with the Elohim and the Kabirim. "Return (says Ihuh), O backsliding children (the two sisters Judah and Israel), for I am a husband to you" (Jer. iii. 14). This backsliding, however, was itself a return to Israel's earlier love—"Israel," that is, as a part of the "common, dim populations" of Syria, Phœnicia or Canaan, and Palestine. The change from Baal to Ihuh is indicated by Hosea (ii. 16, also by Jeremiah iii.) when it is said to Israel, "And it shall be at that day, saith the Lord, thou shalt call me 'my husband,' and thou shalt call me no longer Baal. For I will take away the names of the Baalim out of her mouth, and they shall no more be memorialized by name." The Baalim, like the Elohim and Âbirim, were the Ali, companion gods or powers, that were originally a group of seven, to whom El or Baal was added as the eighth or highest God. They existed in the time of the totemic matriarchate before the husband or the father could be known personally, whether as human or divine. In this passage the deity becomes monogamous, and Israel, as a feminine equivalent for the suppressed goddess, is to be his wife. The language of the "prophets" concerning the whoredom of Israel cannot be comprehended apart from the status of the woman in communal connubium. The whore of later language is the representative of the totemic woman, who might cohabit with seven or any other *appointed* number of consorts. The harlot in mythology was the Great Mother, whose own children were her consorts in the beginning. When the fatherhood was divinized the god became the husband, the one instead of the seven or eight, who were the Ali, Illi, Elohim, Âberim, or Baalim. Israel had consorted with the Baalim, and therefore cohabited promiscuously. And after the one god was made known to her as a father and a husband, she still went a-whoring after the earlier gods. Hence the denunciations of Israel as the whore who would not truly play the part of wife.

Hebraists have surmised, and some Hebrews (known to the writer) have admitted, that the prefix B in B'Jah (B'Jah is Jehovah, Is. xxvi. 4, and B' Jah is his name) is an abbreviation for the name of Baal. If written out fully this would read, Baal-Iah = Baal is Jah. Bealiah is a proper name in the book of Chronicles I. xii. 5, in which we see that Baal-Iah as divinity supplied a personal name. Thus the Baal who is Iah יה would be the Iah who was one of the Baalim; and the earliest Baalim were a form of the seven companions, like the Kabarim and Elohim, which are followed in the book of Genesis by the god named Iahu-Elohim. The one god in Israel is made known to Moses by the two names of יהוה and יה, Ihuh and Iah. Now a priest of On (Osarsiph) would naturally learn at On of the one god Atum-Ra, who was Huhi the eternal in the character of God the father and Iu in the character of God the son, which two were one. In accordance with Egyptian thought, that which was for ever was the only true reality. This was represented by Huhi the eternal. And Huhi is the god made known to Israel by the priest of On. Gesenius derives the name of Ihuh from a root huh, which root *does not exist in Hebrew*. But it does exist in Egyptian. Huh or heh signifies ever, everlastingness, eternity, the eternal. Huhi was a title that was applied to Ptah, Atum-Ra, and Osiris, as Neb-Huhi the everlasting lord, or as the supreme one, self-existing, and eternal god, which each of these three deities represented in turn as one divine dynasty succeeded another in the Egyptian religion. An eternity of existence was imaged by the Egyptians as ever-coming or becoming; hence ever-coming or ever-becoming was a mode of imaging the eternal being. Thus the one god as their Huhi was not only he who is for ever as the father, but also he who comes for ever as the son. This visible mode of continuity by means of coming naturally involved becoming, according to the Egyptian doctrine of kheper, which includes ever-evolving, ever-transforming, ever-perpetuating, ever-becoming, under the one word kheper. Thus the name of an eternal, self-existent being which is יהוה in Hebrew can be traced as Huhi, the name for the one eternal, ever-living, ever-lasting god as Egyptian. And now for the first time we can distinguish the one name, יהוה from the other יה, if only on Egyptian ground. "Iu," with variants in Au, Iau, Aui, and others, is also an Egyptian word, but with no linguistic relationship to the word Huh. Iu is likewise the name of an Egyptian god, as Iu-em-hetep, he who comes with peace, who was primarily the son of Ptah, and who was repeated in the cult of Atum-Ra as Nefer-Atum. In fact, Atum-Ra is both Huhi and Iu as the one god living in truth, the father manifesting as the ever-coming son, who was Iu-sa the son of Iusāas in the cult of On. All that was ever represented to the Jewish mind by the name of Ihuh

(Ihvh or Jehovah) had been expressed to the Egyptian by the word huhi, or, later, hehi. As Egyptian "huh" signified everlastingness, millions of times, eternity, and "Huhi" was also a name of their god the eternal. It had been a title, we repeat, of Ptah, of Atum, and of Osiris, each in turn, in three different cults at Memphis, On, and Abydos. Huhi, then, was the eternal as the father; he who always had been, ever was, ever should be, and hence the everlasting god.

Iu was the ever-coming son, Iu-sa or Iu-em-hetep, the son who comes with peace as periodic manifestor for the eternal father. Thus the One God of the Jews was Egyptian in this twofold character, both by nature and by name.

The change in Israel from the worship of El-Shaddai to the worship of Ihuh, from the Elohistic to the Jehovistic god, corresponds to the change from the stellar to the solar worship in the astronomical mythology. El in the highest was the star-god on the summit of the mountain, who in the Kamite mythos might be Sut, Seth, or Anup at the pole. The pole was represented by the mount, one Egyptian name of which is Sut, denoting standing-ground. The ruler of the pole-star was the lord of standing-ground or station at the fixed centre of the heavens. The highest El was the eighth of the Ali or Baalim. In Hebrew he is called El-Shaddai, commonly rendered the powerful or mighty one. Another rendering, however, of the name is more than probable. This was the most high god, El-Elyon, whom the Phœnicians also called *Israel*. As Egyptian, it was Anup on the mount, or at the pole, the highest of the star-gods or Elohim who preceded the solar sovereignty of Ra. El-Shaddai, who was Phœnician, and had been co-worker with the Elohim in the legends of creation, was succeeded and superseded by the god of two names who is made known to Israel as "Ihuh" and Iahu, or "Iao"=Egyptian Iu. The Egyptian word Iu is also written Ï, with *u* inherent, and has the meaning of coming, come, to come, and is the name of the ever-coming and eternal child, Iu-em-hetep, or Iusa, the coming son. In the Phœnician version the deity Iao = Iu is the coming son, the well-beloved, the only-begotten son of El, who was to be called Ieoud (or יהוד), the supposed, prototype of "something to come" in Christianity (*see* Bryant). The word Iu with these meanings in Egyptian agrees with Iah or Iahu in Hebrew, signifying come and to come. Thus Huhi is equivalent to יהוה, and Iu is equivalent to יה as Ihu or Iao, the two forms of which name are different from each other at the root, but could be applied as two titles of the one god. Iah is portrayed as the god who is operative, audible, and visible in material phenomena. His are the mighty deeds. He is the manifestor for the father, the opener of Amenta in the solar mythos. The Song of Moses shows that Iah was the divine deliverer who triumphed gloriously over the adversaries of the father, as did this deliverer in the exodus from the lower Egypt of Amenta (Ex. xv. 2). Iah is the opponent of Amalek, with whom he makes war for ever, as did Horus with Apap, the eternal enemy (Ex. xvii. 16). Iah is the god who rides as conqueror through the deserts, (Ps. lxviii. 4) and goes forth before his people marching through the wilderness. It was he who led his people "like a flock, by the hand of Moses and Aaron" (Ps. lxxvii. 20). Iah is called upon as deliverer from death and as the saviour from the sufferings of Sheol (Ps. cxvi.). He is the coming one who is looked to and watched and waited for as the redeemer of Israel. It is to Iah the Hallelu-Iah of the Psalmist is raised. In short, *the character is that of God the son, and therefore Iah is one with Iu the son of Atum-Huhi.* Iah is god the son, and the son in Egyptian is the Messu. Thus, Iah the Messu is the Mes-Iah, hence the Messiah in Hebrew. The Messiah as Iah the Messu was the ever-coming son, like Iu, and Iu as Egyptian is he who comes as manifestor for the eternal father.

The duality of Ptah, also of Atum as Huhi the eternal father, and Iu the ever-coming son, is repeated and preserved in the "Pistis Sophia" of the Egypto-gnostics. Ptah is not mentioned by name. But the great forefather is called the father of all fatherhood, the god who was "parentless"; and Ptah is the one god, who, being gotten by his own becoming, was the self-existent and eternal one, Huhi (Eg.), Ihuh (Hebrew), Iao (Phœnician), or Ieou (Egypto-gnostic). The one god in two persons, or, as the Ritual expresses it, with two faces, becomes twain in the father and son. These are called Ieou the greater and Iao the lesser. Ieou the elder is "the overseer of the light"; Iao the younger is the good Sabaoth, who emanates from Ieou as a son from the father (B. ii. 193). Iao is also designated Sabaoth-Adamas, who is the gnostic and Jewish deity Iao-Sabaoth thus identified with Atum-Ra, lord of the heavenly host. The same duality of father and son was figured in the twofold Athamas at Samothrace. "The two great books of Ieou" are mentioned in "Pistis Sophia," which are said to have been written down by Enoch when Jesus "spoke with him from the tree of knowledge and the tree of life, which were the two trees in the paradise of Adam" (B. ii. 246). The paradise of Adam was the garden of Atum, and the Jesus who spoke and uttered the sayings was the wise youth Iu, or Iu-em-hetep, the son of Atum, or Atum in his earlier character of Iu as the son of Ptah.

Moreover, it is not improbable that a version of these is extant in two books of the apocrypha, viz., the Wisdom of Jesus and the Wisdom of Solomon. The expounder of the mysteries in these writings was the Egyptian Jesus, who is the Sayer, word or logos, twice over as Egyptian, once as Iu the son of Ptah, at Memphis, and once as the son of Atum-Ra, Iu-em-hetep, the prince of peace, and prototype of the Hebrew Solomon, at On. The Egyptian Jesus was equally the Egyptian Solomon, the youthful sage, as sayer and teacher of the oral wisdom. When Iamblichus describes the one god who was worshipped at Heliopolis or Annu as "Ichton and Emphe," he refers to Atum in his two characters of father and son or Ra and Horus. Atum was represented at Annu by the fish of the inundation, and also by Iu-em-hetep, the bringer of peace and plenty, as Ichton the fish that typified the saviour to Egypt. And now if for the modern Jews we read the ancient worshippers of Atum-Iu or, still earlier, of Ptah, we shall be able to follow Isaiah in his survey of the great dispersion of the Jewish people over all the earth. "The Lord shall set his hand to recover the remnants of his people which shall remain from Assyria, and from Egypt, and from Pathros, and from Kush, and from Elam, and from Shinar, and from Hamath, and from the islands (or coast-lands) of the sea. He shall assemble the outcasts of Israel, and gather together the dispersed of Judah from the four corners of the earth." (Is. xi. 11, 13.) It is noticeable that the prophet calls the Lord who is to gather the Jews together from all lands by the double name of Iah-Jehovah. Iah is the Egyptian Iu, whose followers were the primeval Jews of Egypt north and south (Pathros), of Æthiopia and Chaldea, of the islands of the sea, and the remotest shores of the earth, including the Jews of Cornwall. These are the prehistoric Jews who are to be known by the name of the god they worshipped. This range will include the black Jews of Africa and India, and all the rest of those whose god we identify with Iu the Egyptian original and prototype of all; Iu as god the son, whether of the father as Atum or as Ptah. No such world-wide dispersion of the Jewish race from Palestine or Judea had ever occurred in the time of Isaiah. It is the religious community, not the race, that will account for the Jews who emigrated to the ends of the earth, and for the names of the Jewish god, who was the Egyptian Iu, Phœnician Iao, Hebrew Iah, Assyrian Iau, Egypto-gnostic Ieou (greater and lesser), Chinese Iaou, Polynesian Iho-Iho, Dyak Iaouh, Nicobar Islands Eewu, Mexican Ao, Toda Au, Hungarian Iao, Manx Iee, Cornish Iau, Welsh Iau (greater and lesser), Hebrew Iao-Sabaoth, Chaldean Iao-Heptaktis, Greek Ia, and IE, Latin Jupiter and Jove.

To follow the Jews as the Aiu of Egypt in their world-wide dispersion, we shall have to think in continents rather than in Petticoat Lanes and Ghettos.

The worshippers of Iao in Phœnicia, of Iau in Assyria, of Iao in Syria, Iau and Hu in Britain, Ia or Iu in Greece, Jupiter in Italy, Iho-Iho in Polynesia, Iau in America were each and all of them Jews in a sense, but the sense was religious, not originally ethnical; and religion does not determine race any more than language does in later ages of the world. There was a religion of the god Iu or Iao in Egypt thirteen thousand years ago. That god was Atum-Iu, born son of Ptah. He was the earliest father in heaven because he was the divine Ra in his primordial sovereignty. He is the god in two persons who was first figured as the sun upon the double horizon = the father in the west, the son in the east. This god went forth from Kam by several names and various routes. Those who worshipped him as Atum became the Adamites, the Edomites, the red men; those who worshipped him as Iao, Iah, or Iu became the Jews in many lands, and these are the Jews of that world-wide dispersion recognized by Isaiah, which did not follow any known historical exodus from Egypt or captivity in Babylon, or migration from Palestine. The Jews were only ethnical at root when the root was the vine in Egypt, or in Æthiopia beyond, and the Jews were one of its branches. They were only ethnical at root when the race was black, whether these were the black Jews in Africa or in India.

From the beginning the Jews were as they are to-day, a religious community. It is the worship of Iu in Egypt thirteen thousand years ago and the going out from thence that will account for the supreme being amongst the Dyaks of Borneo being known to them as Yavuah, which name was not derived from the Hebrew Jehovah, but from the original of both (A. M. Cameron, *Proc. Soc. of Bib. Arch.*). The Dyaks also preserve the tradition of a great ancestor who was determined to construct a ladder that should reach up to heaven, but one night a worm ate into the foot of the ladder, and it fell like the tower of Babel. The Dyaks also have the legend of a great deluge which drowned the chief part of mankind and divided the rest. These two catastrophes mark the endings of two vast periods in time which preceded the supremacy of Atum-Iu in the Zodiac of twelve signs. Thus amongst a people so isolated as the Dyaks they have the god Yavuah and the tradition of the two catastrophes which are represented in the book of Genesis by the destruction of the tower and the deluge of Noah. Naturally the "wisdom" was carried into the island of Borneo with the cult of the god Iaouah, whose worshippers are elsewhere called the Ius or Jews from the Egyptian deity who was Iu or Aiu by name both in the cult of Ptah at Memphis and of Atum-Ra at On. The same god is found in the Babylonian mythology with the name Ia, or Iau = Iah in Hebrew (Pinches, T. G., *Proc. Soc. of Bib. Arch.*). But it is not necessary to suppose the Assyrian god Iau was derived from the Hebrew deity Iahu, or *vice versa,* when there is a common origin for both in the Egyptian god Iu. This is not a matter merely of philology, but of the characters in the mythology. Iau is "the sage of the gods" (*Assyn. Fragments*). He is also described as the divine artisan or art-workman, especially in the character of the potter. This is Ptah all over. He was pre-eminently the potter, and the head of the Knemmu or divine moulders. Further and finally, it was Ptah-Iu who, with his Ali, the Elohim, created the Aarru-garden as a paradise of pleasure in the earth of eternity. And in the Assyrian eschatology it is Iau, "the sage of the gods," who transports the justified spirits after death to the "place of delights," where they are fed on butter and honey and drink the water that gives eternal life (*Records,* vol. xi. 161-2). Our British Druids worshipped a deity of the same name and dual nature as the Egyptian Iu, the Assyrian Iau, the Hebrew Iahu. This divine duality, consisting of the father and the son, was called by them Iau the elder and Iau the younger, corresponding to the gnostic Ieou and Iao.

The god Iu, as son of Ptah, was an astronomical builder and architect of the heavens. Iu the son of Atum was also reputed to be a great builder. As the Kamite Solomon he was not only the prince of peace and the divine healer; he was also said to have *designed the Temple.* The stages of building on earth were reflected in the heavens. The mound-builders were first. They raised the seven mounds of the heptanomis. Shu raised the four pillars of the four quarters. Ptah was the architect who based his building on the pole and the four cardinal points = the four-square tent and tent-staff. Atum, his son, was the builder of heaven as the house, "the Father's house on high" of which the Christian sings. This in the Ritual is called "the dwelling of my father Tum" (ch. 17). It is also said to the deceased, "Tum hath built thy house" (ch. 17, 30). "The double lion-god hath founded thy habitation." Lastly, the temple was designed by Iu-em-hetep the son of Atum, as the builder in the astronomical mythology. Thence the people named after the deity Iu as the Aiu, or later Jews, would come to be recognized in Egypt, the land of temples, as the great builders. And according to Rabbinical traditions the Jews = Ius or Aaiu were the great typical builders. They are said to have excavated the mountains, raised the pyramids, built temples and cities, and surrounded them with walls; divided the Nile into several canals, and constructed dykes against the inundation (Josephus and Philo). One of these great works was the canal of Joseph, *i.e.* the divine architect who as son of Ptah was his sif, Iu-sif = Joseph. Also, if we have to do with Egyptians who are only identified by a religious name, that of the deity Iu, there is no difficulty about their having built the Meskenoth of Tum, or, as it is rendered, the store-cities of Pithom and Rameses, when the great temple of Atum-Iu was originally erected at Annu or On, which according to the divine dynasties followed Memphis in attaining its supremacy. The Jew-name was Egyptian then as Iu, or Aiu, with other variants. Aiu is a form of the word, and Neb-Aiu, the Lord Aiu, filled the office of high priest in the temple of Osiris at Abydos. The Aiu as manes in Amenta are the children of Ra, who was Atum-Huhi as Ra the father and Atum-Iu as Horus the son. The land of Judea or Judah was named in Egyptian. It appears upon the monuments as Iuta or Iutah. Iu is dual, ta is earth or land, and Iuta is the double land or double earth of the Egyptian mythos localized in Judea. The dual kingdom of Judea was derived by name from the dual deity Iu, whose followers in Egypt were the Ius, Iews, or Jews, and given to Joseph in the persons of his two sons, Ephraim and Manasseh. "Joseph shall have two portions" says Ezekiel (xlvii. 13); and these had already been assigned to the two sons of Joseph by Jacob in the book of Genesis. In the mythos the two portions of the double earth were united once a year to form the kingdom of the sif or son, who is Joseph in the Hebrew version and Iu the sif as son of Atum-Ra. The two halves were united by the son in his name of Har-sam-taui, unifier of the double land.

It has been shown that the Hebrew deity Ihuh was god the father in one character and in the other god the son. If the type of these was the bull, this would represent the father, and the bullock or calf the son, as with the bull of Osiris and the calf of Horus. If the lion were the type, the old lion would represent the father, the young lion the son. The same with the ass, which was another type of the deity Iu, the father and the son being represented by the ass and its foal. The symbolism of the lion, the bull, and the ass has its tale to tell concerning Israel and the Kamite origins. The lion was a zoötype of Atum-Iu. He is called the lion-faced in the Ritual. His mother was a lioness. He is addressed as a lion-god (Rit., ch. 28), the god in lion form (chs. 38, 41, 53, 54, 62). It is the same with Ihuh in Israel. The god is described by Hezekiah (Is. xxxviii. 13), as a lion: "As a lion, so he breaketh all my bones." This is looked upon merely as a tropical figure of speech, but it is a figure of fact in the original symbolism. Atum-Iu was the lion of Judah in the Egyptian mythos. The lion origin of Judah's totem was known to Nahum in his inquiry for the lion-spirit of the past: "Where is the den of the lions and the feeding place of the young lions, where the old lion and the lioness walked with the lion's whelp and no one made them afraid? The lion tore in pieces enough for his whelps, and strangled for his lioness and filled his caves with prey." (Nahum ii. 11, 12, 13.) These are equivalent to the lion as Ptah, the lioness as Sekhet Merptah, and Atum as the whelp. Iah roareth as the typical lion: "Thou shalt walk after the Lord, who shall roar like a lion, for he shall roar" (Hos. xi. 10). "The Lord shall roar from on high, he shall mightily roar" (Jer. xxv. 30). "The Lord shall roar from Zion" (Joel iii. 16). "The lion hath roared: the Lord God hath spoken" (Amos iii. 8). Job was hunted by the Lord in the shape of a lion. "Thou huntest me as a lion," says the fearfully-afflicted one (Job x. 16). The Lord was known in Israel by his roaring like a lion, because he had been known in Egypt as the lion-god who was Atum-Ra, the lion of the double force which was represented by the twin lions (Rit., 162, 1). The solar Dionysius was known by the name of "the roarer," and he was also portrayed as a lion-headed god. In the Bakchai of Euripides (1078) he is invoked by the chorus to manifest in his might and appear as a flaming lion. The reason of this roaring in that shape is that the Lord was imaged as a lion on the mount of the lions, which was the Mount Shennu = Sinai, the lion-mount where the Lord was the solar lion—where, in fact, he was the two lions, the old lion and the young one. These are referred to by Hosea. "I will be unto Ephraim as a lion, and as a young lion to the house of Judah. I, even I, will tear and go away; I will carry off, and there shall be none to deliver." (Hosea v. 14.) The solar birthplace in the mythos was upon the mount of the two lions. Horus the son was reborn upon the horizon as "the young lion made resplendent at his birth by the two lions" (Rit., ch. 3). Also it is said that "Judah is a lion's whelp; he stooped down, he couched as a lion and as a lioness." In this description we have the typical lion in the triple form of a lion, the lioness, and the whelp, as the type was portrayed in Egypt. There was a triple-headed lion-god at Meroe with four arms, which may well stand for the dual-natured Atum-Iu as the son of the lion-headed Ptah and Sekhet (Rawlinson on Herodotus, ii. 35). According to the language of the Ritual, this would be the "lion of the double lions," or double force. It is proclaimed by Ezekiel that the mother of Israel was a lioness. As "a lioness she couched among lions and she brought up *one of her whelps;* he became a young lion; the nations also heard of him: he was taken in their pit, and they brought him with hooks into the land of Egypt" (Ez. xix. 1, 5). This is another and a truer version of the mythos euhemerized in Exodus as the story of Joseph and his brethren. The lion was taken in the same pit into which Joseph was cast in the "historic" account, and this identifies the Egypt signified as lower Egypt in Amenta. Joseph is the Iu-sif in Egyptian—that is, Iu the son, who is here represented as the young lion whose mother was a lioness.

The origin of the mother as a lioness was the same as with the sow or the cow. It was totemic and typical. The lioness was a zoötype of the mythical Great Mother, Kefa (or Kheft), who became the Hebrew Chavvah, the genetrix of life and mother of the human race. Sekhet, the Great Mother in her solar form, was also a lioness, and in certain Egyptian texts the goddess Sekhet has been represented as an ancestress of the human race (Lefébure, *Tombeau de Seti,* i. 11, Pl.

4, 5). She also was the mother in Amenta who reproduced the Aiu or Jews, as the children of Ra, for another life. "I know," says the manes, "that I have been conceived by Sekhet and born of Neith" (Rit., ch. 66). This likewise was the divine or mythical ancestry of the Jews; but only the Egyptian wisdom ever could explain the derivation of the race, of either Jew or Gentile, from the lioness. Sekhet was the consort of Ptah, one of whose types is the lion. These two, Ptah and Sekhet, were the parents of Atum, the lion-god in the cult of Atum-Ra; and Atum was the first man and reputed father of the human race, with Iu, the sif, or son, who is the young lion as Joseph. Thus, and in no other way, was man or mankind mothered by Sekhet the lioness, by Kefa, by Chavvah, or by Eve. And in that way only was a lioness the mother of Israel, whose whelp is the young lion as the lion of Judah. The Lord who was a lion as the representative of solar force becomes the "lion-like" of later language. Thus the Egyptian origins of the Jews, their gods, their mythology, and their symbolism were veiled from view, and philology was left without the necessary determinative types and palpable figures of the underlying facts.

The Egyptian deity Iu, the son of Atum-Ra, was also portrayed as a short-horned bull-calf. Not as the god in person, but as a figure to be interpreted by a necessary knowledge of the symbolism. Osiris was designated the "bull of eternity." Atum was the earlier bull-father. His consort was Iusâas, a form of the cow-headed goddess, their divine child being Iu, the su or sif, in the image of a bull-calf; and as here shown Iu is = Jah in Hebrew, as god the son, who is identifiable with Joseph. The difficult passage in Genesis (xlix. 22) might be more correctly rendered, "Joseph is son of the heifer." This he would be as Iu (em-hetep), the sif (son) of the cow-headed Iusāas, who was a form of Hathor, the golden heifer, in the temple of Atum-Ra at On. The god who brought up Israel out of Egypt is not only represented by the golden calf; he is also said to have the horns of the ox or wild bull (Numbers xxiii. 22). Iu was the bull in one character and the calf in the other; and as it was with Iu in Egypt so is it with Iahu in Israel, only we must learn to read the imagery aright in accordance with the Egyptian wisdom, which we are told was so familiar to "Moses." As Kuenen states it, "Ihuh was worshipped in the shape of a young bull. It cannot be doubted that the cult of the bull-calf was really the cult of Ihuh in person." This statement, however, is not in keeping with the present mode of presenting the facts. The existence of types does not of necessity involve a worship of the type. The whole range of sign-language lies between such an assumption and the possible truth. Otherwise stated, the young bullock was one of the types under which the god Iu was represented by the Egyptians and the Israelites. The bullock, for example, was identified with Joseph and venerated as the zoötype of his divinity by certain of the ancient Jews (Kircher, vol. I, p. 197), Joseph being, as herein maintained, a form of Iu the son (sif), with Jacob as a figure of the father-god. The calves of Beth-Aon also point to Iu, the calf-headed god, and the beth or temple of Atum-Ra in Annu, the Hebrew On (Hosea x. 5). It is said by Hosea, "Ephraim is an heifer that is taught, that loveth to tread out the corn; but I have passed over upon her fair neck" (*Ib.* x. 11). Iusāas, the mother of Iu, was the heifer on whose neck, or between the horns of whose head, the sun-god rode. Her son was Joseph as the Iu-sif; and in this passage we have a casting back aimed at the origins after the attempted casting out of the cult. The sons of Joseph are identified with the calves of Beth-On, and Ephraim with the heifer. Covenants also were established in Israel by cutting a calf in twain and passing the contracting persons between the two parts (Jer. xxxiv. 18, 19), which made the type equivalent to the two sexes of the mother and child or heifer and calf, or the calf that was both male and female; also to the duality of father and son.

The Vignettes to the Ritual prove that Atum-Ra the solar god and his son Iu were also represented by the ass. The sun or sun-god goes down to Amenta as, if not riding on, the ass. He is attacked there by the Apap-serpent who devours in the dark (Vignette, Rit., ch. 40). At dawn he rises and is hauled up by the ass, or by the young solar god with ass's ears. Thus we have the old ass and the young, the Hebrew ass and the foal of an ass, on which the sun-god in the later legend rode when he came up from Amenta riding on the ass in the mythology which preceded the eschatology. The ass and the young sun-god also were both named Iu, and Iu was the son of Atum-Ra, the ass being his zoötype. Iu, as Egyptian, is represented by Iao in Phœnician and in Hebrew. Clement Alexander, who was an Egyptian, spells the name of Jehovah as Iau. Thus, "Iu" is the ass in Egyptian, Iao is a name of the god with an ass's head, and Iau is Jehovah, the god of the Jews and the Christians also. Epiphanius asserts that the deity Sabaoth has the face of an ass. He calls it "the gnostic Sabaoth." But Sabaoth was also the Jew-god, or god Iu, who was known by the name of Iao-Sabaoth. The ass-god is portrayed on some of the talismanic stones that were copied by King in his work *The Gnostics and their Remains*. In one of these Iao is ass-headed in the character of Horus grasping the two scorpions as he stands upon the cippus (pl. G, 2). But King, who calls this "the ass-headed Typhon, or the principle of evil," is hopelessly wrong. According to the Egypto-gnostic "Pistis Sophia," Iao-Sabaoth is god the son to Ieou (Ihuh) as god the father, both of whom were forms of the ass-headed deity. And Iao, or Abrakas, is likewise portrayed upon the gnostic gems in the shape of a double-headed ass, which is equivalent to the father-god and son in the same image as Ieou and Iao, Ihuh and Iah, or Huhi and Iu with their duality blended in one figure (King, G. R., pl. B). It represented Horus, or Iu in the cult of Atum-Iu. King knew only of one ass, which to him was a type of the evil Sut or Typhon.

But this was not the ass of Iu, Iao-Sabaoth or Atum-Ra.

In the Museum of the Collegio Romano to-day there may be seen a figure of the ass-headed god who was Egyptian, Jewish, and Gnostic. It is the image of a man extended cross-wise on the Roman cross. The figure is being saluted by a worshipper of the god, who was thus portrayed with the head of an ass. It was discovered some years since scratched roughly on the wall of a room in a house that was buried in ancient times beneath the buildings of the Palatine Hill, and was cut out from the wall and deposited in the Roman

Museum. King, in describing it, tries hard but vainly to make out that the animal is not an ass, but was intended for Anubis, the jackal. He says: "In reality the production of some devout but illiterate gnostic, it is construed into a shocking heathen blasphemy and a gibe upon the good Christian Alexamenos, because they mistake the jackal's head for that of an ass, and consequently imagine an intentional caricature of their own crucifix." There is no mistaking the ass for Anubis. There was no caricature in the crucifix. The ass is a type of the solar sufferer in Amenta, who came to be called the crucified. The Roman or Latin cross is a figure of the longest night and shortest day when the sun was in the winter solstice. The ass-headed god upon the cross is the exact equivalent of Osiris-tat, and in this crude representation we find the divine victim on or as the cross instead of the tat, or instead of being devoured by the "eater of the ass," as in the Vignettes to the Ritual. The adoration of Alexamenos was directed to the god who is portrayed upon the cross, not of the equinox, but of the winter solstice, as the sufferer in Amenta, and as the form of the solar deity who made himself a sacrifice like Ptah, or Osiris in the cross-tree of the tat. (King, *The Gnostics and their Remains,* 2nd ed., pp. 229-30).

It was charged against the Christians in Rome that they also were worshippers of the ass-god. Tertullian in a passage of his reply says to his opponents, "Like many others, you have dreamed that an ass's head is our god, but a new version of our god has lately been made public at Rome, ever since a certain hireling convict of a bull-fighter put forth a picture with some such inscription as this, 'The god of the Christians O N O K O I H T H Σ.' He was portrayed with the ears of an ass, and with one of his feet hoofed, holding in his hand a book, and clothed with a toga" (Apol., 16). Diodorus says, according to the fragment of Lib. 34 preserved by Photius, that when Antiochus Epiphanes, after conquering the Jews, went into the inner sanctuary of God, he found there a stone statue of a man with a long beard, holding a book in his hand and sitting on an ass. This he took to be an image of Moses. We should rather take it to have been the image of the ass-headed god Atum-Iu, who passed out of Egypt as Iao, Iau, or Iao-Sabaoth, the solar god who as lord of hosts in Egypt, before going forth, had attained the status of Huhi the eternal, the one god in spirit and in truth; Ra in the mythology, the holy ghost in the eschatology; Atum-Huhi as the father, Iu as the son, and Ra as the holy spirit. But the ass was not the god, whether of the Egyptians or the Jews, the Gnostics or Christians. It was but a type of the power that was recognized at first as solar, the power that was divinized in Atum, who was Ra in his primordial sovereignty, and whose son was the ass-headed Iao, Iau, or Iu.

But we must make a further digression on account of Joseph as a form of the young solar god in Israel who was Iu, the ass-headed sif or son of Atum-Ra, in Egypt. Not one of the legends in the Hebrew writings attributed to Moses could be understood apart from the mythology from which they were fundamentally derived. Nor does the mythology remain intact in the form of the märchen. The story of Joseph, for example, is a collection of fugitive fragments, each one of which is separately identifiable. Joseph is not simply one of ten or twelve or seventy brethren in the family of Jacob or Israel. Joseph-El as the beloved son of Jacob was divine, and would be a divinity if there were any possibility of all the other sons being human. It is now known that Jacob-El and Joseph-El were worshipped as two divinities in Northern Syria, and it is there we find a remnant of the seed of Israel or Isiri-El, and therefore of Jacob-El whose son was Joseph. But it is not to be supposed that Jacob was a human father, and that Joseph was his human son, who were divinized by adding the divine El as a suffix to their names. This leaves us with nothing but the two divinities to go upon. These probably originated with Iu in Kheb, or Lower Egypt, as Jacob, and Iu, the sif, or son, as Joseph; the two divinities being humanized in the later legends of the Iu, Aiu, or Jews, as was the common way in converting mythos into history. It can be shown that Joseph was a form of the divine, the beloved son, whose father was יהוה in one version of the mythos and Jacob in another. Io or Jo = Iu in the name of Joseph (יהסף) is taken by Hebraists as the equivalent of Iahu; and in Ps. lxxxi. 5, the name of Joseph is written Iahusiph (יהוסף)—that is, Iah the siph or sif, which in Egyptian denotes the son. Also the names יוספיה, that is Joseph-Iah and of Josephiah (Ez. viii. 10) proclaim the fact, in accordance with the use and wont of the Hebrew language, that Joseph is Iah = Iu in Egyptian. In the same way the name of El-Iasaph (Num. i. 14 and iii. 24) identifies the deity of Joseph, and affirms that Iasaph is one with Iah, and therefore *is* Joseph-El. Joseph as son is Iu the sif, or the coming son, in Egyptian. These names show the identity of Joseph and Iu the sif, and denote that Joseph was the son of the same father, who is Jacob in the one version and Ihuh in the other. The descent of the sun-god into the lower Egypt of Amenta is portrayed in the märchen as the casting of Joseph into the pit, and the ascent therefrom in his glory by the coat of many colours. In Egypt Joseph plays the part of Repa to the Ra or Pharaoh. In this character he rides in the second chariot when he goes forth as the Adon, or Aten, over all the land. But as Joseph-El he is the divine Repa, the Horus of thirty years—that is, Iu the sif in the cult of Atum-Ra. At thirty years of age the son as Horus, or Iu the sif=Joseph, took his seat upon the throne beside the father, and went forth as ruler over all the land of Egypt, the halves of which were united when the young god assumed the sovereignty of the double country in the mythos, and is called Har-sam-taui, uniter of the double earth, or earth and heaven, in the eschatology. His relationship to Neith likewise attests his divinity. When the throne-name of "Zaphenath Paneah" = Sif-Neith the living, is conferred upon him he is identified as the son who became the consort of the cow-headed Neith, a form of whom was the goddess Iusâas, the mother of Iu the sif=Joseph, at Heliopolis. This relationship to the great Neith is fulfilled when he becomes the consort of Asenath or Asa-Neith, whose name identifies her as the great goddess Neith, the daughter of Ra, or, as "historically" rendered, the daughter of Potiphar.

As mythical characters, Joseph and Jesus are two forms of one original. Joseph in Israel was a name of the Messiah who was expected as the ever-coming son. Now, in Egyptian there are two names for the coming son: one is Iu the su = Jesus; the other is Iu the sif = Joseph. And when the wandering Jew, named Kartaphiles, became a Christian he is called *Joseph,* and was said to have fallen into a trance once every century, and to have risen again at *thirty years of age.* That is the age of Horus the adult in his second advent; also of Jesus in the Gospels, as well as of Joseph when he became the Adon over all the land of Egypt, the double land or double earth of Egypt in Amenta.

Joseph being identified as a god in Joseph-El, the god Joseph is further identifiable as an Egyptian deity who was Iu, the ever-coming son, both in the dynasty of Ptah at Memphis and also of Atum-Ra at On. It may be seen from Josephus against Apion (B. i., ch. 32) that the Hebrew hero Joseph was the Jewish form of Iu, the sif or son. Iu the typical son was the su or sif of Atum, also of Ptah. In either case he is the resuscitated form of the father who becomes his own son, Iu the sif, as he who is the bringer of peace. The name of Iu the coming son would be written in Egyptian either as Iusa, Iusu, or Iusif. The one form passes into the name of Iesous, the other into the name of Joseph, chief among the twelve sons assigned to Jacob or Israel. The form Iusa may be found in the name of Iusāas, the mother who was great with the Egyptian Jesus or Iusa in the cult of Atum-Ra at On. The divine nature of Joseph-El may explicate a passage from Cheremon, cited by Josephus, who records a tradition that one of the two leaders of the Israelites, in an exodus from Egypt which can no longer be considered historical, was Joseph. Cheremon was one of the most learned men in Egypt, and the contemporary of Apion, against whom Josephus wrote his reply. He was keeper of the rolls and books. He was an Egyptian historian in the library of the Serapæum. He also composed a hieroglyphical dictionary, fragments of which are still extant and have been of service to Egyptologists. Cheremon, therefore, was one of those who knew. He not only asserts that one of the two leaders was Joseph, but also that his Egyptian name was Peteseph, and that he was *a sacred scribe.* Now, as may be seen, the name of Ptah was rendered by Pet in the Greek name of Petesuchis for the Ptah (Putah) of crocodiles; and Joseph = Peteseph in Egyptian is the sif or son Iu, *i.e.* Iusif, whilst Peteseph is the son of Ptah, which he was as Iu the sif of Ptah in the Egyptian divine dynasties—that is, Iu-em-hetep. Peteseph as Iu the son of Ptah (or Ptah the son) was the divine scribe in person who is portrayed in that character with the papyrus-roll upon his knee and the cap of wisdom on his head. The fact of Joseph being the son of Ptah, or Ptah in the character of the divine son, was certainly not derived from the biblical history of the Jews, but it was derived by Josephus from an unimpeachable Egyptian authority, viz., that of Cheremon. Thus, Iu the sif of Ptah, with Moses, is equivalent to the youthful solar god with Shu-Anhur in the exodus from the lower Egypt of Amenta. Of course, Joseph and Moses could not be contemporaries as historical characters according to the book of Exodus, but they could as mythical divinities. And when Moses and Joseph are restored to their proper position as deities there need be no difficulty about dates. As gods they could be contemporaries (see "The Exodus," in Book x). Joseph is the typical dreamer and diviner in his youth. And if Iu the sif of Atum-Ra be not an interpreter of dreams, he was the revealer of the future by means of dreams. One of the Ptolemaic tablets records the fulfilment of the promise that was made in a dream by this god to Pasherenptah concerning the birth of a son (Renouf, *Hib. Lect.,* p. 141). This would be ground enough for the "inspired" writer to go upon in establishing the character assigned to Joseph as the dreamer and interpreter of dreams. The dream of the sun, moon, and eleven stars making obeisance to Joseph shows the astronomical relationship of the twelve to the signs of the zodiac.

Doubtless there was "corn in Egypt," which was at all times *par excellence* the land of corn, but the typical corn-land of the religious mysteries is in Amenta, where the corn germinates periodically from the buried body of Osiris. We need to go no farther than the Papyrus of Ani to see from whence the legend of the seven kine was derived. In the Hebrew märchen it is related that Pharaoh—which Pharaoh is never specified, and this is as it would or should be if Ra, the solar god, is meant—dreamed that seven kine came up out of the river that were fat and well-favoured, and seven other kine that were lean and ill-favoured. When interpreted by Joseph, the seven fat kine are said to signify seven years of plenty and the seven lean kine seven years of famine. The dream was fulfilled in proof that Joseph was an historical personage, and that all the rest of the mythos reduced to märchen was matter of fact. Now, in the Ritual these are the seven cows which are the givers of abundance in the Egypt of the lower earth, through which the river runs as the celestial Nile. This then is the river out of which the seven cows arose, and the country is in the other world, the lower Egypt of the double earth, from which the original exodus was made in the going forth of the manes from Amenta. The land of Egypt, the river and the seven cows, all go together in the mythical representation from which the "history" has been manufactured. The seven cows are associated with the bull in the Aarru-paradise of plenty. The bull was the young solar god as Horus, or the bullock-headed deity Iu, who passed out of Egypt as Joseph, the bull of Israel.

If there ever had been a failure of the Nile for seven years together, the biblical account is none the less a pious fraud (*see* the fraudulent "Tablet of the Seven Years of Famine," *Proc. Soc. of Bib. Arch.*). For the fact is there was no real famine in the land of Egypt. "And the seven years of famine began to come, according as Joseph had said: and there *was famine in all lands: but in all the land of Egypt there was bread. And the famine was over all the face of the earth.* And all countries came into Egypt to Joseph to buy corn, because the famine was sore in all the earth." (Gen. xli. 54-57.) But not in Egypt. That is, not in the Egypt of eternal harvest, where the corn grew seven cubits high with ears some eighty-four inches long. There is no historical sense in which such a statement could be truly interpreted. The mythos only can render it intelligibly. As may be seen in the Vignettes to the Ritual, the seven cows, called the providers of plenty, are depicted in the Aarru-paradise. This is in the lower Egypt of Amenta, and it is a land abounding with corn, the only harvest-field in all the earth of eternity. There was nought but arid desert and the wilderness of sand in the domain of Sut. The Aarru in Khebt was the harvest-field of Horus = Joseph, of the twelve who are his reapers, and the people who are his followers, amongst whom we shall at last discover the Jews as the Aaiu in Egypt.

Joseph in Egypt has been assigned the place of Horus in the Egypt of Amenta. "Joseph was thirty years old when he stood before Pharaoh, King of Egypt," and went forth as the Repa to buy up the corn against the coming famine. This is the age of Horus when he rises in Amenta as Amsu the husbandman, the master of food, or lord of the harvest, to become the ruler for Ra, the divine Pharaoh, with the flail or khu sign in his hand. Pharaoh makes Joseph ruler over all the land of Egypt, second only to himself; that is, according to Egyptian usage, Joseph becomes the Repa to the Ra.

In the Stele of Excommunication "Tum the creator god" is said to be "the duplicate of Aten." This tells us two things. First that the duality of the god, which is expressed by the names of Huhi and Iu, was also expressed by the names of Atum and Aten. Atum was god the father, and Aten the Nefer-Atum, the Repa, or royal son. Thus Iu the sif is Aten = Adon by name, and Aten is the Adon to Atum-Ra, the divine Pharaoh. Now we are told that it is, or was, a practice of the Jews to use the word Adon instead of the word Ihuh in calling on the sacred name. And Adon, we repeat, is the Hebrew equivalent of the Egyptian Aten as a title of Iu, the son of Atum-Ra, or of Atum who was "the duplicate of Aten" in the person of the father. The Aten in Egyptian is the lord, one with the Hebrew Adon, and when Joseph rode in "the second chariot" as lord over all the land of Egypt, and second only to the Ra, the Adon represented Aten the son to Ra, the father who was Atum-Ra or Atum-Huhi the eternal. Atum was adored at On or Annu as the living god who in Egyptian was p-ankhu, the living god. Now when the Egyptian titles are conferred on Joseph, and Pharaoh is said to have called him by the name of Zaphenath-Paneah, whatsoever Egyptian word may be represented by Zaphenath, it is generally agreed by Egyptologists that Paneah or Paneach is a rendering of p-ankhu, the living god, which was the especial title of Atum-Iu in the temple of On. Joseph was thirty years of age when he "went out over the land of Egypt." Horus was thirty years of age when he went forth over all the land of Egypt. Thirty years was the age of full adultship. It is the typical age of the Sheru, the Prince, the Messiah in the Egyptian, Persian, and Christian mythology. Joseph was the Adon of the Pharaoh, the Aten of Atum-Ra, and therefore he was thirty years of age when he went forth as ruler over all the land of Egypt. Joseph as the Aten was the lord over Egypt, with Atum-Ra as over-lord. The divine Ra and Horus were impersonated in the human Pharaoh and Repa: these were previously extant as Atum and Aten, Tum and Nefer-Tum, who were the divine Ra and Iusif in the pre-Osirian religion of the Egyptian Ius who became the unclean, the accursed, the lepers, the outcasts of Egypt in later monumental times. Seek for the Jews in Egypt as the Iu, or Aaiu, and they will be found there in the same character that they assign to themselves as a people suffering terribly from leprosy and other diseases said to have been the result of uncleanness in their religious rites, which are so fervidly denounced in the Old Testament. The conclusion that Joseph was the young solar divinity, Iu the Son of Atum-Ra at On, may be clinched by the story related of Potiphar's wife, which is the same that is told in various other legends of this same mythical personage. The märchen that do exist in Egyptian, as shown by the "Tale of the Two Brothers," prove themselves to be the deposit of indefinitely earlier myth, the tale in this instance being a literary version of the Sut-Horus legend, and of the two brothers, the twins of light and darkness, which is found world-wide as myth or märchen. The tale contains its own evidence of ancientness in the fact that the sun-god invoked is not Ra, but the Horus of both horizons, Har-Makhu, who preceded the earliest form of Ra. The seven Hathors, who are otherwise the seven cows of plenty, are also present with Bata, the bull of the divine company.

The history of Joseph can be partly traced to the Egyptian story of "The Two Brothers," written by the scribe Anna in the time of Seti II, nineteenth dynasty, on a papyrus now in the British Museum (*Records of the Past,* vol. ii, p. 139). In this story we find a form of the Sut-Horus myth reduced to the status of the popular märchen. Sut appears in his later character of Sut-Anup or Anup (to drop the name of Sut). Anup is the elder brother of Bata, who is Horus as the younger brother. Like Horus, he is the bull of the divine company of the gods who went down into Egypt or the dark land of Ethiopia. The double Sut and Horus imaged back to back is repeated when Anup is described as sitting on the back of Bata. "Anup his elder brother sat upon his back at dawn of day," that is, in the twilight which was represented when Sothis rose heliacally, or, as it is imaged, sat upon the back of Horus the young solar god. The dual nature of Child-Horus is repeated in Bata when he says to his consort, "I am a woman even as thou art," and declares that his male soul or his heart is in the flower of the acacia tree. This soul of Bata in the flower of the tree of life can be paralleled in the Ritual, where Horus is the golden Anbu, the flower of the hidden dwelling (ch. 71). Anup is the guide of Bata in the märchen, as of Horus in the myth. Anup is the attendant on Bata in the mountain and his mourner in death, as he is of Horus in the Ritual. Anup is the master of the fields of food, and he ordains that those who are in charge of the food shall be with the Osiris (ch. 144). Bata follows the beautiful cattle, who tell him where the greenest grasses and the richest herbage grow. These are the seven cows who are the providers of plenty, to whom Bata, like Osiris or Horus, is the fecundating bull. The seven cows likewise appear in the same story as the seven Hathors. Bata the strong one can be identified with Horus in the character of Amsu the husbandman, who is portrayed as the preparer of the soil and sower of seed. Bata does the ploughing and other labours in the fields of Aarru, and his equal was not to be found in all the land. Thus the myth of Sut-Horus the twin brothers can be traced in the ancient folk-lore of Egypt, and this can be followed into the "historic" or euhemeristic phase in the book of Genesis, where it reappears as the story of Joseph the beautiful youth and Potiphar's wife. Bata was the bull of the divine company that went down into the Egypt of Amenta. Joseph is the bull or chief one of the children of Israel who went down into Egypt. Bata is the divine husbandman and lord of the harvest. Joseph is the one to whose sheaf the other sheaves bowed down in recognition of his supremacy as lord of the harvest (Gen. xxxvii. 5-8). The seven cows or Hathors are the foretellers of fate consequent on their being the bringers of good fortune. Also the bull of the cows is the diviner of fate. Bata the bull divines and foretells the events that will occur to him. This is the character ascribed to Joseph as the diviner in the biblical version. If the parallel had been perfected, Potiphar, whose name denotes the servant of Ra in Egyptian, should have taken the *rôle* of Anup, who is the servant of Ra. In the Hebrew version we read that "Joseph was comely and well-favoured. And it came to pass after these things that his master's wife cast eyes upon Joseph, and she said, Lie with me. But he refused, and said unto his master's wife, Behold, my master knoweth not what is with me in the house, and he hath put all that he hath into my hand: there is none greater in this house than I; neither hath he kept anything from me but thee. How then can I do this great wickedness, and sin against God? And it came to pass, as she spake to Joseph day by day, that he hearkened not unto her, to lie by her, or to be with her. And it came to pass about this time that he went into the house to do his work, and there was none of the men of the house there within. And she caught him by his garment, saying, Lie with me: and he left his garment in her hand, and fled, and got him out" (Gen. xxxix. 9-12). In the Egyptian folk-tale Bata goes into the house of Anup to fetch seed, and the wife of Anup cast her eyes upon him. "And she spoke to him, saying, What strength there is in thee; indeed, I observe thy vigour every day. Her heart knew him. . . . She seized upon him, and said to him, Come, let us lie down for a little. Better for thee. . . . beautiful clothes. Then the youth became like a panther with fury on account of the shameful discourse which she had addressed to him. And she was alarmed exceedingly. He spoke to her, saying, Verily, I have looked upon thee in the light of a mother, and thy husband in that of a father to me. (*For he is older than I, as much as if he had begotten me.*) What a great abomination is this which thou hast mentioned to me. Do not repeat it again to me, and I will not speak of it to anyone. Verily, I will not let anything of it come forth from my mouth to any man" (*Records,* vol. ii. pp. 140, 141). Joseph being identified as the same character with Bata, it is Bata who will explain that character. Bata signifies the soul of the earth. In the Egyptian mythos this was the sun. "I am Bata," says the manes in the character of the solar god who is renewed and reborn daily as the soul of the earth and multiplier of the years (Rit., ch. 87). He might be reborn under the serpent type, or as the soul of Atum from the lotus, or the soul of Bata from the flower of the tree of dawn. But the myth is not merely solar. In fact, there is no bottom to the solar myth except in the lunar. Anup and Bata must be identified with Sut and Horus as the brothers in the two halves of the lunation before the tale can be correlated and correctly read.

Sut-Anup was the elder brother of the two. His consort was Nephthys, the lady of darkness, who is charged with soliciting the young lord of light. There was some scandal respecting her and Osiris. The typical wanton who seduces or tries to seduce the youthful hero is the lady of the moon, who overcomes or who assails the lord of light. The character is determined in relation to Anup = Sut, the elder of the twin brothers in the mythos which passed into the eschatology and finally survived in the märchen of the two brothers. The story was represented three times over: (1) as mythical, (2) as eschatological, and (3) as a folk-tale, before it was narrated of Joseph in Egypt as Hebrew history or biblical biography. The origin of the mythos rests with the darkly beautiful Nephthys, consort of Sut (or Anup), the power of darkness in the nether-earth. That she had a character somewhat aphrodisiacal assigned to her, which became the subject of the legend, may be gathered from her being a divinity of the Egyptian town Tsebets, called Aphroditopolis by the Greeks. But she has been degraded as a wicked wanton in later representations of the dark lady who was originally the lady of darkness, at first in complexion, afterwards in character. The Semites began it with their scandal-mongering concerning Ishtar (or Shetar, the bride in Egyptian), because she had been the pre-monogamous great mother whose child and spouse were one. The Greeks followed them either directly or indirectly. Plutarch repeats a tale in which it is charged against Nephthys that either she seduced Osiris or he succumbed to her wiles. It is represented in the romance that after Nephthys had become the wife of Anup she fell in love illicitly with Horus, and besought him to stay with her when he came to plough and sow the seed-fields of Amenta. It is as the sower of seed that Bata goes to the house where Anup's wife is sitting at her toilet. He says, "Arise and give me seed, that I may go back to the field." Nephthys is literally the house of seed personified. She carries both the house and the seed-bowl on her head, and her name of Nebthi signifies the seed-house or granary of the earth. The story of Joseph and Potiphar's wife contains a mutilated fragment of this ancient Egyptian märchen reduced from the mythos into a romance. In this Potiphar is Anup, the wife is Nephthys, and Joseph is Bata or Horus, who is called the bull. Bata was the bull, and Joseph is also the bull, in Israel; hence the totem of the tribe of Ephraim was the bull. Bata is the bull of the seven cows which come to him as the seven Hathors, and, to make use of the Egyptian figure, Joseph, likewise is the bull of the seven cows that were seen in Pharaoh's dream. He was also the bull as the adult of thirty years. In the Egyptian story Bata becomes a bull. "And Bata said to his elder brother, Behold, I am about to become a bull with all the sacred marks, but with an unknown history. The bull arrived, and his majesty the Pharaoh inspected him and rejoiced exceedingly, and celebrated a festival above all description; a mighty marvel and rejoicings for it were made throughout all the land. To the bull there were given many attendants and many offerings, and the king loved him exceedingly above all men in the whole land. And when the days were multiplied after this his majesty was wearing the collar of lapis lazuli with a wreath of all kinds of flowers on his neck. He was in his brazen chariot, and he went forth from the royal palace. Bata was brought before the king, and rejoicings were made throughout the whole land. They sat down to make a holiday (and *they gave him his name*); and his majesty at once loved him exceedingly, and raised him to the dignity of Prince of Æthiopia. But when the days had multiplied after this, his majesty made him hereditary prince of the whole land. And the sun-god Horus of both horizons said to Khnum, O, make a wife for Bata, that he may not remain alone. And Khnum made him a companion, who as she sat was more beautiful in her limbs than any woman in the whole earth; the whole godhead was in her." And now a tale is told of this consort of Bata which tends to identify her with Neitochris, that is primarily with the goddess Neith, and thence with Asenath the wife of Joseph. These quotations from the Egyptian tale contain the gist of the following statement. "And Pharaoh said unto Joseph .... Thou shalt be over my house, and according to thy word shall all my people be ruled; only in the throne will I be greater than thou. And Pharaoh said unto Joseph, See, I have set thee over all the land of Egypt. And Pharaoh took off his signet-ring from his hand and put it upon Joseph's hand, and arrayed him in vestures of fine linen and put a gold chain about his neck; and he made him to ride in the second chariot which he had: and they cried before him *Abrech:* and he set him over all the land of Egypt. And Pharaoh said unto Joseph, I am Pharaoh, and without thee shall no man lift up his hand or his foot in all the land of Egypt. And Pharaoh called Joseph's name Zaphenath-Paneah (צפנת־פענה), and he gave him to wife Asenath the daughter of Potiphera. And Joseph went out over the land of Egypt. And Joseph was thirty years old when he stood before Pharaoh the King of Egypt" (Gen. xli. 40, 46). The passage in which Joseph makes himself known to his brethren should be compared with the scene in which the lost Bata reveals himself and says, "Look upon me; I am indeed alive. Look upon me, for I am really alive. I am a bull!" and Bata "reigned for thirty years as king over Egypt." "And Joseph said unto his brethren, I am Joseph; doth my father yet live? And he said, I am Joseph your brother, whom ye sold into the land of Egypt" (Gen. xlv. 3, 4). Joseph also had become a bull or typical adult like Horus the man or god of thirty years. The fact is admitted when it is said that "Joseph was thirty years old when he stood before Pharaoh, King of Egypt." In the solar symbolism the sun as a calf in the winter solstice became a bull in the vernal equinox, where he found his heart, his soul, his force, sometimes imaged as phallic, upon the summit of the tree of dawn. In the human sphere the boy became a bull when he was Khemt as a man of thirty years. In Amenta, Amsu is the bull of his mother, "Ka-mutf," as the anointed Horus, thirty years of age. Joseph, raised to the Repa-ship, also became a bull—that is, a typical adult of thirty years. Asenath we take to be a form of the great Neith, who was represented at On (Annu) by Iusāas the mother of the young bull Aiu (or Iu = Io), who as her sif or son was Iusa. Professor Sayce in his "History of Joseph" says, with an unabashed effrontery, *"What is important"* (in this episode) *"is that the incident which played so large a part in Joseph's life should have been preserved in Egyptian tradition! It became part of the literary inheritance of the Egyptians!*" (p. 36). Thus suggesting that the Egyptians derived their mythology and folk-tales from the Hebrew Pentateuch.

But to resume: the dramatis personæ in the Hebrew books of wisdom are chiefly the father and the son. The father is Ihuh, the self-existent and eternal god, and Iu (or Iusa) is the messianic son as manifestor in the cycles of all time. It is the father that is speaking of one of these periods, possibly a sothiac cycle, who says to Esdras, "The time shall come." "My son Jesus shall be revealed with those that be with him, and they that remain shall rejoice within 400 years." This was long thought to have been a prophecy of a Christ that was to come as an historical personage. But this son of god, whether named Iu, Iao, Iusa, Jesus, or Joseph, could no more become historical than god the father, both being one. And if this divine son could ever have become historical, he would have been Jesus the son of Atum-Ra at On, or, still earlier, Jesus the son of Ptah at Memphis. The "Wisdom of Jesus" in the Apocrypha is, according to the Prologue, the wisdom of two different Jesuses, the one being grandfather of the other. This can be explained by the Kamite mythology and the two representatives of that name in the two divine dynasties of Ptah and Atum-Ra. As Wilkinson remarked, "The Egyptians acknowledged two of this name (Jesus), the first the grandfather of the other, according to the Greeks, and the reputed inventor of medicine, who received peculiar honours on a certain mountain on the Libyan side of the Nile, near the City of Crocodiles, where he was reported to have been buried" (*The Ancient Egyptians,* vol. iii, p. 205). There are not only two with the name of Jesus who represent the sayer for the father god; Solomon is likewise a form of the wise youth who uttered the wisdom in the sayings or logia kuriaka. We are told in the prologue that "this Jesus did imitate Solomon." But Iu-em-hetep, the Egyptian Jesus, *as the prince of peace,* was Solomon by name. Thus the Jesus and Solomon of the Apocrypha, to whom the Wisdom of Jesus and the Wisdom of Solomon are ascribed, were two forms of the Word or Sayer, who was Iu the son (su) of Ptah, and Iu-em-hetep, the prince of peace, otherwise known to the Hebrews by name as Jesus and Solomon.

The most ancient wisdom was oral. It was conveyed by word of mouth, from mouth to ear, as in the mysteries. This consisted of the magical sayings or the great words of power. Following the oral wisdom, the earliest known records of written wisdom were collections of the sayings, which were continually enlarged, as by the Egyptian Jesus, or "the two of this name." The Osirian Book of the Dead is largely a collection of sayings which were given by Ra the father in heaven to Horus the son, for him to utter as teacher of the living on earth and preacher to the manes in Amenta. The wisdom of Ptah the father was uttered by the son, who is the Word in person. The names for the son may be various in the several religious cults, but the type was one, no matter what the name. The sayings collected in some of the Hebrew books of wisdom, such as the book of Proverbs, are spoken as from the father to his son. "My son, attend to my words; incline thine ear unto my sayings" (Prov. iv. 20). "Hear me,

O my son," is the formula in the book of Ecclesiasticus. It has now to be suggested that the mythical or divine originals of this father and son in the books of wisdom were the wise god Ptah and the youthful sage Iu, the sayer or logos, who was his manifesting word as the son. Egyptian literature as such has been almost entirely lost, but amongst the survivals lives the oldest book in the world. This is a book of wisdom, in the form of sayings, maxims, precepts, and other brief sentences, called the Proverbs of Ptah-Hetep, which was written in the reign of Tet-Ka-Ra or Assa, a Pharaoh of the fifth dynasty, who lived 5,500 years ago. The author's name denotes that he was the worshipper of Ptah, and his collection contains the ancient wisdom of Ptah, although it is not directly ascribed to the god or to his son, the sayer, Iu-em-hetep. In this volume Ptah-hetep collects the good sayings, precepts, and proverbs of the ancient wisdom; the words of those who have heard the counsels of former days and the counsels heard of the gods. He addresses the god Ptah for authority to declare these words of wisdom, speaking as from a father to his son; and in reply "the majesty of this god says, Instruct him in the sayings of former days" (*Records of the Past*, 2nd Series, vol. iii, p. 17). Ptah-hetep, then, the author who wrote a book with his own name to it 5,500 years since, assumes the position of the wise god Ptah addressing his son Iu-em-hetep, to whom the wisdom was communicated which was uttered in "the wise sayings, dark sentences, and parables," and collected in such books as the Sayings of Jesus, the Wisdom of Jesus, the Wisdom of Ecclesiastes, the Wisdom of Solomon, the Psalms, and the Book of the Dead. We quote a few of the sayings from Ptah-hetep, which give us a glimpse of the intellectual height attained by the Egyptians 5,500 years ago. "*No artist is endowed with the perfections to which he should aspire.*" "*He who perverts the truthfulness of his way, in order to repeat only what produces pleasure in the words of every man, great or small, is a detestable person.*" "*If thou art wise, look after thy house. Love thy wife without alloy. Fill her belly, clothe her back, anoint her, and fulfil her desires as long as she lives. It is a kindness which does honour to its possessor.*" "*If thou art powerful, command only to direct.*" "*To be absolute is to run into evil.*" "*The gentle man penetrates all obstacles.*" "*Teach the man of great position that one may even do him honour.*" "*If thou hast become great who once was small, and rich after having been poor, grow not hard of heart because of thy prosperity. Thou hast only become the steward of the good things of God.*"

Ptah was the father of Atum-Ra, therefore an earlier god. Memphis was an older foundation than On, the northern Annu. And the wisdom of Ptah-Iu was indefinitely older than the writings of the Aiu or Jews which had been preserved in the library at On and brought forth thence by Osarsiph as the basis of the Pentateuch. But the sayings of Jesus or logia of the Lord did not come to an end with the collection called the Wisdom of Jesus, that was translated "when Euergetes was king," and ascribed to two of the name of Jesus, with Sirach interposed between. The first gospel of the Christians began with a collection of the Sayings of Jesus, fatuously supposed to have been an historic teacher of that name. Every sect had its collection of the sayings that were uttered as the word of God by the Word in person, who was Horus in the Osirian religion, or Iu, the Egyptian Jesus, to whom the books of wisdom were attributed thrice over, once as the son of Ptah, once as the son of Atum-Ra, and once as the son of Ieou in the Pistis Sophia. The veil is being torn away from the eyes of those who were unable or unwilling to see through it, and dead Egypt speaks once more with a living tongue. Explorers are just beginning to find some missing links betwixt the Ritual and those "gospels" that were canonized at last which were needed to complete the argument concerning the Egyptian origin of the Christian legend herein presented, and to demonstrate beyond doubt that the historic rendering of the mythos does but contain an exoteric version of the esoteric wisdom. Only the other day a loose leaf was discovered in the rubbish-heaps of Oxyrhynchus which had belonged to some unknown collection of the sayings or logia of "the Lord," who was not Jesus, a Jew in Palestine, but Jesus or Iu-em-hetep, a god of the Jews in Egypt (*Sayings of our Lord*, Grenfell and Hunt). It was at Memphis, we suggest, the book of wisdom, known to later times as Jewish, originated as the wisdom of Ptah, whose manifestor was Iu the coming son, who was his logos, his word, the teacher of his wisdom and sayer of his sayings. Atum-Ra was born son of Ptah as Iu-em-hetep in his primary form. When raised to the dignity of Ra, Iu-em-hetep, the typical bringer of peace and all good things, was continued as his son. Both Ptah and Atum had the title of Huhi the eternal, and each of them was also a figure of the one supreme god who was both father and son in one person. In the gnostic representation the propator was known to Monogenes alone, who sprang from him. It was also taught by the Egyptian Valentinus that the father produced in his own image without conjunction with the female (Irenæus, Against Heresies, B. I, ch. ii, 1, 4, Ante-Nicene Library). The following brief list will serve to give an *aperçu* of this divine duality in various phases. Huhi the eternal god the father, Iu the ever-coming son; Atum-Ra as father, Nefer-Atum as the son; Osiris the father, Horus the son; Ihuh the eternal father, Iah the messiah or ever-coming son; Jacob-El the father, Joseph-El the son; David the father, Solomon the son; Ihuh the father, Jesus the son (Christian); Ieou the father, Iao the son (Pistis Sophia); Jehovah as the father, Jesus as the son. These are all twofold types of the same great one god in the religion that was established, first at Memphis, with Ptah as Huhi the eternal, the self-existent, lord of everlastingness, "he who is," or the "I am," and Iu-em-hetep as his su, sif, or son, continued in the cult of Atum-Ra at On, and brought forth from Egypt as the religion of the Ius or Jews, who were the worshippers of Huhi the eternal and of Iu the ever-coming messianic son, which dual type was also represented by the old lion and the young one, by the bull and the bullock, and by the ass and the foal of an ass. Moreover, it is recorded in the Hebrew legend that the one god of Israel was made known to Moses under two entirely different names. In two passages the name given is "יה" (Ex. xv. 2 and xvii. 16). Moses says, "Iah is my strength and son." "This is my God and I will praise him." The other name is יהוה, rendered Jehovah. Under both names it is the one lord. Under both names the god is celebrated in the Psalms. Then the name of Iah is dropped altogether, except by Isaiah, who combines the two names under the one title of יהוה־יה, rendered "Jehovah-Jah," or the Lord Jehovah (Is. xii. 2). These two names, we repeat, represent the Egyptian names of Iu = Iah for god the ever-coming son, and Huhi = Ihuh the eternal father, who was the one god as Atum-Ra. Thus Isaiah's *Iah-Jehovah* combines the names of both the father and the son in the name of Israel's one god. And now, as the two characters of Huhi (Ihuh) and Iu (Iah) met in one person and the two names were combined in Iah-Ihuh, it appears probable that both the names were blended in one word to form the divine name of Ihuh (or יהוה) in Hebrew, by compounding those of Iu and Huh, thus, Iu-Huh, as a title of the eternal one. Iu would then be represented by the Ï or *yod* alone, and the final form would be Ihuh, which, with the introduction of the Hebrew letter *vav,* was extended into Javeh and Jehovah for Jewish and Christian use.

An insuperable difficulty was bequeathed to the later monotheists of Israel in the mystery of a biune being consisting of a father and son who were but one in person. This needed a knowledge of the ancient wisdom to explicate the doctrine. How could the one god be two, or the twain one, to the plain and unsophisticated man? There was no abstract conception of any one god in two persons, or three, or 153 (Rit., ch. 141) as a spiritual entity. The origins are rooted in the phenomena of external nature, and have to be interpreted by means of sign-language and the mythical mode of representation. The Jews had got the father and son, and finally knew not what to do with both. The son was a perpetual difficulty in their writings, which repeated fragments of Egyptian mythos in the old dark sayings without the oral wisdom of the Gnostics, and left a stumbling-block that has remained to trip up all good, dunder-headed Christians. Still the son is present, as the anointed Son of God, the Christ that was, who has been all along mistaken for the Christ that was to be and is not yet, although the reign of the son as Ichthus in Pisces is nearly ended now, and the *Pisciculi* are gasping for breath like little fishes out of water. Jewish theologians did their utmost to suppress the sonship of the godhead, as well as to get rid of the motherhood. This was preparatory to the rejection of the sonship altogether when presented in the scheme of "historic" Christianity. They pursued their messianic phantom to the verge of the quagmire, but drew back in time to escape. They left it for the Christians to take the final fatal plunge into the bog in which they have wallowed, always sinking, ever since; and if the Jews did but know it, the writings called Jewish have wrought an appalling avengement on their ignorant persecutors, who are still proving themselves to be Christians, as in Russia, by ignominiously mutilating and pitilessly massacring the Jews. Their god, like the Mohammedan deity, was to be a father who never had a son. To put it in Egyptian terms, they held to their one god Ihuh the eternal, as the fixed and everlasting fact, and dropped the Iu or ever-becoming son, together with the *modus operandi* of becoming, whether astronomical or eschatological, and so they parted company with the followers of Ptah-Iu and of Atum-Iu. Or rather the son was turned into the subject of prophecy, whose ultimate coming was supposed to be fulfilled in the cult of Christianity. Thus the Jews are worshippers of the father, whereas the Christians substituted the son. These are two branches of the original religion in which the one god connoted the father and the son, who was Huhi or Ihuh the eternal, with Iu as the ever-coming cyclical manifestor for the father in the sphere of time.

Celsus casts it up against Moses, as leader of the Israelites, that he deceived them with his magical tricks, and misled them into the belief that there was but one god (Origen, Contra Celsum, ch. 23). For good or evil, however, the one god was established on the ground herein set forth, and this as יהוה the Hebrew god, the eternal, self-existent, supreme one, whose other name is יה, Iah, Iao, or Iu. These are the two lords who constitute the one god in the Hebrew version of the Egyptian doctrine. In destroying the cities of the plain it is said, "The Lord rained upon Sodom and upon Gomorrah brimstone and fire from the Lord out of heaven" (Gen. xix. 24, 25), which is identical with Horus the lord as Har-Tema, the son who avenges his father Osiris in the great judgment and destruction of the condemned, who are overwhelmed in the cities of the *plain* because the occurrence is on the level at the place of equilibrium in the equinox of which there was a yearly representation in the mysteries of Amenta. There may be an attempt at times to conceal the dual personality in the phraseology, as when the Psalmist says, "God standeth in the congregation of gods," "He judgeth among the gods" (Ps. lxxxii. 1). But the writer lets in a flood of polytheism at the same time that he acknowledges the duality of Ihuh. In one psalm the anointed son is *begotten* (Ps. ii.); in another he is *appointed* (Ps. lxxxix.) as the holy one of Israel. In the latter instance it is David who is made the anointed son. Isaiah proclaims the god of Israel to be "the everlasting father" or father of eternity at the same time that he is the "prince of peace" who was the ever-coming son as Horus or Iu-em-hetep, the prince of eternity in the astronomical mythos of Egypt and the prince of peace in the eschatology. "For unto us a child is born, unto us a son is given; and the government shall be upon his shoulder, and his name shall be called פלא" (rendered wonderful), "councillor, mighty God, the father of eternity, prince of peace" (Is. ix. 6, 7). This song, uplifted so majestically by the music of Handel, might have been sung at On, or Memphis, many thousand years ago, as regards the subject-matter, which is purely Egyptian. Atum was the father of eternity, and Iu-em-hetep, the su or son, was the prince of peace, and these two were one. Probably the Hebrew word פלא (pehla) represents the Egyptian pera or pela = to appear, show a great sight, in relation to the messianic manifestor, who was the messu or child, the prince of peace, and who "bore the government upon his shoulder" in a symbolical way peculiarly Egyptian. Atum, in his dual character of father and son, is he who says, "I am he that closeth and he that openeth, and I am but one" (Rit., ch. 17).

This doctrine of divine duality was based upon the Egyptian Pharaoh as the father and the repa or heir-apparent as the son—the ever-coming king in the person of the prince who was always born to be a king. The father was king of Egypt, the son was the prince of

Ethiopia, which was the birthplace of an earlier time and remained the typical birthplace of the young prince of eternity for all time. The messu was the root of the Messiah by nature and by name. The prince of Ethiopia is the messu whence the Messiah is Iu the son, messu or messu-iahu—that is, Iahu as the son or repa. In the mythical representation Horus was reborn each year as the messu, and the rebirth was celebrated by the festival called the Messiu. The repa symbolized the succession of Ra, or the sun, to himself, in a mode of showing that the god or the king never died, but continued for ever by transformation of the father into the son. The transformation was also seen in the old moon changing into the new, and the sun that set symbolically rendered as the old beetle that went underground to hatch its seed and die, to issue forth again renewed in its young. The Pharaoh transformed into his own son and manifestor as the repa, Atum into Iu-em-hetep, Osiris into Horus, Jacob into Joseph, and Ihuh into the Messiah. This transformation occurred in natural phenomena periodically, therefore at the end of some particular cycle of time which was always indefinite for those who knew not the method of measurement astronomically.

The Lord and his anointed as father and son had been already represented at Memphis by Ptah and Iu-em-hetep, at On by Atum and Nefer-Atum, at Abydos by Osiris and Horus of the resurrection. The lord's anointed was the second Horus, Horus the adult, Horus who rose again in spirit after death to manifest the glory of the father with the holy oil upon his shining face which made him the anointed. The Lord's anointed, called the Messiah in Hebrew, the Kristos in Greek, and Chrestus in Latin, is the Messu in Egyptian. Messu signifies the son, the child, or heir-apparent, the prince of Ethiopia. As human he was the repa, son of the Pharaoh. As divine he is the son of god. Messu is also an Egyptian word signifying the anointed and to be anointed. The Lord and his anointed are frequently mentioned in the Hebrew writings. These are the father and son, equivalent to Osiris and Horus his son; also to Ptah and Iu the prince of peace. "The Lord shalt exalt the horn of his anointed" (I Samuel ii. 10). "Here I am: witness against me before the Lord and before his anointed" (I Samuel xii. 3). "The kings of the earth set themselves, and the rulers take counsel together, against the Lord and against his anointed" (I Ps. ii. 2). "The Lord showeth loving-kindness to his anointed" (Ps. xviii. 50). "The Lord saveth his anointed; he will answer him from his holy heaven" (Ps. xx. 6). "He is a stronghold of salvation to his anointed" (Ps. xxviii. 8). "Behold our shield, O God, and look upon the face of thine anointed" (Ps. lxxxiv. 9). "Thine enemies have reproached the footsteps of thine anointed" (Ps. lxxxix. 51), who was the witness and the messenger that showed the way of the Lord in the heavens, in the earth, in the waters and in the nethermost depths of Sheol. The "anointed of the Lord" was the very breath of their nostrils to them who had said, "Under his shadow we shall live among nations" (Lam. iv. 20). "The Lord goes forth for the victory with his anointed" (Hab. iii. 13). This duality of Ihuh and the Messiah or reborn son was the source of a great dilemma to the Jews, and the cause of a conflict betwixt their monotheism and the Messiahship. They knew of a doctrine concerning the Messiah, but were afraid of the astronomical fulfilment being mistaken for the humanly historical, and thus insisted all the more upon the divine unity in its simplicity. In the Ritual, Horus is described as the son who converses with the father. He is thus addressed, "O son who conversest with thy father!" (ch. 32). This character is ascribed to David as the divine son in the Psalms, he who declares, "The Lord said unto me, Thou art my son, this day have I begotten thee" (Ps. ii. 7). In the same psalm the Lord is said to have begotten his anointed son and set him as the king upon his holy hill in Zion. This is the son as the divine avenger of whom it is said, "Kiss the son, lest he be angry and ye perish by the way, for his wrath will soon be kindled." The father says to his son, "Ask of me, and I will give thee the nations for thine inheritance, and the uttermost parts of the earth for thy possession. Thou shalt break them with a rod of iron; thou shalt dash them in pieces like a potter's vessel" (Ps. ii. 7, 8, 9). In the Ritual (chs. 17 and 175), this avenger is the son who "cometh red with wrath as the heir of Osiris seated upon the throne of the dweller in the lake of twofold fire." This is Horus who says to his father after the periodic battle with the evil powers, "I, thy son Horus, come to thee." "I have avenged thee. I have overthrown thy foes. I have established all those who were of thy substance upon the earth for ever." That is when he returns to the father in heaven with his work accomplished on the earth and in Amenta. In the time of Isaiah and of the Hebrew psalmist the type of the son, the chosen one, the servant who became the beloved of the Lord, was extant as a man, not merely as the lamb or the branch. It is the same type in the gospels, which were written with reference all through to the figure that was pre-extant (Ps. ii. 7, 12; Is. xlii. 1; Matt. chap. iii. 1 to 3). Moreover, the same things were said of that type in the earlier as in the later time. He was equally the crucified or suffering Messiah; gall was given to him for meat, and vinegar for drink (Ps. lxix. 21). He was bound in his hands and feet; his garments were parted amongst his spoilers, who cast lots for his vesture (Ps. xxii. 18). All that was fabled to have been historically acted at a later period had been already fulfilled with non-historical significance. It is the same also with the character of John the Baptist as with Jesus in the gospels. In defiance of the fact that the event is contemporary with or had occurred previously in the prophetic writings, the Christian world supposes that the so-called prophecies simply refer to a Messiah who is to come in a "personal and historical character." Thus it is assumed that the "prophecy of Isaiah, "The voice of one that crieth, Prepare ye in the wilderness the way of the Lord! Make straight in the desert a highway for our God. Every valley shall be exalted and every mountain and hill shall be made low, when the uneven shall be made level, and the rough places a plain, and the glory of the Lord shall be revealed" (Is. xl. 3-5; Matt. iii. 3); it is assumed that this was historically fulfilled when the passage is quoted in the gospel according to Matthew and applied to John the Baptist, whereas the alleged history in the New Testament is based upon the supposed fulfilment of this prophecy in the Old. Yet it is only a fragment repeated from the Egyptian mythos, in which Anup was the crier in the wilderness and the guide in the ways of darkness through which the road was made from equinox to equinox in the desert of the under-world. When reduced to their proper level, the elevation of the valley and the lowering of the mountain are but another mode of describing the equinoxes. Anup was the precursor, the forerunner, the prophet of Horus the Lord who came in glory, and the preparer of his way. As such he appears in the opening chapter of the Ritual, where we read, "O openers of roads! O guides of paths to the soul made in the abode of Osiris (the house of heaven with thirty-six gates), open ye the roads! Level ye the paths of the Osiris." That is, bring the lofty low in process of levelling or making the road equal in the mount of the equinox at the coming of Horus the lord. Horus as lord of the two horizons was Har-Makhu, lord of the equinoctial level. At the time of the Easter equinox the path was made level, the valley exalted, and the mountain brought low at the coming of Har-Makhu who revealed the glory of the lord.

If the Jews had only held on to the sonship of Iu, the su or sif, they might have spoiled the market for the spurious wares of the "historic" Saviour, and saved the world from wars innumerable, and from countless broken hearts and immeasurable mental misery. But they let go the sonship of Hy with the growth of their monolatry. They could not substitute the "historic" sonship; they had lost touch with Egypt, and the wisdom that might have set them right was no longer available against the Christian misconstruction. They failed to fight the battle of the gnostics, and retired from the conflict dour and dumb; strong and firm enough to suffer the blind and brutal *Juden-Hetze* of all these centuries, but powerless to bring forward their natural allies the Egyptian reserves, and helpless to conclude a treaty or enforce a truce. The Jews have suffered and been damned along the line of 1,800 years on account of the false belief which they unwittingly helped to foster; and if they should still suffer slinkingly for gross gains instead of turning round and rending their persecutors and helping us to win the battle for universal freedom, when once the truth is made known to them, they will, if such a fate were possible, be deserving of eternal damnation in the Christian hell. The rootage of matters like these lies out of sight, and is not to be bottomed in the Hebrew scriptures, but such passages as those quoted show the existence of a god the father and a god the son. Not a son who is to be begotten at some future period by miraculous interposition of divine power playing pranks with human nature in a female form. The anointed son was then begotten and already extant. It was he who suffered like Horus in one character, and who came like Horus in the other as the arm-lifter of the lord, the avenger red with wrath, to rule with a rod of iron, not on this earth but in the earth of eternity, the Sheol of the Psalms. And on account of this language in the Cursing Psalms, as they have been called, the militant Christians have claimed a divine sanction for all their brutality in going forth with fire and sword to blast the face of this fair earth and slay the utterly astonished natives of other lands who would not or could not accept a doctrine so damnable as a revelation emanating from the most high God. The Psalmist celebrates this son of God, his begettal, his advent, but offers no real clue to the nature of the sonship; and the Christians, knowing nothing of the astronomical mythology or of the Egyptian eschatology, could only conclude that it must be historical. No "Jewish monotheist" could explicate the duality of the deity. The Psalmist celebrates the coming of the Lord, but who the Lord is or what the advent may be it is impossible to tell when the mythical background has been left out of view by the adapters of the ancient matter. As Egyptian, Iu the son is the ever-coming one as the means by which the father of eternity manifests in time and other natural phenomena. As Egyptian, the divine duad of father and son had been Ptah and Iu, or Atum and Iu, or Osiris and Horus, according to the cult through pre-Hebraic and pre-Christian ages. In Israel it might be Jacob-El the father, with Joseph-El as the beloved son; or Abraham with Isaac, the sacrificial son; or Ihuh and David, the divinely-begotten son; or David and Solomon, the wise youth and prince of peace.

It has now to be shown that these two represent the father and his beloved son who are Ihuh and David in the book of Psalms. These are the two lords as the Lord and the Lord's anointed in Psalm cx.: "The Lord said unto my Lord, sit thou at my right hand until I make thine enemies thy footstool. The Lord shall stretch forth the rod of thy strength out of Zion. In the beauty of holiness from the womb of the morning thou hast the dew of thy youth. Thou art a priest for ever after the order of Melchizedek" (Ps. cx. 4). That is the Lord who is the "coming son" in all the so-called prophecies; and David is the son who thus converses with the father as Horus did with Ra, or as Jesus is represented in converse with Jehovah. As a divine personage David is a form of the beloved son; hence perhaps the origin of his name. David, Daoud, or Dood means the beloved; and as a mythical character the beloved one, the Lord's anointed, the Messiah, is the son of Ihuh, not the son of Jesse, *who is not mentioned in the Psalms.* This is the typical character with which we are now concerned, the original in the mythos who afterwards became a subject for the popular märchen. The inscription on the Moabite Stone shows that the Israelites of the northern kingdom worshipped a deity named Dodo or Dod (= David) by the side of Ihuh, "or rather they adored the supreme god under the name of Dodo as well as under that of Ihuh" (Sayce, *Hib. Lectures,* pp. 56, 57). Mesha, the Moabite king, announces that he has carried away the altars of Dodo and "dragged them before Chemosh," Dodo and Ihuh being David and Ihuh as two divinities, or the one god in the dual character of father and son. And if, like Jacob-El, Joseph-El, and Israel, David was a god, it follows that the son assigned to him as Solomon was so likewise. Only a divinity could be the prince of peace. Solomon was also a form of the divine son called the beloved. Hence the prophet Nathan gives him the name of Jedidiah, the "beloved of the Lord" (II. Sam. xii. 24, 25). And the beloved son was the messianic or anointed son.

In addition to the divine duality of father and son which was imaged in Ptah and Kheper, Atum and Iu, Osiris and Horus, Ihuh, and Iah, and the Egypto-gnostic Ieou and Iao, there was a twofold nature manifested in the sonship human and divine. This has been one of the most profound of the ancient and most perplexing of

The Egyptian Wisdom in other Jewish Writings 525

modern mysteries. It is to the Egyptian wisdom we must turn if we would trace the origin of this messianic mystery to the root in nature. But there is no beginning with the solar mythos. As it is said of Jesus, there are three which bear witness that the Messiah came in the water, in the blood, and in the spirit (I John v. 6, 7). As Egyptian, the first was Horus who came by water in the inundation, the second was Horus who came in the blood of Isis, the third is Horus of the resurrection, who came again in the spirit; and, as Horus in these characters, "the three agree in one." The Book of the Dead describes the source and origin of life as water and the water-plants. This was religiously commemorated as a mystery of Amenta. The water-spring was imaged in the tuat of the nether-world, "which nobody can fathom," and the offerings of which are "edible plants" (Rit., ch. 172), the water-plant being a form of primeval food. Thus Horus on his papyrus springing from the water represents the soul of life that came by water in or as primeval food. Hence he was depicted as the shoot. He would now be called the spirit of vegetation, born of water. Horus is also imaged as the child that issues from the plant or from the mother earth. The child = the shoot was typical of an ever-renewing and eternal youth; hence Horus the eternal child. The Egyptian "eternal" was *œonian* and *ever-coming,* whether figured by the shoot or as the child. Horus came by water annually, and brought abundant food. There was famine when the water failed, and therefore Horus as the spirit of vegetation was a kind of saviour to the world. He came from Ethiopia as the messu. The messu in Egyptian is the child, and Horus was the messu of the inundation, the water-born upon his papyrus, and an image of the source and sustenance of life born of a mother who was ever-virgin but non-human. Such is the root origin of the messianic mystery, and also of the mythical virgin and her ever-coming child. But the ever-coming child not only came by water. He also came by blood as Horus who was incarnated in the blood of Isis. Thus Horus of the incarnation was the child that came by blood and was made flesh by her who doctrinally was the ever-virgin mother. This is the elder Horus, the eternal child of her who was known to the gnostics as the eternal virgin. This duality in the sonship of Horus has its origin in his twofold advent and his twofold character, which implied a twofold motherhood. In the first he was the child of the virgin mother as the soul of the mother only. In the second he was Horus in spirit, the beloved only-begotten son of the father in heaven, who was Ra the Holy Spirit. Horus in two of his characters is palpably depicted in the Hebrew scriptures. In the first he is Horus, who in the Ritual (ch. 115) is called the "Afflicted One." This was the Horus of the incarnation, the god made flesh in the imperfect human form, the type of voluntary sacrifice, the image of suffering; being an innocent little child, maimed in the lower members, marred in his visage, lame and blind and dumb, and altogether imperfect. No man upon the cross or in the Tat-tree could ever make appeal to equal this, the most pathetic picture in the world. And Horus, "lord of resurrections" from the house of darkness (Rit., ch. 64), who as the first "of them that slept" woke up in death as the "soul most mighty" and burst the mummy-bandages and rent the tomb asunder and arose as Horus divinized, the victor over death and hell and all the powers of evil, is the most triumphant figure in the world.

A piteous portrait of the first Horus, the afflicted sufferer, is depicted by Isaiah. "Behold, my servant shall deal wisely; he shall be exalted and lifted up, and shall be very high. Like as many were astonished at thee (his visage was so marred more than any man, and his form more than the sons of men)." "Who hath believed our report? and to whom hath the arm of the Lord been revealed? For he grew up before him as a tender plant, and as a root out of a dry ground; he hath no form nor comeliness; and when we see him, there is no beauty that we should desire him. He was despised and rejected of men; a man of sorrows and acquainted with grief; and as one from whom men hide their face he was despised, and we esteemed him not. Surely he hath borne our griefs and carried our sorrows, yet we did esteem him stricken, smitten of God, and afflicted. But *he was wounded for our transgressions, he was bruised for our iniquities; the chastisement of our peace was upon him; and with his stripes we are healed.* He was oppressed, yet he humbled himself and opened not his mouth; as a lamb that is led to the slaughter, and as a sheep that before her shearers is dumb; yea, he opened not his mouth. And they made his grave with the wicked and with the rich in his deaths. Thou shalt make his soul *an offering for sin*" (ch. 53). The character here portrayed for the Messiah is that of the Messu-Horus in every feature, except that he was not "wounded for our transgressions" nor "bruised for our iniquities." The Egyptians were indefinitely older than the Semites, but had never heard of the world being lost by Adam's fall, or its need of an historic saviour who should take the place and act the part of the Jewish scapegoat. The later doctrine of vicarious atonement has been added. That is Semitic, not Egyptian. Osiris of the mysteries was dramatically represented as a victim, but not as a vicarious sacrifice on account of human "transgressions" or "iniquities." Osiris, the good being, gave his life that men and animals might live, which was in providing the elements of water and food. This was commemorated in the sacramental meal, at which his body was eaten as the bread of life and his blood was drunk in the red wine or beer. The doctrine itself is indefinitely older. The Great Mother was imaged earlier still as the giver of life and sustenance in or as the tree by Hathor, who was imaged in the sycamore-fig as the tree of life, which was her body; and by the Cyprian Venus, who was apparently bound upon the tree. In neither case is there any doctrine of the scapegoat, neither as animal, human being, or divine. Horus is said to be the altar and the offering in one, and a form of the altar is the tat. The tat-cross was the tree, whether of Hathor or Horus, of Osiris or Ptah. But there was no sufferer on it or in it who bore the sins of the world. That is a doctrine of barbarous, non-Egyptian ignorance, only fit for cowards, slaves, and criminals. The only substitution in the Osirian religion is when Horus becomes the voluntary substitute for the suffering god the father as a type of divine sonship and an example for all men to follow in the war of good against evil. But there is no scapegoat and no innocent victim of divine wrath, no expiatory sacrifice in the Egyptian eschatology. That was a perversion of the Egyptian doctrine. There is a sacrificial victim as Child-Horus, but it was a voluntary sacrifice.

He comes to earth and takes upon himself the burden of mortality, and is conscious that he has to suffer and die in order that he may demonstrate the resurrection in spirit to the manes in Amenta and to men on earth. He comes as the calf of the sacrificial herd, and in a body that will be eaten at the sacramental meal (Rit., ch. 105). "In his deaths," which are periodic, he comes to an end on behalf of the father in heaven, at whose table he will ultimately rest (Rit., ch. 70). The elder Horus in the Osirian cult is that child of the virgin mother who in a second phase and at the second advent is the father's own begotten and beloved son, who takes upon himself to suffer in the father's and the mother's stead, not only in the phenomena of external nature, but also as a figure of the human soul immersed in matter. This involved the doctrines of the incarnation, the virgin mother, baptismal regeneration, the begettal of the anointed son as Horus of the resurrection, Horus the great judge, Horus the avenger, Horus the spirit glorified in the likeness of the father. He dwelt on earth as mortal Horus in the house of Seb (earth) until he was twelve years of age. He went down to Amenta as the human soul in death, or as the sun of winter sinking in the solstice. He rose again from the dead in search of his father, whom he had not known on earth. The father, as Osiris in Amenta, had been overcome by Sut, the power of darkness. Horus rises in Amenta as the avenger; he rises as "the living soul," Horus who now comes in the spirit (Rit., ch. 5). He comes to see Osiris and to drive away the darkness (ch. 9). He comes as the beloved son to seek for Sut, the adversary of Osiris, in the nether earth, and pierce him to the heart (ch. 11). The teaching of the Ritual is that sacrifice was of a twofold nature. In one aspect of the doctrine it was voluntary, in the other it was vengeful and piacular. This doctrine was brought on at second-hand in Rome as the bloody and unbloody sacrifice, both being associated with *one victim there instead of two*. But as Egyptian there were two, one innocent and one guilty. Osiris or Child-Horus of the mysteries was the voluntary victim of the unbloody sacrifice, and Sut the victim of the vengeful sacrifice that is celebrated in the Ritual on the night of the great slaughter and the manuring of the fields with blood. Osiris was the voluntary sacrifice. He was the god who gave himself in all the elements of life that all his creatures might have life. He came to earth or manifested in the water, and in flesh and blood, in vegetation and cultivated corn, or, more abstractly, as the bread from heaven. For the later providence was imaged in some likeness of the primitive provider. Hence Osiris is depicted as the wet-nurse with a myriad mammæ. The Great Mother as the bringer of plenty might be superseded together with her seven cows, and Isis, the good lady, by Osiris as Un-Nefer, the good being, with whom she was united in one; but still the figure of food and drink remained as an eternal type, when the god gave "the food that never perishes" by the incorporation, or the later incarnation, of himself. This was the voluntary victim who was made a sacrifice in the Osirian mysteries. As represented, he was slain by Sut, the leader of the evil powers, on the night of the great battle. Then follows the vast vengeful sacrifice of Sut and his co-conspirators, who in the form of the Typhonian animals were slain upon the highway of the damned so long as there was any blood to flow.

The vengeful sacrifice is also shown when Apap, the enemy of Ra, is slain. It is said, "Apap is stricken with swords; he is sacrificed" (Book of Hades, *Records,* vol. xii). Horus the child was the typical babe and suckling that was accredited with a revelation beyond the range of human faculty concerning things that were hidden from the wise and understanding. That was in a mystery, not meant for an apotheosis of infants or simpletons and bibliolaters. Horus the human was the child, and the divine Horus was the prince, the repa with the kingly countenance; and these are alluded to disparagingly by Iahu when he says of the people of Israel, "I will give children to be their princes, and babes shall rule over them" (Is. iii. 4). Human Horus came to earth in the character of a little child, a type of gentleness otherwise figured as a lamb or a calf. This typical little child is described by Isaiah in his millennial account of the Messiah who came periodically as the bringer of peace, Iu-em-hetep or Horus, or the Hebrew Mes-Iah, which is equivalent to Mes-Iu the coming child in Egyptian, who is otherwise the Iu-su, son of Atum and Iusāas. "And the wolf shall dwell with the lamb, and the leopard shall lie down with the kid; and the calf and the young lion falling together; and a little child shall lead them. And the cow and the bear shall feed; their young ones shall lie down together; and the lion shall eat straw like the ox. And the sucking child shall play on the hole of the asp, and the weaned child shall put his hand on the adder's den. They shall not hurt nor destroy in all my holy mountain" (Is. xi. 6, 9). This little child was the human Horus in the Egyptian mythos. The tender plant that springs up out of the dry ground, in the prophecy of Isaiah, is also represented both in the Osirian religion and in the earlier cult of Atum-Ra. Horus, the branch, or natzer, was the branch of the unbu or golden bough. The speaker in this character says (Rit., ch. 71, Renouf), "I am unbu of An-ar-f, the flower in the abode of occultation." An-ar-f denotes the abode of the sightless Horus, who was encircled by darkness and obscurity. It was there, in a waste place where nothing grew, that the golden unbu, or golden bough, burst into blossom as the living shoot from out the soil or the annually decaying tree of vegetable life, as offspring of the sun. Child-Horus as the natzer or Messiah was the "tender plant" that literally grew up "as a root out of a dry ground." As the plant of Anrutef he is rooted in the dry desert (Rit., ch. lxxi.; cf. Is. lviii. 11) which precedes the place of emergence from Amenta in the east. The dry ground was intensely actual in Egypt at the time of the winter solstice, when the land was left waterless. It was the season of coming drought that was reflected in the wilderness of Anrutef, through which the suffering sun god had to pass. It was there that Isis sought the water of life which was imaged as her lost Osiris. In this desert Horus suffered his great thirst, and here he sprang up as the tender plant from a root in the dry ground when nourished at the breasts of his mother. He had no form of comeliness, because he was that amorphous product of the virgin that lacked the soul and seal of the authenticating fatherhood which conferred the grace and favour upon Horus the divinized adult. This was the human Horus who was but human in the way already indicated as the maimed, crippled, shapeless, dumb, blind, impubescent product of the mother nature only. It was the ancient Child-Horus who was continued in the catacombs as the little old and ugly Christ. "He hath no form nor comeliness" (says Isaiah), "and when we see him there is no beauty that we should desire him; as one from whom men hide their face he was despised." Or as one who hid his face from men. The man of sorrows who had neither form nor comeliness was but a typical, not a natural man, still less an historic personage who hid his face and opened not his mouth; and the type was identical with that amorphous birth of the gnostic Sophia which she produced when flowing away into immensity until she was crossed and stayed by Stauros, who stopped the issue of blood. Both were the same as the imperfect, inarticulate child of Isis. The tender plant of Isaiah is one with Horus the shoot, who is also called a plant out of the Nun. The Hebrew man of sorrows is thus doubly identified with the human Horus, and only in the human Horus do we reach the genesis in nature of that Jesus who was reputed to have been born of flowing not of concreted blood. For mystical reasons this was the child who never could become a man, and never did; the typical victim of this sacrifice always remained a child. And because the Horus was but a type, he could be represented by the red shoot, the red fruit, the red calf or lamb, the red crown, or the red sun as sufferer in the winter solstice. Various types of this meek and lowly Horus made divine appeal to human tenderness and melted their way to the heart on behalf of the suffering mother and her dear, deaf, dumb, and sightless little one, the child of silence who was her Logos in sign-language.

The duality represented by Horus the Messiah in his two-fold character is described in the Ritual from the root. This is the chapter (Renouf, 115) by which the manes cometh forth into heaven, or the Child-Horus changes into the Arm of the Lord, the mortal Horus into Horus the immortal. The speaker says, "I know the powers of Annu. Doth not the all-powerful issue forth like one *who extendeth a hand to us?* It is with reference to me the gods say, Lo the Afflicted One, who is the heir of Annu! I know on what occasion the lock of the male-child was made. Ra was speaking with Amhauf, and a blindness came upon him. Ra said to Amhauf, Take the spear, O offspring of men. And Amhauf said, "The spear is taken." Whatsoever the meaning of this instruction, the result was that "two brethren came into being. They were Heb-Ra and Sotemanes, *whose arm resteth not*." As Child-Horus, he assumed the form of a female with the lock, which became the lock in Annu. Sotemanes is an image of Horus as the arm of Osiris. This is the arm that takes the spear to wield the weapon mightily. The Child-Horus might be of either sex, and the lock of childhood was worn by him as the type of both sexes. In his condition of blindness Horus of the lock was the afflicted one, but he is still *the heir of Annu*. That is the city where the transformation takes place in the temple. "Active and powerful is the heir of the temple, the active one of Annu. The flesh of his flesh is the all-seer, for he hath the might divine as the son whom the father hath begotten. And his will is that of the mighty one of Annu" (Gr. Heliopolis). This, we repeat, is the account given by the Ritual concerning the origin of the divine duality that was manifested in the double Horus, as the child of twelve years and the adult of thirty years, the wearer of the lock and the victorious lifter of the arm.

Now, Horus in these two characters can be as clearly traced in the Psalms as he is described in the Ritual. As Horus the human, he is the child with the side-lock, the afflicted one, the maimed, dumb, and blind sufferer who is persecuted by Sut. As Horus divinized, Horus the king's heir, "he hath the might divine as the son whom the father hath begotten"—that is, begotten in spirit for the resurrection from the dead. This is he whom the Psalmist celebrates: "My heart overfloweth with a goodly matter: I speak the things which I have made touching the king: my tongue is the pen of a ready writer. Thou art fairer than the children of men; grace is poured into thy lips: therefore God hath blessed thee for ever. Gird thy sword upon thy thigh, O mighty one, thy glory and thy majesty. And in thy majesty ride on prosperously. Thou hast loved righteousness and hated wickedness: therefore God, thy God, hath anointed thee with the oil of gladness above thy fellows" (Ps. xlv. 1-9). This in the original was Horus the anointed, the son of god, the oil of gladness on whose face was typical of his divinity. The person addressed in the 45th Psalm is also recognizable as "the royal Horus," Horus of the beautiful countenance. The Psalmist continues: "All thy garments (smell of) myrrh and aloes and cassia; out of ivory palaces stringed instruments have made thee glad. Kings' daughters are among thy honourable women: at thy right hand doth stand the queen in gold of Ophir" (Ps. xlv. 2, 9). Isaiah has likewise reproduced a portrait of Har-Tema the mighty avenger in his second advent, who came at the end and re-beginning of the period which is called the year of redemption: "Who is this that cometh from Edom, with garments crimson from Bozrah; he that is glorious in his apparel, marching in the greatness of his strength, mighty to save?" "Wherefore art thou red in thine apparel, and thy garments like him that treadeth in the wine-vat?" "I have trodden the wine-press alone; and of the people there was no man with me: yea, I trod them in mine anger and trampled them in my fury: and their life-blood is sprinkled upon my garments, and I have stained all my raiment. For the day of vengeance was in my heart, and the year of my redeemer is come. I looked, and there was none to help; and I wondered if there was none to uphold; therefore my own arm wrought salvation unto me, and my fury it upheld me; and I trod down the people in my anger and made them drunk in my fury, and I poured out their life-blood on the earth" (Is. lxiii. 1-6). This in the original is magnificent; in its perversion it is bewildering, but no bibliolater could possibly have known what it was about. Hence the endeavour to make it a matter of prophecy by means of marginal misinterpretation; a feast of vengeance for good Christians to look forward to at the second coming of their long-belated Lord. It is not prophecy: it has no other meaning and had no other origin than that of the Egyptian mythology and the mysteries of Amenta. Horus in his human personation was the mother's suffering son, the victim as described by Isaiah (chs. lii. liii.) and by the Psalmist as the sacrificial victim in the present, not in a future, near or far (Ps. xxii. 17, 18; xxxi. 5; xli. 9; lxix. 21). After his death, a representative of the Osiris rises again triumphant as the maker of justice visible. He does not merely speak of righteousness. He is the just and righteous judge who does justice in the judgment hall of Maati on the day of doom. As the divine avenger of the suffering Osiris or the human Horus he arises in the person of the red god, who is thus addressed: "O fearsome one, thou who art over the two earths, red god who orderest the block of execution, to whom the double crown is given," as Horus at his second coming (Rit., ch. 17). He comes back in his second advent as the lifter of the arm, great in his glory, as wearer of the double crown, the terrible avenger of the wrongs that were inflicted by the wicked on the suffering Osiris, or on humanity in that appealing and pathetic representative in the god of humanity who gave himself a sacrifice to show the way that others might have life. The way of salvation was revealed by the human Horus being divinized in death, and emerging as an immortal on the horizon of the resurrection, safe beyond the valley of the shadow and the darkness of Sheol. The drama from which scenes are given in the Hebrew writings, as if these things occurred or would occur upon the earth, belongs to the mysteries of the Egyptian Amenta, and only as Egyptian could its characters ever be understood. We have to bear in mind that the typical teacher of Israel is alleged to have been learned in all the wisdom of the Egyptians. Unfortunately, the key of the Mosaic writings was mislaid, and the Bible has become a lock-up of bondage for the prisoners of the Christian faith. Isaiah asks, "Who hath believed that which we have hard, and to whom hath the arm of the Lord been revealed?" To none, we reply, save those who know the god who lifted up the arm in death, who bared the holy arm in retribution, and who wrought salvation with it for the oppressed who suffered from the adversaries in Amenta. Horus-Amsu is the god who uplifts the arm of Osiris the lord, which he has freed from the swathings of the mummy as he rises from the tomb. The buried Osiris represented the god in matter, the earthly half of the divinity, so to say, earth being termed his body and heaven his soul. Hence he is imaged by one arm, one leg, one side. Hence also the typical right and left arms. Osiris buried in Sekhem is represented with the left arm *still bound and powerless.* Horus in his resurrection is the right arm that was lifted when he had burst the bonds of death and got the better of Sut as conqueror of the grave and manifestor in phenomena both natural and eschatological for the father in Amenta, the father of eternity, or the eternal father, he whose son was manifestor by periodic repetition in the sphere of time. The tat-type of support and stability on which all rested in Tattu is said to be the arm or shoulder of Horus in Sekhem (Rit., 18), whose figure with the fan or khu in his right hand will show us how the government was *on his shoulder.* The abstract language of the Jewish writings takes the place of the earlier concrete representation and the Egyptian symbol, which were figures of the facts that dislimn and ultimately fade away in words. Amsu-Horus, who rises from the grave in Amenta with his right arm freed from the mummy-swathe, is designated the "lifter of the arm," and in this connection we may compare a Fijian burial custom. When a hero or distinguished "brave" is buried, the body is interred with the right arm lifted up above the mould of the grave mound. The people passing by, on seeing this, exclaim, "Oh, the hand that was the slayer of men" (Lorimer Fison, "Notes on Fijian Burial Customs,"

Journal of the Anthropological Institute). The natural fact was first rendered in sign-language, and this supplied the type to the mythical or eschatological phase. The Fijian custom shows the figure, straight from nature, of the arm-lifter as the conqueror in life thus imaged memorially in death; Amsu-Horus is the lifter of his right arm as the victor over death. Such a custom is by no means "ghastly" when interpreted by the Egyptian wisdom, but a mode of honouring the brave spirit, which in Amsu-Horus is exhibited as triumphant over death and all the ills of mortality, as the arm of the lord, the conqueror of his father's enemies, triumphant over death and the grave. It was Amsu-Horus who "hath showed strength with his arm," for he has wrenched and raised it from the leaden grasp of the burial-place and the bondage of the mummy, holding aloft the sign of rule and government as the express image of potency personified. Amsu personates the "arm of the lord" outstretched from the mummy of matter. He is called the arm-raiser, and through his potency the other arm bound up in the mummy case is set free, and the Osiris emerges pure spirit, with both arms intact and both feet in motion. "Behold," says the prophet; "Behold, the Lord God will come as a mighty one, and his arm shall rule for him" (Is. xl. 10). In this aspect he comes as the good shepherd. "He shall feed his flock like a shepherd; he shall gather the lambs in his arm and carry them in his bosom, and gently lead those that are with young" (Is. xl. 11). This was Horus the lifter of his arm for Osiris, upon whose shoulder rested the insignia of his government, which included the whip (or flail) and *the shepherd's crook*. As the Good Shepherd Horus tends the sheep of his father, and comes to gather them in his fold. He was personified as the delegated power that drove with the whip and drew them with the *hek* of rule, which became the shepherd's crook. The portrait of Horus the good shepherd, who was likewise the arm of the lord in this picture of pastoral tenderness, was readapted by the Hebrew writer for the comforting of distressed Jerusalem. The character and the picture belong to the Amenta in the Ritual, and these have been represented as if belonging to this earth, whereas the good shepherd and the sheep, the fields of peace and pastures of plenty beside the *still* waters, pertain to hetep, the paradise of peace. Of the "prince of peace," who is proclaimed by Isaiah as *having come* (he came annually or periodically in the mythos), it is said, "The government shall be upon his shoulder" (ch. 9, 6). So was it with the Egyptian prince of peace as Horus the "sustainer of his father." On the night of setting up the tat and of establishing Horus in the place of the dead Osiris Horus takes the government upon his shoulder. It is said, "The setting up of the tat (of stability) means the shoulder of Horus"—that is, the shoulder with which he sustains the government (Rit., ch. 18). In this sense he was the arm of the lord, "the lifter of the arm," called "the avenger of that left arm of Osiris which is in Sekhem." Horus images the mummy-Osiris in the resurrection. With the right arm lifted he wields the sceptre of his power that signifies his triumph over death and hell and the grave; he also bears the sign of government upon his other shoulder. What a portrait of level-browed justice is that of Amsu-Horus, who is described as the god "whose eyebrows are like the two arms of the balance (or scales) upon that day when outrage is brought to account and each wrong is tied up to its separate block of settlement" (ch. 17). This is the judge in person of the son, the god who lifteth up his arm, and who is the arm of the lord made manifest for the execution of justice. And this is the arm of the lord invoked for the same purpose by Isaiah, which alone explains the expression, "Mine arm shall judge the peoples." The veil of words in the Hebrew constantly conceals the wisdom of the Egyptians that lies beyond it in the Jewish scriptures, and this is the rending of the veil. One needs must observe in passing that if the divine victim and the redemption from sin were historical and once for all, these must certainly have already taken place when Isaiah wrote; and if it had been once for all it could not have occurred once afterwards. Besides, the same victim is described in the Psalms as suffering or having suffered as the same sacrifice. And how the Sarkolatræ have gloated and are gloating ghoul-like over this cowardly doctrine of the divine victim suffering in a human form to ransom the guilty with the blood of the innocent, and save them from Nemesis of natural law and the consequences of their own sins. But we have to do with no historical transactions, prophetic or fulfilled. Horus is described in the Ritual (ch. 17) as making his first and second advent in the two characters of blind Horus (An-maati) and Horus the avenger or reconstituter of his father. These two forms of the Messiah, the founder and fulfiller of the kingdom of heaven on behalf of the father, can now be traced in the Hebrew scriptures, especially in the books of the Psalms, Isaiah, Zechariah, and Daniel. Mortal Horus in his humanity was born as the servant. He was the divine heir in the likeness of the child that from the earliest totemic times was born to be a servant or a slave, which was its natural status. He is portrayed as blind and deaf and dumb. This is the coming Messiah described by Isaiah as the servant who is blind and deaf and dumb. "As a lamb that is led to the slaughter, and as a sheep that before her shearers is dumb" (liii. 7). "Who is blind as my servant, or deaf as my messenger that I send? Who is blind as he that is made perfect, and yet is blind as the Lord's servant?" (ch. 42). As was Horus the child, who suffered in his mortality as the servant and was deaf and dumb and blind in the earth of Seb to attain the beatific vision of the Horus perfected in spirit. The blind messenger described by Isaiah is the sightless Horus, whose zoötype was the mole or shrewmouse because it was an eyeless digger underground, and therefore a likeness of Horus in the darkness of the nether earth. Human Horus, called the elder because the first born, and who "had no form nor comeliness," was the virgin's amorphous child. Horus divinized was the god with the beautiful face, who was "fairer than the children of men," and blooming with eternal youth as the type of immortality. In the Jewish traditions concerning the Coming One we find the doctrine of a Messiah in two aspects: in one character he was born to suffer, in the other he was destined to triumph. In the one he is identical with the maimed and suffering

Horus, in the other with the victorious Har-Tema. In the first he was to come as Joseph's son, who would make war on the adversary and himself be slain (as was the elder Horus) at Jerusalem. Then the second Messiah, called the son of David, was to defeat the enemy, called by the Gentiles Antichrist, and, according to the solar imagery employed, consume him with the breath of his mouth. This consummation was to be on the grandly indefinite scale, but the tradition preserves details of the annual representation. When Messiah came as conqueror in the glory of his strength there was to be a reign of nine months. At the end of the nine months, Messiah Ben-Joseph was to be revealed—that is, the sufferer who was foredoomed to fall, and who was followed by the Messiah Ben-David, who was destined to succeed. Now, the annual cycle in the Kamite mythos was divided into nine months and three. The elder Horus was born about the time of the winter solstice, answering to the birth of Christ at Christmas. This is a form of the victim who was slain or blinded by Sut the prince of darkness. Three months afterwards the risen Horus was revealed upon the mount of glory as the vanquisher of Sut. And after his reincarnation it was nine months before the next rebirth at Christmas. Thus the circle was completed both in time and space according to the facts in nature upon which the myth was founded (*Avkath Rochel apud Huls.*, pp. 22, 23, 35, 36; Eisenmenger, *Endecktes Judenthum*), and the two births or advents of Messiah Ben-Joseph and Messiah Ben-David, at the end of nine months, and again at the end of three, are exactly the same as the advent of the elder Horus in the winter solstice and the second coming of Horus triumphant in or following the vernal equinox. So necessary is the mould of the astronomical mythology for understanding the eschatology, whether we call it Jewish, Egyptian, or Christian. It is the ruler for one year in the solar mythos that will account for "the year of the Lord" which was "the acceptable year of the Lord and the day of vengeance of our God" proclaimed in Israel by Isaiah (Is. lxi. 2). But the doctrine of a coming Messiah who came to rule for one year has no meaning apart from the mythos, in which the coming was annual, whether as Horus of the inundation or as Iu the youthful solar god. It was this reign of Messiah on the scale of one year that bequeathed the tradition of the one year's ministry of Jesus re-announced by Luke (iv. 19) from Isaiah. The gnostics Ptolemæus and Herakleon, also the Christians Clement Alexander and Origen, who were both from Egypt, held this view of the reign that lasted only one year. And it was this foundation in the mythical representation which has made it impossible to build the gospel history on any other basis, or to conclusively define any other length of time for "our Lord's public ministry."

Whether written by Paul or not, the Epistle to the Hebrews contains the Egypto-gnostic doctrine of the Christ which was taught by Paul in accordance with "the beginning of the first principles of the oracles of God"—that is, of the divine wisdom which was communicated in the mysteries, and in which Paul was an adept and perfect. This, for example, is a brief sketch of the twofold Horus who suffered as Horus in his mortality and overcame as Horus in spirit, who personates the redeemer from death. This was he "who in the days of his flesh, having offered up prayers and supplications with strong crying and tears unto him that was able to save him from death, and having been heard for his godly fear, though he was a son, yet learned he obedience by the things which he suffered: and having been made perfect, he became unto all them that obey him the author of eternal salvation" (Heb. v. 7). This in the Egyptian was the maimed and suffering human Horus who was saved from death in becoming the anointed son, the glorified sahu, the spirit perfected, the typical initiator into an existence hereafter that was called salvation to eternal life. The change from Horus the mortal to Horus in spirit is plainly described by Isaiah (xlii.). "Behold my servant whom I uphold, my chosen in whom my soul delighteth; I have *put my spirit upon him;* he shall bring forth judgment to the nation. He shall bring forth judgment in truth." The meek and lowly one, the virgin's lamb, the suffering Messiah, was Horus in a maimed and most imperfect human form. This was the typical sufferer for the mother and the servant of the Lord, who in his changed and glorified estate became the only-begotten from the father; his beloved son. The spirit of God was "put upon him" when he was a divine hawk of soul or became dove-headed; and he who was so dumb and gentle that he would not break a bruised reed was transformed into the Horus who as Tema was the terrible judge, the red god, and as Horus-Makheru the judge in very truth.

It was on the mount of glory in the east, the mount that rose up from Amenta, that Messiah in his second advent came in the glory of his father with his angels, who were represented as spirits of fire in attendance on the sun or solar god. This in the annual fulfilment was in the vernal equinox, at the point where the two earths were united in one. It is also said in the Talmud (Talmud, Cod. Sanhedrin, ch. 3, p. 38) that the Messiah called the son of David "will not come till the two houses of Israel shall be extinct." Here the two houses answer to the double horizons in the Egyptian mythos which were united and made one in the new heaven and earth established at the advent of Horus Sam-taui, the uniter of the two houses of the double earth. The following "prophecy" contains an appeal to the father god on behalf of the anointed son. "Give the king thy judgments, O God, and thy righteousness unto the king's son. He shall judge thy people with righteousness, and thy poor with judgment. The mountains shall bring peace to the people. He shall break in pieces the oppressor. In his days shall the righteous flourish, and abundance of peace. . . . All kings shall fall down before him. All nations shall serve him. *There shall be abundance of corn in the earth upon the top of the mountains,* and the fruit thereof shall shake like Lebanon. And they of the city shall flourish like grass of the earth. His name shall endure for ever; *his name shall be continued as long as the sun,* and men shall be blessed in him; all nations shall call him happy" (Ps. lxxii.). The reign of justice, law, and righteousness was renewed at the advent of the prince, the repa or heir-apparent, who came to represent the father god. The maat or hall of justice was erected on the plain as the seat of Har-Tema the great judge. The kingdom or house of heaven was refounded for the father once a year by Horus, or by Jesus, the Messiah-son. It was founded upon the four quarters, which were represented by the four mystical creatures, by four flag-staffs or pillars, or by the four-fold Cross of the tat.

Horus is described in both characters by Zechariah at the second coming. "And they shall look unto him *whom they pierced,* and they shall mourn for him as one mourneth for his only son, and shall be in bitterness for him, as one that is in bitterness for his first-born" (Zech. xii. 10, 11). He is to come in the "day of the Lord," to fight the battle called the battle of Har-Magedon in Revelation, which was fought annually in the astronomical mythology. Har-Makhu was the ancient Horus of both horizons, more exactly of both equinoxes, and most exactly of the double earth that was united annually in one at the eastern equinox upon the Mount of Olives, or Bakhu in Egyptian. Person, place, event, and circumstances are all the same as in the original. This is the avenger Har-Makhu, otherwise described as Har-Tema, executor and executioner of divine justice in the maat upon the mount of glory. And it is to be as in the previous manifestations. They shall look upon him whom they *had* pierced. In the Kamite representation Horus came periodically in the vernal equinox as the king's son, who was called the prince of eternity, the royal Horus, Horus of the kingly countenance, now made judge of all the earth. He took his seat upon the summit; the balance was erected in the hall of righteousness or of maat, where judgment was delivered and undeviating justice done. But this was the annual assizes of "all souls" held in the earth of eternity, not in Judea nor the earth of time. Isaiah foretells that in the great day that will come there is to be "a vineyard of wine": "sing ye of it. I the Lord do keep it night and day." "And in the mountain shall the Lord of hosts make unto all peoples a feast of fat things, a feast of wines on the lees, of fat things full of marrow, of wines on the lees well refined" (Is. xxv. 6 and xxvii. 2, 3). And the coming, which was actual in Egypt, and was celebrated yearly with the Uaka or Nile festival, is to be fulfilled at some indefinite future time that was chiefly known to prophecy as the day of doom and the ending of the world.

The vine and fig were two especial forms of the typical tree in the garden of Hetep, Aarru, or Eden. According to the prophecy of Micah, every man was to sit beneath his own vine and fig-tree in the paradise of peace, with none to make them afraid (iv. 4). But this garden of the gods and the glorified, which is relegated to the future by the biblical writers, had been planted by the Egyptians in a far-off past. The vine and sycamore-fig were two types in the Kamite paradise. In the papyrus of Nu he prays that he may sit under his own vine and also beneath the refreshing foliage of the sycamore-fig tree of Hathor. The garden of Aarru is a garden of the grape, and the god Osiris is sometimes seated in a Naos underneath the vine, from which bunches of grapes are hanging. Moreover, Osiris was the vine, and his son Horus-unbu is the branch. The solar mount was called the mount of glory. This is in accordance with the natural fact. It is the same in the Hebrew writings. The mount of God in Exodus is the mount of glory. It is called the mount of the glory of God: "The glory of the Lord abode upon Mount

Sinai" (Ex. xxiv. 16). The solar nature of the glory is apparent in certain passages. "The glory of the Lord went up and stood upon the mountain which is on the east side of the city" (Ez. xi. 23). This identifies the solar mount of glory. "And in appearance the glory of the Lord was like devouring fire on the top of the mount in the eyes of the children of Israel" (Ex. xxiv. 17). The law was given to Israel on the mount in the shape of the Commandments, that were written on two tablets. This corresponds to the law of maati given in the great judgment hall upon the mount of glory at the place of equilibrium, or the scales of justice in the equinox. The two tablets image the duality of maati, or the twofold law and justice. The mount is identified with the Egyptian judgment-seat by the statement made to Moses in the mount: "Now these are the judgments which thou shalt set before them" (Ex. xxi. 1)—these being the laws distinguished from the Ten Commandments. The maat was the judgment-seat, the great hall, the place or city of truth and righteousness. The scales of justice were periodically erected on the mount, whether at the vernal equinox in the solar mythos or at the pole in the earlier stellar representation. Hence the application of the maat to Jerusalem by Zechariah. "Jerusalem shall be called the city of truth (maati), and the mountain of the Lord of hosts the holy mountain" (Zech. viii. 3, 4). The Lord, he cometh, "He cometh to guide the earth; he shall judge the world with righteousness; righteousness and judgment are the foundation of his throne" (Ps. xcvi. and xcvii.). These are the foundation of maati, truth, righteousness, law, and justice all being expressed by the one word maati. The doctrine of maati could not be more perfectly illustrated than it is in Psalm xlv. 6. "Thy throne, O God, is for ever and ever; *a sceptre of equity* is the sceptre of thy kingdom." From the time of Tum, *i.e.* Atum-Iu, the Egyptian one god was the deity of justice, truth, and righteousness. He is still the god of maat or maati, which has the meaning of law, truth, justice, and right. In this wise the mythos and the eschatology of Egypt were converted into matter of prophecy that was to be fulfilled on earth as the mode of future realization.

The mythical mount is also typical of two different characters, female and male: one was the mount of earth, the other the mount of heaven. The worship of the Great Mother never died out wholly with the children of Israel. The high places, the asherim, the sacred prostitutes, the heifer, the sow, and other types were indestructible, all the Protestantism and Puritanism of the monotheists notwithstanding. Hence we are told, as something very terrible, that Solomon built a temple to Ashtoreth "on the right hand of the mount of corruption" (II Kings xxiii. 13), the mount of the Great Mother. The female nature of the mount of earth was shown when the Lord "covered the daughter of Zion with a cloud in his anger and cast down the beauty of Israel," and is said to have "forgotten his footstool." She was the footstool of Ihuh as a type of the earth-mother, just as Isis is the *seat* of Osiris. There is a general casting out of the divine motherhood by the Hebrew writers, especially under the type of the female mount. For the Lord of hosts was to reign in Mount Zion after the casting out of the woman Wickedness, whose emblem was an abomination in all the earth (Is. xxiv. 23). "Behold, I am against thee, O destroying mountain, saith the Lord. I will make thee a burnt mountain. . . . Thou shalt be desolate for ever" (Jer. li. 25). "O my mountain in the field, I will give thy substance and all thy treasures for a spoil, and thy high places, because of sin throughout all thy borders" (Jer. xvii. 3). This was the mount of earth and of the motherhood, and the seat of the Great Mother in the mount of earth or Jerusalem below is now to be superseded by the throne of God most high in the holy mount of Jerusalem above. The change is described in the book of Zechariah. Jerusalem that was forsaken in one sense, and her mount of the motherhood cast down, is to be restored to Israel, in another character, by the erection of another mount and sanctuary. "Thus saith the Lord: I am returned to Jerusalem with mercies; my house shall be built in it. The Lord shall yet comfort Zion, and shall yet choose Jerusalem" (Zech. i. 17). The mother in the earlier cult was cast out and her seat denounced as the mount of corruption because she had been worshipped and fecundated beneath every green tree on this *mons veneris* of the earth (II Kings xxiii. 13), in all the high places that were consecrated to Ashtoreth and the asherim, as the mount of the mother. This was the hill of Jerusalem on which her whoredoms were committed by the daughter of Zion (Is. x. 32). It is the hill of Esau, and of her "that dwelt in the clefts of the rock" as the old earth-mother, who was now to be swept away in the coming day of the Lord, the mountain that before Zerubbabel was to become a plain for the foundation of a new house of heaven (Zech. iv. 7). The preparations for the building—the four horns or corners, the four smiths, the man with a measuring-line in his hand—show that the new Jerusalem signified is celestial or astronomical. It is to be built by Zerubbabel, whose hands "have laid the foundations of this house." The mount that had been is to be levelled by him and become a plain. This was the mount of the woman called Wickedness, whose emblem was to be removed to the land of Shinar, where her house was to be built, and when it was established she was to be set upon her own base. The new house of heaven or the new Jerusalem is built upon the mountain of the Lord, who is about to bring forth his servant, the Branch. And now we learn that, notwithstanding the historic-looking instructions given by "the word of the Lord to Zerubbabel" concerning the building, the actual builder is the man whose name is the Branch. "Thus speaketh the Lord of hosts, saying, Behold the man whose name is the Branch; and he shall grow up out of his place, and he shall build the temple of the Lord; and he shall bear the glory, and shall sit and rule upon his throne; and he shall be a priest upon his throne, and the counsel of peace shall be between them both" (Zech. vi. 12, 13). As Egyptian, this builder of the temple was Iu-em-hetep, the prince of peace. In one of its various meanings the word hetep signifies gathering and uniting together. Hence hetep is the mount of congregation. This was continued as a Hebrew title of the mount. Isaiah identifies "the mount of congregation," or place of gathering together, as the mount in the uttermost parts of the north—that is, with the summit of rest at the celestial pole (Is. xiv. 13). As is said by the Psalmist, "The wicked shall not stand in the judgment nor sinners in the *congregation* of the righteous" (Ps. i. 5). "In the midst of the congregation will I praise thee" (Ps. xxii. 22). "God standeth in the *congregation* of God; he judgeth amongst the gods" (Ps. lxxxii. 1). The final landing-place in the Egyptian paradise, where the souls of the departed reach an anchorage in the still waters of hetep or peace eternal in the heavens, is a divine district called "the isle of corn and barley" (Rit., ch. 110). This was attainable only at the summit of Mount Hetep, the mount of peace and everlasting plenty in the circumpolar paradise, not on any local mount of Zion in Judea or in Palestine, although it was thus literalized in the biblical prophecies. The great and glorious good time coming for the Egyptians was not in this life nor the present world. It was in the heaven of eternity. It was a picture of the paradise awaiting the blessed dead. This was portrayed twice over; once in the nether earth of the solar mythos, once in the highest, earlier heaven, in the garden of hetep on the stellar mount. The pictures of this paradise in the Hebrew writings, the Psalms, the books of Isaiah, Ezekiel, Micah, Zechariah, and Revelation, were pre-extant long ages earlier *as Egyptian*. What the so-called "prophets" of the Jews did was to make sublunary this vision of the good time in another life. There were already two Jerusalems from the time when Judea and Palestine were appendages of Egypt. Two Jerusalems were recognized by Paul, one terrestrial, one celestial. The name of Jerusalem we read as the Aarru-salem or fields of peace, equivalent to Aarru-hetep or Sekhet-hetep, the fields of peace in Egyptian. Jerusalem below was the localized representative of Jerusalem above, the Aarru-salem or Aarru-hetep on the mount of peace in the heaven of the never-setting stars. The burden of Jewish prophecy, which turned out so terribly misleading for those who were ignorant of the secret wisdom, is that the vision of this glorious future should be attained on earth; whereas it never had that meaning. But the Hebrew non-initiates came to think it had; they also prophesied as if they thought it had. Thus Jerusalem on earth was to take the place of Jerusalem above, and the Aarru-hetep become the Jeru-salem simply as a mundane locality. Jerusalem is to be rebuilt, and to be called the City of Truth, which had been the Maat upon the mount in the Egyptian eschatology (Zech. i. 16; ii. 1, 2, and 10; viii. 3). The bringer of peace is to return and build the temple of the Lord, and the counsel of peace is to be between him and the Lord. And "there shall be the seed of peace; the vine shall give her fruit, and the ground shall give her increase, and the heavens shall give their dew; and I will cause the remnant of this people to inherit all these things" (Zech. viii. 12), "all these things" being the things predicated of the promised land of the mythos, the fields of peace or gardens of Hetep in the eschatology, the abode of the blessed in Jerusalem above. In this new Jerusalem on earth it was to be as it had been in the maat upon the mount, where Atum or Osiris imaged the eternal on his seat who presided over the pole of heaven (Rit., ch. 7). Every man was to speak the truth with his neighbour, and execute the judgment of truth and peace in their gates after attaining the maat. Amongst the Egyptian sayings that have been taken literally by the Jews and Christians is the statement that the meek shall inherit the earth. We read in the Psalms, "Those that wait on the Lord, they shall inherit the land. Yet a little while and the wicked shall not be. But the meek shall inherit the land, and shall delight themselves in the abundance of peace. Their inheritance shall be for ever. But the wicked shall perish. Such as be blessed of him shall inherit the land, and they that be cursed of him shall be cut off. The righteous shall inherit the land. Wait on the Lord, and he shall exalt thee to inherit the land" (Ps. xxxvii). If such promises and prophecies had applied to the lands of this world (which they did not), our English race would have proved itself to have been the most righteous people on earth, and the landless Jews the most utterly deceived by the Lord on whom they waited, like the hungry animal in the fable, when he depended on the word of the nurse who threatened to throw the child to the wolf, and was deceived regarding his supper. It never was *our* earth that the meek or the righteous were to inherit, but the land in the earth of a future life, the land that was promised to the doers of right and the fulfillers of justice on this earth, who became the cultivators in the fields of divine harvest for eternity. In the Egyptian teaching this land of promise, of plenty, and of peace was the land of Hetep, the garden of Aarru, the elysian fields, the paradise of spirits perfected who were the only righteous on the summit of the mount, which had to be attained by long climbing in the life hereafter as well as in the life on earth. That was the only land to be attained by those who waited on the Lord. It was a land of pure delight mapped out in the northern heaven, to be seen through the darkness that covered the earth by night. In that land every worker had his appointed portion given to cultivate and bring forth his share of produce. There were no Feringhees or eaters of the earth up there. But change the venue and pervert the teaching by making this land of promise an earthly possession, as is done all through the biblical writings, and you have an alleged divine sanction and warrant for all the robbery of land and all the iniquity that has been perpetrated against the weaker races of the aborigines by God Almighty's favourite whites. The Jews professed to wait upon the Lord, therefore they were to inherit the land. The Spaniards likewise waited on the Lord, and therefore the lands of the Peruvians and Mexicans were theirs by divine right. So has it been with the English in America, in Australia, in Africa. They who wait upon the Lord once a week, or once a year upon Atonement Day, without atonement, shall inherit the earth. And all the time such teaching is not only utterly immoral, not only ethically false; it never had the significance assigned to it by the Jews and Christians when first taught by the Egyptians. A false bottom has thus been laid by this perversion of old Egypt's wisdom, and on that false bottom have the Jews and Christians built for this world, whereas the Egyptians laid their foundations for eternity.

The Egyptian wisdom, to which the whole wide round of the world is one vast whispering gallery, has been looked upon by the bibliolater as "*the materials that Revelation had to deal with*" (Cobb, *Origines Judaica*)—that is, the wisdom pre-extant, for which the Egyptians had toiled during a dateless antiquity, becomes divine revelation when mutilated and misrendered in the biblical version. For the sounder inference to be drawn from the comparatively late origin of the Hebrew letters is not that the subject-matter of the documents is necessarily

The Egyptian Wisdom in other Jewish Writings 541

late, but that it was preserved in the hieroglyphic language which was read by Osarsiph and his fellow-priests from On, before it was transcribed in the later letters. The truth is that the primary records on which the Bible was based were not a product of the Palestinian Jews. In the original scriptures no mistakes are made by the speaker as to the nature of the promises or the place of performance. In one of the rubrics to the Ritual it is said: "If this chapter be recited over him (the deceased), he will make his exodus and go forth over the earth, and he will pass through every kind of fire, no evil thing being able to hurt him." But this was in making his progress over the earth of Amenta, the land of life, as a manes, and not as a human being in the earth of time. The secret of the whole matter is that in both the Old and the New Testaments the mysteries of Amenta have been literalized and shifted to the human dwelling-place, and the readers have been left groping and wandering in the wrong world.

It is the people of Israel who were in Sheol, not in Palestine, that speak in the following words of Hosea: "Come, and let us return unto the Lord (who is described in the preceding chapter as the double lion); for he hath torn and he will heal us; he hath smitten, and he will bind us up. *After two days will he revive us; on the third day he will raise us up, and we shall live before him.* And let us know, let us follow on to know the Lord. His going forth is sure as the morning; and he shall come unto us as the rain, as the latter rain that watereth the earth" (Hos. vi. 1-3). These were the people of Israel who suffered their captivity in the prison-house of Amenta. They have suffered death from the lion god, who has laid them low in Sheol, but will raise them upon the third day to live with himself. This was the captivity of Job the sufferer from Satan in Sheol, and also the sufferer in the Psalms whose soul is a prisoner bound in Sheol, waiting for deliverance and for the salvation that cometh out of Zion (Ps. xiv. and xvi). It is a captivity that never was historical, in a land of bondage which may be called Babylon, Egypt, or Sodom; but, as Hosea shows, it was a bondage from which the prisoners were set free *after two days—that is, in the resurrection on the third day.* A knowledge of the matter at first hand in the Egyptian rendering will disintegrate the historical captivity and exodus, leaving but little to set foot upon beyond a heap of ever-shifting sand. In Alexandria, about the year 140 B.C., the Sibyl was giving forth her oracles in a farrago of the ancient wisdom, concerning an advent of the righteous king who was to rise up in the east, as all such personages ever had done in the solar mythos, and found his kingdom of perpetual peace. The Jews in Alexandria, being in subjection, cultivated this idea, and did their utmost to convert the mythical Messiah into an ethnical saviour. Their falsely-excited hopes, however, ended in a few desperate endeavours to fufil the supposed prophecies respecting a political deliverer who should free them from the Roman yoke. And the same delusion, mainly born of misinterpreted mythology, lived on afterwards as Christian. More especially *after the alleged historic fulfilment.* It broke out as a belief in the second advent and the establishment of the millennium which had not been historically realized the first time. The Christian opinion most prevalent for many centuries was that the Messiah would come again, like Arthur and other Æonian heroes of the astronomical mythology, and that his kingdom was to last one thousand years. After that the deluge, or the dragon. Christian Chiliasim was unwittingly founded on the periodic return of the ever-coming one who had been Horus or Iu the prince of peace in the "house of a thousand years," an earthly likeness of which was restored for Amen of Nepata by King Harsiatef of the 26th dynasty (Stele, *Records of the Past,* vol. vi, p. 85). This ever-recurring advent was dated for those who kept the chronology, but the ignorant Christian Chiliasts were left literally dateless from their lack of the gnosis. That which had been in the astronomical mythos was yet to come according to the biblical prophecies. In the Kamite eschatology the mountain of the Lord's house had been established at the summit of Aarru-hetep, the paradise of peace, the country that is called the "tip of heaven" (Rit., ch. 99). The house of the Lord upon the mount was the great hall of judgment called the maat, from which proceeded the law and the word of the Lord and the son of God who came to make the word of the Lord truth against his adversaries. "But in the latter days it shall come to pass that the mountain of the Lord's house shall be established in the top of the mountains, and it shall be exalted above the hills; and peoples shall flow unto it. And many nations shall go and say, Come ye, and let us go up to the mountain of the Lord, and to the house of the God of Jacob; and he will teach us of his ways, and we will walk in his paths; for out of Zion shall go forth the law, and the word of the Lord from Jerusalem. And he shall judge between many peoples, and shall rebuke strong nations afar off: and they shall beat their swords into ploughshares, and their spears into pruning-hooks; nation shall not lift up sword against nation, neither shall they learn war any more. They shall sit every man under his vine and under his fig-tree, and none shall make them afraid; for the mouth of the Lord of hosts hath spoken it," "and the Lord shall reign over them in Mount Zion from henceforth even for ever" (Micah iv. 1-8). But whilst the prophet is apparently peering forward into some indefinite future, he is only looking into the *camera obscura* in front, which is all the while reflecting things that lie behind him in a far-off past. Ages on ages earlier the feast of fat things, with the heaps of food, the thousands of geese and ducks, the corn and beer in huge abundance, had been spread in the Egyptian paradise for the eternal feast, with Mount Hetep for the table. This was the heaven of all good things that were imaged as provisions in the land of promise that could not be attained in Jerusalem below, but only at the summit of another life. This was the mount of peace where the Lord of all things rested, he whose name was Neb-Hetep, the lord of peace. That was the land in which there was no more night and the tears were wiped from all faces, and pain and sorrow ceased, and sighing had for ever passed away. A close acquaintance with the Ritual shows that the Ius brought out of Egypt certain writings that contained the Egyptian eschatology, the wisdom in which they tell us their giver of the law was learned. That wisdom of the other world was converted into history for this, and all turned topsy-turvy by changing the earth of eternity into the earth of time and the manes into mortals. In this way the noble, full, flowing river of old Egypt's wisdom ended in a quagmire of prophecies for the Jews and a dried-up wilderness of desert sands for the Christians. And on those shifting sands the "historic" Christians reared their temple of the eternal, which is giving way at last because it was not founded on the solid rock, and because no amount of blood would ever suffice to solidify the sand or form a concrete foundation or even a buttress for the crumbling building.

The secret of the ancientness and sanctity of the writings is that they were originally Egyptian, like the Jewish community. They are not the product of any ground-rootage in the land of Judea. They come to us masked and in disguise. The wisdom of old, the myths, parables, and dark sayings that were preserved, have been presented to us dreadfully defeatured and deformed in the course of being converted into history. An exoteric rendering has taken the place of the esoteric representation which contained the only true interpretation. The past was known to Philo, the learned Jew, who when speaking of the Mosaic writings told his countrymen that "the literal statement is a fabulous one, and it is in the mythical that we shall find the true." To understand their own books, their religious rites, festivals, and ceremonies, the Jews will have to go back to Egypt for the purpose of comparison. The Egyptian Ritual will show them why their New Year's Day is the annual judgment day, the great day of doom; and why it is also the "great day of memorial" for celebrating the creation of the world, as it was in Egypt. Their "great day of atonement" is identical with that on which the Sut-Typhonians and adversaries of Osiris were slain in a bloody sacrifice that was offered up as pleasing to the Good Being, Un-Nefer, who was annually put to death by these emissaries of the evil one and annually avenged by Har-Tema and his faithful followers. The blowing of the trumpet, or Shofar, is the signal for the resurrection from Amenta, or Sheol, and has been so since the vernal equinox entered and the solar resurrection occurred in the sign of the Ram, 4,300 years ago, to say nothing of the earlier stations in precession. The Rabbins have preserved the tradition that the dead are summoned before the divine tribunal to be judged upon the day of doom, which occurs each New Year's Day.

Gleams of the ancient glory are afloat in Jewish eyes that still turn Zionward, still mistaking the earthly for the heavenly vision of the eternal city, a promised land in Palestine for a celestial locality that is still *en l'air* or in the clouds of prophecy. If they were to see the promised land in Palestine to-day, they would not find the eternal city of their dreams at Jerusalem any more than at Rome or Thebes, at Memphis, at Annu, or any other foundation upon which the celestial home of rest was portrayed in heaven or localized in a pattern on this earth. On the other hand, the Jews in their religious mysteries go back to Jerusalem once every year; and once a year Messiah comes to them, from generation to generation as "the persistent traveller upon heaven's highways, who steppeth onwards through eternity" (Rit., ch. 42). The yearning for Zion by these homeless lodgers who are aliens in all lands did not arise from love of country or desire to cultivate its soil. It originated in religious feeling and the following of a heavenly mirage that could be pursued over all the earth and its deserts, independently of locality or of race. This view is also enforced by the persistence of the Messianic craze that yet survives amongst the Jewish victims of misinterpreted mythology, who still await that fulfilment of the impossible which the persecuting Christians fatuously suppose they have secured for all time and for eternity.

www.ingramcontent.com/pod-product-compliance
Lightning Source LLC
Chambersburg PA
CBHW081142290426
44108CB00018B/2418